The Blood of Government

The Blood of

The University of North Carolina Press | Chapel Hill

Government

Race, Empire,

the United States,

& the Philippines

PAUL A. KRAMER

Designed by Eric M. Brooks
Set in Jenson and Seria Sans by Keystone Typesetting, Inc.
Manufactured in the United States of America

The paper in this book meets the guidelines for permanence
and durability of the Committee on Production Guidelines for
Book Longevity of the Council on Library Resources.

Library of Congress Cataloging-in-Publication Data
Kramer, Paul A. (Paul Alexander), 1968–
The blood of government: race, empire, the United States,
and the Philippines / by Paul A. Kramer.
    p. cm.
Includes bibliographical references and index.
ISBN-13: 978-0-8078-2985-1 (cloth : alk. paper)
ISBN-10: 0-8078-2985-4 (cloth : alk. paper)
ISBN-13: 978-0-8078-5653-6 (pbk. : alk. paper)
ISBN-10: 0-8078-5653-3 (pbk. : alk. paper)
1. Philippines—History—1898–1946. 2. United States—
History—1865– 3. Race relations—Philippines. 4. Race relations—
United States. I. Title.
DS685.K73 2006
959.9′03–dc22   2005031380

A portion of this work appeared earlier, in somewhat different
form, as "Making Concessions: Race and Empire Revisited at the
Philippine Exposition, St. Louis, 1901–1905," *Radical History Review*
73 (Winter 1999): 74–114, and is reprinted here with permission.

cloth   10 09 08 07 06   5 4 3 2 1
paper   10 09 08 07   5 4 3 2

For my mother and father,

JUDY & OSCAR KRAMER

Contents

Acknowledgments xi

INTRODUCTION Sliding Scales
Race, Empire, and Transnational History 1

CHAPTER 1 Blood Compacts
Spanish Colonialism and the Invention of the Filipino 35

CHAPTER 2 From Hide to Heart
The Philippine-American War as Race War 87

CHAPTER 3 Dual Mandates
Collaboration and the Racial State 159

CHAPTER 4 Tensions of Exposition
Mixed Messages at the St. Louis World's Fair 229

CHAPTER 5 Representative Men
The Politics of Nation-Building 285

CHAPTER 6 Empire and Exclusion
Ending the Philippine Invasion of the United States 347

CONCLUSION The Difference Empire Made 433

Notes 437

Bibliography 481

Index 511

Illustrations

20 1921 political cartoon in the *Philippine Free Press*

45 Hand-drawn map of the Pacific by José Rizal

49 Photograph of *ilustrados* José Rizal, Marcelo H. Del Pilar, and Mariano Ponce

60 1886 painting *El Pacto de Sangre* by Juan Luna

70 Display of Igorots from Madrid's 1887 Philippine Exposition

107 Illustration from the short story "Itamo, the Insurrecto"

118 "Anti-imperialist" cartoon in the *New York Herald*, July 3, 1898

126 Photograph of trench filled with bodies

142 Photograph of the "water cure" being administered by U.S. soldiers

172 Photograph of U.S. missionaries visiting Filipino prisoners of war

187 Photograph of U.S. and Filipino officials at an elaborate ball

193 Political cartoon from *Public Opinion*, June 1902

202 Photograph of William Howard Taft, Leonard Wood, and U.S. schoolteachers with Filipino children

210 Maps of Northern Luzon circa 1907

219 Photograph of the Bud Dajo massacre of 1906

231 Photograph of Daniel Folkmar supervising Filipino prisoners in Bilibid prison

255 Draft of Felix Resurrección Hidalgo's painting *Through Peace and Liberty*

259 Bird's-eye view of the Philippine exhibit at the St. Louis world's fair

267 Photograph of American visitors with Moros and Igorots at the St. Louis world's fair

270 Photograph of the Visayan exhibit with a solitary American spectator

272 Photographs depicting "the Filipino of yesterday and of today" from the *World's Work*, August 1904

277   Illustration of the "Color Line Problem at the Fair" from the *St. Louis Post-Dispatch*, July 3, 1904

303   Portrait of the first Philippine Assembly

311   Photograph of "A Modern Primary School Building" from Dean Worcester's *Philippines, Past and Present*

315   Photograph of a "Typical Scene in a Trade School"

321   Photographic series depicting the "Educational Value of the Constabulary"

367   Photograph of a headhunter as "A Possible Office-Holder"

373   Photograph in the March 1913 *Filipino People* depicting a "Typical Filipino Home"

399   Map of exclusionary zones in U.S. immigration law, 1928

405   Photograph of a "Positively No Filipinos Allowed" sign in Stockton, California, 1930

409   Photograph of Esther Schmick and Perfecto Bandalan in the *Watsonville Evening Pajaronian*, December 1929

429   Photograph of University of the Philippines student protest from the *Manila Times*, January 31, 1930

Acknowledgments

The research and writing of this book were made possible by the generosity of a number of fellowship programs that allowed me the time to research and write. My thanks to the Smithsonian Institution, the Fulbright Foundation, the Newberry Library, the Bentley Historical Library, the Andrew Mellon and Charlotte Elizabeth Proctor Fellowship programs at Princeton University, and the Dean's Summer Incentive Grant program at Johns Hopkins University. Archivists and librarians too numerous to count helped me identify the materials used in this book. I am especially appreciative of the staff of Hopkins's Milton S. Eisenhower Library, particularly history bibliographers Jeannette Pierce and Thomas Izbicki, and Sharon Morris in government publications. The Eisenhower's dedicated interlibrary loan office allowed me to greatly broaden this project's source base, and staff members have been endlessly patient.

Scholars and friends have been generous with their hospitality during the travels I have undertaken while completing my research. My thanks to Josep Fradera for his hospitality in Barcelona. I owe special thanks to the History Department of Ateneo de Manila University and the University of the Philippines. I am especially indebted to Merce Planta and Marco Lagman for their welcome, and to Megan Thomas for many thought-provoking coffees at Ateneo. Noelle and Leal Rodriguez were the best companions I could have ever hoped to have.

I have also had the great benefit of a supportive academic environment. Since arriving at Hopkins, I have learned enormously from my colleagues in the History Department. I am especially grateful to all the participants in the department's seminar and to the students in my graduate classes, from whom I've learned a great deal. I owe special thanks, for their professional guidance and moral support, to Dorothy Ross, David Bell, Judy Walkowitz, Ron Walters, and Gabriele Spiegel. The smooth functioning of the department in which I work has been due to the energy of the History Department's staff: Lisa Enders, Megan Zeller, Ayana Teal, Eva Gonzalez, the late Sharon Widomski, and Shirley Hipley. My thanks also go to Clayton Haywood and Jamie Bakert for their technical assistance. Harry Marks and James Goodyear, who played key roles in my becoming a historian, have also been supportive colleagues. A number of individuals at Hopkins played crucial roles in the book's final completion. Manuel Cabanilla carefully scanned the images, Rachel Hadler diligently located and helped me secure their copyrights, and Catherine Jones patiently helped with the bibliography.

I have been the beneficiary of many readers' wisdom and critical imagination. The insightful comments of Eileen Scully, Elizabeth Lunbeck, and Benedict Anderson challenged and guided me as I shaped this work. Dan Rodgers was an engaged and supportive adviser while I was at Princeton and remains an inspiration to me as a scholar and teacher. I have been fortunate in having the opportunity to present my research in a number of illuminating workshop settings; my thanks in particular go to Vicente Rafael and David Szanton, Rebecca Scott, and Ann Stoler. I have also learned much from suggestions made by commentators at a number of conferences, including Mary Renda, David Roediger, Susan Schulten, and Robert Vitalis. My thanks to Etienne Balibar for his illuminating summer course at Cornell on theories of race and to the class's engaging students. For their moral support and dialogues with me on this book's themes, I'm grateful to Martha Hodes, Amy Kaplan, Carl Nightingale, John Plotz, and Emily Rosenberg. For their careful, challenging readings of this manuscript, in whole and in part, I'm grateful to Benedict Anderson, Vicente Rafael, Michael Cullinane, Reynaldo Ileto, and Richard Meixsel, as well as to its anonymous readers. For their care and attention in the publication process, I thank Charles Grench, Amanda McMillan, and John Wilson at the University of North Carolina Press, and Maricor Baytion and Esther Pacheco at Ateneo de Manila University Press.

Finally, and most important, I'm grateful to friends and family without whom I could not have completed this project. For their support and friendship, I thank Takashi Yokoyama, Alfonso Leyva, Benjamin Peck, Matthew Shum, Matthew D'Agostino, Rebecca Plant, Sacramento Rosello, James Mokhiber, Victor Osorio, Adilia Sosa, Susan Grossman, Tina Huang, Jonathan Roberts, Joel Walker, Paul Cohen, and Claudia Zatta. Thanks to all my friends in the dance world, especially Susan Leiter and Barbara Bernstein. I am especially grateful to Dirk Bönker, who, as friend, reader, and critic, has helped me craft my ideas here more than anyone else. Melinda Turner has enriched my life with her generosity, playfulness, and salsa in ways that I can only begin to thank her for. My sister and brother, Amy and Andy Kramer, have been endlessly supportive. Finally, I wish to thank my parents, Judy and Oscar Kramer, for their love, kindness, and inspiration. This book is dedicated to them.

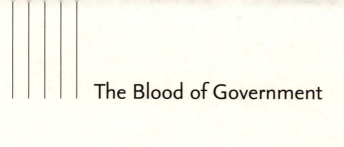

The Blood of Government

Race, Empire, and
Transnational History

On January 9, 1900, Senator Albert Beveridge, Republican of Indiana, stood before the U.S. Senate, defending a war on the other side of the world that refused to end by American command. The previous November, Gen. Elwell Otis had declared victory and an end to major combat operations in the Philippines, where American troops were struggling to impose U.S. sovereignty on the forces of the Philippine Republic. Over the next months, however, much to the frustration of U.S. generals and the McKinley administration, resistance would both vanish and intensify as Filipinos adopted a guerrilla strategy to fight off the invaders. Beveridge was uniquely suited to justify the war before the Senate and "anti-imperialist" critics, having built his early reputation on thundering rhetoric in defense of American empire. Campaigning in Indianapolis on September 19, 1898, for example, he had turned the recent U.S. victory against Spain in the Caribbean into a mandate for global liberation. America's mission-field would be a world contracted by electricity and steam. "Distance and oceans are no arguments," he asserted. The seas did "not separate us from lands of our duty and desire" but bound Americans to them. A half century earlier, California had been "more inaccessible" from the eastern United States than was the present-day Philippines, where U.S. troops had captured the city of Manila from Spanish forces the previous month. For Beveridge, Americans had "world duties" as "a people imperial by virtue of their power, by right of their institutions, by authority of their Heaven-directed purposes." He urged his countrymen to "broaden [the] blessed reign" of freedom "until the empire of our principles is established over the hearts of all mankind." As for criticism that "we ought not to govern a people without their consent," Beveridge asked his audience, "Would not the people of the Philippines prefer the just, humane, civilizing government of this Republic to the savage, bloody rule of pillage and extortion from which we have rescued them?"[1]

Filipinos had not, in fact, greeted the Americans as liberators. When Beveridge addressed the Senate in early 1900, nearly a year into the bloody conquest of the Philippine Islands, he did so as an expert who had himself beaten the oceans argument and traveled through the islands, guided by U.S. military commanders. In this second address, his sense of the Philippines' centrality to the United States' export trade to Asia was heightened, as was his rage at seeing "our mangled boys" on the battlefield, wounded indirectly by "anti-imperialism," or what he called "American assaults on our Government at home." As the war's terrors unfolded and its manifold costs were debated, Beveridge attempted to locate the invasion beyond dissent. Its true meaning, he stated, was "deeper than any question of party politics," than "any question of the isolated policy of our country," deeper even than "any question of constitutional power." "It is elemental," he asserted. "It is racial." Sublimating conquest into liberation meant making race. The American cause was nothing less than that of the "English-speaking and Teutonic peoples" whom God had prepared for "a thousand years" to become "the master organizers of the world," possessors of what he had called, in the 1898 address, "the blood of government." The enemy had also become more focused in Beveridge's imagination as Filipino guerrillas disappeared into villages and forests. He urged his colleagues to "remember that we are not dealing with Americans or Europeans" but with "Malays" corrupted by "hundreds of years of savagery, other hundreds of years of Orientalism, and still other hundreds of years of Spanish character and custom." What "alchemy," he asked, "will change the oriental quality of their blood and set the self-governing currents of the American pouring through their Malay veins?" In a time of empire-building, blood and government were intimately connected. Newly drawn and challenged lines of race would separate and bind those who ruled and those who were ruled.[2]

This book is a transnational history of race and empire in Philippine-American colonial encounters of the early twentieth century, a history of the novel connections and transformations exemplified in Beveridge's addresses. It is, on the one hand, a history of the racial politics of empire, of the way in which hierarchies of difference were generated and mobilized in order to legitimate and to organize invasion, conquest, and colonial administration. Where many prior accounts have emphasized the functionality of race to empire, often as "colonial discourse," the present work highlights race as a dynamic, contextual, contested, and contingent field of power. It is, on the other hand, a history of the imperial politics of race, of the way that empire-building interacted with, and transformed, the process of racial formation. Where historians have often seen colonial racial formations as "exports" or "projections" of prior, "domestic" ones, the present work argues for the necessity of examining metropole and colony in a single, densely interactive field in which colonial dynamics are not strictly derivative of, dependent upon, or respondent to metropolitan forces. This work argues, moreover, that these two histories—of the racial remaking of empire and the imperial remaking of race—are not separable. It was not simply that difference made empire possible: empire remade difference in the process.

Understanding these processes requires situating them within a rapidly changing global field. The last half of the nineteenth century saw a transformation in the character and intensity of global integration: following an array of distinct crises, what had formerly been predominantly regional strategies of self-reproduction became fundamentally intertwined.[3] Nowhere was this accelerating connection felt more strongly than in the colonial world. The early modern Atlantic empires had inaugurated world-spanning networks of commerce and geopolitical rivalry. But in the wake of the Euro-American conquests of the nineteenth century, both metropolitan and colonial elites found themselves even more intensely connected in a single, vertical field of global politics, with actors in each setting irrevocably internal to quests for power, authority, and legitimacy in the other. Colonialism wove metropolitan and colonial imaginaries together in myriad ways, with its wide-ranging participants aware that their destinies in part resided elsewhere. Along the multiple nodes that linked colonizing and colonized societies, simultaneous glances upward and downward along novel axes of power formed new symbolic economies of hope, terror, and identification.[4]

Among the formerly disparate regions of the world whose histories became permanently inseparable during this period were the Philippines and the United States. Contacts between these two societies had been sporadic before the end of the nineteenth century: with little trade or migration between them, each was virtually, if differently, unknown to the other.[5] The force that ushered in their joint twentieth century pushed from the Caribbean, when U.S. intervention in Cuba against Spain in 1898 was accompanied by the launching of the United States' Asiatic Squadron to Spain's largest Asian colony. The U.S. defeat of the Spanish fleet at Manila Bay and the military occupation of Manila in the middle of that year placed the histories of U.S. empire and Philippine sovereignty on a collision course. The two nations' histories would subsequently be fired together in years of brutal warfare and take the violent shape of their crucible. Over the next half century and well beyond it, neither would the Philippines and the United States ever be closed to the other nor would their connection be cut off from the rest of the world. In highly differential ways, oriented to steep gradients of power, each would become part of the other's remaking.[6]

Specifically, this book is about the transnational politics of race and empire. The two categories were never external to each other in the late nineteenth and early twentieth centuries. Empire meant exercising sovereignty and power over peoples denied the rights that were increasingly coming to define the modern nation-state: it meant inventing ideologies to calibrate inclusion in these expanding and hierarchical polities. Among others, race was an epistemology suited to constructing the political exceptions that would qualify and delimit these states' universalistic claims. Race intersected with modern state institutions: by the late nineteenth century, its scientism and the developing apparatus of the modern administrative state were mutually implicated. Race helped give shape to the modern bourgeois family upon which imperial self-definitions were commonly constructed, anchoring the differential powers of women and men in moral, biological, and world-historical frameworks. Where industrial capitalism was brutally reworking relations of power and production, race was capable of mobilizing class-organized workers behind imperial projects of state. In the colonial world, race would justify and structure vertical, authoritarian state-building, denigrating its very collaborators. Its gradations of humanity would also facilitate ultimate forms of exclusion: the extreme violence upon which those states would often be constructed.

This book is about the articulation of race and empire in the making of Philippine-American colonial history. Like works that precede it, it argues that race as a mode of power and knowledge was a core element in the making of formal colonialism in the Philippines.[7] But breaking from earlier accounts, it suggests that the intersections of race and empire were contingent, contested, and transnational in scope. Race was the site of intense struggle in Philippine-American colonial history, between Filipinos and Americans, between actors in metropole and colony, between actors inside and outside the colonial state. This struggle was, at its narrowest, transpacific in scope, involving participants not only in the United States and the Philippines but in Europe and its colonial outposts. These struggles were never detached from their political contexts: rather, the colonial racial-formation process was intimately tied to broader shifts in colonial politics, which it decisively shaped and by which it was shaped in turn.

The result of these struggles was a novel racial formation whose specific contours and texture emerged from a particular local convergence of transnational forces, rather than the "export" of U.S. racial idioms and institutions or the installation of generic "colonial" discourses. Its earliest moment was the encounter between American and Filipino forces with the U.S. occupation of Manila in mid-1898; with the outbreak of war in early 1899, more than three years of imperial conquest structured U.S. racial visions of Filipinos as both tribally fragmented—and thus incapable of "self-government"—and as racially united in support of "savage" guerrilla warfare. Following the unpersuasive declaration of war's end, a civilian colonial state under the Philippine Commission and collaborating Filipino elites organized itself around new forms of knowledge-production, including the generation of novel racial formations. Self-consciously breaking with the army's brutal and homogenizing "race war," the commission and its allies constructed a new racial state organized around an aggressively optimistic colonialism of "capacity." In it, progressive, future-oriented visions of Filipino evolution, maturation, and tutelary assimilation toward self-government under indefinite U.S. control converged to make sense of, and calibrate, the often tense terms of Filipino-American collaboration. This was an inclusionary racial formation that both invited and delimited Filipino political agency in colonial state-building. Its undefined timetables—qualified by rhetorical benchmarks and promises of "progress"—helped legitimate and exceptionalize Philippine-American colonialism before American, Filipino, and international publics.

At the heart of the new racial formation was the bifurcation of the Philippine Islands' population into "Christian" and "non-Christian" peoples. This boundary line had deep roots in the Spanish colonial period, when it had marked one of the central hierarchies of Spanish colonial society, along with *mestizaje* (blood mixture) and territorial nativity. As U.S. colonial rulers "attracted" Hispanicized Filipino elites, both groups articulated a widening gap between the islands' "civilized" peoples and its "non-Christians." Under U.S. colonial rule, this distinction was installed at multiple levels of the colonial state and territorialized in the form of special provinces: a "Mountain Province" to correspond to the animist highlanders of Luzon, and a "Moro Province" for the Muslim populations of the southern archipelago. Unlike the semielected governments of Christian provinces, these provinces would be administered exclusively by appointed U.S. politico-military commanders and would long remain under exclusive U.S. control. Politically, the bifurcation of Christians and non-Christians helped persuade U.S. audiences that the war was over by rhetorically reducing Philippine "savagery" to the non-Christian population alone. It held out to U.S. colonial officials rich resources for a politics of divide and rule: when colonial rule was seriously challenged in the metropole in the mid-1910s, for example, these officials would recast themselves as the "protectors" of non-Christians from Hispanicized Filipinos and of Filipinos from non-Christians. Bifurcation also promised Hispanicized Filipino elites their own "internal" colonial subjects. U.S. colonialists, disparaging the very Hispanicized elites with which they collaborated, had maintained that they were perpetually incapable not only of their own self-government but of the government of non-Christians. Filipino nationalists would counter with nationalist-colonialist assertions of their duties and capacities to rule over non-Christians: they would prove their very readiness for self-government, alongside other measures, through the elaboration of an "internal" empire.

While the racial politics of colonialism would, in this way, fundamentally shape emerging Filipino nationalism, it would also have an impact upon U.S. national and racial identities. While Americans held out fantasies that colonialism would involve one-way Filipino "assimilation," the Philippines was becoming absorbed into U.S. history at the same time. At the Louisiana Purchase Exposition in St. Louis in 1904, the colonial regime organized an enormous tableau meant to place the Philippine occupation —and its subjects—at the core of a narrative of continuous U.S. national-imperial "progress." If the display was meant to showcase Filipino capacities to be assimilated—along bifurcated lines—it was also meant to inspire confidence in the United States' own capacities to assimilate Filipinos without losing its racial integrity. The regime's inclusionary racial formation—necessary to the functioning of Filipino-American collaboration—would, however, collide with more exclusionary domestic racial institutions. At St. Louis, it would be rejected by racist white mobs that assaulted Filipino troops for their overly "assimilated" courtship of white women. More significantly, the mass labor migration of male Filipino workers to the mainland United States in the late 1920s and 1930s—based upon their rights as U.S. nationals—posed these inclusive and exclusive racial formations directly against each other. Where the regime saw Filipino migration as assimilation by other means, organized nativists represented it as an "invasion" by "Asiatics," who must be excluded from the United States, even at the price of Philippine independence itself.

This book, then, is about the imagined community of empire. It is about the mutual imbrication of American and Philippine nation-building across almost four decades of transnational encounters. Asymmetrically and reciprocally, the process by which each emerging national community came to imagine and bind itself unfolded inside the other. At the core of this interconnection was the protean project of justifying and organizing U.S. sovereignty over the Philippines, a project that was widely resisted in both the Philippines and the United States. This project—and opposition to it—led not only to articulations of difference between Filipinos and Americans but also to proliferations of difference among them, forms of difference that were new to both societies.[8]

Connecting Histories

This section offers three different, but overlapping, ways the larger work will represent Philippine-American history as both imperial and transnational history. They will be presented as three prophetic voices, each of which directly confronted questions of race and empire, and each of which opened Philippine-American history outward and joined it to other "continents" of historical experience. As might be expected, they annexed this history to their ongoing concerns. But together, they demonstrate possibilities for the connection of Philippine, American, and world histories. Writing in 1889–90, Filipino intellectual and activist José Rizal y Alonso situates Philippine history within larger transnational frames in a foresighted essay. On the eve of the Philippine-American War in February 1899, British imperial poet laureate Rudyard Kipling locates the U.S. colonial project in the Philippines within the contemporary world of European colonialism. More than a year into that war, black intellectual and activist W. E. B. Du Bois folds an account of the ongoing colonization of the islands into a worldwide survey of the "color line." Each of these voices suggests that while it was geology's work to make the islands, it took politics and ideology to make their histories "insular."

Of the many histories that flow together into the present one, the least insular in many ways is the trajectory of Philippine history. The inhabitants of the islands had long been involved in extensive regional trade that linked them commercially and culturally to other islands and to mainland Asia before the coming of Spain. By definition, "Philippine history" as such was the product of Spanish conquest: far in advance of their own dominion, Spanish imperialists had framed together and narrated a single archipelago under the name of their monarch. While it did not curtail older regional connections, Spanish colonization reoriented them in crucial ways. The galleon trade that the Spanish inaugurated between China and Mexico undermined earlier networks of interisland and regional trade. While its frontiers remained ragged until long after Spanish dominion had ended, the "Philippines" came into being oriented toward Europe, the Atlantic, and an emerging world economy.[9] This orientation inexorably made its way into early Spanish historical accounts of the islands. Philippine historiography in its first forms, organized around narratives of colonization, was inescapably global: as it had in the Americas, Spain had conquered the Philippines in order to bring its "heathen" inhabitants into the fold of Christendom in ways that reflected everlasting glory on Spain. In arguing first for Filipino rights and later for Philippine independence, Filipino nationalists would redraw the global map of Spanish colonial historiography.

No one engaged in this project as energetically as the Tagalog physician, scholar, and activist José Rizal. Rizal's own path revealed in microcosm how profoundly global Philippine history had become by the late nineteenth century. Like many among his class and generation, Rizal had sought educational and political opportunity in Europe in the 1880s and 1890s, escaping an increasingly repressive environment in the islands.[10] Collectively, he and others, in effect, annexed Europe as the Philippine archipelago's one free island, a place where modern education might be pursued, new selves invented or discovered, and Spanish colonialism challenged and reformed. Rizal's attempt to resituate Philippine history in the world occupied much of his political and intellectual work; one of its sharpest expressions was his prophetic 1889–90 essay "The Philippines a Century Hence." Rizal began by imagining a Philippine history before Spain and, therefore, a history that might have escaped Spain. The islands' peoples, whose civilization Rizal would detail in his 1890 translation of Antonio de Morga's chronicle, had become "incorporated" into Spain through violence and disruption. The islands had been "depopulated, impoverished, and set back," and its peoples had forgotten "their writing, their songs, their poetry, their laws." Indeed, they had become "ashamed of what was theirs and national in order to admire and praise what was foreign and incomprehensible."[11] Here, Rizal's historiography, with its confident separation of the "national" from the "foreign," sought Filipino rights through historical insulation.

But Rizal was also profoundly aware that Filipino solidarities were themselves the product of broader forces. Developments in communication, especially the advent of steamers and telegraphs, meant that "the inhabitants move from one island to another," and "naturally communication and the exchange of impressions increases." Scarcity of schooling "forces the youth of all the islands to gather and to learn to get to know each other." Journeys to Europe were the furthest extension of this process, for "abroad the inhabitants of the most distant provinces seal their patriotic feeling." All of these travelers, from "sailors to the wealthiest merchants," upon contrasting "the sight of modern liberties" and "the misfortunes of home," embraced and "call each other brothers." Above all, Spanish disdain for the islands' peoples had forged them together. What he called the "general affront against a whole race" by the enemies of reform had "wiped away the ancient enmities between different provinces."[12]

The overseas travel that Rizal in part credited with the making of Filipino nationality also allowed him to criticize Spanish colonialism from without, drawing on contemporary colonial models from elsewhere. "I am studying all the books that have been published regarding colonies, with the goal of bringing myself up to date on colonization," he wrote to the anthropologist A. B. Meyer at the same moment.[13] While Spanish reactionaries argued against Filipino representation in the Cortes, he observed, the French colonies had delegates. In the British Empire, Parliament was debating representation for its Crown colonies, and other colonies already "enjoy a degree of autonomy." Spain's own colonies, Cuba and Puerto Rico, had had representation for decades. Ultimately, it was a reading of world history that allowed Rizal to deliver a thinly veiled warning. History did not record "any lasting dominion exercised by one people over another, of different races, of strange ways and customs, and of opposed and divergent ideals." As it was impossible "to destroy the inhabitants gradually," if pushed to war, the Philippines would gain its freedom. World history showed that colonies established "to serve the politics or commerce of a metropolis, all conclude by becoming independent." Most striking, Rizal suggested that if this were to come to pass, it would not only jeopardize Spain's remaining colonies in Africa but her very independence in Europe. Collapsing empires might quickly become colonies in their own right.[14]

While Rizal deployed European empires against Spain, how would they intrude on his history before-the-fact of Philippine independence? Following what he anticipated would be "heroic and stubborn conflicts," the Philippines could "rest assured" that neither England, Germany, France, nor Holland would "dare to take up what Spain was unable to hold." The islands would be saved by the colonial division of Africa, which would soon "completely absorb the attention of the Europeans"; the "immense territory offered by the Dark Continent, untouched, undeveloped, and almost undefended," was far more enticing than "a group of poor and hostile islands." In the context of Asia, Britain was "already lord of the Orient," with Singapore, Hong Kong, and Shanghai; Germany "avoids all foreign complications"; the "French spirit" did not "shine in zeal for colonization"; Holland was "content to keep the Moluccas and Java." Nor would the Philippines be threatened by Asian powers. China would "consider herself fortunate if she succeeds in keeping herself intact"; Japan was far more interested in Korea and under diplomatic pressure from Europe, such that it would "not think of outside affairs until she is freed of it."[15]

There remained one other power to consider, in many ways the least relevant to Philippine history to that point. "Perhaps the great American Republic," wrote Rizal, ". . . may some day dream of foreign possessions." Admittedly, it seemed unlikely: in 1890, the U.S. presence in the Philippines was minimal, represented by a handful of merchants and the sporadic visits of naval vessels. An isthmian canal had not opened in Central America, nor was "the territory of the States congested with inhabitants." Colonization of this kind was "contrary to her traditions." But the United States' "interests lie in the Pacific," and the country had "no hand" in the conquest of Africa. From the European perspective, the United States would make a "troublesome" rival "if she should once get into the business." For this reason, Europe would likely prohibit U.S. aggression, "for they know very well that the appetite is sharpened by the first bites."[16]

If one way to connect Philippine-American history outward is by exploring the Philippines' transnational history, a second involves connecting the history of U.S. empire to contemporary European colonialisms. The United States' first empire had been continental in scope, a territorial empire achieved through the violence of a genocidal state and of white settlers against Native Americans, and one that opened up vast land and natural resources for industrial capitalist exploitation. Employing the resources and infrastructure of this first empire, the United States had by the late nineteenth century begun to construct a second, overseas commercial empire of exports, built under the protection of the U.S. Navy, that reached as far as East Asia. Links between both U.S. empires and European states were dense and complex, involving economic competition, naval rivalry, and struggles over geopolitical spheres of influence. At the same time, Americans continued to turn to European precedents for guidance and inspiration. Even as the United States came into its own as a transcontinental and overseas empire, some Americans continued to see themselves as "colonial"—defined as a kind of parochial dependence—with respect to European and especially English patterns.[17]

In 1898, the two "colonialisms" flowed together, as Americans setting out to conquer overseas territories turned to the British Empire for inspiration. Specifically, those who advocated the colonial annexation of Cuba, Puerto Rico, and the Philippines argued that the United States was justified in doing so by deep racial-historical links of common "Anglo-Saxon" heritage. As the world's predominant empire, the British Empire had demonstrated that Anglo-Saxons had both a right and a duty to conquer large portions of the earth's surface; in embarking upon similar tasks, then, the United States was merely fulfilling Anglo-Saxon responsibilities dictated by its racial-historical character. British observers did not hesitate to point out that American "Anglo-Saxonism" was compromised by immigrants and its imperial potential undermined by overly democratic traditions and inexperience at overseas rule. American imperialists responded, in turn, by seeking British advice, approval, and models of colonial rule in what might have been called a colonial manner. Throughout the period of American rule in the Philippines, U.S. colonial officials would circulate in the British colonial world, follow British imperial developments closely, and selectively adapt elements of British imperial policy: U.S. "colonial" imperialism, then, was colonial in two senses.[18]

Such colonialism tended to draw uninvited advice. It came in February 1899, on the very edge of the Philippine-American War, in a work that immediately gave birth to one of the most long-lived metaphors for colonialism in the twentieth century. It was penned by Rudyard Kipling, poet laureate of the British Empire. In biographical terms, Kipling was densely entangled in Anglo-American and Anglo-Saxonist communities who defined their racial membership in explicitly "imperial" terms.[19] As Filipino-American tensions were reaching critical pitch in the islands and the U.S. Senate debated the annexation treaty, Kipling published a poem in *McClure's*, "The White Man's Burden," that generously offered the Americans counsel. If Rizal's essay demonstrated the degree to which Philippine history was world history, Kipling's poem suggested how deeply entangled Philippine-American colonial history would be with the history of European colonialism. The work ricocheted throughout the colonial world, its title quickly becoming one of the central catchphrases and rationales of empire in general, as well as the locus of sustained critique.

The poem urged Americans to take up the responsibilities and sacrifices of what Kipling imagined as Pan-European imperial manhood. He urged Americans to "Send forth the best ye breed" to the Philippines, although the specific imperial mission with which they were charged was fruitfully vague. What was sharply focused was Kipling's sense—against the criticisms of both British and U.S. "anti-imperialists"—that empire meant boundless sacrifice rather than greed and self-aggrandizement and, as such, was an endeavor positively foolhardy in its morality. Among the deepest sacrifices empire entailed was the almost panoptic scrutiny that it subjected its exponents to. The "silent sullen peoples" of the colonies were busy "weigh[ing] your God and you," while other empires would—no doubt uncomfortably—"search your manhood" and deliver their "dear-bought wisdom, / The judgment of your peers." This judgment was presumed to be disappointed: at its feverishly self-righteous core, the poem named the lot of the imperialist as one of radical underappreciation, a toil of "thankless years," earning "The blame of those ye better / The hate of those ye guard."[20] While coupling the U.S. and European colonial projects, Kipling lent both a tragic boundlessness: empire was a martyrdom of infinite regress.

A third way to connect Philippine-American history outward is through the global history of antiracist mobilization. The transnational geography of race-making was at the core of both Rizal's and Kipling's respective prophecies. For Rizal, it was Spain's imperial racial formations that had helped forge Filipino solidarity; for Kipling, it was panimperial whiteness that grounded a global vision of empire as uplift. Race's transnationalism was nothing new to their age. It had, for example, been one of the key structures organizing the Atlantic economies and societies out of which the United States had emerged, particularly through the racialization of African slave labor and the conquest of indigenous peoples in North America. Crossed by slave ships until the early nineteenth century, the Atlantic Ocean bridged transoceanic debates over race, labor, and empire with little respect for national borders. Following emancipation, race would continue to be debated in a "free labor" context, characterized by accelerating industrial transport and communication. By the early twentieth century, race was an organizing principle in a global commerce of ideas and institutions that spanned literary, academic, and political spheres.

One of the forces powerfully internationalizing race during this period was empire. Imperial rivalry involved distant societies in deeper interaction and dialogue than ever before, even as this competition was being conducted in increasingly convergent and mutually intelligible terms. Within the Euro-American world, imperial powers often rationalized their conquests by linking national destinies to broader, shared Pan-European racial solidarities. These solidarities were especially evident in the colonial world, where diverse and otherwise rancorous Europeans and Americans often invented commonalities precisely as they confronted nonwhite opponents. At their most ambitious, these visions sublimated the competition of European powers, the United States, and Japan into a single, outward-moving frontier of "civilization." They also necessarily involved a transnational and interimperial dialogue over the character and fate of those caught on the other side of that line. While the definitions of "self" and "other" that emerged from these racial dialogues were highly varied, and tailored to historical contingencies, they increasingly made empire part of their content and took place on a widened, interimperial terrain.

These developments were clear to some contemporaries. When W. E. B. Du Bois declared prophetically in 1903 that "the problem of the 20th century is the problem of the color line," he was quick to clarify that this meant "the relation of the darker to the lighter races in Asia and Africa, in America and the islands of the sea."[21] In his 1900 address as president of the American Negro Academy, Du Bois had explored the space between "America and the islands of the sea" in detail. While some considered "our race question . . . a purely national and local affair," for Du Bois, a quick global survey revealed that, in fact, "the color line belts the world." (Indeed, in the original formulation of his famous prophecy, the color line was to be "the world problem of the 20th century.") Du Bois then traced the somewhat uneven path of that belt for his audience. The "race question" was playing out in colonial Africa, "the centre of the great Negro problem," where Du Bois had some praise for English colonial rule. Asia also contained "congeries of race and color problems." It was the continent of "the unbridled injustice of conquerors toward the conquered—of advanced toward undeveloped races—of swaggering braggadocio toward dumb submission," although Du Bois applauded English education in India and found in Japan's recent entry into "the ranks of modern civilized nations" "the greatest concession to the color line which the nineteenth century has seen." In Latin America the "color line" had been less clearly drawn, although "the condition of the dark masses" there was "far from satisfactory."[22]

For Du Bois, the "race questions" of the United States and those of the world were becoming inseparably "belted" together by imperial processes. What Du Bois called "the expansion and consolidation of nations" was leading to "countless repetitions" of American conditions—"the inclusion of nations within nations—of groups of undeveloped peoples brought in contact with advanced races under the same government, language and system of culture." The same conditions were being confronted by "German Negroes, Portuguese Negroes, Spanish Negroes, English East Indians, Russian Chinese, [and] American Filipinos." This last reference was especially important. Du Bois identified the "most significant" recent development in the United States as "our ownership of Porto Rico, and Havana, our protectorate of Cuba, and conquest of the Philippines," which constituted the "greatest event since the Civil War." The space between "America and the islands of the sea" was collapsing, and with it, former boundaries between the "race questions" of the United States, the Caribbean, and the Pacific. For Du Bois, this meant a doubling of the "colored population of our land," one that would make "brown and black people . . . a third of the nation." "What is to be our attitude toward these new lands and toward the masses of dark men and women who inhabit them?" he inquired. Du Bois urged that it be one of "deepest sympathy and strongest alliance." "Negro and Filipino, Indian and Porto Rican, Cuban and Hawaiian," he enjoined, must "stand united under the stars and stripes for an America that knows no color line in the freedom of its opportunities."[23] For better or for worse—Du Bois was hopeful—imperial history had annexed the world to the "Negro problem" and vice versa.

Insulating Empire

These voices from the past, with their varied global scales, contrast strikingly with what has been, until relatively recently, the comparative "insulation" of Philippine-American colonial historiography.[24] This fact requires different Philippine and American historiographic explanations. In the Philippine case, the American colonial period has frustrated the traditional narrative of rising Filipino nationalism that provides much of the structure for nineteenth-century Philippine historiography. In this literature, the last three decades of Spanish rule are narrated as a series of crises that ultimately provoke a recognition of Filipino "nationality," one that is ultimately expressed in the Philippine Revolution and the Philippine Republic. By contrast, historians of the American colonial period are faced with the reality of nationalism without revolution or, for nearly four decades, the achievement of independent statehood. Thus, the period is represented as one in which "true" nationalism was "suppressed"—hence the failure to secure the independent state that must be the outer form of nationalism—and false, "official" forms brought forward to displace authentic ones. The class politics of nationalism play an important role in these narratives: Filipino elites, who both led the revolution and entered the subsequent American colonial state, are said to betray "authentic" Filipino nationalism rather than to pursue nationalism—and their own interests—within U.S. colonial structures. The Philippine-American colonial period has been bracketed in the teleology of Philippine nationalism: anything else risks the blurring of "official" nationalism and what is imagined as its untainted opposite.

Within U.S. historiography, the insulation of Philippine-American colonial history is part of a broader project of American national exceptionalism.[25] Since its advent, U.S. colonial rule in the Philippines has frustrated accounts of American uniqueness: ushered in with a war that looked much like Europe's colonial wars, it involved the United States in colonial state-building and international politics of a kind undertaken by European great powers during the same period.[26] Historians were able to rewrite the history of continental empire in North America as "expansion," a term that starkly separated it from European imperialisms. But expansion was predicated on white settler colonialism: in the Philippines, by contrast, narratives of "civilization" through white settlement met their limits. It did not help that U.S. imperialists themselves turned to European and especially British precedents for inspiration, guidance, and justification. The question, then, became how to reassert an American national-exceptionalist narrative that could account for this history. In this effort, historians have traditionally drawn directly on the accounts of U.S. imperial actors themselves. Following their lead, they have minimized the Philippine-American War as an "insurrection," the shadowy aftermath of the Spanish-Cuban-American War. The war's historians also depicted it (as U.S. generals had) as one not of "cruelty" but of restraint and "benevolence." Those who focused on the "postwar" period emphasized not continued violence, authoritarian state-building, and economic exploitation but projects of school construction, public health, and Filipino participation that were presumably their opposites. But the imperial architecture of national exceptionalism went far deeper, relying on the temporal exceptionalism of the 1890s, the analytic subordination of formal to informal empire, and the minimizing of American contacts with European colonial empires. Exploring each of these in turn is necessary to opening up the space for the present work.

The insulation of Philippine-American colonial history has been achieved in part through forms of temporal exceptionalism, especially regarding the 1890s. This account was especially important to some early diplomatic and political histories of what was comfortingly called the United States' "imperial moment" and remains influential in recent cultural histories.[27] In these accounts, the United States acquired its overseas colonial empire after 1898 in a fit of fever-mindedness. The 1890s was a time of "psychic crisis," wrought from the accumulated stress of industrial depression, corporate concentration, labor and populist radicalism, and the end of the frontier. Colonial empire was the natural "outlet" and resolution of these tensions, whose release was manifested as "jingoism," a term that vanishes analytically from later historical time.[28] It was an exceptionalist stage set for an exceptionalist drama: the 1890s needed to be a unique decade because it had to explain and repair an apparent rupture in the fabric of American historical uniqueness. While the exceptionalist chronology of U.S. imperialism was challenged on many fronts—especially by the New Left historians—it is striking that the narrative of the empire-inducing crises of the 1890s continues to inform even the most interesting of the new cultural histories of U.S. imperialism. Whatever their other strengths, these histories also comfortingly, if unpersuasively, limit U.S. empire to a set of exceptional and unrepeatable events in a distant past.

The New Left historians challenged the temporal exceptionalism of the 1890s: the work of William A. Williams and Walter LaFeber, for example, showed that U.S. empire developed over a long arc that simply reached a new height in the late nineteenth century. Where the driving force of U.S. empire was the ongoing quest for overseas markets, the 1890s did not need to be a particularly exceptional decade for explanatory purposes.[29] At the same time, New Left historians deinsulated Philippine-American colonial history to some degree by embedding it in the broader history of informal empire in the late nineteenth century. The Philippines was conquered, in these accounts, to provide a crucial "stepping stone" to Asia and the fabled "China market," making it merely one strategic point in the global fabric of informal empire.[30] But having integrated the Philippines into wider currents of U.S. and world history, the New Left historians simultaneously insulated them: just as the Philippine Islands were geopolitical "stepping stones" to Asia, they were analytical stepping stones to other historical problems. The "informal empire" that was their focus subordinated the United States' formal empire and exceptionalized it. The Philippines was the anomaly that proved the rule of U.S. "open door" imperialism; Philippine history did not matter in and of itself but only in so far as it bore weight in the larger architecture of informal empire.

While narratives of informal empire integrate Philippine-American history in longer trajectories, it is telling that nearly all works that specifically approach Philippine-American colonial history treat the year 1898 as a sharp temporal border. Historical consciousness follows the flag. In U.S. accounts, which have traditionally focused on military and diplomatic actors and events, the Philippines has been, for analytical purposes, invented by Dewey's arrival at Manila Bay. Philippine historical consciousness also follows its flags. Within Philippine historiography, 1898 saw the advent of Philippine independence in the form of the short-lived Philippine Republic, the principal end point in the teleology of Philippine nationalism. As the present work hopes to show, crossing between Philippine and U.S. histories means crossing 1898 to reveal the myriad ways that what is bounded as the "Spanish colonial" period flows into the "American colonial" period that followed in its wake.

Along with the insular 1890s and subordination to informal empire, Philippine-American colonial history has traditionally been insulated from the history of contemporary European empires for purposes of comparison and connection. In its most extreme form, the claim has been made that the United States was not comparable to European empires. The formal/informal divide has often been employed to make the United States stand out typologically from European cases; in this sense, the New Left historians were national-exceptionalists, seeing the United States' informal empire as unique and sharply contrasting with Europe's contemporary formal empires. Where attempts at intercolonial comparison have been made, they have often served to further insulate U.S. imperialism by exceptionalizing it. Rather than an exception by type, the United States becomes an exception by pattern of rule: U.S. colonialism was "ambivalent," "tutelary," or even "democratic," in contrast to a European colonialism presumably its opposite. Historians have projected this exceptionalism backwards onto their historical actors, who are said to have completely rejected "European" precedents in the making of their colonial empire. This obscures the uncomfortable fact that U.S. imperialists often took inspiration, in complicated ways, from the world's other empires, especially the British Empire. Exposing some of these connections between empires, as this work hopes to do, will hopefully enhance understandings of the historical construction of exceptionalism. Imperialists themselves had powerful investments in, and machineries to produce, persuasive national-exceptionalist narratives of colonial rule. Indeed, many of the tropes that dominate historical writing on these themes to this day are artifacts of the history they purport to describe. Breaking with national-exceptionalist accounts of U.S. empire, in other words, enables an understanding of the ways in which national-exceptionalist ideologies were themselves produced on imperial terrain.[31]

Race and the Politics of Recognition

At the historical intersection of race and empire was a politics of recognition. While physical force always lay behind claims of imperial sovereignty, recognition was a logic of legitimation with hegemonic potential, requiring at least two distinct, contracting parties of differential power. Within the realm of recognition, the relations of power between them were defined not by the hegemon's outright political exclusion of the less powerful but by its ability to establish and adjust standards or criteria for inclusion. In this way, the politics of recognition was not only formally inclusionary but participatory: it required the subordinates to acknowledge, learn, and demonstrate their "assimilation" of the standards of the more powerful in order to gain certain powers and resources, defined perpetually as revocable privileges rather than inalienable rights. While the hegemon was, in theory, compelled to cede some power when its criteria were absorbed and realized, under the politics of recognition it would, by definition, never cede the authority to evaluate, to interpret or change standards, or to adjust the relationship between those standards and the granting or withholding of power. Indeed, the subordinate party's acknowledged "success" in achieving these criteria affirmed and strengthened the hegemon's evaluative power.

In the colonial setting, imperial powers stood to gain a degree of legitimacy from the politics of recognition, rationalizing processes of collaboration by providing formal criteria for political participation and inclusion and, in at least some cases, a timetable for the devolution of power that could make the empire's illusions of impermanence plausible. Where successful, it also directed resistance by colonized people toward channels already made safe by the regime: political opposition could be directed toward the gathering of "evidence" or "proof" that the regime's standards had been achieved; this removed any single standard from the arsenal of disenfranchisement but simultaneously affirmed its larger logic. But colonized peoples were not left powerless by the politics of recognition. Its very existence spoke to the limits of physical force and the necessity for legitimation. While imperial powers retained the power to recognize, it was the actual or potential resistance of the colonized that compelled them to recognize. The politics of recognition was especially attractive to collaborating elites who could both follow its stipulations and employ them to accelerate or delay the counterimperial transfer of sovereignty in ways that bolstered their own power. While imperial powers could arbitrarily alter their criteria for recognition, these alterations made them vulnerable to charges of tyranny or hypocrisy not only among the colonized but in the broader international arena in which the empire's own recognition was at stake.[32]

The politics of recognition hinged on the maintenance of justifiable hierarchies of difference that legitimated varying degrees of disenfranchisement. Among the most powerful and flexible of those hierarchies in the modern world, if far from the only ones, were hierarchies of race. Race has long been a staple of the historiography of U.S. empire.[33] But much of this literature reinforces rather than undermines the "insularity" of Philippine-American history, in at least two ways. The first of these might be called the historiography of "export" or "projection," which claims that Americans simply applied racial formations drawn from the "domestic" United States, especially those directed against Native Americans and African Americans, to the world beyond the United States. "Export" describes historical actors as having been able to recognize difference wherever they went, failing to account for their frequent bewilderment, argument over, and reinvention of difference in new contexts. Where historians have begun to explore the contextual, contingent, and plural character of racial formations in the United States, the metaphor of "export" suggests that race is discrete, uncontested, impervious to context,

This 1921 cartoon in the *Philippine Free Press* offers an ironic, modernist critique of race within the context of Philippine-American colonial history. It represents the Philippines as a skeptical observer of diverse U.S. portrayals of Filipinos, specifically as a critical reader of the Republican-sponsored anti-independence report by Leonard Wood and William Cameron Forbes, one who does not recognize himself in the regime's past images. The cartoon suggests that by that time Filipino critics had developed a sharp, self-conscious sense of the imperial politics of recognition, as well as a sense of their own power to assess and engage with U.S. colonial representations and to earn the nervous solicitation of colonial officials. From McCoy and Roces, *Philippine Cartoons.*

and unchanging in historical time. It sets historians to work looking for familiar patterns and processes drawn from "domestic" contexts, ironically cleaving, in the very act of "transnational" departure, to U.S. history's traditional boundaries. "Export" has particular difficulty accounting for historical change: where U.S. racial politics in the 1880s and 1890s was undergoing revolutionary transformations, from Jim Crow to the Dawes Act to Chinese exclusion, for example, historical change is made to stop at the water's edge in 1898. Not unlike late nineteenth-century notions of the frontier as a moving line of unchanging "civilization," export imagines the world outside the United States as a set of open ports, virtually uninhabited by historical agents, malleable to Americans' static perceptions and desires. That much of this literature casts itself as critical of empire only sharpens the irony of its essentially "imperial" framework. Promising to connect U.S. history outward, export, in practice, insulates it.[34]

If export makes colonial racism the mere projection of domestic projects, a second approach, "colonial discourse," involves nearly the opposite problem, that of reducing any colonial racial formation to the outcropping of generic, archetypal racial formations found elsewhere in the colonial world. Colonial discourse has already received diverse criticism. Its ahistorical character—the tendency to prefer long arcs of continuity over disjunctures, discontinuities, and contingencies—has long been one source of such criticism. Some have criticized its homogenization of what were diverse imperial actors and contradictory agendas both within colonies and between metropoles and colonies. Others have highlighted its flattening of divisions between racial modes in the interest of representing stark, dualistic hierarchies of self/other and colonizer/colonized.[35] Still others have emphasized its frequent functionalism: colonial discourse is often represented as the organic expression of a seamless imperial project of military conquest, political control, and economic exploitation. Necessary to this functionalism is its analytic exclusion of colonized peoples whose engagement—in whatever complexes of collaboration, resistance, and mediation—is deemed analytically unnecessary. Given the long-term tendency toward national exceptionalism in U.S. historiography in general, and accounts of empire in particular, a colonial-discourse model might seem to open up space for an interimperial historiography, but it in fact closes down such options: if "export" collapses colony into metropole, "colonial discourse" collapses colony into colony, precisely preventing the historical reconstruction of interimperial connections. If colonies spontaneously gave rise to the discourses they required, this obviates the need to reconstruct the complex dialogues and exchanges that gave distinct colonial discourses their common elements.

In contrast with both these perspectives, this work proceeds from the assumption that race is irreducibly a system of power, and that as a result, the process of race-making takes its shape from, and in turn lends shape to, specific socially and historically constituted political projects. As a means of organizing power, what has made and continues to make race effective is precisely its protean and opportunistic character. While never strictly derivative of them, race is deeply embedded in other hierarchical categories of difference, such as gender and class, upon which it relies and to which it in turn lends strength.[36] Indeed, its political force at any moment in historical time derives from what Ann Stoler has called its "tactical mobility," the ease of movement between its "own" terms and a political culture's other explanatory structures.[37] What might be called its historical mobility, or social reproduction, can only be sustained through a continual and contested process of what Michael Omi and Howard Winant have called "rearticulation," in which racial idioms are translated into other evolving cultural terms, racializing those terms in the process.[38] Both kinds of mobility—tactical and historical—make possible race's malleable, contingent, and contextual character, allowing it to reach and haunt the densest connection points in a political culture.

This sense of the contingencies of race suggests the limits of both "export" and "colonial discourse" for comprehending the imperial construction of race and the racial construction of empire. In the novel contexts of empire, new forms of race developed, often destabilizing existing racial formations in the process. While imperialists often sought to represent global power as the seamless "expansion" of the nation, empire in its formal and informal varieties often meant rupture and discontinuity. Never unitary even in its national frames, race-making in imperial settings was shaped by confrontations with new cultural groups, in unprecedented types of encounters, which raised original and often troubling questions about the character of the nation itself. Among other tasks, it had to organize and justify practices of rule, marking often unstable hierarchies that could legitimate, and calibrate, degrees of disenfranchisement and violence. While older racial idioms sometimes played a role in capturing these new realities, they frequently did so in translation, owing their eventual forms as much to newly developing "host" languages of difference as their older "guest" languages. Other occasions saw the self-conscious abandonment of earlier modes of race and the construction of entirely new racial ideologies and practices. The result was a multilevel pluralism of colonial racial formations, with diversity not only between nationally defined colonial systems but between colonies in a single nation's empire, and ultimately within individual colonies, where competing colonial agendas were organized by different racial visions and vice versa. Rather than being part of a homogenizing "colonial discourse," these distinct relational framings of colonizer and colonized might better be seen as particular imperial indigenisms, reflecting their culturally, politically, and historically specific settings.[39]

In its many manifestations, imperial race-making was a fundamentally gendered process, as has been highlighted in some of the richest new cultural histories of empire. Empire became the ground for reconstructing gender as well as racial politics, as men and women in metropole and colony competed for power. Colonial wars gave rise to new imperial-masculinist formations that measured "self" and "other" in degrees of power, honor, and physical courage. Imperial nationalists often refigured the nation in masculinist terms, finding critics of empire insufficiently "manly." Colonial state-building was itself a masculinist project that reconstructed patriarchy, grounding colonial hierarchies in the purportedly deficient masculinity of indigenous elites; its subjects were often imagined as the "children" of benevolent or disciplinarian "fathers." Metropolitan women often attempted to construct a woman's empire, asserting their rights by speaking on behalf of colonized women, often against colonized men. Gender was also remade by masculinist nationalists who were as eager to diagnose the vulnerabilities of their societies to colonial rule as they were to shore up the patriarchies it threatened. Imperial race-making and gender formation coalesced in preoccupations about purity, reproduction, and contamination, in the question of how the nation was to preserve itself in interactions beyond its borders. This preoccupation congealed in fears that white women would degenerate in the colonies, that white families could not reproduce themselves beyond the nation's borders, that nonwhite men migrating to the metropole would sexually threaten white women and the nation's racial integrity. As in the race-making to which it was closely attached, the gender formations of empire were neither exports nor generic colonial discourses, but contextual and contingent.[40]

Among the forces promoting the colonial reconstruction of race, perhaps none was so immediate as the agency and mediation of indigenous peoples. As scholars have often noted, the politics of empire did not involve "colonizers" and "colonized" peoples defined in this way before the fact, but rather consisted of the struggle to define the very boundary line between colonizer and colonized, as well as the relations across it. Marking, stabilizing, and institutionalizing this line was often complicated by the fact of physical resistance to colonial rule. But it was equally challenged by the accommodation and opposition of indigenous elites, who had their own quarrels with, and hopes for, colonialism. These elites brought their own understandings of themselves, their societies, and the broader world to the arena of colonial politics; as part of the intellectual labors of collaboration, they often interposed themselves as authorities between colonizing elites and the masses, providing elements of local knowledge that helped structure developing imperial-racial accounts, even as they rationalized their own privileged position in the social order. They were also, within limits, able to remake the emerging terms of colonialism in their own image. Elites' mediation and selective appropriation of colonial knowledge shaped their ideologies, finding diverse ways into projects of nation-building.

While partly determined by the actions of indigenous peoples, imperial race-making was never confined to the geographic or cultural space of the colony. Rather, empire became intertwined with national identities in the metropole, as colonial soldiers returned home laden with war, as domestic elites rationalized national-imperial sacrifice in terms of new and dangerous enemies, and as freshly constituted imperial publics—sometimes aware of themselves as such, other times not—debated the meanings of global power for the nation. Nor did "indigenous" peoples themselves remain indigenous: the colonial-capitalist incorporation of new regions destabilized local economies and facilitated transportation and communication linkages in ways that promoted out-migration not only to colonial cities but to other colonies and to the metropole. Imperial race-making came "home" both in the broadened imaginaries of metropolitan subjects and in their often undesired "domestic" encounters with colonized peoples. In both cases, the intersection of metropole and colony was often tense. Indeed, as colonial politics on the micro level consisted in the often problematic distinction of colonizer and colonized, imperial politics on the macro level involved attempts to distinguish metropole from colony. Understanding these historical developments means comprehending these spaces not as distinct and interacting but as mutually constitutive, part of what Mrinalini Sinha has called a single "imperial social formation," bound by creative and disruptive processes of differentiation.[41]

The impossibility of racial "export" and the reconstruction of race in colonial settings was sometimes witnessed and registered by anxious historical actors: Europeans in the colonial world inevitably confronted new, alien, and often threatening forms of difference they could not fully comprehend. Take, for example, John T. MacLeod's short story "The Sliding Scale," initially published in the *Philippine Free Press* and later in an anthology. MacLeod, a British subject, had been born in Canada and traveled to the Philippines in 1880 to work in a merchant house; according to a society biographer, he was one of the "representative men" of Manila, equally well-liked by Britons, Spaniards, and Filipinos.[42] As his writings illustrate, MacLeod was fascinated and troubled by the intermingling of "races"—and of racial formations—in the Philippines. "In the blending of the peoples, the admixture of the races, the play of the white and brown, there is presented the most fascinating study here extant," he wrote. MacLeod was especially intrigued by the figure of the "mestizo," both the Chinese mestizos who played a prominent role in the islands' economy and the American mestizos he expected would be the inevitable outcome of U.S. colonization. The theme presented him an exciting, perhaps even sexually exciting, undertaking, as it "pushes its fingers right down into the very roots of man's being—into his moral nature, the realm wherein the great tragedies of life are enacted, the realm wherein the deep undercurrents of our existence are forever surging to and fro."[43]

MacLeod's story "The Sliding Scale," set in the late nineteenth century, is about the difficulty and danger involved in recognizing race in the Philippines. It begins as the tale of a Chinese mestizo named José, the son of a Catholic Filipina and a prosperous Chinese merchant, who, in the interest of moving up in society, changes his name to the Spanish "Palma." José, nicknamed "Pepe," is "a bright lad, squat in stature, nose slightly flat and stubby, features somewhat irregular, but withal rather smart and presentable in appearance." Sent to England to study commerce and English at the age of nineteen, José settles into college and quickly adopts an English gentleman's dress and manners; "enveloped in an attractive glamour," he charms the lovely Adelaide, a professor's daughter. Wooing her as they overlook the Thames at one point, he notes the difference between the scene stretched before them, with its "strongly contrasted colors," and the land of his birth, where "nature has blended all shades of light and color as only nature can, in a manner which the art of man cannot possibly imitate."[44]

Adelaide is entranced, and they soon marry, but the honeymoon is short: showing off his wife like a piece of merchandise in Paris and slinking off into the city alone at odd hours, José gives Adelaide a "first glimpse of an oriental's attitude toward his wife," and "the first crack in the veneer of José's acquired polish" is exposed. Adelaide's situation worsens upon her arrival in Manila. At the docks, they are greeted by José's family, and it is only then, upon seeing José's father, that she recognizes her husband's race: he is "Chinese," a realization that nearly causes her to faint. Confusion and betrayal twist through her as she suddenly reassesses her husband: "Why had Pepe never told her that his father was a China-man? How did he come by his Spanish name? . . . She had read of half-brained missionary women who had married Chinamen—but for her the thought of her new relationship was too awful!"[45]

Adelaide is ushered into a cloistered life in José's family home, a shabby, dreary, and sullen place where she is under constant surveillance. Even during her only temporary escape, carriage-riding on the Luneta prome-nade near Manila Bay, she is stared at and marked by Filipinos as "Palma's English wife," and "she could imagine their making other remarks of a not altogether complimentary nature." But it is on one of these rides that she happens pleasantly, through a kind of racial kismet, onto Mr. Robert Ramsey, British commercial agent and a former London acquaintance. When Ramsey at first does not come calling, Adelaide is disappointed, "still in ignorance of the big social gulf existing at that time between the Europeans and the half breeds, so difficult to bridge over." Through a Filipino courier, however, Ramsey is able to sneak Adelaide a stiffly af-fectionate letter, and they come to meet regularly and clandestinely on Ramsey's boat, where Adelaide confides her loneliness, desperation, and fear. "'I can only go on and suffer,'" she cries. "'There's no escape but death.'"[46]

Shadows gather when José catches Adelaide at the end of a rendezvous (and a very chaste kiss), threatens to kill her, and in a rage, strikes her. She collapses, grows ill, and is nursed back to health by José's family, but a cholera epidemic sweeps through the area. Deceptively, José offers Ade-laide medicine and, too late, she realizes she has been poisoned. She screams out, naming her murderer, but "[t]he struggle was soon over, and what mortally remained of the once pretty Adelaide was but a mass of twisted, disheveled humanity in a heap," and to make things worse, "in the middle of a disordered bed." Without ceremony, Adelaide's body is tossed unmarked into a burial pit with thousands of others. But rumors of José's vile act spread, and he is compelled to move to Japan, where he takes the name Ikura and is naturalized as "a son of Nippon." His sympathies, however, remain Filipino. In fact, readers are told, he is credited as being "a recognized agent in Japan of the Filipino insurgents," and "with trying to enlist the sympathies of Japan in favor of his countrymen." Presumably, the author relates ominously, "he is still there ready to help in making any new trouble he can."[47]

"The Sliding Scale" opens a small window onto the historical perception of racial formations intersecting uneasily. Its narrative of mistaken racial identities, of dangerous male racial hybrids from the periphery who disguise their true identities in the metropole and threaten the racial-sexual purity of white female victims, bears a surface resemblance to Bram Stoker's *Dracula*, published thirteen years earlier.[48] It also draws on classic, cautionary miscegenation fables, warning of José and Adelaide's "disordered bed" and unimaginable offspring, would-be children of racial "light" and "dark." The consummation of their marriage is, and can only be, a poisoning. Faced with the cliff-edge of racial impurity, Adelaide's constitution—true to form—opts for virtue, and she expires, a lesson to readers.

But MacLeod's story used existing conventions to represent what he believed to be a problem distinct to the colonial Philippines, the collision between two incompatible racial formations. On the one hand, there is an "Anglo-Saxon" fixed standard of racial "purity" and aversion, in which individuals of a race both naturally cohere with one another and contend with other races, and racial essences are manifested by outward cultural signs; it is feminized to convey its innocence, purity, and vulnerability. On the other hand, there is the "sliding scale," or *mestizaje*—its aggression masculinized—in which racial lines are sacrificed to expedience, and cultural markers skid loosely back and forth over their "racial" origins: a Chinese merchant gains social advantage by taking a Spanish surname, his mixed-race son acquires a layer of English cultivation, and when it suits him, becomes Japanese. These latter maneuvers are associated not only with deception but with political revolution, the overturning of the social order itself. In the end, the racial scale of Mr. Ramsey, the exporter, fails; Adelaide is tragically subsumed within *mestizaje*: her body tossed among abandoned corpses, Adelaide's own carefully tended identity is also lost, "mixed" with thousands of others, unrecognizable.

Book Outline

In its explorations of race, empire, and the politics of recognition, this book contains six primary thematic emphases, each of which is highlighted in, if far from confined to, specific chapters. First of these themes is the Philippines' status as a twice-colonized country and the centrality of the Spanish colonial period for understanding Philippine-American colonialism. Specifically, it was Spanish colonial racial exclusions of the nineteenth century that fundamentally shaped protonationalist assertions, which I explore in Chapter 1. The Spanish colonial regime and society had been highly stratified from its advent. On the one hand, colonial privilege was marked by categories of territorial nativity (peninsular versus creole) and *mestizaje*, or "blood" mixture, between Spaniards, Chinese, and *indios*; on the other, there were divisions between the Hispanicized Catholic world and the unconquered world of animists and Muslims on the colony's frontiers. Racial exclusion became sharper in the nineteenth century, with "natives" denied representation in the Cortes after 1815 (alone among the remaining Spanish colonies) and closed out of religious academies and higher positions in the Philippine clergy, and Spanish colonial rule was defended increasingly in racial terms, using imperial-indigenist descriptions of the islands' inhabitants that cast them as "childlike," "savage," "indolent," and "superstitious." Spanish racist attacks, in turn, gave rise to criticism by those beginning to gather themselves under the term "Filipino." The Propaganda movement of young activists in Europe blasted Spanish racial disdain with criticisms of cynical ideological manipulation and with efforts to gain recognition of Filipino "advancement" and "civilization." This history was fundamental to early structures of Filipino nationalism and provided Filipinos a critical awareness of how racial politics might be used against their aspirations. At the same time, Filipino claims made in the name of Hispanic civilization pushed those who remained unconquered—animists and Muslims—outside of the emergent nation in the making.

A second element in colonial race-making was the Philippine-American War as the foundational moment of twentieth-century Philippine-American history. As I discuss in Chapter 2, the Philippine-American War developed into a "race war." The racialization of Filipinos by U.S. troops, however, was not a foregone conclusion. U.S. soldiers occupying Manila in late 1898 were, in some cases, prepared to see Filipinos as their rough equals and the Philippine Republic as a legitimate state. The outbreak of the war in February 1899 altered the structure of perception dramatically: faced with the necessity of redefining Filipinos as an enemy, U.S. soldiers racialized them with terms such as "gugu," the root of the later term "gook," as well as adapting older racial vocabularies. This process accelerated during the transformation of the war into a guerrilla struggle after November 1899, when the dispersion of the Filipino army and its disappearance into forests, mountains, and villages suggested to U.S. soldiers and policy makers the "savagery" of both Filipino soldiers and civilians. Filipino leaders shared the Americans' sense of guerrilla war as less than civilized but insisted that its use was tactical rather than racial. During the latter stages of the war, racialization facilitated a widening of violence that included the torture and killing of prisoners, indiscriminate destruction, and the "reconcentration" of rural populations into over-crowded village centers where disease claimed tens of thousands of lives. The war left a deep imprint on subsequent colonial state-building, which would proceed through a dialectic of violence and attraction. It also continued to shape future racial formations, establishing the versatile and persistent problem of "savagery" in Philippine-American relations.

Third is the role of Filipino-American collaboration in the making of the Philippine-American colonial state. Historians have long emphasized the crucial roles that indigenous collaborators played as mediators of colonialism at a variety of levels.[49] An attention to the complex and shifting links that tied specific Filipino elites to U.S. colonial officials has also characterized much of the recent literature on the political history of the American colonial period. These ties were also important to the reconstruction of race in the fragile and self-conscious "postwar" period, as I explore in Chapter 3. At the municipal, provincial, and insular levels, collaborating Filipino elites were essential to "pacification," mediating between U.S. colonial authorities and the Filipino masses, promising stability in exchange for access to new structures of colonial power. The civilian Philippine Commission and other U.S. officials turned to these elites for basic knowledge regarding the nature of Philippine society and history. At the same time, collaboration shaped the content of emerging racial formations: as the problem of how far Filipinos would be allowed to advance in the colonial state became paramount, race was mobilized to explain Filipino deficiencies and capacities and to narrate slow, gradual progress along lines of assimilation and tutelage. Where the war had foregrounded discourses of radical otherness, this was an elastic, inclusionary racism capable of subtle readjustment as long as an indefinite future could be colonized to contain it. The new racial formation also internalized wartime discourses of savagery, projecting them onto "non-Christians," especially Cordilleran animists and Muslims of the southern archipelago. The result was a bifurcated racial state in which distinct modes of colonial administration accompanied narratives of parallel colonial progress: Filipino Catholics, recast as "Christians" and "civilized" by their juxtaposition to "non-Christians," represented as "savage," were moving steadily, if indefinitely, ahead in evolutionary time under U.S. colonial control.

Fourth is the tension between metropolitan and colonial perspectives on empire. Scholars have long paid attention to disjunctures between the interests, agendas, and ideologies that opened up between metropole and colony within imperial systems. Tensions over the structure of authority, funding priorities, questions of legal coherence, and racial and cultural perceptions often drove deep wedges between colonial governments and the metropoles in whose name they ruled. These tensions are explored in my discussion of the Philippine exhibition at the 1904 Louisiana Purchase Exposition in St. Louis in Chapter 4. Philippine participation in the fair was initiated by the insular government as an exercise in colonial propaganda, an effort to persuade domestic U.S. audiences of a concluded war, of the benevolence of U.S. efforts, and of the bifurcated path of Filipino progress. The display's construction, however, revealed the limits of the emerging collaborative relationships upon which it depended. The exposition board's most difficult task proved to be translating its diverse messages, drawn from a radically different colonial context of inclusionary racism, into terms comprehensible to U.S. audiences in light of exposition conventions. While it sought to represent the sharply divided path of Filipino progress through separated "villages" of Christians and non-Christians and with marching Constabularymen and Scouts, the exposition board found that fairgoers reoriented these divergent tracks into a linear, progressive framework. Prior wartime images encouraged audiences to recognize only "savages" as Filipinos; this cast any "civilized" Filipinos that were recognized as such as the work of five years of U.S. colonialism. American "misrecognition" of Filipinos along these lines, alongside other tensions, would alienate rather than attract collaborating Filipino elites.

Fifth is the complex dialogue between colonial ideologies and nationalist mobilizations. The process by which nationalists absorbed and transformed colonial frameworks has by now become a staple of the historiography of nationalism. Scholars working in a number of colonial and postcolonial settings have demonstrated the ways in which nationalism was a "derivative discourse," reversing rather than entirely abandoning colonial idioms.[50] Chapter 5 explores the interaction between U.S. colonial ideologies and the Filipino nationalisms that engaged, challenged, and transformed them in the years surrounding the inauguration of the first Philippine Assembly in 1907. As Filipinos achieved promotions inside the colonial state, their "progress" heightened the question of their "capacity" along several different dimensions. U.S. colonial officials held that Filipino capacities—for labor, for production, for self-government—remained latent, but developing, under U.S. control. Filipino nationalists countered by arguing that their capacity had been demonstrated precisely by their collaboration in colonial state-building. Filipino "assimilation" also raised debates regarding the status of the Filipino "nation": U.S. colonialists claimed they were "building" a nation, especially through English-language education and a "material development" policy of export-oriented infrastructure. Filipino nationalists asserted that, under their auspices, the nation was reemerging out of the ashes of the revolution. Struggles during and after the founding of the Philippine Assembly highlighted the politics of national "representation" in several senses, as Americans and Filipinos struggled over both decision-making authority and the question of how to represent the nation symbolically.

Sixth is the intersection of the politics of colonialism, nationalism, and migration. Throughout the colonial world, imperialists faced the problem of "containing" their colonies in terms of human movement, of streamlining the outward movement of "civilizing" elements and the lateral, intercolonial movement of laborers, while protecting the metropole from threatening colonial refluxes.[51] Chapter 6 explores these issues from the era of World War I into the early 1930s. The mid-1910s saw a number of key transitions in Philippine-American colonial relations. Under Woodrow Wilson and the Democrats, Congress passed the Jones Act, which eliminated the Philippine Commission and promised "eventual independence" for the first time; the U.S. colonial bureaucracy undertook a "Filipinization" process that placed far more state power in the hands of Filipino elites. Postwar languages of "self-determination" fired new visions of independent Filipino nationhood. The political struggles surrounding these changes brought the racial politics of colonialism into sharp focus:

U.S. imperialists mobilized the image of "non-Christians," sometimes employing them as exemplars of incomplete civilization, but more frequently as the inevitable victims of "Christian" depravity in the absence of U.S. protection. Filipino nationalists often countered with nationalist-colonialist claims: civilized Filipinos would demonstrate their capacity for independence precisely through their ability to conquer, rule, and uplift the savages in their midst. Meanwhile, both the war and immigration-restriction acts of the early 1920s had spurred Filipino labor migrations to Hawaii and the mainland United States, which raised the specter—both on the West Coast and in Washington, D.C.—of a racial "invasion." The fear that the United States might be conquered by its own colony went to the heart of Philippine-American colonial history toward its close. To the extent that nativists formed part of the independence movement during this period, Philippine independence should be seen less as an early act of "decolonization" than as the triumph of an exclusionary racial formation over the colonial regime's inclusionary racial premises.

This work emphasizes the profound historical persistence of the Philippine-American War, an interpretation that runs against the grain of its oblivion in U.S. historical memory. The war's much-debated end point itself suggests the ways it overflowed officially declared temporal boundaries, yet the division of labor between military historians of the conflict and historians of colonial politics has tended to obscure connections between "war" and "peace." In strict terms of large-scale Filipino physical resistance to U.S. sovereignty, the war was ended in a highly piecemeal fashion, declared "over" several times before its official close on July 4, 1902. Colonial officials and Filipino revolutionaries both knew that many more battles would be fought, waged by the Philippine Constabulary—formally a civilian police force but whose main tasks were military—and those now labeled "ladrones," or bandits. The legacies of war would be a scarred countryside and the loss of family members to both disease and violence. The ongoing war that refused to end would shape the "postwar" government erected in its midst.

Even after a functioning hegemonic state had been assembled, however, the war continued haunting colonial politics at various levels of remove. Languages of aggressive "uplift" and benevolence that long outlasted the war should be seen not as expressions of inherent U.S. values—as they often are—but rather as direct responses to the wartime criticism of U.S. brutality, corruption, and immorality. The new icons of the colonial state were the inverse of wartime realities: English-speaking Filipino children as the shadow of unnumbered dead Filipino civilians; marching Constabularymen as the shades of invisible, elusive Filipino guerrillas. When U.S. colonial officials advanced an "official" nationalism to stave off more radical forms, it was profoundly shaped—one might almost say determined—by what they imagined as its frightening revolutionary antecedents. Filipino nationalists made selective use of the war, mobilizing its memory in their speeches in making claims against U.S. colonialism and for Filipino common sacrifice and struggle in the cause of freedom. Perhaps it was some memory of the U.S. invasion that inspired the nightmares of U.S. nativists in the 1920s: that if Filipinos were not excluded from immigration, hordes of Filipino laborers would ultimately conquer the United States.

While its canvas is broad, this study, like any other, is defined by its limits. In its attempt to reconstruct large-scale transpacific historical spaces, it by necessity largely neglects the divergent, local factors within Philippine provinces and municipalities that shaped colonial politics. While it attempts to establish interimperial connections between Philippine-American colonial history and European colonialism, it does not attempt a comparative analysis that would take these colonial empires as discrete "cases" whose structures might be delineated and juxtaposed. Similarly, this work does not explore either comparisons or connections between the Philippines and other formal U.S. colonies such as Puerto Rico, important work that is already under way.[52] The work is based on a wide variety of primary sources in both U.S. and Philippine archival and library collections, but they are nonetheless limited to Spanish- and English-language sources. These limits point in different ways to the vast future research that remains to be done and to which this work hopes to contribute.

The Philippines and the United States were, prior to the late nineteenth century, part of each other's "boondocks." This term, originally *bundok*, a Tagalog word for mountain or remote area, was brought into U.S. consciousness by soldiers returning from guerrilla war, layered with connotations of bewilderment and confusion. The existence of this term—for a liminal, border region—tells us something about the history that followed. The world crossed over into American English at the very moment that Philippine and U.S. histories became inexorably internal to each other. Its very presence in English suggests, in brief, precisely why neither Philippine nor U.S. history can afford to conceive of the other as boondocks, as marginal to their core concerns. Historians are only now beginning to trace the myriad complex transits that surround this small linguistic crossing, by moving beyond the conventional conceptual borders of the Philippines and the United States, which for over a century have not captured their connected histories. This work will have succeeded if it points the way toward an elusive goal: a history without boondocks.

Spanish Colonialism and the Invention of the Filipino

*In the conscience of everyone, with the exception
of those who for some type of atavism of schooling are seized
by antiquated preoccupations, there is the notion that genius
is cosmopolitan; that knowledge is not bound to any privileged
race; that color does not presume talent, just as the habit
does not make the monk.*

    La Solidaridad, 1889

*When [the Spanish colonial government] has to ask us
for something, it puts a human nature in our bodies, and
takes it away when we ask for representation in the Cortes,
freedom of press, rights, etc.*

    JOSÉ RIZAL, 1887

We begin our story not in Manila or Washington but in Madrid, beneath the trees of the Parque del Retiro, where, in summer 1887, the Spanish state put its largest remaining colony, rather defensively, on display before Spanish and European publics at a grand Philippine Exposition. In doing so, the Spanish state was participating in an emerging European imperial tradition, the use of colonial and metropolitan resources and institutions to mount elaborate spectacles that would simultaneously advertise national glory and sovereignty and colonial goods. But the exposition was also specifically attuned to Spanish and Philippine political realities. Liberal Overseas Minister Victor Balaguer had pressed for the exposition as a neomercantilist effort to interest Spanish investors and merchants in Philippine trade that was being increasingly lost to British and German companies. He was also eager to showcase the Philippines as a self-consciously modern colony, in an effort to challenge symbolically, if not politically, the overarching power of the Catholic friar orders that continued to monopolize power in the archipelago. The exposition's two ornate pavilions, one a Crystal Palace (modeled on London's

1851 Victorian exposition) and the other a Palace of Industry, were well stocked with geological, mineralogical, and meteorological displays that reflected Spanish scientific knowledge of the islands and, by extension, the colony's modernity and suitability for business. The exposition, for Balaguer, would deepen, widen, and tighten the fraying ties between Spain and its farthest imperial extension, ties that were seen as increasingly problematic in the wake of ongoing rebellions in Cuba. In retrospect, he recalled that the event had "rectified the opinion of some, opened new horizons for many, taught things that had been ignored," and "awakened curiosity and study." It had also, he believed, "embodied in the nation mutual sentiments of love between those islands and the metropolis."[1]

At least some visitors to the exposition were, however, not so persuaded that "mutual sentiments of love" had been awakened. Global integration was placing imperial spectacles in front of unanticipated and undesired audiences. By 1887, Madrid had, along with other European capitals, small "colonies" of elites from the islands, engaged largely in the pursuit of higher education in subjects closed to them in the Philippines itself. Although many of them were becoming versed in the very scientific discourses in which the exposition traded, these *ilustrado* (enlightened, educated) elites had been neither consulted in the making of the exposition nor invited to its formal events, facts that offended their sense of entitlement and honor. Demanding recognition, they felt themselves ignored and misrepresented. Most outrageous to some was the transport and display of approximately thirty actual "natives," housed in "typical" dwellings. This group, which contained several animists and Muslims, was widely seen as a deliberate effort by Spanish colonialists— despite the promise to "rectify" Spanish opinion—to promote images of the islands' backwardness and savagery. Even in anticipation of the event itself, Evaristo Aguirre, a creole from Cavite, suspected "a Machiavellian spirit set on domination and exploitation." Ministers would "take notes," journalists "invent witticisms, stories, and anecdotes," and missionaries lecture the public on the "docile, apathetic, and ignorant character of that people."[2]

The *ilustrados'* encounter with the Philippine Exposition was one decisive moment in a two-decade-long campaign for recognition, the subject of this chapter. The Philippines had been the Spanish Empire's great political exception from the 1830s onward, its inhabitants denied any representation in the Spanish Cortes, unlike Cuba and Puerto Rico. Even as Spain itself underwent political upheavals and liberal challenges, the islands continued to be ruled by a repressive politico-military state and the reactionary friar orders. Where it was challenged, the Philippines' political exceptionalism within the Spanish Empire was defended predominantly on racial grounds: if the Philippines was excluded from representation, it was because the islands' peoples were uniquely undeserving of it, its ostensibly Catholic *indios* (natives) mired in superstition, its "savage" *infieles* (infidels, i.e., animists and Muslims) entirely untouched by the saving hand of the church. By the late nineteenth century, however, the Philippines' isolation from liberal currents would be challenged by the *ilustrados*, who would argue for Philippine "assimilation," the political normalization of the islands within the Spanish Empire through the extension of metropolitan political and legal institutions, including representation in the Cortes.

Seeking Spanish rights, the *ilustrados* would chart and unravel the dense fabric of Spanish imperial racial formations that justified the status quo. This meant interposing themselves as authorities between the islands' peoples and the Spanish imperialists who deprecated them. Writers in what came to be known as the Propaganda movement would seek Spanish and broader European recognition of Philippine sociocultural development in ways that both undermined and confirmed Spanish colonial hierarchies. The Propaganda writers both satirized Spanish imperial racism and held Philippine peoples up favorably to some of its standards. Their starting point was that Spanish colonial illiberalism was the result— deliberate or not—of misrecognition. Where Spaniards saw lazy, primitive savages in need of military repression, Catholic evangelization, and coercive labor control, they should instead recognize the Philippines' peoples as "overseas Spaniards," their "civilization" illustrated by their education, artistic achievement, eloquence in Spanish, and loyalty to Spain. What Spanish imperialists called the "abyss" between the islands' peoples and Spaniards was bridged by the legend of a "blood compact," which bound the two through shared blood. This glancing, rather than frontal, attack on Spanish imperial racism, by predicating political rights on sociocultural features, would also exclude certain Philippine peoples from an "assimilated" Philippines. The *ilustrado* quest for Spanish recognition, in other words, delimited the boundaries of who would ultimately be recognized as "Filipino."

The energies of the Propaganda campaigners would have unintended consequences: when the activists encountered intensified Spanish racial-imperial defenses and failed to achieve their political goals, they would become increasingly alienated from Spain. When revolution broke out in the islands in 1896, its leaders would take up many of the concepts the reformist Propaganda movement had developed in defense of the islands' inhabitants, including the category of "Filipino" itself, in their effort to construct the "imagined community" of an independent Filipino nation. That identity would be transformed again by the search for international recognition of the Philippines as an independent republic.

Race and Spanish Colonialism

The dramatic Philippine transformations of the late nineteenth century had their roots in both metropolitan and colonial tensions. Beginning with its colonization of the archipelago in the early sixteenth century, the Spanish had ruled the Philippines as a political extension of Latin America, subject to the Laws of the Indies and extensive Catholic evangelization. In economic terms, the Philippines was treated primarily as an essential commercial entrepôt in the highly profitable galleon trade between China and Mexico, revenues from which funded the Spanish colonial state. External and internal shocks impacted upon and altered this system in the eighteenth and nineteenth centuries. The British takeover of Manila in 1763 demonstrated the relative weakness of Spanish control and of Spain's monopoly on Philippine trade. Spanish American independence in the first half of the nineteenth century dealt a crippling blow to Spanish mercantilism; Spain was unable to maintain its traditional monopolies and isolationist policies and was forced to open the Philippines to greater extraimperial commerce. At the same time, Spanish domestic politics in the first three-quarters of the century involved volatile shifts between liberal and reactionary regimes. Liberals in power challenged the authority of the Catholic religious orders, through their secularization and the confiscation of church property. But the loss of Latin America made liberals aware of the fragility of their remaining colonies and led to policies of retrenchment: the Philippines, which had had parliamentary representation in the Cortes during three constitutional periods prior to 1837, was excluded from representation subsequently. Unlike Spain's other colonies, Cuba and Puerto Rico, which would continue to be represented, the Philippines would, for the remaining six decades of Spanish rule, be the politico-legal exception, the last of Spain's colonies to be ruled through modified versions of the Laws of the

Indies and a series of "special laws" that pertained to no other part of Spain's dominion.[3]

Spanish colonial society in the islands by the nineteenth century was highly racially stratified, with colonial difference marked in terms of territorial nativity, *mestizaje* (blood mixture), and religious "civilization." On the one hand, racial difference was associated with territorial nativity, with "peninsular" Spaniards—those with bilineal Spanish ancestry and European nativity—at the pinnacle of colonial society. Philippine "creoles," or "Philippine Spaniards," blessed with bilineal Spanish ancestry but corrupted by their colonial births, were beneath them and often resentful of their lesser status. The ranks of the friar orders were drawn exclusively from both "Spanish" communities, which also monopolized—with few exceptions—all governmental positions above the level of *alcalde mayor* (mayor). A second mode of difference was measured in blood mixture. "Spanish mestizos," the children of Spanish men and *indio* women, were relatively few in number, compared with other mestizo groups, and would become prosperous through both landholdings and as economic middlemen between *indios* and European commercial houses, although they would also be objects of racial scorn and social exclusion. Chinese mestizos were far more numerous, with Chinese-*indio* intermarriage encouraged by Spanish authorities as a means of Catholic evangelization. By the late nineteenth century, they were prominent among the islands' economic elites, having taken advantage of their unique position between rural small producers and urban merchants to profit enormously from the growth of export trade. A third line of distinction divided those who were inside and outside Hispanic Catholic civilization. There were the Chinese, whose commercial success and resistance to conversion made them suspect to both Spanish authorities and *indios*. On the territorial frontiers of the Spanish colony, there were the *infieles*, the still-unconquered highland animists of Luzon, often collectively referred to as "Igorots," and the "Moros" of the south, Muslims whom Spaniards had named by borrowing a term used to describe the Muslims that Catholic Spain had fought in its reconquest of the peninsula. Those who were "inside" Hispanic Catholic evangelization and "unmixed" in blood, the masses of lowland peoples, were called *indios*, a term adapted from the New World context.[4]

Racial distinctions between these communities were embedded in, and defended by, the institutions of church, state, and market. The line between Spaniard and non-Spaniard was most sharply exercised in the realm of state or church positions. Racial lines also were institutionalized in racialized systems of taxation, forced labor, and economic exclusion. Regulations exempted both Spaniards and Spanish mestizos from the tribute, or *polo*, the annual, compulsory six-week period of labor on public works, which *indios* were forced to provide; Chinese mestizos were taxed double the rate of *indios*, and the Chinese higher rates still, with the latter community also banned from agriculture. The colonial courts racialized justice, requiring the testimony of six *indios* to balance that of one Spaniard. The racial origin of a defendant was to be taken into account as a complicating factor in guilt since, as the 1887 Penal Code put it, the offense of the guilty must be punished "and not the condition of inferiority that nature has endowed him with." Especially in urban areas, there were elaborate patterns of residential segregation. Before 1768, Spaniards were prohibited from residing among *indios* unless they were married to one; prior to the nineteenth century, only Spaniards and their permanent household servants were allowed to reside in Manila's walled Intramuros district, pushing mestizo elites into the suburbs of Binondo, Ermita, Trozo, and Quiapo. The Chinese were subjected to the strictest segregation, with mandated residence in *parianes* (ghettos) in Manila and other urban areas. Ghettoization was closely correlated with racialized violence, with Chinese *parianes* routinely attacked and destroyed in the eighteenth and nineteenth centuries. The racial politics of state position, taxation, labor, and residential segregation were emphasized in everyday rituals of deference and submission. Upon meeting or passing a Spaniard, non-Spaniards were to remove their hats as a gesture of submission; upon meeting a Spanish friar, they were to remove their hats, kiss the friar's hand, and kneel before speaking.[5]

The first struggles over racial-imperial exclusion involved parish appointments. The "protection" of the Philippines from liberal reform was the concession Spanish liberals made to the overarching power of the Catholic religious orders in the islands. Since the Spanish conquest, the friar orders had been the regime's principal representatives and the immediate face of colonialism before Spain's Philippine subjects, overseeing conscription, imprisonment, health conditions, elections, and other state functions. They maintained a monopoly on education in the colonies, emphasizing tertiary education in theology, philosophy, canon, and civil law. They were also among colonialism's chief economic beneficiaries, the landlords of much of the islands' valuable land. Because the liberals relied on the friar orders, the latter were exempted from liberal decrees that devastated the church's power in the metropole. These same exemptions also produced a heightened reactionary sensibility among the friars, who were able to imagine themselves as the last bastion of an unreconstructed order.[6]

In the late 1860s, conflict erupted when Philippine priests challenged friar supremacy over local parishes. Following the expulsion of the Jesuits from the Philippines in 1768, efforts had been made to replace Spanish religious parish priests with Philippine secular priests. But especially following Mexican priests' participation in the independence revolution, Philippine priests were viewed with suspicion and their parishes increasingly handed over to the Spanish friar orders. When the Jesuits returned in 1859, they were assigned at the expense of Philippine clergy, who lost wealthy parishes in Manila. A movement among the clergy, led first by Father Pedro Peláez and subsequently by Father José Burgos, led a campaign against the turnover of parishes.[7]

The priests' arguments resembled those made later by the Propaganda movement: Philippine priests were not corrupt, incompetent and disloyal, as the friars held, but responsible, intellectually capable, and dedicated servants of church and crown. "If in our days we do not see more Filipinos outstanding in learning," Burgos wrote in an 1864 "Manifesto of Filipinos," strikingly redefining a Spanish colonial term for creoles, "let this not be attributed to their character nor to their nature nor to the influence of the climate nor much less that of race, but rather to the discouragement which for some years now has taken possession of the youth." Why should native-born youth struggle toward the priesthood, Burgos asked, only to see their "most noble aspirations wither away under the destructive influence of scorn and neglect?"[8] The priests' campaign had been encouraged by the Revolution of 1868 in Spain, which brought reformist officials to power, but when reactionaries retook control in 1871, it met stiff reaction. When in January 1872 a mutiny broke out in the arsenal of Cavite, colonial authorities purged the islands of perceived subversives, deporting priests, lawyers, and businessmen and executing Burgos and his colleagues.

The 1872 repression both signaled and greatly exacerbated tensions between the Spanish colonial state and the growing *ilustrado* class. From the advent of Spanish conquest, Spanish colonial authorities had operated through *datus* (chiefs), who were appointed as *gobernadorcillos* (local governors) or *cabezas de barangay* (village heads), and in this capacity collected tribute, worked closely with parish priests on Catholic instruction and festivity, and coerced manpower for the Spanish armed forces and *corvee* labor system, or *polo*. Over time, these positions of local authority rotated among members of a well-defined elite class, closely tied to state authority: the *principalía*. As the Spanish sought to rationalize land policy through registration, the *principalía* was ideally positioned to become a powerful landed, as well as bureaucratic, class, particularly as export trade developed in the nineteenth century. While dependent upon the *principales*, the Spanish colonial state and friar orders also suspected their loyalty and ambition; the *principales* resented the limits placed on their promotion in the colonial state and the clergy and sought avenues for advancement. The lack of Spanish secular priests had resulted in the training of Philippine secular priests whose parishes had become, as Burgos's protest had shown, an important element of *principalía* power and identity.

The *ilustrados* emerged as the urban, educated element of the *principalía* in the late nineteenth century. This new class was made possible by the Educational Reform Law of 1863, which provided for a system of compulsory primary education with free instruction in Spanish language and grammar, Christian doctrine, arithmetic, geography, agriculture, music, the history of Spain, and courtesy. These schools were administered by parish priests and became another mode of *principalía* power and mobility; *gobernadorcillos* helped monitor them, and *principal* families contributed to their construction. By the 1870s, the Spanish tertiary educational system had also expanded, with new colleges of medicine and pharmacy, for example, enabling young *principales* to pursue educations in Manila and to enter the professions, much in demand in the rapidly urbanizing world of the capital. This younger generation defined its elite status less in terms of traditional state and landed power than by its education, urbanity, cultivation, and "civilization."[9]

The growing friction between *ilustrado* aspirations and Spanish exclusions can be witnessed in the early career of the brilliant Tagalog physician, scholar, novelist, and essayist José Rizal. Rizal had been born to a wealthy and educated family in Calamba, sugar growers on land rented from the Dominicans. The family had ties to Burgos, and Rizal would attribute his own developing consciousness to the post-1872 repression. Rizal's extraordinary scholarly, literary, and linguistic talents would emerge early during his studies at the Jesuit Ateneo Municipal. In 1880, at age nineteen, he won a prize for his poem "To the Youth of the Philippines" in a literary contest sponsored by the Artistic-Literary Lyceum of Manila, open only to *indios*.

In the poem, Rizal praised the rising generation, whose "prodigious genius" was the "fair hope of my fatherland!" This fatherland was, importantly, not Spain but the Philippines. In that "ardent region," Spaniards, with "pious and wise hand," offered a "resplendent crown," not to what *ilustrado* reformers would later call the islands' "overseas Spaniards" but to what Rizal called "the son of this native soil."[10]

But winning cultural recognition only heightened a sense of political exclusion. The following year, Rizal triumphed in another literary contest, this one open to the islands' population as a whole, beating various peninsular journalists and friar professors. At the award ceremony, Governor-General Primo de Rivera apparently presented Rizal with a gold ring, awarded to "one who had honored Spain in this distant land." Walking one subsequent evening, however, Rizal had failed to salute a passing lieutenant of the Civil Guard, who then struck and wounded him. Rizal had indignantly gone to the palace of the same governor-general that had honored him to demand justice but was rebuffed. The lesson would remain vivid. Cultural recognition and political power did not connect: even an *indio* who triumphed over *peninsulares* in literary contests could be attacked with impunity by any petty Spanish state thug.[11]

Travel, Comparison, and Criticism

Such encounters were not confined to Rizal. During these years, Spanish authorities suspected indigenous elites of subversion and insurrection and subjected them to harassment and persecution. At the same time, elite Philippine families were becoming increasingly aware of the limits of the colonial educational system in a world of modernizing industry and commerce. Together these factors contributed to an *ilustrado* strategy of exit: the educational, economic, and political aspirations of *ilustrado* youth would be pursued in Europe. Cut off from "civilization" by the friars, the *ilustrados* would follow it to its source, inventing a European-Philippine world in the process. This out-migration was enabled by advances in steamship technology that joined Europe and Southeast Asia in new ways. The opening of the Suez Canal in 1869 had greatly shortened the voyage between Spain and the Philippines, for example. The old route from Barcelona had taken the traveler through Cadiz into the Atlantic, down the west African coast, around the Cape of Good Hope, and eastward across the Indian Ocean, taking approximately four months. The new route cut directly through the Mediterranean into the Indian Ocean, reducing the trip to just four weeks. Speedier travel brought new liberal and radical influences to the Philippines—in the form of Spanish exiles—and brought aspiring *ilustrados* to Europe.[12]

Travel did not simply transplant or extend *ilustrado* consciousness but transformed it. As some noted, travel itself could loosen one's conceptual categories and make one's perceptions of the world, and of oneself in it, temporarily molten. "What emotions, such varied sensations agitate the heart at every step when one travels in a strange and unknown land," Rizal marveled in an 1882 essay entitled "Travels." "There everything is new: customs, languages, faces, edifices, etc., everything worthy of observation and meditation." Travel could give rise to a "revolution" in perception: through it, one became able to "examine up close that which one had previously judged without seeing." Travel potentially gave one critical traction by folding multiple societies into an expanded frame of reference, summoning what Rizal would call "the specter of comparisons." At the same time, it lent the traveler independent authority and made possible the forging of one's own standards of recognition. "[A]t one stroke," through "direct observation and firsthand knowledge," one "ceased to be the echo of the opinions of others, in order to express one's own."[13]

While travel might melt down one's perceptions, *ilustrados* hoped to recast them in a specifically European mold. On one level, *ilustrado* travel to Europe was a dramatically widened extension of earlier elite patterns: rural elites had long sent their sons from the provinces to Manila—the insular metropole—for both education and social prestige. But travel to Europe was also different, not merely a form of political escape but of *ilustrado* self-realization. In the *ilustrados'* imagination, Europe would be the Philippines' one free island. Study in European universities would provide them the technical skills with which to modernize the Philippine economy. Cultivation in European cities would transmit skills of bourgeois self-presentation necessary to gain both personal and political recognition. Europe beyond Spain would supply a fulcrum from which to criticize Spain from within "civilization."

For Rizal, the meanings of Europe had become clearer with the aid of an American interlocutor. Leaving Paris on July 4, 1889, following a visit to the Paris Exposition, Rizal found himself crushed into a tiny, overheated train compartment with three Americans, two Frenchmen, and an Englishman. Two of the Americans were silent, but the third, "with the appearance of an American humbug," spoke "for the two and for himself." This man, with a "boastful mien," editorialized constantly throughout the

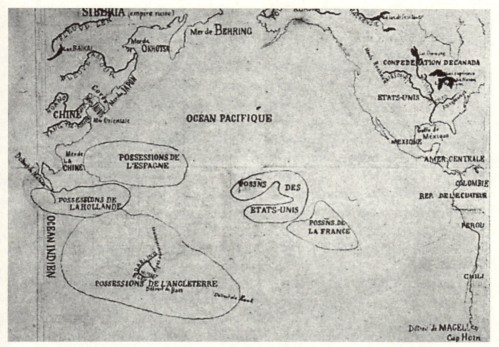

This hand-drawn map of the Pacific by José Rizal illuminates one corner of the cosmopolitan consciousness of the scholar and activist. Travel provided Rizal and other ilustrados the means to reimagine themselves and the Philippines in a global context. In this map, Rizal reveals a preoccupation with a multi-imperial landscape of Asia and the Pacific that includes Dutch, German, British, French, Spanish, and U.S. colonies; it can be seen as an accompaniment to the 1889–90 essay "The Philippines a Century Hence," in which Rizal reviewed the chances that another foreign power would take the islands following the fall of Spain, including what he considered the remote possibility of a U.S. colonization of the Philippines. From Craig, Lineage, Life and Labors of José Rizal.

trip. He had found everything in Paris "unsatisfactory": the "exposition, Eiffel Tower, streetcars, omnibus, cafés, restaurants, buildings, etc." It had been "nothing comparable with New York." To his chagrin, Rizal found the nation in the man. Rizal had recently crossed the United States and had observed "more than once," for example, that "the North American is wont to use hyperbolic language," though "not as much as the Spaniard": Andalucía was "the *most beautiful country* in the world," for example. When Rizal's companion complained that St. Paul in London was "'the dirtiest place in the world I have ever seen,'" Rizal observed wryly that "he must have seen little of the world and even of his own country," for filthier places could be found "without going outside New York." Rizal was beginning to be "annoyed by the fury of the traveler" and was going to relate "what I have seen and endured in America," when "by magic" the American stopped talking. Rizal appears to have seen all the Americans with him through the lens of science fiction, noting that they had "long beards exactly like those I saw as a child in the illustrations in the book of Jules Verne." But at this moment, he whimsically imagined, of his antagonist, that "my man's verbosity, being a good Yankee, came from the steam of a boiler inside his body." Indeed, Rizal envisioned him as "a robot created and hurled to the world by the Americans, a robot with a perfect engine inside to discredit Europe and make the Great Republic triumph, a machine fed with the very steam of locomotives, etc."[14]

Rizal used the occasion of the American's silence to launch into probing self-reflection on the meanings of Europe for him. Why had he felt so compelled to defend France, whose people had slighted him in other ways? "Is it the blood of Quixote that boils in me which drives me to defend my very enemies when I see them unjustly attacked?" he asked himself. While Rizal speculated that it might have been the "coffee or chicory," the incident also suggests how profound an investment Rizal and other *ilustrados* had in European civilization, despite their criticisms. The crass American "robot" had provided Rizal one point of triangulation between the Philippines and Europe: confronted with American disdain of Europe, Rizal could be Europe's defender, responding from "within." As he had hoped, travel across North America had also allowed Rizal to haunt both Europe and the United States with his "specter of comparisons." From this "cosmopolitan" vantage point, the American's perspective collapsed into pathetic provincialism.[15]

For *ilustrados*, "specters of comparison" would provide critical tools with which to undercut claims of Spanish colonial greatness. If the crass

American's robotic task had been to discredit Europe, *ilustrado* tactics often involved using the rest of Europe to discredit Spain. In particular, they looked to the British Empire as a model of benevolent, liberal colonialism, a model reinforced by the *ilustrados'* use of Hong Kong as a political refuge since the repressions of 1872. Britons appeared to pay attention to their colonies, unlike Spaniards. "There is no English newspaper that does not dedicate some columns daily to the movement of its possessions," read an editorial in the Propaganda newspaper *La Solidaridad*. "[T]he day is rare wherein they do not discuss some matter that directly affects Britannic subjects on the other side of the ocean." Indeed, Spain's European rivals were developing what ought to have been Spain's own colonial resources in the Philippines. "The British press and that beyond the Pyrenees dedicate brilliant pieces to the fertility of that soil," read the founding editorial of *La Solidaridad*. While "Spain sleeps, all its agricultural, industrial, and commercial interests there, with the exception of those of a monastic character, are defeated by foreign commerce."[16]

This critical comparison was paralleled by Spanish colonialists' comparisons of their own methods to those of rival powers, which attempted to explain, diagnose, and remedy Spain's global decline relative to the rest of Europe. Although not in isolation, the preeminent British Empire attracted much of this agonized admiration. Some Spanish imperialists saw in the British Empire the successful commercial exploitation of colonies. Others emphasized the more sustained preparation of British colonial civil servants, based on actual knowledge of colonial conditions. According to the columnist Pablo Feced, "[t]he English and the Dutch study and familiarize themselves with the races they dominate"; the Philippines, by contrast, was "not well-known in Europe nor even in our own peninsula." Others saw in the British Empire appropriately repressive and autocratic regimes that had lessons for apparently lax Spanish colonial practices. One Spanish writer was quoted as approving of the policy of Britain's Southeast Asian colonial officials who "fix everything . . . [with] the *stick*" and invited *ilustrado* activists on a hypothetical walking tour of these British colonies, where "they would have seen chain-gangs . . . fixing the streets to the rhythm of blows by policemen."[17]

While animated by hopes for Spanish recognition, *ilustrados* were forced to confront a popular Spanish insistence on their otherness that was shocking and painful. According to many, metropolitan Spaniards did not recognize the *ilustrados* as "overseas Spaniards" to whom they were tied by language, religion, and nationality; when Spaniards did, they often failed to recognize this status as conferring either rights or respect. On the contrary, the *ilustrados* encountered numerous instances of insulting racist ridicule. The Philippines, alongside other colonial themes, often cropped up comically in theaters, coffeehouses, social halls, and games.[18] "When the dictionary is exhausted of Cuban resources, of the question of tangos, blacks, little black women, and mulattoes, the customs for evoking laughter are directed, it seems, to the Philippines," wrote Antonio Luna in his bitterly satirical "Madrid Impressions of a Filipino." Luna described the everyday marking of his racial difference in the metropole. "My pronounced Malayan build . . . excites the curiosity of the sons of Madrid in a flagrant way," he wrote. A young seamstress "turns her head two or three times to look at me and to utter, in a voice loud enough to be heard: Jesus, how horrifying! He is Chinese. He is an Igorot." Boys small and large, "not content with this," shouted "like savages Chinese!—Little Chiiinese!—Igorot!!" Lurid, racist Spanish attention was a constant, pressing reality. "In the theaters, in the promenades, in gatherings," he wrote, "everywhere always the same general inspection of my person, the smile of mockery mixed with the half-arrogant, half-stupid stare." In that moment, Luna ceased to recognize Spain as part of Europe, "doubting that I live in the capital of a European nation" and imagined himself instead in "Morocco, in the dangerous districts of the Riff."[19]

Such ridicule produced a highly self-conscious sensibility among overseas *ilustrados* and placed high stakes on the everyday politics of self-presentation. As colonial subjects in the metropole, eager to gain recognition as overseas Spaniards, they would reflect and act on these pressures in different ways and to varying degrees. They would move uneasily within the boundaries of racist discourses, exemplary of their "race" before the eyes of a curious and skeptical Spanish public, even as they attempted to undermine Spanish racial assumptions. Most overseas *ilustrados* embraced the role of exemplars: as evidence of the Philippines' civilization, what better "exposition" than they themselves? As individuals, their educational, literary, and artistic achievement, social graces, manliness, and honor would, they believed, bear witness to a broader capacity for assimilation, equal rights, and political participation.

But this task of representation came with costs, which at least one writer depicted as a kind of feminine anxiety: only men granted recognition, while it was women who struggled to achieve it. When one *La Solidaridad* editorial set out to describe "that disorganized move-

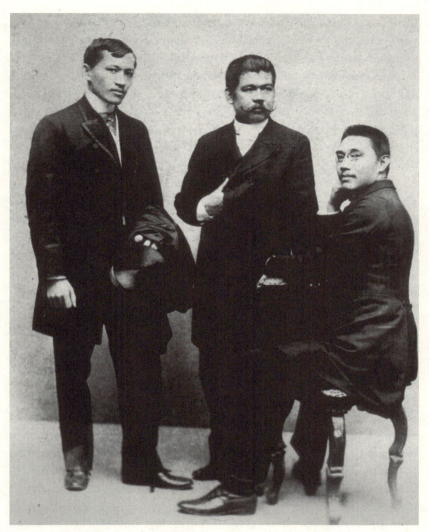

This late nineteenth-century portrait of three principal figures involved in the overseas journal *La Solidaridad*, José Rizal, Marcelo H. Del Pilar, and Mariano Ponce (from left to right), conveys a powerful sense of *ilustrado* manhood, bourgeois self-stylization, and "civilization." Like the journal itself, the portrait presented a challenge to Spanish imperialists who represented the inhabitants of the islands as "savage" and incapable of exercising political power in either the Philippines or the Spanish Cortes. Reproduced with permission, from the private collection of Ramon N. Villegas.

ment of a people which begins to emerge from its ancient existence to take part . . . in the concert of civilization," it tellingly described the Philippines as a debutante. The Philippines, represented by the Filipino colony in Europe, was like "a young woman making preparations to attend a grand ball: her activity is indefinite." Specifically, her "desires and aspirations" were directed toward presenting herself in "a dignified manner to that great world," although she was "uncertain of the ways and means," and "from there arises her vacillations."[20]

Although their actions were not "indefinite," expatriate *ilustrados* embraced a variety of strategies to achieve recognition before Spanish and European publics. They sought concrete ties to liberal political figures that might aid their cause. Liberal figures in the Overseas Ministry, while reliant on the friars, were also eager to undercut what they viewed as their overbearing power. *Ilustrados* in Spain cultivated these connections in public organizations such as the Asociación Hispano-Filipino, as well as in the ranks of Spanish Masonry, a key institutional site of nineteenth-century Spanish liberalism. Masonry in Spain and *ilustrado* activism would be closely linked, with *ilustrados* joining lodges with Cubans and Puerto Ricans, as well as founding a predominantly *ilustrado* lodge called "Revolución." Masonry provided *ilustrados* with organizational ties to Spanish liberals and officials; Propagandists would both circulate reform petitions inside the lodges and send them to key ministry officials whom they addressed as Masonic brothers. The order may also have supplied a vision of antiracial community: while *ilustrados* organized their own lodges in Spain, they also, importantly, were members of predominantly Spanish lodges from which they had been excluded in the Philippines.[21]

Ilustrado activists also widened the potential circle of sympathizers through extensive and ambitious publishing enterprises, in the form of Spanish-language or bilingual Spanish-Tagalog pamphlet literature and newspapers. This effort began with the short-lived 1882–83 *España en Filipinas* but intensified with the arrival in Barcelona of Marcelo H. Del Pilar, agent to Spain of the Manila-based committee of Propaganda. With others, Del Pilar founded *La Solidaridad*, a "Democratic Fortnightly" published in Barcelona and subsequently in Madrid between 1889 and 1895. The newspaper drew on, and provided a literary and political platform for, the greatest talents within the overseas *ilustrado* community, with Del Pilar its editor, Rizal a frequent contributor, and dozens of correspondents from Spanish cities and elsewhere in Europe. *La Solidaridad* was an expression of *ilustrado* liberalism and hopes for assimilation, a Spanish-language vehicle for *ilustrado* argument and eloquence in an uncensored environment that was made to stand in stark contrast to the repressive colonial regime. Meant to enfold sympathetic Spaniards and *ilustrados* into an imagined community, its pages were populated with supportive Spanish and European liberals. It was self-consciously cosmopolitan: while its editorials focused largely on Spanish parliamentary debates on the status of the Philippines, its news columns carried items from the rest of continental Europe, from the United States, and through telegraph relays from the Filipino colony in Hong Kong, from the Philippines itself. Its circulation also radiated outward from Barcelona and Madrid, to Filipino colonies elsewhere in Europe, and ultimately to Hong Kong and the Philippines, where bribes and other strategies moved it past Spanish censors.[22]

These publications ably inserted *ilustrado* expertise into what even many Spaniards admitted was a stunning metropolitan ignorance of the archipelago. Victor Balaguer had lamented that "Spain did not even know" the Philippines, while it was at the same moment the subject of "persevering studies" in "foreign lands." Journalists and scholars who published works on the Philippine Exposition often conceded that they described the Philippines against an almost completely empty backdrop. D. E. Maisonnave, in his conclusion to a popular newspaper guidebook to the exposition, wrote that those who had not been to the islands had, prior to the event, only "a vague idea" of the Philippines. The reason, he believed, had been that "the criteria of those writers that have spoken of that part of our territory are so opposed" that it had made it "difficult to see and get to know" it. Spanish physical anthropologist Manuel Antón lamented that "not even a single insignificant fact" could be presented regarding the islands' anthropology. While Spain's Museum of Natural History had only "a few dozen crania and some photographs," those of Paris and Dresden had "thousands of specimens of Philippine anthropology." The vagaries of Antón's own scientific annotations reflected this gap: the islands contained, for example, "four distinct races, more or less confused and mixed at some points."[23]

Expatriate *ilustrados* were among the most persistent critics of Spanish "ignorance." "[M]y surprise knew no bounds before the complete ignorance that these people generally have of the Philippines," wrote Antonio Luna. "There are newspapers which mention with the greatest geographical certainty: 'Our Asiatic possessions, our colonies on the Asian continent,' ideas similar to those of that minister who mistook the badly named *indios* (natives) of the Philippines for Indians of the Pampas." Those who were slightly more informed would "dare to digress upon tobacco, abaca (for abaka), the friar, or the Igorot, or would make improvised speeches about the 'exuberant natural resources of those virgin lands' and would introduce the 'If I were there' plan to modify the Spanish colonial administration, etc., etc." Luna found himself at one point playing jokes on a dim priest by claiming to be from the Philippines, "near China, province of Japan, north of Siberia." Rizal concurred, writing home in 1883 of Spaniards' "false knowledge" of the islands, with many people "so ignorant" that it was "not strange that they take us for Chinese, Americans, or mulattoes." Many people, "even the young students," did not know "if the Philippines pertains to the English or the Spanish." One person had apparently "asked one of our countrymen if the Philippines was very far from Manila." The fiery orator and correspondent Graciano López Jaena complained that "[o]ur possessions in Oceania" were "unfortunately, little known here [in Spain]," with few even able to "recognize them on the map." Most people believed the Philippines to be "located on the American continent" or to be "a fiefdom of the Chinese Empire." The sheer distance, he speculated, and "the almost absolute ignorance that prevails with respect to the Archipelago" had allowed "certain pens to write and relate strange, stupendous things about the Spanish people beyond the seas."[24]

Confronting Race

But if the Spaniards were ignorant, they also held up as experts metropolitan racists whose vitriol against Filipinos was matched only by that of the friars. Spanish colonial ideology would rely on imperial-indigenist representations of the Philippine population that rooted and justified Spanish rule in Filipinos' own failings. Most prominent among the architects of Spanish imperial-indigenism was the "certain pen" to whom López Jaena referred, the columnist Pablo Feced Temprano, pen-named "Quioquiap," one of the Spanish reading public's chief sources on things Philippine in the late 1880s. Having fought against the Carlists, Feced had left for the Philippines in 1884 to take charge of a farm in Camarines Sur, owned by his older brother, a magistrate and *alcalde mayor*. Beginning in 1885, he began contributing essays with his impressions of Philippine society, culture, and politics to the *Diario de Manila* and to the republican Madrid newspaper *El Liberal*, many of which he would gather into an 1888 collection, *The Philippines: Sketches and Brushstrokes*, published in Madrid. Feced's perspective in the essays is that of an embittered settler, impressed only by the sheer backwardness around him, hassled by Spanish officialdom, but, most of all, surrounded by his racial inferiors. In tone, he was a sort of Spanish Rudyard Kipling, an ironic, on-the-ground authority, combining venomous racism against Philippine "natives" with satires of Spanish colonial society and governance, especially where it tended toward "assimilationism." Indeed, Feced's work should be seen as a response to a rising assimilationist campaign: if his humor conveyed a certain light confidence, his virulence and frequent attacks on assimilation suggest embattlement.[25]

While racism runs in a thick vein through his writing, Feced's major premises appeared in the 1887 essay "Them and Us." In it, he describes natives of the Philippines as radical others. When naive Spaniards arrived in the Philippines (including each new governor-general), he wrote, they often recognized Filipinos as rough equals and dismissed obvious signs of difference between themselves and "natives," saying, "The Filipino is a Spaniard; he is our compatriot." But this sensibility did not last long once they had "placed their foot in the dirty and deserted streets of the Pearl of the Orient." The small size of the islands' men and their hairlessness relative to Spaniards showed them to be children lacking in virility; their nakedness and agility made them monkeylike; as laborers they were indolent; as thinkers they were superstitious. Feced called on racial anthropology to authenticate "the anthropoid ancestors of these people." Everyday observation, confirmed by natural science, pointed to an enormous and insurmountable "abyss between *them* and *us*."[26]

But to Feced's frustration, these facts of nature were receiving less and less political respect. Take, for example, the Philippine Exposition itself, whose goal had been "that the Spaniard get accustomed to seeing in the Filipino nothing *but a brother*" and that Filipinos learn to see in Spain "a caring mother," struggling to "elevate them to the height of the most cultured and civilized peoples." Spanish officials had been misled by their own ignorance and by the deceptive "works of propaganda" mounted by the *ilustrados*, who had "ignore[d] at least three-quarters of the *indios*" on display at the exposition. The vast majority of these *indios*, he maintained, had had "no idea what culture and civilization are," nor did they "suspect that they are our brothers." Under Propaganda influence, he noted with alarm, negligent Spanish officials were failing to enforce racial hierarchy.

While "[c]onventional and artificial law" could attempt "to erase those differences," he cautioned, nature was "unopposable in its power" and "throws to the ground every officious edifice."[27]

AS LONG AS THE Propaganda project was oriented toward assimilation, its central challenge was to achieve recognition by undermining the racial logic of Spanish colonial exclusion.[28] It was a mark of the determination and intellectual vitality of Propaganda writers that their criticisms took many forms, exploiting the numerous internal tensions and inconsistencies in the ideological fabric of Spanish colonial rule. Political inclusion, *ilustrados* hoped, could be achieved by aligning Philippine "facts"—to which they believed they had unmediated access—to Spanish sociocultural criteria. Perhaps metropolitan Spaniards might recognize the islands' inhabitants on the basis of *ilustrado* proficiency in Spanish or the success of Catholic evangelization. Perhaps they would recognize the *ilustrados'* bourgeois manners and conspicuous consumption. With sufficient evidence of this kind, the claims of racial-imperial exclusion would, in theory, crumble. While they sought recognition that they believed would lead to enfranchisement, overseas *ilustrados* struck out against Spanish racism with a range of arguments.

Some Propaganda writers confronted Spanish racism dismissively: racial thinking was simply outdated. For one *La Solidaridad* editorialist, racism was the artifact of an era thankfully left behind by the evolutionary march of progress. The belief that "genius is cosmopolitan" was "[i]n the conscience of everyone," excepting "those who for some type of atavism of schooling are seized by antiquated preoccupations." This majority, he wrote, held that "knowledge is not bound to any privileged race; that color does not presume talent, just as the habit does not make the monk." Del Pilar observed similarly that "[i]n these times of culture," it was "needless to talk about the relations of anthropological superiority and inferiority." What Del Pilar called the "constant manifestation" of the "superiority of races taken for inferior," as well as the "inferiority of superior races," made for an "indestructible logic" that undermined "unjust past depictions of indolence."[29]

Propaganda writers also pointed to inconsistencies in the political application of Spanish racial ideologies as evidence of their false universalism. Del Pilar observed wryly that while Spanish exclusions from citizenship were meant to apply to Filipinos as a race, they were in fact territorially exercised, since a Filipino traveling to Cuba, Puerto Rico, or Spain could exercise political rights there, "in spite of his alleged primitive state." In an ironic May 1887 editorial, Rizal presented a Spanish colonial problematic torn between the necessities of denying and conceding *indios'* basic humanity. Different authorities could not agree, in brief, on whether to recognize Filipinos or not. On the one hand, there was the much-cited authority Father Gaspar de San Agustín, who "only concedes us half a soul, saying that we are the descendants of monkeys." The problem was that "[o]ur most excellent governors are not of the same opinion." These officials taxed *indios* and exacted military service from them, "and we die for the government almost in the same way as other men who are acknowledged to possess a soul." If Filipinos were soulful enough to be sacrificed in Spain's colonial wars, "unfortunately . . . some idealists believe that the soul's existence creates an exigency for certain rights." Rizal had captured the arbitrary and contradictory character of the Spanish Empire's politics of recognition: "When it has to ask us for something, it puts a human nature in our bodies, and takes it away when we ask for representation in the Cortes, freedom of press, rights, etc."[30]

While such responses challenged race at the level of theory, Propaganda writers also gathered empirical evidence of the high "civilizational" achievement of so-called inferior races, including Filipinos. Introducing a new feature entitled "Celebrated Filipinos," *La Solidaridad* editorialized that "it wounds us to our very soul to see how the sons of that vast Philippine Archipelago have been ridiculed and outraged, negating their every intellectual capacity." They had been regarded as "inept and incapable of any culture and process, incapable of education, anthropoids, quadrupeds, grown-up children with thin bodies and thin wit, pygmies without energy, etc., etc." Even worse, "those who continue insulting us," the friars, were "the very same people called upon to defend us and to elevate us to the height which we justly deserve." Against these discourses, the new feature would present "in broad strokes, the life and contracted merits of the Filipinos who have most distinguished themselves among others."[31]

It was a measure of *La Solidaridad's* cosmopolitanism that its editors found evidence of the merits of "inferior" races in far corners of the world. It found an ally, for example, in Frederick Douglass, whose biography, reported through relays in New York, was summarized in a report following Douglass's death in 1895. True to the dominant U.S. interpretations of Reconstruction at that moment, the account owed something to contemporary American white supremacy, emphasizing freed peoples' "acts of savagery" upon emancipation. But the biography was also a warning to Spaniards, implicitly casting potentially rebellious *indios* in the role of enslaved African Americans. Treated "like dogs," denied education (as were Filipinos), the slaves had eventually given "free rein to their long-suppressed passions of vengeance and hatred." Douglass had argued that without education or citizenship, no other result was possible, "convincing even those most opposed to negroes." Douglass, in other words, was an African American *ilustrado*, leader of his own Propaganda movement, arguing for assimilation before his own colonial overlords.[32]

Ilustrados also often sought recognition in civilizational accomplishment, especially in the fine arts. When two *ilustrado* painters, Juan Luna y Novicio and Felix Resurrección Hidalgo, won prizes at the 1884 Exposition of Fine Arts in Madrid, for example, the victory was broadly symbolic for overseas *ilustrados* and their Spanish allies. A celebration, hosted by the Tagalog writer and socialite Pedro Paterno, was attended by Spanish liberals, republicans, and leftists, and telegrams of congratulations sent from the development and overseas ministers were read. The evening's centerpieces, however, were toasts by López Jaena and Rizal that turned the artists' victories into vindications of Filipino ability. López Jaena stated that "[t]he brush of Luna and the palette of Hidalgo have given one more irrefutable proof that ability and genius are not the exclusive patrimony of those races who call themselves superior and who make a boast of being the depositories of intellectual capacity, and of their development in civilization."[33]

Rizal was more subtle and less direct. The victory belonged both to the Philippines—who had "given the precious stones"—and to Europe, which had "provided the polish to them." The banquet was an expression of "that mutual embrace of two races who hold each other in love and affection," united for four centuries and looking forward to their fusion into "one single nation in the spirit, in their duties, in their outlook, in their privileges." But if Rizal's address appeared more conciliatory, it was simultaneously more subversive, imagining a Philippine future without Spain. He flattered his colonizers with their evaporation, speculating that if Spain's flag "should disappear," "her memory will remain, eternal and imperishable." After all, he asked, "[w]hat effect does a piece of red and gold cloth have, what can guns and cannons do, where a sentiment of love and affection does not spring forth; where there is no fusion of ideas, unity of principles, concordance of opinions?"[34]

If, for the Propaganda writers, people of color had shown superior achievement, racial hierarchies were also undermined by the critical, empirical study of European societies. As they struggled to achieve recognition from the larger world, *ilustrados* overseas learned something traveling colonial subjects would learn everywhere: it was easier for imperialists to maintain the fiction of the metropole as utopia at a distance of thousands of miles than close at hand. After all, the imperial politics of recognition only worked as long as the empire could live up to its own standards. When Propaganda writers reversed a Spanish maneuver—generalizing about a society from the servant classes—imperial pretensions dissolved. "Most Spaniards, priests as well as officials, judge us according to the behavior of the servants, etc., . . . with whom they deal," Rizal wrote to his friend and fellow Propaganda writer, the Austrian anthropologist Ferdinand Blumentritt in August 1888. "Heaven help me! If I had to judge Spaniards by what I have seen in Madrid of servants, criminals, bullfighters, and job-seekers, what judgment would I have to pronounce on them?" Biased Spanish judgment of Filipinos was no more authoritative, then, than that of "an educated Tagalog who, traveling through France and Germany, judges the French and Germans by stable girls, domestic servants, waiters, and coachmen." Rizal was, of course, the traveling Tagalog in question, having explored rural France and Germany on foot. Picked up by the German police for "visiting cities, towns, and the smallest and most insignificant villages" and "establishing certain personal relationships" there, Rizal would conclude that European peasants— passive, superstitious, and backward—were commensurable with Philippine ones.[35]

Blumentritt especially delighted in reversed comparisons that held Europeans to the very standards they subjected their colonies to, standards that they could often not meet themselves. "Many Malayan dialects have a literature that is grander and richer that those possessed by certain Latin nations," such as Romania, he wrote. Where were Spanish, French, English, and German alphabets to match those found among the islands' peoples by the Philippines' first colonizers? "Were not the Malayans superior on this score to the majority of European nations that today march *at the head* of civilization?" These reversals were especially sharp with regard to parliamentary representation. If the criterion was intelligence, "[t]he entire principality of Bulgaria does not possess the number of men that know how to read and write that there are in the province of Manila alone, even deducting the number of Europeans." The fact that Sardinia had a lower literacy rate than the Philippines, with its reputed *"immensity of savage races,"* did not stop Sardinia "from electing its delegates to the Italian Parliament without harm." The Bocches of Austria were at the "same state of civilization" as the Philippines' Igorots; "although barbarous," the Bocches "descend from their villages and hills to Catarro and Risano to make use of their right to vote."[36]

If the achievement of "colored" peoples around the world and the comparative mediocrity of the European lower classes undermined Spanish racial logic, the widely admitted "backwardness" of at least a segment of the Philippine population required alternative explanation. This backwardness, especially accusations of Philippine "superstition," was deflected back onto the friars, who were blamed for inculcating a ritualistic Catholicism heavy in magical thinking. López Jaena confessed that the Philippines was "extremely backward," but this was not due to the "refraction of culture" or "the ineptitude of our race for progress," but to the friars, who "found in the *indio* an inexhaustible vein for exploitation" by "submerging him in ignorance and fanaticism." The common charge of "indolence" was similarly recast. For Gregorio Sancianco, author of an early socioeconomic criticism, indolence in the Philippines was a political myth: blaming *indio* behavior for the lack of agricultural production was a way to curtail educational and public works efforts and to justify harsh labor practices. The discourse had been merely "a pretext to commit disgraceful abuses which discredit the Spanish name as well as ruin the poor Filipino farmer."[37]

Rizal extended Sancianco's argument further in his 1890 essay "On the Indolence of the Filipino." If in the Middle Ages the devil was blamed for all misfortune, in the Philippines "indolence is blamed for one's own faults and those of others." Unlike Sancianco, though, Rizal believed that indolence was real, explainable, and exaggerated. There were climatic causes to indolence—were not warmer, southern European nations like Spain more indolent than colder, northern European ones like Germany?—no better demonstrated than in the indolence of Europeans in their tropical colonies. "Surrounded by numerous servants, never traveling by foot but always in a coach," Rizal observed, they needed their servants "not only to pull of their boots for them but even to fan them!" But the indolence of Filipinos was primarily the by-product of Spanish colonial history, what Rizal called "a fatal contest of circumstances." Rizal showed how the Spanish galleon destroyed the islands' vigorous internal industry and commerce. Spanish use of natives in colonial wars drained communities of their productive power; not knowing "if their fields would be their graves or if their crops would feed their executioner," Filipinos experienced "discouragement." *Encomenderos* (planters) enslaved the natives, the corrupt state extracted enormous bribes for commercial and industrial licenses, and the friars had enriched themselves by cultivating in *indios* spendthrift habits such as the purchase of expensive ritual equipment. Any native who rose in education, business, or the professions was instantly suspected of subversion. Given the howling absence of incentives, one had to be crazy not to be indolent in the Philippines. Against this backdrop, the political use of indolence was revealed to be, as it was for Sancianco, "the pretensions of some white Christians, who want to make the Christian of color into a kind of driving force, more intelligent and less costly than steam power."[38]

Even as they undercut logics of racial difference and exclusion from multiple directions, Propaganda writers sought to construct cultural and even racial bridges across Quioquiap's "abyss" between Spaniards and Philippine natives, bridges that might ultimately convey political rights. One of the principal arguments along these lines turned on what Propaganda historians called the "blood compact" that, in important ways, made Spaniards and Philippine peoples one in "race." According to their accounts, as well as those of Spanish historians, it was ancient Philippine custom to seal treaties of alliance or friendship by mixing the blood of leaders. Such a compact had been struck between the Spanish explorer Miguel López de Legazpi and indigenous leader Sikatuna. Unlike many elements of Propaganda argument, the blood compact subverted rather than sought recognition. Recognition required two parties: if Spaniards and Filipinos were indistinguishable, then the former could not "recognize" the latter; if anything, the compact was a moment when Legazpi had been forced to recognize native tradition. While both Spanish and Propaganda historians agreed on the event's occurrence, it came to play a disproportionately important role in the Propaganda historical project and would inspire the painter Juan Luna, who depicted it in an 1886 painting, *El Pacto de Sangre*, for the Ayuntamiento (government seat) of Manila. After 1896, the blood-compact narrative would play a role in the ideological founding of the revolutionary organization, the Katipunan.

For the Propaganda movement, the blood compact symbolized the unity of Spain and the Philippines, their equality as contracting parties, and the mutual obligations between them, borne by common blood. "It is now three centuries since the blood of Legazpi and of Sicatuna [*sic*], mingled in a cup which both men drained in sign of eternal friendship,

This prize-winning 1886 painting, El *Pacto de Sangre*, by the Ilocano painter Juan Luna represents the "blood compact," one of the founding myths of Spanish liberal imperialism and assimilationism. In it, an assertive Rajah Sikatuna (modeled by José Rizal) incorporates anxious-looking Spanish explorer Legazpi (modeled by T. H. Pardo de Tavera) into a peace pact by mixing their blood together and drinking it. The legend was used to argue that shared blood between Filipinos and Spaniards should convey wider rights to the former, while making an act of racial mixing the founding moment of Spanish-oriented Philippine history. Reproduced from Roces, Felix Resurrección Hidalgo and the Generation of 1872, with permission, Lopez Memorial Museum.

ratified their oath to fuse from that day forward into one ideal the aspirations of Spain and of the Philippines," Del Pilar began one pamphlet indicting the friars. But passing centuries had not only seen that "fusion" fail but "strengthened the domination of the monasteries." Friar abuses and other forms of Spanish exploitation constituted a withdrawal from the compact's obligations, making separatism morally defensible.[39]

Faced with everyday indignities, however, Propaganda writers knew the blood compact was likely to remain persuasive only at a metaphorical level and turned to cultural resources better able to sustain their identity as overseas Spaniards. Perhaps most important of these was the Spanish language. As Vicente Rafael has shown, the friar orders' conversions process had since the sixteenth century relied on translations of the Mass and other key rituals into indigenous languages. This process had led to the assimilation of Spanish Catholic rituals into indigenous cultural forms. As a result, Spanish was retained as an exclusive language of colonial rule, with highly restricted access to Spanish-language education. Following the 1863 educational decree, secular elementary schools had been inaugurated for *indio* and mestizo students, but friar opposition and political instability left them underfunded and incapable of attracting Spanish-speaking instructors. According to Barbara Gaerlan, however, the late nineteenth-century in-migration of Spaniards and their marriage into *principalía* families increased the linguistic Hispanization of the Philippine upper class, even among those without Spanish ancestry. The children of these elites learned Spanish in the home, whether directly from Spanish-speaking mothers and grandmothers or through tutoring by relatives or a local Spanish priest. A Spanish-language milieu had been reinforced by *principalía* socializing with Spanish civil and religious officialdom. By the close of the century, Spanish was a strong second language in the homes of the very elite of society. Comfort with Spanish, in turn, had prepared the *ilustrado* youth to pursue formal friar training at the secondary and tertiary levels.[40]

Within the universe of print, many early Filipino publications were bilingual, dating back to Del Pilar's short-lived 1882 *Diariong Tagalog*; Spanish would emerge as what Rafael calls "a secondary language for translating the primary languages of the archipelago." As such, Spanish would be imagined not only as a possible bridge across Philippine cultures but as a means of communicating demands vertically through the Spanish colonial hierarchy. Propaganda writers would place the intensification of Spanish instruction near the center of their demands for reform and attribute its blockage to the friars. As Rafael shows, by learning the colonizer's language, the islands' peoples were, like the friars, able to speak in the language of the other. *Ilustrado* public eloquence in Spanish would vividly connect them to sympathetic Spaniards, who might tie rights to a common language. It might also, however, cause surprise rather than recognition. Antonio Luna wrote of a Spanish woman's surprise at his command of Spanish. "'I am surprised that you speak it much as I do,'" she had stated. "It is our official language," Luna had replied, "and that is why we know it." "'But, dear God!'" she had exclaimed. "'Spanish is spoken in your country?'" Perhaps, Luna suggested, "we are thought to be little less than savages or Igorots." Perhaps "they ignore the fact that we can communicate in the same language, that we are also Spaniards, that we should have the same privileges since we have the same duties."[41]

Ilustrados also seized on resources of manhood. Spanish racists' depictions of *indios* relied on specifically gendered aspersions: the islands' men as feminine, childish, physically weak, and cowardly; its women (generalized from the lower class) as unsuitably modest. If *ilustrado* responses were varied, they were all shaped by these racist, gendered discourses: gentlemanly bearing, swordsmanship and dueling, feasting, romantic rivalry and womanizing were all demonstrations of masculinity before each other, skeptical Spanish publics, and audiences in the islands. So, indeed, were the debates entered into by Propaganda writers, often represented as a kind of manly intellectual duel with Spanish enemies. López Jaena described his effort, as others would, to "vindicate the good name of the Philippines before the public" against the "slanders and unfair aggressions inflicted by Quioquiap's pen." When Luna's satiric "Madrid Impressions" was attacked by otherwise sympathetic republican journalist Celso Mir Deas, Luna went to Barcelona to demand satisfaction—and recognition—through a duel, a challenge that, when not accepted, found its way into Luna's subsequent articles.[42]

In both literal and intellectual dueling, what was at stake was honor, often cast as the defense of women, actual or metaphorical. While they had begun with appeals to "Mother Spain," Propaganda writers increasingly saw themselves as defending the virtues of "Mother Philippines" from her many detractors. Both conceptions of nation and gender owed a great deal to the Hispanic Catholic cult of the Virgin Mary, as well as to the actual mothers of Propaganda writers, many of whom were powerful inspirations for their sons. While inspired by real and metaphorical mothers, however, Propaganda writers tended to view women as abstractions rather than as agents, passive and vulnerable repositories of virtue in need of protection by active men. Their responses to Spanish attack made claims for *indio* equality in explicitly masculinist terms. López Jaena noted ironically that Quioquiap's *indios*, with "'those frail, naked bodies,'" had "fought in a manly way" beside Spaniards against Chinese invaders and "demonstrated their *energy*, their *valor*, their *virility*" in fending off the British. The unsubtle claim sought to demonstrate *indio* manhood and loyalty, and suggesgted that Spanish colonialists, in relying on *indios* for their defense, might lack masculinity themselves.[43]

Rizal's toast of the painters Juan Luna and Felix Hidalgo suggested that while Propaganda writers were reimagining the historical and political relationship between the Philippines and Spain, they had also begun to imagine a Philippines without Spain. Unable to publicly express such a Philippine future without grave consequences, they would do so in a reimagined Philippine past, specifically through revisionist history. For one, history was a site where nations were built in the nineteenth-century European imaginary. As they studied in European universities, *ilustrados* had encountered exercises in historical scholarship that traced the roots of present-day nations back to primordial customs, traditions, and institutions. A shared history was one foundational "invented tradition" that an aspiring nation must possess. But Propagandists also chose history because it was the terrain of their critics, who often cited earlier Spanish chroniclers to confirm their prejudices against—presumed unchanging—*indios* in the present. These accounts were, conveniently, virtually the only surviving written sources regarding the early colonization period. One of the most authoritative sources had been the 1720 report of Augustinian friar Gaspar de San Agustín, who claimed fifty years in the islands. Apparently drawn largely from experiences with his servants, the work was a scathing imperial-indigenist attack on native culture and society that would cast a long shadow, emphasizing natives' laziness, stupidity, and impertinence to their Spanish betters. "[I]n the *conventos* and houses where they are servants," he had written in frustration, "they break so many things that one would think they did it on purpose."[44] San Agustín was refuted by other missionaries, in particular the Jesuit Juan José Delgado, but he would nonetheless survive as an authority into the nineteenth century.

Propaganda writers set out to invent a new Philippine past in a variety of ways. This involved, in some cases, flights of imaginative fancy. In the late 1880s and early 1890s, for example, Pedro Paterno composed a number of historical works, such as his 1887 *Ancient Tagalog Civilization*, which claimed that the islands' precolonial inhabitants had been both Spanish and Catholic in their culture, in all but name, prior to the arrival of Spaniards. Revision might also, on the other hand, rely on the discovery and interpretation of new sources. Rizal had sought an account of early Philippine society with a pedigree sufficiently venerable to match San Agustín's and found it in the British Museum, in the still earlier *Sucesos de las Islas Filipinas*, by Dr. Antonio de Morga, published in Mexico in 1609. The text was in many ways ideal for Propaganda purposes: it paid close attention to indigenous customs and was the only major Philippine chronicle not written by a Spanish missionary, its author being a member of the Real Audiencia (the islands' supreme court). While working in the museum, Rizal hand-copied the rare document, later bringing out an annotated edition in Paris. Using Morga, Rizal was able to answer Spanish racist attacks, connecting Morga's descriptions to a critical narrative of cultural decline. Rizal affirmed Spanish characterizations of natives, especially in terms of indolence and superstition. But through Morga, he demonstrated how advanced, preconquest Filipino industries, religion, and civilization had been destroyed by Spanish domination and argued that the negative qualities often attributed to natives by Spaniards must be seen in light of a history of colonial devastation. The Morga chronicle in Rizal's hands, in other words, turned conventional Spanish histories on their heads: instead of *indio* backwardness being the justification for Spanish colonization, it was its most virulent effect.[45]

If Propaganda history gave the Philippines' peoples a united past, folklore scholars provided a usable present. Folklore societies had proliferated throughout Europe in the late nineteenth century, as the rising middle classes wrapped their newfound political authority in the garb of invented traditions. Folkloric custom could lend historical legitimacy to bourgeois nation-states; middle-class pedigree could be marked geographically on a landscape of monuments and temporally in genealogies and cycles of patriotic celebration. In one sense, the collection of folklore was different in colonial settings: here, the persistence of folklore was often registered as colonial failure, tradition that had escaped the grindstone of civilization. But folklore might also be made to justify continued colonial conversion or uplift. In the Philippines, for example, the documentation of *indio* customs and beliefs had a long history by the late nineteenth century. For centuries, Spanish writers, especially the friars, had scrutinized the *indio* cultures through the lens of conversion as vestiges of a pagan past to be collected for ridicule and eradicated for the greater glory of Christendom. Like history, the "folkloric" could be used to establish authoritative colonial knowledge, indexing native incapacities in concrete, empirical detail.

While the friars denegrated Philippine customs, others set out in search of a new "Philippine folklore." Chief among these was the Ilocano journalist Isabelo de los Reyes, who would energetically collect and publish Philippine customs in a number of works in the 1880s and 1890s. With his *ilustrado* roots in a landowning family from Vigan, De los Reyes would study in the Vigan seminary before moving to Manila in 1880 to attend the University of Santo Tomas and enter the world of journalism, Masonry, and reform. By his own account, his project began with his alienation from the friars' folkloric project: while at the seminary, he had once been asked by a Spanish priest to collect Ilocano "superstitions" as signs of backwardness. De los Reyes's training in paleography and access to Santo Tomas's library enabled him to embark on studies of Ilocano history and culture, and it was not long before he was the islands' chief correspondent with Spanish folklorists as well as scientists such as Blumentritt. In 1885, upon a request from Spanish correspondents, he issued his "Call for Folk-lore," a manifesto calling for Philippine folklore research. "More than the European nations," he wrote, in a striking and offhand comparison, "this country" needed "to gather traditions, customs, legends, superstitions, etc., so that later scholars can make comparisons with them." These studies "would have as their object the unraveling of the thousand mysteries that are locked in the past of these peoples." De los Reyes cast his net over an immensity of Filipino creativity: "ways, customs, ceremonies; familial, local, or provincial shows and fiestas, rites, practical beliefs, superstitions, myths and children's games, idioms, tongue-twisters, turns of phrase from each locality, nicknames, wisecracks, children's sayings, the names of places that are not mentioned on maps."[46]

Deploying the Philippine historical past and folkloric present against Spanish detractors meant making implicit and explicit decisions about the communities and boundaries of defense. The *ilustrado* diaspora in Europe and the Propaganda campaign were together giving rise to new forms of identification. Take, for example, the racial divide—sharply marked in the Philippines—between Spanish mestizos and *indios*, the former held to be superior on the basis of their partial Spanish ancestry. To some degree, these tensions played out in the *ilustrado* colonies of Europe, as when some *indios* challenged what they considered mestizos' arrogant presumption of leadership in a new Propaganda journal. But these tensions were also reduced by circumstances in Europe. Spanish racists had much to say against both groups on racial grounds; in the context of alienating encounters with Europeans, such as that recorded by Antonio Luna, the mestizo-*indio* divide seemed increasingly to be an "internal" one, narrower than the "external" gulfs that separated the overseas *ilustrados* as a whole from the Europeans around them. "Partisans that we are of the unity of races, we protest against that division of races between mixed-bloods and pure natives," wrote one editorialist in *La Solidaridad* in 1889. Revealing the continued hold of these distinctions, he went on to note that he did "not consider mestizos superior, or *indios* inferior," because "if creoles and mestizos must be held up in all branches of knowledge, one has to hold up *indios*, in a marvelous way, as they shine in the purest heaven of the arts, sciences, and letters." In some cases, divisions by racial mixture broke down, and entirely new terms arose to encompass the overseas *ilustrado* community. Describing the "colony" to Blumentritt, Rizal stated that it contained "creole young men of Spanish descent, Chinese mestizos, and *indios*, but we call ourselves only Filipinos."[47]

The Boundaries of the Filipino

Who was this "Filipino," this new person? The term had previously been a racial one, used in Spanish colonial society to denote creoles of Spanish descent: "Filipino" preserved the Spanishness of "Spaniards" who had never seen Spain. But Rizal and other overseas *ilustrados* broadened the term for diasporic and propaganda purposes to contain, and mitigate, their diversities of race. It was a term of convenience, but it was also an insurgent category that could be used in assertions of civilization and claims to recognition and politico-legal assimilation. In *ilustrado* publications like *La Solidaridad*, it was often used as an adjective modifying "people"—"*el pueblo Filipino*"—but it also emerged as a noun, particularly when describing the widespread talents and capacities of the islands' peoples or the grievances they had in common. One piece complained that Manila's Spanish press debated unfairly, "accusing the enemy if he is Filipino, and silencing him if he is a foreigner." Writing in 1889, one editorialist assured his readers that "the Filipinos adore Spain." "Our Filipinos," wrote Antonio Luna, "already know the most intricate declensions of classical Latin."[48]

But where were the boundaries of the "Filipino"? Where the *ilustrado* diasporic experience had led some to challenge notions of *mestizaje*, the Propaganda campaign also radically heightened the salience of Hispanic culture that the *ilustrados*—but not all of the islands' inhabitants—shared. Where *ilustrado* activists held up their civilization before Spain and Europe more broadly in a quest for recognition and assimilation, Philippine peoples that could not measure up to these standards became increasingly problematic. While Propagandists were highly critical of the Catholic friar orders in the Philippines, ultimately their notion of civilization derived to a large degree from a secularized account of Hispanic Catholic evangelization. The edges of the Filipino would still cleave largely to the borders of Spanish Catholic conquest and conversion: the animists and Muslims of the archipelago, never defeated by the Spanish, would not for the most part be embraced within the emergent category of the Filipino. The attempt to blur or eradicate the line between peninsular and overseas Spaniards through evidence of civilization, the core of the Propaganda effort, would in this way darken the line between those inside and outside Hispanic Catholic influence.

The impact of the campaign for recognition on the *ilustrado* social imaginary can be seen in the developing Propaganda visions of Philippine history. As Filomeno Aguilar has shown, in establishing its Philippine counterhistory, the Propaganda writers drew on Ferdinand Blumentritt's theory of "wave migrations" to account for hierarchies of difference in the Philippines. According to this theory, pre-Hispanic Philippine history consisted of three successive "invasions," each of which had retreated inland in the wake of the next. The invasions came in an evolutionary, progressivist sequence: a first wave of Negritos had been the most "barbarous" and had quickly retreated into the mountains; a second wave of "invading Malayans" had succeeded them, mixed with them, and acquired "barbarous" elements; only a third wave of Malay invaders, with "a higher civilization and milder morals as compared to the first Malay wave," were identified as the ancestors of present-day *indios*.[49] It was precisely the favorable, "racial" features of this third wave that had made it more susceptible to Hispanic Catholic evangelization and civilization. The barbarism of contemporary animists and Muslims was due, then, to the mutually reinforcing effects of their prehistoric "savagery" as the descendants of the first two waves of migration and their active repulsion of Christianity. In their efforts to gain political and cultural recognition from Spanish authorities, the overseas *ilustrados* would recognize themselves in only a small portion of their reconstructed Philippine past.

But not all *ilustrado* writers agreed that Hispanic Catholic civilization should be the defining core of emergent Filipino identity. Perhaps because of his geographic proximity to the Luzon highlands, perhaps because of his own Ilocano alienation from imperial Manila's Tagalogs, perhaps because of his populist politics, De los Reyes stretched the boundaries of the Filipino further than any of his expatriate counterparts. His Filipinos were defined in ways that subverted hierarchies of urban and rural, elite and popular, and even Catholic and animist religious cultures. In an 1885 essay, he famously described himself as the "[b]rother of the forest-dwellers, the Aetas, Igorots, and Tinguianes." In another essay, "The Origins of the Races," he took to task European theorists, including Blumentritt and his wave migration theory. He minimized the distinctions that these thinkers believed were fundamental and cast them as the by-products of social environment. What he called the "insignificant differences" between "the partly civilized Ilocano, the Tinguian who wears pants and jacket, the pacified Igorot who though still naked has lost his unsociable and cruel nature, and the runaway fugitives with their savage customs" were "simply the effects of the places where they live." Different groups "appear civilized or savage" depending on their proximity to "places frequented by Spaniards or civilized Ilocanos."[50]

But this more inclusive notion of the Filipino would remain marginal. De los Reyes's declaration of brotherhood with the "forest-dwellers" would open him to ridicule. Instead, overseas *ilustrados* sharply marked the difference between themselves and the unconverted "others" for whom they were sometimes "misrecognized." They used historical evidence of Filipino service in Spain's colonial wars against animists and Muslims as evidence of their loyalty and civilization. In his "Madrid Impressions," Antonio Luna, writing self-consciously as "a Filipino," expressed his outrage when, in a Spanish play, an "Igorot" character was made to speak Tagalog. Hounded in Madrid by jeering children calling him "Chinese" and "Igorot," he mocked their ignorance, scoffing that for most of them, "Chinese, Igorots, and Filipinos are one and the same." This was a mistake that he himself did not make: those who should rule the islands should know them, and knowing them meant recognizing lines of difference and drawing them where they belonged.[51]

The contested borders of the Filipino were illuminated by diverse *ilustrado* responses to the 1887 Philippine Exposition in Madrid. Initially, at least some *ilustrados* in Spain appear to have been broadly supportive of the effort, in many ways an enactment of assimilationist hopes. "We do not deny that this [exposition] will produce positive results for the development of Philippine commerce, industry, and agriculture," wrote López Jaena, for example. But many were critical of their exclusion from the planning and execution of the exposition: an event that might have been a powerful symbol of, and means toward, recognition had taken shape right before their eyes without their having been consulted. In the absence of other forms of representation, *ilustrado* critics imagined the exposition as a kind of symbolic parliament that allowed all colonial interests except Filipinos to represent themselves. "In this Exposition all have their place of honor," wrote López Jaena, ". . . except the Filipinos [*los filipinos*], the genuine Filipinos, those of the indigenous race." If these former groups had "vested interests to protect in those latitudes," excluded Filipinos had "equally great and perhaps even higher interests to defend, as they concern their own country, customs, and traditions."[52]

The Spanish failure to recognize the *ilustrados* had led inevitably to their failure to recognize Philippine cultural artifacts. Asserting his own expertise, López Jaena claimed that the exposition had paid a price for Filipino exclusion in authenticity. One Spanish collector, Juan Alvarez-Guerra, was "not Filipino," nor did he "know the natives, their ways, and customs thoroughly, even having resided in the Philippines a long time." As a result, inappropriate materials, such as Japanese and Chinese objects, had been included "in a mixed-up heap" with Philippine ones. "If true Filipinos had been included in the Executive Commission," he asserted, "certainly they would not have advised" it to include these items, which "blemish the Exposition."[53]

Ultimately, the displayed "objects" about which *ilustrados* had the most to say were people.[54] *Ilustrado* fears had been raised in October 1886 by the announcement that Filipino artisans would be sent to Madrid to demonstrate their craftsmanship. Some had predicted that such displays would be used to discredit the islands' inhabitants in general, and especially the *ilustrados* themselves, before Spanish and broader European publics. Rizal wrote Blumentritt in mid-1887 that he had hoped, five years earlier, for a Philippine exposition along *ilustrado* lines, one that featured modern Philippine industry and "not an Exposition of Human Beings so the indolent inhabitants of Madrid might amuse themselves with this display of our country folk as a curiosity!" Although the exposition would contain industrial exhibits, its planners also transported to Madrid eight Igorots, eight Moros, two people from the Marianas, two from the Carolines, and about twenty-four others, including Negritos, from the Philippines.[55]

This engraving from *Exposición de Filipinas*, a Spanish volume commemorating Madrid's 1887 Philippine Exposition, features a scene of displayed Igorots. The exposition was a neomercantilist effort by the Spanish colonial state to tighten links between metropole and colony in political and economic terms. The display of *infieles* like the Igorots enraged many *ilustrados* either for reasons of mistreatment or because they believed such "backward" groups were being used deliberately to misrepresent the Philippines' peoples and undermine their own quest for cultural and political recognition.

Some Spaniards expressed hostility at the display of human beings as beneath European standards of humanitarianism. Others expressed their disgust for both the exposition organizers and displayed peoples. Father Pascual Barrado, a Jesuit who had spent some years in the Philippines, recounted insulting remarks by Spanish spectators made in the presence of the display's indigenous cigar-makers; the ignorant visitors had been surprised when one of them responded in perfect Spanish. Barrado himself expressed revulsion at "the most humiliating and repulsive degradation" of the people of the exhibit, who "hide in their miserable huts through whose windows the spectators stare at them as if they were wild animals shut up in their cages."[56]

Ilustrado fears of "misrepresentation" appear to have been realized by the lessons taken from the exposition by Spanish visitors. Orienting spectators in anticipation of the display itself, the newspaper *El Resumen* had, upon the arrival of the Filipino artisans, noted that "[i]n the majority of them one sees the stamp of stupidity and imbecility; the feeble ray of intelligence which may be glimpsed through their slanted eyes reveals neither surprise nor astonishment, but rather fear of strength." In his introduction to a commemorative volume by the newspaper *El Globo*, D. Emilio Castelar suggested the exposition's human displays might help anthropologists "contemplate variations of the human species that bring prehistoric times to the eyes." They might also experience "samples of monosyllabic languages that call to mind the fitful articulations of the human voice as they draw closer to the cries of lower species."[57]

In their response to the exposition at least some Spanish Catholic officials confirmed *ilustrado* suspicions. Archbishop Pedro Payo wrote to Balaguer, for example, of his hopes that displayed natives would "modif[y] somewhat certain ideas generally admitted concerning the inhabitants of these islands, even though these natives are far from representing completely the diversity of races which people this Archipelago." Payo hoped the exposition would allow, "at least in imperfect fashion," a "study . . . of the *indio* who can be called civilized, those who form part of the mountain tribes, and the Moros, who are so refractory to European customs and usages." Augustinian Father Salvador Font saw the exposition as the necessary, disparaging response to an emerging, affirmative *ilustrado* scholarship on Philippine prehistory. Whatever "the Paternos and Rizals" might say, he wrote, "[i]n the Philippine Exposition of Madrid we have seen in its actuality the Igorot civilization."[58]

Ilustrado responses to the displays varied. Some *ilustrados* extended their own recognition. "The colony is not as wild as was painted for us when we contemplated it, from very far away, exclusively by map," wrote López Jaena. "The Igorots are neither savage nor irrational, as an historian of those provinces told us." They were "susceptible to modern civilization," some being "somewhat enlightened" and others "of notable intelligence," such as the party's leader, who "speaks Spanish correctly, has a vast knowledge of geography and commerce, [and] knows Latin, Ilocano, and other dialects."[59] On the basis of this recognition, López Jaena then made the suffering of his "compatriots" on display a metaphor for the neglect and broken promises of the Spanish Empire. Housing conditions for the exposition's "Filipino colony," for example, were inadequate to the Madrid climate. Confined to "a tiny barrack with wooden walls inside and covered outside with galvanized iron," packed in "like canned sardines," the displayed peoples complained of severe chills. López Jaena called on exposition officials to relocate them to comfortable apartments nearby and to make good on earlier promises to provide everything the colony might need, including wages with which they might purchase necessities. He also demanded that officials end their effective arrest, for the colony was prohibited from venturing more than twenty meters beyond the barracks, and "[t]he repression of their personal liberty makes this colony's condition more distressing." All of the colony's members were apparently "eager to see the town" but were unable to take advantage of the cosmopolitan explorations Propaganda writers themselves had enjoyed. Along with others, one young woman, Antonia de los Santos, a seamstress, fluent in Spanish, Chamorro, and other languages, "showed grand yearnings to visit the establishment of the *Singer machines* . . . where there are peninsular compatriots of her class," but she was forbidden. Material neglect, crushed civil liberties, restricted education: there was perhaps no more succinct *ilustrado* expression of assimilation unjustly denied.[60]

But others concerned themselves less with the physical comfort and survival of the displayed peoples than with what they considered the cynical misrepresentation of the islands' peoples for political purposes. Some *ilustrado* visitors suspected a conspiracy organized by the friars, whom they accused of deliberately mounting displays of "savage" peoples to influence Spanish imperial politics. "What was the idea which inspired the Central Committee of Manila, presided over by his Excellency the Archbishop in sending these poor people to this Capital?" inquired an editorial in *España en Filipinas*. "To mislead the opinion of our governments, or that of society concerning the state of civilization of the inhabitants of the Philippines, in order that in view of such rude specimens, no reform or liberty might be possible among that people for a long time?" Some affirmed the savagery of some of the displayed peoples but turned it into an accusation of the very failure of the friars as civilizing agents. According to the editorial, "a certain collectivity exists there with an interest in maintaining this kind of darkness in the intelligence of the inhabitants of the Archipelago for the purpose of a more efficient and more facile exploitation of them."[61]

This approach to those outside Hispanic Catholic civilization by those beginning to define themselves as Filipinos can be described as nationalist colonialism. While strains of López Jaena's humanitarian solidarity and De los Reyes's more inclusive framework would remain, Filipinos undertaking political reform and, later, colonial collaboration would often define themselves against animists and Muslims. Nationalist colonialism was fundamentally shaped by the imperial indigenism it was invented to confront. It affirmed imperial-indigenist categories of difference, in this case, between those inside and outside of Hispanic civilization. But where imperial indigenism emphasized the savage elements of a colonized population for purposes of disenfranchisement, nationalist colonialism countered by minoritizing, or even rhetorically eliminating, those elements. Authoritative demonstrations of knowledge of their "own" population—superior to the knowledge possessed by the colonizer—was a crucial part of the nationalist-colonialist project. The colonizers' misrepresentation of the colonized was understood by nationalist colonialists as part of a broader failure of colonial knowledge. Ultimately, nationalist colonialism "internalized" empire by arguing that those who were civilized among the colonized—in this case, the Hispanicized Filipino descendants of a "third wave" of invaders—had the capacity, right, and duty to rule over those who were not civilized. The justification for, and means toward, national self-fulfillment would be found in internal empire.

From Assimilation to Revolution

The Propaganda movement and its campaign for recognition and assimilation reached its peak in the early 1890s and collapsed thereafter. The final, and failed, effort was for representation in the Spanish Cortes, which had been part of the *ilustrado* reform agenda since the early 1880s. In early 1890, Del Pilar convinced a liberal deputy, Francisco Calvo Muñoz, to call for an amendment to a new universal suffrage law that would provide for three Philippine deputies, to be chosen by a limited electorate restricted to officeholders and those paying over fifty pesos a year in taxes. When the electoral commission rejected the amendment, Calvo Muñoz had spoken out in its defense but had been stymied by fellow liberals, including Overseas Minister Manuel Becerra, who supported the measure in principle but declared the moment inopportune; more time was needed to eradicate the "ignorance" of potential Philippine voters.[62]

Rizal countered sharply in *La Solidaridad* that Becerra had matters reversed: parliamentary representation and a free press would themselves erode "ignorance," and not the other way around. But Del Pilar took advantage of even this opening to promote the cause in *La Solidaridad* and in fetes of the Asociación Hispano-Filipino, eventually drawing up, with Calvo Muñoz, an independent bill to guarantee the Philippines sixteen deputies. The July 1890 fall of the Liberal Sagasta government and the rise of Conservatives under Antonio Cánovas, however, eliminated any chances for the bill's passage; Del Pilar nonetheless circulated petitions in favor of Philippine representation inside Masonic lodges; in August 1891, the Asociación petitioned the Cortes to allow Philippine representation. When the Liberals returned to power in December 1892, they were hesitant to entertain Philippine representation; Del Pilar presented a petition of 7,000 signatures in February 1895, and in March, Deputy Emilio Junoy presented a bill for Philippine representation. Two weeks later, however, the Liberal government again collapsed, and the return of the Conservatives doomed any opportunity for this centerpiece of assimilation to be realized.[63]

Liberal betrayal and Conservative opposition, within an overall climate of racist hostility, produced disillusionment and alienation from Spain among *ilustrados*. Spain was increasingly derecognized as a potential interlocutor; the "blood compact" narrative of connected histories gave way before aspirations of insulation and separation. Antonio Luna's series "Madrid Impressions," published in 1890–91 in *La Solidaridad*, skewered Spanish morals and customs, with Luna privately declaring his purpose as nothing less than "to overthrow the idol, smashing its pedestal to pieces." Rizal complained of Madrid's decadence, corruption, and immorality. Del Pilar missed "the graciousness, the sincerity, and cordiality of our oriental customs," expressing bitter thanks to the friars for isolating the Philippines from Spain's venomous influence. The friars should be blessed "for having saved our race from the penetration of the customs of the colonizer," he wrote. As a result, "our virtues have been preserved," including "our love for order, our hospitality, that spirit of eminent charity." Del Pilar confessed that he had come to Spain "with very flattering predispositions," but "each day I go on acquiring the very sad conviction of the incompatibility of this race with sentiments of honor." The Spanish were "as selfish as they are frivolous, without ideals, with no other conviction than their own personal and momentary convenience." Spanish racism was at the root of Spain's corruption; the peoples of the Philippines were merely Spain's most recent victims in its long history of oppression, beginning with the Muslims and Jews who had founded Spanish culture and then been expelled from Catholic Spain. Against the grain of assimilation, he sadly acknowledged that "we will learn nothing from this accursed race, and accursed must be that race which treated with cruelty its fathers."[64]

Spanish intransigence and *ilustrado* alienation led to sharp debates over tactics that ultimately resulted in fatal divisions within the overseas community. While Del Pilar wished to continue the metropolitan campaign, Rizal increasingly felt that recognizing Spaniards as interlocutors was a futile exercise; his own failed attempts to protect his family from eviction from Calamba would underscore this. Rizal had been skeptical of the appeal to Spain for some time. In 1887, he had written Blumentritt that "[t]he peaceful struggle must remain a dream, for Spain will never learn from her earlier colonies in South America." Quioquiap was crude but "honest"; he wanted "political separation, and he is right," while Filipinos desiring "Hispanization" were "wrong."[65] Rather than petition Spain, he believed, Propaganda writers should continue their campaign of education among Filipinos, preparing them for the day of their liberation. These tactical differences were exacerbated by intense personal rivalries; when Rizal pressed to secure formal leadership of the Madrid colony over Del Pilar and lost, he abandoned Madrid and *La Solidaridad* and ultimately returned to Hong Kong and Manila, from where he would be exiled to Dapitan in 1892 for the publication of his subversive novel, *Noli Me Tangere*.

Rizal's ambivalence regarding the notion of Filipinos as overseas Spaniards, his enthusiasm for an autonomous collective identity, and the shift in his locus of activism toward the Philippines can be seen in the short-lived collective he attempted to form in 1889. The proposed organization's goal was to inspire self-discipline, mutual aid, education, and "the propagation of all useful skills, be they scientific, artistic, literary, etc. in the Philippines." Rizal also urged the new group to study its native land as the first step toward ultimate self-rule. "The knowledge of a thing prepares its mastery," he wrote. "We are the only ones who can come to that perfect knowledge of our country, because we know both languages, and besides we are informed of the secrets of the people in whose midst we are educating ourselves."[66]

Rizal chose to name the new group "Los Indios Bravos," or "the brave natives." The name was in some ways incidental to larger shifts in Rizal's thinking, but its circumstances are nonetheless telling. Here, as before, Rizal's evolving sense of self and politics was shaped by encounters with the United States during European travels. While visiting the Paris Exposition of 1889, he and his companions had attended a performance of Buffalo Bill's Wild West Show. While they did obligingly die to make room for white history, Buffalo Bill's Indians also seized stagecoaches, held off invading cowboys, and performed elaborate riding tricks.[67] Rizal was apparently impressed with the Indians' boldness and skill, and he turned an American spectacle into a Filipino pun. Adopting the phrase "Los Indios Bravos" meant reversing "assimilation" by making "overseas Spaniards" into *indios*, appropriating a Spanish term of derision in the process. The choice of "brave" to modify *indios* reflected a masculinizing imperative: these were not Quioquiap's weak, passive, and effeminate *indios*, but what Rizal would call a "close-ranked phalanx" capable of great discipline, energy, and achievement.[68] Rizal was appropriating one Spanish name for the colonized. He was also, in at least symbolic terms, making a statement about tactics, rejecting the peaceful, literary petitioning that was starkly missing from Buffalo Bill's tableau.

While *ilustrados* abroad became increasingly alienated, revolution was stirring in the islands by the mid-1890s. Peasant revolts of varying intensity had plagued Spanish colonial authorities throughout the nineteenth century, breaking open most commonly where taxation, labor, and military policies violated peasant notions of their traditional rights. As Greg Bankoff shows, during the 1870s and 1880s, Spanish colonial police records listed a proliferation of petty rural crimes: theft, arson, tax and *corvee* evasion, and vagrancy, among others. The destabilizing effects of capitalist land relations in the countryside and growing peasant dissatisfaction with tenancy, forced labor, and local corruption were all factors in the use of these weapons of the weak. On more than one occasion, hard-pressed peasants threw their strength behind charismatic leaders who, in turn, animated their forms of political understanding into anticolonial action. Resistance also began to gather in urban areas: beginning in 1892, a new revolutionary organization, the Katipunan, led by Andrés Bonifacio, had formed among urban clerks and artisans in Manila. In August 1896, the Spanish authorities' discovery of the conspiracy touched off a premature revolt and triggered the Philippine Revolution.[69]

While the revolution's immediate causes were rooted in socioeconomic tensions in the colony, its history was also entangled in the Propaganda movement in complex ways. As Reynaldo Ileto has shown, many of the ideological structures of the Katipunan movement came from Philippine transformations of Catholicism: the social, historical, and political vision of the Katipunan was deeply indebted to millennial Catholicism and, specifically, the *pasyon* (passion) narrative of Christ's redemptive suffering. The *pasyon*, widely performed throughout the archipelago, provided a common narrative capable of organizing large numbers of revolutionaries. It also relied fundamentally on a notion of mutual, familial obligation: having subjected its child "Filipinas" to corrupt, friar rule, Mother Spain had surrendered her right to reciprocal loyalty.[70]

But while they mined deep Philippine moral traditions, Bonifacio and other Katipunan leaders also indigenized the works of the cosmopolitan Propaganda movement, which, smuggled in through Hong Kong, had circulated widely in the islands over the previous decade. In his circulars and manifestos before Tagalog *Katipuneros*, Bonifacio made wide use of the blood-compact legend that Del Pilar and others promoted in Europe; his poetry lyricized a glorious pre-Hispanic Filipino civilization whose details Rizal had dug out of the British Museum. Where the Propaganda movement had recognized differences in class and education, however, the Katipunan created a broad, horizontal space of equal membership that leveled social distinctions marked not only by wealth but by education and race. The movement did not speak in Spanish, the language of colonial elites, but in Tagalog, the language of Manila's masses. "There shall be no discrimination between rich and poor, learned and unlearned," declared a set of "Instructions Concerning Admission into the Society." "All shall be equal and regarded as brothers by each other." In place of the hierarchical definitions of knowledge and education imposed by the Spanish, Katipunan doctrine held that all its members, high and low, were characterized by their "good minds," evidenced by their ability to maintain a balanced *loob* (spirit) even in the face of fearful obstacles. Honor was not the possession of kings or those "having a white complexion" but of those who were truthful and loving of country, "although born in the forests and knowing nothing but [their] own language."[71]

Given the localized political institutions and solidarities and the ethnolinguistic diversity of the islands, the early suspicion by non-Tagalog peoples that the revolution was a "Tagalog rebellion" was perhaps unsurprising. In fact, there was reason to suspect this within the revolution itself. Katipunan leaders like Bonifacio addressed themselves directly to Tagalogs and used Tagalog as the movement's lingua franca; the largest Katipunan chapter, located in Tondo, was named Katagalugan; townspeople at Imus greeted the victorious revolutionary general Emilio Aguinaldo in September 1896 with the cry "Long live the Tagalogs!" But as Leonard Andaya shows, revolutionary leaders also used the term "Tagalog" expansively to denote all of the islands' peoples. "Katipunan had for its object," wrote De los Reyes in 1898, "the development of the Tagalog race (under this name Tagalog), all of quasi-Malay origin are included, that is to say, all the natives of the country." Given the extremely limited and elite-reformist use of "Filipino," "Tagalog" was the most likely term of address, capable of both building a mass base at the revolution's seat and broadening the insurgency outward from Tagalog areas. In a 1902 manifesto, revolutionary Macario Sakay would define "the Tagalog archipelago" as the "barrios, towns, and provinces of the Philippines," including "Jolo, Mindanao, the Visayas, the Ilokos, and other lands which are truly Tagalog."[72]

It was in this context—in the space opened up by the broadened "Tagalog"—that the Propaganda term "Filipino" emerged and spread within revolutionary discourse. Strikingly, given his Ilocano regionalist pride, even De los Reyes accepted the interchangeability of "Tagalog" and "Filipino" in revolutionary discourse (the latter term used more commonly in the Spanish language). In a Tagalog speech given at Cavite in August 1898, Aguinaldo stated that "all of us Filipinos" were "sons of a single mother, the Mother of the Philippines." "[A]ll the natives, all the Spanish mestizos, as well as all the Chinese mestizos of the Philippines," were "sons of God in this land"; God himself had "united with a single aspiration the intelligence and will of the whole Philippine archipelago." Others sought to define and disseminate to literate audiences a newly widened concept of "Filipino." Revolutionary adviser Apolinario Mabini defined it systematically as a solidarity that transcended region and religion in his June 1898 bilingual Spanish-Tagalog *Decalogue*: "The country is not only the province, nor the pueblo, much less is it even the place where one has been born; it is formed by all the provinces, all the pueblos, and all the places in which a Filipino may have been born, whatever the beliefs he may profess or the dialect he may speak."[73] Despite its novelty, the new terminology was employed broadly enough to be noted by curious outsiders. German naval lieutenant-commander Paul Hintze, who visited an "insurgents' club" called the Ateneo Rizal in July 1898, referred to Felipe Buencamino, the new republic's minister of justice, as "a *Filipino*, to use the name invented as a new national denomination for the natives of the northern part of the Philippines, including Spaniards, Chinese, and mestizos of any kind."[74]

Even as it struck out for independence, however, the Philippine Revolution reiterated many of the terms of the earlier assimilation movement. Like that earlier movement, it was critical of Spanish racial divisions. "We make no racial discrimination," read an 1897 manifesto from Aguinaldo. "[W]e call upon all who possess honor and the sense of personal dignity; the Filipino, the Asiatic, the American, and the European all alike suffer; and we invite all those who suffer to aid in lifting up a fallen and tortured people." The people of the Philippines aspired to a government "in which will take part the most capable, the most worthy in virtues and talents, without regard to their birth, their wealth, or the race to which they belong." But the revolution was also self-consciously eager to promote its "civilization" in an effort to gain international recognition. In that same manifesto, Aguinaldo rehearsed a long list of friar and Spanish wrongs, then cried out in frustration, "Oh civilization and culture!" "We fling back into their teeth the name which our enemies give us," he stated. The Philippine Revolution would "show the world that we are worthy of having our own government—our own country, as we have our own language."[75]

Spaniards in the metropole were apparently taken aback by the revolt. Given Spain's generosity, patience, and tutelage, what had gone wrong? Why do the Filipinos hate us? some asked. There were at least two sets of answers, the first of which blamed the friars themselves for creating the conditions for revolt. Perhaps surprisingly, some charged the friars with the insufficient exercise of racial hierarchy. "Why are there *Filibusteros* [insurrectionists]?" asked correspondent Manuel Alhama. Alhama placed primary blame on the friar-dominated educational system for overeducating natives. "When they emerge from the seminary," he chided, "they consider themselves just as priestly and consecrated as the priests and friars of the white race and just as worthy as they are of respect and consideration." Felipe Trigo, writing in June 1897, agreed. "You can't have it both ways," he put it plainly. A nation's intentions toward its colonies might, on the one hand, be "generous," with the aim "to thoroughly civilize the indigenous colonial population." Such a nation should, however, not be surprised "when the colony, having attained its majority, tries to emancipate itself from the tutelage of the mother country," as the histories of North America, Mexico, Santo Domingo, and most recently, Cuba, had shown. On the other hand, a nation might be "egoistic" and "block" the introduction of civilization, "as does the perspicacious and practical England in its Asian possessions." Although the friars had sought to pursue a policy between civilizational inclusion and exclusion, there was "no middle way possible."[76]

A second, and popular, answer to the question blamed the revolt not on the spoiling of children but on the inherent disorderliness of beasts. The bellicose theatrical production *The Philippines for Spain*, launched in June 1897, which pit heroic Spanish forces against savage Tagalogs in the battle for Cavite, contained stage directions on the "repugnant appearance" of the enemy, which one character described as orangutans, suited for the Barcelona zoo. Popular journalist Luis Taboada stated that news of revolt revealed "the state of exaltation in which some monkeys from that archipelago find themselves." Tagalogs, it seemed, in their desire to "imitate their brother simians in Cuba," had taken up arms with the cry of "'Death to men! Long live free monkeys is a free jungle!'" He then satirized the Propaganda movement, telling the story of a Filipino named Silvestre (wild, savage) who had come to Madrid to study and spent much of his time sitting in a tree in the Parque del Retiro. Upon his landlady's request, Silvestre began to behave like a man, but before long he was "asking for the emancipation of the champanzee [sic], the vote for the gorilla, and the right to hold public office for orangutans over the age of twenty, provided they present certification of good conduct." Silvestre had ultimately returned to the Philippines and joined the rebellion, becoming one of its "most illustrious heads" due to his landlady's positive influence. But "Silvestre remains a monkey on the inside," Taboada reminded his readers.[77]

Spanish reaction in Manila was yet harsher. Speaking before the Military Club in Manila, Rafael Comerge, its president, called for genocidal war in the interest of civilization. The "cannibals of the forest are still there," he said, "the wild beast hides in his lair." The hour had come to "finish with the savages." "Wild beasts" should be "exterminated." "Destroy! Kill!" he urged his audience, to "frantic applause." He insisted that Spanish officers "[d]o not pardon"; Spanish soldiers were "the right arm of Spain" and must "execute; exterminate if it be necessary." In calling for exterminist racial purging, Comerge violently severed the blood-compact narrative of connected bodies. "Destruction is the purport of war," he stated. "[I]ts civilizing virtue acts like a hot iron on a cancer, destroying the corrupt tendons in order to arrive at perfect health." Spanish forces must "[a]mputate the diseased member to save the body." Comerge would later receive a Grand Cross of Military Merit for the speech.[78]

The revolt failed. Spanish missteps in repression had animated mass opposition, especially the execution of Rizal in December 1896, which rapidly transformed him into what Spanish philosopher Miguel de Unamuno called "the saint of the Philippine Malays." Although sustained by widespread support, the revolution had been hobbled from the start by lack of preparation and the loss of the element of surprise. Katipunan revolutionaries were badly funded and badly armed, most wielding bolos against heavy Spanish arms. Internal divisions split the movement down its center; in a power struggle between the factions of Bonifacio and Aguinaldo, then a rising young leader from Cavite, Aguinaldo had Bonifacio shot. While personal and regional loyalties played a role in the split, Aguinaldo's ascendancy also represented a shift in class and ideological leadership. Where Bonifacio had represented an egalitarian ethos, Aguinaldo represented the *principal* class and stood for a more conservative, elitist republicanism.[79]

By July 1897, Aguinaldo had been forced into retreat. In defiance, he declared an independent Philippine Republic at Biak-na-Bato in November 1897, with its constitution copied directly from the Cuban constitution. General Primo de Rivera, whose troops had experienced high casualty rates, was receptive to a truce. With the intervention of Paterno, Aguinaldo signed the Pact of Biak-na-Bato in December; in exchange for amnesty, an indemnity of 1.7 million pesos, and the promise of Spanish reform, the revolutionaries would surrender their arms, and he and other revolutionary leaders would accept exile to Hong Kong. Both sides violated the terms: Aguinaldo raised money and arms in Hong Kong in preparation for a continuation of the revolution; and rather than reform, Spanish officials intensified repression in the islands. At least some Spanish Civil Guards in Manila took Comerge's award-winning advice to heart in March 1898 when, upon hearing of a boisterous discussion among Visayan sailors in a tavern in San Nicolas, a contingent of guards massacred nearly one hundred of them to prevent a presumed "conspiracy" from erupting in insurrection.[80]

The direction of Philippine history would at this moment be jolted by events in the Caribbean. As the transplanted Cuban constitution in Southeast Asia suggested, the leadership of the Philippine Revolution was well aware of the ongoing fortunes of the latest war for Cuban independence, which had broken out in 1895. The former Philippine governor-general, Valeriano Weyler, had been sent to Cuba by early 1896, where he had undertaken an aggressive policy that included the "reconcentration" of rural populations, which had taken a vast toll in human life. The Cuban war increasingly attracted attention in the United States: outrage at Spanish atrocities and a sense of imperial opportunity came together in lurid press reports and in a Republican party platform calling for U.S. intervention to rid the hemisphere of a corrupt European power. Pressure by U.S. ministers in September 1897 obtained from Spain promises of a moderated campaign and of Cuban autonomy, but Spanish loyalists rejected the agreement the following January, and Cuban revolutionaries demanded full independence.[81]

War and diplomatic news from Washington, Madrid, and the Caribbean made its way quickly to Hong Kong, where the revolutionaries debated the implications of what they understood to be a coming war between the United States and Spain. They concluded that such a war constituted an opportunity and sought formal recognition of the revolution by the United States. On November 3, 1897, Felipe Agoncillo, Aguinaldo's foreign minister, approached the U.S. consul in Hong Kong, Rounseville Wildman, with the prospect of an alliance in the case of war, including a U.S. supply of arms and ammunition and recognition of the revolutionary government; the State Department refused the offer. On February 17, 1898, however, just two days after the explosion of the U.S. battleship *Maine* in Havana harbor, the revolutionaries were surprised and encouraged to find a U.S. naval squadron land in Hong Kong. They were confident that the U.S. vessels were on their way to Manila Bay to confront the Spanish fleet and hoped that they would do so as the advance force of Philippine liberation.

Encountering the U.S. Empire

The arrival of that U.S. naval squadron was predicated on three decades of explosive American industrial and imperial growth. Since the end of the Civil War, the United States had expanded and consolidated into a continental empire of conquered subjects, migrant settlers, raw materials, and industrial products. At the center of its architecture were the railroads—linked transcontinentally after 1869, the same year in which the Suez Canal had been opened—which simultaneously pioneered modern corporate organization, made available new natural resources for extraction and development, opened up new consumer markets, and promoted dependent white colonization. By the mid-nineteenth century, white migrants had pushed west toward the Pacific in vast numbers; earlier treaties notwithstanding, the federal government forcibly removed eastern Native American peoples westward and established the reservation system to isolate them in arid and undesirable regions far from white settlements. Nomadic peoples in the West put up the greatest resistance to white encroachment and were conquered through genocidal wars by the U.S. Army in the 1870s and 1880s, a process aided by the telegraph, repeating rifle, and Gatling gun. By the end of the latter decade, Native Americans would find it difficult to maintain possession of the reservations themselves. The railroad, and the industries it gave birth to, in turn attracted diverse, novel working populations from around the globe. On the East Coast and in the Midwest, southern and eastern European migrants poured into the United States by the millions to labor in factories and mills. The West was still more dramatically altered, seeing the entry of Chinese and Japanese laborers in mines, lumber camps, farms, and on the railroad. Native American genocide and the wrenching social transformations of rapid industrialization were the preconditions of vast economic growth: U.S. resources in minerals, lumber, cattle, petroleum, and agriculture pushed the United States to the front ranks of the global economic powers by the end of the nineteenth century.

The U.S. empire had long burst over its continental limits by the time the U.S. census declared the land frontier closed in 1890. The United States' transatlantic ties were long-standing, developing out of the nexus of the early modern European empires, and would intensify with improvements in steamship travel and cable communication. Europeans would continue to provide much of the capital necessary for U.S. industrial growth and continental empire and, despite traditions of national exceptionalism, Americans would continue to look to Europe for cultural legitimacy and political models in many areas.

The American view across the Pacific was also transformed in this era. Until the nineteenth century, many Americans saw the Pacific, through the lens of missionary activity, as a place of teeming heathens ripe for conversion. U.S. trade in the Pacific dated back to the eighteenth century, but by the late nineteenth century, American encounters with the Pacific became increasingly commercialized and industrialized. American merchants took advantage of the treaty port system forced on China following the Opium Wars; in 1854, Commodore Matthew Perry had forcibly opened Japan to international trade. In many ways, the "westward course of empire" across the continent already had embedded in it the promise of a second, transpacific commercial empire. China's fabled market of consuming millions had attracted investors to the railroads and, particularly during depressions, industrialists hoped to supply Asia's masses with textiles and machine goods.

Until the last years of the century, the U.S. state presence in Asia would remain thin. American naval forces on the Asiatic Station showed the flag in China, Japan, and Korea while in the Eastern Pacific, and ships on the Pacific Station cruised the coasts of North and South America and as far west as Hawaii and Samoa. The U.S. missionary, investment, trade, and naval empires overlapped most in Hawaii, where the descendants of American missionaries had, following an 1875 reciprocity treaty, come to dominate the islands' economy through sugar plantations. The U.S. Navy also saw the islands as crucial for both defensive and commercial purposes and had obtained exclusive use of Pearl Harbor as a naval station in 1887. In 1895, the American planter elite would overthrow the Hawaiian monarchy with the aid of the U.S. Marines.[82]

FOR MANY PHILIPPINE REVOLUTIONARIES, however, the arrival of the U.S. naval squadron had meant "liberation," at least at first. Aguinaldo asserted these hopes eloquently in manifestos and proclamations in early 1898: the United States loomed larger for purposes of emulation and assimilation the closer it appeared to be allying with Philippine independence. "[L]et us second the avenging and humane action of the Republic of North America," he stated, and "learn from it, accepting its counsels and prescribed forms, the manner of living in order, peace, and liberty, copying its institutions, which are the only suitable ones for nations which desire to reconquer their personality." Just before Commodore Dewey's squadron left Hong Kong for Manila Bay to engage the Spanish fleet, Aguinaldo would declare to his audience that the Americans, "not from mercenary motives, but for the sake of humanity and the lamentations of so many persecuted people," had "considered it opportune to extend their protecting mantle to our beloved country." Aguinaldo expressed that the junta was "very much afraid" that his audience "may be induced to fire on the Americans." It was the Spaniards that Filipinos should combat, he urged, not the Americans, "your liberators." Filipinos might be enjoined by the Spaniards to fight the Americans, but this would be a grave mistake. Why "defend those that have despised you and even in public speeches asked for your extermination—those that have treated you little better than savages?" Filipino military service to Spain—upheld by Propaganda writers—was now reimagined as needlessly sacrificed "Philippine blood." Filipinos had been made to fight against the English, "who in any case would have made better rulers than the Spaniards." They had also warred against peoples of Mindanao and Sulu, "on the pretext of making us believe these people are our enemies, when in reality they are our brothers—like us, fighting for their independence." Enough of "this Spanish tutelage," he concluded, invoking the name of "our immortal José Rizal" as "the greatest patriot our country has seen." In the coming days, Filipinos should "assemble in numbers" "where you see the American flag flying." The Americans "are our redeemers."[83]

Ultimately, the Spanish government had failed to recognize Propaganda writers' claims to equal rights as "overseas Spaniards." In the process of articulating their demands, Propaganda writers had invented the "Filipino," a category that cut across Spanish colonial racial lines and territorialized membership in a national polity. Filipinos, they had argued, shared a common history of pre-Hispanic civilization and, despite the efforts of the friar orders to squelch them, capacities for artistic, literary, and intellectual endeavor and political expression. These assertions, the foundations of the assimilation effort, would also ground the Philippine Revolution that succeeded it. But they would also bound it: the promotion of Philippine civilization had involved differentiating, minoritizing, and exceptionalizing Muslims and animist groups that did not meet Spanish or broader European social-evolutionary standards. Anticolonial struggle had, in this way, given rise to a nationalist colonialism that reinscribed internal categories of difference in an externally oriented campaign for reform.

The question, as of early 1898, was whether the United States would recognize the Philippine Revolution and Filipino "civilization." Rizal would likely have been skeptical. On his way to Europe in 1888, he had traveled eastward across the Pacific, meeting up with the western edge of North America in late April and crossing it by railroad over the next two weeks. He was apparently little impressed and impatient, his diary hastily noted, as if the continent itself were an obstacle to be overcome. Writing from London to his friend Mariano Ponce in July, he noted that he had seen "the largest cities of America" with their "big buildings, electric lights, and magnificent conceptions" and concluded that while "[u]ndoubtedly America is a great country," it still had "many defects."[84]

He was, for example, a critical observer of U.S. racial politics from the moment he landed. On April 29, he had written in frustration to his parents from onboard the ss *Belgic*, anchored outside of San Francisco harbor due to quarantine-related delays. "Here we are in sight of America since yesterday without being able to disembark," he wrote. The cause was more than 600 Chinese passengers who, having joined the ship in Hong Kong, were reputed to have smallpox. Rizal was doubtful. The "true reason" for the delay was that, "as America is against Chinese immigration and now they are campaigning for the elections, the government, in order to get the vote of the people, must appear to be strict with the Chinese, and we suffer." During his travels, additional racial exclusions met his comparative eye. Because "[i]n some states the Negro cannot marry a white woman, nor a Negress a white man," he concluded there was "no real civil liberty" in the United States. U.S. nativists, he noticed, also confused Asian migrants in their expansive racial hostilities. "Because of the hatred of the Chinese, also other Asiatics, like the Japanese, being confused with them, are likewise disliked by the ignorant Americans."[85] The question was what, if any, difference these particular American "defects" would make when U.S. soldiers arrived to "liberate" the Philippines.

The Philippine-American War
as Race War

There is no question that our men do "shoot niggers"
somewhat in the sporting spirit. . . . Undoubtedly, they
do not regard the shooting of Filipinos just as they would
the shooting of white troops. . . . The soldiers feel that
they are fighting with savages, not with soldiers.

H. L. WELLS, 1900

The warfare that has extended the boundaries of
civilization at the expense of barbarism and savagery has
been for centuries one of the most potent factors in the progress
of humanity. Yet from its very nature it has always and
everywhere been liable to dark abuses.

THEODORE ROOSEVELT, 1902

On February 9, 1899, an editorial in the *New York
Times* raised a dangerous crisis of recognition that had broken open in
Philippine-American relations over the previous week. The piece, titled
"The Status of the Filipinos," promoted the Senate ratification of the
Treaty of Paris, which would formally transfer sovereignty over the Philippines, Puerto Rico, and Cuba to the United States. With that treaty,
Spain's former subjects in the Caribbean and the Pacific would become
"dependent people under a military government established by the President." The problem was that over the previous half year in the Philippines
"several thousand of these new dependent peoples of ours" had "gone
through the motions of setting up a Government at Malolos." American
troops had been greeted as something less than liberators. On the contrary, Filipinos had decided "we are invaders of their land" and, in the past
week, had "taken up arms against us." What was the status of the "rebels"
at this strange moment of transition? As "Spanish subjects not yet dena-
tionalized," they were not yet external to Spain and thus could not be
"regarded as the public enemy." At the same time, as Congress had not yet

established their status, they were not yet internal to the United States and did "not as yet owe us allegiance." The only way to resolve the paradox was to exchange ratifications with Spain: the passage of formal, legal sovereignty from Spain to the United States would legally invent an "insurrection," with the revolutionaries' status becoming "that of insurgents against their own Government." At the same moment, the "name and nature of their offense" would change. While Americans might recognize and "look with leniency" on rebels who "had been persuaded to consider themselves an independent nation resisting a foreign foe," once "our sovereignty" was established "the fiction of an independent Government at Malolos" could not be tolerated any more than "we tolerated it at Richmond some years ago." Formal annexation by treaty would simultaneously dissolve the United States' foreignness in the Philippines, turn imperial war into civil war, and convert the soldiers of the Philippine Army into "insurrectionists." Ridding Filipinos of their "delusions" would be "painful work" but necessary for the "peace" of what the editorial preemptively and prematurely called "our domain."[1]

The Senate would take the editorialist's advice, inventing the "Philippine Insurrection" in the process. While it was not the absolute beginning point of Philippine-American history, the war between the United States and the Philippines dramatically changed the histories of both societies and the history of their interconnection. Within U.S. military history, the war was the United States' first of many troop deployments in Asia in the twentieth century and delivered the United States an important, if vulnerable, site for the projection of force.[2] Within the history of the United States' "informal empire," the war led to the acquisition of naval bases and coaling stations that facilitated U.S. commercial penetration into the region. As a moment in U.S. political and cultural history, the war prompted significant debates on American national exceptionalism, the meanings of "empire," and the racial and political implications of colonial war and occupation.

The war marks an equally important set of transitions in Philippine history. For Filipinos, the war meant trading—after an eight-month interval of embattled political independence—one imperial antagonist for another. In military terms, it involved the continuation of the revolution against a newly arrived and ill-prepared force. Socially, it meant widespread destruction, dislocation, and death that would cast a long shadow over the coming decades. Politically, it led to the reconsolidation of urban and rural elite structures that more radical sectors of the revolution had challenged, as former revolutionary leaders came to negotiate with the U.S. invaders over terms of peace and collaboration. Where Philippine history crosses over into U.S. historical consciousness, the "Philippine Insurrection" is nearly always rushed through on the way to a regime of benevolence and uplift. In the present account, by contrast, the latter cannot be understood without the former: the war's patterns of violence and race-making set many of the terms for subsequent colonial state-building and Filipino-American politics. The ragged outer edge of the war in chronological terms—it was declared to be over many times before its actual close—was representative of the way the conflict shaped the "post-war" order. Born in violence, the United States' colonial period of the next five decades would be characterized by a tense and brutal dialectic of force and "attraction."

Specifically, this chapter sees the Philippine-American War as race war: a war whose ends were rationalized in racial terms before domestic publics, one in which imperial soldiers came to understand indigenous combatants and noncombatants in racial terms, one in which race played a key role in bounding and unbounding the means of colonial violence, and in which those means were justified along racial lines.[3] While race has long been an emphasis of the war's historians, both in terms of troop conduct and domestic U.S. debate, this chapter emphasizes the contingency and indeterminacy of the process by which the United States' racial-imperial ideologies took shape.[4] Rather than featuring the "projection" or "export" of preexisting formations, the war prompted, and was in turn fundamentally structured by, a process of racialization in which race-making and war-making were intimately connected.

This contingency was due to the entanglement of race-making in the ongoing problematic of recognition. Both sides in the conflict sought to justify their ends in the war, and their means in fighting it, before American and international publics. Defenders of the Philippine Republic argued that their war was one of national liberation and self-defense and sought recognition for Philippine independence in terms of Filipino socio-cultural standing and "civilization," in ways similar to the earlier Propaganda movement. On the United States' side, the promotion of the ends of imperial war led to two interconnected processes of racialization. In the first, American imperialists racialized themselves as "Anglo-Saxons" in order to legitimate the controversial U.S. war as racially and historically inevitable: Americans were inheritors of Anglo-Saxon virtues, foremost among them the capacity for empire-building. Where "anti-imperialists" claimed, often in national-exceptionalist terms, that the war was contrary to U.S. republican traditions, imperialists would counter that racial-exceptionalist traditions of Anglo-Saxon empire-building went deeper. In the second, American imperialists would, in the interests of derecognizing the Philippine Republic, racialize Philippine society into a set of fragmented and warring "tribes" that were "incapable" of nationality. What might otherwise appear to be an emerging nation and state in the islands was merely the illegitimate will-to-power of a single tribe of Tagalogs over the others. As projects to justify the ends of U.S. imperial war, the Anglo-Saxonizing of the United States and the tribalization of the Philippines were mutually constitutive.

Each side would also seek recognition of its cause in its means of fighting. On the Philippine side, it was hoped that powerful, "civilized" countries might acknowledge the republic if its forces fought a civilized war, waged in conventional formations, demonstrated discipline, and treated prisoners humanely. War would be a Propaganda movement by other means. American soldiers, officers, and policy makers acknowledged a similar relationship between civilization and war. But within the Euro-American world, patterns of warfare were important markers of racial status: civilized people could be recognized in their civilized wars, savages in their guerrilla ones. This interconnection meant that race-making and changing strategies and tactics moved together in a dark, violent spiral. When Filipino forces adopted guerrilla tactics after 1899, for example, Americans recognized in it the work of savages rather than soldiers: not just another set of tactics, guerrilla war was the inherent war of preference of "lower races." This racialization of guerrilla war raised the central question of whether Filipinos, in waging a savage war, were owed the restraints that defined civilized war. Many U.S. soldiers and officers answered this question negatively.[5] In numerous settings, guerrilla war developed into a war of racial exterminism in which Filipino combatants and noncombatants were understood by U.S. troops to be legitimate targets of violence. The heart of the United States' emerging imperial racial formation was rich in contradictions: the people of the Philippines did not possess enough of what Gen. Arthur MacArthur would call "ethnological homogeneity" to constitute a nation-state, but they did have enough to be made war upon as a whole.[6]

Tensions of Recognition

The forces that pushed the Asiatic Squadron out to Manila Bay were complex and continue to be debated by historians.[7] As early as late 1897, officers in the Navy Department and Naval War College anticipating war with Spain had drafted war plans that included the temporary occupation of Manila in order to deny Spain revenue, to provide a base of operations, and to gain leverage for a more favorable peace settlement.[8] These war plans were compatible with, if they were apparently developed independently of, a political elite aggressively committed to overseas empire, advocates of a "large policy," such as Assistant Secretary of the Navy Theodore Roosevelt and Senator Henry Cabot Lodge, Republican of Massachusetts. In late 1897 and early 1898, both men pressured President William McKinley to see geopolitical opportunity in the war with Spain: by seizing Spain's largest Asian colony—in whole or in part—the United States would gain a strategic foothold from which to wedge open China's markets, a rationale for building up U.S. naval strength, and the recognition and respect of the world's imperial powers.

February 15, 1898, provided large-policy advocates the opening they had hoped for, when the USS *Maine* exploded mysteriously in Havana harbor, where it had been sent to hold American options open and to protect the property of U.S. citizens. An investigatory commission suspected Spanish weapons of mass destruction, and the *Maine* disaster was assumed to be the work of Spanish treachery by interventionists in the McKinley administration and in the imperialist press. While the advocates of intervention called for the "liberation" of Cuba, just ten days after the disaster, Roosevelt ordered Commodore George Dewey and the Asiatic Squadron to depart San Francisco for Hong Kong to await further instructions. Following a U.S. declaration of war, Dewey was to proceed to Manila Bay to engage Spanish naval forces there.

Looming war between Spain and the United States finally gained Filipinos elements of the recognition and reform from Spanish authorities that Propaganda writers had sought since the 1880s. Rumors of a westbound U.S. Navy and a sudden need for Filipino allies to defend the islands loosened the Spanish reform imaginary, at least in instrumental terms. With blood from the San Nicolas massacre hardly dry, the new governor-general, Basilio Augustín, inaugurated both a Filipino militia and a consultative assembly, staffed by conservative Filipino elites.[9] With others, Archbishop Bernardino Nozaleda hastily reknotted previously irrelevant ties of blood and history, calling on *indios* to fight off the Americans, "who lack the Catholic faith of Spain," who have "not the maternal blood, nor the noble magnanimity, nor the community of interests of history, dating back to more than three centuries." Americans, unlike the Spanish, did not have "the mixture of blood that circulates through the veins of many of us," blood that "in a hundred glorious deeds" had been shed "in our common defense, united by a common brotherhood, the sons of the mother country and of the colony." Americans would establish "an insuperable barrier . . . between [you] and your vainglorious masters."[10]

Exiled revolutionaries were divided and willing to play both sides. The end of April 1898 saw Miguel Malvar in Hong Kong negotiating with Spaniards for autonomy and Emilio Aguinaldo in Singapore negotiating with a U.S. consul for recognition of Philippine independence. From late March to early April, Aguinaldo had a number of meetings with Captain Wood, acting on behalf of Commodore Dewey, who had urged him to return and continue the revolution, assuring him that Americans would supply him with necessary arms. By Aguinaldo's account, Wood had stated that the United States was "a great and rich nation and neither needs nor desires colonies"; he would not put these commitments in writing without Dewey's approval.[11] Later that month, Aguinaldo received yet more enthusiastic assurances from the U.S. consul at Singapore, E. Spencer Pratt, who summoned him to a private meeting. Again according to Aguinaldo, Pratt urged him to continue the revolution, citing the advent of war between Spain and the United States; he held up the Teller Amendment, disallowing a permanent Cuban colony, as evidence that the United States had no intent to occupy the Philippines. Like Wood, he would not commit these promises to writing. Pratt arranged for Aguinaldo's travel back to Hong Kong, where he might meet with Dewey himself; before leaving, Aguinaldo arranged for Pratt to purchase arms for the revolution.

The United States declared war against Spain on April 25, and Dewey was ordered to proceed immediately to Manila Bay to engage the Spanish squadron. Where Aguinaldo had hoped Dewey would recognize the revolution by carrying him back to Manila Bay triumphantly in his flagship, he discovered upon arrival in Hong Kong that Dewey had left without him. The U.S. consul in Hong Kong, Rounseville Wildman, informed Aguinaldo that Dewey had left instructions for him to arrange for Aguinaldo's return to the Philippines; Wildman also agreed to purchase arms for the revolutionaries, although a second shipment never materialized despite completed payments.

On May 1, the U.S. Asiatic Squadron utterly destroyed the Spanish naval forces at Manila Bay, and the revolutionaries in Hong Kong debated strategy. Aguinaldo wanted a written promise of recognition from Dewey but also felt compelled to establish a revolutionary government quickly before his rivals could. The exiles were deeply suspicious of U.S. intentions, as reflected in a late-April circular sent to Manila with José Alejandrino, who had been allowed to travel with Dewey. The present situation, stated the circular, was "exceedingly dangerous for the Philippines." Having engaged in discussions with the consuls and Dewey, the exiles had "infer[red] that they are trying to make colonies of us, although they said they would give us independence." It was "advisable to simulate belief at the same time equipping ourselves with arms." A part of the revolutionary forces would "aid the Americans by fighting with them in order to conceal our real intentions," while "part will be held in reserve." If the United States "triumphs and proposes a colony we shall reject such offer and rise in arms."[12]

While Dewey had severed the transoceanic cable, and the character of his victory remained unclear in Washington, McKinley ordered U.S. troops to be sent to the Philippines. Mobilization efforts in the Spanish-Cuban-American War attempted to balance the competing demands of state National Guard units for participation and the War Department's desire for sufficient manpower and an efficient, trained force. An initial plan for the expansion of regular forces to 67,000 and the use of only 60,000 volunteers failed, and McKinley called instead for 125,000 volunteers, undermining any hopes for an orderly mobilization or a trained fighting force. During the chaotic period that followed, new volunteers would be sworn into federal service through an additional oath of enlistment to serve for the duration of the war. The first three expeditions left San Francisco to great fanfare between May 25 and June 27; by late July, nearly 11,000 U.S. soldiers had arrived. Among them were fifteen state volunteer units, who would remain in the islands until mid-1899, when they would be replaced by regular army units. Officers and ordinary soldiers admitted complete ignorance regarding the character of the islands or their people; they were also unclear as to the exact nature of their mission.

THE VICTORIOUS DEWEY held Aguinaldo at arm's length until mid-May, sending a cruiser to bring him to Manila. The content of their meetings remains unclear, the controversy hinging on different understandings, and manipulations, of the symbolism of recognition. Aguinaldo claimed Dewey had honored him as a general, urged the lifting of a Philippine flag, and promised U.S. recognition of Philippine independence. Dewey had supplied arms to the revolutionaries upon their landing in Cavite on May 19. On the twenty-sixth, Secretary of the Navy John D. Long cabled Dewey warning him to avoid "political alliances with the insurgents or any faction in the Islands that would incur liability to maintain their cause in the future"; on June 3, Dewey answered that he had complied.[13] At the same time, Dewey had "given [Aguinaldo] to understand that I consider insurgents as friends, being opposed to a common enemy."[14]

Aguinaldo quickly mobilized forces throughout the region to resume the aborted revolution. In doing so, he was extremely aware of the tenuous diplomatic position in which the revolution found itself and urged a "civilized" war on Spanish land forces. The quest for recognition must continue in the context of war. "[I]n respect to our conduct," he wrote in a May 21 proclamation, he had informed Dewey and "other nations" that "we shall carry on a modern war." When a Spaniard surrendered, "he must be pardoned and treated well," so that subsequently "you will see that our reputation will be very good in the eyes of all Europe, which will declare for our independence." If "we do not conduct ourselves thus," he warned, "the Americans will decide to sell us or else divide up our territory, as they will hold us incapable of governing our land."[15] Aguinaldo's predictive sense and success in controlling his troops were conveyed in a subsequent report by U.S. consul O. F. Williams. While Spaniards in the campaign had "cruelly and barbarously slaughter[ed] Filipinos taken in arms" and "often noncombatants, women, and children," Williams observed, victorious insurgents would "spare life, protect the helpless, and nurse, feed, and care for Spaniards taken prisoner and for Spanish wounded as kindly as they care for the wounded fallen in their own ranks." In doing so they were, of course, "following American example."[16]

Aguinaldo took advantage of his consolidation of revolutionary forces to declare the Philippine Islands independent at a ceremony held on June 12 in Cavite, three weeks after the first U.S. expedition's departure from San Francisco. Such a declaration might galvanize the Filipino populace behind Aguinaldo's leadership and simultaneously raise the stakes in negotiations with the United States and other powers, from the recognition of belligerency to the recognition of independent statehood. The "Act of the Proclamation of Independence of the Filipino People" was a bold statement of the "independence of our territory" and the "recovery of our sovereignty." Witnessed by "the Supreme Judge of the Universe" and protected by "the *Mighty and Humane North American Nation*," the "inhabitants of all these Philippine Islands" asserted their right to be "free and independent," with "every political tie" between the Philippines and Spain "completely severed and annulled." It acknowledged "the Dictatorship" established by Aguinaldo, "the Supreme Chief of the nation," which "this day commences to have a life of its own."[17] The "life" of this nation was heralded with the performance of a newly written national anthem, and the Philippine national flag was unfurled for the first time.

The ceremony's success in gaining recognition was ambiguous. Commodore Dewey politely declined an invitation but sent a colonel of artillery, J. M. Johnson, who witnessed the ceremonies and signed the declaration as a witness, "the only foreigner" present.[18] Statements of recognition flowed, however, freely from the consuls, Pratt and Wildman. Just days before the declaration, on June 8, a delegation of Filipinos had gone to Pratt's office—decorated simply with a U.S. flag and a portrait of Aguinaldo—and "serenaded" him. Dr. Isidoro de Santos expressed gratitude for Dewey's "moral and material support" through Pratt, "the genuine representative of the great and powerful American Republic." He hoped that "persevering in its humanitarian policy," the United States would "continue to support" Pratt's agreement with Aguinaldo, "that is to say, the independence of the Philippine Islands, under an American protectorate."[19] The *Straits Times* reported Pratt's response the following day. He recalled how, after one hour's meeting, he had decided that Aguinaldo was "the man for the occasion" and arranged his meeting with Dewey, hailing Aguinaldo's "co-operating on land with the Americans at sea."[20]

Wildman was even more exuberantly committed. "Your work and ability has been fully recognized by not only the people of the United States, but by the entire civilized world," he wrote Aguinaldo July 25. He urged

Aguinaldo to "stand shoulder to shoulder with our forces" and to prevent "any small differences of opinion and fancied slights" from keeping his troops from "freeing your Islands." Wildman reported ominous word of a European scramble for the islands, which would "require all the power of the United States and Great Britain to keep your Islands in tact [*sic*] and to hold you as the first man in them." He assured Aguinaldo that he had "vouched for your honesty and earnestness of purpose to the President of the United States and to our people, and they are ready to extend their hand to you as a Brother, and aid you in every laudable ambition." Recalling that the United States had liberated Cuba rather than intervening "for the love of conquest or the hope of gain," he promised that "[w]hatever the final disposition of the conquered territory may be," Aguinaldo could "trust the United States that justice and honor will control all their dealings with you."[21]

In step with contemporary, preprofessional U.S. diplomatic practice, Pratt and Wildman were in essence independent operators, embracing the rush of history, exaggerating their own authority, and cutting deals opportunistically.[22] The State Department belatedly imposed its will. Secretary of State William R. Day rebuked Pratt for failing to "avoid unauthorized negotiations with the Philippine insurgents." Pratt's speech had "occasioned a feeling of disquietude and a doubt as to whether some of your acts may not have borne significance and produced an impression which this Government would be compelled to regret."[23] Tensions between metropolitan mandates and local compromises would continue until the outbreak of a second war. Dewey and Thomas Anderson, commander of U.S. Army troops, both had instructions not to communicate directly with Aguinaldo. But Anderson had actively sought Aguinaldo's cooperation, particularly in the delicate matter of the removal of Filipino troops from Cavite so that it might be occupied by U.S. troops. On July 4, 1898, he wrote that he and his forces had "entire sympathy and most friendly sentiments for the native people of the Philippine Islands." Referring to Aguinaldo as "your excellency," he explained that in occupying Cavite, he did "not wish to interfere with your residence here and the exercise by yourself and other native citizens of all functions and privileges not inconsistent with military rule."[24] Aguinaldo, suspicious of the arrival of U.S. troops, demanded a written request that would formally recognize his government but ultimately agreed to move his troops prior to the written agreement; the request was never submitted.

Competitive State-Building

As Aguinaldo and others feared, the arrival of U.S. Army expeditions from late June through late July turned the balance decisively against their recognition. With additional troop strength, U.S. commanders felt less need for Filipino allies against the Spanish and more concern for the question of how to keep the "insurgents" outside of Manila when it fell. This latter preoccupation emerged in secret dialogues between U.S. and Spanish officers who, understanding their desperately weakened position, agreed to surrender in a prearranged battle in mid-August with the as-surance that Filipino troops would not be allowed to enter the city. U.S. officers alerted Filipino forces that the coming battle was to be entirely between Spaniards and Americans. On August 13, Anderson sent a tele-gram to Aguinaldo warning tersely, "Do not let your troops enter Manila. On this side of the Pasig River you will be under fire."[25]

That day, U.S. troops stormed the city, facing ineffectual Spanish fire; U.S. commanders charged their soldiers with keeping Filipino forces outside the city, but without engaging them. At one point outside Intra-muros, or "Walled City," Filipino forces encountered U.S. troops, which pushed them aside; in some instances, Spaniards caught between them rushed to the U.S. lines for protection. The surrender agreement dis-solving Spanish authority in the islands—Spain's final official act fol-lowing over three hundred years of colonial rule and the United States' first—marked a racial distinction between Spain's "European" and "na-tive" troops.[26] Spain's flag was hauled down, and the U.S. flag was raised over Manila, to remain there until the Japanese occupation in 1941. De-spite their sense of triumph, American troops were unsettled by condi-tions that were, in the words of Iowa volunteer Joseph Markey, "the most singular in war's history." Manila was "a city occupied by victorious troops, the enemy walking peacefully in the streets, while the supposed allies are armed and at the very outskirts of the city."[27]

The exclusion of Filipino troops from Manila was reflected in the first U.S. declaration of sovereignty over the Philippines: the instructions McKinley had given to General Merritt on May 12, which Merritt had translated into Tagalog and Spanish and circulated only on August 14. The instructions, which formally governed Filipino-American relations during the negotiations at Paris, preemptively claimed for the United States a wide degree of sovereignty in the islands. The Philippine Republic, its officers, and its army did not appear in them. In that manufactured vacuum, U.S. commanders were charged with guaranteeing the security of persons and property in the Philippines. They were to be given rights to all public property and were to enforce existing Spanish laws until revoked by the occupying power. They were to publish proclamations explaining that the United States' intention was not to make war against Filipinos but to "protect them in their homes, in their employments, and in their personal and religious rights." In the case of disorder, they were authorized to replace Filipino officials with officials from the United States and to establish courts of justice. They were charged with protecting, so far as it was possible, churches, schools, and monuments; transportation systems could be seized but not retained. Taxes formally remitted to the Spanish government would be paid to the occupation government toward its expenses; private property seized would be paid for "at a fair valuation."[28]

In the tense period between the U.S. occupation of Manila and early the following February, the Philippines found itself between two colliding declarations of sovereignty: Aguinaldo's declaration of June 12 and McKinley's, circulated after August 14. During that period, Manila and its outskirts were characterized by competitive state-building between Filipinos and Americans: both the Philippine Republic and U.S. Army forces in occupied Manila struggled to construct states to fill in the outlines of their respective declarations with political facts on the ground. Philippine state-building had a two-month lead on U.S. imperial state-building. Following the Declaration of Independence, Aguinaldo had moved quickly to build a viable state, formally renaming the "Dictatorial Government" a "Revolutionary Government," issuing the terms for municipal and provincial governments and courts, establishing an executive cabinet, and providing for a future congress to be elected by an elite male suffrage. State revenues were to be drawn in through citizenship certificates, bonds, sliding-scale taxes, and land seizures. In July, the new state inaugurated an official organ, *El Heraldo de la Revolución*, which published circulars, orders, and revolutionary speeches; it, along with the semiofficial newspaper *La Independencia*, was meant to be a concrete and mobile representation of the Philippine Republic's sovereignty before audiences both within and outside the archipelago, symbols of, and means to, a Filipino "imagined community" united by news and literary association.[29] Republic state-building continued in full force following the U.S. occupation of Manila. In August, local governments were ordered to reopen schools; a "Literary University" was established. That month, Aguinaldo ordered the seat of government moved to Malolos, fearing an armed clash with the Americans in Manila. In the middle of September, the first Philippine Congress was convened at Malolos: the congress, which drafted a constitution based in part on those of Belgium, Mexico, Guatemala, Costa Rica, Brazil, and France, was an elite-dominated institution that enfranchised and won over influential *ilustrados* fearful of a revolutionary government dominated by military executives and the "ignorant" masses beneath them.[30]

The Philippine Republic took explicit steps to prevent U.S. advances in the game of competitive state-building. Officials passed a law requiring foreign travelers to carry passes signed and secured from high government officials; foreigners engaged in the shipping business would have to have permits to operate; laws prohibited Filipinos from contracting with foreigners without government consent; no laborers but Filipinos could unload cargoes. The new state also prohibited any foreign vessel from landing troops on Philippine soil.[31] At the same time, Aguinaldo and other Filipino leaders strategically invoked American precedents in the interests of winning U.S. recognition. Speaking before the Malolos congress, Aguinaldo dispatched Spain by lamenting that it had once been "a kingdom well-known for goodness like the great North American nation," an "honorable friend" who showed "the greatness of her government to the world," by "aiding the enslaved countries to rise to their feet, and not colonizing them for her advantage." He then declared Philippine independence by borrowing and adapting the Monroe Doctrine against the United States itself. "[N]ow we witness the truth of what the famous President Monroe said, that the 'United States is for the Americans,'" he said. "[N]ow I answer that 'the Philippines is for the Filipinos.'"[32]

U.S. military commanders also extended their control through competitive state-building in Manila and elsewhere. Inside the city, they took over policing and criminal justice and inaugurated sanitary campaigns that would protect U.S. forces from disease, advertise the United States' "benevolence," and through its close ties with spies, yield intelligence. These efforts also involved the enlistment and cultivation of *ilustrado* elites in the city who were, in many cases, eager to find a potential counterweight to the revolution. In their relationship to the Philippine Army on the edge of the city, U.S. commanders' demands tested the limits of their sovereignty, calling for the release of the Philippine Army's Spanish prisoners, for example, which Aguinaldo refused. U.S. commanders were also aggressive in seeking territorial concessions, calling for the abandonment of two suburbs that they maintained were formally inside the boundary lines of Manila. Gen. Elwell Otis stated that failure to comply would result in "forcible action."[33] Otis followed Aguinaldo's withdrawal with yet another demand on the strategic suburb of Pandacan; following protests, Aguinaldo again pulled back his forces, although he successfully resisted the establishment of a U.S. hospital there.[34]

Filipino state-building had transnational dimensions, with recognition sought through international diplomacy. Aguinaldo appointed diplomatic emissaries to travel to European capitals and to Washington to lobby for the recognition of the Philippine Republic. These agents launched legal and historical arguments for the sovereignty of the Philippine Republic and the impossibility of the islands' legitimate transfer from Spain to the United States. These claims were forcefully expressed by Felipe Agoncillo, the representative of the Philippine Republic sent to the United States to lobby on behalf on Philippine independence. In his January 30, 1899, "Memorial to the Senate of the United States," Agoncillo asserted that the United States' formal recognition of the Philippine Republic had already been established by U.S. consular and naval dealings with Aguinaldo's government. By the time of the United States' declaration of war, he claimed, the army of the Philippine Revolution had advanced sufficiently against Spanish forces that Spain had no legal title or right to cede the islands to the United States. Furthermore, Filipinos had successfully undermined Spanish control, as rebellions in lowland areas had broken out "continuously with greater or less fury for the past hundred years." Including Muslims and animists within the boundaries of the new Filipino polity, he noted that "a large number of my countrymen" had "never been subdued by Spanish power." Agoncillo backed this legal-sovereignty argument with facts on the ground, in the shape of a map showing Americans in control of 143 square miles of the islands, and Filipinos, 167,845 square miles. Agoncillo also appealed to the United States' own history and political institutions, inviting American attention "to several notable and exact American precedents" and urging "the Republic of America" to "adhere to the teachings of international law as laid down by some of its founders."[35]

Whether undertaken in the form of competitive state-building, external diplomacy, or publication, many of the revolutionaries' campaigns for recognition were waged in the language of "civilization." During mid-1898, Filipino leaders had emphasized the favorable treatment of Spanish prisoners as outward demonstrations of the revolution's civilization. The republic's publications also frequently tied sovereignty to claims of social-evolutionary standing. Agoncillo himself published an essay entitled "Are the Filipinos Civilized?" for a popular American magazine in May 1899, answering affirmatively.[36] This brand of argument was common in *La Independencia*, whose editors saw it—much as had the editors of *La Solidaridad*—as a means of projecting Filipino civilization toward the outside world. In their first issue, the editors described "Our Program" as "demonstrating the ideal and the supreme aspiration of the country," "publicizing the priorities of our government," and "requesting recognition of our independence from other nations, grounding ourselves in the capacity of the race, in the deeds that outwardly reveal our culture and in the vitality that we demonstrate in governing 26 provinces with more than 3 million inhabitants."[37]

Cultural evidence of such "capacity" poured off the pages of *La Independencia*. Its banner head promised "Literature, Arts, Commerce, Economic Questions, News from Abroad, Drawings, Chronicles of Art, War Notes, Correspondents in all the provinces of the Archipelago, London, Paris, Madrid, Singapore, Hong-Kong and Saigon."[38] The paper featured articles on "The Culture of the Filipinos" and descriptions of "Our People" and simultaneously attacked "Campaigns of Hate" and "Racial Hatreds."[39] During late 1898 and early 1899, it defended the sovereignty of the republic through reports of successful rule in the provinces and the humanitarian treatment of Spanish prisoners and exposed suspicious U.S. maneuvers. At the same time, it highlighted treatises on "modern" government, including civil service reform, municipal budgeting, public instruction, moral reform, public hygiene, and "the spirit of association."[40]

The other face of *La Independencia* looked anxiously inward; while the newspaper itself was meant to reveal "the union of the Filipinos," its editors admitted that the popular classes had been "distanced" and that print propaganda was needed to ground Filipinos "into a single soul." As one editorial ominously suggested, displaying "capacity" before European and U.S. audiences necessitated government without dissent and the sacrifice of democracy and popular participation. Precisely because Filipinos were often depicted as "*savage* and *uncivilized*," it was necessary for "all classes" to "demonstrate that there is sensibleness and nobility among our people." Accusations from without could foreclose possibilities for internal conflict. The editorial urged that in their political behavior, Filipinos demonstrate that "we know how to govern and be governed without quarreling or factions, with perfect discipline and order as if we had been habituated to this life from ancient times."[41]

While U.S. officers on the ground continually attempted to use the revolution without recognizing it, at least some of the "civilizational" campaign appears to have been convincing. Dewey informed Washington that he viewed Filipinos as "far superior in their intelligence and more capable of self government than the natives of Cuba."[42] General Anderson cabled Washington conceding "with all deference that we have heretofore underrated the natives." Filipinos were "not ignorant, savage tribes, but have a civilization of their own." Though "insignificant in appearance," they were "fierce fighters, and for a tropical people are industrious."[43] Even following the outbreak of war, Gen. Charles King, writing in a Milwaukee newspaper, asserted that "[t]he capability of the Filipinos for self-government can not be doubted." Their leaders were "highly educated"; the population was "industrious, frugal, temperate" and could "look out for themselves infinitely better than our people imagine." Like Dewey, he believed they ranked "far higher than the Cubans"; they were also superior to "the uneducated negroes to whom we have given the right of suffrage."[44]

Filipino-American Encounters

On the ground, relations between Filipinos and American soldiers were as varied as the questions of recognition they raised. U.S. soldiers in occupied Manila found themselves in an enticing, disturbing, and illegible Filipino urban world; Filipinos unsure of the invading army's status were wary of the Americans in political terms but eager for their business. Most social contacts were commercial in nature, with Filipinos and Americans first meeting each other haggling over food, transport, liquor, and sex. Clashing interests, failed translations, mutual suspicions, and questions of jurisdiction sometimes erupted into animosity and conflict, especially where U.S. soldiers became drunk and disorderly or failed to pay their debts. Soldiers commonly characterized Filipinos on the whole as filthy, diseased, lazy, and treacherous in their business dealings, sometimes applying the term "nigger" to them. One anonymous black soldier, reflecting back on this period, stated that the subsequent war would not have broken out "if the army of occupation would have treated [Filipinos] as people." But shortly after the seizure of Manila, white troops had begun "to apply home treatment for colored peoples: cursed them as damned niggers, steal [from] them and ravish them, rob them on the street of their small change, take from the fruit vendors whatever suited their fancy, and kick the poor unfortunate if he complained."[45]

As more than one soldier made clear, one of the chief sources of rising American animus against Filipinos was a crisis of martial masculinity.[46] U.S. soldiers sent west during the Spanish-Cuban-American War had thrilled at the idea of killing Spaniards in manly combat, only to see their quest for martial glory culminate in a "sham battle" in mid-August and a quick armistice. Disappointment at the loss of genuine combat opportunity was compounded by strict orders not to engage Filipino troops. The time required for treaty negotiation and confirmation was paid for on the ground in American masculinist angst. Some American troops ably shifted their attention from Spanish to potential Filipino antagonists.[47] Irving Speer noted hopefully in late August that he and others had been told "that there were other city [sic] still held by the Spaniard[s] and that we would see plenty of fighting before we left the Islands also that the Fipilinos [sic] were getting ugly at not being allowed to enter the city." By early November, he observed that the "men [were] getting more disatisfied, now that peace is almost sure between Spain and the U.S."[48] The soldiers "all want to fight, and would be terribly disappointed and chagrined if they didn't get what they came over here for," wrote Claude Myers to his parents in January 1899. "Besides, if we are going to get into trouble, we want to get into it now, while we are feeling that way." If the soldiers were "held back too long," he feared, "that feeling might wear off."[49]

If an abstract desire for war fueled U.S. hostilities, so did Filipino assertions and U.S. orders not to engage. According to Speer, when Filipino troops would advance, "our outpost would fall back," and soon Filipino soldiers "thought we were cowards, and began to insult while on guard[,] call us all kinds of names and dare us to stand our grounds."[50] It was bad enough that "the people in the city call us cowards and the spaniard women spit on you as you pass beneath her window or through [throw] dirty water on you."[51] Close to American military interlocutors he would soon flatter with a campaign book, Karl Irving Faust blamed the war on Filipino soldiers' "continuous insults," which Americans had "endure[d] . . . with patience." This "restraint" had been wrongly interpreted by the Filipinos as "manifestations of cowardice," making them foolhardy. Meanwhile, American restraint boiled into ferocious anger. "Upon the part of the rank and file of the Americans," Faust recalled, "and doubtless, also, upon the part of many of the officers, there grew up a feeling of intense personal hatred of their tormentors, and an earnest desire to be turned loose upon them and kill them."[52]

As U.S. troops' animosity intensified, Filipinos developed suspicions of the U.S. military presence in the islands in which circulating rumors of race played an important role. Where U.S. forces had deliberately left their ultimate intentions ambiguous, Filipinos filled this gap with their knowledge of the United States' domestic racial history. "One of the stories that received universal acceptance," reported General McReeve, "was that ever since the Americans had liberated their negro slaves they had been looking around for others and thought they had found them at last in the Philippines."[53] Two naval officers reported that many Filipinos they encountered "have been prejudiced against us by the Spaniards," charges "so severe that what the natives have since learned has not sufficed to disillusion them." Two points in particular had stood out regarding "our policy toward a subject people": "that we have mercilessly slain and finally exterminated the race of Indians that were native to our soil and that we went to war in 1861 to suppress an insurrection of negro slaves, whom we also ended by exterminating. Intelligent and well-informed men have believed these charges. They were rehearsed to us in many towns in different provinces, beginning at Malolos. The Spanish version of our Indian problem is particularly well known."[54]

One black veteran reported during this period that when Filipinos were "told of America's treatment of the black population," they were "made to feel that it is better to die fighting than to become subject to a nation where, as they are made to believe, the colored man is lynched and burned alive indiscriminately."[55] Correspondent Frederick Palmer blamed the outbreak of war, in part, on precisely these suspicions. Once Americans had allowed Aguinaldo and his compatriots, who were "familiar . . . with the position of the colored man in our Southern States," to become "convinced that their lot was to be that of the 'nigger,'" the Filipinos had begun to isolate U.S. troops. "All prominent Filipinos" that Palmer had spoken with had agreed: "If the status of the negro, as they understood it, was to be theirs in the new system, they would have to leave the islands anyway, and they had concluded to make a fight before going."[56]

Parallel to the rising hostility and suspicion was a kind of competitive sociability among Spaniards and Filipinos for U.S. recognition. In occupied Manila, U.S. soldiers found themselves drinking and card-playing with the Spanish soldiers they had defeated; U.S. officers were invited to the homes of high Spanish officials and wealthy Spanish merchants, presumably learning much about the indigenous population of the islands in the process. At the same time, Manila's Filipino elites actively courted the U.S. officials in their midst with what were for the Americans awe-inspiring demonstrations of hospitality. The result, in the interval between wars, was a striking amount of recognition, as U.S. soldiers came to know individual Filipinos and their families and visited their churches and homes. Up until the very brink of war, American soldiers frequented Filipino concerts, dances, ceremonies, and dinners, often recording their admiration for Filipino grace, generosity, and artistic achievement in their diaries and letters. One striking example was a poem presented at a Thanksgiving dinner in Manila in November 1898, which recalled the recent fall of Manila and expressed the soldiers' thanks:

> We're thankful that the City's ours, and floats the Stars and Stripes;
> We're thankful that our cause is one that from these Islands wipes
> The degenerate oppressors of a brother human kin
> Who now—beneath "Old Glory"—a nation's place may win.[57]

There were dark signs here: the U.S. flag as the sole guarantor of liberty; passive Filipinos as objects of U.S. redemption; the sense that Filipinos still had a "nation" to win ahead of them "beneath 'Old Glory.'" As later colonial history would show, "brothers" were not necessarily equals. But what was striking in light of future developments was that Filipinos were still "human kin."

Filipino-American sociability and its impact on the politics of recognition can also be found in the short story "Itamo, the Insurrecto: A Story of the Philippines," published in December 1898 in a short-lived U.S. Army magazine in Manila, *Soldier's Letter*. At the story's beginning, the narrator, an American soldier stationed near Manila before its fall, finds "[a]ll things on the Island of Luzon . . . new and strange," especially the mysterious Filipino soldiers outside the city. Making his way to the Filipino lines, he encounters "great disappointment" in the shape of Itamo, an "insurrecto": short in stature, his uniform "a collection of rags," his use of a Spanish Mauser sporadic and inaccurate. After the fall of Manila, the narrator finds himself in the Alhambra Café, where he is eagerly greeted by "a handsome native, dressed in the height of eastern fashion . . . with regular features. . . . [H]is bronze skin made a fine contrast to his white clothes, white shirt, collar and tie." It takes the American a moment to recognize "the dirty, half-fed, native soldier of the trenches"; indeed, he "marveled at the transformation." The two strike up a friendship, the narrator tells us, "wandering through the narrow, crooked streets sightseeing, and he delighted to show me his own people."[58]

The narrator loses track of his friend and is later sent on a mission into the countryside where, riding at night, he is overtaken by three armed natives. Two mistake him for a hated Spaniard, but the third man, the narrator's "lost friend" Itamo, quickly recognizes his American companion and warns his compatriots away; when they refuse, he engages one of them in battle. The battle is "a magnificent exhibition of skill"; Itamo defeats his antagonist, only to be stabbed by another, whom the narrator then shoots and kills.[59] While recognition here was still highly limited—Itamo's sacrifice for the American is taken for granted, for example—the narrator's collegiality with the "insurrecto" is still striking in light of what was to come.

Given the wide latitude of McKinley's instructions, Americans and Filipinos also met as members of rival states-in-the-making, as U.S. soldiers consolidated military control over Manila and its municipal government—from sanitation to law enforcement—and Filipino soldiers extended the republic's control in the wake of Spanish defeats. Competitive statebuilding, sociability, and the question of recognition all converged in the inland expedition of Luzon taken by two naval officers, William Wilcox and L. R. Sargent, in November and December 1898. While the two men's task was "of a very indefinite nature," it was fundamentally a problem of recognition: they were to determine whether the institutions controlling the Filipino countryside constituted a state and, if a state, whether it was hostile or not to two wandering U.S. naval officers. As Sargent put it, they were "to proceed as far to the northward as the character of the country and the attitude of the natives would permit, and to return only when forced to do so."[60]

If border control was a state's measure, then the Philippine Republic was up and running: Aguinaldo offered the two friendship and verbal consent but no written passports. As a result, the two set out relying on local *presidentes*, who provided them local passports, carriers, and safe passage between towns, although at least one had hesitated to give assistance in fear that "any incident" might "create a wrong and injurious impression of the good faith of the Philippines."[61] Wilcox noted, of elaborate balls and operas staged in their honor, that he had never "been treated with more kindly hospitality." Sargent, however, observed that Filipino responses to them varied to a frustrating degree between "the coldest suspicion" and "the most demonstrative hospitality." Some members

This illustration from the short story "Itamo, the Insurrecto," written by a U.S. soldier in the Philippines in late 1898 and published in the *Soldier's Letter*, suggests the complex interactions and perceptions of U.S. forces in the islands before the outbreak of the Philippine-American War, some of which were conducive to U.S. recognition of Filipinos. In the story, a U.S. soldier dismisses the dirty "insurrecto" Itamo whom he meets in a trench, then befriends the same man—mannerly and properly dressed—when they meet again in a Manila café. The story thematizes issues of misapprehension and argues that Filipino insurgents were civilized and deserving of recognition. Reproduced from the *Soldier's Letter* with permission, Lopez Memorial Museum.

of the *principalía* may have seen great advantage in winning over two naive Americans; others may have seen in them only the opening wedge of an invasion. At one town they might be greeted "by the ringing of the church bells and the music of the band, and at the next by the critical cross-questioning of the local authorities."[62]

In either case, local officers of the republic lost no chance to represent to visiting Americans their authority and popular support. Wilcox and Sargent were regularly treated to elaborate Filipino patriotic celebrations, stirring declarations of independence, and impressive military drills. "At that time the enthusiasm of the people was tuned to the highest pitch," reported Sargent. "In every village, every man was training in arms. Companies were formed of boys, from eight years of age upward." He had witnessed the "impressive ceremony" that transferred control from a military officer to an elected official in a "simple and efficient" civil government. The new governor "declared the purpose of the people to expend the last drop of their blood, if necessary, in defending the liberty thus gained against the encroachments of any nation whatsoever." Many times villagers had gathered in the large room of the Presidencia where the two men were quartered and "put their whole hearts into the songs in which their patriotism found vent."[63] When asked about the Philippines' status, "leading townspeople" had answered in unison that they would "accept nothing short of independence."[64]

But even as Wilcox and Sargent worked their way across Luzon, the unstable political window through which they were traveling began to close. As steamers and telegraph lines brought word of the Treaty of Paris from Hong Kong newspapers, Wilcox and Sargent faced stiffer restrictions. "Already the hope was fading that freedom from Spain meant freedom of government," wrote Sargent. "The feeling toward Americans was changing, and we saw its effect in the colder manner of the people, and in their evident desire to hustle us along the most direct road to Manila."[65] The party came under greater scrutiny and was detained or forced back, subject to a new regulation that travelers not "carry arms, nor approach within 200 meters of a fortification, not make any plans, or take photographs of them."[66] Their final report, written upon their return in December, was a curious hybrid that, on the one hand, took note of tactical and logistical questions appropriate to war and, on the other, recognized the legitimacy of the republic, the fervor of Filipino revolutionary aspirations, and the varied capacities of the Filipino people. Perhaps on these latter merits—perhaps due to bureaucratic inertia—it was issued into the public record as a Senate document only in 1900, a year and a half after it was originally filed.

While Wilcox and Sargent were traveling in the Luzon provinces, U.S. and Spanish commissioners in France settled the disposition of the Philippine Islands, culminating in the signing of the Treaty of Paris on December 10, 1898. McKinley's intentions for the islands from May through October remain difficult to discern: he used vague and ambiguous rhetoric in public addresses but had unambiguously sent thousands of troops to the islands as a potential occupying force.[67] He appears to have initially favored the seizure of only a coaling station in the islands and had become persuaded that the taking of Luzon would be necessary to secure it. The decisive month appears to have been October, when McKinley stumped for candidates in the Midwest and used the opportunity both to tutor and test political audiences on the Philippines. On October 28, McKinley had cabled the commissioners at Paris that they must press for the entire archipelago, as the cession of Luzon alone would leave the rest of the islands subject to Spanish authority and to potential great-power contention, neither of which could be "justified on political, commercial, or humanitarian grounds."[68]

While the U.S. commissioners at Paris had differed on a proper course, they successfully pushed for what Spanish negotiators bitterly called the "immodest demands of a conqueror."[69] With the United States occupying Manila and the Philippine Revolution spreading, Spanish representatives were left with few options and accepted a U.S. offer of $20 million for "Spanish improvements" to the islands, signing the treaty on December 10. While in Manila and its environs questions of recognition had been ambiguous over the previous months, they had been stark at Paris: no Filipino representatives were recognized in treaty negotiations, and the islands' inhabitants, their rights and aspirations, and the Philippine Republic that acted in their name had played a minimal role in Spanish and U.S. discussions.

McKinley effectively closed the first chapter in the recognition debate in his statement of December 21, with Wilcox and Sargent scarcely out of the woods. Authored by Elihu Root and later known as McKinley's "Benevolent Assimilation" proclamation, it narrated the American destruction of the Spanish fleet and the Treaty of Paris, laid a claim to U.S. sovereignty over the entire archipelago, and sketched a bare-bones military government with improvised ground rules for the maintenance of property rights, taxation, and tariffs. McKinley seemed most concerned, however, with the recognition of U.S. sovereignty by Filipinos. In an effort to extend U.S. power "with all possible despatch," U.S. military commanders in place were to announce "in the most public manner" that the Americans had come "not as invaders or conquerors, but as friends, to protect the natives in their homes, in their employments, and in their personal and religious rights." It should be the military's "paramount aim" to "win the confidence, respect, and affection of the inhabitants of the Philippines by assuring them in every possible way that full measure of individual rights and liberties which is the heritage of free peoples, and by proving to them that the mission of the United States is one of benevolent assimilation, substituting the mild sway of justice and right for arbitrary rule."[70] Most significantly, the proclamation was a formal derecognition of the Philippine Republic and established the relationship between the United States and Filipinos as that of sovereign state to passive, individual subjects. The term "assimilation," by which the address would come to be known, held more than a hint of malice: the very fact that it required the adjective "benevolent" to soften it suggested more or less directly that there were kinds of assimilation that were not. It was also a striking reversal of the Propaganda use of the term. Where *ilustrado* activists had used it to call for Philippine rights like those enjoyed in Spain, McKinley's declaration imposed exceptional forms of sovereignty unlike those that defined the United States.

December and January saw passionate Senate and public debate on the question of the treaty's ratification. McKinley campaigned by touring in the South, asserting U.S. sovereignty and "duty" in the Philippines in advance of ratification. Senators attached various resolutions to the treaty: that would deny the United States the power "to acquire territory to be held and governed permanently as colonies" under the Constitution; that stated the United States' goal was to prepare Filipinos for self-government; that stipulated Filipinos should be granted independence as soon as a stable government was established; and that would detach ratification from endorsement of a future colonial policy.[71] It was a highly, but not exclusively, partisan debate, with annexationists, many of them Republican, speaking out in the name of the United States' duty, the extension or nonretraction of the flag, commercial opportunities in Asia, and the "uplift" of Filipinos. "Anti-imperialists," many of them Democrats, called "imperialism" a threat to the United States' domestic freedoms and racial integrity and condemned the belief in Filipino "assimilation" as folly. While the sides were closely matched, Republican political bribery and William Jennings Bryan's support for the treaty (ostensibly on the grounds that it would allow the Senate to grant Philippine independence with a simple majority) pushed it to an extremely narrow passage on February 6.

One factor in the treaty's ratification may have been the outbreak of war in the islands between U.S. and Philippine forces. Both sides had feared the political implications of war: treaty advocates feared ambivalent senators might hesitate to annex a colonial war; treaty opponents despaired that it would be impossible to argue for lowering the flag where U.S. soldiers' blood had been shed. January had seen a series of abortive negotiations between Aguinaldo and Otis; the latter had seen them as a stalling tactic that would permit the arrival of additional U.S. forces. On February 4, U.S. sentries fired on Filipino troops outside Manila, and hostilities, long awaited on both sides, erupted. Nonetheless, the outbreak of war surprised and horrified domestic American observers, who believed U.S. Army reports of Filipino aggression as its trigger.

Why do they hate us? some asked. For some, the fact of conflict itself ended the debate on Filipino recognition. "The Filipinos have chosen a bloody way to demonstrate their incapacity for self-government," wrote the *New York Times*, "but it has been effectual." Special hostility was directed at Filipinos' failure to recognize the Americans as liberators. The *Times* could not comprehend Filipinos' ingratitude in launching an "insane attack . . . upon their liberators." Unwilling to attribute much agency to Filipinos themselves, it blamed the "disastrous effect" of U.S. "anti-imperialist" propaganda, which had convinced Filipinos of a "plot to put the yoke of a fresh vassalage on their necks." As a result, "blood has been shed, sedition fomented, hatred and distrust engendered"; what it called "our long task" in the Philippines had become "more difficult." "We meet these people now not as pupils at school," it observed, "but as armed rebels in the field." Nonetheless, the military's task was, "with all needed firmness" and "force proportioned to the degree of resistance," to educate Filipinos, who must be "made to understand that they must recognize our authority and obey."[72]

War for Recognition

The first few months of combat saw U.S. forces defeat and overrun the republican army outside of Manila and capture several important cities, especially Malolos, the republic's capital, Panay, and Iloilo. Filipino military casualties were high, and in the case of the latter city, naval bombardment resulted in massive destruction and loss of civilian life.[73] Land-ing in Iloilo after the bombing, Thomas Osborne confronted impressions that would "never grow old to my memory." "Every house in town was burned," he wrote, "and I saw dead women, dead horses, dead men, dead dogs, dead cows and many burned people," some with "both legs shot off others with one arm torn off and their carcasses lying partly in the fire and partly out."[74]

In important ways, the first period of the war continued the struggle over recognition, as each side attempted, in its combat, to persuade the other side of its "civilization." U.S. Army policy sought to achieve Filipino recognition as well as submission. General MacArthur emphasized in his field orders that "one of the most important duties of American soldiers to assist in establishing friendly relations with the natives" was "kind and considerate treatment in all matters arising from personal contact."[75] General Henry Lawton told a subordinate that pacification would require the U.S. Army to "impress the inhabitants with the idea of our good intentions and destroy the idea that we are barbarians or anything of that sort."[76] However profound the failure of recognition had been at the level of diplomacy, the U.S. Army still recognized its enemy sufficiently to fight in conventional ways. This approach came to be known as the "friendly policy," a term that emphasized the voluntary and benevolent nature of "civilized" war.

At the same time, the U.S. government advanced what came to be known as the "policy of attraction," aimed at achieving the recognition of Filipino elites. It was undertaken most energetically by the Philippine Commissions, the first of which arrived just one month into the war, on March 5. The commission, under Cornell president Jacob Gould Schur-man, was composed of a diplomat, two military officers, and one scientist. It was charged with advisory and investigative responsibilities, but its second incarnation, under William Howard Taft, would be given legisla-tive and executive functions and emerge as the core of the "postwar" government. Once settled into the Audiencia, former home of the Span-ish Supreme Court, the commission's daily sessions became the central ritual of urban, wartime collaboration, where informants, especially il-ustrados, exchanged testimony favorable to U.S. sovereignty for political patronage.[77] While the commission prided itself on its consultation with "men of all classes," its itemized list of interlocutors was striking for its lack of breadth: "bankers, brokers, merchants, lawyers, physicians, rail-road and shipowners, educators, and public officials."[78]

Over the next year, the commission built an authoritative record of affairs in the Philippines aimed at defending U.S. retention of the islands, while "attracting" key sectors of the Philippine elite. It also developed a compelling account of the revolution in dialogue with these elites: the "insurrection" was the work of a small faction, usually a "single tribe" of Tagalogs, and would evaporate with the conciliation of elites, accompanied by symbolic efforts at "benevolence." As one "attracted" Filipino put it, one should deal with the rebellion as one would deal with a stubborn donkey, "with a rattan in one hand and a lump of sugar in the other."[79] By May, the policy of attraction appeared to be yielding important political results: the defection of key *ilustrados* and their taking up posts in the military government, especially Benito Legarda, Felipe Buencamino, Trinidad H. Pardo de Tavera, and Cayetano Arellano; the inauguration of Pardo de Tavera's proannexation newspaper *La Democracia*; and the displacement of Apolinario Mabini's irreconcilable faction within the republic by more conciliatory elements.

In carrying out its own policy of "attraction," the U.S. Army extended recognition to Filipino military units, eventually organized as the Philippine Scouts. In doing so, it was adopting Spanish colonial precedents: the Spanish colonial army had recruited Macabebes from Pampanga province to serve in its colonial militias in campaigns against bandits, animists, and revolutionaries, as well as in foreign campaigns. The U.S. Army was also acting on broader traditions of European and American imperialism. As Capt. Charles Rhodes noted in a 1902 essay, Britain and other colonial empires had used native forces in crushing colonial resistance, nor had the United States "disdained to use native against native" in its wars for the continent. The recruitment of the Scouts had been the initiative of Lt. Matthew A. Batson, who in July 1899 had requested permission to recruit a single company of "Macabebe Scouts" as guides; their assistance to U.S. forces overcame initial suspicions by U.S. commanders, who ordered the recruitment of more units in late 1899 and 1900, as both guides and combat forces.[80]

Filipino units became a military necessity as resistance to U.S. control outlasted congressional authorization for the U.S. volunteer army, which returned to the United States by July 1901, leaving only U.S. Regulars and Scouts. As recruitment of Filipinos was extended in the context of guerrilla war, it was also centralized and standardized. Until July 1901, collaborating Filipino units had been civilian contractors with the U.S. Army's Quartermaster Department. By early 1902, new congressional legislation and army regulations established a unified system of Philippine Scouts, composed of fifty companies for a total of approximately 5,000 men under the direct control of the U.S. Army. It would play a crucial role in the eventual suppression of the "insurrection," especially in terms of local geographic, linguistic, and social knowledge.[81]

But where the U.S. Army attracted Filipino military forces, it recognized them as members of "tribes." Scout recruitment was heaviest in Pampangan and Ilocano speaking areas, and thinnest among Tagalogs. In organizing units, U.S. officers followed Spanish precedent in segregating soldiers within units by tribe—as well by prohibiting each "tribal" company from engaging in operations within their home region. The July 1901 reorganization of the Scouts had replaced earlier military-geographic designations—such as the 3rd and 4th District Scouts—with tribal ones, such as the Ilocano Native Scouts. For U.S. commanders, winning the war would mean fomenting and attempting to direct race war between specific Philippine tribes. Indeed, the recruitment of Macabebes had been consciously undertaken not only because of their reputed loyalty and prowess in fighting for a prior colonial power but also because of their "racial" animosity toward Tagalogs, which some called their "hereditary enemies." According to one newspaper report, Macabebes' hatred for Tagalogs was "a wonderful kind of hate," with "no reason, no palliation."[82]

At the same time, U.S. officers hesitated to recognize the Scouts fully, suspecting their courage, fearing desertion and the sale of U.S. arms to insurgents, and blocking the promotion of Filipinos to officer positions. Some feared that "race" might trump "tribe," that U.S. efforts to promote and harness conflict between tribes might give way before a race war uniting all Filipinos against Americans. Batson recalled that when he had initially asked General Otis for permission to recruit Macabebes, Otis had told him he expected they would "'put a bolo in your throat.'" The "general feeling among American officers," he wrote, "was that every Filipino was really an insurgent," a sentiment that had resulted in "the oppression of thousands of innocent natives."[83]

As the Americans sought Filipino recognition of their authority, Filipino spokesmen also continued the struggle for recognition in the midst of war, promoting Filipino civilization to the wider world as a claim for independence. "We, the Filipinos, are civilized, progressive and peace-loving people," asserted Galiciano Apacible in a Spanish-language memorandum written from Toronto in June 1900, translated and published by the Anti-Imperialist League, called "Al Pueblo Americano" (To the American People). Apacible urged Americans to "weigh our statements against the fallacies that Imperialism employs to mask its designs." These statements bore striking resemblance to the claims mounted by Filipino Propagandists as early as the 1880s. As evidence of Filipinos' right to self-government, the author invoked many witnesses who had spoken "with an impartial spirit of observation" of

> our exceptional culture, of our capacity to achieve every advancement, of the two centuries of well-received literary education that we bear, of the small number of illiterates found among the inhabitants of the islands, of the men of science and art, judges, military officers, and high dignitaries of the Church, sons of the Philippines, that in Europe, especially in Spain, were recognized for their true merit, achieving high positions, academic laurels, honors of all kinds.[84]

Filipinos had demonstrated these capacities best in the establishment of the Philippine Republic. Rather than giving in to revolutionary excess, Filipinos had established an orderly governing infrastructure, one that made science, technology, and education the hallmarks of civilization. Under the republic,

> all the administrative mechanisms, disturbed by the recent conflict, were reorganized, the mails, telegraphs and railroads functioned regularly, electric lighting was established in some communities, a new University was created, four institutions of secondary education and numerous primary schools and, in sum, the new nationality embarked upon a path of ordered evolution that promised a most smiling future.[85]

"The imperialist cannons can boast they have disrupted all this!" he wrote. This had not been inevitable: indeed, U.S. soldiers after Dewey's victory had "applauded the new oceanic nation, at the same moment that ours acclaimed liberating America." That had been "the time of beautiful fiction"; now the hour of "cruel disenchantment" had come. While Filipinos had expected to find liberation in America's shadow, America had merely "plagiarized" Spain's "boastful tyrannies." Filipinos had been compelled to demonstrate their right to independence through righteous war. "[I]f our conditions of culture and character makes us worthy of independence," he wrote, Filipinos had earned this right even more so by "the high motives that always inspired our rebellious actions."[86]

Along with demonstrating their "culture and character," some Filipino leaders conceived the struggle as explicitly antiracial. One anonymous address, "To the Filipino People," captured by the U.S. Army, affirmed Filipino bravery and sacrifice and laid claim to divinely granted freedoms. "We are living on one planet under the same celestial vault," it stated, "and if we differ in color, it is because of the distant latitudes in which we are, and this difference in no way signifies any superiority of the one over the other."[87] Foreign Secretary Apolinario Mabini urged his countrymen to "revindicate our own sovereignty" and to disbelieve promises of deliverance by outsiders like the Philippine Commission, who must not be trusted, "above all when separated by the impassable abyss opened by race hatred." Even if the U.S. Constitution followed its flag with "the rights and liberties of American citizens," he warned, "race hatred will curtail these prerogatives." Annexation to the United States in whatever form, Mabini maintained, would "unite us perpetually to a nation whose manners and customs are distinct from ours, who hate mortally the colored race, and from which we shall not be able to separate ourselves except by means of a war."[88]

Race-Making and Annexation

Race was a central issue of debate, as the administration struggled to defend the war and annexation before U.S. publics.[89] It was, in particular, pressed by U.S.-based "anti-imperialist" societies that had been inaugurated in 1898 and banded together into the Anti-Imperialist League.[90] The league, which organized chapters in Boston, Washington, Chicago, and numerous other smaller cities, drew on diverse political roots, many of them in earlier reform movements, from civil service reform leagues, to single-tax leagues, to abolitionism.[91] Anti-imperialism did not fit neatly into the party system, comprising a loose coalition of conservative and white-supremacist Democrats and an older generation of liberal Republicans. During treaty negotiations, their hope was to turn U.S. public opinion against Philippine annexation, using extensive lobbying and educational campaigns; following the outbreak of war in February 1899, they had criticized the U.S. invasion as unjust in both ends and means.[92]

Some anti-imperialism was directed at achieving, and connecting, the sociocultural recognition of Filipinos and the political recognition of the Philippine Republic. The anti-imperialist publication *Facts about the Filipinos*, for example, relied on tropes and authorities similar to those used by the Propaganda movement, citing Blumentritt at length in foregrounding the islands' "Christianized and Long Civilized Malays." Describing the inhabitants' architecture, clothing, agriculture, and industries, Blumentritt declared the Philippines' Malay population "a highly gifted and ambitious people, who deserve and will continue to deserve the sympathy of civilized Europeans." Among their virtues were hospitality, artistic achievement, and "a self-control which resembles that of northern peoples," as demonstrated in their disciplined fighting against both Spain and the United States. A subsequent issue hailed Filipinos' "Intellectual Attainments and Education," citing such key Propaganda reference points as the paintings of Juan Luna y Novicio and the *Sucesos de las Islas Filipinas* by Antonio de Morga. This recognition was, however, always predicated on sharp, hierarchical distinctions between "civilized" and "uncivilized" peoples, the latter of which were always exceptionalized and minoritized.[93]

Much anti-imperialism, however, was not based on recognition of Filipinos or the Philippine Republic.[94] Especially early on, more insular anti-imperialisms predominated, which saw Americans as empire's only victims and imagined this victimization as the United States' racial "corruption" by potential colonial subjects. The diversity of this racial anti-imperialism reflected the broad range of anti-imperialist politics.[95] Carl Schurz, for example, asserted that colonial empire posed two related threats to the United States: if colonial subjects were denied political rights, it would inevitably undercut those rights for Americans; if they were granted political rights, the political agency of "backward races" would destroy U.S. institutions. The new subjects were "exclusively of races to whom the tropical climate is congenial," including "Malays, Tagals, Filipinos, Chinese, Japanese, Negritos, and various more or less barbarous tribes in the Philippines." While some were "quite clever in their way," most were "utterly alien to us"; their tropical environment made them "incapable of being assimilated to the Anglo-Saxon." If incorporated, they would remain a "hopelessly heterogeneous element" in the population, and the "homogeneousness of the people of the republic, so essential to the working of our democratic institutions," would be "irretrievably lost."[96]

Mrs. Jefferson Davis's form of anti-imperialism was a southern, white, paternalist one that argued on the basis of the "Negro problem" that the nation should protect itself by refusing an additional "white man's burden." While she understood the Philippines to be "a sort of human mosaic" of "tribes, nationalities and races"—"impossible to classify"—she was certain that among them were "several millions of negroes" that

TROUBLES WHICH MAY FOLLOW AN IMPERIAL POLICY.

This "anti-imperialist" cartoon by Charles Neland, published in the *New York Herald*, July 3, 1898, represents one unsatisfying resolution to the paradox of an empire-building republic. Congruent with other wartime images, the Philippine population as a whole is pictured as "savage." The perils of granting these savages political representation are illustrated when the Philippine "representative" to the House, voting with his spears on an appropriation bill, sends the rest of the legislature into flight. The cartoon suggests that Filipino "incapacity for self-government" could threaten the United States' own political institutions. From Neland, *Cartoons of Our War with Spain*.

should not be annexed to the United States' still unsolved "negro problem." Imperial war would compel the United States to rule over a resentful population of Philippine "negroes," "more ignorant and more degraded
than those in our Southern States."[97]

Anti-imperialist racism was also articulated by those concerned with
the racial rights of white laborers, who directed their attention to the
threat of potential in-migration of Filipino workers that might erode the
labor rights and racial integrity of white workingmen. Samuel Gompers
feared that colonialism meant the annexation of "coolie" labor standards
that would undercut the hard-won freedoms of white workers and prophesied that the nation would be inundated by new and undesirable tides of
"aliens." "If the Philippines are annexed," he asked, how would it be
possible to prevent "the hordes of Chinese" and the Philippines' "semi-
savage races" from "swarming into the United States [and] engulfing our
people and our civilization?" How to "close the flood gates" against immigrants "coming from what will then be part of our own country?"[98]

The racial meaning of war and annexation was also debated in the
African American press.[99] Some black editorialists argued that the new
colonial annexations would provide a new outpost of Jim Crow, explicitly
challenging arguments for "benevolence." As the *Washington Bee* put it, if
blacks were "denied their rights in this country, the same conditions
would obtain in the Philippines when once the whites got control."[100]
One writer noted sardonically that when "one of the great Christian
countries" found land it desired, it was "quickly seized with a commendable desire to spread the benign influence of civilization over the natives,"
but "what a remarkably small number of natives are left after this process
of civilizing has been completed!"[101]

Many critical editors made equivalences between imperialism and Jim
Crow, urging their readers to break with traditional Republican alle-
giances and encouraging young black men to refuse Philippine military
service. "The policy of the national administration in dealing with the
Filipinos is the same as that of the Democratic state administrations in
dealing with the colored people in the southern states," said the *Richmond
Planet*.[102] The denial of republican government to Filipinos was, in the
words of one editorialist, "the same old fear of 'nigger dominance' albeit it
is to be 8000 miles away."[103] Another writer turned this connection the
other way around, condemning what he called "North Carolina imperialism," when William Jennings Bryan failed to intervene to prevent that
state's Democrats from disenfranchising blacks. "Does Mr. Bryan's zeal

for 'consent of the governed' extend to native American citizens or is it limited to Malays?" the author inquired.[104]

Some turned the imperialist language of "liberty" inward, arguing that imperialist charity should begin at home. Chicago lawyer Beauregard F. Mosely stated that "[t]he expansion we are sadly in need of is wise laws, free schools in Alton and everywhere which black and white may attend, [and] the death penalty for lynchers." Here was an "expansion" "besides which the dream of the 'Expansionist,' with his few beggarly islands, is a pitiful thing."[105] The *Cleveland Gazette* observed wryly, of the U.S. military campaign against the Boxer Rebellion, that "[f]rom a race standpoint there are plenty of 'Boxers' (Red Shirts, Ku Klux and the like) in the South who are greatly in need of the presence of soldiers."[106] The *Indianapolis Recorder* noted similarly that it was "a sinful extravagance to waste our civilizing influence upon the unappreciative Filipinos, when it is so badly needed right here in Arkansas."[107]

Some black leaders made the still more controversial move of declaring solidarity or even identity with Filipinos. "[T]here is some analogy between the struggle which is now going on among the colored people for constitutional liberty and that of a similar race in the orient and hence a bond of sympathy naturally springs up," wrote the *Washington Bee*.[108] Noting that the islands' inhabitants were "dark races," the *A.M.E. Church Review* suggested that Filipino resistance and black mobilizations in the United States were both part of a larger, global pattern:

> If we further consider that almost all the other movements involving the existence and integrity of weaker governments are against the dark races in Africa and Asia, and add to that the domestic problem of the American Negro, we are struck with the thought that a startling world movement has begun which is no less than the stirring of the spirit of civilization and [progress] among the dark-skinned races, to lead on, doubtless, to an adjustment which shall in the cycles change the present relation of oppressor and oppressed to that of coadjutors in the world's redemption.[109]

The *Cleveland Gazette* stated that Filipinos were "foreign members" of blacks' own racial household.[110] Some papers, however, especially the *Indianapolis Freeman*, challenged these connections, urging blacks to support the Republican Party and the war as an expression of "patriotism." "Imperialism and race issues have no connection," the *Freeman* stated.[111] "The strife is no race war," it had declared earlier. "It is quite time for the

Negroes to quit claiming kindred with every black face from Hannibal down. Hannibal was no Negro, nor was Aguinaldo."[112]

The task of rationalizing the war in its ends and means before the American public led to the active production of a novel, imperial-racial formation by the war's defenders. This formation had a dual character, simultaneously and reciprocally racializing Americans and Filipinos in new ways. Its first half racialized the U.S. population as "Anglo-Saxons" whose overseas conquests were legitimated by racial-historical ties to the British Empire. Opponents of the treaty and the war frequently argued that while the U.S. continental empire had involved the legitimate unfolding of republican institutions into empty (or emptied) space, the Philippine annexation constituted a disturbing departure from the United States' exceptional and exemplary political traditions, one that would ultimately undermine the nation's moral and political foundations. This apparent violation of U.S. historical laws was answered with extralegal claims of racial essence. Specifically, the war's advocates subsumed U.S. history within longer, racial trajectories of Anglo-Saxon history that folded together U.S. and British imperial histories. The Philippine-American war was a natural extension of Western conquest, and both taken together were the organic expression of the desires, capacities, and destinies of Anglo-Saxon peoples. "Blood," in the phrase widely used in this context, "was thicker than water," specifically the Atlantic that separated American and British "cousins." Americans, as Anglo-Saxons, shared Britons' racial genius for empire-building, a genius that they must exercise for the greater glory of the "race" and to advance civilization in general.[113] Anglo-Saxonist racial exceptionalism was given its most resonant expression in February 1899, when Rudyard Kipling published "The White Man's Burden" in *McClure's*. The poem condensed racial destiny and humanitarian martyrdom, recasting Americans as a "race" with an inevitable imperial destiny.

If the advocates of war attempted to racialize the U.S. population as "Anglo-Saxon" in defense of empire, they simultaneously racialized the Philippine population in ways that would legitimate U.S. conquest of the islands before domestic and international skeptics. Just as the Spanish had, the Americans would develop their own imperial indigenism aimed at denying Filipinos political power on the basis of attributed sociocultural and racial features. Specifically, the Philippine Republic would be derecognized as nothing more than the will to power of what was called a "single tribe" of Tagalogs. Conventional evolutionary theory held that societies, in evolving from savagery to civilization, moved in political terms from "tribal" fragmentation to "national" unity and toward the elusive goal of "ethnological homogeneity."[114] To successfully recognize tribes—marked by language, religion, political allegiance, or other features—was to disprove a nation's existence. Enumerate a society's fragments, and what might otherwise have looked like a nation became merely the tyranny of one tribe over others; what might have appeared to be a state became instead a problem of imperial "assimilation."[115]

The "tribalization" of the republic would rhetorically eradicate the Philippine Republic as a legitimate state whose rights the United States might have to recognize under international law. This argument was forcefully advanced by the Philippine Commission's report, whose first installment was issued in January 1900, and which represented the most influential effort to reduce the Philippine Republic to what came to be called the "single tribe" of the Tagalogs. The report's section entitled "The Native Peoples of the Philippines," written by University of Michigan zoologist Dean C. Worcester, began by admitting disputes over the civilization of the islands' people: "The most diverse and contradictory statements are frequently met with concerning the inhabitants of the Philippine Islands, at present collectively known as 'Filipinos.' Some writers credit them with a high degree of civilization, and compare them to the Pilgrim Fathers or the patriots of '76, while others regard even the more highly civilized tribes as little better than barbarians."[116]

Worcester set out to "reconcile views which are apparently contradictory" based on their investigation of Philippine conditions.[117] After a brief review of opposing views, he presented his conclusions, which drew heavily on Blumentritt's wave migration theory. The Philippine population consisted of "three sharply distinct races," the Negrito, the Indonesian, and the Malayan.[118] Early migrations by the Negritos, a group "near the bottom of the human series," had been displaced by invasions of Indonesians and Malayans with superior racial constitution and civilization.[119] Out of these three races had sprung "numerous tribes, which often differ very greatly in language, manners, customs, and laws, as well as in degree of civilization."[120] Worcester's migration theory, unlike that of the Propaganda movement, did not emphasize an exceptional "third wave" predisposed to assimilation and civilization but rather the chaos, multiplicity, and backwardness produced when successive migration waves crashed on Philippine shores.

The argument of tribal anarchy, based on Blumentritt's theory, became the centerpiece of arguments against Filipino self-government. The very scientific framework that *ilustrados* had used to exceptionalize themselves as a civilized wave of migration was now being used to deny the islands' peoples as a whole self-government on the basis of their fragmentation. "The most striking and perhaps the most significant fact in the entire situation," began the section of the commission's report entitled "Capacity for Self-Government," "is the multiplicity of tribes inhabiting the archipelago, the diversity of their languages (which are mutually unintelligible), and the multifarious phases of civilization—ranging all the way from the highest to the lowest—exhibited by the natives of the several provinces and islands."[121]

While Worcester admitted it was "extremely difficult to arrive at anything approaching a correct estimate of the numbers of even the more important civilized tribes," the report was a powerful representation of the commission's ability to encapsulate the Philippine population by scientific means and gave birth to one of its most widely employed "facts": the number eighty-four as the total number of Philippine "tribes." In future debates, the figure, meant to convey impossible plurality, would echo through imperial argumentation in defense of the commission's central ethnological and political conclusion: "The Filipinos are not a nation, but a variegated assemblage of different tribes and peoples, and their loyalty is still of the tribal type."[122]

Worcester would be followed quickly into the "tribes" question by anti-imperialist and Filipino nationalist publicists. In 1900, for example, Filipino nationalist Sixto Lopez was asked by the New England Anti-Imperialist League to produce "a brief statement of the facts" on the tribes, "as a native of the country, and as one who has given some attention to the ethnography of the Archipelago, both by personal research and by a study of the best works on the subject." For Lopez, the commission's findings had been "entirely incorrect." The number eighty-four had been the product of "imagination, bad spelling, translation, subdivision, and multiplication." The commission had badly transcribed already inaccurate Spanish records, mistaken the mountain peoples for lowland villagers, confused racial groups for language groups, and exaggerated the differences between these languages. "It would be just as absurd to regard the Americans as one tribe and the 'Yankees' as another," he wrote, "and then to increase these two tribes into four or more by misspelling the word 'Americans,' or by translating it into French." To imagine that tribal anarchy would result without U.S. control, he asserted, was "as absurd as to suppose that the inhabitants of Massachusetts would rend the men of New Hampshire or Rhode Island." Lopez also answered the charge that the islands' linguistic pluralism would lead to chaos by reminding his readers that the population of most countries possessed the ability to speak more than one language "with perhaps the exception of the United States."[123]

Lopez's defensive homogenization of the Philippine population led him to minimize and exceptionalize animist and Muslim groups along nationalist-colonialist lines. Ninety-five percent of the Filipino population, he claimed, "belong to one race and all of them are Christian people practicing the morals and arts of civilization." The "so-called 'tribes'" were actually a small minority, analogous to "the uncivilized or semi-civilized remnants of the Indian tribes still inhabiting certain parts of the United States." Filipinos could not be Indians, in other words, because they had "their own" Indians. At the same time, Lopez refuted charges of "barbarism" against these groups; in reality, non-Christians had "a religion and a code of morals of their own." Like the Propaganda writers, Lopez and his anti-imperialist allies feared that Filipinos were being misrecognized as savages by American audiences. When the anti-imperialists published his family story, they did so in order to introduce Americans to "the interior of a Filipino household, disabusing them, to a large extent, of the idea that the Filipinos are people of a distinctly inferior race, to be likened to our Indian tribes."[124]

Race-Making and Colonial Warfare

Even as the Filipino leadership cast the war as an expression of civilization, part of an increasingly desperate bid for international recognition, U.S. soldiers racialized the "insurrection" with striking speed and intensity. What had been diffuse and fragmented prewar animosities congealed into novel racial formations at the very center of U.S. soldiers' popular culture, capable of defining a wartime enemy and organizing and motivating violence against it. "A lively hatred of our newly declared enemy was the one enthusiasm of the camp," wrote a corporal in the Montana regulars in July 1899.[125] The race-making process is vividly illustrated by terminological shifts in the diaries and letters home of U.S. volunteers in the early months of the war. Although the linguistic starting points and end points differed, many soldiers progressively racialized their terms for the insurgents specifically, and Filipinos generally, although in few cases did these terms entirely replace other terms like "insurgent" or "native."

Andrew Wadsworth, for example, a twenty-eight-year-old sergeant in the First Nebraska Volunteers, had observed shortly after arrival in Manila that "the natives are bright and intelligent as the average run of people" and admired their art, musicianship, and industriousness. Three months later, as tensions sharpened between U.S. and Filipino troops, Wadsworth's assessment darkened. "I didn't even like a negro, but they are pretty good people after seeing the natives that live here near the sunset," he wrote. Writing home from "the Field" two weeks after the beginning of the war, he wrote that "it was a hot time going over some of the ground. . . . [It] swarmed with the indians but we didn't do a thing to them." Within another two weeks, his racism was more matter-of-fact. "[H]ave forgotten whether I have written any of you folks since we commenced to chase niggers," he wrote offhandedly, "have no doubt read in the papers what we are doing."[126] Despite rising tensions, Earl Pearsall of the same unit had recorded in his diary on January 5, with some regret, that "the insurgents have not been as friendly lately as they have been for they have not visited our camp for three or four days." The day war broke out, he imagined that "the dusky fellows don't care for any more of this warfare with the Americano." Less than three weeks later, however, he thrilled that U.S. artillery had "put the black rascals over the hills." Early in March, he reported being "attacked by the 'Gugos'" on the Mariquina road.[127]

For the first two weeks of the war, Oregon volunteer William Henry Barrett referred to the enemy exclusively as "natives" or "Philippinos," as when "[n]atives [were] driven from their trenches and forced back all along the line." Just over two weeks later, he recorded that other companies had "chased out the niggers [and] run them across the swamps into Malabon."[128] South Dakota volunteer Louis Hubbard, a leader in his unit's regimental band, had accepted the gift of a sword from "one of Aguinaldo's sergeants" in December 1898 and recruited a Filipino musician, "the finest clarinetist I ever heard in my life." Two weeks into the combat, angered by reports of Filipino atrocities against U.S. troops, he wrote that "[t]hey are just like any savage." In mid-March he recorded the hope for a speedy charge on Malolos, "for the quicker we get there and get these 'gugos' of[f] the face of the earth the quicker we will be ready to start for home."[129]

This racialization process drew the attention of U.S. journalists and

The original caption for this photograph of a trench filled with bodies, which appeared in Neely, Fighting in the Philippines, reads: "The American Artillery did wonderful execution in the battles with the insurgents. In a trench at Santa Ana the Tagal dead lay in piles. The group shown in the picture consisted of thirty-eight bodies" (112). Photographs of dead Filipinos were common trophies among U.S. journalists and soldiers. Albert Sonnichsen wrote in his memoir of "the heaps of dead and dying natives . . . photographed by our people, and exhibited with such mottoes as: 'Can the ——d Regiment boys shoot? You bet they can. Count the dead niggers'" (quoted in Roth, Muddy Glory, 53).

soldiers on the scene. Even prior to the war, some observers understood rising hostility as the inevitable surfacing of latent "race differences" on both sides. "After the first glamour which surrounded our troops," soldier-correspondent John F. Bass reported to *Harper's* as early as late August 1898, "a glamour due to an exaggerated and almost childish idea of the liberty and freedom we were bringing to the Philippines, the race differences have made themselves felt, which antagonize the natives and exasperate our men."[130] H. L. Wells noted that U.S. troops saw the enemy in racial terms. "Undoubtedly, they do not regard the shooting of Filipinos just as they would the shooting of white troops," he wrote in mid-1900, following the advent of guerrilla war. "The soldiers feel that they are fighting with savages, not with soldiers."[131]

This "lively hatred" was not, however, a projection or an export, but a new racial formation developing on the ground. Its novelty was evidenced by the consistency with which reporters—imperialist and anti-imperialist—felt compelled to explain it to their domestic readers, as above. The new formation was strikingly illustrated by the appearance of a new term, "gu-gu," or "goo-goo," in U.S. soldiers' discourse, almost certainly the linguistic ancestor of "gook."[132] Veteran Charles A. Freeman, writing in the 1930s, noted that "[o]f recent years the world [*sic*] has been shortened to gook, but gu-gu persists in Philippine fiction and fact written by Americans, and applies to the lower class Filipino."[133] If the term had a sinister future, its origins remain speculative. One of two plausible explanations—far from incompatible with each other—roots the term in local dynamics: the term came from the Tagalog term for a slippery coconut-oil shampoo, pronounced *gu-gu*, which may have been used to convey a sense of the enemy's elusiveness.[134] A second account suggests the term was born at the intersection of immediate sexual tensions and racialized U.S. popular culture. According to Freeman, among the songs sung by U.S. troops on the long voyage from San Francisco had been a minstrel tune with the chorus "'Just because she made dem goo-goo eyes.'" When American soldiers first "gazed into the dark orbs of a Filipino *dalaga* [young woman]" on arrival, they had commented to each other, "'Gee, but that girl can make *goo-goo* eyes.'" Filipino men had taken the term as an insult; when American soldiers learned this, "it stuck, and became a veritable taunt."[135]

Whatever its specific origins, "gu-gu" formed part of a distinctive Philippine-American colonial vocabulary that focused hatreds around a novel enemy and lent American troops a sense of manly, insider camaraderie. The newness, immediacy, and localism of U.S. soldiers' racial formation were suggested by the quotation marks and parenthetical explanations soldiers commonly included near terms like "gu-gu" in their letters and diaries, especially early in the conflict. On occasion, soldiers explained these terms to what they imagined to be befuddled family members at home. Peter Lewis, for example, promised in November 1900 to write home again about his "fights with the 'Guggoes' as the Filipiones [sic] are called."[136]

The other common term assigned to the enemy by U.S. troops was "nigger." "Our troops in the Philippines . . . look upon all Filipinos as of one race and condition," wrote Henry Loomis Nelson, "and being dark men, they are therefore 'niggers,' and entitled to all the contempt and harsh treatment administered by white overlords to the most inferior races."[137] Frederick Palmer, sympathetic to the war effort, was amused by the soldiers' "good-natured contempt" toward "the little brown man" but regretted the use of the term "nigger," which "too often" included groups that were above it, however marginally: "If a man is white; if he speaks English; if he knows his lines as we know them, he is as good as anybody on earth. If he is white and yet does not understand our customs, we insist that he shall have equal rights with us. If he is any other color too often we include him in one general class called 'nigger,' a class beneath our notice, to which, as far as our soldier is concerned, all Filipinos belonged."[138]

On the surface, the application of the term "nigger" to Filipinos suggests the export of domestic U.S. racial formations. But in other ways it appears that the term itself was being transformed in the colonial setting. As with "gu-gu," soldiers felt compelled to explain its colonial meaning to family members, as when Corporal William Eggenberger observed in March 1899, of Filipino clothing, that "it is nothing to see a niger (we call them nigers) woman pretty near naked."[139] In some cases, U.S. soldiers ridiculed their comrades who used it, as when John Jordan poked fun at white Southern soldiers. "It must have been very embarrassing to men almost entirely from Georgia, Ala., Miss. and Florida to be whipped and captured by 'niggers,' " he wrote of one recently defeated unit. "The Capt. is from Miss. and I have no doubt it will be an unpleasant recollection to him especially when he returns to Natchez."[140]

Just as colonial warfare was promoting the invention of new terms like "gu-gu," it was proving capable of dislodging, reframing, and transforming older terms like "nigger." When Peter Lewis of New York was sent in January 1902 to supervise a thousand Filipino women allowed out of a reconcentration camp to collect palay, he described the scene as being like "the American niggers picking cotton."[141] It was striking that he felt compelled to modify "nigger" with "American"; it suggests that, without it, he was afraid his family might mistakenly think he was referring to Filipinos and not African Americans. One black soldier complained that white soldiers "talked with impunity of 'niggers' to our soldiers, never once thinking that they were talking to home 'niggers.'" When reminded that "at home this is the same vile epithet they hurl at us," these soldiers "beg pardon and make some effiminate [*sic*] excuse about what the Filipino is called."[142] While these white soldiers may have been deliberately taunting black soldiers, it may have been that, in the colonial context, "nigger" was becoming strangely detached from its older moorings.

Black troops fighting in the islands had much to say about the race war emerging around them.[143] "You have no idea the way these people are treated by the Americans here," wrote Sgt. Patrick Mason, excluding himself from this category. "The first thing in the morning is the 'Nigger' and the last thing at night is the 'Nigger.'" Some like Sgt. Maj. John W. Galloway accused whites of "establish[ing] their diabolical race hatred in all its home rancor in Manila . . . to be sure of the foundation of their supremacy" under civil rule. Unlike white soldiers, Galloway noted, black soldiers did not "push [Filipinos] off the streets, spit at them, call them damned 'niggers,' abuse them in all manner of ways, and connect race hatred with duty." Filipinos ably exploited the U.S. Army's race war by making direct racial appeals to black soldiers on the basis of what one black soldier, quoting a Filipino, called the "affinity of complexion." William Simms had been struck by a question posed to him by a little Filipino boy, to the effect of "'Why does the American Negro come . . . to fight us when we are much a friend to him. . . . He is all the same as me and me all the same as you. Why don't you fight those people in America who burn Negroes, that make a beast of you?'"[144]

More coordinated appeals to black troops appear to have been suggested by exiles in Hong Kong, better connected to British and U.S. news sources. In August 1899, Paula Pardo reported having received instructions from there "advising us to make big placards with large letters, in English, to be placed in the frontier trenches" that would "remind the Black Americans of the offenses committed and that continue to be committed against their race by the white Americans and, above all, the recent executions carried out on their black brothers."[145] Filipino troops did place hundreds of pamphlets near black units; one was addressed "To the Colored American Soldier" and stated that "[y]our masters have thrown you into the most iniquitous fight with double purpose—to make you the instrument of their ambition and also your hard work will soon make the extinction of your race. Your friends, the Filipinos, give you this good warning. You must consider your situation and your history, and take charge that the blood of . . . Sam Hose . . . proclaims vengeance."[146]

The Politics of Guerrilla Warfare

If one way to rationalize a war of aggression was to declare the enemy state a "tribe," one way to end it was simply to declare it over by fiat. November 1899 saw the war's first end by U.S. proclamation. General MacArthur reported the U.S. mission accomplished, saying that there was "no organized insurgent force left to strike at," and declared that all future resistance be characterized as "banditry," and the killing of U.S. soldiers, murder.[147] General Otis cabled Washington stating that the revolutionaries had been dispersed and that the "claim to government by insurgents can be made no longer under any fiction."[148] In fact, Filipinos had undertaken a strategy of guerrilla war. Disbanding the regular army in the wake of defeats, Aguinaldo divided the country into military zones, each under a guerrilla commander, preparing for a regionally dispersed set of smaller campaigns through locally raised *sandatahan* (guerrilla) units. It was hoped that in these scattered settings, tropical disease, impassable roads, and unfamiliar conditions would weaken the American advance, while geographic knowledge and village-level support would sustain guerrilla ambushes and surprise attacks against isolated American patrols.[149]

A key advantage of this kind of war for Filipinos would be the potential disappearance of Filipino combatants into the rural population. As the Filipino army reorganized, the Luzon villagers that Wilcox and Sargent had met singing patriotic songs and marching in formation would sustain the guerrilla effort with food, money, and information. A network composed of the friends and relatives of guerrilla officers within the *principalia* collected taxes and crops from villagers (not always willingly), established secret Katipunan societies, and formed their own intelligence systems, often supplying the guides, interpreters, and municipal officials upon whom the U.S. Army relied. Eluding the surveillance of U.S. post commanders and soldiers, revolutionaries funneled supplies to the guerrillas, hid them in civilian clothes, and informed them about American strategies and troop movements.

This guerrilla campaign, in turn, altered the command structure, tactics, and knowledge requirements of the U.S. Army. General Otis decentralized his forces to match the Filipino army, splitting the army into four departments, his plan being to advance outward into the hinterlands, fighting back Filipino rebels and garrisoning the towns that supported them. In these regional settings (eventually more than 600 scattered posts), often cut off from Manila contacts, local commanders would by necessity take on greater autonomy and be forced to adapt their tactics to local crises. Reliable intelligence was a scarce commodity. "The troops were more than able to annihilate, to completely smash anything that could be brought against them," reported Colonel Arthur Wagner, ". . . but it was almost impossible to get any information in regard to those people."[150]

Guerrilla war involved not merely a set of tactics but a set of understandings: about the nature of combat, about the means to victory, about oneself as a combatant, and about the nature of the enemy. For Filipino officers, schooled exclusively in European conventional warfare, it was largely unfamiliar, although at least some Filipino soldiers had encountered it while collaborating with the Spanish Army against Muslims and animists. By 1900, it was still unfamiliar enough to require explanation.[151]

Filipino strategists drew on anticolonial guerrilla struggles elsewhere in the world. Isabelo de los Reyes, for example, published an article on guerrilla war in the March 1900 *Filipinas ante Europa*, by "a valiant and enlightened Filipino lieutenant" who had fought in Cuba.[152] Filipino commanders also took inspiration (most likely unreciprocated) from the Boers' struggle against the British Empire. Juan Villamor, advising Gen. Antonio Luna in Ilocos, claimed to have taken his guerrilla model from the Boers in their struggle against the English, most likely learned of through Hong Kong newspapers. In a speech to raise troops in February 1900, Villamor noted that this warring style, "such as we are starting today," was "characteristic of a small nation when fighting a big one" and had produced "the most surprising successes" in South Africa.[153]

One possible explanation for Aguinaldo's delay in adopting guerrilla tactics may be the symbolic politics of war and preoccupations with "culture and character." The most obvious reason for this delay was political. As the republic's officials well knew, guerrilla war was at once a decentralized war that empowered local commanders at the expense of the center and a people's war that involved mobilizing the energy of, and handing power to, a rural base. This base was, in turn, largely mistrusted by Aguinaldo's cadre and was itself often ambivalent about the question of whether republican "independence" and *kalayaan* (freedom) were the same thing.[154] But it was also, perhaps, not so easy to let go of the quest for recognition. In its bid for international recognition, the republic's self-representations to the world had nervously held it to a standard of civilization in which war played a significant part. Officials of the republic agreed with the Americans that, among many other things, civilized societies adhered to the laws of civilized warfare. The military drills witnessed by Wilcox and Sargent had drawn on a vocabulary of republican martial order imbued with notions of a civilized fighting force; the republic's newspapers of 1898 had foregrounded the organized, hierarchical character of the Filipino army and the favorable treatment of its Spanish prisoners as advertisements for its broader civilization.

Guerrilla warfare, by contrast, meant scattered organization, loosely disciplined troops little distinguishable from savages, a reliance on rural supplies little distinguishable from looting, and forms of concealment and deception that violated Euro-American standards of masculine honor in combat.[155] Emilio Concepción, a captain fighting in Namatay, later recalled that, for reasons of honor, he "was vacillating for some time" before he reorganized his troops into guerrilla units. "In reality, when I took that step, I had thought about it well for some days before, because in principle I believed that if I made myself a guerrilla fighter, I would stop being a revolutionary, and at that time for me the title of revolutionary was much more glorious."[156] By winning a conventional war, the Philippine Army would win the world's support for independent Philippine statehood; victory in guerrilla battle, however, might mean losing the war for international recognition.

While Filipino commanders believed guerrilla war was undesirable, they also believed it could serve as an effective intervention in U.S. politics; localized struggle could have transnational effects. One of the most striking aspects of the Filipino guerrilla campaign was the way that it was imagined by its leaders as an intercession into the 1900 presidential campaign, specifically on behalf on William Jennings Bryan's candidacy, which had made anti-imperialism its centerpiece. "It would surprise you what a close watch these [Filipino] people keep on American politics," Lt. Samuel Lyon wrote home in March 1900, about congressional debates on the

Philippine bill. "[E]very disloyal sentiment uttered by a man of any prominence in the United States is repeatedly broadcast through the islands and greatly magnified."[157] U.S. military censors expressed frustration at Filipino newspapers' "old tactics of translating the most virulent articles in the American press . . . to foster the belief among the people that the majority of Americans were in favor of their demands."[158]

The U.S. election cycle was, in fact, a crucial factor in shaping Aguinaldo's strategy, even as he retreated into the mountains of Luzon. From mid-1900, Filipino commanders emphasized the need to maintain enough resistance to make the price of empire high and to aid Bryan in his quest to make the Philippine-American War "the paramount issue."[159] "The presidential election which is being held at present in North America seems like a ray of hope for the cessation of this war," stated Aguinaldo in an October 1900 proclamation, "inasmuch as Mr. Bryan promises to recognize the independence of the Philippines, provided he is elected president of the North American Republic."[160] Filipino hopes for the election were known even to common U.S. soldiers. "[T]he niggers are getting more active all over," wrote William Eggenberger in September, "it is just before election and they want to make a showing[.] [T]hey think if bryan gets elected they will get their independence but they will get left."[161] William Carey Brown claimed to have found among one revolutionary leader's papers a "carefully folded . . . picture of—Mr. William J. Bryan!"[162]

Such claims ought, of course, to be met with skepticism. Real or imagined Filipino support for Bryan's candidacy was especially appetizing for the war's partisan defenders in the United States, who used it to confirm the "treason" of their opponents. Apparently, one was either with the administration or with the savages. The *New York Tribune* blamed Bryan's candidacy itself for the persistence of the revolt and named the Nebraskan as "more the leader of these people than Aguinaldo."[163] The 1900 Republican campaign book promised "Evidence That the Insurrection Was Encouraged and Kept Alive by the Utterances of Mr. Bryan and His Political Associates" in the shape of fragments of proclamations and manifestos.[164] In sometimes odd and striking ways, the war's proponents made Aguinaldo and Bryan equivalents as representatives of anarchy and misrule. S. B. M. Young, for example, told Adj.-Gen. Henry Corbin in November 1900 that "Bryan and his friends—the enemies of good government . . . gave us considerable trouble through their brother anarchists in the mountains of Northern Luzon."[165] That same month, writing Theodore Roosevelt from the Philippines to congratulate him on McKinley's reelection, Young observed that "[t]he attack on you by the Tagalogs of Colorado is on par with actions of the brown Bryanites of Luzon."[166]

If on the Filipino side, guerrilla war was U.S. electoral politics by other means, on the American side, it was both novel and disturbing. It meant dispensing with hopes for gallant rushes at the enemy and hunkering down for a protracted campaign that was both boring and anxious, with soldiers isolated from other units, in a largely unknown terrain, unable to recognize the line between "amigos" and hostile peoples. It was little surprise that the most lasting term the war introduced into American English was "boon-docks," drawn from a Tagalog term for "mountain" or remote area, which came to be associated with distant, bewildering unknowns.[167]

"Uncle Sam's cohorts set down in the Philippines at the beginning of the century saw in everything, something new, strange and utterly incom-prehensible," recalled one veteran years later. "The enemy existed unseen in the dripping jungle, in the moldering towns and in the smoky clearings on the hillsides, and since a natural prudence bade him not risk any open encounter, the enemy was not to be found. But they existed nonethe-less."[168] Even as U.S. soldiers relied on Filipinos as guides, translators, car-riers, and providers of food and intelligence, they found the task of distin-guishing Filipino soldiers from "amigos" in garrisoned towns a frustrating and dangerous one. Erwin Garrett put the problem succinctly in verse:

"Amigo" to your face, forsooth,
Or when you spend the dough,
But a red-handed "katipunan" when
You turn around to go.[169]

Many U.S. soldiers racialized Filipino tactical deception. As Jacob Issel-hard recalled in his memoir, local villagers, "with that particular faculty of all Orientals to say one thing and meaning [sic] another, professed to be 'mucho amigo' (good friends) to our faces, while secretly aiding the insur-rection with all the means at their command." Those who stepped for-ward as guides, for example, "would invariably and purposely get lost on a trail which led either to nowhere or into well prepared death traps."[170]

The collision between Filipino revolutionary and U.S. Army perspec-tives on guerrilla war can best be witnessed in a brief written exchange in late August 1900 between Gen. James Franklin Bell and Apolinario Mabini.[171] Bell was writing Mabini to pressure him to reconcile himself to United States rule and to declare himself against continued guerrilla resistance, as had an increasing number of revolutionaries. His argument hinged on the difference between "civilized" war and its opposites. War, he began, could only be justified by a combatant where success was possible; as soon as defeat was certain, "civilization demands that the defeated side, in the name of humanity, should surrender and accept the result, although it may be painful to its feelings." Combatants who strayed from this principle "place themselves in a separate classification" as "incompetent in the management of civil affairs to the extent of their ignorance of the demands of humanity." In this specific case, the end of conventional war and the dispersal of the Philippine Army meant that continued Filipino resistance was not only "criminal" but was "also daily shoving the natives of the Archipelago headlong towards a deeper attitude of semicivilization in which they will become completely incapable of appreciating and understanding the responsibilities of civil government." Civilization meant pacification and the acceptance of U.S. sovereignty: "The Filipino people can only show their fitness in this matter by laying down their arms."[172]

Mabini countered with a brilliant riposte. Bell's starting point, he noted, was simply the claim that might made right, that the United States' war was "just and humanitarian" because its army was powerful, "which trend of reasoning not even the most ignorant Filipino will believe to be true." If in real life, he noted, "the strong nations so easily make use of force to impose their claims on the weak ones," it was because "even now civilization and humanitarian sentiments that are so often invoked, are, for some, more apparent than real." No one deplored more deeply the "guerrilla and ambush system" the Filipinos had been "forced to adopt"; Mabini had always considered "the fight that offers equal risks to both combatants more noble and more worthy of men." But the Filipinos had been left no choice. The very laws of war that authorized strong nations' use of "powerful weapons of combat" against weak ones were those that "persuade[d]" the weak to engage in guerrilla war, "especially when it comes to defending their homes and their freedoms against an invasion."[173]

Guerrilla war was, in other words, tactical rather than ethnological: in this "extreme case," the laws of war "implacably order the weak people to defend their threatened honor and natural rights under pain of being called uncivilized and uncapable of understanding the responsibilities of a proper government." Civilization meant neither capitulation nor conciliation but resistance to submission. Indeed, for Mabini, resistance itself— even through guerrilla war—was the only mark of a civilized people. The Filipinos, he wrote, "fight to show to the United States that they possess sufficient culture to know their rights even where there is a pretense to hide them by means of clever sophisms."[174] Earlier, Mabini had written, along the same lines, that "[a] humiliating peace is tolerated only in uncivilized countries."[175] Asserting the logic of recognition, Mabini hoped the revolution would in this way "remind the Americans of the struggle borne by their ancestors against the Englishmen for the emancipation of the colonies which are now the free States of North America." At that moment, the Americans had been "in the same place which the Filipinos are in today." Contrary to what some believed, Filipino resistance was "not motivated by hatred of race, but by the same principles sealed with the blood of [the Americans'] own ancestors."[176]

Almost immediately following McKinley's presidential victory in November 1900, U.S. commanders felt at greater liberty to widen the boundaries of violence, which General MacArthur achieved through a mass-circulated proclamation dated December 20. In content, it was a highly expedient interpretation of General Orders No. 100, the Civil War–era regulations on the conduct of combat; MacArthur selected those provisions he felt "most essential for consideration under present conditions." The proclamation was meant to "instruct all classes" and was circulated widely: the army distributed 10,000 copies to the Department of Southern Luzon alone, and copies of it were printed in Tagalog, Spanish, and English in the *Manila Times*, the first English-language daily in the islands.[177] MacArthur had assumed, wrongly, that Filipino military leaders "probably had never before been informed of the existence of such a law" and boasted that its "educational" effect had been "immediate and far-reaching."[178]

Here, MacArthur ran into the problem of the resistance's status: to share the "laws of war" with Filipinos might appear to recognize them as the army of an actual state. Accordingly, he "reject[ed] every consideration of belligerency of those opposing the Government" and directed the document both at combatants and "noncombatants, native or alien, residing within occupied places." In those locations, the U.S. Army owed protection only to those Filipinos who demonstrated "strict obedience" to U.S. commanders. Noncombatants who in any way aided Filipino combatants, through "secret communities," collecting supplies, recruiting men, or sharing military information, would from then on be seen by the U.S. military as indistinguishable from combatants.[179]

In broadening the enemy in this way, MacArthur invoked a category from the General Orders: "war rebels, or war traitors." Any such person residing in an occupied area and engaging in acts that were "inimical to the interests of the occupying army" would be punished "at the discretion of the tribunals of the occupying army." The terms themselves embodied the contradictions of the United States' claims to sovereignty, which the *New York Times* had foreseen: "war" recognized the enemy as a state, while "rebel" and "traitor" incorporated the enemy as a force against "its own" government. MacArthur's proclamation defined these terms in ways that embraced the entire population in areas of combat as potential targets of punishment. It did not recognize intimidation by insurgents as a legitimate cause for cooperation: compliance with the rebels without reportage to the U.S. military "creates the presumption that the act is voluntary and malicious." Neither did he accept defenses based on ignorance of insurgent activity, which due to "a common language," must "be of knowledge to a large part of the resident community."[180] Assuming that all Filipino villagers in garrisoned areas had information regarding the guerrillas, those who failed to share it "offer themselves as easy victims to be plundered and murdered" and "expose themselves to the danger of being classified and tried as war traitors against the United States." "War rebels" who slipped back and forth, to and from combat, "divest themselves of the character of soldiers" and if captured were "not entitled to the privileges of prisoners of war."[181]

These changes of status would authorize alterations in the practical apparatus of repression. MacArthur warned journalists in Manila that any article published in a "martial environment" that could be "classed as seditious" by its intention to "injure the army of occupation" would subject its authors to "such punitive action as may be determined by the undersigned." In additional orders, MacArthur commanded that all "prisoners of war" captured "in the field, or arrested in the towns," would be held in custody "until the cessation of hostilities." He also ordered the deportation to Guam of "prominent and popular agitators," including Mabini. The indefinite incarceration or deportation of prisoners was a self-consciously terror-generating strategy. There was "no doubt" that what MacArthur called the "legitimate employment of strong human emotions" had been "very instrumental in bringing about final results."[182]

Racializing Guerrilla Combat

Race was at the core of the U.S. Army's effort to rethink and redefine the enemy in a context of guerrilla war. Mabini was right that, in waging guerrilla war, Filipinos risked "the pain of being called uncivilized." Throughout the colonial world—including the republic's leadership—races were characterized in part by the way they made war. The General Orders No. 100 that MacArthur had drawn upon had themselves relied on racial-historical dichotomies between civilized and savage war.[183] While "barbarous armies" and "uncivilized people," for example, offered no protection to civilians, the "inoffensive citizen" was protected in "modern regular wars of the Europeans, and their descendents in other portions of the globe." While the General Orders authorized retaliation by "civilized nations," when taken too far, this principle quickly devolved into "the internecine wars of savages."[184]

By these lights, those who waged guerrilla war were, by definition, savage: Filipino warfare, therefore, did not take this form out of ignorance or strategy but because of race. Conventional wisdom to this effect issued from the top of the U.S. military hierarchy in the Philippines. "War in its earlier form was an act of violence which, from the very nature of primitive humanity and of the forces employed, knew no bounds," General MacArthur had declared in the December 1900 proclamation. "Mankind, from the beginning of civilization, however, has tried to mitigate, and to escape, as far as possible, from the consequences of this barbarous conception of warlike action."[185] The Filipinos, in refusing these boundaries, had shown themselves to be less than civilized. "The war on the part of the Filipinos," wrote Secretary of War Elihu Root, "has been conducted with the barbarous cruelty common among uncivilized races."[186]

Racial terms were also useful in making sense of the guerrillas' mass support as the U.S. effort ground to a mid-1900 halt. Late in December 1900, General Robert Hughes reported to the War Department that "[t]he situation is still very dark. . . . The whole population has been rank insurrectos from hide to heart, and all have been contributing to the support of the cause in one way or another according to their ability."[187] In his October 1, 1900, report, MacArthur sought to account for what he called, with begrudging respect, the "almost complete unity of action of the entire native population." His conclusion was that Filipino participation was neither rational nor political. "[T]he adhesive principle comes from ethnological homogeneity," he stated, "which induces men to respond for a time to the appeals of consanguineous leadership, even when such action is opposed to their own interests."[188] General Young concurred. "The keynote of the insurrection among the Filipinos past, present and future is not tyranny," he stated in an April 1901 address, "for we are not tyrants. It is race."[189]

Where all hearts were those of insurgents, legible from their "hides," race became the sanction for exterminist war, the means by which earlier distinctions between combatants and noncombatants—already fragile—eroded or collapsed. As long as support for the rebellion was imagined as political—as a matter of decisions, interests, and incentives—within a pluralistic Filipino polity, the task of the U.S. Army was to "persuade" Filipinos of various sectors to accept U.S. sovereignty. That this persuasion might take terrible forms was something that U.S. officials readily acknowledged. But no such persuasion was possible where "ethnological homogeneity" governed over reason, where hides determined hearts. The Filipinos were one united "race"; its "savagery" placed it outside the bounds of "civilized" warfare: the two explanatory halves converged, pincerlike, into racial exterminist war as the only means to "peace."

On the ground, racial terms like "gugu" and "nigger" both reflected and enabled a broadening of the enemy. In their letters and diaries, U.S. soldiers sometimes attached them to descriptions of combat status—such as "nigger army"—which, in effect, made them racialized terms for "insurgent." In some cases, they continued to distinguish combatants and noncombatants, referring to the latter as "natives" or "Filipinos." But in other cases, soldiers used both "gugu" and "nigger" to refer explicitly to noncombatants. "At meals [sic] times there are always a lot of little 'gugus' around, each with his tin can, begging scraps to eat," wrote Perry Thompson.[190] Peter Lewis described how "the Niggers keep going to Church" on Easter.[191] When Eggenberger received curfew orders "to make all niggers to put out lights after 9 oclock and arrest all niggers caught out after 7 oclock," he enforced it by thrusting his rifle's bayonet through the outside walls of noncompliant civilians' homes.[192] If a "nigger man" was unfortunate enough to stroll through camp while U.S. soldiers were feeling lonely, "he generally feels the weight of our heavy government shoes for we hate the sight of them."[193]

Racial terms and exterminist sentiment were at the center of the most popular of the U.S. Army's marching songs, which marked the Filipino population as a whole as the enemy and made killing Filipinos the only means to their civilization.

Damn, damn, damn the Filipino
Pock-marked khakiac ladrone;
Underneath the starry flag
Civilize him with a Krag,
And return us to our own beloved home.[194]

One Nebraskan soldier boasted to his parents of his comrades' bold, aggressive fighting spirit, restrained only by officers' reticence. "If they would turn the boys loose," he wrote, "there wouldn't be a nigger left in Manila twelve hours after."[195] Henry Hackthorn explained to his family that the war, which he regretted, had been avoidable, but "the niggers got in a hurry." "We would kill all in sight if we could only receive the necessary orders," he wrote.[196] Frank Jackson was angered by an American public convinced that "we are nothing but murderers that march out occasionally and kill all the niggers we see!" he complained. "I wish that might be so for the world would be much better off without these lazy black devils."[197] Eggenberger reported happily in March 1900 that collaborating Macabebe troops had killed 130 "ladrones" without one escape. "[L]et the good work go on[.] [W]e will have the damn bug eaters sivilized [sic] if we have to bury them to do it," he wrote.[198]

Racial exterminist impulses were also in evidence in U.S. soldiers' descriptions of violence against prisoners and civilians. The American torture of prisoners—some fraction of which appeared in soldiers' letters, newspaper accounts, and court-martial proceedings—was often, if not always, justified as a means of intelligence-gathering. The most notorious form of torture by the American side, if far from the only one, was the "water cure," in which a captured Filipino was interrogated while drowned with buckets of filthy water poured into his mouth. The scale of its practice and the frequency of death remain difficult if not impossible to establish. Later blamed almost exclusively on the United States' Macabebe Scouts, it was in fact the tactical expression of the military policy of attraction, undertaken in many cases by U.S. and Filipino forces working together both secretly and with the tacit approval of U.S. officers. In the context of guerrilla war, the water cure would simultaneously cure Filipinos of their unknowability and Americans of their ignorance.[199]

Despite later claims that distanced U.S. soldiers from torture, U.S. soldiers not only carried out the water cure but apparently did so in a jocular manner. In 1902, Albert Gardner, in Troop B of the First U.S. Cavalry, composed comic works that made light of torture in a way that suggested familiarity and ease. The first, playing with the torture's name, was a mock-testimonial patent-medicine advertisement addressed to "My Dear Doctor Uncle Sam," by a certain "Mariano Gugu."[200] The author complained of a recent bout of "loss of memory, loss of speach [sic] and other symptoms" of a disease called "insurectos"; among other things, he "had forgotten where I placed my Bolo and my rifle."[201] He had been miraculously cured with "only one treatment of your wonderful water cure." "No hombre's shack is complete without a barrel of it," he concluded in a postscript.[202] More striking still was Gardner's original marching song, "The Water Cure in the P.I.," which made no mention of interrogation but simply urged U.S. soldiers to commit torture as an expression of U.S. imperial patriotism. Torture and liberation would be expressions of each other. The song form itself suggests singers and possible public performance:

> Get the good old syringe boys and fill it to the brim
> We've caught another nigger and we'll operate on him
> Let someone take the handle who can work it with a vim
> Shouting the battle cry of freedom
>
> [Chorus]
> Hurrah Hurrah We bring the Jubilee
> Hurrah Hurrah The flag that makes him free
> Shove in the nozzel [sic] deep and let him taste of liberty
> Shouting the battle cry of freedom.[203]

A subsequent verse promised to teach a captured "nigger" that liberty was "a precious boon" and pump him until he "swells like a toy baloon [sic]."[204] Another hailed "[t]he banner that floats proudly o'er the noble and the brave" and urged the men to continue "till the squirt gun breaks or he explodes the slave."[205]

Along with torturing them, U.S. soldiers also killed Filipino prisoners. Rumors of "no-prisoners" orders were common. Arthur C. Johnson of the Colorado Volunteers, for example, reported as early as February 1899 that Manila's prisons were already overflowing, and "the fiat is said to have gone forth that no more prisoners are to be taken"; he anticipated that "the Filipino death list promises to correspondingly increase." "They say our boys raised the cry of no quarter," Willis Platts wrote on the second day of the war, "([I] am glad of it) and disregarded the numerous white flags because of many treacherous deeds." Nearly two months into the war, George Telfer recorded his one line of thought while "jumping trenches—seeing mangled bodies, writhing figures, and hearing groans everywhere": "'Guide right.' 'preserve touch.' 'Advance' 'Lay Down' 'Forward'—'Kill' 'Kill'—'Take no prisoners.'"[206]

Specific instances of the killing of prisoners were recorded by U.S. soldiers. Thomas Osborne was sent out in search of five men, and when

This is a photograph of the "water cure," one mode of torture and interrogation used by U.S. soldiers and their Macabebe allies during the Philippine-American War. Water would be forcibly pumped into the open mouth of a Filipino prisoner, in an effort to compel him to provide information regarding the guerrilla army. The very fact that a portrait of it was created—one that itself includes casual spectators—suggests both the status of atrocity as spectacle and the complacency with which this torture was conducted, despite vigorous denials of its practice. Reproduced with permission, Jonathan Best Collection.

they were captured, "nor [sic] did we take them prisoners for our guns were anxious to be fired so we left them to be buried next morning."[207] Pvt. George Osborn wrote that while holding a prisoner on a captain's instructions, "a fellow by the name of Lynch said to him to (vamos) (meaning to get away) and when he had run about 20 yds they shot him." When the captain later asked where the prisoner was, "Lynch said he tried to run away and we shot him[.] [T]he Capt. said all right."[208] William Eggenberger reported hearing at one point that the "niggers" would kill "all the [American] prisoners they capture from now on, and of corse [sic] we will ring [sic] all the damn necks of the ones we capture too."[209] He recorded several occasions of shooting prisoners attempting to "escape" but later confessed that "[w]hen we capture a suspicious nigger, we generally loose him in the swamps, that is he is lost and he isn't lost but he never shows up any more. Turn about is fair play. They do it to us and we do it to them, they killed three of our fellows with out mercy but we have taken a very sweet revenge and a very clear revenge to them to[o]."[210] The most notorious wartime executions by U.S. forces were not of prisoners but of collaborators. Filipino and Chinese guides, interpreters, and carriers were essential to U.S. operations, in constant proximity to U.S. soldiers, and the most immediate objects of scrutiny and suspicion; they were highly vulnerable scapegoats when U.S. operations went sour. When Marine Maj. Littleton Waller's forces became lost, sick, and starved following a scorched-earth campaign across the island of Samar in 1901, he ordered the summary execution of eleven Filipino porters.[211]

The ultimate form of exterminist war was the killing of acknowledged noncombatants. As early as April 12, 1899, an entry in Chriss Bell's diary took derecognition to its furthest extension: Filipinos had already "caused so much trouble & murdered so many of our boys" that U.S. soldiers "recognize them no longer but shoot on sight all natives. Natives will not or cannot understand kind & civilized treatment. If you treat them as equals they will think you are afraid of them & murder you."[212] On the second day of the war, Bell recorded that insurgents "did so much shooting from the bamboo huts that an order came to fire the huts as the men advanced. This was done & men, women and children suffered." A few weeks later, Albert Southwick described shooting indiscriminately into forests and residences. "[T]he 'nigs' were so well hidden and using smokeless powder," he wrote home, "it was almost impossible to find any of them, but we filled the trees with lead. . . . [W]e sent a shot into every clump of bush and houses, thick leaved trees, or anything that looked like a place for a 'nigger' to hide." Willis Platts related how he and others would "fire into a house and when the natives would run fire at them and generally they tumbled." Having shot into one hut, though, he recorded his relief at finding a number of people unhurt who had "lain flat" but later "witness[ed] the painful sight of many women shot." Two months later, his sympathies had apparently eroded, the term "amigo" emptied of all but bitter irony. After one fight, his troop had been so "encouraged" they had "scattered out and burned every house anywhere near and whenever 'an amigo' showed up generally put him to sleep. . . . I know of quite a number they killed, even shot at many myself."[213]

One of the most banal and brutal manifestations of racialization was U.S. soldiers' imagination of war as hunting. The Manila occupation and "friendly policy" had frustrated martial masculinity; the metaphor of the hunt made war, at last, into masculine self-fulfillment.[214] All at once, a language of hunting bestialized Filipinos, made sense of guerrilla war to American troops, and joined the latter in manly fraternity. "I don't know when the thing will let out," wrote Louis Hubbard one week into the war, "and don't care as we are having lots of excitement. It makes me think of killing jack rabbits."[215] John F. Bright described one advance near San Juan Bridge: "As we advanced they would jump up like rabbits only a few feet from us, dead game ready to sell their lives as dearly as possible, but we shot them down before they could do any damage."[216] Gen. S. B. M. Young wrote in November 1900 that he had "sufficient troops now to make a fox hunt for these Dr. Jekel and Mr. Hide [sic] amigos and assassins."[217]

On occasion, racist terms explicitly linked hunting to exterminism. "There is no question that our men do 'shoot niggers' somewhat in the sporting spirit," admitted H. L. Wells. "It is lots of sport to hunt these black devils," wrote Louis Hubbard just three weeks into the war, inspired by revenge.[218] Private George Osborn of the Sixth Infantry wrote home from Negros on January 15, 1900: "Just back from the fight. Killed 22 niggers captured 29 rifels [sic] and 1 shotgun and I tell you it was a fight. . . . [W]e just shot the niggers like a hunter would rabbits."[219] In April 1899, Lieutenant Telfer wrote from Marilao that nighttime scouting raids were his men's only relief from the boredom of guarding a railroad, and that it was "great fun for the men to go on 'nigger hunts.' "[220]

The most notorious orders of indiscriminate killing were Gen. Jacob H. Smith's late October 1901 instructions to Marine Maj. Littleton

W. T. Waller, following Filipino revolutionaries' successful surprise attack against U.S. soldiers at Balangiga on the island of Samar, to make reprisals against the entire population of the island. "I want no prisoners," he had directed. "I wish you to kill and burn." Smith ordered "all persons killed who are capable of bearing arms in actual hostilities against the United States." When Waller had asked the general for clarification, Smith stated that he considered any person over the age of ten "capable of bearing arms." The interior of Samar must be made "a howling wilderness!" The direct result of these instructions was systematic destruction and killing on a vast scale. One marine wrote home that he and his comrades were "hiking all the time killing all we come across."[221] Another later recalled that "we were to shoot on sight anyone over 12 years old, armed or not, to burn everything and to make the Island of Samar a howling wilderness."[222] While Capt. David D. Porter later explained that he believed Smith to have meant "insurrectos" only, he recalled that marines at the time had understood that, with the exception of those who had taken an oath of allegiance, "everybody in Samar was an insurrecto."[223]

Justifying Torture and Exterminism

If racialization encouraged U.S. soldiers to broaden the war toward exterminism, race also legitimated this process from above, undermining moral and legal claims against U.S. soldiers accused of wartime atrocities in the halls of American governance, in press debates, and in courts-martial. Race would not only justify the ends of the war—especially as the necessary response to Filipino savagery and tribal fragmentation—but would be used to justify many of the "marked severities" employed by U.S. soldiers to bring it to its desired conclusion.

Little if anything of the cruelties of the war became known to the U.S. public prior to early 1902, in part due to rigorous censorship of foreign correspondents by the U.S. Army.[224] By mid-1902, however, the American press—particularly Democratic and independent papers—became more emboldened, particularly as editors learned of General Bell's "reconcentration" program in Batangas. Some critical press attention was due to the energetic efforts of anti-imperialists like Herbert Welsh, who resourcefully culled for republication references to the water cure and other atrocities in hometown newspapers and sent agents to interview returning soldiers firsthand. These efforts would culminate in the publication of the pamphlet *"Marked Severities" in Philippine Warfare*, a compilation by Moorfield Storey and Julian Codman of descriptions of U.S. atrocities attributed to U.S. soldier-witnesses, with attempts to connect atrocity to administration policy.[225]

These propaganda efforts coincided with a Senate investigation between January and June 1902, initiated by Senator George Hoar, Republican of Massachusetts, to "examine and report into the conduct of the war in the Philippine Islands, the administration of the government there, and the condition and character of the inhabitants."[226] The Senate hearings would force open small windows onto U.S. Army conduct, although their potential challenge was blunted by Senator Lodge's able maneuvering of the hearings into his own, prowar Committee on Insular Affairs, which was closed to press and public, and where sympathetic witnesses and lengthy War Department reports would predominate. The anti-imperialist publicity campaign that would reach its height in April–May 1902 would be met by a determined administration counteroffensive, as Lodge, army officers, and ultimately President Roosevelt would answer charges of military misconduct.

In both the press and the Senate hearings, the army's defenders repeatedly held that atrocities were rare; that where they occurred they were swiftly and thoroughly punished; and that testimony to the contrary was exaggerated, partisan, cowardly, and traitorous. But racial arguments, of at least four varieties, were crucial to defending the war's means, just as they had been to the justification of the war's ends. The first variant claimed that the Filipinos' guerrilla war, as "savage" war, was entirely outside the moral and legal standards and strictures of "civilized" war. Those who adopted guerrilla war, it was argued, surrendered all claims to bounded violence and mercy from their opponent. Capt. John H. Parker employed this line of argument in a November 1900 letter to Theodore Roosevelt complaining that the U.S. Army should not "attempt to meet a half civilized foe . . . with the same methods devised for civilized warfare against people of our own race, country and blood."[227] The point was made plainly during the Senate hearings, when General Hughes described to Senator Rawlins the burning of entire towns by advancing U.S. troops as a means of "punishment," and Senator Joseph Rawlins inquired, "But is that within the ordinary rules of civilized warfare?" General Hughes replied succinctly, "These people are not civilized."[228]

In their effort to depict Filipino combat as savage, the war's defenders made much of what they considered evidence of a Filipino "race war" against whites. Racial exterminism by whites, it seemed, was merely the inevitable, progressive working out of history; race war took place only when nonwhites resisted white domination, in violation of the natural order.[229] Evidence of a Filipino race war was found in what was represented as an early 1899 military order by Gen. Teodoro Sandiko, a document reputedly captured by U.S. soldiers.[230] In it, Sandiko allegedly commanded Filipinos inside the U.S.-occupied city of Manila to revolt in preparation for an invasion of the city from the outside by the army of the republic: not only U.S. soldiers but all "whites" inside the city were to be killed. While evidence of U.S. racial exterminist atrocities was cut off by censorship, the "Sandiko order" was widely promoted in the American press as early as April 1899 as a sign of Filipino savagery. "The war has developed into a race war," wrote John F. Bass of the order in *Harper's Weekly*. "After this let no one raise his voice to favor Aguinaldo's government or army." There was "no choice of methods" ahead, only the need for a "strong military government, untempered by mercy." Use of the "Sandiko order" as a justification for the ongoing war intensified with the presidential race of 1900, finding its way into vice presidential candidate Theodore Roosevelt's speeches and even into the Republican platform.[231] The Filipinos' race war, it appeared, contrasted sharply with the war of civilization waged by the United States.

If the first argument defined U.S. actions as outside the moral and legal frameworks of civilized war, a second one distanced American atrocities from U.S. initiative: Civilized men might reluctantly adopt savage methods to defeat savages, but they could do so without surrendering their civilization; guerrilla war was tactical for whites, ethnological for nonwhites. This argument required emphasis on racial solidarity between domestic U.S. audiences and American soldiers. Maj. Gen. S. B. M. Young accused those who had claimed "that our soldiers are barbarous savages . . . and not fit to be considered as civilized," as "abusing their own flesh and blood" for political advantage.[232] He found the anti-imperialists more traitorous even than the Civil War's Copperheads had been; the latter, at least, had been defending "kindred," where the current war had been "against a cruel and vindictive lot of savages, who were in no way related to us."[233] Henry Cabot Lodge expressed a similar sentiment in an address before the Senate. "One would suppose from what has been said here in debate," he stated, "that it was an army of aliens and mercenaries; that we had out there in the Philippine Islands some strange foreign force which we had let loose upon that helpless people." But this was not the case: Americans at home should respect a blood compact with their imperial soldiers abroad. "Why, Mr. President," Lodge declared, "those soldiers are our own. They are our flesh and blood, bone of our bone, flesh of our flesh."[234]

If U.S. atrocities were not a matter of race, they must be a matter of emulation: Americans appropriated what little savagery they had undertaken from their immediate surroundings. "What is it which has led them to commit these atrocities which we all so much regret and over which we sorrow?" Lodge spoke climactically. "I think I know why these things have happened. I think they have grown out of the conditions of warfare, of the war that was waged by the Filipinos themselves, a semicivilized people, with all the tendencies and characteristics of Asiatics, with the Asiatic indifference to life, with the Asiatic treachery and the Asiatic cruelty, all tinctured and increased by three hundred years of subjection to Spain."[235] In most cases, the role of "Asiatic treachery" and "cruelty" was played by Filipino insurgents, but in some cases, it was admitted that Americans had learned their lessons in savagery from the Macabebes with whom the U.S. Army was collaborating closely. Where forced to concede that Americans soldiers had participated in torture, apologists claimed they were merely mimicking or assisting Macabebes. Torture by whites, then, was not morally or racially essential but temporary, contingent, and contextual.

The "Asiatic" roots of U.S. atrocities were given powerful emphasis in Senate Document 205, *Charges of Cruelty, etc., to the Natives of the Philippines*. Submitted in February 1902 by Secretary of War Elihu Root to satisfy senatorial demands for investigation and prosecution of "cruelty and oppression exercised by our soldiers toward natives," the document's first part contained 57 pages of investigation against U.S. soldiers, for cases that Root assured his audience had been "either unfounded or greatly exaggerated."[236] Its second part, a massive 370 pages, contained two years' trial records for military tribunals convened to try cases against Filipinos "for cruelty against Filipinos."[237] These were not, importantly, Macabebes abusing peasant supporters of the revolution but "insurgents" torturing and assassinating "amigos" of the United States. Taken together, the reports left little doubt as to the race of "cruelty."

A third argument attributed U.S. atrocities entirely to Macabebe collaborators organized into Scout units. While the emulation argument suggested that Americans were merely subject to the tutelage of savages, this third argument was that atrocities had been committed almost entirely by cooperating Filipino troops over whom American officers had little or no control. Call it a policy of outsourcing savagery: where the Macabebes had been hailed as "Filipinos in Uncle Sam's Uniforms" during their recruitment, they were represented during atrocity investigations as a kind of mad unconscious that could neither be dispensed with nor fully harnessed.[238] In response to reports that Macabebe units had looted the town of Magallanes and raped women there, for example, General Lloyd Wheaton noted that they were "in these outrages, conducting themselves in their usual and customary manner."[239] Brig. Gen. Frederick Funston strongly denied his own troops had committed the "water cure," but it was "common knowledge" that Macabebes had done so "when not under the direct control of some officer," and it was "utterly impossible to prevent a few offenses of this kind." Responsibility went only as far as race. Funston had "never heard of its having been administered to a native by a white man."[240]

A fourth argument, that of "degeneration," made U.S. atrocities the by-product of civilizational meltdown. Inextricably a medical, racial, gendered, moral, and sexual discourse, "degeneration" had attained its greatest explanatory power at this moment on a vast, Euro-American and interimperial scale.[241] Discourses of "degeneration" had been common throughout the war, emerging from anxious discussions of tropical heat, disease, and exhaustion, as well as contact between "races."[242] It was unsurprising, then, that it came to play a key role in rationalizing U.S. atrocities: rather than "emulating" their human and physical environments, American soldiers had collapsed into them. The most vivid use of "degeneration" along these lines was made by Dr. Henry C. Rowland, who had served in the Philippines as acting assistant surgeon in the U.S. Army in two separate terms of service. Rowland's account of "Fighting Life in the Philippines," published in *McClure's Magazine* in 1902, sought to explain the "obedient fulfillment of cruel and savage orders by exactly such men as we see about us every day." He invented three hypothetical U.S. soldiers named Tom, Dick, and Harry and set them on a path reminiscent of Joseph Conrad's *Heart of Darkness*, published three years earlier. Once in the islands, the three witness the progressive degeneration of their company. One sergeant "suddenly seized with acute dementia" opens fire on his comrades; a corporal beats a Filipino "without the slightest discoverable cause"; another is caught "deliberately attempting the murder of a native."[243]

For Rowland, the cause of these disorders was a fatal tension between the soldiers' racial essence and their immediate environment, a tension whose danger was (perhaps like a guerrilla combatant) that it was "unsuspected" and would "smolder along until it finally bursts into a flame of suicidal, or homicidal, mania." To a disturbing extent, this essence was subject to deep alteration and deterioration when transplanted into new, unfamiliar settings. "[U]nder certain unaccustomed conditions," he wrote, "it is possible for men to behave in a manner entirely foreign to all prehabitual impulse as the result of unusual influences upon which they have no gauge."[244]

Over the course of Rowland's tale, Tom, Dick, and Harry are remade in the image of their surroundings as the harsh physical conditions of the tropics mesh poisonously with the realities of guerrilla warfare. Cut off from home, with letters arriving less and less frequently, the soldiers' civilized restraint, mercy, and gentility erode. Having found their trusting comrades "hacked and dismembered," they no longer look upon "friendly natives" with "kindly toleration" or "play with the brown babies." They devalue Filipino life, giving it "equal value to that of a sheep-killing collie"; a trench of dead Filipinos "awakens no more feeling than the wreck of a cattle train." Eventually, they decide that "the only chance of pacification lies in wholesale cataclysm; an inundation of human blood that will purge the islands of treachery." By the time the three find two company members—"*parts* of them"—in the jungle, they have already concluded that Filipinos are "vermin only to be ridded by extermination." The story concludes with the killing of Dick and Harry and with Tom's summary execution of captured "niggers."[245]

The unit's moral "degeneration" is, Rowland explains, a mirror of its surroundings. Cut off from civilized associations, they are imprinted with—indeed penetrated by—their savage surroundings. Here, perhaps, was an eerie reversal of the water cure, in which Americans were being forced to consume the Philippines against their will. "They have seen savage sights," wrote Rowland, "they have eaten the food of savages; they have thought savage thoughts; the cries of savages are ringing in their brains." In such circumstances, "we hark back along the trail until we reach a point that coincides with our environment—a point where the treatment of a primitive condition will not be warped by misapplied modernism." While carried out by Americans, then, the killing of prisoners was not American—nor civilized—at all but, in fact, Filipino. "Their lust of slaughter," Rowland wrote suggestively of his American protagonists, "is reflected from the faces of those around them."[246]

But the narrative of exculpatory degeneration did not go unchallenged.

It was parodied, for example, in Poultney Bigelow's sharp, ironic, mid-1902 essay, "How to Convert a White Man into a Savage." The piece was a brief paraphrase of an after-dinner conversation Bigelow claimed to have had in the West Point mess hall with a "blue-eyed, fair-haired youngster" recently returned from the Philippines. Bigelow had inquired whether American soldiers were torturing Filipinos, and the man casually described forcing prisoners to walk ahead of U.S. troops to trigger jungle booby traps. "Yes, it's brutal," he concedes. "[I]t's revolting to a white man; yet we're ordered to do it; if we don't we are guilty of military insubordination; if we do we are branded as cruel!" But such tactics were also the only viable path to victory; specifically, he maintained, the U.S. military must

> make war upon the whole population and to conduct it with so much determination that the whole Philippine population will recognize the fact that they are dealing with a force that must be obeyed.
>
> War then resolves itself into a wholesale devastation. Every house that can harbor a native must be burned, every store of food must be carried away or destroyed; every animal that can assist the enemy must be shot (notably the water buffalo), and, harder still, every man, woman and child must be regarded as an enemy.

Bigelow's point was clear: it was not Filipino collaborators or a Philippine environment that "converted" white men into savages but U.S. military tactics in a brutal, unjust war. Bigelow closed his essay by urging a revision of school histories so they might teach not merely "the gaudy and glorious side of warfare" but "the dark and monotonous murder which is sometimes an ally in imperial progress."[247]

Fictions of Victory

The war's second end was declared in a public ceremony in front of the Ayuntamiento in Manila on July 4, 1901, with the formal transfer of all executive governmental functions from the military to the civil government under the Philippine Commission and William Howard Taft, who was inaugurated as the United States' first "civil governor" in the islands. The shift of authority had begun the previous September 1, when the military had handed over legislative and some executive powers to the commission. The capture of Aguinaldo the previous March had been a serious blow to the revolution and led to the surrender of a number of key revolutionary generals. The July 4 transfer marked one of what Taft called the "successive stages in a clearly formulated plan" for making the islands "ripe for permanent civil government on a more or less popular basis."[248] According to the *Manila Times*, the city had "never been decorated so much, and the profusion of flags, bunting, palms, lanterns and pictures in the house decorations was a marked difference from past Fourths."[249] An editorial in the *Manila Times* cheered that "all races" could celebrate the event, which marked a "dividing line" between "the past of war and the future of peace." The choice of Independence Day had been felicitous, as the United States' own anti-imperial revolution had "made it possible to extend the liberties of her stable republicanism to these Eastern peoples in their day." Filipinos would one day recognize that "America's Fourth is their Fourth," once they came to "regard their conquest in a gratiful [*sic*] spirit, as an act necessary for their own good."[250]

The ceremony itself revealed the relative absence of this spirit and the blurriness of the dividing line between war and peace. With seating for only six hundred, the day's celebration was guarded by four hundred U.S. and Filipino policemen "distributed around the square to keep order and regulate the crowd," which even the *Manila Times* felt had "appeared too great a show of force." Taft noted that the transfer of legislative power the previous September had only pertained to "pacified provinces" and warned against exaggeration of the commission's success in organizing provincial and municipal governments. The current, celebrated handover of authority to civilians was itself "provisional." "Armed insurrection" continued in "four or possibly five" of twenty-seven "organized" provinces and in portions of others, where the military governor would continue to have executive power; "unorganized" provinces were "not ready for civil government" at all.[251]

The war continued unbidden by the Americans. Ultimately, the strategy that would crush the remaining resistance involved implementing MacArthur's December 1900 instructions most harshly by waging war against the entire rural population in hostile areas, a strategy represented best by the policy of reconcentration undertaken from 1901 to 1902 in numerous locations. The policy aimed at the isolation and starvation of guerrillas through the deliberate annihilation of the rural economy: peasants in resistant areas were ordered to relocate to garrisoned towns by a given date, leaving behind all but the most basic provisions. Outside of the policed, fenced-in perimeters of these "reconcentration camps," troops would then undertake a scorched-earth policy, burning residences and rice stores, destroying or capturing livestock, and killing every person they encountered.[252] Americans had first become aware of this tactic during the final Cuban war of independence, when its use by the Spanish general Weyler had inflamed righteous American outrage and tilted the United States toward intervention against Spain. "This cruel policy of concentration," President McKinley himself had observed in his first message to Congress, while rationalized "as a necessary measure of war and as a means of cutting off supplies from the insurgents," was immoral, requiring the U.S. government to issue a "firm and earnest protest." "It was not civilized warfare," he stated. "It was extermination."[253]

By late 1900, however, Americans were getting reacquainted with the concentration camp, not for the last time. While at least some Filipinos had turned to the Boers for inspiration, Americans were accommodated to the new concept by articulate British spokesmen hailing the policy's necessity and effectiveness in South Africa. Speaking in New York in December 1900, for example, one year before General Bell's first reconcentration orders in Batangas, the twenty-six-year-old parliamentarian, writer, and lecturer Winston Churchill, speaking on the ongoing war against the Boers in South Africa, defended the British "policy of removing country people into the towns." In a comparison many might have found less than flattering only a few years earlier, he noted that "the present situation in South Africa seemed to him to resemble that in Cuba" prior to 1898. In the South African case, the policy had been brought on by the Boers themselves, who, fighting without uniforms, had made it "hard for the British to distinguish between combatants and noncombatants," and thus radical, geographic separation was required. While "less comfortable" than they would have been otherwise, Churchill assured his audience that reconcentrated populations had "not been subjected to unnecessary hardship."[254] The American press followed the lead of Churchill and other British imperialists along these lines. In October 1901, the middle-class reform journal *Public Opinion* reprinted a piece from the London press presenting the camps—"which have lately aroused so much controversy"—as orderly, hygienic, and as "cozy and comfortable as circumstances will permit."[255]

Two months later, the U.S. military was constructing camps of its own, accepting at least part of the "dear-bought wisdom" of its imperial peers. It became the preferred strategy of Gen. James Franklin Bell, who had debated with Mabini the previous year on definitions of "civilized" war. Bell had been sent to Batangas in November 1901 to put down stubborn guerrilla resistance under General Malvar, having successfully "pacified" Ilocos earlier that year by concentrating civilians in selected towns. His rationale at the time had been that the only way to split guerrillas off from their civilian infrastructure was to make war directly upon the latter. Once the people "realize what war is"—through starvation, burning, and terror—they would end their support and bring the war to a close. Writing from Batangas at the outset of his reconcentration program there, Bell dismissed the "[n]atural and commendable sympathy for suffering and loss" but, quoting General Orders No. 100, maintained that a "short and severe war" was preferable to a "benevolent war indefinitely prolonged."[256] Facing an insurrection, it was "impossible to wage war efficiently and at the same time do abstract justice in operations unquestionably essential."[257] Distinctions between combatants and noncombatants were inconvenient. "It is an inevitable consequence of war that the innocent must generally suffer with the guilty," he noted in an early order. "Military necessity frequently precludes the possibility of making discriminations."[258]

THE LAST ACT OF the administration's mid-1902 political counteroffensive against anti-imperialist critics was the third and (almost) final declaration of the end of the war. On July 4, 1902, President Theodore Roosevelt issued a proclamation declaring the Philippine-American War officially over, as if cued by John Philip Sousa himself. It stated that the "insurrection against the authority and sovereignty of the United States" was "now at an end," and that peace had been established throughout the archipelago, "except in the country inhabited by the Moro tribes," to which the proclamation "did not apply." It accused Filipino combatants of "many acts in violation of the laws of civilized warfare" but granted "pardon and amnesty" to unpunished "insurrectionists" and their supporters. Anyone seeking this pardon would be compelled to take an oath to "recognize and accept the supreme authority of the United States of America in the Philippine Islands" and "maintain true faith and allegiance thereto," doing so "voluntarily, without mental reservation or purpose of evasion."[259]

As had previous declarations, Roosevelt's 1902 statement failed to persuade some remaining insurrectionists. War's end remained a beleaguered fiction that broke down in unflattering reversals: by 1905, parts of the provinces of Batangas, Cebu, Bohol, Samar, Cavite, and Albay would be returned to military authority due to continued Filipino resistance. The commission's June 1903 Reconcentration Act extended the war in tactical terms by authorizing use of the wartime measure by civilian authorities in areas "infested" with "ladrones." Liberal use would be made of this in subsequent years, in Albay and Bicol in 1903 and Batangas and Cavite in 1905.[260] The Philippine Commission would pass specific, separate acts shifting authority from the military to civilians, officially "ending" the war in these regions in silent, piecemeal fashion until 1913. Warfare was only beginning in the Moro regions of the southern archipelago, and resistance to U.S. control would continue there for more than a decade. A *Washington Post* editorialist attempted to turn into a virtue the regime's repetitious failure to end the war by fiat. The war had been "brought to an end on six different occasions" since the first declaration of U.S. victory, it noted, but "[a] bad thing cannot be killed too often," it suggested.[261]

Ending a war that refused to end on its own meant making it invisible to American publics. In November 1902, the Philippine Commission passed the Brigandage Act, which, even more than Roosevelt's address, ended the war by command, defining any remaining Filipino resistance to American authority as "banditry" or "ladronism" rather than "insurrection." Parallel to the passage of this act was the inauguration of a Philippine Constabulary, an insular police force under commission control, which would in many ways function as a colonial army in police uniform, waging war in areas otherwise designated as "pacified." If, as the *New York Times* noted in 1899, the ratification of the Treaty of Paris had efficiently turned imperial war into insurrection, the Brigandage Act conveniently turned insurrection into crime. Returning U.S. soldiers, freed up by the transfer of military power to the Philippine Scouts and Constabulary, were perhaps the most potent, if illusory, signs to American audiences of an insurrection well ended.[262]

Two public addresses meant to end the war in the Philippines rhetorically stamped it with official U.S. meanings. The first of these, directed at Amerian audiences, affirmed race war as a historical necessity. Theodore Roosevelt's 1902 Memorial Day speech at Arlington National Cemetery was both one of the final interventions in the administration's mid-1902 propaganda campaign and, as the first such address in the cemetery's history, a sign of the way that empire would become a foundation for national institutions. According to the *Boston Morning Journal*, an estimated 30,000 people attended, hearing a set of "harmonious" speeches in which the war in the Philippines was "most prominent." Roosevelt had "never delivered a speech that more impressed his hearers." Turning to the

Philippines after Civil War invocations, "[t]here was indignation in every word and every gesture." U.S. soldiers in the Philippines—"your younger brothers, your sons"—were bringing to completion "a small but peculiarly trying and difficult war" on which turned "not only the honor of the flag but the triumph of civilization over forces which stand for the black chaos of savagery and barbarism." Roosevelt formally acknowledged and regretted U.S. atrocities but claimed that "a very cruel and very treacherous enemy" had committed, for every American atrocity, "a hundred acts of far greater atrocity." Furthermore, while such means had been the Filipinos' "only method of carrying on the war," they had been "wholly exceptional on our part."[263]

Roosevelt condemned the army's critics—those who "walk delicately and live in the soft places of the earth"—for dishonoring the "strong men who with blood and sweat" had suffered and laid down their lives "in remote tropic jungles to bring the light of civilization into the world's dark places." These were men, unlike their armchair counterparts, engaged in the heavy work of race and history. "The warfare that has extended the boundaries of civilization at the expense of barbarism and savagery has been for centuries one of the most potent factors in the progress of humanity," Roosevelt said. While "from its very nature it has always and everywhere been liable to dark abuses," to avoid such wars would show Americans to be "cravens and weaklings, unworthy of the sires from whose loins we sprang." Victory over the "Aguinaldan oligarchy" had been the only "effective means of putting a stop to cruelty in the Philippines." Now a regime of benevolence and uplift could begin.[264]

Much less survives of a second public statement, circulated in the Philippines at war's end. This statement erased and denied race war before Filipino audiences, and as such, can be read as an early charter of the "postwar" regime. Upon his departure after three months in command of forces in Linao, David J. Gilmer, a black captain in the 49th U.S. Volunteer Infantry, felt compelled to confront the question of race directly in a widely circulated letter. The existence of the letter suggests that the Filipino experience of race war, compounding earlier rumors and suspicions, had left Filipinos highly suspicious of American intentions as an occupying power. Gilmer felt uniquely qualified to allay these fears, as the self-conscious ambassador of an empire without race. With "the visible Negro blood that flows in the veins of my body," Gilmer claimed to be the last who would "sanction the cause of your oppressors." Praising 204 Filipinos who had recently taken the oath of allegiance to the United

States, he called his country a "true democracy," with "the majority" of its legislators "opposed to the oppression of human and religious rights." There was, it was true, a "rabble" in the United States that "runs riot at times," but "[y]ou need not have any fear of that class of Americans, for they cannot reach you." To Filipinos who may have suspected that this "rabble" had, in fact, arrived, Gilmer urged his Filipino readers to be as nonracist as their American occupiers. Against the notion that "all white men are unfair to the Negro races," he urged the people of Linao to teach their children "to judge men according to the deeds of the individual and not by the color of his skin."[265]

OVER 4,000 U.S. TROOPS and an estimated 50,000 Filipino troops were dead. Approximately 75 percent of U.S. deaths had been from noncombat causes; the wound rate among U.S. troops was 2.3 percent, the mortality rate 3.3 percent.[266] But U.S. sovereignty was purchased mostly in the lives of Filipinos, especially through losses to epidemics. While Americans had feared tropical "degeneration," American troops had brought with them numerous diseases uncommon in the islands; "hikes" and interisland naval transport spread these as well as illnesses contracted in the islands between formerly isolated Filipino populations.[267] The destruction of villages led to their abandonment by Filipinos and dislocation into harsh, remote mountain environments; the burning of rice stores and the killing of livestock produced malnutrition on a vast scale that, in turn, provided almost ideal conditions of vulnerability to disease. The policy of "attraction" and close interactions between American troops and Filipinos in garrisoned towns, used as evidence of benevolence, also provided efficient vectors of disease transfer. Even more perfect, however, was "reconcentration," which brought together malnutrition, overcrowding, unsanitary conditions, and social dislocation in a formula for mass disease and mortality. The specific loss of human life, while staggering in scale, is still unknown: Glenn May finds a disturbing "150,000 missing Filipinos" in the Batangas region alone.[268] According to Ken De Bevoise, "reconcentrated" Batangas may have had the highest mortality rate not only in the Philippines but in the world at that moment.[269] The estimate of 250,000 Filipino war deaths appears conservative.

The war had brought the Philippine Revolution to a cataclysmic, temporary end. Along with the Spanish-Cuban-American War, it had ushered the United States into the ranks of the world's colonial powers. On the Filipino side, it had been a war for national liberation and *kalayaan*, a continuation of the anticolonial 1896–98 struggle against the Spanish Empire. By seeking to project an image of civilization, the Filipino struggle had also continued, in military form, the campaign for recognition undertaken by the Propaganda writers of the late nineteenth century. On the American side, it had become a race war. Over its course, many Americans came to understand their enemy, the nature of the fighting, and their political, historical, and moral rationales for fighting it in racial terms, a war against the "half-devil" that Rudyard Kipling had warned would perpetually test imperial greatness. Race war in the Philippines had turned not on racial projections but on a novel, colonial-racial formation suited specifically to the tasks of colonial conquest, guerrilla warfare, and ultimately for many soldiers, exterminism. But the day belonged to those who regarded Filipinos as Kipling's "half-child." The war's end, or near end, left Americans with a problem still more complex than bringing a race war to virtual conclusion: that of waging racial peace.

Collaboration and
the Racial State

The Commission says . . . that the Filipino is refined,
cultivated and honorable, but governmental authorities in
the United States, including the President, allude to the
inhuman manner in which warfare has been conducted in the
Philippines against the Americans . . . that the fighting of the
Filipinos was barbarous and that of semi-civilized savages.
*   It is difficult to reconcile the two descriptions.*

EDGAR BELLAIRS, 1900

There is far more difference between the Igorrote of Benguet
and the Tagalog of Manila than between the latter and
ourselves.

EDITH MOSES, 1908

Somewhere between an American parade, a Filipino
fiesta, and a British imperial durbar, the opening and dedication of Manila's Santa Cruz bridge was pompously undertaken in March 1903, celebrating the "first outward and visible monument to American progress in
the Philippines." By that year, the project was simply one element in the
U.S. colonial regime's ongoing reform of the capital, aimed especially at
commercial infrastructure, sanitary improvement, and police surveillance.
But the bridge carried special symbolic weight that spoke to the peculiar
predicaments of a colonial state still literally under construction. In reporting the occasion, Manila's English-language press and American colonial officials shared a somewhat obvious metaphorical vocabulary. The
structure "not only bridges the Pasig," reported the *Manila American*, "but
a chasm that has existed between the native Filipinos and their American
fellow-citizens." The hope was for a one-way crossing, so that "over this
bridge may come the hearts and minds of the former."[1]

The ceremony was a ritual of recognition, one that enacted harmonious
connection across some of the widest political chasms of the early Ameri-

can colonial era: not simply between Americans and Filipinos but between the U.S. Army and civilian officials and between American commercial interests and state officials. At the appointed hour, army engineer Lieutenant Brown presented the bridge to Municipal Board president Herrero, who accepted it with gratitude in Spanish (with an English interpreter) and led Mrs. Ide, the wife of a Philippine commissioner, by the hand to christen it. A parade then crossed, led by the municipal police chief, followed by infantry and artillerymen. Capital followed in the wake of force, in the shape of seventy members of the American Chamber of Commerce, "dressed in white, and presenting a striking illustration of the spread of American commerce." Following capital, there was collaboration: two hundred "embryo politicians" of the state-sponsored Federalista Party, "with banners expressive of the most florid patriotism," backed by Constabulary patrols. Here, in the midst of a churning commercial entrepôt, was a fragile, dreamlike moment. In it, Philippine-American colonial society was an ordered phalanx of functional, connected parts—civilians sandwiched between soldiers, Filipinos behind Americans—moving in a common, progressive direction, enabled and organized by the fruits of modern science and technology. "Never before have these various classes mingled in a common interest as they did today," reported the *Manila American*.

> To each spectator it was "our bridge"—a fetich which will make Manila more truly a community than it has ever been before. Never until now could anyone have expected to see the American Chamber of Commerce, representing solid business interests and fervid Americanism, standing along the curb and giving "three cheers and a tiger" for the city's brown guardians. Such incidents serve to teach the Filipino that he is a brother and not a serf.[2]

The ritual would demonstrate how significantly the political, and racial, texture of American colonial politics had changed since the formal declaration of the end of the Philippine-American War. The new colonial state, with the Philippine Commission at its hub, would have civilians at its helm, although it would retain strong military elements. It would draw strength from, but also be challenged by, an American colonial civil society of merchants, businessmen, and adventurers. Most of all, it would be a regime of collaboration between Americans and Filipinos, one in which U.S. officials recognized provincial and metropolitan elites as unequal political partners. The process had, of course, begun during the war itself. Continued repression and the promise of amnesty had attracted both rural and urban elites away from the revolution and toward the U.S. military state. But the system of collaboration would become more extensive and formalized under the civilian regime, both more autonomous from Washington and more deeply rooted in Filipino social structures.

The new political configuration necessitated a new racial formation to organize and legitimate it. The broad-gauged, in some cases exterminist, racism of the U.S. military during the Philippine-American War was ill-suited to the more subtle arts of compromise, feint, and manipulation that would characterize Filipino-American power-sharing under the Philippine Commission. What was needed was a racial formation that could somehow persuade its Filipino participants that they were "brothers" and not "serfs" and simultaneously explain to them why they were unready for the rigors and responsibilities of self-government. It must also be able to explain to racist anti-imperialists why the assimilation of Filipinos would be successful and pose no threat to the United States itself. The result was an inclusionary racial formation that brought metaphors of family, evolution, and tutelary assimilation into a gradualist, indeed indefinite, trajectory of Filipino "progress" toward self-government.

The new formation had at its core a division of the Philippine population into Hispanicized and non-Hispanicized peoples, a dividing line that was also one of the central sociocultural divisions under Spanish rule. Hispanicized Filipinos and those the regime called "non-Christians" would be disenfranchised for different reasons: the former were condemned for their "superstition" and "cacique" politics; the latter for their "savagery," technological backwardness, and lack of Christianity. This represented in many ways an internalization of wartime discourses of savagery and their displacement from the Hispanicized Filipinos that had fought against U.S. invasion onto non-Christians. It also necessarily meant the transformation of savagery from a politico-military to a religio-cultural category.

The civilian regime's racial formation would be institutionalized as a bifurcated racial state in which imperial-indigenist categories would inform distinct patterns of administration. Christians and non-Christians would be ruled by different means, organized around what Lord Lugard would later, in a very different context, call "dual mandates."[3] Differences would be embedded in the colonial administration through the establishment of two "special provinces," the Moro Province and the Mountain

Province, which would promote the racialization of territory and the territorialization of race. In Christian regions, the colonial state would grow out of linkages with Hispanicized elites who would be granted highly restricted, elite male suffrage; in non-Christian regions, "paternal," nonelectoral systems of authority that empowered U.S. politico-military officers would predominate. The bifurcated racial state was also in evidence in ambitious state projects like the Ethnological Survey and the 1903 Philippine Census, both of which harnessed the emerging collaboration system to the project of making the Philippine world legible to Americans. The United States' recognition of Hispanicized Filipinos through the structures of collaboration would widen the perceived racial gap between Catholics and non-Christians.

Colonial State-Building

The fact of conquest did not itself determine the political and legal principles by which the United States would rule the Philippines. The Treaty of Paris of 1898 had not addressed the status of the territories ceded by Spain to the United States, leaving the decision to the U.S. Congress. From mid-1898 through the years of the Philippine-American War, debates unfolded in the United States among legal scholars, jurists, and public officials on the character of U.S. sovereignty in Cuba, Puerto Rico, and the Philippines and the proper modes of its exercise. As Lanny Thompson has shown, discussion revolved around several possibilities. Some argued for the doctrine of *ex proprio vigore*, which held that the Constitution applied to the new territories "by its own force": in popular terms, the Constitution would "follow the flag." This meant that continental models of territorial incorporation employed in North America must necessarily apply to the new, overseas territories, which would eventually become "incorporated" as politically equal states of the Union.[4]

But the *ex proprio vigore* approach was attacked, and defeated, on the grounds of race. Indeed, the explicitly racial character of U.S. territorial models was illuminated by their rejection in the case of the new territories. As many critics explained, empire-building across the continent had not been "imperialism" at all, but "expansion" in which white settlers had unfolded their race-given "capacities" in racially empty (or emptied) space. Territorial "incorporation" had been the constitutionalism of a white settler colonial state. The Constitution did not follow the flag; lagging somewhat behind it, the Constitution followed the race. The new acquisitions from Spain were different: for reasons of racial environmentalism (the inevitable "degeneration" of whites in the tropics) and land scarcity (what was often called "thickly settled populations"), there would be few if any white, republic-laden settlers. At the same time, the islands' majority populations were "incapable of self-government" on racial grounds; to enfranchise them, pushing the Constitution dangerously beyond the boundaries of the race to which it exclusively applied, would only endanger the islands' inhabitants and, worse, imperil the white continent over which they would share power. The momentum of racial-imperial republicanism, which had been carried as far as Hawaii by white missionaries and sugar planters, had run out. The United States now faced an "imperial" problem, defined by what legal scholar Frederic Coudert called "the domination over men of one order or kind of civilization" by "men of different and higher civilization."[5]

Opponents of *ex proprio vigore* launched a doctrine of incorporation that would become the dominant politico-legal framework for the United States' colonial empire. Its goal was to insulate the United States politically from its new colonies, while protecting continental North American territories from otherwise unlimited, "plenary" congressional power. As set out by Abbott Lowell, the doctrine sharply distinguished "annexation" from "incorporation." Possessions "acquired by conquest or cession" did not automatically become "part of the United States" but could become so if granted this status by "legislative or treaty-making authorities." These authorities could decide to "incorporate" the possession—so that most constitutional restrictions applied to it—or decide that it was "not to form part of the United States," in which case they did not apply. Beginning in 1901, the Supreme Court would employ and legitimate the incorporation doctrine in the Insular Cases, which dealt with the legal status of the inhabitants of the "new possessions." In *Downes v. Bidwell*, Justice Edward White declared that "in an international sense," Puerto Rico was "not a foreign country," but that it was "foreign to the United States in a domestic sense," because it had not been "incorporated" into it but was "merely appurtenant thereto as a possession." The Philippines, Puerto Rico, and Cuba prior to 1902 would, therefore, be "unincorporated territories," under the sovereignty of the United States but outside its body politic.[6]

While legal "unincorporation" appeared to solve problems of race and republicanism, it left unresolved the question of how the new territories would be incorporated within the U.S. national state. The answer was expediency, as U.S. military authorities on the ground in Puerto Rico,

Cuba, and "pacified" areas of the Philippines took over complex, non-traditional, "civilian" functions of government. "The War Department found itself without adequate machinery to handle this new work," recalled Clarence Edwards. In response, it inaugurated a new division that would develop into a Bureau of Insular Affairs, headed by Edwards, to handle correspondence and memoranda regarding civil affairs administered by the U.S. military in the new territories. As U.S. military dominion widened and deepened, the bureau was empowered to hire its own staff of specialists and clerks, about seventy-five by mid-1904.[7]

The bureau was, according to Edwards, the "clearinghouse for all questions as between the government of the Philippine Islands and the government of the United States." Among many other tasks, it studied and recommended colonial policies to the secretary of war, purchased and shipped supplies to the Philippines, assisted in appointments to the Philippine Civil Service, reviewed the expenses of the colonial government, acted as the insular government's lobbying arm in Washington, and served as the central liaison between the regime and the American public, with its "uninterrupted stream" of public inquiries regarding the islands.[8]

The bureau would shape policy by a host of indirect means, through the colonial legislation it recommended to the War Department, through the continual influence it exercised through its choice of appointees, and through its framing of colonial questions to Congress and the concerned public. It would measure its success in its ability to protect the insular governments from most domestic pressure other than its own. "The study of successful colonial governments," wrote Edwards, showed that they are "generally administered by a separate department of the home government." It was evident to anyone, he said, that such a system must also prevail in the Philippine case to prevent a chaotic administrative scramble between executive agencies.[9]

In brief, it was the job of the Bureau of Insular Affairs to keep the new colonial governments as "insular" as possible in political terms. Edwards emphasized the importance of guarding their autonomy from domestic politics. "[T]he government of the Philippine Islands is in the Philippines," he wrote, and was meant "to govern under the broadest constitutional limitations, agreeable by analogy to the essential principles upon which our own government is established." Where European colonial offices often had far broader administrative and executive powers over specific colonial governments, the bureau's task was merely to lay down general policy rules, secure personnel, define their powers, and, quoting

Secretary of War Elihu Root, to "'hold them responsible for the conduct of government in the islands with the least possible interference from Washington.'"[10]

If the government of the Philippines was to be "in the Philippines," the islands' unincorporated status meant that, like the other new dependencies, it would receive its government through a separate, congressional "Organic Act," rather than by territorial precedents. While the Organic Act for Puerto Rico had been passed in April 1900, a Philippine act awaited the outcome of the war and the plausibility of civil government itself. By mid-1902, resistance to U.S. control had faded, and the circle of actually existing provincial and municipal governments under the Philippine Commission's auspices had widened. When the Philippine Organic Act was approved on July 1, 1902, just three days before Roosevelt's amnesty declaration, it built upon the president's prior executive orders and instructions to the commission. In effect, congressional action chased presidential directives by a year: by mid-1902, the Philippine Commission had, without the Organic Act, been exercising most legislative and executive control in pacified areas of the islands for nearly a year, in theory if not always in practice.

Nonetheless, the Organic Act provided greater shape, coherence, and legitimacy to the emerging civilian government than had been previously possible. Its authors denied any intent to occupy the islands permanently, entitling it "An Act Temporarily to Provide for the Administration of the Affairs of Civil Government in the Philippine Islands, and for Other Purposes."[11] It defined the institutions, powers, responsibilities, and limits of the civil government, delineated the inhabitants' political status, rights, and duties, and provided detailed rules regarding the disposition of land, mineral rights, and government franchises. Consistent with the Treaty of Paris and the islands' unincorporated standing, persons residing in the Philippines who had been Spanish subjects on April 11, 1899, and their children were not U.S. citizens but "citizens of the Philippine Islands," excepting those who had elected to preserve their allegiance to Spain.[12] These Philippine citizens were granted a bill of rights that included due process of law, freedom of religion, and freedom of speech (which had been previously crushed under a Sedition Act), but not the right to a jury trial or the right to bear arms.

Most controversially, the act contained provisions for a future Filipino assembly. When "the existing insurrection" in the islands had ended and the president certified a "general and complete peace," the Philippine

Commission would carry out a census of the population. Two years following the census's completion and publication, were peaceful conditions to continue in areas "not inhabited by Moros or other non-Christian tribes," the president would call for a "general election" of delegates to a "Philippine assembly" of between fifty and one hundred members, which would share power with the Philippine Commission as the lower house of a bicameral legislature. Two "resident commissioners" would be sent by this legislature to the United States and would be "entitled to an official recognition as such by all departments." Lest there be any fear, these "representatives" would come to Washington without rights to vote or debate and would thus not be fully incorporated into the U.S. congressional process.

ON THE GROUND IN the Philippines, a civilian government needed civilian employees, which raised the question of how they were to be identified and hired. The Philippine Commission insisted on establishing a civil service system, still new to the United States, as the basis of the islands' colonial state.[13] The commission believed it would likely be "very difficult" to identify "honest, competent Americans" with the necessary "spirit of the missionary task," but without such a system, the U.S. government was "foredoomed to humiliating failure." A system based on "competitive examination," it was hoped, would "secure the selection of the finest candidate" and offer "equal opportunities for all." It would also help legitimate the regime and fulfill its larger objectives of political tutelage, as a civil service "regulated by justice to all applicants" and "directed solely to the welfare of the community . . . cannot fail to commend to [Filipinos] a republican form of government." Immediately upon their assumption of legislative powers in September 1900, the commission enacted Act No. 5, to establish an "Efficient and Honest" civil service system. The act appointed a civil service board, which would establish civil service rules for the insular and provincial (but not municipal) administrative levels of the colonial state, including the classification of positions, qualifications for applicants, and examinations. Examinations were given in either English or Spanish in both Manila and the provinces, where regional examining committees were established. They would also be given to applicants in the United States by the Bureau of Insular Affairs.[14]

Over the next several years, the Philippine Civil Service Board would build up the administrative branches of the new state. By September 1903, 9,366 candidates had been examined, 66 percent of them in Spanish—the vast majority Filipinos—and the rest in English. The board's instructions were to give preference in hiring, where qualifications were equal, first to Filipinos, second to honorably discharged U.S. soldiers, sailors, and marines, and third to other U.S. citizens. The appointment during this period of nearly 60 percent of candidates who passed the exams suggests both the difficulty of attracting applicants and the weakness of claims to a "competitive" system. Of the 2,919 appointed, 53 percent had taken the Spanish-language exam; despite the stated preference for Filipinos, applicants who passed the English-language exam were over 15 percent more likely to be hired than those who had passed the Spanish-language exam.[15]

Despite civil service regulations, corruption thrived in the colonial state-building process. Reconstructing the islands required the widespread granting of government franchises and contracts to private entities, and the first wave of American civilians in the Philippines had not been civil service employees, but what William Howard Taft called the "venturesome business spirits that thrive best in times of trouble and excitement," who had followed in the wake of the invasion with the hopes of supplying the U.S. Army and the postwar government. In particular, Taft noted a marked increase in attendance levels at the hearings of the commission once it achieved the right to let out contracts and licenses. Once "those gentlemen who were spending the islands' funds" realized "that there was some power at least in the Commission," he reported to the Senate, the meetings were "thronged with persons interested in legislation, and the Filipinos began to come to the civil government for assistance and advice."[16]

In some cases, U.S. Army officers and soldiers inaugurated contracting businesses that served the commission government. As educator and anthropologist David Barrows wrote to a businessman friend in 1902, some men in the islands had already made "a great deal of money," although "the means they have employed would in most cases not be followed by yourself." The greatest profits often came from government building contracts, where state officials' desire for rapid work met the hopes of U.S. entrepreneurs. In effect, U.S. contractors profited from their race, nationality, and language as middlemen between the colonial state and labor recruiters and local enterprises, especially Chinese-owned businesses. "It is possible to get a government bid for a round sum, and sublet the contracts to Chinos for half or less of the amount received," Barrows explained. Barrows did not believe that "there is any corruption on the part of the Army officers who let these contracts," but the government wanted "the work done and done quick and the contractors of course are very willing to take advantage of the government's need."[17]

The emerging civil service would struggle, not always successfully, with this other mode of colonial politics. Apart from contracting-related corruption, there was the outright stealing of government resources, especially by provincial treasurers (a position that was reserved for Americans because of their superior "honesty"). The *Manila Sunday Sun* complained in October 1903 that "[d]ishonest government employees" had "not failed to furnish at least a weekly sensation for many months past," especially in the form of theft and embezzlement. During each of the fiscal years ending in June 1903 and 1904, the civil service "involuntarily" terminated the employment of nearly 10 percent of all Americans in the colonial civil service. Nonetheless, some Americans insisted such behavior was entirely exceptional. Mrs. William H. Taft wrote years later that the U.S. mission in the Philippines had been "based upon the highest principles" and that she found it "particularly painful" that "a little band of white men in Bilibid prison" had demonstrated "venality and breach of trust." Some U.S. officials congratulated themselves that the investigation and punishment of American corruption illustrated superior U.S. political morality, furnishing Filipinos "a spectacle which they had never enjoyed during the Spanish regime." But others understood this enforcement to be, in fact, Filipino in origin: U.S. policing of the civil service was necessary in order to prevent the popular, and disastrous, delegitimation of the state. "[I]n no part of the world does rumor of injustice, or fraud, and of underhand methods in the administration of public office, receive so much credit as in the Orient," lamented one U.S. official.[18]

While they minimized the wide-ranging activities of corrupt American officials, the civilian government successfully promoted American teachers as its true representatives. Of all the icons of U.S. colonialism, there was none more vivid or long-lived than the arrival of the USS *Thomas* to the islands on August 21, 1901. The ship, which carried 509 Americans intending to become teachers in a still-unbuilt Philippine public school system, became instantly freighted with hopes for an occupation of "uplift."[19] Adeline Knapp wrote lyrically of "a white ship in mid-ocean, her forefoot set toward the Philippines, her deck thronged with young men and women actuated for the most part by high ideals and a genuine desire to be helpful." The teachers' task was "to carry on the education that shall fit the Filipinos for their new citizenship." But it was also their charge to close "a chasm" between Americans and Filipinos "which must be bridged by a common knowledge and sympathy." Like the Santa Cruz bridge, the *Thomas* would close a gap between Americans and "a people who neither know nor understand the underlying principles of our civilization," yet who "for our mutual happiness and liberty, must be brought into accord with us." Importantly, the ship's arrival—made representative of the essence of Philippine-American relations—set the United States apart as a national-exceptional case, placing it above an abstract world of lesser empires. If reconcentration had made the United States seem dangerously like Spain and Great Britain, the teachers arriving on the *Thomas* would, some hoped, restore the fabric of U.S. national exceptionalism. "Never before in the history of the world has any country sent out a body like this," wrote Knapp, cautioning the teachers to make good on this claim by quelling "all desire for exploitation of the opportunity" and "all dreams of personal gain."[20]

Morality, education, and national exceptionalism converged in the name the voyagers adopted for themselves: the "Thomasites." By making U.S. teachers into missionaries, the term—soon used for U.S. public schoolteachers in the Philippines in general—connected the journey to much older trajectories of Protestant evangelism in Asia, while moralizing and exceptionalizing U.S. colonialism.[21] But the civilian project of uplift was intertwined with the ongoing war, despite denials. There was perhaps no more vivid example than the *Thomas* itself. Originally a British ship named the *Persia*, it had been bought by an American commercial company and converted into a transatlantic cattle transport in the mid-1890s. Prior to serving as a vehicle of uplift, the *Thomas* had been a ship of war. In July 1898, the U.S. government had purchased it, and soon after the outbreak of the Spanish-Cuban-American War, it had been used to move troops, horses, and supplies to Cuba and Puerto Rico. The following year, in fall 1899, it made its first trip to Manila as a troop transport. By the time of its most famous, mid-1901 voyage, laden with teachers, it had already made six other, now long-forgotten journeys, burdened with U.S. soldiers. At the same time, at least ten of the Thomasites were veterans of the invasion, proudly heralded by their comrades for their "pioneer spirit" in returning to the country "they helped to reclaim from misrule and industrial waste." There was also rhetorical continuity, measured in the frequency with which the Thomasites referred to themselves as a kind of occupying "army." According to Knapp, the ship "bore no armed force," but its passengers were nonetheless a "great army of instruction," its soldiers "scattered over the insular field fighting each his battle with what might is given him."[22]

The Thomasites and other civilians often described their task as "regenerating" the islands and their people: if degeneration had been a chief U.S. war anxiety, regeneration was one of the principal hopes for its aftermath.[23] It did not hurt that this discourse was continuous with military representations of the war as a regenerating force. Even as U.S. soldiers had destroyed rice, killed cattle, and torched entire villages, they had found plentiful evidence of regeneration in the more limited projects of rural school-building and public health. Some American civilians touring the islands would also emphasize the war's revitalizing impact. When Edith Moses, wife of Commissioner Bernard Moses, was allowed to tour Batangas, where U.S. military destruction had reached its outer limits, she corrected what she assumed would be her family's negative impression of the region under General Bell. "You have heard the sensational rumors of the 'harrying of Batangas,' the reconcentrado camps, and the 'Weyler-like methods of General Bell,'" she wrote. But evidence of the U.S. military's regeneration of the islands abounded for her. In "all parts of the Islands," she wrote, "the ravages of war" were "soon repaired." She noted that the nipa houses she witnessed were "almost all new" but showed little curiosity about the fate of their predecessors. Most strikingly, given her own recent arrival to the islands, she claimed, based on unspecified evidence, that the islands' villages "really looked more prosperous than before the war."[24]

Other Americans were aware of how difficult this claim was to defend. The war had left the Philippine economy in ruins and its rural society in chaos. Six years of war had meant the destruction of farmland and the abandonment of agriculture. Midway into the war, an epidemic of rinderpest had swept the islands, killing an estimated 90 percent of draft cattle and water buffalo. The collapse of agriculture had meant malnutrition and disease among Filipinos on a mass scale; reconcentration had involved the decimation of whole towns and villages. A deadly cholera epidemic would sweep through the islands between 1902 and 1904. An estimated quarter-million Filipinos were dead, and tens of thousands displaced, many of them migrating to Manila and other large urban centers. In the context of rural crisis, active resistance continued to thrive.[25]

Collaboration and Divided Colonizers

Faced with economic collapse and political instability, the commission and its agents faced the formidable problem of constructing a "postwar" society in the midst of ongoing war. The need to create a self-consciously postwar order was, on the one hand, the product of domestic U.S. politics. Republican officials knew that the best way to quell domestic anti-imperialist dissent was to formally declare an end to the war at which this dissent was directed; maintaining anti-imperialist silence meant sustaining the fiction of a war concluded in victory. But a postwar period was also a necessity vis-à-vis the two political fronts upon which the civilians would battle for political control in the Philippines itself. First, there was the difficult struggle against the U.S. Army: to the civilians' dismay, the U.S. military—politically invested in an ongoing war—in many cases refused to recognize the legitimacy or authority of civilian officials who had been formally given powers in "pacified" areas. It did not help in the least that it was often difficult, if not impossible, to determine which areas were pacified. The commission's second front was against Filipino elites; just as it had to persuade U.S. soldiers to subordinate themselves to civilians, it had to convince Filipino elites that their interests lay with U.S. dominance rather than with war and that there was a meaningful distinction between these two conditions. Both cases involved political reliance upon the opponent, attempts to wrest authority from them, and rhetorical differentiation that would separate U.S. civilian leaders from their adversaries.

The central organizing principle of the postwar state, one that would continue throughout the American colonial period, was the recognition of Filipino elites and Filipino-American collaboration. Such cooperation represented another key continuity with the war, which had wound down through a series of on-the-ground settlements with the *ilustrado* and *principal* classes. In very practical terms, the best way to guarantee stability was to surrender large portions of the state to powerful Filipinos who had formerly resisted the U.S. invasion. Provincial and rural elites had, after all, sold their resistance to the Americans in the coin of political power and might presumably find additional ways to subvert the state if it were denied them. To guarantee its own stability, in other words, the new colonial state had to demonstrate successfully to influential Filipinos that they were "brothers and not serfs." What this meant in practical terms

While meant to convey the "benevolence" of U.S. civilians, this photograph of U.S. missionaries visiting Filipino prisoners of war at Fort Santiago in mid-1901 suggests the interpenetration of violence and "uplift" in the early U.S. colonization. While efforts were made to delineate sharply the war and its aftermath in time, "benevolent assimilation" of the kind represented here would emerge out of the war years. The new regime would involve both missionaries and secularized mission discourses; importantly, it would involve many women as teachers and "official wives" and have a radically different gender politics. From Condict, Old Glory and the Gospel in the Philippines.

was the rapid absorption of these elites into the new structures of governance at the municipal, provincial, and insular levels.

Drawing on wartime improvisations, the colonial state was built in a highly decentralized manner, from local governments toward the center. At the local level, those who met stiff suffrage requirements were permitted to elect municipal councils consisting of *presidentes* and the headmen of barrios. These councils in turn elected the provincial governor (technically their superior), who served on a provincial board with two appointed officials: a treasurer and a supervisor of public works.[26] In practice, this structure allowed the civilians to build sources of authority outside the highly centralized military institutions that still predominated. It also, most importantly, rooted the new American colonial state in entrenched rural power structures, surrendering local colonial politics to the *principales*, guaranteeing them control over municipal councils and provincial governorships and satisfying their desire for control of their constituents and labor forces. At the same time, this structure allowed American appointees to retain fiscal authority.

Collaboration also occurred at the insular level. The civilians organized a new, postwar architecture of repression in the form of a Filipino-ranked and American-officered Philippine Constabulary; together with the Philippine Scouts, continued from the war, it directly connected young provincial elites to the state. They also ushered in a one-party state by recognizing and sponsoring the Federalista Party, whose platforms supported American colonial annexation and, at first, eventual statehood. In practical terms, the party was a patronage network that allowed Americans to establish linkages with cooperative *ilustrados* and place them in official positions. Like local elections, the Federalista Party also helped give life, in the midst of ongoing violence and devastation, to the illusion of a slowly emerging democracy.[27]

The politics of Filipino-American collaboration generated new forms of dissent among both Americans and Filipinos. The U.S. military on the ground actively resisted the transition of authority to the newly arrived commission; while these tensions had roots in Washington bureaucratic politics, they played out in transfers of power at all levels of the colonial government. "When first the civil government was established," reported the journalist Edgar Bellairs, a strong ally of the military in these struggles, "the very natural differences that were certain to arise, began to take place throughout the Archipelago between the outgoing military officers and the incoming civil authorities." Taft described the emerging two-front political conflict with a mix of irony and surprise, recounting of his arrival in Manila, "I cannot describe the coldness of the army officers and army men who received us any better than by saying that it somewhat exceeded the coldness of the population." To Taft's chagrin, MacArthur had offered "no social recognition of the presence of the Commission here." Mac-Arthur greeted the commission, for example, by initially providing it office space in a location other than the Ayuntamiento, the current seat of governmental authority, before finding rooms in that building that were reportedly cramped and inconvenient.[28]

Similar dynamics were experienced at the provincial and municipal level where army officers were forced to share power with, then surrender it to, civilian officials. Tensions over succession were problems of recognition: were soldiers recognizing civilian officials or the other way around? Soldiers were reluctant to withdraw, believing themselves to be the only potentially effective force for the maintenance of order. "The attitude of the Army . . . is decidedly hostile to the provincial and municipal government in this province and to civil government in these islands in general," reported Cornelius Gardener, a major and provincial governor in Tayabas, in late 1901. "It is openly stated that the Army should remain in charge for the next twenty years." Potential conflict was heightened by the policy of maintaining military officials at their local posts even as they devolved power on civilians who were formerly their subordinates. "The man who gave up the reins of power," observed Bellairs, "frequently turned them over to some man he had known, and for whom he had a certain amount of contempt." In a context of confusing overlaps in jurisdiction, Filipinos took advantage of spaces opened by military-civilian succession. Some rural Filipinos continued to call on familiar military authorities to adjudicate disputes that, when taken up, undermined civilian authority and called down angry reprimands from Manila; in other cases, Filipinos petitioned for a rapid transfer from military to civilian control.[29]

In establishing their authority in Manila and beyond, commission officials confronted not only the military but an emerging, militarized civil society of what came to be known as "Manila Americans." This community consisted of American merchants who had scrambled to the islands during the war to supply the commercial needs of the U.S. Army, as well as U.S. soldiers who had left the military to exploit such opportunities after the fighting. Connected to the U.S. military and to the war by both their histories and interests, the Manila Americans were highly suspicious of the commission and its authority, as reflected in the English-language journals they inaugurated as some of the central institutions of colonial civil society. Manila's American newspapers regularly charged commission officials with overly rosy assessments of ongoing "pacification," with arbitrary, authoritarian rule, with "carpet-bagging," and with empowering Filipinos who were, at best, corrupt and, at worst, still savage "insurrectos" at heart. They urged the continuance of military government and actively opposed Filipino-American collaboration, insisting on the employment of Americans over Filipinos in civilian government positions.

Taft would attempt to persuade this community through suasion: speaking before the Union Reading College in Manila in December 1903, for example, he urged Manila Americans to opt into the commission's vision of gradual self-government for Filipinos. But the commission would also use coercive power to draw lines around permissible debate. On November 4, 1901, it passed Act No. 292, a "Sedition Act"; section 9 banned the formation of any secret society "having as its object, in whole or in part, the promotion of treason, rebellion or sedition, or the promulgation of any political opinion or policy." Section 10 made it unlawful "for any person to advocate orally or by writing or printing or by like methods the independence of the Philippine Islands or their separation from the United states, either by peaceful or forcible means." While directed at Filipino conspiracies, the act was first used to prosecute a Manila American, E. F. O'Brien, the editor of the *Manila Freedom*, for a critical editorial; O'Brien was found guilty of sedition, fined $1,000, and sentenced to six months in jail.[30]

Manila's divided colonial civil society of Americans encapsulated the fragmented landscape of its formalized social life, as described in 1902 by Bellairs. American society's earliest axis was the Army and Navy Club, which during the war had been "the centre of social life of Manila," especially for high military officials. When authorities associated with the commission arrived, they established a second, parallel structure, "a distinctively civil club under American management, as distinct from the Army and Navy"; its name, The University Club, set its 120 or so members apart by class and education. While divided along lines of authority, both these clubs shared elite status and membership; the most recent addition to the clubs, however, was the broad-based "American Club," with approximately 1,000 members, in which "social qualifications cut no figure in election to membership"; it was open to any man who was "an American . . . of good character and average intelligence." Bellairs pointed out, approvingly, that across Euro-American social life in Manila, "the

Filipino is a small quantity," and there was "scarcely any communication between the two races." Of course, there were social events between high U.S. officials and prominent Filipinos, but "there all social communication may be said to cease."[31]

The commission also faced the serious dilemma of ongoing Filipino hostility and the beginnings of an organized "postwar" resistance within the regime's own political framework. While the commission's conciliatory efforts would attract important elements of the elite, the war's brutality had left widespread suspicion throughout the populace that the new regime would, despite its rhetoric, approach Filipinos as "serfs" and not as "brothers." Some apparently generalized from the experience of reconcentration or the abuse of Manila's rig drivers by American customers. Taft reported to the Senate committee, for example, a conversation he had had in Batangas with a "Filipino gentleman" who recounted a dialogue with his *carromata* (carriage) driver on the way from his estate to Manila. "'When the American Government is established here and the Americanos are in control,'" the servant reportedly asked the *ilustrado*, "'how far shall I be allowed to go out of one mile square, for I understand that it is the regular policy of the American Government to keep us in a certain area. Secondly, what kind of a cart, wagon, or carromata shall I have to help pull, because I understand the Americans are buying up all the horses in the Philippines with a view to killing them, so that the Filipinos shall be made the beasts of burden.'"[32]

Filipinos openly challenged the new colonial state through organized protest that tested the regime's rhetorical promises of an open public sphere. The first years of the occupation, for example, saw the advent of organized labor politics. Bellairs reported that strikes by organized workers had caused a "considerable amount of annoyance to business in Manila." There had, for example, been a "considerable strike" in the printing business, one of the rapidly growing sectors of the economy, with rising demand for not only newspapers but government forms, licenses, and reports. Two hundred workers, under the leadership of Isabelo de los Reyes, had walked out demanding a 25 percent raise in wages. Depleted of funds, the workers had returned to work within a week, but De los Reyes had also organized a strike among dockmen and lightermen, "with the result of a great interference with shipping." These latter workers had "demanded the same as they would be paid in the United States for the same work."[33]

Filipino resistance to the regime also took the form of an emergent, critical press that would investigate and expose state abuses and corruption, ironize official discourses, and assert the capacity of Filipinos while developing new, expressive literary forms. This tendency was most identified with *El Renacimiento / Muling Pagsilang* (Rebirth), founded in September 1901 by Rafael Palma, which would, over the next nine years, draw on, develop, and project some of the Philippines' most talented literary, intellectual, and political voices, including Fernando Maria Guerrero and Teodoro M. Kalaw. The bilingual Spanish-Tagalog newspaper was a critical counterpoint to the "Americanista" publication *La Democracia*, official organ of the regime-backed Federalista Party. *El Renacimiento*'s political crusades included attacks on the continuance of reconcentration, the corruption of the Constabulary, and the economic exploitation of the Philippines by government and business. Contributors to the newspaper also resisted the "Americanizing" impulses of the regime, campaigning for the use of Spanish as the official language of the Philippines and romanticizing the Philippines' "Latin" tradition as a preferable alternative to the grasping materialism of American "Anglo-Saxonism."[34]

Filipino resistance of this kind illuminated the sharp edges of American-granted "freedom" in the islands. As the commission had done with the Manila Americans, it made clear that its promises of openness were directed only at a narrow spectrum of "responsible" Filipino opinion. The Sedition Act met its greatest challenge in Filipino revolutionary melodramas. Formally prohibited from displaying Katipunan flags onstage, for example, actors temporarily constructed and dismantled flag images composed of fast-moving actors, delighting popular audiences. The most prolific and subversive of the authors, Aureliano Tolentino, went so far as to haul down the U.S. flag onstage himself. The plays, which came to be known by the name of the law that sought to prevent them, as "Seditious Plays," were repressed wherever discovered. U.S. soldiers started riots and destroyed stage equipment; the plays' authors were arrested, fined, and imprisoned. Tolentino was found guilty on the grounds that, through his play, he had instigated others to "meet together for unlawful purposes" and to "incite rebellious conspiracies and riots and to stir up the people against the lawful authorities."[35] The repressive Sedition Act, together with the active promotion of *La Democracia*, which advocated Filipino surrender and collaboration, created the illusion of a broad-based Filipino-American consensus at the advent of a "postwar" civil society.[36]

Defining a "Postwar" State

In the interest of blunting Filipino resistance and anti-imperialist opposition, the civilian regime worked hard to distinguish itself from its military predecessor. It was able to do this through both sociological and discursive strategies, which were themselves connected. First, civilians had the advantage of recognizable shifts in personnel. The gender of the civilian regime, for example, was markedly different. The arrival of American women to the islands—as schoolteachers, as nurses, as "official wives" to military and civilian officials—marked a central boundary line in the marking of colonial time.[37] War had been defined in terms of brutal, racialized confrontation between men; the arrival of American women signified not only a margin of safety but a transformation of colonial politics from war to suasion. As in the Thomasite case, the presence of American women also helped fold novel U.S. colonialism into older, legitimated trajectories of female missionary evangelism in Asia. The gender roles of civilian men were also different, invested in notions of masculine honor, duty, and restraint that were often self-consciously set apart from the army's unbounded violence.

If the gender of the civilians distinguished them, so too did their class. The two criteria were, of course, connected, with only well-heeled, prestigious officials capable of supporting their wives in the islands in the required manner. Civilian officials often boasted that they had drawn from the nation's finest talent in staffing the new colonial state. While many of the new officials were aspiring middle-class professionals, Ivy League schoolteachers were held up as examples well beyond their proportional presence, and the regime worked hard to draw less attention to the many former U.S. soldiers who had entered civilian positions with their prior class standing sadly intact. Much to the chagrin of colonial civil service builders, the civilians' claims to "quality" would be constantly undermined by a colonial state too frugal to pay salaries that would draw the "best men" to the colony. Especially early on, Filipino elites, especially of the *ilustrado* class, remained unpersuaded that their U.S. counterparts in collaboration were worthy of their social and political recognition.

If the sociology of the civilian regime set it apart, its discourses and social practices did so as well. Foremost among the new civilian discourses was that of rule by "expertise." This was hardly surprisingly in light of contemporary developments both in the United States, Europe, and its colonies, where government by "experts" was emerging as the touchstone of modern administrative statecraft. In the United States, expert government was a self-conscious strategy of reform, funneling the "best men" toward public matters over which it was believed they ought to exercise control by virtue of superior intellect and character and displacing more corrupt, if sometimes more democratic, politics. Generated by industrial society, the knowledge of scientific experts mirrored the new corporate order and would be used to apprehend and control it. But in the colonial context, "expertise" had special political tasks to perform on the emerging fronts of U.S. colonial politics. Employed against the army, it defined the new regime as superior on the basis of its capacity to produce and authorize knowledge about the Philippines and its people, knowledge suited to the tasks of collaboration. Directed against the anti-imperialists, it had to construct a narrative of superior local knowledge, uplift, and national exceptionalism to defeat ongoing investigations. Against the Filipino elite, it had the somewhat more difficult task of exalting Americans as superior in Philippine knowledge to Filipinos themselves.

As Taft's Philippine Commission took shape, the scarcity of American experts on the Philippines was starkly evident. There had been only a handful of Americans in the islands before 1898, mostly the agents of U.S. commercial houses. "I feel these fair islands are no place for the permanent residence of an American," one of them, Joseph Earle Stevens, had complained in his memoir. "We seem to be like fish out of water here in the Far East, and as few in numbers."[38] But one American was able to successfully translate pre-1898 expertise into colonial authority. Dean C. Worcester was a young zoologist at the University of Michigan who had accompanied zoologist J. B. Steere on a collecting expedition to the islands in 1887 and returned in 1890. On both trips, he had gained something of a colonial education, as his party was hosted by Spanish officials and planters and housed in town tribunals, elite private homes, or the domiciles of families removed in their honor. Laborers forcibly drafted from the local population by his hosts served as carriers and guides. Worcester later related some of the conventional wisdom regarding Filipino laborers he had learned from a sugar planter: "Too much kindness is very likely to spoil him," he wrote, "and he thinks more of a master who applies the rattan vigorously, when it is deserved, than of one who does not." When a convict named Paradiso, leased to Steere by a Spanish official, was accused of stealing five pounds of gunpowder, Worcester and his colleague Frank Bourns interrogated him with thrashings from "a nice piece of Michigan hickory."[39]

In mid-1898, Worcester had seized the opportunity to turn such experiences into expertise. Following Dewey's victory at Manila Bay, he had swiftly published six articles on the Philippines in major American magazines and secured a contract from Macmillan to compose a description of the islands, on firm deadline. After six weeks of furious editing, he had refashioned his letters home into an adventure travelogue, *The Philippine Islands and Their People*. Published in October, the book sold quickly enough to require four monthly printings. In a work otherwise dedicated to derring-do, zoological specimens, and Spanish corruption, Worcester wedged in long editorials about the islands' peoples and their prospects for self-government. Calling those "who lump the whole population of the Philippines as barbarians and savages" "grossly in error," Worcester ranked "more than eighty distinct tribes," from the "lowest" Negritos—"incapable of civilization"—through the Moros, "pagan" Malays, and "civilized" Malays. While he admitted having spent little time with lowland groups, Worcester concluded strongly that "[w]ith all their amiable qualities it is not to be denied that at present the civilized natives are utterly unfit for self-government."[40] The book was widely and positively reviewed, with the *Outlook* commenting that it had "come forth most seasonably, to satisfy the general hunger for reliable and recent information" regarding "the hitherto unknown lands and peoples of which we have just been put in control."[41]

Despite claims of a "pure" colonial civil service, Worcester's appointment to the commission had been the result of more or less pure academic machine politics. When Worcester learned through Bourns, still in the islands, of rising tensions between U.S. and Filipino troops and potential Filipino support for U.S. annexation, he passed the news and his recommendation—the sending of additional U.S. troops to prevent Filipino military consolidation in the islands—to President McKinley personally. Worcester's mentor, University of Michigan president James Burrill Angell, who had close scientific and political ties in Washington, arranged the meeting. McKinley was apparently impressed with Worcester and asked him to serve in the Philippines, first as a personal representative, then as a member of the commission, at a salary of $5,000 per year plus expenses, a great improvement over his academic salary.[42] Just before his departure with the commission, the *New York Times* described

Worcester's book as a "standard reference work"; he was part of a team that was "excellent from the standpoint of expert knowledge."[43]

However new and provisional its own knowledge of the Philippines, the Philippine Commission was able to cast an aura of expertise over the entire colonial state. Like domestic industrial commissions, it was organized around elaborate rituals of data-gathering, especially hearings, to which select members of the Filipino and European elites of the Philippines were invited, exchanging information for political recognition and patronage. The commission would also sponsor a great deal of scientific research during its first years, establishing scientific institutions and conducting surveys of the Philippines' agricultural, forestry, and mineral resources, as well as "ethnographic" data. Worcester would expand his power on the commission as its political sponsor and administrative architect.[44]

The commission saw the production of expert knowledge as central to colonial success. As Rizal had observed, "[t]he knowledge of a thing prepares its mastery." In his 1903 Union Reading College speech, Taft noted that for U.S. merchants to succeed in the islands, "native tastes must be studied" and "close examination made into the question of who of the natives may be safely trusted." An "intimate knowledge" of "native customs and native desires as well as of the language of the country" was also necessary. This kind of knowledge was especially necessary in order to solve the islands' vexing "labor question." To U.S. officials and investors who complained of the "indolence" of Filipino laborers and house servants, Taft urged that an investigation be conducted "systematically." "To get the best out of the Filipino servants," he stated, "one must know them and must study their traits." His sense of the importance of knowledge in colonial labor relations was consistent with his broader sense of colonial politics: "before satisfactory labor can be obtained from [the Filipino], he must be under the control of a master who understands him."[45]

Congruent with the logic of collaboration, civilian American officials also recognized Filipino experts as a way to build bridges to the *ilustrado* elite. No single Filipino in the early Taft regime would occupy the ideological intersection between the American colonialists and *ilustrados* as fully, or translate it as adeptly into political power, as Trinidad H. Pardo de Tavera. Pardo was less expert than scholar, a medical doctor, linguist, bibliographer, and archetypal *ilustrado*, born in 1873 of parents from two of the most distinguished families in Manila. Educated at the Jesuit Ateneo de Manila and the University of Santo Tomas, he completed his medical degree at the Sorbonne in the mid-1880s, while distinguishing himself as a Philippine linguist and folklorist and gaining membership in European academic societies. In his social background, circuits of travel, and scholarly enthusiasms, Pardo was exemplary of the overseas *ilustrado* community. But unlike his Propaganda movement contemporaries, he had few oppositional instincts and gravitated toward shifting centers of authority. When revolution broke out in the Philippines in 1896, he remained aloof, joining a conciliatory "consultative assembly." Appointed director of diplomacy in the Malolos government on October 1, 1898, he lasted only a month before breaking with Aguinaldo over the appropriate policy toward the United States.[46]

In ideological terms, Pardo's politics were in many ways those of a laissez-faire liberal, wary of state power, hostile to religious conviction and authority, and committed to modern science and technology as the engines of progress. In the late nineteenth-century context, these beliefs had been potentially subversive of Spanish colonial authority and especially friar rule. The question in 1898 was whether Filipinos or Americans would institutionalize them. Pardo, doubtful of Filipino capacity for self-generated "progress," had answered the question in the Americans' favor in the wake of the U.S. occupation of Manila. Parlaying his own expertise into political patronage, he was appointed to a U.S. Army Board of Health established by Maj. Frank Bourns in late September 1898, even before formally abandoning Aguinaldo's government. In May 1899, following the outbreak of the Philippine-American War, he inaugurated *La Democracia*, a daily newspaper whose pro-American editorial opinion earned him the favor of U.S. military authorities. By December 1900, he had co-organized the Federalista Party, whose platform initially called for eventual U.S. statehood for the Philippines, and whose central activity was to accompany the Philippine Commission through the provinces negotiating the surrender of revolutionary leaders. Pardo would become a crucial nexus between provincial rural elites and the insular government, funneling the sons of *principales* into state positions. Even before the war's end, the commission would reward the Federalistas with official recognition and patronage in its state-building efforts; Pardo, Benito Legarda, and José de Luzuriaga would earn appointments to the Philippine Commission.[47]

The first front of commission expertise was the U.S. military itself, as the civilians challenged the legitimacy of army knowledge. Here, the newcomers were at a decided disadvantage, several intrusive years behind their military rivals in apprehending Philippine reality. As a result, they high-lighted the military's failure to learn about the Philippines and empha-sized their own status as potential experts, bearers not of actual knowl-edge, perhaps, but of a superior mode of knowing. Civilian officials, for example, argued that the military continued to employ the half-baked, and now irrelevant, generalizations that had guided it in war. In a letter to Secretary Root, for example, Taft himself complained that General Mac-Arthur "regards all the people as opposed to the American forces and looks at his task as one of conquering eight millions of recalcitrant, treach-erous and sullen people." Maj. Cornelius Gardener reported to the Senate committee that such assumptions were damaging the delicate fabric of early collaboration. "[T]he failure of inexperienced, lately appointed lieu-tenants commanding posts to distinguish between those who are friendly and those unfriendly," he testified, "and treating every native as if he were, whether or no, an insurrecto at heart," meant that "favorable sentiment . . . is fast being destroyed and a deep hatred toward us engendered." For David Barrows, the postwar military, increasingly isolated from Filipino populations, was also perilously ignorant. "[T]he army in the provinces where civil government exists is no longer in a position to form the most reliable judgments," he wrote to a patron. "The soldiers no longer leave the posts; the officers rarely go beyond their quarters. . . . They have no more official relations with the natives nor do they have in most cases any longer acquaintance with them. Under these circumstances rumors are magnified and uneasiness is likely to prevail when no real danger exists."[48]

But if expertise was one way to deflect military authority, it was also a way to win ground in domestic U.S. debate, undermining anti-imperialist claims with increasingly detailed renditions of the Philippines. Among other publications, the commission would exercise its greatest influence through its published annual reports to the War Department. The first, heavy volumes, for example, overpowered readers with long transcriptions of testimony, cross-referenced tables and charts, and reproductions of Worcester's photographs of the islands' infrastructure, resources, and "na-tives."[49] The cumbersome tomes were probably not read widely, but their publication was itself a news item, and the reports would become the standard citation on the Philippines in American newspapers and weekly magazines. According to a *Harper's Weekly* editorial, the report was "by far the most important contribution that has been made to our knowledge of the situation in the archipelago." Its conclusions were "not a mere matter of opinion, but are supported by a large mass of evidence." In brief, the article stated, the report had concluded that Aguinaldo, who had never been guaranteed American support, had provoked a war with the United States in the name of a falsely named "republic"; only a firm, tutelary administration would successfully instruct Filipinos in the ways of self-government. For the *Harper's Weekly* editorial, the commission's "authoritative" account had closed the "Philippine question" for good. "There can be no room for argument, it seems to us, about these fundamental propositions," it concluded. The figure of Worcester himself was central to the report's credibility as "the highest authority that we have on the condition of civilization, as well as on the natural history, of the archipelago." Carried in the reports, Worcester's word as scientist on the spot easily displaced the ephemeral words of critics. "The testimony of such a man," it read, "is worth a worldful of sentimental and academic literature and mere political talk."[50]

But civilian officials were also able to steer U.S. public opinion in their favor by making experts out of American travelers. Where the army had censored and threatened to deport foreign correspondents during the war, civilian officials now invited American legislators, journalists, and men of affairs to travel and observe the Philippines firsthand as pacification proceeded and interisland transport was consolidated. In a near-total domestic vacuum of knowledge, traveling in the Philippines, protected by the American colonial state, itself came to constitute a certain kind of expertise. But how much was one really seeing? As Arthur Griffiths warned, even self-conscious anti-imperialists hoping to gather ammunition by visiting the islands had not been impervious to manipulation on such trips. "Men came to the Philippines at their own expense and at the expense of the government for the sole purpose of studying the Philippine situation from the Filipinos' standpoint," he wrote. "After being wined and dined at the various officers' clubs in the principal parts of the archipelago, hearing speeches by Filipinos prepared for the occasion, as a minister prepares his sermon to conform to a certain text, they return 'knowing the Philippine situation' but in truth loaded with hearsay."[51]

Griffiths's fears were borne out in an October 1901 description of the visit of a number of "Congressional sightseers" to Manila. Eavesdropping on a conversation between Manila Americans and congressmen "beneath the shady palms" of the Army and Navy Club, one Manila reporter overheard Congressman Edgar Weeks, Republican of Michigan, express skepticism about his colleagues' capacities for unbiased observation, particularly those of the anti-imperialist persuasion. Twenty times, Weeks claimed, he had heard his colleagues admit to seeing the Philippines through their prejudices. One had, prior to his trip, stated before Congress that "'seventy-five per cent of the Filipinos were fit for self government and everything that I have seen here confirms that opinion.'" Weeks's colleagues would "take home bolos and spears and shields, and . . . useless nicknacks, as samples of what these people can do, and laud their cunning workmanship while not able to point to a single useful thing they make, or know if they are industrious." Conceived in prejudice, such impressions, voiced with "trumpet tongue" back home, would do "more harm than good to the public."[52]

Weeks contrasted this ignorance with his own insight, acquired, he believed, far closer to the surface of Philippine reality. The truth of the Philippines was not in the curio market, he claimed, but in remote domestic interiors. "The way to know a man is to see him at home," he asserted, "to see if his house is orderly and neat, if good books and papers are read by him and if his family is well cared for." By unknown means, almost necessarily with the aid of colonial officials, Weeks claimed to have had access to such spaces and concluded, apparently unencumbered by his own prior impressions, that "not ten thousand of the Filipinos are fit for self government and not one percent of the population are intelligent enough to take part in it." Anti-imperialist travelers to the Philippines might make claims of Filipino self-governing capacity, but they could do so only as what Weeks dismissively called "sightseers." By contrast, Weeks could ground his retentionist argument in the presumably deeper and more authentic reaches of Filipino culture, made accessible to him by the colonial state.[53]

Cultures of Collaboration

If the civilians employed discourses of expertise to distinguish themselves from their military forebears, they set themselves apart just as sharply through their practices, specifically by collaborating in new cultures of Filipino-American sociability, what might be called "fiesta" politics. During the first several years of the commission's rule, war's end was signaled by the holding of rituals of recognition. While some of these were held in public, like the bridge dedication, many more were conducted privately, such as balls, dances, and ceremonies hosted and attended by both Americans and elite Filipinos. The most elaborate of these were held in Manila, but as commission members toured the provinces establishing governments in pacified areas, town elites welcomed them with expensive and intricate festivities, often featuring parades, speeches, and the erection of ceremonial arches. Filipino-American sociability signaled the changing gender of colonial politics: where the war had been driven by both men and masculinist politics on both sides, Filipino-American sociability foregrounded women's tasks and expertise, especially the maintenance of households and social "standards." In a very real sense, the shift placed the responsibility for demonstrating civilization—by both Americans and Filipinos—in women's hands. Filipino and American women also came to occupy new places within the colony's symbolic politics. It became one of the centerpieces of commission balls that Taft would ask leading *ilustradas*, beginning with the hostess, to dance the *rigodon*; leading *ilustrados* would in turn dance with Mrs. Taft.

The symbolism was highly charged for both Americans and Filipinos. For Americans, it signaled a sharp break with ongoing military encounters as well as with domestic U.S. racial forms. Contrasted with war, Filipino-American sociability signified peace or was itself understood as pacification. When General Bell danced with the daughters of elite Lipa families, Edith Moses believed that "he did more 'pacifying' that night than he had accomplished during his entire campaign." Fiesta politics and Filipino-American dancing was meant to convey social equality and promises of political equality. It was "difficult to make the Filipinos believe in our theory of political equality," Moses believed, when "so many Americans are disposed to emphasize by their conduct the idea of social inequality." For the Filipino elites involved, it signaled social recognition, opportunities for conveying civilization as bourgeois style, and opportunities for incorporating Americans into networks of obligation. Despite civilian self-congratulation, social equality nonetheless had its racial and gendered limits for both sides. Moses noted approvingly that there was "naturally a certain shyness on the part of the Filipino men about asking the American women to dance."[54]

But there were sharp limits to fiesta politics as the civilian regime struggled to achieve a hegemonic position over the military. While according to James LeRoy, Taft's secretary, the civilian regime often included Filipinos in its social practices, in their "informal affairs" in Manila, Americans and Europeans "betray a tendency quietly to 'draw the colour line,'" with whites "'flock[ing] by themselves' to a large degree" in their private dealings. LeRoy believed this was especially true of military officers and their wives. At a commission ball in 1899, for example, "officers whose wives had joined them did not think of meeting any residents but some of

This photograph of an elaborate ball pictures one of the central rituals of Filipino-American collaboration, at the core of what can be called "fiesta" politics. Where the racial formation of the war years was characterized by radical exclusion, fiesta politics played an important role in the civilian regime's inclusionary racial formation, which promised Filipino elites highly qualified political power and gradual devolution. Where U.S. officials danced with the wives of Filipino officials, they constructed a novel symbolic politics of cross-racial empire-building that was at odds with wartime politics and, in many ways, at odds with domestic U.S. racial formations. From Guerrero, Under Stars and Stripes.

the wealthy Spanish 'left-overs' on anything like terms of social equality."
One army wife, upon visiting the commission and learning of its plans,
apparently "exclaimed in horror: 'Why, surely you don't propose to visit
these people and invite them to your own home just the same as you
would white people!'" Few American "army women" had any Filipinas on
their calling lists, and in the provinces, "they often take it on themselves to
caution American women sent out as teachers against mingling with the
people of their towns."[55]

This social exclusion extended to institutional sponsorship. The founders of the Woman's Hospital in Manila attempted to exclude Filipino
patients "as well as to keep off the list of patronesses the names of Filipino
women." The board of ladies that founded the American Library in Manila, built in part with funds from the Philippine treasury, "made very
strenuous protests against having it also thrown open to Filipinos for a
share in its management and use." They had employed languages of nationalism and martial honor, contending "that it had been established as a
monument to American soldiers who lost their lives in the Philippines,
and that it was unfitting that Filipinos should have anything to do with it,
though Philippine taxes might support it."[56]

Even where the fact of fiesta politics might be agreed upon between
U.S. civilians and Filipino elites, its specific elaborations were fraught
with political tension. Fiestas were, above all, rituals intended to efface the
uninvited character of the U.S. presence in the Philippines. When Americans hosted parties, they were inviting Filipinos to collaborate in the new
state; when Filipinos hosted, they were recognizing the commission's
power. But hospitality was also politically open-ended. Where Americans
could dominate through sheer force, they could not universalize modes of
hospitality and were forced to recognize and adapt to Filipino customs.
Moses noted, for example, that "[t]he table etiquette is somewhat difficult
at first" but that she was learning manners "in Filipino style" and wrote
proudly at one point that she had "acquired the proper society speeches."
As before the war, cultures of hospitality led to reassessments of Filipinos;
Moses noted that the grace of provincial Filipinos "places these inhabitants of distant pueblos within the ranks of civilization in respect to
formal politeness." Indeed, Americans were often disappointing by contrast. "I think our people are too offhand with the Filipinos," Moses
lamented. Somewhat parallel with the larger invasion to which they were
attached, many Americans visited houses "where they are unbidden."
Filipinos also made strategic use of cultures of hospitality, sometimes to

the chagrin of their American guests. Moses complained that, on one occasion, "we were obliged to drink the health of the 'American nation and the Filipino people, one and the same,'" a toast that reproduced the legend of the blood compact. On another, a Filipino "lady of gracious manner" had said to a U.S. general, soon to return to the United States, with impeccable form, "'Well, general, so you are really going away. I can't tell you how sorry we are. It is a shame for you to leave us.'" All present, including the general, understood her meaning. The general responded, with less grace, that it was "'always flattering to hear such things, even when they are said for politeness only,'" and doubly so when "'they come from the heart.'"[57]

Colonial sociability was also rimmed with danger. In general, Manila's emerging elite social life was meant as a sign of peace that was highly embattled from the start. Moses lamented Manila's lack of entertainment apart from social functions; on account of martial law "compelling persons to have passes or to be at home in the evening," there were "no performances." An 1899 newspaper article, "Socials in the Gate City of the Orient," described emerging social traditions among the Manila Americans: evening carriage rides on the Luneta, a chain of receptions, parties, and club smokers, and outdoor sports like golf and tennis. "The attempted insurrection in the city during the week," it noted offhandedly, "did not affect the social features. The promptness of the military, in illustrating how thoroughly the city is protected, filled every heart with confidence." The sense of palpable danger was only intensified by Filipino-American social interaction. Since its goal was to win the hearts of actual or potential "insurrectos," it meant direct encounters with those who had been invited in order to draw them away from ongoing war. The politico-military status of one's social partners was often unclear, and it was not always easy to recognize a "pacified" collaborator. Moses reported one gathering attended by Aguinaldo's foreign minister, who was "turning or turned to our side." At one point, Moses found herself traveling with an "insurrecto general who two weeks ago was in the mountains fighting our men" and who was "now our guest and apparently our warm friend"; Moses hoped he had "no bolos and no bad intentions." After a visit to see skilled bolo makers at work, Moses was plagued by nightmares of insurrection. "[V]isions of the bolo makers persisted in coming to my mind," she wrote. "I heard insurrectos whispering under my bed and coming up the ladder." While such fears interrupted American enjoyment, some Filipinos may have cultivated them as a source of entertainment. Moses observed that "[s]ome people think the rumors of uprisings are often started by natives for the fun of seeing the soldiers turn out."[58]

Collaboration politics was not only characterized by the United States' construction of Filipino culture but also by Filipino constructions of U.S. culture. One of the features of fiesta politics most commonly observed by Americans was Filipinos' employment of identifiably "American" imagery. This was often recognized as "assimilation": how else could one measure the progress of assimilation than by the appearance of "Americanisms" among Filipinos? But such adoption gave Filipinos possession of this imagery, enabling them to rework it along unforeseen lines. Among others, Edith Moses chronicled a number of these moments, observing Filipinos' particular attraction to the language and imagery of American independence and liberty. Greeted by a typical bamboo arch in July 1900, she recorded among the mottoes it carried "Viva La Independencia!" along with "Viva America y Filipinas!," "Viva La Protectoria!," and "Viva La Amnestia!" One of the more subversive arches featured "pictures of President McKinley and Aguinaldo enclosed in a double frame of greens," which explicitly made them equivalent heads of state.[59] On another occasion, in Antique, the community built four arches, one of them three stories high, "with a balcony from which two little girls dressed as Goddesses of Liberty waved American flags in welcome." Following an English-language welcome address by the *presidente*, the party passed under the second arch, while "doves decorated with red, white, and blue ribbons were let loose."[60]

The uneasiness that such appropriations could cause was illustrated when the party arrived at a great square where stood a statue, "a Goddess of Liberty . . . presumably enlightening the world with a torch that looked like a big club." The statue was standing on a pedestal bearing the names of Washington, Lincoln, McKinley, and Taft, whose misspelling Moses mocked. The figure had been a saint "brought from an interior town and dressed up in secular garments for the occasion," including an American flag draped around its waist. Moses thought the image "an extraordinary creature"; Taft registered his discomfort by using it as the prop for an impromptu educational lecture. According to Moses, he stated that the statue was "well timed in its application to this province and these islands." But "liberty was a force much misunderstood." It did not mean "license to do everything" but "that condition which prevails under a government organized to secure such liberty to the individual as was consistent with law and order." As this occasion illustrated, Filipino efforts to use American imagery were sharply curtailed by the realities of U.S. power on the ground. Moses noted, for example, that at a public school Fourth of July celebration, "patriotic songs were sung and the Declaration of Independence was read in Spanish and English," but that a Filipino orator had been arrested subsequently for advocating similar sentiments. "No one commented on the incongruity."[61]

Calibrated Colonialism, Inclusionary Racism

If the new civilian colonial state had differentiated itself from the military project to which it remained firmly attached, it faced an equally formidable ideological task in framing its relationship to the Filipino elites upon which it relied. Specifically, there were two fundamental questions that civilian officials would be compelled to answer, both of them central to Filipino-American collaboration. First was the question of what terms should be used to comprehend and delimit Filipino participation in the colonial state. Second was the question of the timetable of American rule. The U.S. military had answered the first question in war-ending terms: Filipino elites that put down their arms could continue to exercise traditional, local power in pacified areas but remained highly suspect. The army had not been compelled to answer the second question: it had measured time by anticipating (and promoting) what remained remote triumphs, but once secured, occupation was imagined as stretching indefinitely into the future, the only way to honor shed American blood and a raised American flag.

The civilians' answers to these questions were organized around two principles: calibrated colonialism and an inclusionary racial formation. Each developed under pressure from both domestic anti-imperialists and Filipino elites, both of which insisted on a gradual surrender of power to Filipinos as the mark of progress. Calibrated colonialism involved the setting of criteria by which Filipinos would be recognized as having the capacity to responsibly exercise power in the colonial state and establishing credible, if illusory, markers in time that would signal devolutionary progress in the regime under construction. It could succeed only as long as freedom could be both reliably promised and endlessly deferred. As such, it was a colonialism predicated on the endless colonization of the future: by establishing temporal benchmarks whose marking was still an exclusive American preserve, calibrated colonialism could persuasively generate what might be called the illusion of impermanence.

The other feature of civilian ideology and practice was an inclusionary racial formation that both invited and delimited Filipino political participation. Inclusionary racism involved praise for Filipino capacity even while lamenting present ability; it hailed Spanish Catholic evangelization for its "civilizing" work while lamenting its "feudal" legacy. It placed Filipinos on a slow-moving track toward the future, identifying key social, cultural, and intellectual milestones toward this end, but constantly marking tragic insufficiency in the present. It heralded an imperialism of process whose keywords—promise, progress, possibility, capacity, and development—were intended to mask the very empire from which they issued. The optimism of the inclusionary racial vision regarding the capacity of Filipinos was held up as one of the colonial regime's distinctive—indeed, exceptional—features.[62]

The new racial formation was closely tied to new political practices. The regime of collaboration, both symbolized and enabled by fiesta politics, meant that anything like a formal racial bar in official circles would be practically impossible. Although Americans would exercise greater authority, they would nonetheless share power, compromise, and inevitably struggle with Filipinos inside the colonial state on terms of highly qualified equality. Such relations, however hierarchical, ran roughshod over any strict racial line. "Officially, there can be no colour line in Manila," declared James LeRoy. It was suggestive of the racial formation's novelty that LeRoy felt compelled to explain it to domestic U.S. audiences. He found its root in colonial politics, observing that on-the-ground political pressures, especially from assertive Filipino elites, had essentially forced greater openness upon their putative masters. "Under American rule," he explained, "the very force of political necessity" had "compelled the recognition of the native families of prominence." The result had been a "consequent relaxation of the social rule," which left "less place than there once was for caste feeling." What he called "the exigencies of political expediency" had thus made for "a freer *régime*." LeRoy wished to believe this was partly "because of the nature of American institutions," but he acknowledged that it was "partly in spite of the fact that the new rulers are, in general, stronger in prejudices based on race and colour than were the Spaniards."[63]

Many observers noted clashes between inclusionary and exterminist racisms. According to the reporter Bellairs, the commission found the Filipinos "refined, cultivated, and honorable," while government officials in the United States, presumably reading military reports, believed them

**THE SENATE PHILIPPINE BILL OFFERS GREAT INDUCE-
MENTS TO THE BAD FILIPINO.** — *Minneapolis Tribune*

This cartoon from the Minneapolis Tribune, reprinted in Public Opinion of June 1902, casts the Philippine Bill, then being debated in the Senate, as an offering of "benevolent assimilation." The cartoon suggests the ways that the war itself shaped racial ideologies: "civilized" Filipinos are those who have embraced peace; "savage" ones continue to fight. The cartoon also literalizes the vertical promises of colonial "uplift"; interestingly, "civilized" Filipinos rather than Americans are the agents of this benevolence, suggesting both emerging collaboration networks and a desire to make U.S. empire invisible.

to be "semi-civilized savages" on the basis of their "barbarous" fighting. "It is difficult to reconcile the two descriptions," he admitted. In testifying before the Senate in 1901, Taft attempted to reconcile the two by adopting what might be called a social-constructionist approach to race. The difference between military and civilian accounts of Filipinos, he observed, was the context of their encounter. MacArthur and the army had come in contact with "the natives who are in an actual state of war," while the commission met "the natives who are interested in civil government." Given this fact, Taft argued, "it could not be otherwise than our relations with the natives, our confidence in them, our opinion of their capacity to learn self-government should be different from that of the military officers engaged in actual war." For LeRoy, military racism had been enhanced by military-civilian tensions. "[T]he loss of power through the merging of military into civilian government has increased the hostility of narrow-minded army officers to the native," he wrote. "One present in the Philippines during this transfer of governing power could see a bitterness against the natives crop out that had not been expressed, and often not felt before." Similar opinions were reflected more or less exactly in Robert F. Morrison's comic poem in the *Manila Sunday Sun*:

> I'm only a common soldier-man in the blasted Philippines;
> They say I've got Brown Brothers here, but I dunno what it means.
> I like the word Fraternity, but still I draw the line;
> He *may* be a brother of William H. Taft, but he ain't no friend of
>   mine.[64]

While inclusionary racism did differ from its wartime predecessor, its exponents also self-consciously constructed it as a radical alternative to more violent and exclusionary racial formations in their midst. Indeed, justifying the racial hierarchies at the core of civilian "inclusion" depended upon the repeated articulation of what could be represented as less favorable options. Civilians like LeRoy, in other words, had clear stakes in representing themselves as morally superior to those Americans who could not imagine political coexistence with Filipinos. They accomplished this by defining "race prejudice" narrowly, as more public, "social" forms of dishonor, insult, and harassment. Race would not revolve around questions of power but of etiquette; exclusion in the Philippines was imagined to be a reactionary, atavistic holdover from domestic hatred of "Negroes." The goal was a racial formation whose central claim was its nonracialism. Colonial officials like LeRoy put forward the notion of a tragic and unnecessary export of U.S. racial idioms in order to mask the racial formation they were in the process of constructing. LeRoy provocatively suggested that colonialism in the Philippines was a "step of transcendent importance," in part because it "draws us into a field in which ultimately our prejudices may broaden out, and in which our provincialisms must disappear."[65]

LeRoy, for example, contrasted the civilian regime's approach with what he called the "'nigger' theory" that some Americans had brought to the islands. In a 1902 article titled "Race Prejudice in the Philippines," he claimed that some Americans had "carried into the Philippines a petty race prejudice" that was "the offspring of past provincialism and the inheritance of slavery with its residue of settled problems." Under its influence, American colonialists were "betraying a tendency to swagger under the 'white man's burden,' sometimes in the garb of commercialism, sometimes in the raiment of science." It was, for example, "the usual thing" for Americans in the islands who "imbibed a contempt or dislike for the people" to "betray in their conversation the fact that their theories of the situation are based upon popular notions at home as to negro shortcomings and incapacity."[66]

LeRoy's point was that such "exports" were illegitimate as elements of a U.S. colonial-state ethos in the making because they would completely undermine Filipino-American collaboration. Even the water cure, he claimed, implausibly, did less overall to make enemies of Filipinos than "a studied attitude of contempt, an assumption of racial and individual superiority, and the constant disregard of their petty personal rights and of the little amenities that count so much with them." While military success "always depends upon force," he wrote, the success of civilian government "must rest upon conciliation." Articulating and supplanting unofficial "nigger theory" with an official, inclusionary racial formation, LeRoy asserted the central axiom of the new, inclusionary racial state. Filipino-American conciliation and collaboration meant that "the employees of the civil government are obliged to consult native feelings and native interests, no matter what may be their personal prejudices."[67]

In some cases, the assertion of inclusionary racism, and the U.S. national exceptionalism to which it was connected, was aided by non-American onlookers. Mrs. Campbell Dauncey, for example, British resident in the Philippines and the wife of a sugar planter, negatively contrasted the new civilians' racial ethos and its recognition of Filipino elites with how she viewed appropriately violent and hierarchical British colonial racism. "[T]here is socially no marked colour-distinction here as in every other country in the world," she complained. Dauncey had been told that the United States did "not pose as either 'white' or 'ruling' in these islands, preferring, instead, to proclaim Equality, which seems a very strange way to treat Malays." "Equality" was policy in Manila social life, where "[t]he white men are friendly with many of the Mestizos, and dance with their pretty daughters," and were "occasionally foolish enough to marry the latter." More disturbing still, it was manifested in the operations of the state. Dauncey was, for example, scandalized to learn that a white customer had been "heavily fined" by the police for striking a Filipino clerk who was "impudent."[68]

If "nigger theory" did not serve the new civilian politics, what theory would? Inclusionary racial politics meant, first and foremost, rewriting Filipino deficiencies to suit new political realities. This meant a new imperial indigenism that refined the criteria for denying full Filipino self-government. While tribal fragmentation would continue to be an important discourse—and one that underwent key transformations—the criteria shifted during this period toward more specific questions of political behavior, morality, and intelligence. While the use of macrolevel criteria like language diversity remained, closer attention was paid to the character of Filipino elites and their relationship to the Filipino masses. This was unsurprising, given the increasingly intense nature of Filipino-American contact and exchange during collaborative state-building. In a context of tense power sharing, Americans were reflecting on their lesser partners in colonialism, as well as drawing much of their reflection from their partners' accounts of themselves. The most consistent and begrudging of their observations were those of Filipino political agility and immorality, which claimed the elites were, as Taft put it, "as ambitious as Satan," and by their very nature "deceptive, venal, corrupt, [and] exploitative." Filipino leaders were "the most magnificent liars that it has been my luck to run across," Taft had written, less than a month after his arrival, a fact he discerned from the ease with which they "change from one side to the other," that is, from the policy of attraction itself. Not only dishonest, they regarded public office "as a personal perquisite and an opportunity for that which the Orientals tersely call 'a squeeze.'"[69] American colonial officials adopted and redefined the Spanish term cacique to condemn the political practices of those whom the U.S. colonial state was simultaneously recognizing.[70]

But the disparaging of elites was only one component of the remaking of "incapacity": the other was the representation of the Filipino masses as ignorant, superstitious, passive, and lazy. A little over one month into his stay in the islands, Taft had written Root that the Philippines was inhabited by "a vast mass of ignorant, superstitious people, well intentioned, light-hearted, temperate, somewhat cruel, domestic and fond of their families, and deeply wedded to the Catholic Church." Some other observers emphasized religious irrationality. David Barrows, for example, described the Filipinos he had encountered as "stirred with religious emotions and beliefs which they only half comprehend—routed to political aspirations which they know nothing of at all." For others, Filipinos were incapable of reason itself. According to Maud Huntley Jenks, the wife of a government anthropologist, a logical edifice would have to be constructed for them by others. "It looks to me as though it will take fifty generations of 'line upon line' and 'precept upon precept' before these natives will know enough to govern themselves," she wrote. "[M]any of them seem to be very stupid. The men here in the house, who teach in Manila schools, say the natives can't reason."[71]

The incapacity of both Filipino elites and masses was allegedly rooted in habits of mind. American evaluations of Filipino popular culture were one index of these habits and, therefore, an important site of colonial race-making. Filipino drama, for example, was the subject of a detailed investigation by Arthur Stanley Riggs, a naval officer and a correspondent and editor of the *Manila Freedom*, who lived in the islands from 1902 to 1904. For Riggs, Filipino theater was evidence of Filipino incapacity, what he called the "[d]eficiencies and limitations of the people." Riggs's first chapter included a "brief historical review of the social and literary characteristics" of "the Filipino Tribes, there being no Filipino Nation."[72] Promoting the discourse of Filipino fragmentation, Riggs was struck by what he called the "strange lack of cohesiveness" in Philippine society; there was "a distinct sense of units rather than of a coherent whole blended and fused together." If there was no such nation, there was also "no Filipino literature," the opinions of Filipinos "not withstanding." Literature and other forms of creative expression were potential signs of intellectual achievement and deserving of recognition, but what Filipinos took as "a genuine native literature," Riggs dissolved into a number of "foreign influences," especially Spanish and Chinese. Filipino mythology, he noted, was "not chaste, nor of a purely Filipino or Malay origin or character," but had been "singularly adulterated" by "foreign influences" that "disfigured it with their ineradicable stamp." He accused those who wrote of a glorious pre-Hispanic Filipino past of cynical deception; the real Filipino was best revealed through present-day theater, which artlessly "discloses the native character in a white light" and in the process gives Filipinos' enemies "a new weapon to bury in the breast that conceived it."[73]

Riggs himself took up the weapon: Filipino drama showed Filipinos to be "[b]arren to bleakness in literature, void of that finer feeling and sense of fitness which makes for a high conception of life and its possibilities to both individual and people." The lack of traces of pre-Hispanic culture exposed "the mental nakedness of the people 'half-child, half-devil.'" Present-day plays were saturated with superstition, a feature Riggs found "representative" even of elites. "Even the educated men of the better class show at times an ignorance or a deliberate stupidity that is amazing," he wrote. The plays were "intensely emotional . . . without the slightest show of restraint"; they contained "strange involutions and distortions" rather than "any simple, straightforward presentation of fact or argument." It was notable that Riggs enlisted an "expert," anthropologist Albert Ernest Jenks of the regime's Ethnological Survey, to support his appraisal. Jenks's opinion of the plays, which Riggs had provided him, was "of the greater value since it comes from a government officer, as most of officialdom is unremittingly laudatory of the native." Jenks reported in January 1904 that the plays bore many "glaring defects and crudities" and revealed "the pitiful shallowness of the native mind" and its "lack of inventiveness." Any "racial progress" revealed not Filipino creativity but the heroism of the friars, to whom Riggs rendered thanks "for many services and courtesies at their willing hands." As with other Americans during this period, Riggs was fascinated with the assimilation project of Spanish evangelization that had inaugurated this evolution. His account of the Spanish contained hopes for the Americans. The "hardy exploring priests," he wrote, had found the natives "plastic as wax, externally, malleable to the tools of the spirit, and almost as tractable and docile as they were easily influenced and attracted."[74]

Colonial Fraternalism, Evolution, and Tutelary Assimilation

If the Filipino masses were superstitious, passive, and ignorant, if Filipino elites were venal, corrupt, and abusive, what was a colonial state to do? What was the inclusionary racial narrative of postwar colonialism in the Philippines to be about? Three interlocking narratives and metaphors went into the making of this inclusionary racism: familial, evolutionary, and tutelary-assimilationist. All three provided necessary frameworks for hierarchical participation and a progressive, if indefinite, time frame for political change. Each recognized Filipinos but predicated that recognition on Filipinos' demonstration of sociocultural features that only Americans could determine and evaluate. Each marked a path into the otherwise uncertain colonial future by drawing necessary, concrete calibrations. The unevenness of their deployment, and their inconsistencies when juxtaposed, were part of their collective power, if they also opened up spaces for resistance. At the same time, their underlying homologies—especially by promising and withholding authority—sustained the hegemony of inclusionary racism and the imperialism of process.

What made each of the narratives powerful was its success in colonizing the future. Filipino incapacities were deep obstructions in the present, but not immutable. "While there is to-day a palpable unfitness for self-government among [Filipinos]," Taft himself put it, "there is in them a capacity for future development, for future preparation for self-government." Each of these narratives came with its own progression into that future: children matured, the backward evolved, students learned. Each of these required outside authorities to accredit or deny progress. When asked to provide more specific timetables for U.S. colonialism, Taft and other colonialists drew boundaries far into the future. Filipinos would "need the training of fifty or a hundred years before they shall even realize what Anglo-Saxon liberty is," Taft wrote, for example.[75] Oftentimes, American officials turned to an expansive language of "generation." There were, for example, Maud Jenks's necessary "fifty generations" of education. Taft believed it would take "at least two generations" to "educate" Filipinos for self-government. "Generation" used in this way combined an open-ended sense of time, a logic of family reproduction, and a neo-Lamarckian hope that self-government might be bred in.

Discourses of family were central to the new inclusionary racial formation. The idiom was encouraged, but not determined, by the arrival of American women and the establishment of new U.S. colonial domestic settings that included, in some cases, young children. Family was a metaphor of inclusion and belonging but also one of hierarchy, of natural inferiors and superiors. In its elaborated form, the colonial state as "family" cast Filipinos on the whole as children; as such, they were credulous, irresponsible, undisciplined, unruly, and gendered as boys; they were also "educable," reinforcing the colonial state as "school." The colonial state sought graduated timelines for colonialism, which children's progressive maturation to adulthood could provide. But if they agreed Filipinos were "children," Americans in both the Philippines and the United States divided sharply over the broader organization of the colonial "family." Most Manila Americans, for example, especially those close to the military, defined Americans as Filipinos' metaphorical "fathers"; in this mode, the framing of colonialism as family was impelled by the desire to make the ongoing brutalities of war morally invisible by recasting them as legitimate, patriarchal, disciplinary family violence. Officials associated with the Philippine Commission, by contrast, represented themselves as Filipinos' elder "brothers"; the result was what might be called colonial fraternalism, most succinctly expressed in the term for Filipinos attributed to Taft, "little brown brothers." While often taken as a generic expression of colonial condescension, this term needs to be seen in the specific context of an emerging inclusionary Philippine-American racial politics. It invited Filipinos into an imagined household of U.S. empire; it remade them from "black"—the color often attributed to them during the war, into the softer "brown." The metaphor of "brotherhood" did not need to convey actual or potential equality, but it was nonetheless the most potentially subversive of the terms—a fact noted by the Morrison poem above—which made the two other modifiers necessary. While naturalizing and moralizing colonialism, familial metaphors were also problematic in racial terms: it remained unclear how American "fathers" ended up with Filipino "children," or how Americans became the elder siblings to "little brown brothers."

Of the three, evolutionary metaphors were the most abstract, confidently grounding the contested historicism of U.S. colonialism in widely held metanarratives of staged, progressive development. During the late nineteenth and early twentieth centuries, social-evolutionary historicism had reached the pinnacle of its authority within U.S. social science and public culture as a mode of narration and legitimation.[76] But "evolution" had specific functions to achieve in the Philippines: most important, evolution grounded social processes in natural-historical time, which rooted U.S. colonialism in inescapable forces. Where anti-imperialists had challenged the legitimacy of colonialism as a violation of U.S. historical traditions, evolution promoted an alternative—and primordial— historical narrative. But as in other spheres, U.S. colonialists did not simply export existing U.S. social-evolutionary frameworks but rather reworked existing Philippine ones. U.S. colonialists drew on earlier wave-migration theories in casting Philippine history on the whole as a series of racial invasions by progressively more civilized elements; Spanish colonial history, for all its depravities, was recast as the steady, gradual retreat of savagery in the wake of a more progressive Christianity. Within the imagined present and future of U.S. colonial history, Filipinos as individuals would progress still further in evolutionary time. The specific axes of movement varied: they would "evolve" from ignorant peasants to English-speaking students; from filthy urban denizens to sanitary subjects; from recalcitrant to disciplined laborers. Philippine society would also evolve as a whole: from the tribal chaos and fragmentation that was said to have characterized pre-Hispanic and Spanish colonial time, to the emergence—far in the future—of a nation characterized by "homogeneity," forged by transportation and communications infrastructure and by English as a common language.[77] Not all the inhabitants of the Philippines were placed on the same evolutionary track: while evolution was said to characterize U.S. colonial time, Christians and non-Christians were progressing not only at different rates but in different directions. Evolutionary colonial progress, in fact, might widen rather than diminish difference among the islands' inhabitants.

More than any other, the new colonial state's defining metaphor would be tutelary and assimilationist, one that cast the colonial state in its entirety as a school and made its task the active transformation of Filipinos in an unsteady and necessarily indefinite movement toward "Americanism." Tutelage and assimilation were anchored in the actual construction and organization of schools during the first years of the Taft regime and the increasing number of American teachers. By 1904, there were hundreds of new school buildings erected at the center of villages throughout the archipelago; voluntary contributions by local elites for construction purposes rooted these novel institutions in Filipino power structures. The metaphor's greatest practical beneficiaries were the private English-language schools that sprung up in Manila and other cities, promising to train bright and enterprising young Filipinos in English for the civil service exams. The state as school, in other words, made sense in part because attending school facilitated entree into the state as a civil servant.

But the metaphor's power far outstripped the existence of actual public or civil service schools. There was virtually no state arena of Filipino-American interaction—from office clerkships to forced road labor—that was not conceived of as "education." On one level, it sublimated the wartime hatred that had often justified violence in the name of "teaching"

This photograph of William Howard Taft (*far right*), Leonard Wood (*back row, center*), and American schoolteachers with Filipino children evokes the regime's defining self-justification as a tutelary enterprise predicated on an optimistic assessment of Filipino "capacity." The civilians reimagined previously savage Filipinos as "little brown brothers" to be guided sternly into adulthood or as neat, orderly students to be educated and disciplined. By means of imagery such as this, the regime was able to cast itself as the core of a national-exceptionalist project of benevolent colonialism. From Hollnsteiner and Ick, *Bearers of Benevolence.*

Filipinos "a lesson." But "tutelage" was also a shorthand for "benevolence" and "uplift," the very messages the regime wanted to send to both Filipinos and domestic U.S. audiences. Even U.S. soldiers, officials emphasized, had opened schools in the garrisoned towns they had occupied during the war. Education organized the colonial state's myriad tasks into a single one: providing Filipinos the necessary, if elusive, political rationality required for successful self-government. If assimilation was the regime's long-term goal, tutelage was its process and policy. This pervasive metaphor—colonialism as tutelage in self-government—applied equally well, if differently, to still "incapable" Filipino elites and masses. Collaborating Filipino elites would receive "practical instruction" from the U.S. officials with whom they would share power in provincial and insular governments. In the new, American-run public school system, children of the Filipino masses would gain the manual and industrial training, literacy, discipline, and work ethic with which they might eventually exercise responsible "citizenship."

English-language instruction was central to the metaphor of colonialism as tutelage. The decision for English as the primary language of the state was partly structural. On the ground, there were small numbers of Americans who could speak Spanish with the elites of Manila and other cities, and none who spoke any other Filipino languages that might take them farther into the countryside or further down the class scale. A regime so heavily reliant on Filipino collaborators, it might have been argued, should have opted to train the comparatively few Americans in Filipino languages, rather than the far more gigantic project of training Filipinos in English. But, as many observers pointed out, neither the U.S. government nor the academy had the capacity for training potential U.S. civil servants in Filipino languages.[78]

The choice of English was also profoundly ideological, becoming invested with political and moral force in at least two ways. First was the notion of English as the linguistic counterpart of nation-building. What had been one of the central rationales of the U.S. invasion—that proliferating tribes were a sign of the impossibility of Philippine nationality— was now emerging as an organizing regime problem. If the Philippine Republic had been merely a Tagalog conspiracy, as many Americans believed, a genuine Filipino nation could only be constructed through the inculcation of a common language. Spanish might have presented itself as a candidate for the language of Filipino nationality, as the second language of much of the Filipino elite, especially in urban areas. But here, a second ideology was essential, one that invested English with transformative, liberating power. The inherent political superiority of English had been emphasized during the Anglo-Saxonist mobilizations that had proven so important during the annexation debate. English was not only the means to national unity but the necessary vehicle for tutelage. Only English could convey Anglo-Saxon morals and institutions of self-government, transforming its users.[79]

English-language instruction became one element in the regime's broader national-exceptionalist claims. Explaining why American colonial civil servants were neither trained nor examined on Philippine languages, Everett Thompson, a civil service board examiner, noted the "radically different principle underlying the *raison d'etre* of the Philippine government" relative to India, Java, and Indochina. These colonies were "governed as sources of strength and revenue to the home power" and lacked an impulse "magnanimously to uplift" or "train the inhabitants for citizenship or to change their language or customs." As a result, European officials in them, "to better administer the necessary affairs of government," became "thoroughly imbued with the genius, the language, the laws, and customs of the subject peoples." "With the Philippines," he wrote, "all this is different." Since the Philippine government existed "primarily for the Filipinos," the "permeating spirit of the Philippine civil service is the training of the Filipino in the best methods of government." Filipinos compelled to speak English might become "thoroughly imbued" with the Anglo-Saxon genius, rather than the other way around. English might also have the more mundane benefit of encouraging compliance with the colonial state. "In mastering the English language the Filipinos not only fill their minds with a knowledge of its literature," wrote Thompson, "but are thus the better prepared to appreciate the high aims and purposes of the present government."[80]

There was no better condensation of the projects of tutelage and assimilation than the *pensionado* program, inaugurated in 1903, which would eventually send approximately 300 Filipino students to the United States for government-funded higher education. After receiving four years of college and living with American families, the *pensionados* would be required to return to the Philippines as teachers, engineers, or other civil servants for five years. The program arose out of the desire for higher-level Filipino civil servants and the complete absence of secular higher education in the Philippines capable of meeting American standards of expertise. It was also hoped that it would introduce "assimilating" Filipinos to the United States as advertisements for the regime's benevolence. It resembled empire-building educational programs elsewhere; indeed, U.S. officials compared it to "the efforts of the British Government to educate the people of India by sending them to England, and of the Japanese Government in behalf of its own people in sending them to notable foreign schools."[81]

If the *pensionado* program was about reorienting the rising elite generation toward American customs and loyalties, it was also about putting forward the best and brightest Filipino youths before American eyes as symbols of successful assimilation. The requirement of high-school graduation, a goal achieved by only those few families that could sustain children in school, tended to deliver upper-class candidates. Where a poor but talented student might have squeaked through, Taft's instructions to provincial governors made clear that "[e]ach student must be of unquestionable moral and physical qualifications, weight being given to social status." William Sutherland, the program's first supervisor, would later recall that the program's goal was "to make a favorable impression" on Americans "who mostly thought theretofore that Filipinos wore gee strings and slept in trees."[82]

If narratives of tutelage, family, evolution, and assimilation made headway in the Philippines, it was only because they were ideologies familiar and acceptable to select Filipino elites, some of whom emphasized that Filipino progress could only be achieved through U.S. colonialism. These elites were recognized and promoted by the colonial state and given a platform in official publications and in opinion journals in the United States.[83] Such ideological congruence was most visible at the insular level, where collaboration between Americans and Filipinos allowed and required a mutual shaping of political discourses. T. H. Pardo de Tavera best represented the Filipino side of this dialogue in the early years of the Taft regime. His vision of Filipino progress through colonialism, and especially through U.S. secular education, was articulated, for example, in a 1906 address given before American and Filipino teachers entitled "The Filipino Soul." In it, Pardo criticized "conservatives" who would "preserve our customs and traditions" so that "our social conscience, poetically styled the Filipino soul, may remain unchanged." Only "uncivilized countries," he claimed, remained "immutable and petrified before the moving forces of history." As when barbarous Europeans long ago had become civilized by submitting to conquering Romans, Filipinos should submit to the tutelage of the "Anglo-Saxon race," the "trustee and the dictator of the highest civilization that we have ever known of."[84]

Like the American architects of inclusionary racism, Pardo stated that he did "not believe that race-inferiority is a matter of permanence or of anthropology" nor "an inherent or a natural condition of any race." Indeed, it was those who advocated a "Filipino soul" that were overcommitted to "racial" thinking. These "anthropo-sociologists" failed to acknowledge the "absurdity" of essential racial hierarchy, denying, for example, the historical rise and decline of races between positions of superiority and inferiority. Japan presented Pardo a "striking example" of social transformation through adoption of European ways; he prophesied that the day was "not far distant" when Philippine progress would "present one more practical example to the sociologists who deny the existence of inferior races, because our culture will also shed a luster on this world side by side with that of Japan."[85]

Also like his American counterparts, Pardo sought to legitimate the U.S. occupation by indigenizing it, making it the historic extension of the late nineteenth-century *ilustrado* diaspora and Propaganda reform movement. Filipinos abroad in that period had sought "to acquire a new spirit, a new mentality," rather than to cling to a "Filipino soul." There was a certain irony, then, that "now that the civilization which we want to seek outside our country" had "come to visit our own homes in the form of the Anglo-Saxon public school instruction, a strange reactionary spirit and puzzling attitude of mind struggle to drive it away." Those who claimed that colonial education would undermine Filipino nationalism had to deal with an awkward historical fact: colonial education had historically promoted nation-building. "The Filipinos educated in Spanish schools in the Philippines, under a strictly Spanish system," he noted, "were the individuals who brought about the revolution which ended Spanish sovereignty in the Philippines." While it might seem that the "movement for Philippinism" emerged from the "uneducated classes," it was in fact the work of the educated, "whose souls had been 'profoundly adulterated.'" It was European-educated Filipinos that had learned "to respect the race, venerate the customs of the ancestors, discover the beauties of Nature in the Islands (in which other people found nothing but objects of ridicule and scorn), admire the land, and dream of the country's redemption." Pardo believed U.S. colonialism would continue this process. English-language education would create an awareness of "the oneness of our rights, the singleness of our duties, the harmony of our aspirations, and the unanimity of our ideals." Communications networks would spread civilization across physically isolated provinces, and "in place of heterogeneity, there will spring a homogeneity of ideas." Interregional contact and communication would "give rise to a sentiment of national fellowship which, in truth, hardly exists today."[86]

While tutelage and assimilation found some Filipino advocates, they also produced American skepticism and anxiety. It would remain one of the regime's central tasks to persuade doubting domestic U.S. publics that Filipinos could be Americanized. Tutelage and assimilation were both fantasies of one-way cultural connection without unanticipated reflux: the colonized would learn from the colonizers without, in turn, teaching them; the colonized would become more similar to the colonizers without transforming them. If the new regime empowered Filipinos who believed in assimilation, there were nonetheless many American skeptics who feared what it might mean for the United States itself, as in Rebecca Taylor's 1903 critical essay, "Disposition of the Philippine Islands." Taylor's piece can be seen as taking up where Henry C. Rowland's wartime account of the tragic "degeneration" of U.S. troops had left off. It evaluated the regime's policy of assimilation, which she defined as "nothing less than incorporation into the body politic." Pushing the metaphor to the point of extremity and dark satire, Taylor defined assimilation in digestive terms, in the process revealing just how important unincorporated status had been. Taylor redefined McKinley's "benevolent assimilation" to mean that the "Philippine prey must be captured by the great assimilating body, and devoured—ground to powder by the military force composing the strong teeth of that body; that Filipino mincemeat must be moistened by saliva of superior brand—spat upon, if you please, the mouth of the big assimilating body fairly 'watering' at the prospect of an Oriental meal. Down the American esophagus the mass must go."[87]

Once devoured, the Philippines would become "'flesh of our flesh and bone of our bone.'" But the process would not merely change the Philippines. During actual, physical digestion, "[t]he assimilating body is also changed by the character of the substance assimilated. The purity of the blood, the strength of the muscles, the quality of the brain, the tension of the nerve, the texture of the skin, the temperature, and even the moral nature are strongly influenced by that which is assimilated." This would operate as well in the political sphere. In "assimilating the Filipino, the

American people must accept the change that will be wrought in the national body by the very nature of the case." Continuing her striking description of digestive imperialism, she stated:

> This fine pulp must be passed through the Taft pylorus into the American duodenum, to be acted upon by the various superior fluids, notably American gall, after which the political villi will dip down into the Filipino-American chyle . . . and finally the refined emulsion, when mixed with American blood, will pass to the heart of the nation, whence it will be pumped through the American arteries to all parts of the assimilating body, building up the new America.[88]

Taylor predicted that, before assimilation was completed, the United States would have had "several centuries of frightful indigestion." More seriously, the nation would itself have been fundamentally disfigured. Americans would "scarcely recognize" the nation "because of its Oriental diet, so foreign to our American system," she wrote. An empire of recognition might become unrecognizable to itself. "We will find ourselves Malayed Americans, even as they shall have become Americanized Malays. It remains to be seen how far the change will improve either."[89]

Hispanicized Catholics and "Non-Christian Tribes"

The U.S. colonial racial state was not constructed from a uniform administrative blueprint but was divided into "dual mandates" whose implications would prove profound for subsequent Philippine history.[90] This bifurcated state was built upon an imperial indigenism, one of whose fundamental features was a racialized construction of religion, specifically an account of the radical, typological difference between Hispanicized Catholics and what were called non-Christians.[91] Where Americans' imperial indigenism recognized Filipino elites in lowland areas, it recognized them as Catholics, partly civilized by centuries of Spanish influence. The bifurcated racial state involved an internalization of wartime discourses of savagery: the recognition of Catholic Filipinos was predicated on the displacement of the characteristics that had been attributed to the warring Filipino population as a whole—especially savagery and tribalism—onto non-Christian peoples. This bifurcated racial formation confirmed the relative civilization of Filipino Catholics, who would contribute to official knowledge of non-Christians and, especially, their distinction from Christians. "There is far more difference between the Igorrote of Benguet and the Tagalog of Manila," wrote Edith Moses, reflecting a new discovery, "than between the latter and ourselves."[92] The dichotomy would have deep institutional implications. The Philippine colonial state would undertake what anthropologists Felix and Marie Keesing would later call "a dual task," with Hispanicized Filipinos governed within one set of political institutions, evolving toward self-government, and non-Christians governed by U.S. politico-military commanders. The territorialization of race and racialization of territory would come together in the formation of two special provinces, the Moro Province founded in Mindanao and Sulu in 1903 and the Mountain Province in Northern Luzon, established in 1908, each of which would be, in the words of the Keesings, a "dependency within a dependency."[93]

American officials approached non-Christians in light of an increasingly favorable recognition of the Spanish colonial state and its legacy, adopting many of the structures of Spanish colonialism. The American colonial state had, for example, inherited the built environment of Spanish office buildings, prisons, military barracks, and forts; the commission itself had taken up residence in the Ayuntamiento, the former seat of Spanish secular authority. Somewhat to their surprise, U.S. officials had found a great deal to respect in Spanish colonial law and adopted the former power's civil and criminal codes, with changes made to procedural and sentencing laws. The most serious political engagement with the Spanish colonial past, however, was the settlement of the friar lands question. In 1902, Taft and a diplomatic commission visited the Vatican to arrange for the purchase of the friar orders' rich agricultural lands and, in this way, to diffuse one of the most long-standing and volatile Filipino resentments. While the mission was meant to displace the friars politically, it was also an admission of the church's power, a power that would be manifested throughout the American colonial period, especially in questions of education policy and missionary activity. The Philippine Commission would, on more than one occasion, remove American officials who were too outspoken against either the church hierarchy or Catholicism as a whole.[94]

Where Americans in the Philippines disparaged Spain, along the traditional lines of the Black Legend, as an oppressive, exploitative, feudal power, they also found themselves praising Spain's Philippine legacy, especially its conversion of "savages" to Christianity. Where Filipino

These maps of Northern Luzon show the provinces into which the region was divided under Spanish rule (left) and U.S. administration (right), with the American colonial state's new Mountain Province (shaded gray) created in 1908. The province represented one of the projects of the colonial government as racial state. The outlines of its subprovinces, based upon Dean Worcester's "ethnographic" delineation of "non-Christian tribes," sharply distinguished Hispanicized from non-Christian groups in racial and administrative terms, allowing limited Filipino self-rule in "Christian" provinces and subjecting the latter to exclusive U.S. rule.

Catholicism had been reduced by imperialists to a veneer of Spanish feudalism during the war, it was now made Filipinos' unique gift to Spain's American successors, who "inherited" a "semi-civilized" people with a demonstrated capacity for assimilation. In this, U.S. national exceptionalism was made to resonate with Philippine Christian exceptionalism: only the Filipinos had been blessed with such benevolent masters; only the Americans had been provided with such precivilized subjects. According to James LeRoy, who was elsewhere critical of Spanish rule, Spain was due "the highest praise" for its early accomplishments, for it had achieved "what no other European nation has ever done in the Orient," the development of "a whole people spiritually," and had done it "without crushing the people under her heel." Recognition of the virtues of the Spanish Catholic past was made part of the symbolic landscape of Manila when the U.S. military government erected on the Luneta, one of "the most prominent sites in the whole archipelago," a bronze statue of Spanish explorer Miguel López de Legazpi and Augustinian friar Andrés de Urdaneta salvaged during the occupation of Manila. In his dedication, Taft called the Philippines under Spain "a Christian mission rather than a colony" and praised "the enterprise, courage, and fidelity to duty" of those Spaniards who had "braved the then frightful dangers of the deep to carry Christianity and European civilization into the far-off Orient."[95]

The official recognition of lowland, Hispanicized elites and praise for Hispanicization also involved the simultaneous recasting of those peoples that had remained largely outside Spanish-Catholic colonization. The Spanish had referred to these groups as *infieles* (infidels) and, in the case of Muslims, as *moros*. It was a sign of how far Americans had gone in adopting local, Spanish-colonial, and Filipino categories that they borrowed these terms; *infiel* became, in awkward translation, "non-Christian," a term rarely if ever used in domestic U.S. contexts. These groups were, in turn, represented as being organized into "tribes." During the war, the entire Philippine population had been represented as tribal—indeed, the war itself had been blamed on one of the islands' "eighty-four" tribes—but as lowland, Hispanicized elites were recognized by the colonial state, Catholic Filipinos were seen as less tribally fragmented, and the term "Christian tribes" faded accordingly. With lowland Catholics now on a gradual evolutionary trajectory toward self-government, they were no longer members of tribes, but elements of a hypothetical nation in development that might eventually be united through collaboration, assimilation, and tutelage. With the detribalization of Catholics, the term "tribe" came to cohere most to animists and Muslims, converging in the term "non-Christian tribe," which suggested the uncivilized, fragmented, and antinational character of the peoples they described.

But as the commission government consolidated and attempted to establish its authority in the Luzon highlands and in the southern archipelago, it faced the problem of defining these tribes for purposes of governance. During the war, "tribe" had been nothing more than an abstraction, the polemical opposite of "nation." But state-building on the Philippines' frontiers required a clearer sense of the non-Christians, especially their territorial boundaries, political and economic organization, and religious and linguistic self-definitions. To investigate these questions, the commission inaugurated a "Bureau of Non-Christian Tribes" in October 1900.[96] Renamed the "Ethnological Survey" in 1901, its task was consistent with the regime's mode of basing colonial policy on "expert" knowledge. Its establishment simultaneously conveyed the ambiguities of the tribes, the novel state investments in clarifying them, and the deepening administrative division between Catholics and non-Christians. Its staff, headed first by University of California anthropologist David P. Barrows, was to "[c]onduct systematic investigations" with reference to the non-Christian tribes "in order to ascertain the name of each tribe, the limits of the territory which it occupies, the approximate number of individuals which compose it, their social organizations and their languages, beliefs, manners and customs, with special view to determining the most practicable means of bringing about their advancement in civilization and material prosperity."[97]

While the bureau was charged with defining the tribes authoritatively, officials would debate their status long into the American colonial period. This fact pointed both to the new racial formation as a site of struggle and to the local contexts in which colonial knowledge was being forged. "Great confusion exists as to the classification and geographical distribution of the non-Christian tribes inhabiting this area," wrote Worcester in a 1906 paper titled "Non-Christian Tribes of Northern Luzon" in the *Philippine Journal of Science*. In his introduction titled "The Peoples of the Philippines" for the 1903 Census Report, Barrows reiterated Sixto Lopez's complaint that "[e]rrors in nomenclature prevail everywhere in the Islands," with "three or four different terms . . . applied by different localities or towns to identical peoples." According to Barrows, Blumentritt had credited 82 distinct tribes; Father José Algué and the Jesuits, working on an ethnological report for the commission, had declared the existence of 67, and census enumerators had decided on 116 tribal designations, "which had to be explained and reduced to system."[98] Ultimately, officials debated the applicability of the concept of "tribe" at all. Barrows concluded, based on fieldwork in Northern Luzon, that if a "tribe" meant a political unit, then tribes were "unknown in this Archipelago," a striking admission from the former director of a bureau named for precisely such entities. Condensing highland populations into "culture areas," Barrows concluded that tribal organizations of the kind "we find among the North American Indians" were "far beyond the capacity of the Filipino of any grade."[99] By contrast, Worcester stood behind the concept of "the tribe," which he defined more broadly as a "division of a race" that shared characteristics such as physical features, ornaments, agricultural methods, and marriage customs, without constituting either a political unit or a single dialect. While the anthropological validity of Worcester's definition of "tribes" was questionable, his position would give him the authority to set them quite literally on the map.

Hispanicized Filipinos were involved in the colonial state's construction of the non-Christian tribes. The Bureau of Non-Christian Tribes' first publication was a reprint of T. H. Pardo de Tavera's Spanish-language "Etymology of the Names of the Races of the Philippines," which purported to recognize the islands' true ethnological divisions. "After the fable of the 1,500 islands that make up the Philippine Archipelago," wrote Pardo, "comes that of the 'hundreds of races that, in Babylonian confusion populate the islands,' as one lyrical geographical writer wrote of this country." Affirming Blumentritt's theory of the islands' three principal races—Negritos, Indonesians, and Malayans—Pardo expressed frustration at accounts that conflated "political groupings that are in no ways different from each other."[100] Pardo was not the only Hispanicized Filipino who participated in the shaping of the state's new racial grid. One intriguing example of Hispanicized Filipinos attempting to adjust their relationship to non-Christians in their midst was a petition sent to Pardo by the municipal council of Kainta, "requesting that the name of that town be changed to San Andrés, under the pretext that in that town there exist a tribe of blacks, and when Kainta is spoken of, it is supposed that everyone in Kainta is black." In a letter to a friend in the region (probably the provincial governor), Pardo criticized the petition in light of the common accusation that "whites make differences between themselves and those of color"; here, Tagalogs were guilty of the same thing. Pardo believed this would be "a bad measure" involving "a pretext that not only is not worthwhile, but which must not be invoked by the Tagalogs." Extending his own scholarly recognition to the blacks, he claimed that, having successfully resisted Spanish conquest, they were, in fact, "more civilized than the Tagalogs." The results of the exchange are unknown, but it did reveal the sense among at least some Hispanicized Filipinos that the state should be an instrument for marking the distinction between Christians and non-Christians more deeply.[101]

While the perspectives of Hispanicized Filipinos were considered in the state definition of the tribes, domestic U.S. models of tribal governance were rejected. Elihu Root had stated in his instructions to the commission that in its dealings with "the uncivilized tribes of the Islands," it should "adopt the same course followed by Congress in permitting the tribes of our North American Indians to maintain their tribal organisation and government." The appointment to the Bureau of Non-Christian Tribes' first directorship of Barrows, whose research treated the Coahuilla Indians of California, also suggested commensurability between Indian and non-Christian policy. But as with LeRoy's criticism of "nigger theory," models of Indian policy were perceived as inappropriate for the Philippine context, unsuitable for "export." In late 1901, Barrows was assigned his first mission as chief of the bureau, to make a six-month tour of Indian reservations, schools, and academies in the United States and to report to the commission on the feasibility of Indian policy as a model for Philippine efforts. He came away deeply skeptical about the possibilities for extending Indian policy to the non-Christians of the Philippines.[102] He criticized both the reservation policy for its isolation of tribes and also the 1890 Dawes Act, which had opened Indian reservation land to white settlement, dismantled tribal political recognition by the federal government, and promoted Indian assimilation through individual landholding and citizenship. While conceived with "excellent intentions," he wrote, the act had "not brought forth satisfactory results," leading to the transfer of Indian lands by deception and exacerbating Indian poverty. "My belief," he wrote to Worcester, "is that we will not find in the policy of the Government in treating with Indians a model which can be generally followed in handling the wild tribes of the Philippines."[103]

Special Provinces

The racialized division between Hispanicized Filipinos and non-Christian tribes would become central to the territorial and administrative division of the Philippines under U.S. colonial rule. Specifically, the commission would bifurcate its governance into two fundamentally different modes: in predominantly Catholic areas, provincial governments would be partly appointed and partly elected by local *principales*, while in areas that were primarily non-Christian, in the Cordillera Central of Luzon and in the Sulu Archipelago in the south, power would be far more centralized in the hands of appointed U.S. governors, who would then recognize "traditional" authorities at the local level. This approach resulted in the formation of two special provinces, a Moro Province in the south in 1903, and a Mountain Province in Northern Luzon in 1908, which would remain almost exclusively ruled by Americans until the era of "Filipinization." There were important differences between both the state structures and cultural discourses that pertained to the Moro and Mountain Provinces, but they also had much in common. Where lowland politics had been commonly characterized as a kind of colonial fraternalism, commentators often referred to the more authoritarian and militarized rule of the special provinces as "paternal." Both provincial governments effectively insulated their respective regions—approximately one-half of the total territory of the Philippines—from the potential control of Hispanicized Filipinos, setting them apart from the devolutionary track of calibrated colonialism and facilitating a versatile, archipelago-wide politics of divide and rule. Bifurcated state-building, and the racial formation that helped organize and legitimate it, would have profound effects on both U.S. colonialism and Filipino nationalism: one of the cores of U.S. colonial ideology and Filipino nationalism would be the Philippines' "peripheries."

American control of Northern Luzon had been mandated by U.S. officials' desire to develop a sanitarium and hill station in the Cordillera Central, as well as to open up the region to mining and commercial agriculture. Never conquered by the Spanish, the Cordillera was inhabited by diverse ethnolinguistic groups engaged in subsistence rice farming, organized politically into independent *rancherías*, with varying trade contacts with lowland groups, especially Ilocanos. After initial ethnographic surveys, including expeditions by the Bureau of Non-Christian Tribes, the commission extended its authority into these regions in a highly improvised manner, adapted to the character of the specific "tribes" that inhabited them. In general, power was highly concentrated in the figure of a single American governor who combined civil and military authority and who was answerable only to the secretary of the interior; these governors in turn appointed *presidentes* and councils from local headmen, with whom they also had to compete for authority. Among their other functions, these governors prioritized the repression of intervillage warfare as well as the construction of local roads through coerced labor. As local governments were established and tested, the framework for an overarching regional structure took shape. The Special Provincial Government Act and Township Act of 1905, which pertained to non-Christian areas outside of the Moro Province, established a flexible structure that reflected the regime's larger calibrated colonialism in microcosm. The "least civilized" *rancherías* would be governed initially by headmen appointed by the governor but ultimately by officials elected through male suffrage once it was determined that they had "progressed."[104] By summer 1908, the commission had inaugurated the Mountain Province, a single administrative unit directly under Worcester's control, consisting of seven subprovinces that cleaved closely to his map of the region's tribal distinctions.[105]

The explicit goal of establishing the Mountain Province was to insulate the Cordillera politically and economically from lowland Filipinos. In economic terms, U.S. officials sought to control access to the region's rich mineral resources, especially its gold and copper, as well as the rice, sugar, tobacco, and cotton that grew in its valleys. It was telling that the highland administration's system of "Igorot Exchanges" was intended to bridge Cordilleran communities through trade but cut them off from lowlanders. But the reason for the divided state structure was fundamentally political: it meant exclusive American control of a region that could serve as a counterweight to the anticipated challenge of organized lowland politics. As Dean Bartlett put it, "the wild tribes were safely removed from the field of insular politics and placed under the control of the Philippine Commission."[106] Institutional division here relied upon an imperial indigenism that recast highland non-Christians as weak, passive, and easily preyed upon by their ostensibly more "civilized" Christian neighbors. Under the Spanish, wrote Worcester, Christian Filipinos "took advantage of [non-Christians'] ignorance and timidity to impose on them in many ways, robbing them of their horses and cattle, and sometimes even of their crops." Under his regime, by contrast, the non-Christians were "not to be subjected to the municipal officials of Christianized towns, at whose hands they have in the past suffered so much oppression and whom they cordially hate."[107] Instead, American officials would constitute a "protective" state that would defend the victims in an ongoing, internal race war. U.S. officials' hopes for a structurally divided polity reached a pinnacle in one plan for a highland military academy that would, according to colonial official William C. Forbes, "kill two birds with one stone," achieving the goal of "civilizing that number of worthy savages," while turning out "an army of thirty thousand men at practically no cost." This force would, unlike lowland Filipino units, be "absolutely loyal under any combination of circumstances" and "could be relied upon not to be swayed by politicians." If the U.S. Army in the islands were to be preoccupied with "repelling invaders" from the outside, the highland force would "prevent insurrection" domestically.[108] It could, in the worst case, perhaps facilitate an American reconquest of the Philippines from the highlands downward.

The southern Philippines had also never been fully incorporated into the Spanish colonial state. Mindanao's vast interior was sparsely populated and difficult to reach, and powerful, militarized polities under the Muslim *datus* actively resisted the imposition of Spanish control. During the Philippine-American War, U.S. army officials had sought to keep the *datus* out of the war, signing the Bates Agreement with the Sultan of Sulu, Jamal-ul Kiram II, that guaranteed the latter tribute payments and noninterference with Moro laws and customs, in exchange for recognition of U.S. sovereignty in the region. The U.S. military felt no obligation to uphold the agreement, however, and abrogated it once Moro neutrality was no longer necessary. In June 1903, the Philippine Commission formally created Moro Province, an administrative unit consisting of five districts, each under a governor and a board. As in Northern Luzon, the administrative character of these districts was determined by their "tribal" character; each was in turn divided into predominantly Christian "municipalities"—administered as were municipalities elsewhere—and Muslim and animist "tribal wards," where district governors exercised wide-ranging executive and legislative functions and appointed local authorities. Whereas in Mountain Province governance would remain in the hands of the commission, in Moro Province control would be retained by the U.S. Army until 1914 under a succession of military governors. These governors would establish U.S. control by declaring nonintervention with Islamic traditions and by pitting *datu* against *datu*. They would also impose it by force, through a series of merciless military campaigns and the establishment of Constabulary and army outposts in strategic locations. U.S. Army control progressively extended through telegraph lines and, as in the north, through road-building organized around coerced labor. Simultaneously, the state promoted the development of the abaca, timber, and rubber industries, as well as regional trade that would make it independent of Manila-based commerce.

Whereas Mountain Province had been institutionally cut off from Filipino control, as Patricio Abinales demonstrates, Moro Province was a military colony separated from insular politics as a whole, even from the control of the Philippine Commission.[109] This was facilitated by centralized military institutions whose systems of recruitment and decision making were autonomous from Manila. The provincial government's success in generating revenue through taxation and customs collection also made it far less subject to interference. Some settlers even envisioned the formal detachment of Mindanao from the rest of the Philippines to perpetuate exclusive U.S. military and economic control. As in the north, rationales for regional autonomy were predicated on forms of imperial indigenism. In some cases, as in the Cordillera, there was emphasis on the exploitation of animists either by Christians or Moros.[110] In the south, however, it was the Moros' warlike character that was emphasized by officials. As a "martial" race, it was argued, Moros would only respect U.S. military authority; where respect broke down, only the U.S. Army had the power to suppress rebellion and establish control. Army officials raised the specter of Muslim-Christian war; again, the U.S. colonial state was cast as protective, but here it guarded ungrateful Christian Filipinos from barbaric Moro antagonists. One district governor, for example, chided local Christians for abusing the "protection" of the U.S. colonial state and failing to realize that "[i]f you were governed by the Moros you would never stop running until you reached the water's edge, and then you would be compelled to swim to safety."[111] Faced with such intractable hostilities, it seemed, only the U.S. military could guarantee order and stability.

The face of order in the special provinces was most notoriously revealed in the massacre of an estimated 1,000 Taosug Muslims by colonial troops on March 2, 1906, at the extinct volcano Bud Dajo in Sulu. Alienated from their sultan and prominent *datus* and the Americans who backed them, the Taosugs had escaped to the lava cone of the volcano, a natural fortress. Governor Leonard Wood responded by sending 800 soldiers up the side of the mountain, where they launched an attack with mountain guns, rifles, bayonets, and grenades. After four days, what came to be known as the "Battle of Bud Dajo" was over; while U.S. forces suffered the death of 20 troops and some 70 wounded, all the Taosugs were killed. Wood's dispatch to the secretary of war testified firsthand that "no man, woman, or child was wantonly killed." A "considerable number of women and children were killed in the fight," however, because Moro women "wore trousers and were dressed and armed much like the men

This photograph, taken at the site of the Bud Dajo massacre of 1906, circulated rapidly in the United States despite efforts to destroy it. The killing of an estimated one thousand men, women, and children occurred when U.S. and Filipino troops fired on Taosug villagers attempting to escape the control of *datu* collaborators and colonial forces trapped them in an extinct volcano cone. The event suggested the heavy ongoing costs of imperial "nation-building." From Villard, *Fighting Years*.

and charged with them," while children "had been used by the men as shields." The event became a scandal in the United States, particularly when a photograph taken at the site was reprinted in American newspapers. One week after the massacre, President Roosevelt sent a telegram to Wood to "congratulate" him and his men "upon the brave feat of arms wherein you and they so well upheld the honor of the American flag."[112]

The Colonial Census

The racial formation of the new civilian state—its scientistic, expert ethos, its tutelary-assimilationist rationales and collaborationist means, its struggle for pacification and logic of devolution, and its administrative demarcation of Christians and non-Christians—would all come together in the Philippine Census of 1903, the administrative and social-scientific expression of emerging Filipino-American political relationships in all their complexity.[113]

First and foremost, the census was a key marker of political time in the formal establishment of a civilian regime, yet another formal, if embattled, declaration of the end of the Philippine-American War. Section 6 of the Organic Act of July 1, 1902, had mandated that the president order a census "whenever the existing insurrection in the Philippine Islands shall have ceased and a condition of general and complete peace shall have been established therein." As such, the advent of the census meant the formal ushering in of a "postwar" political era. But the census would also mark transitions inside this new era, tracing out hypothetical stages in the granting of self-government to Filipinos. Section 7 of the act stated that two years following the completion and publication of the census, pending continued peace, the commission was to inform the president, who would, in turn, authorize the commission to "call a general election for the choice of delegates to a popular assembly."[114] The census, then, was a highly visible promise directed at both Filipino and American audiences. Aimed at Americans was the promise of a regime based on scientific expertise, one that, unlike European colonial governments, possessed a measurable timetable for self-government. Directed at Filipino elites was the promise of gradually extended state power—specifically, legislative authority—in the unspecified, political future.

If the census as a symbol of future state devolution took hold among Filipino elites, it was in part because census-taking itself followed the boundaries of the collaborationist state so closely. This was out of logistical necessity. Given the vast diversity of Filipino languages, almost none of them known to American colonial officials, Spanish was decided upon as the language of the census reportage. But the selection of "a sufficient number of intelligent Filipinos able to read, write, and speak the Spanish language as well as the various dialects of the people, to serve as enumerators and special agents, was by no means a trivial undertaking." Based on Spanish population estimates, American census planners assumed the project would require 6,000 enumerators for the "civilized" population alone, in addition to more than 1,000 "special agents." They also estimated that of approximately 7 million Christians, not more than 1 percent constituted an "educated class" capable of conducting the census successfully. These were, in most cases, precisely the *principalía* who had been recognized as municipal and provincial authorities in the American colonial state. The census, then, would overlap precisely with the shape of the state itself. In order to employ "the official class" throughout the islands, census director J. P. Sanger noted, it was decided to make "all insular, provincial, and municipal officials, and such officers and enlisted men of the army serving in the Philippines, and Philippine scouts, as might be designated by the commanding general, eligible for appointment as supervisors, special agents, and enumerators."[115]

Reliance on emerging networks of collaboration was also political. A census "on the American plan . . . would not have been feasible" unless the provincial governors, municipal *presidentes* and councils, and *principalía* "were connected with it, so that it might have behind it the support of those classes of the population so influential then and now with the masses, or common people."[116] In November 1903, provincial governors were notified that they had automatically been appointed census supervisors—at a salary increase of $150 per month—and ordered to collect available maps, prepare enumeration districts, and appoint local enumerators.

The census served to integrate the emerging bureaucracy at insular, provincial, and municipal levels. Against most of the grain of colonial state-formation, the initiative necessarily emerged from the center outward. The process began when the "governor-supervisors" were summoned to Manila in December 1903 for two weeks of training in census procedure. While the elections of July 1907 have been identified as the first moment of truly integrated, postrevolutionary "national" politics, the summoning of provincial officials to Manila in December 1903 was a highly significant, if less heralded, point of encounter between political elites from around the archipelago. It demonstrated, on the one hand, the very local character of the colonial regime, as its elites assembled inward from the provinces. At the same time, it began the process, intensified with the election of 1907, of nationalizing those elites. The governor-supervisors were received by Taft and instructed on how to draw census maps with tentative enumeration districts; they practiced filling out census blanks and were assigned districts, including "special enumerators" for "all the wild tribes . . . except those for Mindanao and the Sulu archipelago."[117] Knowing special agents and enumerators would require similar instruction, census officials ordered the governors to summon *presidentes* to meet them in mid-January to pick up census pouches, portfolios, and blanks and to receive instruction so they could, in turn, instruct enumerators in the municipalities. Where the *presidentes* were illiterate, they were instructed to bring a literate member of the *principalía* to assist them.

While the census was meant to map and confirm the realm of "peace," resistance to census-taking suggested the relative shallowness of this fiction. Precautions taken to provide some census-takers with armed escorts suggested that, far from marking off the boundaries of established peace in time and space, the census was pressing its way into sometimes hostile territory, testing new systems of collaboration in the process. In areas inhabited by Moros, the census was carried out by the army. Elsewhere, "it was believed that the army, including the Philippine Scouts, the Constabulary, and the police, were amply able to cope with these marauders, or at least keep them within reasonable bounds while the census was being taken." In at least some cases, census-takers were nonetheless targets of armed resistance. In Cebu, for example, three enumerators were attacked by "ladrones," although as Sanger retold it, the story resulted in proof of Filipino loyalty to the United States when one of the enumerators "stood off his assailants and saved his schedules. Such devotion indicated a very high sense of honor and duty." As this case indicates, while the census was meant to mark symbolically a shift in political time, it was in practice carried out as a political litmus test, with the absence of resistance—or the strength of Filipino collaboration—standing as evidence of consensus. "The fact that no such opposition was made," Sanger wrote of one town, "is conclusive evidence of the friendly attitude of the *principalía* in all the towns, and hence of the masses, toward the census." But Sanger's own ambivalent description of Filipino defenses against "ladrones" left some doubt in this regard. "[T]he Filipinos universally detested these disturbers," he noted, ". . . whatever their feelings might be toward the Americans."[118]

While armed resistance was unusual, more subtle forms of resistance were widespread and, by all accounts, far more difficult to overcome. The majority of this opposition apparently derived from Filipino memories of the Spanish census, which, according to Sanger, "was notoriously hateful to the Filipinos, being regarded as the basis of taxation and conscription." In a few locations, "attempts were made to prevent a census by circulating malicious reports as to its object, which was alleged to be taxation." As a result, census officials did everything possible to advertise differences between Spanish and American census goals. For example, in Iligan, an enumerator named Kennon found that "[o]ne of the sultans of the district refused absolutely to give any information whatever . . . not even his objections." Kennon discovered, however, that the man opened up some-what once Kennon was able to communicate that the census had nothing to do with taxation, as it had under the Spanish. More at ease, the sultan then claimed he had "feared that we wanted to make them dress like white folks and Filipinos; that we wanted to make them wear shoes and hats and cut off their hair." Kennon included the story didactically, "to illustrate the difficulty often experienced in getting into communication with the peo-ple," the central task of the collaborationist regime.[119]

The census was an expression of the new racial state in its simultaneous employment of, and denigration of, Filipino habits of mind within the census-taking process. While the census plan was "quite simple" and its schedules "easily understood," for example, Sanger noted that "their prac-tical application proved to be beyond the ability of many of the enumera-tors and special agents, and even of some of the supervisors." While he suggested that this was "not due so much to a want of intelligence as to a lack of experience," his explanation of these lapses suggested otherwise. A number of Filipino census-takers "were apparently incapable of reasoning from analogy or of applying the instructions to any case not covered by them directly, or of taking the initiative in meeting emergencies or in providing remedies." This did not necessarily reflect "on the natural ca-pacity of the Filipinos, because there is plenty of that," but illustrated "a Filipino trait" of "mistak[ing] ability to theorize freely for practical knowledge." Due to these problems of rationality, many of the governor-supervisors had left Manila erroneously believing that they understood census procedure; "mistakes more or less serious were made," although the most serious of them had been discovered and corrected in time.[120]

Sanger suggested they might have been prevented by greater centralized supervision by himself and his assistants but that the limits of transport and communication had made this an impossibility.

The content of the census also contained evaluative information about Filipinos gathered from numerous witnesses, laying bare the peculiar failings that made them, at least for the moment, "incapable" of complete self-government. Sanger was somewhat delicate in introducing these features, noting that they had been "obtained from persons who, on account of personal contact with them, were thought competent to express an opinion." While a great deal more might be written, "any opinion which may be formed regarding them, unless based on experience and close observation, would prove of very little value." Among their chief assets as potential citizens was subservience to authority; Hispanicized Filipinos were said to be generally "subordinate to lawful authority," and under competent officers, they made "excellent soldiers, and will, in the course of time, it is believed, make good citizens." But they lacked sufficient rationality, illustrated by "the superstitions which seem to permeate the entire race." These interfered greatly with everyday life and caused "much unnecessary anxiety and suffering" and sometimes "serious crime." Sanger held out hope, however, that these obstructive beliefs would "disappear as the people become more intelligent and rational and therefore less inclined to believe in bogies of any kind."[121]

Most important, though, the census—like the rest of the colonial state apparatus—formally installed the administrative difference between Christians and non-Christians, making Hispanic "civilization" the most important state racial boundary line in the process. Non-Christians were formally placed outside the trajectory of devolutionary political time. The census's founding protocols stated that the project was to begin when peace had been established outside of non-Christian areas. The legislative assembly would be inaugurated two years after its publication, assuming "recognition of the authority of the United States" had continued "in the territory of said Islands not inhabited by Moros or other non-Christian tribes." Furthermore, that assembly would inherit part of the authority formerly invested in the commission "in all that part of said islands not inhabited by Moros or other non-Christian tribes." But the census also marked the difference in terms of its procedure. "Such a wide difference in the state of the people suggested a variety in methods of census procedure," wrote Sanger. He emphasized the special difficulties of conducting the census among non-Christians. "In dealing with the Christian or civilized peoples it was decided to follow American methods of census taking," he wrote, "and in the enumeration of the wild, or non-Christian peoples, to follow any plan found practicable." The "greatest caution" had been called for "in dealing with all the non-Christian tribes," in order to avoid "raising suspicions and active opposition." In some cases, armed parties that had been organized as escorts were "instructed to use force, if necessary, to protect the census officials." Happily, however, with only one exception, "no hostile attempt was made to prevent the work of the census of the non-Christian tribes."[122]

While Filipinos' intellectual flaws had been exposed by the census, Americans nonetheless heralded the project as a Filipino triumph, consistent with the Taft regime's logic of tutelage in self-government. "I have dwelt on the organization and operations of the census at length," explained Sanger, "because this is said to be the first attempt, on the part of any tropical people in modern times, to make an enumeration of themselves." Of the 7,627 persons engaged, all but 125 (118 Americans, 1 Japanese, and 6 Chinese) had been Filipinos, so "it may be said, in all sincerity, that it was a Filipino census of the Philippine Islands." If the census had been a successful test of Filipino "capacity," it was also meant to serve as evidence of the uniquely uplifting, educative, and integrating character of the colonial state. Succinctly expressing the narratives of tutelage and benevolent assimilation, Sanger stated that

> under the guidance of a free, just, and generous government, the establishment of more rapid and frequent means of communication, whereby they can be brought into more frequent contact with each other, and, with the general spread of education, the tribal distinctions which now exist will gradually disappear and the Filipinos will become a numerous and homogeneous, English speaking race, exceeding in intelligence and capacity all other people of the Tropics.[123]

The virtues of the state, however, clearly outweighed those of the Filipinos. In his conclusion, Sanger made the political message of the census explicit, emphasizing that "it will be very apparent to the reader that the great need of the Philippines is moral, material, and industrial improvement, rather than political advancement, for which they are not as yet prepared." The direct targets here were anti-imperialist critics. While his conclusions were "apparent to any honest and intelligent investigator of Philippine conditions," efforts had been made "to create a very different impression." Like the commission's hearings and published reports, the census was meant to close debate by introducing irrefutable expertise, having "sought the facts by all available means." The census would have "achieved a lasting and beneficial purpose" if it succeeded "in settling these questions beyond reasonable doubt," "terminating false reports and hurtful agitation in the process," and "making plain the duty of the Government as well as of all patriotic Americans toward the Filipinos."[124]

BY 1903, THE Philippine Commission had succeeded in the contradictory tasks involved in building a Filipino-American colonial state. Lacking sufficient "machinery" for an administration staffed with a majority of Americans and confronting ambitious Filipino elites eager for a state of their own, the commission had recognized and empowered Filipino collaborators at all levels, from the municipalities to Manila, and sought maximum autonomy from domestic U.S. politics. Although army officers reluctantly surrendered power, the commission had successfully weathered the tensions of succession. It had established its expertise as the rationale for its rule, against military, anti-imperialist, and Filipino opponents. New political circumstances called especially for different visions of race. As one expression of its expertise, the civilian leadership had developed a new vision of Filipinos, casting them not as a "savage" bloc to be routed and suppressed as a whole but as a divided population of "little brown brothers" deserving of American benevolence and tutelage. This new vision required dispensing officially with the exclusionary and exterminist racism to which at least some Americans remained prone but that was incompatible with the success of collaboration. It meant developing an inclusionary racial formation built on interlocking metaphors of family, evolution, and tutelary assimilation. These racial formations—meant to rationalize collaboration—developed in dialogue with Hispanicized Filipino elites. Indeed, the recognition of these elites helped sharpen the dividing line—already present in the Spanish colonial period—between them and those "outside" Hispanic civilization, the islands' animist and Muslim populations. The new racial formation was, as a result, bifurcated at Catholicism, with Catholic Filipinos on one evolutionary track and non-Christians on another. As in the nineteenth century, Hispanicized Filipinos would often insist on the rigorous distinction between themselves and non-Christians, and their accidental and deliberate confusion by Americans would be a constant source of friction throughout the American colonial period. Where Catholic Filipinos were given administrative authority over non-Christians, it was part of a promise, and a test, of devolved colonialism. Because non-Christians were outside the trajectory of devolution, they could also be used as a lever for retentionists where Hispanicized Filipinos were seen to be insufficiently capable of taking up "the white man's burden" for themselves.

But a colonial state's success was not only to be measured in its incorporation and manipulation of local elites but in the success with which it could promote its message and rationalize its existence in the metropole. As Sanger had observed, the Philippine Census had been one significant step in this direction, if a limited one. This was, it seemed, a task better suited to an exposition. Europeans had been staging colonialism in their capital cities since the mid-nineteenth century and, indeed, colonialism had even overtaken some of these events, resulting in special "colonial expositions." Expositions, in theory, offered a vast landscape for enacting the distant and alien colonial dramas, inviting, in the present case, mass participation in what were relatively exclusive fantasies of uplift, tutelage, and assimilation. They also offered possibilities to continue the ritual work of the Santa Cruz bridge, connecting Filipino and American collaborators by familiarizing Filipinos with American society and, at the same time, providing them an intimidating view of their colonial masters' industrial supremacy. But building an actual bridge across the Pasig, or a metaphorical one between Americans and Filipinos in the Philippines, was also different from building a bridge between the emerging Philippine colonial state and metropolitan U.S. society.

Mixed Messages at the
St. Louis World's Fair

*In furtherance of this determination to hold our reins of
government they have gone into the remotest corners of the
islands, gathered together the lowest types of the inhabitants
and brought them to this country to exhibit them in an
attempt to justify their paternal grip on the islands.*

VICENTE NEPOMUCENO, 1904

*The problem is how and where to draw the color line on the
Filipinos who have been brought to the Fair.*

St. Louis Post Dispatch, 1904

By April 1903, a small but important part of St. Louis's
Louisiana Purchase Exposition was taking shape in the bowels of Manila's
Bilibid prison, constructed by the Spanish colonial state as a safe and final
home for its heretics, dissenters, and rebels. The U.S. Army had taken
control of Bilibid during its occupation of Manila in 1898; during and after
the Philippine-American War, it had filled its dank cells with "insurrectos" whom it could not persuade to declare loyalty to the United
States. As the architecture of the colonial racial state emerged—as manifested in such projects as the census—Bilibid was discovered to have a
unique role to play in its outlines for two distinct reasons. First, it was
a monument either to the geographic breadth of Filipino resistance or
to the long, brutal arms of the respective Spanish and American colonial states, or both, that no other existing institution in the archipelago
boasted such a vast diversity of racial "types." As Daniel Folkmar, a physical anthropologist employed by the Bureau of Non-Christian Tribes, put
it, Bilibid offered "an unexcelled collection of the leading ~~tribes~~ [sic] peoples from Northern Luzon to Mindanao." Second, there were the repressive conditions of the prison itself, which Folkmar believed highly conducive to anthropological study. Folkmar had been approached by David
Barrows, formerly of the bureau, and Gustavo Niederlein, secretary of the

Philippine Exposition Board, who believed that "the conditions found in Bilibid should be utilized in the interests of the Exposition and of the scientific work of the Bureau."[1]

Specifically, Folkmar had been charged with measuring, photographing, and plaster-casting the heads of prisoners for display in St. Louis. The project was funded by the exposition board and supervised by Barrows, but Folkmar attributed its success to the "hearty co-operation of the Warden" and other prison officials. He had been allowed to use the jail's photographic equipment and was given a workshop and a team of prisoners (mostly Americans) as his assistants. "The conditions of the work were so favorable that the Prison might with reason be called a great anthropological laboratory," he noted. For one, the prison context proved effective in compelling would-be scientific subjects to submit to examination. "It is needless to say that it was easier to handle the prisoners than would have been the case on the outside," he wrote, "since they thought themselves required to submit to the processes of plaster-casting and disrobing for photographs, as in the case of the ordinary prison regulations." But as Folkmar labored "with a strange fascination and conflicting emotions," he acknowledged that violence always lay behind the prison's ideal conditions. Some years later, he recalled one evening in which he had gone out "to hunt up natives of a certain type in a big crowd that was gathered around the main entrance" of the prison and noticed "that the machine gun standing above them was trained down upon the crowd." Folkmar came to learn that there was "some sort of mutiny threatened" and was urged by the warden to lock himself in his shop in case of violence. "It was after I left that a similar crowd was mown down like grass under the fire of the same machine gun," he noted.[2]

This chapter suggests some of the ways that events such as the 1904 St. Louis fair emerged out of colonial institutions and dynamics like those at Bilibid. Most historical accounts of world's fairs take into account only the metropolitan structures that shaped them, especially the agendas and activities of civic and entrepreneurial elites. By contrast, this chapter will explore the Philippine exhibit at St. Louis at the tense intersection of metropolitan and colonial histories like Folkmar's. The massive display— the largest at St. Louis and one of the largest colonial exhibits to that time—did convey hegemonic messages about race, capitalism, and U.S. national superiority. But it also filled forty-seven acres with elaborately crafted spectacles designed to convey to U.S. audiences messages tailored to a certain moment in the development of the colonial state: that the

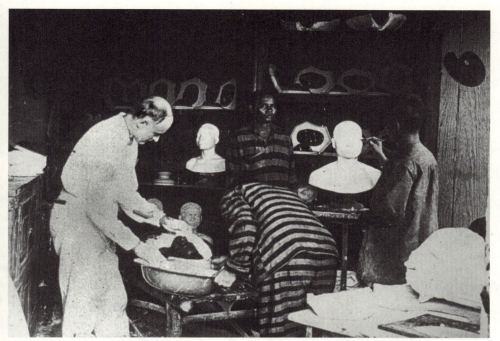

This photograph of anthropologist Daniel Folkmar supervising Filipino prisoners in his physical anthropology laboratory at Bilibid prison suggests the intersections of colonial state, racial knowledge, and exposition culture. When the Philippine Commission authorized participation in the 1904 Louisiana Purchase Exposition at St. Louis as an advertisement for a "postwar" Philippine occupation, Folkmar was charged with producing anthropological studies and plaster busts of the Philippine population; Bilibid prison provided what he considered an ideal environment. The image suggests the need to approach exposition-building as colonial history as well as metropolitan, urban history. Reproduced with permission, National Anthropological Archives, Smithsonian Institution (#98-10096, Folder 759, USNM Manuscript and Pamphlet File).

Philippine "insurrection" was over; that under U.S. control, a highly diverse set of Philippine "natives" were on parallel paths to progress; and that tariff reform and export-oriented capitalism were necessary to maintain and accelerate this process.[3]

The organization and collection of displays was, like the census, made possible through—and contributed to—ongoing state-building processes in the Philippines, especially the recognition of Filipino elites. Americans knew that Filipino cooperation in the making of the exhibit was absolutely necessary; the process would also potentially convey prestige to Filipino elites and cement ties between them and U.S. colonial officials. The project was cast as having the added benefit of being an effective means of assimilation. By participating in their own "exposition," Filipinos would expose themselves to and absorb American ways, customs, and loyalties.

As the exposition board charged with organizing the exhibit soon discovered, however, neither Philippine nor U.S. society proved as easy to manipulate as Bilibid prison (which had itself not proven so easy to control). There were fundamental questions of authority and recognition to be resolved. Would the exhibit be in the charge of metropolitan or colonial authorities? What role would Filipinos, the necessary organizers and mediators of the collection process, play in the exhibit's conceptualization? There were basic questions of spatial organization. Where would Philippine materials belong in the dense symbolic tapestry of the fair? Would the Philippines be "incorporated" into the United States or remain "unincorporated"? There were basic problems of possession: to whom would the collected exhibits, purchased almost exclusively with the taxes and revenues of the colonial state, actually belong? Perhaps most of all, there were problems of communication. Controlling the means of representation did not mean controlling modes of interpretation. American audiences would view the exhibit through lenses prepared for them by prior wartime representations of Filipinos, by St. Louis journalists, and by the expectations they drew from long-standing exposition conventions. Filipino participants and spectators also took away their own, sometimes unintended, messages. These readings tended to undermine U.S. colonialists' boundless faith that proximity always bred loyalty and one-way assimilation. In compelling Filipinos to expose themselves before American audiences, U.S. officials were inadvertently exposing more of the United States to Filipinos than they might have liked.

War and Exposition

The impact that colonial factors had on the making of metropolitan expositions became evident in the first successful attempt to mount a Philippine exhibit at a U.S. exposition, for the 1901 Buffalo Pan-American Exposition, carried out during the Philippine-American War. The eventual contents of that display would be fundamentally shaped by the context of war. According to one account, the fair's commission had been "anxious to have on the grounds a typical Filipino village inhabited by genuine natives—men, women, and children." But such hopes had been curtailed by the realities of ongoing warfare in the islands. Government officials with whom the commission consulted appeared uninterested, suggesting that such a display would cost $150,000 to $175,000, a sum, they believed, "greatly in excess of what would have been necessary in more peaceful times." The organizers were nonetheless "anxious to have an exhibit of some kind," claiming that "the sentiment of the people demanded it." They appropriated $10,000 to procure a more limited exhibit of "purely ethnological specimens" and placed these funds in the hands of the Smithsonian Institution for the purposes of collection.[4]

The decision to enlist the Smithsonian suggested the problematic status of the Philippines at that particular moment. Typically, colonial states collected their own displays at international expositions, but the U.S. Army was precisely in the process, still incomplete, of crushing a prior state and imposing its own. Just three years earlier, the Philippines could have appeared as part of Spain's colonial exhibition (although Spain's ongoing suppression of the Philippine Revolution might have prevented it). Were the Philippine Republic not engaged in defending its very existence, it might have mounted its own display as representative of its nationality and civilization. As U.S. officials' anticipation of "more peaceful times" suggested, at some indefinite point in the future, the islands might appear as part of a U.S. government exhibit. But in late 1899, there was no state on the ground capable of organizing such a display.

Smithsonian officials had been attempting to gain access to the Philippines from the advent of the U.S. occupation. Just three weeks after the Spanish surrender, the acting chief of the Bureau of American Ethnology, W J McGee, began a persistent and largely unsuccessful attempt to maneuver the Smithsonian into position as the dominant engine of colonial investigation.[5] McGee suggested to his superiors that the bureau's legal constitution be amended to include the phrase "and other aborigines of American territory" and that an additional $12,000 appropriation be made for insular studies but was unable to convince the congressional appropriations committee to widen its jurisdiction. But the Smithsonian could carry out colonial studies by other means. In January 1899, John Wesley Powell, chief of the bureau, suggested that the Smithsonian's work be extended to the new territories through close association with the State Department and with diplomatic and consular personnel who might be able to forward information about "natives" and antiquities.[6]

Together, the Pan-American Exposition and the Smithsonian would organize an exhibit in the absence of an on-the-ground colonial state. With the exposition funds, McGee directed the bureau's "ethnologic translator," Frank Hilder, to travel and assemble a Philippine exhibit under the auspices of the U.S. government exhibit, which would be displayed at Buffalo and later pass into the hands of the U.S. National Museum through a newly formed "Special Committee on Outlying Possessions." Hilder, the bureau's only Spanish speaker, was a former colonel in the British army and saw his collection project as commensurable with colonial investigations undertaken by the British Empire. "We have learned a great deal during the present century," he wrote, "as to the best methods of dealing with barbarous people and now we have presented to us a similar problem in the territories that have fallen into our hands by the fortunes of war."[7] As it had in the British Empire, he believed, a museum collection would contribute to the kind of knowledge required for successful empire-building.

By January 1900, Hilder had received formal approval for his expedition and directions that made him the collecting agent of the U.S. government as a whole. The following month, he set out for San Francisco and sailed to Manila, arriving at the end of March and setting briskly about his work. He engaged Penoyer Sherman, a young photographer and assistant to Dean Worcester, and began six weeks of extensive travel, negotiation, and haggling. U.S. Army resources were central to this work. The secretary of war had already approved the use of military transports to move exposition materials, and upon Hilder's appointment, the military was sent circulars "advising all officers and enlisted men of the army of the U.S. . . . and requesting them to co-operate with these gentlemen in securing objects of interest for this Exposition."[8]

But even with military support, Hilder faced tremendous wartime obstacles. Along with widespread disease there was the lack of mobility, which made him dependent on Manila's markets. Second was the effect the devastation of the war had taken on agricultural and industrial production: Hilder had been sent to collect the fruits of fields that had been burned, abandoned, and covered with the bodies of its farmers. Sherman reported that it was a "bad time for collecting certain articles, as for instance, medical herbs." Hilder related that this was because Filipinos were refusing to collect herbs for drug stores, "on account of the great danger of being shot while seen hunting around in the woods." The fear proved to be worth heeding. Sherman reported to Hilder at one point, "[y]ou will be sorry to hear that the native who brought the weaving machine for me has been murdered by the insurgents. . . . Many are captured outside Manila by ladrones, as a result but few curios find their way here."[9]

Hilder's greatest problem, however, may have been the U.S. military itself. Military officials who had pledged to cooperate with him did so reluctantly for reasons of competition; General Otis had himself been ordered to make "a collection of war relics, arms &c" for the War Department. Even worse, many desirable items had been quickly snatched up by what Sherman called "the curio crazy volunteers." "[C]urios are getting more expensive every day," he wrote, "all the army officers wives (and hundreds are now here) are collecting without rhyme or reason, and unless a man can go himself and pick and choose he will get unmercifully cheated." The military police, responsible for confiscating rebel goods, had amassed artifacts, but "every officer is running his own collection, and so there is nothing on hand!"[10]

Facing sharpened competition, Hilder and Sherman were still able to gather a collection of "upwards of a thousand pieces." Not surprisingly, the collection was weighted toward industrial and agricultural products and captured armaments. If medicinal plants had proven impossible to obtain during wartime, the advance of the Americans had produced a crop of weapons taken from the Filipino rebels. In exchange for the cooperation of the War Department, Hilder had been instructed to collect "trophies of the war," including "'[c]lothing worn by the Filipinos, insignia of rank of all soldiers, such as shoulder straps, knots, cords, swords, sabres, knives, pistols, belts &c &c.'" Hilder continued to pressure Otis and finally received permission to collect artifacts directly out of the arsenal, yielding among other items one of the insurgents' bamboo cannons held together with telegraph wire.[11]

If the wartime context produced a stockpile of Philippine weapons for

American museums, it also widened the field for the collection of Filipinos' bones. By April, Sherman had already contracted with a Captain Parker to provision the museum with skulls. After Hilder's return to Washington, Sherman continued to collect, reporting, "I have eight skulls to go to you, and with request that you let me know if more are desired." The commodity was not "to be had in Manila or suburbs," he wrote, "and it was only by sending way out for them that we got any at all." Frustrated at having failed to obtain an Igorot skeleton—"simply because I had no good way of getting far enough north"—the young collector suggested the possibilities for a dovetailing of military and scientific goals. "What ought to be done," he wrote Hilder, "is for the Natl. Museum or the Smithsonian to get an order on the Military authorities here notifying some one here every time an igorrote or negrito was to be hanged so that the agent would have time to make arrangements to secure the brain, skull or whatever else was wanted. Some *fine* material could be secured in that way."[12]

By June 1900, Hilder was back in Washington beginning to label and organize the exhibit, while Sherman continued to ship new material. He was at work until March the following year, when he fell ill and died abruptly of pneumonia. Nonetheless, the Pan-American Exposition and the government's "Colonial Exhibit" opened in spring 1901, giving its audience a first exposition of the territory being conquered. One visitor reporting on the display noted that Hilder had done "remarkably well under the circumstances." Although it lacked live natives, the display illustrated "every phase of native life." Its primary emphasis was on industrial items, such as hats, canes, and looms, and agricultural tools, but there were also many "[f]orcible illustrations" of weaponry, including bolos and krises that were "enough to give one an inspiration of fear."[13]

As if to deliver the earliest possible packages of "uplift," U.S. military organizers of new public schools in Manila—the only place such schools had opened—had provided Hilder with photographs from about forty schools along with examples of student work. At least one response suggested that such displays might succeed in conveying a sense of Filipino assimilation. Charles Spahr, an official in the New York Anti-Imperialist League, had been impressed by the samples, especially by English-language work that demonstrated Filipino children's "remarkable talent for acquiring a foreign language." Indeed, the strongest impression Spahr had taken away from the exhibit was "the similarity of the civilization shown to [that of] our own people." Filipinos and Americans were similar even in the way they were sometimes misrecognized in transnational contexts. He knew of American friends, for example, who had traveled to Europe and encountered "cultivated" people who had nonetheless "thought that an American was at least part Indian." These "misconceptions of America" were "not much more grotesque than certain prevalent misconceptions of the Philippines." As Spahr pointed out, the exposition form itself heightened possibilities for misrecognition. "[I]n all such collections," he observed, prophetically, "the desire for the peculiar and picturesque is likely to get the better of the desire for the fairly representative."[14]

Colonial Display as State-Building

By 1902, Philippine-American statelessness was no longer the problem, although the colonial state still faced formidable obstacles. There was ongoing Filipino military resistance and tension between civilian officials and the army. In the United States, anti-imperialist critics continued to raise questions about American policy, and Congress remained reluctant to enact tariffs preferential to the colony. Confronted with these issues and eager to promote successful civilian rule in the islands—and the end of war—Governor-General Taft, President Roosevelt, and Secretary of War Root decided in spring 1902 upon a costly appeal to the metropolitan U.S. public, one that began with an initial $250,000 appropriation from insular funds. They would use the insular government's new political, technological, and informational resources, currently under construction in the Philippines, to build an immense advertisement for civilian rule in the colonies. Taft made plain the agenda of gaining recognition for the commission's government during a trip to St. Louis in April 1902.

> We are more deeply interested in that Exposition than any others. This Exposition comes at a critical point in the history of the Philippines. We are at a point where there prevails misinformation, misunderstanding, and an unconscious misrepresentation regarding us. Nothing, I think, can bring the two peoples together to promote friendly and trade relations between the States and the Archipelago so well as such an exhibit as I hope we will be able to make at your exposition.[15]

Looking ahead optimistically, Taft believed such an exhibit would put Philippine resources before the eyes of American consumers and investors and represent the islands as a pacified and positive investment climate in need of lowered tariffs. Within the context of an ongoing war (whose outcome was still unknown), it would also demonstrate symbolically a control of the islands that American troops were still, in fact, carving out. But Taft was also aware that, just as it would put the Philippines on display before American eyes, the exposition would unfold the United States before its new Filipino subjects, providing them an intimidating vision of its benevolent might and reconciling them to its colonial rule. In this sense, he was acknowledging the need to persuade Filipinos to recognize U.S. power. Soliciting the exposition company for an additional $100,000 for the exhibit, he noted that the goodwill engendered would "demonstrat[e] to the Filipinos the friendliness and sympathy of the United States." He also "made it clear that in his opinion the encouragement given by the exposition to the Filipino participation would be a very great influence in completing pacification and in bringing Filipinos to improve their condition."[16]

Taft's efforts to find domestic outlets for colonial propaganda paralleled initiatives from within the exposition. From its earliest planning stages, St. Louis elites had encouraged the participation of the new colonial governments, sensing an insatiable hunger for information about the nation's novel "possessions" that would summon the imaginations and billfolds of the consuming public. A few years earlier, wrote one official, there had been "little interest either on the part of Americans in the Far East and Australia, and Hawaii, or on their part for America." But "now the situation is entirely changed," as America was "looking across the Pacific as never before." This observer predicted that Asia would supply the most popular foreign concessions. "The great percentage of attendance at the fair will care more to see exhibits of the Philippines, China, and other Asiatic countries," he wrote, "than they will those of Europe and South America."[17] Organizers and concessionaires wanted to be in a position to satisfy and amplify, as well as profit from, this anticipated demand.

In making a central place for empire, exposition planners were adapting European cultural precedents. In aesthetic terms, the decision to have the colonial state mount a gigantic exhibit dedicated to its benevolence in the new "dependency" was not a statement about U.S. national exceptionalism but its opposite. European countries had long displayed their colonies at expositions, as public stages upon which to dramatize before metropolitan audiences the benefits of distant colonial wars and governments.[18] By 1904, such colonial displays had long been a central and anticipated element of European exhibition aesthetics and politics, beginning with the legendary 1851 Great Exhibition at London, with its famed Indian exhibit, and developing in scale and sophistication over the decades, parallel to (and informing) the widening politico-military and territorial claims of the European imperial powers. By the 1880s, there were expositions predominantly dedicated to colonialism, as was the Colonial Exposition at Amsterdam in 1883. Philippine colonial officials, War Department officials, and exhibition planners were all aware of, and drew on, these traditions. The exposition board's chief organizer, Gustavo Niederlein, was a German botanist and veteran of colonial expositions; he accepted the Philippine appointment following work for a French colonial exhibition.

If the exposition would, in theory, give political momentum to colonialism, the display would necessarily be constructed through new state machineries of empire. This became clearest in the process of negotiating with potential exhibitors from foreign governments. The fair was not merely symbolic of imperial developments but relied upon the growing network of consular officials and commercial agents that had made possible the growth of American trade and political power in Asia. In the fall of 1901, the exposition management, after conferring with the president and the secretary of state, "invited men of national and international reputation and extended experience in the diplomatic service" to act as U.S. government representatives in negotiations with foreign states. The State Department would send letters to its foreign ministers and ambassadors with requests that inquiries about the fair be filed with their host governments. "The Department will make it clear that the Exposition is to be one of international importance," reported the *World's Fair Bulletin*. "It will tell foreign governments of the big appropriation by Congress which has been made for the Fair, and that it is directly under government patronage. It will be made clear that the Fair, to a great extent, is a government institution."[19]

The blurred line between formal diplomacy and exposition recruitment can be seen in the career of John Barrett. Born in 1866, Barrett graduated from Dartmouth, entered a career in journalism, and traveled widely. As early as 1890, according to a brief biography, the young man had "recognized the importance of America's interests in the Far East" and become "identified with the progressive interests of the Pacific Coast." He was appointed the U.S. minister to Siam in 1894 and from that post began exhaustive studies of the "commercial and practical possibilities of other Asiatic countries," such as China, Japan, and the Philippines. At the outbreak of the Spanish-Cuban-American War, he had resigned his position and traveled to the Philippines as a special war correspondent, performing this task "with the particular approval of the State, War and Navy Departments." On his return to the United States, Barrett found himself "a recognized authority on Asia," widely published, and a frequent guest speaker.[20] Barrett's combination of extensive travel, diplomatic service, and business acumen made him the exposition planners' ideal candidate for the fair's "commissioner general" for Asia.

Barrett's task was not easy. Over twelve months and thousands of miles of travel in Asia and the greater Pacific, he had to persuade high officials in foreign governments that the costs of mounting impressive displays, and of their own travel to the fair, would be repaid in expanded commerce and greater international recognition. More difficult still, he had to sell Asian diplomats on the exposition itself as a setting for respectable cultural diplomacy. Barrett encountered substantial resistance on this last point. According to one report, there existed "a degree of prejudice among officials against expositions in general," and "all of them had at first either been averse to participation or declined to take part." While unspecified, this reluctance was "due to unhappy experiences in the past." On these occasions, Barrett countered by assuring his hosts that his effort was "to secure only high class participation on the part of Asiatic nations, and to discourage attempts to promote demoralizing or unwholesome features under the guise of worthy concessions." It was a policy with which "Asiatic monarchs and statesmen . . . heartily sympathized." Returning in spring 1903, Barrett declared his mission a success, with fifteen Asian countries committing over $2 million toward exposition displays.[21]

As in Barrett's case, the organization of the Philippine exhibit would be undertaken by the developing colonial state, under the leadership of metropolitan exposition experts. In November 1902, the commission appointed a Philippine Exposition Board responsible for the financing, organization, collection, assembly, and publicity of the insular exhibit, with an initial appropriation of $250,000. Its commissioner would be Dr. W. P. Wilson, a professor of botany at the University of Pennsylvania, prominent member of several Philadelphia-based scientific societies, and director of the Philadelphia Commercial Museum, which promoted U.S. foreign trade through the collection, display, and promotion of industrial and commercial goods.[22] Just as Barrett had, Wilson moved between diplomatic and exposition roles, having served as commercial attaché to the Pan-American Congress the previous year. As Wilson's assistant and "special commissioner," with the specific task of organizing the Philippine collection for the exhibit, the commission appointed Niederlein, an experienced collector who had represented the Commercial Museum at earlier expositions and in 1900 had been commissioned to classify colonial products for the French Ministry of Colonies.[23] Given the colonial regime's options, the choices of Wilson and Niederlein were notable for their metropolitan character and commercial emphasis. Most obviously, they were not American civil servants serving in the Philippines, as they might have been, but well-connected high officials associated with one of the nation's largest museums.

In these decisions and in its invitations, the exposition board made clear that it saw the exhibit first and foremost as "industrial" and "commercial." This was consistent with Taft's own hopes, which included the reduction or elimination of U.S. tariffs on Philippine products as the means to greater trade and state revenues. The result was an emphasis on the Philippines as a modern zone of production and, to a lesser extent, consumption and on Filipinos as laborers and consumers. This priority was clear in Niederlein's outline of the exhibit, which was to be a "great show of Philippine natural wealth" and "Philippine economic and social life." Among his intended publics, he prioritized "the capitalist and enterprising pioneer"; the exhibit should have special buildings for agriculture and forestry and one for "industrial and ethnological exhibits," including "a full exhibit of foreign goods imported to the Philippine Islands." It would also contain a "pueblo-market place" in which "the various Philippine industries will be presented in full process" and in which "the native tribes" would sell and buy. "Native manufacturers" would make sinamay, tinampipi, piña, and jusi cloth, while others would demonstrate the making of "hats and mats and other fine braided ware . . . cordage, essential oils, cigars and cigarettes, pottery, wood carving, gold and silver smith work, etc." Plantations of rice and tobacco, abaca, and piña plants would be "continually worked by the natives, before the visitors."[24]

In assembling materials for exhibition, the exposition board would turn first to the insular, provincial, and municipal governments that were simultaneously taking shape as the circle of pacification unsteadily widened. Just before the board's founding, Taft had issued a circular letter to all the chiefs of insular bureaus and to provincial and municipal officials "requesting them to assist Mr. Niederlein in every way as [a] commissioner of the insular government." The board also worked actively to take advantage of other state projects, such as the census, meeting with provincial governors who had been summoned to Manila in late 1902 to learn census procedures. Through the Bureau of Insular Affairs, the board requested that the secretary of war instruct the military in the Philippines "to order all men of the islands to cooperate with the exposition," to guarantee an exhibit that would "demonstrate in every detail the historical events and the achievements of the American Army in both military and administrative capacities."[25]

Along with enlisting government agents as collectors, the insular government facilitated collection by exempting exhibitors from taxes, granting free postage for small exhibit packages, and providing free telegraph privileges and free transportation on U.S. Army transports and Coast Guard vessels. For board members and colonial officials, exposition participation was state-building by other means: in lending their assistance and labor to the task, Filipinos would demonstrate their loyalty to the United States. As Niederlein put it, Filipino participants had given "a good proof of their high-spirited patriotic pride," which had induced them, "in the midst of extreme misery," to make a "supreme sacrifice" so that "the resources and conditions of their country might appear in a dignified manner before the civilized world."[26]

Beyond officials, the board would make direct appeals to the *ilustrado* class as a whole. The decision to place two prominent and well-connected *ilustrados* on the board was crucial to this strategy. Pedro Paterno, socialite and negotiator of the Treaty of Biak-na-Bato, was brought on to enlist his social networks; Leon Maria Guerrero, pharmacist and scientist, was enlisted for his extensive natural-historical knowledge. The Federalista organ *La Democracia*—read by Filipino officials and *ilustrados* in general—pushed exposition circulars, instructions, and calls for participation onto its front pages. In addition, the board sent out more than 116,000 letters and more than 51,000 pamphlets with collection and shipping instructions in Spanish, Tagalog, Visayan, Ilocano, Bicol, Pampangan, and Pangasinan. Approximately 20,000 posters were circulated, made "in imitation of World's Fair posters," bearing "the pictures of Presidents McKinley and Roosevelt, and Jefferson, Napoleon, Rizal, and Governor Taft."[27] First, the board offered these participants the exposure of exportable goods before an American public. The board's circular advertised St. Louis to Filipino would-be participants: the city was "the fourth manufacturing city of the world" and would be visited during the exposition by "the buyers of all the important houses of all the nations of the world."[28] The board also offered recognition, cultural prestige, and semi-official patronage in the form of a loosely sketched "scientific" society for which participants would automatically qualify. The society, which would title itself "Philippine Academy of Science, Art, Trade, and Industry, or the Philippine Geographical, Economic, and Scientific Society, or Philippine National Museum of Commerce and Industry, Natural History, Ethnography, Art and Science," would, it was hoped, attract *ilustrado* participation by flavoring "patriotic pride" with intellectual pretension.[29]

In spite of these inducements, Niederlein and the exposition board found many Filipinos reluctant to participate. "At the beginning the Board failed in many endeavors," Niederlein was forced to admit.[30] Like the Asian statesmen courted by Barrett, Philippine commercial and political elites were not convinced it was in their interest to participate in the regime's exposition, and Niederlein and his associates "met with many rebuffs."[31] Of those offered membership in the "Philippine Academy of Sciences," for example, "scarcely half a dozen of the invited professional men . . . helped to collaborate or offered their services." Committees of art, women's committees, and the press committees were "[s]imilar failures."[32] This was likely due to emerging political tensions between the insular government and the elites upon which the board was relying, tensions of which Niederlein was probably unaware.

Among these early failures had been the initial noncooperation of provincial and municipal Filipino officials. Indeed, the exposition illustrated a tug-of-war between insular and provincial governments in which Niederlein and the board were closely identified as "insular" agents. The tension went to the very heart of the colonial state. The exposition, like the colonial state more generally, relied fundamentally on Filipino collaborators. As one observer, a Professor Lyon, put it, "a thousand years" of exposition expertise could "do nothing creditable without the intelligent and earnest cooperation of the citizens of these islands."[33] But recognition of Filipino elites did not mean trusting them; indeed, the United States' power to recognize authorities in the Philippines was predicated on Filipino "incapacities" in which "corruption" featured prominently. Should the exposition board direct money to provincial governors, or allow local funds to be used for the collection of artifacts, the board feared, much of it would end up in the hands of "caciques."

As a result, Niederlein complained, the exposition board had had to comply with the rules of the insular purchasing agent and auditor, and provincial boards were not empowered to budget funds for collection, so that "the most effective way of obtaining exhibits was closed." While denied funding for collection, provincial boards may also have been withholding cooperation for broader political reasons: Niederlein pointed out that the provinces had also been denied $100,000 they had "unanimously requested" from the commission "to overcome the immense difficulties against successful work . . . produced by rinderpest, surra, cholera, and locusts, ladronism, and the consequences of former revolutions."[34] Through the board, the insular government was, in effect, making demands on provincial governors that it refused to fund or trust and pushing on them exposition tasks they felt were irrelevant to more pressing concerns.

A veteran of international expositions, Niederlein found himself completely at sea. "All other systems and ways for obtaining the necessary collections were tried," he wrote, "one after another and then together," but "in this country and under the existing conditions not with the usual results." The board turned somewhat desperately to a number of new strategies. "Nothing was left undone," Niederlein reported. Key figures were encouraged to lend "moral influence" to the undertaking, including Emilio Aguinaldo. Most ambitiously, the board inaugurated a "Permanent Museum" in Manila where, it was promised, the collections were to be housed and made available to predominantly Filipino audiences following the exposition. In such a museum, local manufacturers would be able "to exhibit their cigars, cigarettes, artistic furniture, gold and silver ware, products of art, or of domestic industries, etc."[35]

The relationship between the "museum" and the exposition remained vague: once mounted in Manila, it would at some point be transformed into a "preliminary exposition" that would eventually be transported to St. Louis but, presumably, returned. The strategy apparently achieved results. At its opening, the museum already contained "thousands of selected exhibits, obtained from over a hundred exhibitors."[36] Along with promised material benefit, the museum provided a setting for fiesta politics. In the names of the civil governor, the commission, and the exposition board, more than 2,000 invitations were issued for its ceremonial opening in February 1903, held on George Washington's birthday. The event, attended by top insular officials, was apparently "a great success," eliciting "favorable comments" that "greatly influenced the Filipino people at large to make further contributions."[37]

The board also won cooperation by appealing to more pecuniary motivations, against its initial inclinations. Ultimately, a solution would be found in the release of "unlimited funds, to be used at the last moment in obedience to the law when no more gratuitous contributions could be expected." The board persuaded the exposition company to grant it all the royalties from commercial concessions in the Philippine exhibit, which brought in an "estimated" additional $1 million. It subsequently leveraged an additional $100,000 from the company, in the form of a loan that the insular government promised it would repay if Congress failed to. The commission also doubled its funding for the project, to $500,000. Throughout 1903, these funds were released with an abandon that suggested the board's desperation and the victory of expedience over wariness. The board sponsored "a number of collectors and men willing to gather exhibits in their spare time throughout the islands" and "advanced money to such private parties as school teachers, scientific collectors, and college principals."[38]

The central government had lost its battle with the provinces. The board "proposed to give the provincial governors pecuniary aid," asking them to state "the amount required to collect creditable exhibits in their provinces for the museum and the world's fair." Niederlein confessed that this method had been necessary to success and defensively noted that it had been undertaken "on a business basis." The board eventually voted to provide each provincial governor with 500 pesos, but it was a sign of continued suspicion that in May 1903 an executive order was issued recalling all unspent funds to the treasury, while governors were authorized to spend immediately the rest of their funds for "exhibits of exceptional merit." While "large amounts of new exhibits arrived," this retreat was a sign of the insular government's relative weakness with regard to provincial authorities. Attempting to impose central, insular power, the board had illuminated its reliance on local collaborators.[39]

Tensions of Representation

But who would be recognized to represent the Philippines at St. Louis? And who would have the power to decide? Both metropolitan and colonial organizers agreed that Filipino martial forces were crucial "representatives." As early as December 1902, exposition president David Francis had written to the secretary of war that, while he already understood that the Philippine exhibit would include "several hundred representatives of Filipino tribes," the fair "very much desires that a battalion of four companies of native Filipino troops be camped on the Exposition Grounds." Conveniently, the seventy-five acres set aside for military organizations were adjacent to the reservation for the Philippine exhibit, allowing them to play a key role in the spectacle. There were also cost and logistical advantages, as "the preserve of Filipino troops would materially aid in the policing of the Philippine exhibit reservation."[40] Colonial officials debated amongst themselves, however, whether to bring Constabularymen or Scout troops. Maj. Gen. George Davis of the U.S. Army recommended the better-paid and, he believed, better-disciplined Constabulary; he also suggested that sending the two forces together would result in tensions over pay differentials. Taft believed the Scouts were suitably disciplined and would "present a most soldierly appearance, especially if they are put under a competent Army officer who shall have charge of them and who can exercise that Army discipline over them which is so useful in a large city like St. Louis."[41]

One essential question was which of the ethnically organized Scout companies to bring. Davis had, for example, cautioned against bringing Tagalogs, "the most numerous and the most dangerous to the peace of the islands," warned that it would be "inexpedient or unwise to mingle the Macabebes and the Tagalogs," as "these two tribes are not on pleasant terms."[42] By the middle of 1903, four companies had been selected—one Macabebe, one Ilocano, one Visayan, and one Tagalog—whose "tribal" pluralism sent conflicting messages. On the one hand, it suggested an effort to break down tribalism by pooling from diverse groups; on the other, it plainly illustrated the state's role as an instrument for institutionalizing tribal distinctions. Within these units, a far stricter selection process than normal was employed, paradoxically, to guarantee a representative demonstration unit. When the companies were gathered in July at Caloocan, they were drilled, questioned, and inspected by U.S. officers, and individual members were specially selected for their discipline. The First Provisional Battalion, created for world's fair service only, eventually consisted of 1,369 Filipino enlisted men and 59 American officers; it continued to drill until February 1904, when it was moved to Manila and subsequently sent to San Francisco.

Some argued that the most "representative" Filipinos would be those already recognized by the colonial state, collaborating political elites who could serve in an honorary capacity at the exposition. One version of the idea was put forward in June 1903, when Col. E. J. McClernand, former governor of Cebu, recommended that "representative men—leaders—[be] sent to St. Louis from the Philippines . . . from the different islands." Such elites' "immediate contact" with exposition visitors would have a "much better and more lasting effect than the mere presence of some of the Philippine Scouts, or Constabulary." While McClernand was not opposed to troop displays, they would not do as much "to enable the American and Filipino to study and know each other, something very much to be desired." Collaborating Hispanicized Filipinos were imagined not only as displays but as spectators undergoing assimilation: witnessing St. Louis and its technological wonders would contribute to their tutelage in duty and loyalty. "[T]he impressions made on the more intelligent natives," he advised, "will be used to better advantage on their return home."[43]

But the idea of bringing an "honorary" body of elites was potentially troublesome in political terms. International expositions in the late nineteenth century were powerful sites for the recognition of the status of states in the international order. As with Barrett, invitations to participate were granted only to recognized states—and to their recognized heads—often through diplomatic channels. That recognition, in turn, authorized those states to represent themselves through official delegations that were empowered to conduct actual diplomacy. Such exhibits could include demonstrations of a state's colonial projects, but colonies did not, by definition, send delegates; they could not represent themselves but must be represented. If it decided for a body of Filipino elites, the exposition board would blur genres: in line with the United States' claims that the Philippines was not its colony but a polity under tutelage, its exposition would contain within it a delegation closely resembling diplomats—learning the arts of diplomacy through observation—without formally recognized diplomatic powers. This was a fine line, however, that collaborating elites might choose not to recognize.

When it drafted authorizing legislation, the exposition board did decide to include five "honorary commissioners," who were to be "representative Filipinos." This commission was to travel to St. Louis and serve officially at the fair in a representative capacity; if desired, members would also have "the right to visit Washington to pay respects to the President of the United States."[44] By 1903, the commission had increased the delegation to between thirty and fifty members. Its objective was twofold: to expose the collaborating elites to an impressive, intimidating vision of American power as well as to represent the Philippine people before American audiences.

Who was to be recognized as part of this select class of representatives was, however, complicated in light of sudden shifts in the colonial regime. These were triggered by tensions over internal revenue policies and Constabulary abuses, but most decisively by Taft's decision to leave for Washington to take up the position of secretary of war in late 1903 and his replacement by the far less accommodating commissioner Luke Wright, formerly secretary of commerce and police. A former Confederate soldier from Tennessee, Wright dramatically altered the terms of collaboration, calling for a regime based on "business principles," which for him meant more "efficient" control of the government by Americans. His defense of Constabulary excesses, his refusal to engage in fiesta politics, and his open social exclusion of Filipinos from official functions alienated the regime's Federalista collaborators.

The shift from Taft's to Wright's patronage system manifested itself in the personnel chosen for the honorary commission. Michael Cullinane suggests that some of the commission's members had been selected by Taft prior to his departure; of sixteen commissioners from Manila, all but five were prominent Federalistas, and the delegation was headed by Pardo and Legarda. But Wright appeared to have had some influence in selecting its members: of twenty-six provincial representatives, only six can be identified as Federalistas. The shape of the honorary commission showed, in other words, how slippery the question of Philippine representation was: even as the exposition board attempted to assemble a seamless picture of Philippine-American cooperation, the alliances upon which U.S. power was based were shifting in emphasis toward the provinces and toward a new stratum of the Filipino elite.[45]

By far the most controversial representational decision was to send "non-Christians" to St. Louis.[46] By that time, the display of "savage" peoples had become a staple of anthropological displays at Euro-American expositions. Niederlein's rationale for such displays had from the beginning been one of "scientific" service. In 1903, he reported that the board planned to bring Igorots, Tinguians, Moros, Negritos, and other groups to the fair, which, together with Folkmar's casts, would "furnish the student of comparative anthropology with invaluable material for study." In March 1903, following reports of Niederlein's trip to the southern Philippines to secure Moro "villages" for the fair, what he called "a long and hot discussion" had taken place in the Filipino, Spanish, and English press "about the feasibility of sending non-Christian tribes to the world's fair."[47] The contours of the discussion suggest the very different histories in which the project was embedded in the minds of Filipino and American observers. For at least some Filipino critics, the effort brought to mind the 1887 Philippine Exposition at Madrid with its "Igorots": just like the Spaniards they had displaced, the Americans were using the islands' non-Christian peoples to cynically misrepresent Filipinos on the whole as savages requiring indefinite colonial rule. These critics often argued, as had some at Madrid, in nationalist-colonialist terms that reaffirmed imperial dichotomies of civilization and savagery even as they projected them internally: non-Christians must not be representative of the Philippines, while Christians should.

One of the strongest expressions along these lines was an editorial by Lauro Mataas in *El Renacimiento* entitled "Another 'Retiro' Exposition?" It began by recognizing Niederlein's efforts to collect a " 'genuinely Filipino' " exhibit of industrial goods that would attract capital, much needed for the "well-being and progress of the country." It praised the display of the "artistic culture of the Filipino people, without rival in the Orient," which would bring "unfading laurels." But Mataas "openly censure[d]" the plan to exhibit Aetas, Igorots, and Moros, which would not only "obscure all the successes that our artists and our industrialists can achieve at the St. Louis Exposition" but "ruin all our hopes of political progress, [and] advancement in liberal institutions beneath American domination." It would present Filipinos before the United States, "from whose generosity and justice we hope for benefits and improvements," "not as cultured, progressive beings, deserving of wide political concessions," but rather "as perfectly characterized savages for whom the quantity of 'self-government' granted in the 'Philippine Bill' is too much." Such a display might threaten civil government itself by showing Filipinos deserving only of "a purely military regime that restrains our cannibalism with an iron hand, and missionaries to let us know of the existence of a God and the most elementary notions of European culture."[48]

"Let us recall the precedent of the Exposition of the Retiro," Mataas suggested. Rewriting that earlier history, he had his Propagandists gain much ground with their "unceasing" assertion that "our advances and our culture demanded freer institutions"; support for the extension of Spanish laws to the archipelago and representation in the Cortes was "almost unanimous." But then had come the "unfortunate" exposition whose organizers, "ignorant or badly intentioned," had converted it into a display of savages. The reaction had led to a shocking reversal, as exposition attendees asked themselves how they could confer rights and representation to such savages. All political progress had been "paralyzed"; voices for reform had been "drowned" out by the drums the "savages" had used in their "war dances." The present situation under America was "analogous" to that under Spain: the question was whether "we are or are not cultured enough to obtain political concessions, if we are or are not semisavages." The St. Louis fair, "visited by millions," would be a crucial political battleground. Depending on what they saw there, the American people, "the only judge and master," would or would not "impose on its legislators to govern us as cultured beings and as men of civilization." Should, then, the exhibit contain Moros, Igorots, and Aetas, or art and industry, "which could be mistaken for those of European residents in the Philippines or of some 'Europeanized' Filipinos"? Filipinos should be allowed to participate and compete in the exposition alongside other "civilized" peoples and not as a "class of aspirants for the grand diploma of honor in savagism."[49]

Mataas's argument hinged on questions of an exposition's purpose and the Philippines' status. In criticizing the proposed non-Christian exhibits, he rejected the notion of the Philippines as a colony whose savage people should be displayed. Expositions, he claimed, were mounted to compete for honors, to attract capital and seek markets, and to present "before the eyes of the world the advances and progresses that the country has realized." The proper comparison for the Philippines, and model for it, was not with colonial societies but with more "civilized" states. "Russia sends the best of its industry and of its art," he wrote, "but not its semi-barbaric Eskimos." Japan sent its manufacturers, "not its decadent Ainus"; China sent its "exquisite embroideries and silks," but "not its bloody Boxers!" The rules of display that organized the United States' national exhibit should apply equally to the Philippines. The Americans, after all, had "surprised the world with its industrial and scientific advances" at the 1900 Paris Exposition, and not presented "its miserable Apaches." The Philippines was a tragic exception among civilized societies. "Only we, by some strange privilege," he noted bitterly, ". . . take advantage of as many occasions as are offered us to be represented before the civilized world by the most uncultured that inhabit this soil."[50]

The controversy also turned on different prospective readings of American audiences and, ultimately, on broader theories of reception. While exposition board officials believed there was no danger that the American public would mistake Christians and non-Christians, Mataas expressed skepticism about what he called these "flattering optimisms." Confronted with such displays, Americans' attention would be "undoubtedly dedicated" to it, "because the new, the strange, the exotic would attract more curiosity." Experience showed that "the shocking and the ridiculous strongly impress the spirit before any other thing"; such a "deep and intense" impression then served as "the foundation for judgments." The exhibit might, as Niederlein suggested, be viewed from a "purely scientific perspective." But how many "impartial and dispassionate" spirits would see it in this way? Apart from a few thousand, most viewers would "go by the expeditous path of social and political reflection" and generalize instead about "our lack of culture and our incapacity for the exercise of self-government." Mataas wearily cited past histories to support this prophecy. "We know much of the judgments and opinions from 'abroad,'" he stated. "They judge us and have judged us always by the exception."[51]

Bringing Race and Empire Home

At first glance, the long, marching phalanx that left the entrance of the St. Louis world's fair at 10:30 A.M. the morning of August 13, 1904, bound for the fair's "Philippine Reservation," looked like an invasion. The opening event of the fair's "Philippine Day," held on the sixth anniversary of the U.S. military occupation of Manila, featured what the *St. Louis Post-Dispatch* called, in a banner headline, "The Biggest Military Parade" in the first three months of the fair. Seated in carriages, Secretary of War Taft and Gen. Adna Chaffee led three divisions of marching troops on a path that wound through the fairgrounds over the next hour, heavy with U.S. cavalry as well as infantry and artillery units. But perhaps like the U.S. occupation itself, the invasion of the Philippine Exposition was represented as something more benign. There were, importantly, "natives" recognized among the invaders: Philippine Constabularymen, Philippine Scouts, and members of the honorary commission of *ilustrado* politicians. The parade ended at the Philippine Reservation's Constabulary parade ground with a number of speeches, at which point, as the *Post-Dispatch* put it, the "natives" took their turn as "hosts."

In some ways, neither the parade nor exposition spectators had to travel far to encounter the Philippines: the exposition board had managed to incorporate Philippine displays into many of the general government exhibits, a configuration that powerfully conveyed integration and the irreversibility of colonialism: the Philippines, woven into the symbolic fabric of the United States, was not something that could simply be detached. In the final blueprint, however, the Philippine Exposition was a self-contained unit, largely freestanding in both geography and semantics. As early as September 1901, exposition and Philippine officials had decided that the Philippine exhibit would not be placed inside the U.S. national government building. "The Philippine exhibit might seem in a general way to be associated with the special Government display," read one report, "but it is now planned to have the Philippines participate by themselves."[52]

The isolation of the Philippines was built into the exposition's built landscape. During his initial survey of the proposed ground in September 1902, Niederlein had sought a "'district of varied character'" and had been pleased with the grant of a "dense primeval forest, thick with tangled underbrush and oak."[53] He ordered that the symbolic space of the Philippines be carved out of these woods rather than built on previously cleared ground. In effect, this process reenacted fantasies of the colonial transformation of nature, civilization carved out of savagery. The perceived need to keep Filipinos in the "natural" environment from which they had incompletely emerged meant placing the Philippine Exposition on the opposite side of the fairgrounds from the temples of fine arts, industry, electricity, and manufactures, as well as the national and state government exhibits, clustered among the exhibits for agriculture, horticulture, forestry, and plant industry. As a consequence of the exposition board's own requirements, the Philippines remained at a fascinating (or for the footweary, a tiresome) distance, a place unlike other places, including the United States.

This isolation was reinforced during the Philippine Exposition's widely attended opening ceremonies. The opening on June 17 was a triumphant spectacle in spite of numerous construction delays and postponements. Its twenty exhibit palaces and one hundred huts and lodges were thrown open with a parade of 1,100 Filipinos led by exposition officials, marching beneath a grandstand filled to its capacity of 3,000 in spite of a rainstorm. Staging a march of evolutionary progress, fair officials were followed by Philippine Scouts and Constabulary and their marching bands, followed in turn by "savage" and "semicivilized" peoples. But rather than fully incorporating the Philippines into the symbolic space of the United States—through a parade outside the Philippine exhibit—the event had established the colony as something apart from the United States itself. In this instance, the isolation of the Philippines was an effort to preempt attacks from the Board of Lady Managers. "The parade was confined within the limits of the Philippine territory," one article reported, "as the scant garb of the Igorrotes and the other tribes precluded a big display in the civilized sections of the Exposition."[54]

At certain points, the Philippine Exposition and its elements succeeded in standing in for the larger St. Louis fair, breaking into larger symbolic arenas. The Constabulary band, for example, would serve in a wide range of functions inside and outside the Philippine Exposition, such as opening each day's activities. It was in these settings that the empire was brought most significantly into the fair, with the new territories and their progress becoming the story of the nation's own advancement across successive frontiers and through evolutionary time. In his address at the fair's inauguration day ceremonies, Taft, now secretary of war and introduced as the personal representative of the president, attempted to cast a Philippine meaning over the entire St. Louis fair, linking the Philippine occupation to the nation's imperial history and weaving together the still-unopened Philippine Exposition and the larger fair. After a brief historical sketch of the Louisiana Purchase and its consequences, Taft turned his attention to "another and a different kind of expansion." While "forced upon us without our seeking," the Philippines, like the Louisiana Purchase one hundred years earlier, presented the American people with a unique chance to test their "fearlessness and sense of duty." In closing, he called the centennial "the beginning of the great Philippine problem" and invited the audience to visit the Philippine Exposition, for which "the government of the Philippine Islands felt justified in expending a very large sum of money." The exhibit's aim, he said, was "to make the people who come here to commemorate the vindication of one great effort of American enterprise and expansion understand the conditions which surround the beginning of another."[55]

"Vindication" consisted of several different but connected ideological efforts. First of these was the symbolic conclusion and political neutralization of the Philippine-American War. Military officials took the opportunity to publicly defend the U.S. Army's conduct. During Philippine Day opening ceremonies, Gen. Irving Hale of the Army of the Philippines stated that "[t]he war with Spain and its sequel in the Philippines . . . was unsought and undesired; but, like every duty well performed, it has been and will be an honor and benefit." (The fact that Hale himself could not yet fully consign the "sequel" war to the past tense apparently went unobserved.) Moving Spanish-Cuban-American War clichés westward, Hale noted that the Philippine-American War had "unified our own country, blending the blue of the North and the gray of the South into the khaki of the Orient." Fair ceremony and reportage emphasized the end of hostilities in the Philippines and the substitution of harmony and Filipino subordination. Again and again, the *Post-Dispatch* marked encounters between Americans and Filipinos as the meeting of former enemies, now reconciled through Filipino fealty. "U.S. Generals Meet Old Foes Filipino Day," read the *Post-Dispatch*'s front-page headline on August 13. "Secretary Taft, Gens. Chaffee, Merritt, Funston, Bates and Others Join in Festivities at Fair with Chiefs of Tribes Lately Hostile." These encounters were not represented as diplomatic exchanges between equals but as moments of Filipino awe. "Filipinos See Impressive Array," read one headline, describing a parade of marching U.S. troops. "The Filipinos were allowed to see everything," the article stated, "and to be properly impressed with the great display of soldiery."[56] To drive the point home, the exposition board commissioned Paris-based painter Felix Resurrección Hidalgo, whom Rizal had praised at the Philippine Exposition in Madrid for demonstrating Filipino artistry, to paint a work for the entryway of the government building's art display: *Through Peace and Liberty* was an allegory that featured the wild maiden Filipinas handing an olive branch upward toward the gentle, armored Columbia surrounded by fluttering angels.

One essential symbolic "pacification" of the islands involved the erasure of Hispanicized Filipinos as revolutionary combatants: they were to be represented only as collaborators in colonialism, not its opponents. The parading invasion force that left the fair entrance for the Philippine Exposition on August 13 contained core representatives of the new, Hispanicized Filipino collaboration structure. The honorary commission, which rode in carriages behind Taft's own, "showed their delight at the honors showered upon them," while a battalion of Constabularymen and the bands of both the Scouts and Constabulary marched in among U.S. cavalry and infantry. Toward the very back, "[t]he 100 Filipino students who are visiting the Fair brought up the rear, carrying a Philippine banner." Overshadowed by U.S. power, the joint forces of the American and Hispanicized Filipino colonial state were together invading the Philippines, represented as a non-Christian place. Upon the parade's arrival, the *Post-Dispatch* noted, "the stockades of the villages bent under the weight of unclad Igorrotes and gorgeously-clad Moros who were peeking over to be properly impressed." Over the course of the fair, reports identified former rebels who were meeting with U.S. generals, not as Hispanicized revolutionaries, but as Igorot and Moro chiefs. On Philippine Day, for example, American generals and veterans would meet with "their former enemies, the savage Moros and Igorrotes." The following day, a headline recounted how Taft and his generals had "Felicitate[d] with Chief Antonio [of the Igorots] and Datto Facundo [of the Moros], Whose Bolos Were Lately

Where resistance continued to plague colonial authorities, one of the main purposes of the Philippine exhibit at the St. Louis world's fair was to advertise the notion that war in the Philippines was over. Along these lines, the board commissioned famed, Paris-based Filipino painter Felix Resurrección Hidalgo to paint a work for the government building's art display. Through *Peace and Liberty*—in draft form here—featured the "savage" maiden Filipinas moving upward toward, and handing an olive branch to, a patient, forgiving, and armored Columbia, surrounded by fluttering angels. The remaking of both the Philippines and the United States into female figures was meant to represent the temporal shift from "war" to "peace" in gendered terms. Reproduced from Roces, *Felix Resurrección Hidalgo and the Generation of 1872*, with permission, Lopez Memorial Museum.

Raised against Them."[57] This discourse drew on wartime themes of Filipino savagery but projected them onto non-Christians and erased the Philippine-American War as a conflict between Americans and Hispanicized Filipinos. It also signaled what, for many Catholic Filipinos, would be a disturbing substitution of non-Christians for Hispanicized Catholics in American understandings of the Philippines.

If the erasure of Hispanicized Filipino combatants was one essential move in the political elimination of the war, another was the replacement of U.S. combatants with proxy warriors, as took place during the Philippine Exposition's mock battles. Mock battles were a staple of world's fairs; a synthesis of world's fair subgenres, the Philippine Exposition almost demanded such a display. Accordingly, on August 4 (and again on Philippine Day), Scout troops enacted what the Post-Dispatch called a "Real Sample of Philippine Fight" in the woods near the reservation grounds. Scout commander Major Johnson divided the Scout battalion into two camps. One acted as "insurgents," "hiding in the woods south of the reservation" and wearing uniforms like those "which the American troops learned to know in the days of Aguinaldo." The other, "representing American troops," pitched tents in an encampment and "pass[ed] the early evening playing cards in their camp." Insurgent aggression, in the form of a rifle shot at Americans (an interesting reversal of the war's actual start), was followed by a call to arms, and a detail of mock "Americans" was sent into the woods. The resulting clash, involving the entire Scout detachment, "show[ed] the way American soldiers had to fight in the islands," with blanks used in the rifles "to make the engagement realistic and properly noisy," if less sanguinary.[58]

The staging of the all-Filipino mock battle appears strange in light of the large number of actual U.S. troops at the fair that might have been temporarily detailed. Perhaps it was that the exposition board had easier access to Scout troops through colonial military authorities. But if authenticity were at issue, could not the Bureau of Insular Affairs have pressured the War Department to send a unit of U.S. soldiers? Perhaps exposition planners feared that U.S. soldiers and Philippine Scouts (some of them former "insurgents") were a bit too close to actual battles. Whether deliberately or inadvertently, the mock battle, organized in this way, had the resultant benefit of giving the controversial violence and atrocity of U.S. military action a Filipino face, which was one important step toward erasing memories of U.S. aggression entirely.

The exposition's second goal, only possible in light of the war's erasure, was the dramatic representation of Filipino assimilation in process. The most important actors in this performance were the Constabulary and the Scouts: if progress would come partway through the schoolhouse, one of its main engines was still martial, the progress of moving lines of regimented troops. The martial script of assimilation played out in the numerous services the Scouts provided the fair. In practical terms, they engaged in much of the labor needed in the construction of the Philippine exhibition from imported materials and were also conscripted into assembling other portions of the fair, which lessened the exposition's reliance on organized workers. Once the fair began, the Scouts' main function was to demonstrate their efficiency, precision, and discipline. The battalion staged daily drills, and its marching band held daily concerts; an estimated one million people saw them. One security guard found "rather strange the interest taken in those Filipinos" by fairgoers and commented that "everybody that passes wants to know where they are. . . . Where are the little brown men?"[59]

At least some spectators recognized the troops' accomplishments, a recognition often predicated on racial surprise and skepticism. The *Post-Dispatch* noted that the Scouts' "soldierly bearing, intelligent countenances and obliging ways won praise from the visitors"; they were "polite as Frenchmen and speak Spanish as fluently as their native dialect." Even more striking were signs of assimilation: "Many speak English and are all uniformed in Khaki like the soldiers of Uncle Sam." Capt. James Munro of the U.S. Cavalry noted that their camp was "a model of cleanliness" and their "discipline was perfect," with their drill "precision itself."[60] There was no higher recognition than their assignment as escorts to visiting dignitaries: the battalion would eventually conduct twenty-four escorts of honor, including those of the governors of twelve states, prominent exposition officers, and President Roosevelt himself.

Far less prominent in the narrative of assimilation were about one hundred *pensionados*, between the ages of thirteen and nineteen, who arrived for one-month's stay at the fair in early August, brought to accomplish at least three of the regime's goals for the Philippine exhibit. First, they would help guide disoriented visitors to specific parts of the exhibit, mediating the visitors' experiences by stationing themselves in various Philippine buildings and, as the *Post-Dispatch* put it, "explain[ing] the exhibits and also . . . themselves in the English tongue." Second, like the honorary commission (but unlike the non-Christians), they were imagined as spectators who would be overawed by the fair in general and by its demonstrations of American power and superior civilization. The *Post-Dispatch* made clear that the students arrived "not as a foreign exhibit, but as students learning all they can from the exhibits shown."[61]

But if the students were not a "foreign exhibit," they were, third, an exhibit of the Filipino capacity for, and American success at, assimilation. The reaction of fair visitors and the *Post-Dispatch* to the students' arrival suggests the odds they were up against in this regard. The *pensionados* arrived at Union Station in St. Louis "[g]iving vent to a genuine college yell," in what the newspaper called "an unintelligible mixture of English and Spanish." But their arrival was loaded with other meanings: it is unlikely that any other college students disembarking at St. Louis that summer summoned a crowd; the sight of the students descending from the train had been "a surprise to the crowds at the station, who gazed with wonder at the little people, who made so much noise." A *Post-Dispatch* reporter was surprised but willing to admit that the students were "gentlemanly and courteous," although he attributed these traits to "the year they have spent in this country." Indeed, the *pensionados'* success in "readily learning American customs" had, perhaps dangerously, obscured their race and made them difficult to recognize as Filipinos at all. "All were clad in neat, fashionable clothing," the *Post-Dispatch* noted, "and it was only from their talk and complexion that their nationality could be told."[62]

If Scouts and *pensionados* represented assimilation, the exhibit sought to emphasize the bifurcated character of the racial state: the regime of assimilation would be divided into Christian and non-Christian parts. The fundamentally split character of the Philippine population was central to the very architecture of the exhibit. The exposition's internal organization reproduced the dichotomies of the fair as a whole in miniature; it was, as some called it, an "exposition within itself," or "a wheel within a wheel."[63] The larger fair was spatially organized around stark divisions of racialized evolutionary time, with civilized palaces of industry and art set apart from baser and more riotous pleasures. The Philippine exhibit internalized this same structure. At its center were government buildings dedicated to industry, agriculture, education, and the arts. A circular road, meant to represent the Luneta that stretched along the Manila waterfront, surrounded this core with bandstands, restaurants, and lantern slide displays. As in the larger fair, civilization receded outward from a center. Outside the Luneta road were the exhibits of "villages," with those of non-Christians near a conspicuous base of Philippine Scouts. Niederlein's plan to use the existing forest had emerged

This bird's-eye view of the Philippine display reveals its structure as an exposition within itself, with the Philippines' divided population as its central problematic. Visitors entered through inherited Spanish colonial means, crossing the Bridge of Spain and peering down from the Walled City of Manila. Entering the main grounds, they faced a central, "civilized" plaza containing the Government, Fine and Liberal Arts, and Educational and Fine Arts Buildings and an elegant "Manila House." The Visayan Village, representing the islands' Hispanicized peoples, was placed nearby. Rimming these were the islands' "uncivilized" peripheries: the Negrito Village to the far left, the Igorot Village beyond it (guarded by the Philippine Scouts' Model Camp), the Bagobo Village to the right, and the Samal and Lake Moro Villages along Arrowhead Lake. Reproduced with permission, Missouri Historical Society, St. Louis.

from a desire to illustrate a plurality of Filipino tribes. The "rolling character of the ground" as it stood provided "a grand opportunity for separating the various villages and tribes of the Filipinos." As Filipinos "differ in habits and customs," he wrote, "the best effect would be obtained by keeping them separated."[64]

The bifurcated nature of assimilation—with its parallel tracks of progress—was evident in the symbolic heart of assimilation itself, a "Model Schoolhouse." The centrality of the nipa and bamboo structure to the overall ritual cycle of the exhibit reflected its primacy to colonial state ideologies: in St. Louis as in the Philippines, the United States was not oppressing but "tutoring" Filipinos, imparting American ways and moving Filipinos forward in evolutionary time. The school's principal drama was a set of classes held by Pilar Zamora, a Tagalog normal-school teacher, which fairgoers could observe from a raised platform behind the seated students. According to exposition president David Francis, the model schoolhouse exhibit was popular, often drawing over 2,000 attendees in a single day; a register of visiting teachers eventually contained some 13,000 names.[65] But the model schoolhouse dramatized tutelage along strictly bifurcated lines that reflected colonial racial formations: an initial class was held exclusively for children from the Visayan village and a second for children from diverse non-Christian villages. The Philippine colonial state, it seemed, was a single engine of assimilation that separated groups on either side of Hispanic Catholic influence and moved each of them forward in different directions.

Unintended Responses

Despite the Philippine Commission's hopes and its massive investment of resources and infrastructure, the Philippine Exposition would be interpreted as a failure by the colonial regime even before its close. This fact has been obscured up until now by the metropolitan terms of analysis to which the display has typically been subjected. Viewed from the perspective of Philippine colonial officials, the exposition failed to accomplish its three principal political goals: to convince the American public of civilian control and the terms of assimilation; to promote Philippine exports through tariff reform; and to persuade elite Filipinos of U.S. power and good intentions. In all three areas, results fell far short of expectations and, in some cases, involved reversals. This points, first, to tensions between the propaganda efforts of the insular regime and the fair's promotional goals. Second and more broadly, it suggests the difficulty and even impossibility of "importing" race: the racial formation that had organized colonial collaboration in the Philippines—long on assimilation, tutelage, and the bifurcated state—broke down in a context of commercial display and metropolitan racial formations.

The calamities were not problems of either attendance or attention. While it is impossible to gauge precisely, from available evidence it appears that the Philippine exhibit was one of the most frequently visited sites at the fair. "The Filipino exhibition was one that attracted a great deal of attention and gave much satisfaction," recorded a Mason on holiday. "On the way out here," recalled Mrs. Campbell Dauncey of travel to the Philippines, "I met a German who had been to St. Louis and who told me that the two chief exhibits were the Boer War and the Philippine section." Edmund Philibert visited the Philippine Exposition on at least three separate occasions, hurrying off at one point "as fast as possible" to witness the Scouts' regular drill. Edward Schneiderhahn recorded in his fair diary, "Considered the whole Philippine Reservation a special event." The Philippine troops' musical drill had been "most interesting," and he had returned to see this latter spectacle, "which had been the delight of every World's Fair visitor," at the fair's closing. Indeed, the Philippine exhibit as a whole "proved the high civilization already attained."[66]

Some visitors were greatly impressed by the exposition's narrative of assimilation; at least one saw it as a positive model for domestic U.S. racial politics. When humorist and social critic Marietta Holley's fictitious Samantha visited the Philippine Exposition, she came away as stirred by the "uplift" of the Filipinos as she was struck by its contrast with Americans' approach to the "Negro problem." For Samantha, the exhibit "sings of an ignorant, oppressed race changed into an enlightened prosperous one," a song that "comes floatin' into my ears over the wide Pacific." Samantha urged Uncle Sam to do as well by his "dark complexioned" children, "stole away from their own land to be slaves and drudges for his white children" and living right on his "very doorstep," as he was doing for those "six thousand milds [sic] off." If some of the "disgraceful seens [sic]" carried out "right under your dear old nose" took place "amongst your adopted Philippine children or even amongst your protejays [sic] in Turkey or China," she observed, "you would send out a warship at once."[67]

One of the most common impressions audiences took away was of a stark contrast between the Philippines' "civilized" and "savage" inhabitants. Indeed, visitors were encouraged to do so by the exposition board's propaganda. One promotional guide issued by the board described morning at the exposition as a study in extremes. While in one section, "one hundred bare-limbed Igorot often sacrifice and eat a dog," nearby "a bugle sounds reveille, and four hundred well-trained soldiers in the blue of the United States Army hustle from their tents." As the booklet framed it, "[t]he yells of the dog-dance have scarcely ceased before the blue line is formed for roll call." In case the difference was not yet clear, the booklet stated that "[t]he Igorot represents the wildest races of savages, the scouts stand for the results of American rule—extremes of the social order in the islands." Alfred Newell reported that the exhibit showed "the condition of the savage tribes" and "the most advanced civilization"; in brief, it showed "the nature of the Philippine problem in all its phases." Mark Bennitt reported that the exhibit had familiarized Americans with "the various and incongruous tribal elements of the Philippine population, differing in race, language and religion," and "representing many stages of social progress from the lowest types of head-hunting savages to the best products of Christian civilization and culture."[68]

For Schneiderhahn, the exhibit, and specifically troop displays, had definitively proved "the high civilization already attained." But this perception posed a potential problem: it suggested that the display's civilized Filipinos were not the product of prior Hispanic-Catholic civilization but of less than five years of American assimilation. Indeed, in the eyes of many viewers, there were not two lines of parallel progress—one Christian and one non-Christian—but a single one, with Americans civilizing what had previously been an entirely savage Philippine population. That this was the case was not surprising. The islands had been featured in domestic U.S. newspapers and public debate most intensely during the war, when the racialization of guerrilla warfare had led to military representations of the Philippine population as wholly savage. These discourses had fundamentally shaped metropolitan debate and left the widespread impression of a savage Philippine population that, once pacified, would have to be civilized as a whole. Press coverage of the islands had declined since the declared end of the war, the very moment when a new racial formation, which placed a premium on Filipino assimilation and divisions between Christians and non-Christians, had begun to emerge. Indeed, it was precisely the civilian government's perceived failure to communicate its novel messages to the U.S. public—including racial ones—that had led it to mount a display in the first place.

Long before the advent of the fair, lurid representations of Filipinos as savage had made their way into U.S. popular culture. During the Philippine-American War, political cartoonists had often represented Filipino insurgents using images drawn from blackface minstrelsy, or stereotyped images of African or South Pacific savages.[69] One mundane example of this imagery in a commercial context was a booklet published circa 1901 by George H. Allen, advertising manager of the New York–based Cedarine-Allen furniture polish company. Entitled *Among the Filipinos*, with the sardonic subtitle *A Story for Very Young Folks, Older People Will Not Care to Read It*, the booklet was a satiric reading primer supposedly chronicling episodes from Allen's trip to the Philippines that year with photographs and an easy-to-read text broken down by syllables.[70] Its first page introduced "Uncle George," an American traveler and the text's author, in a photograph of a flooded Philippine village, struggling to budge a mired carabao and cart. Praising the "nice city," the author wisecracked, "Is it not a SHAME to Op-press These Peo-ple with A-mer-i-can Civ-i-li-za-tion?" The following page featured a photograph of Uncle George seated on a carabao, with a lasso tightened around the neck of a startled-looking Filipino man dressed in a nipa skirt. The primer explains: "Has Un-cle George Caught a Fish? No, Un-cle George Has Not Caught a Fish. He Has Las-so-ed a Wild Ig-or-ot-te Chief. The Ig-or-ot-tes Are Tribes of Wild Men Who In-Fest The Jun-gles and Woods A-round Da-gu-pan."

On the third page, Uncle George threatens to shoot the mock-Igorot dead. The final page, however, intended for "older people," was a conventional advertisement for Cedarine polish, with no mention of either Igorots or the Philippines. But as Allen made clear in a letter to wholesaler-distributors of Cedarine, the "Igorot" was intended to become something of a company icon. When handling orders for bottles of Cedarine larger than two gross, the company would send retail purchasers 500 copies of Allen's booklet, along with "a stuffed, life-sized Filipino" for their shop windows.

If the exposition board was competing with earlier shop-window "expositions" of Filipinos, it also sought to steer clear of "midway" conventions. A long corridor of smaller-scale exhibits running along an outer edge of the fairground, the midway had for at least twenty years provided a chaotic counterpart to the stately, neoclassical harmonies of a fair's central temples, serving as home to the incomprehensible and uncontrollable. In stark contrast to the civilized frontage of the fair's central pavilions, the midway (called the Pike at the St. Louis fair) was a sensationalist world of exotic cultures, scientific miracles, and human disasters; the display of foreign peoples and human oddities was one of its most profitable touchstones. Moralistic resistance to midway excess had long been a ritual of middle-class self-definition, a means by which new elites could segment, by class and taste, civic events with capacious appeal. Early on, the fair's Board of Lady Managers had passed resolutions "regarding the so-called 'Midway' features," warning that such displays must be appropriate to respectable, female viewership.[71]

How to guarantee that colonialism would be "respectable" in exposition terms? The proposed display of "exotic" peoples came dangerously close to the midway, whose rank commercialism, according to a fair reporter, "tended to make such collections of people merely a popular show, and to allow the exhibit to degenerate into a money-making scheme." Exposition board officials appear to have worked as hard as possible to distance the exposition from the midway and its excesses. Wilson's formal complaint to the director of works that a proposed saloon to be erected at the entrance to the Philippine Exposition would be "unsightly" was, no doubt, aimed at protecting the exhibit's respectability. W J McGee, head of the fair's Anthropology Department, was convinced of the need to separate serious scientific displays of "primitive" peoples from more haphazard commercial exploitation. "[T]he ethnological display at St. Louis should constitute an integral (and important) portion of the exposition proper," he wrote, "and . . . should by no means be relegated to the place of a midway feature."[72]

At least some exposition board officials believed, with *El Renacimiento*, that the only way to mount a respectable display would be to exclude non-Christians entirely: such groups might otherwise be misrecognized as "typical" Filipinos. In this, they revealed a sensitivity to Hispanicized Filipino categories that had characterized the larger Taft regime's cultural politics. Public presentations made during the fair labored to emphasize the central ethnological tenet of the bifurcated racial state: the stark difference between Philippine Christians and non-Christians. During the exposition's inaugural address, Father José Algué, a Spanish Jesuit scientist and collaborator in the colonial regime, emphasized "that there were 7,000,000 Christian Catholics in the islands," a point he apparently feared might be missed in the rush to see non-Christian tribes. Col. Clarence Edwards of the Bureau of Insular Affairs stated outright that "he hoped the Igorrotes and Negritos would not be taken as fairly representing the inhabitants of the Philippines. The insular exhibit has been . . .

duty bound to make a full ethnological exhibit, but the Igorrotes were no more representative of the Philippines than the most savage Indians are representative of Americans."[73] This comment echoed fears that Edwards would later voice in private to Taft. "Experience has shown," he would write in 1913, ". . . that it was rather unfortunate that we should have inserted in the printed reports of the Commission the various pictures of the aborigines or savages in the Philippines." Rather than convey the commission's intended message of an evolving Philippines beneath America's uplifting influence, the photographs had unintentionally stoked racist anti-imperialism. "I have often heard it remarked in Congress," he wrote, "that from the looks of the people in these photographs we ought not to bother much with the Philippines."

> When I told them the idea was merely to present the unusual types,— that the great body of Filipinos are of a much higher class they say "one certainly would not get that idea from a casual glance at the Commission's reports," in other words, that the representation of Igorrotes, wild Moros, etc., would give as false an impression of the people of the Philippines as would a representation of Indians and Negroes properly represent the inhabitants of the United States.[74]

Exposition officials had ultimately decided that non-Christians could and should be included in the exhibit: American audiences would, they believed, take in the display proportionately, absorb its parallel narratives of Christian/non-Christian evolutionary progress, and not mistake non-Christians for the Philippine population as a whole.

They were wrong. Expositions were driven by economies of spectacle, and among exhibited Filipinos, it was not the modern, civilized, producing and consuming Filipinos that attracted the most attention but non-Christians. When, facing delays in construction, the exposition board had opened completed portions of the exposition to the public free of charge on May 1, thousands of spectators rushed to the exhibit. "All Roads Led to Filipinos," stated the *Post-Dispatch*. "The non-Christian tribes were the magnets which drew them more than anything else," it stated. "Manila architecture" had been viewed "with interest," but "the crowds lingered longest" around the "native villages." The Igorot village was visible through bamboo poles, and "throughout the day men and women were standing thick about the stockade with their faces pressed into the interstices looking at the almost naked savages."[75]

As this suggested, it was the "nudity" of Igorots that best condensed spectacle, commercialism, and late-Victorian sexual repression. The widespread circulation of the Igorots as representatives of "naked savagery" intensified with efforts to suppress such imagery. By June 1904, the *Post-Dispatch* reported, "influential persons had intimated to the war department that the attire of the Igorrotes might be criticised." Upon making a visit to the fair on June 25, Edwards ordered the Igorots clothed in pants. While hoping to avoid criticism on the subject of propriety, Edwards was also said to be concerned that "the savages have been attracting more attention than the educated Filipinos who wear clothes." The order backfired, serving, in effect, as an official advertisement for the exhibit: the morning following the announcement, the Philippine Exposition saw the sudden in-rush of an estimated 2,000 visitors. "The visitors openly declared their purpose was to see the natives as they are at home," reported the *Post-Dispatch*, "and not as the United States government would have them."[76] In evaluating its decision, the War Department consulted the exposition's Board of Lady Managers, since the greatest objections to the Igorots had been made on behalf of female viewers. The board recommended to the War Department that the Igorots be allowed to continue to wear their G-strings, and after a nervous exchange of correspondence between top officials, President Roosevelt himself gave his permission.

While the Constabulary band won recognition for both its musical performances and tight drills, it was the Igorots that triumphed in newspaper coverage, memoir, and scrapbook. When admissions revenues were tallied at the fair's end, the Igorot concession had brought in just over $200,000, half of all admissions revenues for "tribal" exhibits and over four times that of the Visayan display. The Igorot exhibit's success was encouraged by the St. Louis newspapers' relentless hunger for sensation, abundantly fed by Igorot "nudity" and scripted dog-eating. In perhaps the single most disastrous move of the exposition board, its promotional agent had generously invited a crowd of newspaper humorists and cartoonists to the Igorot village for a demonstration of a ceremonial dog-feast: the event apparently turned journalistic stomachs but supplied a half-year stream of Igorot-related, dog-eating or nudity jokes. The Igorots—and the Philippine exhibit as a whole—were being dragged onto the midway. In September, for example, the Pikers' Club of the New York exhibit sponsored a minstrel show benefit with "[s]everal of the officials and dignitaries of the World's Fair . . . present." According to one there, "[t]he hit of the night was made by Miss Terious Asia, the Igorrote hostess," who sang satiric songs that mocked the Congress and the Board

This photograph of American visitors with Moros and Igorots in the Philippine exhibit's "village" at the St. Louis world's fair suggests the popularity of these exhibits within the broader display. While the position of the "non-Christians," both beneath and surrounded by American viewers, supports hierarchical spectatorship, the status of the Americans themselves as objects of display, and their close physical proximity to Filipinos, suggests the fragility of these boundaries in exposition culture. Reproduced with permission, Missouri Historical Society, St. Louis.

of Lady Managers; the Igorot character had been named after a midway concession.[77]

Newspapers used Igorots' encounters with both "savage" and "civilized" peoples to parody genteel, upper-class culture. In May, when the Sioux chief Big Horn was led to the Igorot village by an anthropologist, one newspaper reported it as "the first exchange of international courtesy between the savage peoples at the World's Fair." In June, when Wilson refused to allow the Igorots to accept an invitation to attend a church ice cream social, headlines read, "Igorrotes Suffer Social Setback." The whimsical juxtaposition of high-class sociability and Igorot savagery was enacted at an August breakfast attended by hundreds of East Coast manufacturers, sponsored by the Missouri Athletic Club. Offered a morning swim, the manufacturers' clothes were to be secretly removed, forcing them to attend the meal only in a bath towel, a meal consisting of "heart of dogwood blossoms," "dogberries and cream," "dogfish," and "Collie steak." Tables were to be decorated with stuffed dogs, each one "flanked by a design of crossed Igorrote bolos and war clubs"; the meal was to conclude with "a tom-tom parade around the tables, the last feature being the Igorrote dog-dance."[78]

One of the main implications of crushing attention to the "Igorots" was the relative invisibility of "civilized" Filipinos. William Sutherland, supervisor of the *pensionado* program, admitted in mid-1906 that "much of the good impression that should have remained with the thousands of visitors to the Philippine exhibition was lost or at least prejudiced by an unfortunate arrangement of the native Filipinos who were part of the Philippine reservation." The mistake had, in part, been one of proportions: that of those natives displayed, "only a relatively small number, the Visayans, belonged to the civilized or Christianized races of the Islands," and their exhibit had been "unattractively presented." It had also been due to the machinery of profit: "each race or tribe was separated off into its own inclosure, with a separate admission fee to each." Confronted with this commercial decision, visitors had flocked to better-advertised concessions, which had "the 'tom-toms' going at all hours, and which made much of the uncouth habits of certain of the tribes." Defending itself against the accusation of intentional deception, the Philippine Exposition Board noted that the advertising departments "have avoided official mention of [dog-eating] and have endeavored to call attention to the more worthy characteristics of the natives." "It is not true that the savages have been unduly exploited at the expense of the more dignified exhibits," it claimed, "but no amount of emphasis on the commercial exhibits, Constabulary drills and Scout parades has distracted attention from the 'dog-eaters' and 'head-hunters.'"[79]

Fair audiences rushed to the Igorots not only out of salacious interest, or because the display most closely resonated with their prior imagery of Filipinos, but because they were collecting on what expositions as a whole promised, visually and experientially: grand narratives of evolutionary progress toward civilization. But "progress" was difficult to make into spectacle. Within exposition forms, progress was communicated through extreme, even impossible, juxtaposition and contrast, the neoclassical palaces of industry and art standing always over, and at a remove from, the huts of the world's natives. At expositions, global history was cut to the cloth of industrial process: the savage past was the raw material that civilization would destroy in the process of its own making.[80]

But how to display the "process" of remaking natives? The naked native was spectacle; the "native in process" was not, and thus ran the risk of becoming unrecognizable. Indeed, if the Igorots' highly publicized nudity had made them extremely visible, Visayans and other Christians were practically invisible within exposition conventions. Describing an Igorot schoolboy he conversed with at the fair, Alfred Newell observed that "[c]lad in Western clothes, he would look like a dark American mulatto." Other Americans overlooked civilized Filipinos as either black or "foreign" attendees to the Philippine Exposition who—if their status as consumers and spectators was itself sometimes a problem—were not imagined as part of the Philippines, whose pure "savagery" was therefore preserved. Sutherland lamented later that after the exhibit "to many the word 'Filipino' became synonymous with 'Igorot, Moro, Negrito, Tinguian, Bagobo,' and the like." When a *Post-Dispatch* reporter noted of the *pensionados'* arrival that they did "not dress as one would imagine after visiting the Philippine exhibit at the Fair," he made clear the extent to which savagery had already rendered Filipino civilization either suspect or invisible.[81]

Equally troublesome was the way audiences collapsed the bifurcated narrative of progress into a single one. Presented with the imagery of contrast, audiences tended to place its parts into a narrative, evolutionary sequence. As a result, where civilized Filipinos were recognized as part of the exhibit—and not as foreign or black visitors—they tended to be seen as merely demonstrations of "the high civilization already attained" by former savages under less than five years of American tutelage. This, in

While exhibit planners sought to emphasize Filipinos' "civilized" standing as an argument for successful collaboration, exhibits of Catholic, Hispanicized Filipinos appear to have received less attention than hoped. In this photograph, one lone American spectator approaches the Visayan exhibit, with its reconstituted Catholic Church. More than one Catholic Filipino complained that it was non-Christians that had drawn U.S. audiences and attributed this fact to a deliberate plot by exhibit planners. Reproduced with permission, Missouri Historical Society, St. Louis. Photography by Jessie Tarbox Beals.

turn, made Filipino civilization the exclusive result of American influence; it reduced the evolutionary-historical distance between Igorots and "Filipinos" to almost nothing, making Visayans the short-term future of Igorots and Moros, and Igorots and Moros the immediate Visayan past. Mrs. Campbell Dauncey suggested sardonically that viewers presented with the exhibit's juxtaposition of Catholics and non-Christians had folded the separate evolutionary tracks of the racially bifurcated state into a single, connected one. It had conveyed the sense that the islands' inhabitants were "a race of naked cannibals and savages" who were "suddenly being transformed into the educated *Mestizo*, who goes to college in America and returns here [to the Philippines] to write seditious articles and talk his head off."[82]

Hispanicized Filipinos either visiting the Philippine Exposition or hearing of it through networks of friends and associates had much to say about these developments. St. Louis belonged to radically different histories for its various participants. For exposition planners and municipal boosters in St. Louis, the historical reference point for St. Louis was clearly Chicago, with its World's Columbian Exposition of 1893. For the Philippine Exposition Board, it was most likely London and Paris, with their nineteenth-century colonial expositions. For Hispanicized Filipinos, as in the *Renacimiento* editorial, it was often Madrid, where Propaganda movement critics had exposed Spanish colonial duplicity. The moral failures of colonialism were identified in the deliberate deception of the public as to the "true" nature of the Philippine population, puncturing Spanish and American claims of benevolence. In some cases, critics sought the recognition of Filipino civilization by drawing a darker, deeper line between Catholic and non-Christian Filipinos; the problem with U.S. colonialism was that it symbolically emphasized non-Christians more than they deserved. Here, Filipinos employed nationalist-colonialist arguments for why the Catholic Filipino elite should be allowed to represent itself in symbolic, if not necessarily in parliamentary, terms. Empowered to do so—with or without other kinds of authority—they would represent themselves and the Philippine population more responsibly, minimizing— or even eliminating—the representation of non-Christian groups on the grounds of both ethnography and expedience.

In mid-August, for example, Teresa Ramirez, a Visayan woman, filed a formal protest on behalf of herself and other Visayans with the exposition board's chief of publicity over a passage in one of the Philippine exhibit's guidebooks. The objectionable passage referred to the model schoolhouse

THE FILIPINO OF YESTERDAY
A Negrito, one of the aborigines of the Philippines

AND OF TODAY
A Pilipino scout, trained by American soldiers

This illustration of "the Filipino of yesterday and of today," from a report in the World's Work on the Philippine exhibition at the St. Louis world's fair, conveys the problem the colonial state confronted in conveying its racial-imperial messages. Where the regime had hoped to communicate a bifurcated racial formation in which Hispanicized Christians and non-Christian peoples were both distinct and ruled differently, audiences tended to collapse these distinctions into a single narrative of evolutionary progress in which Filipinos had recently all been "savages" (like the figure on the left) and were only becoming "civilized" (like the Scout figure on the right), under U.S. control. From Newell, "The Philippine Peoples," World's Work, August 1904.

where Catholic and non-Christian children were given instruction daily. "'Within a trim little nipa and bamboo cottage in the rear of the Manila building,'" it read, "'50 little savages, recruited from the various villages, gather each day and are taught to fashion English letters on big blackboards.'" Here, objected Ramirez, was an important difference without a distinction. The model schoolroom had been properly bifurcated— Visayans received instruction from 9:00 to 10:30 in the morning, and Igorots, Moros, and Negritos from 10:30 to 11:30—but exposition publications had not. "'In reading over the Philippine Exposition book, I noticed you say that all the pupils that go to the Model School are savages,'" read the letter, reproduced in the *Post-Dispatch*. "'But not all, I think, because . . . I have seen that the Visayan people are more polite than some of the Americans that come around.'" Ramirez exclusively defended the reputation of the Visayans, suggesting that if the chief of publicity himself visited the Visayan village's market, church, and theater or saw the reaction of American audiences when Visayans sung the "Star-Spangled Banner," "'you would not be able to say those words.'" Indeed, Ramirez denied her own recognition to the American accomplishments she had witnessed at St. Louis. Visayans were, for example, able to do "'much more fancy work than some of your people here,'" including jusi, piña, and sinamay embroidery and woven hats, mats, and carved goods. Ramirez had heard many Americans, upon witnessing these crafts, say, "'Did you ever!'" taking this to mean "'that some of the Americans can't beat the Visayan people.'" She had observed that "'most of the people ask so many foolish questions'" and were also rude, turning their backs after receiving an answer, "'without saying good-by or thank you.'" She closed the protest on behalf of "'all the Filipinos in our village [who] are very angry to be called savages and ask me to have you change it.'" Some were "'so mad,'" she warned, "'they won't go to school no more.'"[83]

The most vocal expressions of nationalist colonialism came from *pensionados*. As the self-conscious front line of Hispanicized Filipino self-representation in the imperial metropolis, they had been selected for their very respectability and carefully policed their behavior and self-expression in the United States, constantly reminded to do so by colonial authorities. A *Post-Dispatch* reporter sitting in on a *pensionado* lunch hour in August noted, with surprise, that "the scene is much like what one might see in the dining hall of any university," with the same "good-natured chaffing and bantering, the same unflattering nicknames." A party of students just coming in from guide duty, however, was "weary with answering visitors." "'How ignorant people are here,' growled one. 'Some of them think America discovered the Philippines,' murmured another. 'A lady asked me if I liked wearing clothes.' "[84]

The *pensionados'* shock and dismay at the way the "Igorots" had overtaken public attention would deepen as they either witnessed or heard reports of displays touring the United States in the wake of St. Louis, attempting to capture the feverish and profitable mania for Igorots. "It seems as though the Filipino people have before them a long lifework in attempting to counteract the impressions spread broadcast through America by those who so thoughtlessly exhibit savages belonging to our wild, uncivilized tribes in the islands," wrote a *pensionado* editorialist wearily in mid-1906. He did not enjoy explaining that he remained "ignorant of that delicacy which we may politely denominate 'fricaseed canine,'" nor that the University of Santo Tomas was older than Harvard, nor that "there is a larger percentage of Christians in the Philippines than in this country." Not long before, one of his colleagues had been disgusted to see displayed in a little Vermont town "a miserable, deformed semblance of humanity" advertised as "Laduca, the Wild Filipino Woman." There were "'Filipinos'"—the quotation marks were his—at Coney Island, Portland, Los Angeles, "all on exhibition for visitors at 10 cents apiece." In terms of realism, the writer's counterpoint was to capture a few geese and take them to the Philippines to exhibit as "True Specimens of 'Americanos!'"[85]

In one instance, a nationalist-colonialist critique of the Philippine Exposition became the vehicle for broader critiques of U.S. colonial policy. In an interview with the *Post-Dispatch* conducted through an interpreter, Honorary Commissioner Vicente Nepomuceno denied recognition of American benevolence at the Philippine Exposition, declaring it "shrewd political work" and "nothing more than a coup of Machiavelism [sic] on the part of the Republican administration." Nepomuceno was a Cagayan attorney and professor of secondary instruction who had served in the Philippine Republic as a provincial governor and subsequently entered the American regime as a judge and provincial *fiscal*.[86] For him, the exposition was "but a foil seeking to justify in the public mind the administration's insincerity toward the Filipino." In their "determination to hold our reins of government," officials had "gone into the remotest corners of the islands, gathered together the lowest types of the inhabitants and brought them to this country to exhibit them" in order "to justify their paternal grip on the islands." The appointment of an honorary commission had been an inadequate response to Filipino opposition: "the damage had been done; the impression had gone abroad that we are barbarians; that we eat dog and all that sort of thing, and no matter how long we stay here we cannot convince the public to the contrary."[87]

For Nepomuceno, nationalist colonialism was merely the entering wedge of a broader critique of U.S. colonial policy, reflecting tensions in the transition from Taft's to Wright's rule. Nepomuceno complained, for example, of an order that would make it mandatory that every Filipino officeholder speak English by January 1906, an impossibility that he claimed would, in effect, drive Filipinos from all government positions. Indeed, as it was, the American regime had "overloaded us with an army of employees, the majority of whom are neither needed nor wanted." Far from improving the Philippines, American rule had set it back, considering "the enormous debt that has been piled on us," while "a prohibitive tariff has shut out all commerce and dwarfed our revenue." These criticisms of American machinations were confirmed by the Philippine Commission's deliberate passage, during the honorary commissioners' absence in St. Louis, of a controversial tax reform law.[88]

The next day, Nepomuceno's tirade was refuted by Benito Legarda, one of the chairs of the Honorary Commission. While he maintained that Nepomuceno should not have "spoken so vigorously," Legarda conceded to his nationalist-colonialist terms, agreeing that "many Filipinos think the Philippine village exhibit is out of proportion" and confessing that "I should like it better if a higher class of Filipino life were shown." His defense of the exhibit was somewhat halfhearted: that the Philippine government did "not go beyond the proprieties in making its village attractive." He went on to defend the exhibit on purely economic grounds: "It must be remembered that the Philippine exhibit represents an enormous outlay," he stated, "and there must be some means for recovering some of the investment. The exhibition of savages is attractive; civilised peoples would not be attractive. There would be no novelty to it." What was notable about Legarda's supposed rescue of the exhibit, however, was the degree to which he echoed Nepomuceno's criticism of American colonial policy. "Americans have not kept their promises to the Filipinos," he stated. Millions of dollars of promised mining and natural resource investments had failed to appear, and where honorable American officials had been promised, in actuality, "they are not, as a rule, of either a high or a very desirable class . . . not of credit to their home country, and of no benefit to the Philippines."[89]

While "civilized" Filipinos criticized their relative invisibility—often seeing it as deliberate—when they were noticed, in at least one prominent case, they might be taken as a profound threat. The thrill of the Igorot spectacle derived in part from the fact that its danger was, ultimately, safely contained within the village grounds themselves. Civilized natives were both less recognizable as natives and had the freedom to stroll the fairgrounds openly, both of which facts made them more elusive. "All were clad in neat, fashionable clothing," the *Post-Dispatch* had noted of the arriving *pensionados*, "and it was only from their talk and complexion that their nationality could be told." This elusiveness became perilous in the case of the Philippine Scouts and what the *Post-Dispatch* provocatively called "An Unexpected Phase of Cosmopolitan Development."[90]

Toward the end of June 1904, certain Philippine Scouts had been observed strolling around the fairgrounds in the intimate company of young, white, female admirers and accepting their invitations to social gatherings. As the *Post-Dispatch* noted with some horror, this meant that Filipino troops at St. Louis were "now accepted as . . . social equal[s] in a widening circle" and considered "superior in attraction to the other uniformed men at the Fair." Indeed, the article speculated ominously that "it will not be strange if some of the Philippine soldiers, when they sail away, leave American brides behind, as American soldiers returning from the Philippines leave Philippine brides behind." In stating the essence of the dilemma, the *Post-Dispatch* shed surprising insight on the colonial problematic more broadly. "The problem," it observed, "is how and where to draw the color line on the Filipinos who have been brought to the Fair. To what extent, if any, shall the tanned tribesmen of the tropics be permitted to associate with their white assimilators? If they are to be permitted to sip sparingly of the social delights, how is it to be expressed upon them that thus far they may go and no farther?"[91]

For the exposition board, such associations were viewed as positive contributions to the goals of assimilation. This had been especially true in Manila and colonial capitals where the consolidation of Filipino-American political alliances had taken shape. Although fears of miscegenation haunted the imaginations of many Americans in the Philippines, the open social association of elite Filipinos and Americans had become a characteristic feature of the civilian regime. It was this colonial logic of assimilation that lay behind the board's aesthetic and political decisions regarding Filipino troops at St. Louis. Making the acquaintance of Americans at the fair, Filipino troops would adopt American

St.Louis Color Line Problem at the Fair.

Filipino Soldiers Aspire to Figure in Society

Little Brown Men Are Popular

This drawing from the St. Louis Post-Dispatch, July 3, 1904, accompanied an anxious article on the mutual attraction of Philippine Scouts and white American female visitors to the fair. For colonial officials, fraternization between Scouts and American women was a favorable index of one-way assimilation they hoped the fair would accomplish; for white supremacist mobs, it constituted a terrifying sign of collapsing racial-sexual boundaries that must be policed by violent means.

tastes, customs, and duties and gain a wider and more intimidating sense of their imperial sponsors. The board's reported response to brewing racial conflicts demonstrated just how different the regime's collaboration-based racial formation was from metropolitan ones: given the Filipino troops' exemplary loyalty, military discipline, and evidence of civilization, "it is the proper thing for them to associate with white people on terms of equality."[92]

Mobs of white men at the fair, however, did not recognize this inclusionary racial politics. Where Samantha had seen a hopeful template for the "Negro problem" in visions of Philippine "uplift," these men brutally insisted on applying the former model to the latter. For them, the vision of Scout troops with white women did not carry colonial messages of assimilation but signaled alarming ruptures of Jim Crow racial strictures. In this, they were demonstrating just how much the "universal exposition" was rooted in the particularities of contemporary St. Louis, with its Jim Crow laws and newspapers stocked with lurid tales of "Negro crime." St. Louis had drawn its color line firmly through the fairgrounds: black attendees at the fair registered outrage at their exclusion from restaurants and water fountains, for example, and after a public outcry were granted a special "bureau." In taking the colonial regime's terms of assimilation seriously and redefining them to include social and even sexual domains, the Scouts were violating the central precept of Southern, white, male self-possession: the monopolization of white women by white men as a means of controlling both them and the nonwhite men perceived to threaten racial-sexual boundaries.[93]

This threat would be met by open violence. On July 3, white men at the fair were reported to have been incensed upon seeing the couples and to have begun to act on their anger. "White men scowl and mutter 'niggers' and soulfully yearn to punch the heads of the presumptuous soldiers," read one report, "and not infrequently jostle and jeer at the colored cavaliers." On July 6, twenty U.S. marines stationed at the fair set out at midnight to attack the Scout camp and "teach the Filipinos to let white women alone," only to be intercepted by the fair's guards, with whom they scuffled. The following evening, they regrouped, attacking several Scouts in the company of white women near the midway display entitled "Mysterious Asia." According to one report, the resulting melee eventually involved 200 men.[94]

The following week, the marines' vigilante actions earned the formal approval of fair officials, when exposition guards forbade a half-dozen

Scouts to leave the fairgrounds in the company of white women. Accordingly to the *Post-Dispatch*, "[a] large crowd cheered the action of the police." The Scouts' female companions, in contrast, repeatedly came to their defense. On the first occasion when the Scouts emerged with "the marks of rough treatment, a crowd composed mostly of women, surrounded them and expressed sympathy for them." Nonetheless, the change in policy, which apparently originated from the Scouts' commander, was a defeat for the exposition board. In a sense, the effort to suppress the Philippine-American War at the exposition had failed: where Filipinos would be substituted for Americans during the staged combats, the melee between white marines and Filipino Scouts suggested an ongoing battle.[95] With the U.S. invasion of the Philippines scarcely over, white men at St. Louis had fought to guarantee that the United States would not be invaded by Filipinos.

Exposition by Other Means

As the fair wound to a close in the late fall of 1904, the exposition board would revisit the question of the exhibit's proper owners. They would do so in light of a progressive drop-off in receipts about which War Department officials were "very much disappointed." An exhibit aggressively cast as "industrial" had failed disastrously as a profit-making venture. Whereas at the height of the season, the exhibit had brought in $8,000 per day, in the month of October, it had fallen to only $5,000, and by November had sunk further, to approximately $3,500. Items for sale in the exhibit, such as publications, had been failures from the beginning. "Very little was realized by the Board from the sale of the handbook," admitted exposition official A. L. Lawshe. According to Wilson, there were approximately 6,000 remaining handbooks and other publications in government warehouses, "making a total of at least fifteen thousand pounds mostly in original cases having never been opened."[96] The first victims of these shortfalls were the inhabitants of non-Christian villages; whereas the original plan had been to dismantle the displays before the onset of cold weather, Wilson decided to leave them standing until heaters were required to maintain what were imagined as minimal living conditions.

While incoming revenues dropped, at least some of the exposition board's budget appears to have been siphoned off through corruption. Civil service regulations had been suspended in the exposition's legislation, allowing "agents" to be hired under dubious circumstances. During the busy months of preparation, board appropriations were quickly channeled toward myriad exposition expenses, making precise accountability difficult and presenting multiple opportunities for graft. In September 1904, for example, Capt. Ira Keithley, formerly in charge of the Constabulary at the fair, abruptly disappeared shortly after a federal warrant charged him with embezzlement of insular government funds. The funds, intended to pay Constabulary salaries, were suspected of having been used to pay off Keithley's horse-racing debts instead. By the time the money was missed, he was believed to be on his way to Mexico with a sum estimated at over $4,000.[97] It is probable that other such losses went undiscovered. The board's final budgetary estimates, issued to the press toward the end of the fair, varied from $1 million to $1.5 million.

When ticket sales were tallied, the exposition board was forced to confront a net loss of $600,000. Edwards saw the positive in this and was quoted as saying that the government had been "very well satisfied" with the expenditure in light of "the results in the way of acquainting the American people with Philippine conditions." Organizers sought to make up at least some of the loss by selling off as much of the exhibit as possible. Edwards noted that, in an abrupt change of plans, "it had been decided to take nothing except the natives back to the islands." The fiction of a "permanent" museum for Manila was made complete, its hypothetical holdings sold off in the United States. Philippine articles for sale included "pictures and statuary, articles of gold, silver, ivory, shell, brass, bronze and bone, silks, pineapple and hemp fibre cloth, mantillas, lace and embroidery, beadwork and fine samples of wood carving from Bilibid prison in Manila."[98]

While the board sold off some exhibits, it was simultaneously negotiating to have large numbers of them transferred to the American Museum of Natural History in New York. It had decided as early as late 1902 that the exhibit belonged in the United States rather than in the Philippines, a decision confirmed in a January 1905 agreement to dispose of the exhibit so as to "bring the greatest measure of benefit to the commercial, education and social interests of the people of the Philippine Islands." The decision was seen as a cost-cutting measure; housing the exhibit in the United States meant storage of "material for exhibition at any future exposition in which the Philippine government . . . may desire to participate." The Smithsonian and the Philadelphia Commercial Museum, which were also competing for the materials, pledged to transfer rights to the whole of the Philippine materials to the American Museum, in exchange for the return of some future portion of them at no cost. The American Museum agreed to pack and remove the exhibit from the St. Louis fairgrounds, to distribute its duplicate items to "a number of the leading educational institutions and Museums of the United States," and to arrange with the War Department to prepare an adequate Philippine exhibit for the Lewis and Clark Exposition in Oregon, at no cost to the U.S. national government.[99]

As part of its agreement, colonial officials reserved the right to temporarily withdraw specific exhibits for the regime's own display purposes. But, in fact, the exposition board's agreement with the American Museum was disastrous for institutions in the Philippines, especially for proposed museums there. The majority of the materials intended for the Philippine museums had been sent to St. Louis. Toward the end of the fair, colonial government anthropologist Albert Jenks had been assigned to designate remaining portions of the ethnological material to be returned to Manila as the basis for a museum. The effort proved to be a calamity for the Ethnological Survey and for hopes for an insular museum. Of those items that were eventually transported to the bureau offices in Manila, many arrived without labels; many others were lost in transit. Plans for a museum in Manila were shelved in 1906.[100] In the end, the exposition's chief success appears to have been separating Filipinos from the artifacts they had laboriously created and collected over the prior two years. At the close of the exposition, the exhibits went eastward to New York, and nearly all the Filipinos—apart from the *pensionados*—headed west to the Philippines. To the dismay of colonial officials, a few others who did remain did so for commercial exposition purposes that continued to project the wrong messages, as a few midway impresarios took Igorots on the road to state fairs and vaudeville venues.[101]

While a handful of displayed Filipinos continued to travel on the midway, they would also continue to circulate in published form. When Taft had attempted to mobilize the exposition, it had been only the most ambitious part of a wider search for metropolitan engines of colonial promotion. Taft had, for example, also worked to disseminate the findings of the 1903 census as widely as possible in the United States, a process that would help popularize *National Geographic Magazine* as a staple of U.S. culture. Specifically, Taft took advantage of the opportunity to reach out to the amateur scientific community. In February 1905, he was approached by his second cousin, Gilbert Grosvenor, then in his fourth year as editor of the official organ of a struggling and little-known

Washington-based geographical society. The National Geographic Society had been founded in 1888 as a tight-knit society of professional scientists and amateur enthusiasts, drawing heavily for its membership on the national government's emerging scientific bureaucracy in Washington, such as the Geological Survey and the Bureau of American Ethnology. By 1899, it had only about 1,000 members. Facing mounting deficits in the late 1890s, the society's new president, Alexander Graham Bell, had attempted to raise funds by expanding the subscription base for its publication outward from Washington and beyond the scientific establishment by offering subscribers membership in the society itself.[102]

In April 1899, just two months into the Philippine-American War, Bell had hired Grosvenor as the magazine's editor. Seeking to widen the appeal of both the magazine and the society, Grosvenor had pursued photographic reproduction, taking advantage of new and inexpensive photo-engraving technology and the availability of photographs taken by agencies of the national government, what Grosvenor described as "striking gold in my own backyard." The move had been disputed by the society's hard-core professionals, who "frowned on photographs unless they were 'scientific'" and warned Grosvenor that "'the excessive use of pictures and anecdotes is discouraged.'" But photographs had carried the day when Grosvenor published a stack of photographs of Tibet sent to him by a Russian explorer to fill an eleven-page hole in the January 1905 issue. Grosvenor had been congratulated by society members and was elected to the Board of Managers shortly thereafter.

It was in February 1905, just two months after the close of the fair, that he would come upon his second "pictorial windfall," when Taft approached him with the photographs taken by the Philippine Census. The magazine had, in a sense, followed the flag after 1898, capitalizing on, and generating public interest in, regions of the world newly relevant to the United States: it had, for example, run maps of Cuba, Puerto Rico, and the Philippines in its 1899–1900 issues. But when "Mr. Taft had distinctly said 'photographs,'" Grosvenor later recalled, ". . . that word had become as musical to my ear as the jingle of a cash register to a businessman."[103]

With the census materials at its core, the April 1905 issue of the magazine boldly proclaimed "A Revelation of the Filipinos." Coming in the wake of the exposition, it could be seen as either a retrospective guidebook or a print exposition for those unable to attend. It would, perhaps, be a form more amenable to the regime's political messages than the exposition itself had been. Cleaving to the Taft regime's rhetoric, the issue reported the "Surprising and Exceedingly Gratifying Condition of their Education, Intelligence, and Ability," based on census information, and the "Unexpected Magnitude of their Resources and Possibility for Development." Fully embracing his photographic strategy, Grosvenor selected thirty-two full-page plates, containing a total of 138 pictures: of rural scenes, Spanish churches, "native" dwellings, agricultural processes, census supervisors, and "non-Christian tribes." The issue's tremendous success surprised even its advocate, sending the society back to its presses to publish further editions. The society had begun 1905 with 3,400 member-subscribers and would end it with 11,000. When Taft himself was invited to speak in May, he confessed that he had expected to address "a few ladies and gentlemen" informally in a parlor, rather than the large audience he encountered at the Rifles' Armory.[104] Reciprocity between the geographic society and the Philippine colonial state would continue. The Philippine state provided resources—lecturers, authors, photographers—necessary for expanding the society's global purview to the Philippines; the society, in turn, provided current or former officials a sympathetic platform for advancing their views in the heart of Washington and, through the magazine, outward to thousands of middle-class readers. Not for the last time, formal colonialism would help shape the lenses through which Americans saw the broader world.

With printed Filipinos in circulation and actual Filipinos in retreat, St. Louis elites may have sighed in relief. After all, viewed from a certain angle, an exposition was a vast invasion, the world's multitudes funneling inward to a single, "cosmopolitan" point. It was the reason that maintaining an exposition's internal frontiers—especially between colonies and nations and between savagery and civilization—was so essential. Whatever messy social relations unfolded at an exposition, its formal grid conveyed the fantasy that a collapsing world would nonetheless retain its underlying order; indeed, expositions were governed by the hope that the world's true divisions might sharpen and clarify in microcosm. There was also the hope that this order might be transmitted outward when the impossible condensing process inevitably reversed itself, when the facades came down, the money was counted, and the natives scattered.

But as public readings of the exhibit against the grain of the exposition board's intentions suggested, audiences could not be manipulated so easily. Where the board had hoped to convey the colonial regime's novel racial formation, with its bifurcated tracks and tutelary means, to win Filipino recognition of U.S. power and Americans' recognition of civilian competence and progress, audiences had come away with the notion that the islands' civilization was less than five years old, and that beneath the new uniform of every marching Scout was a recently tamed savage. The disproportionate attention paid to non-Christians, prophesied by Filipino nationalist editorialists, suggested the regime's failure, rather than its success, as an engine of assimilation. The exposition had also sharply illustrated the failures of one of assimilation's central myths: that proximity between Filipinos and Americans would necessarily breed Filipino respect for and loyalty to the United States and adaptation to its ways. Like American audiences, alienated *pensionados* and *ilustrados* had taken away unanticipated lessons from the exposition: that the Americans, like the Spaniards, could not be trusted to represent accurately the Philippines and, especially, to recognize crucial distinctions between Christians and non-Christians. In subsequent years, they would take these lessons further, insisting on the right to represent, and to differentiate, themselves.

The Politics of Nation-Building

The six thousand little brown men who wear the red-trimmed
khaki have in three years grown into an efficient compact body
of alert, erect, English-speaking soldiers, who are proud of
their service.

Manila Times, 1904

What teacher would not feel proud of his pupils if he
finds that they answer to the requirements of his plan and
seem able to carry out the object he had in view in less
time than expected?

PABLO OCAMPO, 1908

On the evening of October 24, 1912, Maximo Kalaw, resident commissioner and law student at Georgetown University, took the podium at the Lake Mohonk Conference of Friends of the Indians and Other Dependent Peoples. Set in a resort in upstate New York, the annual conference hosted the highly constrained and self-satisfied conscience of the U.S. empire in its continental and overseas projections. Begun in 1883, the conference was an annual occasion at which missionaries, reformers, policy makers, and officials engaged in dialogues regarding the character and consequences of Indian policy within a largely Christian paternalist framework. In the wake of 1898, its membership had voted to expand its mandate—and its title—in tandem with national "expansion" to include "other dependent races." From that date, the conference reserved sessions for "affairs" in Puerto Rico and the Philippines. Colonial officials cycling back to the United States on sabbatical or following retirement, missionaries returning from service in the field, and journalists and travelers eager to convey their impressions converged each year to collectively debate and mold conventional wisdom regarding "our new possessions." These debates, however, took place within strict boundaries: the conference's platform each year included planks that affirmed the accomplishments of these respective colonial states in often ringing terms.[1]

Like other Filipinos who had spoken at the conference previously,

Kalaw inevitably did so as a "representative man" of the Philippines whose deportment, demeanor, and speech would be carefully scrutinized and made to reflect on Filipinos as a whole. The role of representative was itself embedded in the racist organizational terms of the conference, whose subjects became "dependent" in part through the conference's insistence that their "Friends" had legitimate claims to speak on their behalf. But if Kalaw was by definition "representative" before Mohonk's smug moral vacationers, he was simultaneously the representative of those Philippine assemblymen who had elected him resident commissioner, a position established by the Philippine Commission in 1907. Two resident commissioners from the Philippines would serve as representatives to the U.S. House of Representatives, to be selected by the commission and the Philippine Assembly every two years. Here, at the core of metropolitan authority, limits on Filipino sovereignty were made clear once again, with the commissioners empowered to participate in floor debate but not to vote.

In his speech on "The Filipino Youth and the Independence of the Philippinos [sic]," Kalaw would herald a new Filipino nation fired together under conditions of U.S. colonialism. He spoke on behalf of "the rising generation of Filipinos," those who were being taught to speak and write in English, who played baseball and tennis, "who are . . . to use a misleading term—being 'Americanized.'" Kalaw's central goal was to counter the conference's resolution of the previous year—"that my people have no common aims"—with arguments for Filipinos' "united aspirations." In doing so, he would turn to history. "In order to know the thoughts and ideas of these rising Filipinos," he stated, ". . . it is most necessary that we should know what spirit and ideals have animated them throughout their life and struggles." On the one hand, Filipinos' unity was primordial, rooted in geography—what he called the "compact triangular mass" of islands—and their common Malay "race," such that, prior to the coming of the Spaniards, they had possessed "a civilization of their own, a uniform degree of culture, racial customs, and traditions." On the other, Filipino nationality was colonial, the by-product first of Christianization and subsequently of "the dissemination of European culture and civilization." What Kalaw called "national feelings" had "formed through the medium of the Spanish language and on a basis of European standards and ideals." Finally, unity had been forged in the crucible of anticolonial struggle, "a united protest against common wrongs and injustice, a united struggle for freedom." That revolution was not over, despite American claims. Although it had been crushed militarily by the Americans, the spirit "which animated their fathers and elder brothers in that bloody struggle" still animated the new generation "in their present work for the freedom of the country."[2]

Was "the independence battle-cry" to be "drowned and forgotten amidst the influx of American culture and civilization?" Kalaw provocatively suggested the contrary: the deeper the contacts between Americans and Filipinos, the more Filipinos would long for their independence, prompted precisely by American traditions. "Speaking your own language and reading the books written by your own people," he said, "the young Filipinos can appreciate better your national characteristics and your political institutions." Contact with Americans, especially teachers, had familiarized young Filipinos with "personal characteristics" like "self-reliance" and "love for freedom." The English language itself was "the most forceful language for the expression of free thoughts and free actions," containing "masterly pleas for freedom" by the likes of Jefferson, Burke, and Byron. In brief, American tutelage was itself productive of Filipino nationalism and demands for liberty. "Education brings, above all things," he stated, "a stronger union among a people, a greater consciousness of kind—a more perfect nationalism. And nationalism always manifests itself in a vigorous protest against the foreign yoke." In a striking prophecy that might have flustered more than a few attendees, Kalaw predicted that "[t]hirty-eight million educated [Javanese] would in a moment destroy the Dutch rule in Java. Three hundred million educated Indians would at once free India from English control." Once the "eyes of a people" were open to "the swelling movement of democracy and republicanism," they would never "prefer an alien government to an independent government of their own."[3]

Kalaw's tone was increasingly characteristic of Filipino political assertions inside and outside the colonial state. The period from the St. Louis world's fair to the presidential election of Woodrow Wilson in 1912 was one in which Filipinos asserted new claims to power, taking advantage of the end of censorship, the advent of provincial elections, and the collapse of the Federalista political monopoly. The culmination of this process was the inauguration in 1907 of an elected Philippine Assembly as the lower house of a bicameral Philippine legislature, in which the Nacionalista Party would predominate beneath the Philippine Commission. It was also a period in which U.S. colonialists reorganized the colonial government in ways that simultaneously incorporated Filipinos into higher reaches of the state and centralized power in American hands. U.S. colonialists attempted to displace nationalist demands onto a depoliticized economic sphere, claiming that a "material development" policy of infrastructure, export, and extraction was needed before any "political" considerations could be entertained. At the same time, they actively cultivated and attempted to co-opt and control the emerging forces of Philippine nationalism.

The collision between Filipino demands and U.S. retrenchments raised fundamental questions about the character of the Philippine nation. Working under the premises of calibrated colonialism, the regime's agents understood the goal of the colonial state to be the long-term building of a Philippine nation from a previously fragmented population of which the Philippine Republic—as the tyranny of a "single tribe"—had been symptomatic. U.S. authorities insisted that only they had the power to build and recognize a true Philippine nation; as Filipinos were tutored in self-government, Americans would attempt to control its representatives and forms of self-expression. This fully realized nation, to be completed in the indefinite future, consolidated the United States' innumerable other colonial gifts to Filipinos into a single one; it would also set the United States apart as an exception, morally superior to colonial empires that did not promise their subjects their own, eventual nationality.

But this "nation-building" process was fraught with tension. While U.S. authorities insisted that they were building a Philippine nation for the first time, Filipinos insisted that, as the Philippine Revolution and Philippine Republic had already demonstrated, the Philippine nation was only theirs to make. Where U.S. imperialists held that they could not only rule the Philippines but "represent" Filipinos, Filipino nationalists asserted that only they should be empowered to represent the Philippines in political and symbolic terms. The tension between U.S. and Filipino visions of nation-building produced a multivalent discourse on "capacity" that maintained the politics of recognition and helped redraw lines of race and sovereignty inside the colonial state. U.S. colonialists insisted that Filipino capacities—for technical knowledge, for self-discipline, and especially for labor—were growing under U.S. tutelage but still failed to reach the bar of nationality. Only Americans could recognize Filipino capacities for self-government as they matured. Filipinos often responded by asserting Filipino capacity in the present and the past in order to claim the existence of a Philippine nation in the present and the future. Filipino participation in the U.S. colonial state was, in this view, not simply evidence of U.S. benevolence and passive, one-way Filipino "assimilation" but the mark of an active, Filipino capacity for self-government.

Central to these debates was the status of non-Christians in the Philippine nation-in-process. U.S. colonial officials had isolated non-Christians administratively through a bifurcated state: as Hispanicized Filipinos gradually achieved self-government, they would do so only in "Christian" regions, while American-appointed officials continued to exercise exclusive rule in fully half of the islands' territory identified as "non-Christian." With the rise of the Philippine Assembly, Filipino politicians would attempt to secure greater control over these areas, while U.S. colonialists used the divided state to compare American and Filipino "capacities" for effective rule, always to the detriment of the latter. Employing an imperial indigenism that imagined Christian and non-Christian groups as fundamentally antagonistic, they painted U.S. colonial rule as "protective," the only force in the islands capable of preventing civil war and internal race war. While Filipino politicians resisted attempts to detach non-Christian regions politically from the insular government that was increasingly in their hands, they also actively fought what they perceived to be U.S. colonialists' attempts to negate Filipino capacities through the strategic exposition of non-Christians to the U.S. public. For the purposes of many Hispanicized Filipinos, the non-Christians could not represent themselves, nor, with respect to the outside world, should they be represented.

Alienation and Resistance

The period following the St. Louis fair opened with growing Filipino alienation from the Philippine Commission under its new governor-general, Luke Wright, and from broader U.S. premises of benevolence, uplift, and tutelage. Where Kalaw saw the Filipino assimilation of U.S. culture as a potential source of freedom, others forged a Filipino identity against U.S. imperialist pretensions. This process was visible, for example, among *pensionados*. The *pensionado* project had been predicated on the fantasy of the one-way absorption—imagined as a kind of conversion—of American customs, tastes, and loyalties. But on more than one occasion, *pensionados* had—as at St. Louis—taken advantage of their unique position, experiences, and language abilities to advance different narratives of life inside the United States. Some turned their critical gaze on U.S. institutions. One *pensionado* using the name "Partridge," for example, who had lived in Washington for a number of years, had sent letters written in Spanish to *El Renacimiento* in Manila that satirized metropolitan American society. His essays from 1906 were selected for republication by the editors of the *pensionados'* short-lived, Washington-based magazine the *Filipino*, under the title "America as Seen by a Filipino."

While its author's familiarity with Antonio Luna's "Madrid Impressions of a Filipino" is unknown, the similarities between the two are notable. What struck Partridge most in the United States was the way Americans fell short of his standards of humility. Americans' "vociferous pride" was expressed with such "astonishing garrulity" that, he believed, they would lengthen the day to twenty-five hours "in order that they could continue to enlarge upon and boom all the aspects of their conceitedness." Partridge cited numerous personal incidents that suggested his familiarity with bourgeois domestic spheres in the United States. Just as Congressman Weeks had probed Filipino domestic interiors in search of evidence of "incapacity," Partridge was finding much to criticize in U.S. households. In one, a woman had fished for compliments "unblushingly" regarding her embroidery, while her sister chased praise for her nephew, just "'graduated from a physical culture school,'" with a shocking "want of modesty." But these were not isolated incidents. "One hears innumerable anecdotes" regarding this trait, he wrote, "in family circles, among friends, in the discussion of national and even international affairs." At base, it came down to the following assumption, writ large and small: "The United States first and the rest of the world afterwards."[4]

This "idiosyncratic American pride" was not the result of what Partridge called "recent conquests in the field of worldly regard," although these conquests had "further contributed to their unbearable petulance of today." Recently, for example, aristocrats Mr. and Mrs. Longworth had taken credit for stopping a revolution in Cuba by making their honeymoon there. But pride in and of itself was not a problem. In a democratic society, he maintained, pride was "a rich mine of initiative and energy," and the "continual struggle" between individuals "causes initiative and means of improvement to become newer, more perfect and to multiply for the benefit, not only of the individual, but of the nation as well." In this sense, there was a great deal to admire in America, land of "daring strugglers, overflowing with faith and constancy to earn not one cent but a million." But "excessive conceit blinds [Americans] and causes them to become the victims of ridicule by reason of their most offensive petulance."[5]

There was no better evidence of this, he held, than American perceptions of the Philippines and Filipino responses. "The proud American sees in the Philippines a colony," he wrote, and thus denied it "the same rights and privileges as the colonizing nation." Arriving in the islands, Americans "with few exceptions" carried with them a "triple pride": "innate pride, the pride born of being a colonizer, and the pride arising from the superiority of race." But sooner or later, Americans of this stripe met with "disenchantment" and loss of Filipino recognition. "The Filipino, instead of applauding him for all his acts, and of admitting him, and of respecting him, censures him, considers him an equal only when not as an inferior in certain aspects." Partridge generously agreed not to bother his reader by addressing "the segregation of races, race conflicts, jingoism, and . . . the yellow press" in the United States. "The effect of this disenchantment," he added mischievously, "you are better acquainted with there than I here."[6]

This "disenchantment" had made itself manifest in the breakdown of the first Philippine-American alliance system, triggered by Taft's departure for Washington and Wright's assumption of the position of governor-general. Wright had neither the tact, patience, nor understanding with which Taft had conciliated Filipino elites. While he delivered many of Taft's familiar tropes, his rhetoric and actions signaled what was, for Federalista collaborators, a threatening revision of the terms of collaboration. Wright called for a regime of "business principles," by which he meant the more "efficient" control of the government by Americans.

The result was a dramatic shift in the regime's patronage system. In Wright's eyes, Taft's war-ending policy of "attraction" had preferred Filipino applicants for government posts over resentful Manila Americans; Wright would balance the odds in favor of what he called "equal opportunity for all." Under Wright, government patronage shifted from Taft's Federalista base to a yet more conservative community of U.S. businessmen, Spaniards, and friars. Wright was also unwilling to engage in fiesta politics or the broader politics of recognition; he and his wife openly snubbed Filipino elites socially and refused to acknowledge their demands for political participation. Most frustrating for a wide spectrum of Filipinos was Wright's enthusiasm for harsh, repressive measures by the Philippine Constabulary, including the revocation of habeas corpus for Cavite and Batangas in January 1905. The Constabulary's warlike responses to continued resistance suggested to many *ilustrados*, including prominent Federalistas, that its power was irresponsible and arbitrary. Together with fiscal and other political conflicts, these tensions gave colonial politics what some observers called an ominous "racial" cast. By 1905, Federalista politicians were joined by other groups in opposing the Wright regime. When Taft returned in August 1905 to investigate the situation with a party of congressional leaders and social *prominenti*, he and his advisers found the Filipinos they consulted unanimous in their opposition to Wright.[7]

For Helen C. Wilson, an anti-imperialist reporter who visited the islands, among the chief causes of "resentment and exasperation with the American regime," which "characterize[d] the attitude of the Filipino people," there was "none more potent than the constabulary."[8] The Constabulary was to aid in the consolidation of civilian government at the provincial and municipal levels, which also meant that it was to fight the remnants of the still-unended Philippine-American War in provinces where rebels—now labeled "ladrones"—continued to resist U.S. sovereignty. In practical terms, the Constabulary's resources had been almost completely dedicated to counterinsurgency, becoming a paramilitary force that employed many of the same tactics that U.S. military forces had during the war. The Constabulary's status as a kind of army in police uniform was made clearest when, during its campaigns against ladrones, it incorporated into its ranks Philippine Scout units formerly under U.S. Army control. As during the war, the Constabulary cultivated a network of spies to pass information regarding ladron activity. The flip side of intimidation was corruption, as Constabulary officers and men supplemented their official incomes with protection money or outright theft. In October 1903, for example, two Constabulary officers in Mindanao had seized a small interisland steamer and headed for Borneo with $6,000 in Constabulary funds, seizing a number of ships and killing four Filipino crew members who attempted to overpower the fugitives.[9]

One of the most vivid signs that the war had not yet ended entirely was the Constabulary's repeated reliance on tactics of "reconcentration." The June 1903 Reconcentration Act empowered the governor-general to authorize provincial governors to reconcentrate rural populations who ostensibly supported banditry. The Constabulary would make ample use of this tactic, repeatedly reconcentrating rural populations in the "postwar" era. Reconcentration was one focal point of Filipino press opposition to the Constabulary and the Scouts. In March 1902, for example, *El Renacimiento* condemned a reconcentration plan for Batangas by Col. D. J. Baker that included the arrest of prominent citizens in order to "*augment* respect for the government and *deaden* the terror caused by bandits" by offering these elites "protection." The newspaper stated, to the contrary, that Baker's formula seemed "more dangerous to public contentment and order" than that which it was meant to combat. The fear reconcentration would create could only produce a respect that was "hypocritical" and "little enduring or effective for producing the harmony that is sought."[10]

Three years later, the paper blasted the commission's approval of the reconcentration of Cavite. It appeared that "the generous congressional spirit that clamored so indignantly against Weylerian procedures in Cuba" did not apply to the Philippines. First, reconcentration had "all the appearance of an injustice," as it was applied "more toward the peaceful than to those in arms." Second, reconcentration would (paraphrasing General Grant) leave "discomfort and sentiments of rancor that would be forgotten either late or never." Indeed, it might give rise to additional *bandolerismo*." The poor, "especially the general mass," did "not reason: it feels"; what it felt most sharply in reconcentration was "hunger, ruin, annoyance, discomfort." Add to this a "predisposition to distrust determinations from above . . . a sediment left by the past struggle," and one had a "terrain fertilized for all those bad thoughts." He who "sows coldness gathers wrath and hatred," it warned.[11]

Prompted by Filipino reportage of Constabulary "abuses and outrages," Helen Wilson investigated one camp at Bacoor, just ten miles outside Manila, in July 1905, reporting her findings to the *Springfield (Mass.) Republican* early the following year. Wilson arrived to find the two villages of San Nicolas and Ligas, comprising 500 people, forced by the Constabulary into an overcrowded, disease-ridden camp, where they had been confined for five weeks. While reconcentration was most frequently justified as "a war measure employed against a hostile people," the Constabulary had here isolated two "peaceful and law-abiding" towns to deny resources to Cornelio Felizardo, a former revolutionary officer who had acquired the same "glamour" that had given "the notorious James boys immunity for so many years." No shelter or food had been provided to the villagers, and their improvised bamboo and nipa housing had left them exposed to the elements and prone to dysentery and malaria, while "evidences of food were eloquently meager." Thin children with bloated abdomens reminded Wilson of "the pictures of reconcentration in Cuba and famine in India"; one dying child was "so white and bloodless" that "it was hard to believe that he was the son of a brown woman." In the wake of "the publicity given to the place by the Renacimiento articles," an ill-informed Filipino sanitary inspector had been sent. Wilson's concerns, however, were similar to the regime's: reconcentration camps were building the wrong kind of nation. First was the question of tutelage: "What conceptions of citizenship, of sovereign law, or individual rights," she asked, were villagers learning from the Constabulary's "absolute and arbitrary control"? Second was the "already acute labor problem," and the camp's promotion of "demoralizing idleness." As the Cuban case showed, reconcentration "increases the number of the idle and destitute" and "lowers the efficiency and moral standards of the people."[12]

The increasingly rancorous tone of colonial politics under the Wright regime was widely, if variably, perceived as racial in tenor. Anthropologist Elsie Clews Parsons, who accompanied her senator husband to the islands with the Taft party, saw Americans' racial arrogance as scuttling Filipino-American sociability. "Race snobbishness seems to be the source of much of the present discontent in the Philippines with the American administration," she wrote. "Between this native aristocracy and the Americans in Manila there is at present little or no social intercourse although the natives have a deep sense of hospitality and are devoted to social festivity." American women in Manila were particularly at fault, some having "never been inside a Filipino house"; the president's celebrity daughter Alice had invited no Filipino ladies to her receptions and, where Filipinos did attend, "no resident American women danced with Filipino partners except in the case of one square dance."[13]

James LeRoy, who also accompanied the Taft party, agreed. "We have lost ground in the last year, so far as the political situation is concerned," he stated bluntly to the 1905 Lake Mohonk Conference. Once again, "we have been displaying this same race prejudice, and we shall only regain that ground as we conquer that feeling . . . and by putting the right spirit into the force of our American subordinates." The problem was both one of etiquette and of ideology: both reflected a lack of recognition for Filipino elites. What LeRoy called "a large proportion of officials and employes [sic]" were "not sympathetic toward the Filipino . . . do not believe in the Filipino's capacity to develop and . . . are unfit for the work in which they are engaged." LeRoy claimed that many Manila Americans desired a more "paternal" and "practical" policy, quicker to both display and employ force. Behind this hope there lay, "almost inevitably," the assumption that "those peoples, dependent peoples, or what you may call them," were "inherently and permanently deficient" and "really incapable of progress." Decreasing faith in Filipino capacity for progress, in turn, meant less "patience in studying either his history or his present aspirations, or in listening to what sometimes seems very foolish talk on his part." While the Bureau of Education had succeeded in "getting hold of the people," the Constabulary, by contrast, was still without the "sympathetic contact with the people which it should have." LeRoy reminded his audience of the dangerous consequences of such "pessimism." "We have not given to the Filipinos political concessions wholly out of hand," he stated. "In part we gave them because they made us give them, with their knife at our throat."[14]

Others found Americans' racial arrogance positive and nonexceptional. "Although we Americans as a rule have dilated much in popular discourses upon the doctrine of equality," stated Cornell political economist Jeremiah Jenks, also at the 1905 Lake Mohonk Conference, "it still remains true that the question of race prejudice is a very important one in most social and political relations in all countries." Alongside the Philippines, Jenks's examples came from regions where "the inhabitants have customs that are decidedly different from those of the dominant country, and especially if the people belong to a different race or color," such as British India, or the Federated Malay States, or Dutch Java. Jenks turned LeRoy's account of race on its head: "race prejudice" was imperial honesty, expressed wherever colonial rulers perceived "with great clearness the weaknesses of the people of the dependency." Jenks believed that this sometimes resulted in "harsh treatment" by rulers and attempts to deal "fairly and gently," accompanied by "a certain contempt." But he emphasized that the "contempt of the rulers" was "matched by that of the ruled," especially where the latter saw themselves as superior in "intellectual culture, religious training, or social customs." Malay chiefs, he noted, had a "feeling of superiority in refinement and culture" when compared with a "brusque Englishman or Dutchman." Educated Filipinos had a "natural feeling of race superiority," which "most people who have had any education feel"; the "excesses of our soldiers" had inclined them early on to approach Americans in general with disdain. The race prejudice of the "native," then, was his arrogant and mistaken response to the failure of colonizers to police class within their ranks. Anglo-Saxon race prejudice was, by contrast, merely the result of an admirable "truthfulness in speech."[15]

Filipino assertions and the increasingly oppositional tone of colonial politics contributed to a culture of fear and paranoia among colonial Americans, especially in Manila, whose American population lived in constant fear of Filipino uprising and read its arrival from sometimes remarkably slight evidence. Suspicions of impending "race war" were powerfully reinforced by the local impact of regional politics, especially during and after the Russo-Japanese War. After the 1902 Anglo-Japanese accord, U.S. strategists had seen Japan as a potential ally in containing Russian power in East Asia. The United States had declared strict neutrality in the conflict, but Japanese victory raised the specter of a powerful, imperial state in the region with ambitions that might include nearby U.S. colonial interests. On his way to the Philippines on his investigative trip, Taft met with Japanese prime minister Taro Katsura and negotiated a framework to preserve the status quo in the Far East, gaining Japanese assurances that it harbored no aggressive designs on the Philippines in exchange for the United States' affirmation of Japanese sovereignty over Korea.

It did not help the Manila Americans' sense of security that at least some Filipinos were asserting themselves through the vicarious victories of "Oriental" states over Europeans, reinforcing the sense of a darkening racial line in Philippine-American politics. Japanese military successes against Russia had an electrifying effect throughout the colonial world, as colonized peoples seized on the Japanese Empire's triumph and, through racial lenses, made them accomplishments of the "darker races" as a whole.[16] The impact of the Japanese victory was felt throughout Asia. Charles Elliott, former secretary of commerce and police and an associate justice of the Philippine Supreme Court, wrote in 1917 that Japan's defeat of Russia "gave great impetus to the nationalist feeling which was manifesting itself in all of the countries of the Far East."[17] In the United States, where African Americans were mobilizing against Jim Crow terror, W. E. B. Du Bois wrote that the war had broken the "foolish modern magic of the word 'white'" and raised the possibility of a "colored revolt against white exploitation."[18]

Filipinos had followed what *El Renacimiento* called "the great conflagration of the Far East" with great interest. Just days after the first battles, the newspaper speculated on the broader consequences of victory by either Russia or Japan, "two powers distinguished by their race." The former outcome, it prophesied, would advance "the dominance of Russians, and Europeans in general, in Asia" and lead to "the colonization of that immense continent," a development that suited "neither Filipinos nor the U.S. government in the Philippines." In the latter case, "European influence in the Far East will be weakened [if not] annulled, immediately [uniting] Japan and China to proclaim the principle of 'Asia for the Asians.'" In its conclusion, the editorialist concluded that for both "the Philippines and . . . the North American government," "the triumph of

Japan is preferable to that of Russia." Russia was dominated by "absolutist" ideas; Japan, by contrast, while it had "its ambitions," was "not a nation that is known for being tyrannical and oppressive." Following the Japanese victory, eighty-eight Filipino students at the School of Law drew up and signed a congratulatory message, which they presented to the Japanese consul.[19]

Such assertions triggered widespread American fears of intertwined Filipino insurrection and Japanese invasion, fears that would remain endemic to American colonial society. The Secret Service of the Philippine Constabulary focused increasing attention on Japanese migrants living in the islands, imagining them as the advance guard of the Japanese Imperial Army rather than the farmers they appeared to be. Rumors circulated that pro-Japanese Filipino societies were recruiting among former revolutionary leaders. Special scrutiny was imposed on Filipinos either living in or traveling to and from Japan. An "Oriental Society"—described as having Siamese, Chinese, Korean, and Japanese as well as Filipino members—was reported to have begun in Tokyo and to have featured "anti-American" statements at its meetings, including one in summer 1908 held in honor of José Rizal. Ex-revolutionary Antonio Ricarte, living in exile in Japan, was continually imagined to be plotting an invasion with Japanese financial and military aid. Unwilling to admit to Filipino originality even in conspiracy, William Cameron Forbes insisted upon close ties between Japan and leading Filipino critics, cabling the secretary of war in September 1909 that he was "convinced that the hostility of the Renacimiento is inspired by Japanese influence with the object of prejudicing the Filipino people against the Government"; El Renacimiento editor Teodoro Kalaw, for example, was "one of the most decided Japanese sympathizers."[20]

While U.S. colonial officials expressed concern that Filipinos might take inspiration from the Japanese Empire's victory against a "white" power in the region, Filipinos were also drawing encouragement from black assertions against white supremacy in the United States. One illuminating incident in this regard involved the 1910 heavyweight championship boxing match between Jack Johnson and Jim Jeffries. The fight itself, held in Reno, Nevada, on July 4, 1910, had been heavily promoted within the United States and internationally as a "race war" in the ring, with Johnson, the black racial "menace," confronting Jeffries, the "Great White Hope." When Johnson defeated Jeffries in the thirteenth round, the news sent shockwaves of joy and rage across the United States; racial violence broke out in U.S. cities, and state and city governments, particularly in the South, banned the screening of the fight film, condemning its "brutality" and its imagined capacity to stir blacks to acts of violence-inducing "insolence."[21]

The lead-up to the fight had been closely followed on Manila's front pages, and audiences hungrily awaited the transpacific crossing of motion pictures. "Manila is a city given over to cinema," wrote Pedro Quinto in the *Renacimiento Filipino*. "And few cinematographic films have been so warmly desired in this capital as that of the famous Jeffries-Johnson boxing match." Filipino audiences were upset to learn, then, that Manila's Municipal Council had almost immediately banned the screening of the film: this particular moment in U.S. racial politics would, quite literally, not be exported or projected to the Philippines. While the council's reasons were not reported to the press, Filipino editorialists were quick to supply their own. "The punches thrown in Reno by the black boxer Johnson have reverberated in Manila, wounding the delicate ear-drums of our Municipal Council," read another editorial slyly. The reason for the council's ban was "not a mystery for many": "The victor is a negro. The vanquished is not." Had the outcome of the "Olympian struggle" been different, it noted, "we would have already tired of witnessing its incidents across a white sheet."[22]

Quinto narrated the fight's proceedings and embarked on an exploration of its broader significance for Filipinos and for the world at large. Somewhat disingenuously, he stated that Filipinos were "strangers to the peculiar antagonism between the white and the negro" and were "outside the circle in which dance the happiness and enthusiasm of the 'victors' and the ire and disappointment of the 'defeated.'" While "we do not participate in the sentiments of one or the other," the "tremendous blow" at Reno had "importance for Humanity." It had "no precedent" in the history of the United States, where blacks were treated to "special justice" in the hands of angry mobs and where the "very idea" of a black man raising his hand against a white man was considered a "monstrosity." But Johnson's victory had been meaningful on a broader, even global, scale, having "shake[n] up the moral sense"; it might promote "civilization, social justice and . . . the religion that preaches constantly to love one's neighbor as oneself." Specifically, Johnson's triumph "must rip to pieces the ancient prestige of a race that up to now has preached and maintained that its superiority was above argument." Tyranny, which was "essentially human," needed a "special environment" in which to prosper, in which "the weak . . . bow down before the strong, and where there are men who believe themselves by 'divine right' superior to the rest." Tyranny necessarily arose from inequality of power: when men felt themselves "equally strong and equally exposed to fall," probabilities of tyranny were reduced and "mutual respect . . . the best guarantee of liberty" was cultivated. Johnson had struck a blow against tyranny by forcing the world to recognize "not only his equality, but also his superiority over his adversary." By destroying notions of black inferiority, Johnson had undermined one of the foundations of tyranny in general. Johnson had done "a service to Humanity," in making Jeffries "bite the dust," by "showing where effort and 'training' can take individuals and peoples," and by "making seen, in a salutary way, that nothing on earth is stable."[23]

Colonial Democracy

The crisis of the Wright regime provoked important changes in the structure of Philippine-American colonial politics. In the short term, Taft's investigation resulted in Wright's ouster and reassignment to the ambassadorship of Japan. To prevent this act from emboldening Wright's opponents, Taft simultaneously removed T. H. Pardo de Tavera, who had been a vocal opponent of Wright, from the Philippine Commission. In the longer term, the crisis ushered in a shift in American clientelist strategies away from the sponsorship of Manila-based *ilustrados*, the backbone of the Federalista Party, who had been instrumental in ending the war, toward the recognition of a younger generation of emerging provincial politicians. The opening of provincial governorships to election by municipal governors was the first step in bridging local factional politics and insular state politics. For some, it suggested the fulfillment of U.S. promises of evolutionary self-government. In practical terms, it gave rise to the figures who would come to dominate the emergent Nacionalista Party, and through it, Philippine politics, at least two of them—Sergio Osmeña of Cebu and Manuel Quezon of Batangas—for four decades.

As the older collaboration system collapsed and a new one emerged, there developed a multisided struggle over the meanings of "nationbuilding." As censorship receded and a postwar Filipino press developed, languages of nationalism had reemerged as a defining feature of colonial politics. Where such rhetoric had proven frightening to the early civilian state, it would be increasingly cultivated and transformed by U.S. colonial officials. Indeed, if "assimilation" had been the rhetorical touchstone of the first alliance system between Taft and the Federalistas, "nation" would emerge as the axis of the second, and far more durable, alliance system between subsequent civil governors and the Nacionalista Party, which would dominate the next four decades' politics. Working closely with the Nacionalista leadership, U.S. colonial officials would find much to like, and little to fear, in their public discourses of nationalism, as long as they did not threaten U.S. sovereignty.

As they struggled for power within the colonial state, Filipino nationalists and U.S. colonialists often sharply disagreed on the specific meanings of "nation-building." Filipino nationalists often located the Philippine nation in the historical past and in recent and present-day struggles, from the Philippine Revolution to political mobilization under the colonial regime. In this view, Filipinos had built and were building their own nation, within and against the structures of Spanish and U.S. colonialism. The only appropriate recognition of this nationality was the devolution of power to Filipinos, in whole or in part. U.S. colonialists, by contrast, sought to embed Philippine nationalism in the structures of calibrated colonialism and the ongoing politics of recognition: for them, Filipino nationality was not a reality in the past or present but was the unachieved goal of the U.S. regime. Americans alone would be able to build the varied capacities Filipinos required before Filipino nationhood could be declared, and Americans would be exclusively empowered to recognize these capacities. Where for many Filipino nationalists, present-day Filipino nationality demanded political autonomy or even independence, many U.S. colonialists sought to displace these demands onto the economic sphere: nation-building was a long-term infrastructure and education project that would require an indefinite period in which to realize itself.

PHILIPPINE LEGISLATIVE POWER in the assembly proved to be a central flash point of the cultural politics of nation-building. American officials had been highly ambivalent about the possibility of an elected Philippine legislature within its colonial government, and the provision for one had been included by a narrow margin in the Organic Act of 1902. The assembly had been authorized, however, in a way that safely embedded it in the politics of recognition and the structures of the bifurcated state, leaving the timing of its inauguration up to American judgment, specifically the completion and publication of the census and the guarantee of "stability" in Christian regions of the archipelago. Once the clock had run out on each of these potential stalling tactics, U.S. colonial officials organized and conducted the first assembly election in July 1907. While the election undoubtedly opened the state to new sources of agency, it nonetheless advanced a colonial democracy.

It was, first of all, "colonial" in that many of its potential leaders and voters had been killed in a war of imperial conquest only a few years earlier. The "stability" stipulation tied the advent of assembly elections to the successful completion of the Constabulary's continuing campaign of terror and reconcentration in the countryside. Elections were held only in Christian provinces, deepening the racial territorialization of politics. Within these regions, suffrage was restricted to men literate in Spanish or English who had held office in either the Spanish or U.S. regimes, in effect enabling only *principales* and *ilustrados*, approximately 1.4 percent of the Philippine population, to participate as electors. Elected officers were investigated by the Constabulary's Secret Service for ties to ladrones, agitators, and revolutionaries, collected into a "Personal and Police History of the Deputies of the First Filipino Assembly."[24] Prior to the assembly's inauguration, the commission spent panicked days cramming through legislation that it presumed Filipino legislators would obstruct. The assembly itself was given limited legislative powers, subject to commission amendment or veto; after 1909, Congress granted the commission the power to continue previous budgets to prevent possible assembly filibustering.

In terms of election results, Filipino electors—94 percent of whom voted in 1907—provided a sharp rebuke to the first Filipino-American alliance system, delivering only sixteen seats to the Federalistas and fifty-nine to the emerging Nacionalista Party, with a platform containing a call for "immediate independence." But despite the fear of a radical break that the election had provoked among Americans in the islands, the assembly's political experience was striking: one-quarter of its members had held office under the Spanish, three-quarters under the Malolos Republic, and 90 percent under the American regime. On the whole, the Nacionalistas were younger than the Federalistas and had power bases in provincial capitals rather than Manila. Unlike the Federalistas, who had grown into their politics during the late Spanish period, the Nacionalistas were more likely to have been raised in the idioms and institutions of U.S. colonialism and were thus better prepared to use, adapt, and challenge them. Rising Nacionalista leaders also had close ties to U.S. colonial officials, especially Sergio Osmeña to William Cameron Forbes, and Manuel Quezon to Constabulary chief Harry Bandholtz. Philippine "nationalism" in this mode would often fail to coincide with Philippine independence. Despite the language of "immediate independence," the Nacionalista leadership would, over the next decades of its dominance, prove highly ambivalent in its efforts to secure an end to U.S. sovereignty.[25]

Competing public interpretations of the Philippine Assembly illustrated the conflicting meanings of nation-building. Filipino nationalists viewed the advent of the assembly not as simply another colonial test but as the inauguration of national political self-recognition and even the fulfillment of the Philippine Revolution. As Reynaldo Ileto has shown, Filipino leaders' addresses before mass Filipino audiences regarding the assembly gave shape to radical understandings of independence and freedom. Osmeña, for example, gave epochal meaning to the assembly in a May 1910 speech to an audience in Bulacan, emphasizing the continuity of past and present Philippine history. "[W]e are here to bond the present with the past," he said. Osmeña engaged in flag politics, noting of the hall "the absence of that which we would all like to see," the Philippine flag, "which our brothers defended" and which Osmeña had seen fly in the town during "the difficult days of yesteryear." The Filipino nation was not to be born in an indefinite future of American tutelage but had already been forged in a past of revolutionary struggle. "We did not win in arms," he said, "but when ours fell, weak and poor, and in the middle of general disaster, in which confusion narrowed the horizon between darkness and agony, in which it seemed as if the world would end and we would all disappear, a people lifted itself, never to fall again: the Filipino People."[26]

Osmeña then cast his own labors, and those of the assembly, as the historical extension of the revolution, impelled by the same desire for "national liberation." The "sacrifice of blood" in the "unequal struggle" had not been in vain. "The war concluded," he said, "the struggle, covered with a new form and defending the same purposes, invaded the field of ideas, the field of right, the field of the Law." Just as the revolution was "neither the work of a single man nor sustained by the effort of only a few, but rather of the whole Filipino people," the survival of its ideals required "an institution whose life persists across new dangers and difficulties." The assembly was, in other words, "the daughter of the Philippine Revolution"; no participant in the revolution could attack the assembly if he "remains loyal to his ideals."[27]

If Osmeña interpreted the assembly as the political fulfillment of the Filipino nation, Secretary of War William Howard Taft attempted to cast

Dominated by a new elite of Nacionalistas, the Philippine Assembly, the first of which is shown here, struggled with the commission over jurisdiction and the right of representation in symbolic and political terms. Where U.S. officials had previously monopolized the power to authorize representatives, images like this one evoke broader nationalist efforts to identify and hold up the Philippines' "representative men." Hidalgo's Through Peace and Liberty, from the St. Louis fair, a vision of Filipino submission, hangs at the back of the chamber, suggesting the narrow confines within which the assembly's political challenges would take place. By 1916, the legislature would replace it with a heroic portrait of José Rizal. From Worcester, Philippines, Past and Present, vol. 2, facing p. 738.

it within the politics of recognition, as only the latest of an indefinite series of colonial tests. Returning to the Philippines to inaugurate the legislature as a representative of President Roosevelt, Taft faced an unenviable task: to reassert U.S. imperial sovereignty in the face of elected Filipino representatives, the majority of whom belonged to a party declared in favor of immediate independence. The result was a mixture of false apology, lecture, and threat. The apology came in response to Filipino demands that he declare a firm U.S. policy regarding its sovereignty over the Philippines, especially its duration. Taft stated that these matters were, by treaty, still in the hands of Congress and therefore not for him or Roosevelt to determine. "How long this process of political preparation of the Filipino people is likely to be is a question which no one can certainly answer," he said. But Taft believed the question itself unworthy of asking: it was unwise "to fix a certain number of years in which the experiment must become a success and be completely realized."[28]

That said, Taft adeptly positioned himself, and the larger regime, as the best alternative among innumerable bad ones. On the one hand, U.S. colonialists confronted critics who believed suffrage had been "put . . . into the hands of the Filipino people before they have shown themselves to be industrially and in other ways capable of exercising the self-restraint and conservatism of action which are essential to political stability." On the other hand, there were anti-imperialists who had "encouraged a sullenness on the part of many Filipinos and a lack of interest in progress and development of the existing government." The "constant agitation for independence" had been bad for "material development," scaring off capitalists who believed an independent Philippines "would not be permanent and stable." As a result of the efforts of these latter types (but not, apparently, the former), "during the educational process there has been a continuing controversy as to the political capacity of the Filipino people."[29]

Second, there was a lecture on the virtues and accomplishments of U.S. colonialism to date, one that foregrounded the obstacles confronted rather than the greatness actually achieved. There had been rinderpest, disease, the friar lands controversy, and widespread "ladronism." There had been "the dependence for a time upon men as government agents who had come out in a spirit of adventure to the Islands," some of whom proved "not to be fitted either by character or experience for the discharge of responsible public duties." But in recent years, there had been marked improvement in areas of hygiene, education, and justice. Two years earlier, complaints against the Constabulary had been "numerous, emphatic and bitter," but investigation and reform had yielded results. Taft blunted the potential impact of the election by reasserting its status as a tutelary process, another project in the regime-as-school. Suffrage by those "who have qualifications of education or property that prove intelligence and substance" was "likely to teach the electorate useful political lessons." It made the exercise of power a "useful training ground," while "the power to be exercised is subject to such limitation as not to be dangerous to the community." While highly bounded, limited suffrage had been a concession to Filipino revolutionary politics; Taft conceded that "the granting of the franchise was most useful in producing tranquillity among the people."[30]

Third, there was an explicit threat. Filipinos should not mistake the assembly for national independence or complete self-government but should see it, rather, as yet another moment in the unfolding of calibrated colonialism, an indefinitely extended test of capacity before American arbiters, one in which Americans would continue to recognize, or deny recognition to, political actors and behavior. "There are still many possible intervals or steps between the power you now exercise and complete autonomy," he cautioned. As procedure and legislation developed along "patriotic, intelligent, conservative and useful lines," assemblymen would "show more emphatically than in any other way your right and capacity to take part in the government and the wisdom of granting to your Assembly, and to the people that elected you, more power." Those whose sole aim was "to hold up the government to execration, to win away the sympathy of the people in order to promote disturbances and violence," by contrast, had "no proper place in this Assembly." If the elected majority turned out to be "a body of irreconcilables determined to do nothing but obstruct the present government," it would indeed be "discouraging." Would the assembly successfully cooperate with American authorities, he asked, or would it "by neglect, obstruction and absence of useful service, make it necessary to take away its existing powers on the ground that they have been prematurely granted?" "Upon you," Taft concluded, "falls this heavy responsibility."[31]

Filipino Nation-Building

Alongside the exclusive sphere of assembly politics, Filipino nationalists sought to affirm and build the Philippine nation, as Rizal had, through historical organization, investigation, and publication, seeking to authenticate Filipino nationality by anchoring it in the past. One of the most prolific and determined of these historians was the journalist Manuel Artigas y Cuerva, formerly chairman of the Philippine Revolutionary Committee in Barcelona. By his own 1912 account, Artigas had spent six years in Spain during both the Philippine Revolution and the Philippine-American War, "fighting for our liberties with pen." Upon his return to the Philippines in 1902, he had realized "the urgent necessity of remaking the History of the Philippines." Besides numerous gaps, there were in extant works many "regrettable inaccuracies" that "distort our most celebrated achievements." He saw that "our things continued to be entrusted to foreign hands, and of course, they were shown from points of view that were certainly far from those which should prevail." A "tyrannizing system" persisted that "stigmatizes all that is Filipino," with the "intention of placing our people in the worst of positions, to ridicule it before the eyes of foreigners." It was the same "Machiavellianism" that presented Filipinos as "incapable beings, in need of mentors, without whom it would be difficult, if not impossible, for them to manage their own affairs." In this, there was complete continuity between the Spanish and U.S. empires; Artigas called it "[t]he old foreign ruse from times past."[32]

How, then, to stop these "fanciful censures"? Artigas answered, as had Rizal, that "our history" was the answer. It would "reveal the character of our people, making known the principal leaders of the country, [and] describing in what way we campaigned for our rights." Filipino history must convey "quite clearly . . . what we have been, what we are, and what can be hoped of us." Historical production would aid the assertion of what P. L. Stangl, secretary of a new Philippine Historical Association, called "Filipino nationality." "According to some writers," Stangl noted in August 1905, "such a thing does not exist, nor is there a safe foundation on which to build up one," especially due to "a diversity of dialects and languages in the Archipelago," which was "proof of decentralization and lack of homogeneity, so essential, they claim, to a nationality."[33]

Stangl countered these arguments with tools of historical comparison. Foreign deniers of Filipino nationality "forget apparently all the lessons of history," especially of their own countries. "[I]f the splendid system of railroads were suddenly swept out of existence," he inquired, apocalyptically, "and not replaced by any but the most primitive methods of communication, how many generations would be required before each State of the [American] Union had its own dialect, yes, even separate language?" Even with "almost perfect communication between practically every corner of the country," he wrote, "look at the local dialects actually existing in the United States: the Hoosier, the Georgia cracker, the mountain whites of the Carolinas or Kentucky, Pennsylvania Dutch, etc." For Stangl, nationality was a spirit that transcended language. A unified German Empire had been possible in 1871 despite the fact that the "Low German of Hanover spoke what was a foreign language to his countryman the Bavarian," because in all there "burned clearly the same patriotic fire that made him proud to call himself by the larger name of German." For Stangl, "that same fire burns in every Filipino heart, clear down to the confines of Moro land in Mindanao, from Aparri in the north, the sense of a Filipino nationality." This national feeling could "break through barriers of speech," barriers that were "less in extent than those between the components of the German empire today" among the seven Christian tribes "which comprise nearly the entire population and are alone to be considered in this connection."[34]

Stangl then turned to an exploration of early Philippine history, hypothesizing that the relative absence of traces of other Asian civilizations in the islands' "speech, customs, arts and trades" itself pointed to an earlier indigenous culture. "Had this national spirit not existed during all that time as strongly developed," he speculated, Ferdinand Magellan "would have found here a Javanese or Ceylonese Buddhist, a Chinese, Siamese, Annamite or Japanese civilization." Instead, he had found "a distinct, peculiar, purely indigenous one, which persists to this day notwithstanding almost four centuries of Spanish domination." To be sure, this civilization was "[o]verlaid by much that is exotic" and "greatly changed in externals," but it remained "integral in essentials."[35]

In arguing for deep historical continuities, Stangl reversed the U.S. colonial logic of assimilation: across the centuries, the Filipino had "assimilated" outside cultures to his own by extending his own recognition, "select[ing] those elements of the civilizations he came in contact with that were to him most valuable, that appealed to his progressive spirit, and fusing them into his own." Aware that most Americans saw Filipino assimilation as a one-way process toward "Americanization," Stangl clarified that, in the present, the result was "a Filipino, not an American. . . . A modernized, americanized Filipino, but none the less a Filipino." Spain had "failed" in the islands because it had never recognized Filipino nationality. "May those who succeeded her in the task learn the lesson early," he cautioned, "as learnt it must be ultimately."[36]

At least some of the historical project of nation-building was directed to recognizing, collecting, and promoting what were called "representative men" from the present and past, as in the promotion of "national" heroes. In January 1905, for example, José Katigpak had written an article for *El Renacimiento* containing "Notes of Travel" from Paris, which praised the pantheon of French national heroes. Felipe Buencamino, writing to the newspaper two days later, heartily endorsed the idea of a Philippine national pantheon as one solution to "our problem of regeneration." Along with "invigorating our economic life by means of mercantile, industrial and agricultural associations," the only way to make a country "free, great and happy" was by "invigorating patriotic sentiment by means of words and deeds." Buencamino suggested that "a patriotic and national subscription" be opened and that a site for the structure be designated by the Manila city government. Alongside such hypothetical "nation buildings," Filipino elites gathered themselves into published pantheons. The first assembly elections would be accompanied, for example, by a *Historical Album of the First Philippine Assembly*, with biographical details and photographs. In 1917–18, Artigas would issue a *Gallery of Illustrious Filipinos*, containing biographies and portraits, dating back to "the first days of Spanish domination," of those "sons of the country" who had, in Artigas's eyes, "reached some post of distinction in society."[37]

U.S. Nation-Building

While Filipino intellectuals would challenge U.S. colonial representations of Filipino nationlessness, U.S. colonialists would displace the Philippine nation into the indefinite future, making it the entirely hypothetical end point of U.S. colonialism. The only true path to nation-building was through empire-building. For them, the Philippine nation did not exist and could only come into existence through the heroic, self-sacrificial labors of American colonialists. This strategy of imperialist deferral took shape simultaneously with the advent of Filipino nationalist politics. One of its chief elements was a major restructuring of the colonial state, through the 1905 Reorganization Act. Authored in the name of fiscal responsibility, bureaucratic consolidation, and procedural standardization, the act greatly centralized and Americanized political authority in the islands. Specifically, it routed power toward Manila and away from the provincial governments, which were at least partially in Filipino hands, giving the insular executive secretary the power to oversee provincial finances and eliminating provincial health and public works boards in favor of new, central bureaus based out of Manila. Its second element was what came to be called the policy of "material development": regime priorities would focus on the construction of roads, bridges, harbors, and other infrastructure essential to opening the Philippine economy to export-oriented exploitation.

Both the Reorganization Act and the material development policy were principally the work of William Cameron Forbes, secretary of commerce and police under Wright and governor-general after 1909. Forbes presented the outlines of the policy in a 1908 address at Lake Mohonk titled "What Had Best Be Done for the Material Advancement of the Philippines." Bypassing almost entirely the recently elected Philippine Assembly, Forbes turned instead to a description of the islands' transportation, sanitation, and agricultural production. Having established "most of those reforms of general administration, executive, judicial and legislative," he stated, the state should undertake ". . . constructive work . . . with the object of stimulating industry and promoting development." These measures included lowering U.S. tariff barriers to Philippine products to give them greater access to U.S. domestic markets, increasing investments in railroad and steamship lines, improving irrigation, inoculating of carabao, and lifting legislative obstacles to large-scale land and mining investment, all of which would attract much-needed foreign capital.[38]

While cast in a politically neutral, technocratic language, Forbes's material development policy had implicit retentionist ends. The Philippine nation must be built by American expertise in the form of roads, bridges, and harbors before any significant transfer of authority to Filipinos could be considered. All "political" questions would be deferred—and displaced—onto the economic sphere. At the same time, the material development policy was meant to create Filipino and domestic U.S. political ties that would shore up the colonial state. In funneling resources from the center to local development projects in the provinces, the policy helped cultivate emerging U.S. alliances with provincial elites. Its hopes for attracting U.S. capital to the Philippines through infrastructure improvements were directed at powerful U.S. investors that might be introduced onto the metropolitan stage of Philippine-American colonial politics as a well-positioned lobby for indefinite retention.

One of the discursive by-products of the material development project was the conceptualization of the nation itself as a colonial edifice. This was reinforced by the undertaking of a large amount of actual building, which was, in most provincial areas, the most intensive marker of the presence of the U.S. colonial state. "Schoolhouses, provincial buildings, markets, port works, warehouses, libraries, and hospitals all sprang into being," remarked Forbes later with pride. As in the "construction" of the state of which they were a part, in the making of these buildings "nothing between temporary and permanent was permitted," with a preference given to reinforced concrete. Despite Filipino funding and labor committed to the construction of schools, these structures and others were meant to contrast sharply with "native" buildings. This nation was being constructed from the top down, by a state that stood architecturally apart from its subjects.[39]

The material development policy saw Americans and Filipinos making increasing reference to politics using metaphors of architecture, engineering, and construction. In his introduction to a 1907 album entitled *The Representative Men of the Philippines*, for example, society biographer Frank E. Jackson dedicated the work to those "pioneers" who were "laying the foundation of the great structure which shall finally stand complete in strength, majesty and beauty—fit guerdon for the foremost republic of the earth and worthy of the admiration of all other peoples."[40] Forbes's vision of the state-as-building was most refined and consistently repeated. There was little that Forbes liked that he did not refer to as "constructive." "There was an immense amount of constructive work undertaken by the various members of the Commission," he wrote of the early days of the colonial state, for example. Official reports, he lamented, "rarely portray the great constructive work" of the Constabulary. The work of the Bureau of Health had been "constructive and educational." Speaking in 1908, Forbes stated that future policy should aim to "model and refine the structure from time to time," rather than "to originate and build anew." Not surprisingly, he imagined the indefinite temporal reaches of U.S. colonialism as a kind of travel along an endless path, with Filipinos "helped step by step on the road to self-government and prosperous development" at one point and "advanced on the road to nationality" by American schoolteachers in another.[41]

The project of developing a language of nationalism that remained safe for the imperial politics of recognition turned on the concept of capacity. Questions of capacity had from the beginning been among the most important in the politics of recognition: Americans retained the power to recognize Filipino capacities and exchanged colonial power for Filipino recognition of, and fulfillment of, their standards. A notion of capacity—or more specifically, its absence—had been explicit in wartime debates

A MODERN PRIMARY SCHOOL BUILDING.
Contrast this structure with the native houses near it.

This photograph, printed in Dean Worcester's mammoth 1914 apology for the colonial regime, codes "progress" in the language of the built landscape. The regime's promise of political tutelage and material upbuilding take physical shape in the figure of a bright, angular school building under construction. The caption urges the reader to hold this U.S. imperial architectural form against the presumably inferior "native houses." Here is U.S. imperial nation-building made visible: the implication is that a Philippine nation could only grow inside such structures and that both school and nation were at war with the Philippine landscape around it. From Worcester, Philippines, Past and Present, vol. 1, facing p. 338.

on the legitimacy of U.S. annexation: colonialists held that Filipinos as a whole were either permanently or temporarily "incapable of self-government." It had been crucial in organizing the civilian regime, specifically in drawing the delicate line between U.S. and Filipino sovereignty inside the colonial state: because of this, the term developed into one of the state's principal political-cultural fault lines.

"Capacity" found its power in being protean: it could mean—and often meant all at once—capacity for self-discipline, for loyalty, for rationality, and for communication, each of which pointed toward capacity for self-government and nationality. In each of these modes, discourses of capacity were powerful interventions in what might be called the temporal politics of nationality: they perpetually situated Filipino nationality in the future, something to which Filipinos might rightly aspire and to which they might be guided under U.S. tutelage, but which resided neither in the past, present, or immediate future. All of these discourses were also, in different ways, gendered. The United States had represented Filipinos as misbehaving male children to be disciplined through violence, recognized as "little brown brothers," and through the workings of education and collaboration, assimilated to semi-manhood. The discourse of capacity was that of a watchful elder brother or father overseeing an increasingly potent, but potentially troublesome, male adolescent. As in their constant fear of revolts, U.S. colonial officials were often preoccupied with providing "healthy" outlets for potentially reckless youth, real and metaphorical. "There is nothing more important to the young man and woman of healthy mind and body than a healthful outlet for the excess of physical vigor that normally surges within them," wrote Forbes, for example, of physical education programs. Filipinos' capacities more generally were to be admired, cultivated, and directed, but also tamed.[42]

One of the most important Filipino capacities that U.S. colonial officials measured, judged, and ostensibly hoped to increase was that for technical and scientific knowledge. From the advent of the colonial state, one of the chief rationales for delimiting Filipino state participation had hinged on questions of knowledge and mentality. For many Americans, Filipinos displayed problematic habits of mind: whether due to "Oriental" predisposition or Spanish Catholicism, or some poisonous combination of both, Filipinos were believed to be unusually superstitious in ways antithetical to proper self-government. The technocratic spirit of the material development program sharpened these perceived boundaries between American and Filipino modes of thought in ways highly serviceable to retentionism. Compounding Filipinos' racial predispositions, it was argued, Spanish colonial education had neglected science and technology in ways that left even highly educated Filipinos without the capacities and credentials Americans needed to recognize. Forbes noted, for example, a "lack of skilled Filipino engineers, electricians, machinists, and lino-type machinists" for the regime's printing plant, requiring the presence of costly U.S. "experts."[43]

These technocratic criteria, by refusing to recognize Filipino intellectual accomplishment, locked even highly trained Filipinos into subordinate positions in the logic of tutelage. "[O]f necessity," Forbes wrote, "a complete and general Filipinization of the [civil] service had to wait for the slow work of education." To qualify for "scientific and technical positions," for example, young Filipinos had to pass through the entire educational system, whose upper reaches were still under construction, or even entirely hypothetical. "In view of these facts," Forbes wrote, "it cannot be said that the rate of Filipinization of the public service was unduly retarded." Given this definition of expert knowledge, the "expertization" of the state meant, for the foreseeable future, Americanization. Often with difficulty, the Forbes regime recruited and employed costly American civil and mining engineers, surveyors, scientists, and architects to head colonial state agencies, to train Filipino subordinates, to supervise and evaluate their evolving capacities, and to decide on promotions. Forbes believed that the policy of "advancing men from the lower positions, and testing them well before their permanent promotion was determined," was in line with the general plan of "giving the Filipinos sound training in self-government."[44]

In practical terms, the Filipino capacity that mattered most to Forbes and other advocates of material development was that for labor. Filipino labor had long been one of the regime's central preoccupations, given limited insular revenues and the desire to attract U.S. and other foreign capital to the islands. Under Spanish propulsion, notions of the "lazy native" common throughout Southeast Asia—lounging in tropical largesse or hampered by Malay "blood"—materialized in the "indolent" Filipino unwilling or unable to bear the many "burdens" of civilization. On the islands' thorny "labor question," colonial officials walked a tightrope: attributions of Filipino laziness frightened away foreign capital, but claims of energetic Filipino labor—so closely tied to notions of thrift, property, and self-restraint—could easily be mistaken for recognition of Filipino capacities, perhaps including those for nationality and self-rule. The most common rhetorical maneuver was to attribute indolence to physical weakness brought on by faulty sanitation and nutrition. Where early public health efforts had intended to protect Americans from diseases assumed inherent to Filipinos, aggressive public health programs were increasingly undertaken with the goal of making Filipinos into more productive laborers. In an era of material development, building the Philippine nation meant building Filipino bodies into vigorous, laboring forms. Writing in the *Atlantic Monthly* in 1909, Forbes noted, somewhat architecturally, that "one of our great movements" was "the upbuilding of the physique of the Filipino people," who were "too poorly nourished, and too much weakened by disease," to "do the work which an able-bodied and healthy people ought to do."[45]

There was still the problem of motivating such labor, for which purposes the commission turned to the coercive arms of the state: Filipinos would be compelled to build the nation to American specifications. Act No. 1511, passed July 13, 1906, established a *corvee* labor system that required every able-bodied man in the islands to labor five days each year in road construction or maintenance, or to pay the equivalent sum at the local cost of labor. The commission anticipated opposition and sought to make the law "less offensive to the Filipinos" by putting it into effect only after it was endorsed by provincial boards, which would be elected the following year. To the commissioners' surprise, however, "not a single provincial board accepted this law"; it was "too similar to the odious Spanish law under which so many abuses had been committed." Indeed, the bill was so unpopular that when Laguna's provincial governor, Juan Cailles, had made an "earnest effort" to gain its passage, "he nearly went down to defeat." Nevertheless, pressure placed on local officials by provincial and central authorities to maintain infrastructure led to de facto forced labor that was acknowledged and unopposed by the central state. Forbes noted, for example, that in anticipation of visits by high officials such as the U.S. secretary of war, *presidentes* would call upon the citizens for "'volunteer labor'" on road crews, with municipal police "freely used to induce the able-bodied men of the town to volunteer for this sort of service." In Forbes's journal of October 25, 1907, he observed that "[w]e always suspect their 'voluntary' labor is brought about by a somewhat free use of the municipal police, but as the result is roads, it is not necessary to analyze too closely all the steps leading up to them." Sometimes this willful ignorance had tragic costs. In 1918, for example, the Constabulary would force 1,500 Ifugao men down from the mountains to work on an

TYPICAL SCENE IN A TRADE SCHOOL.
In institutions like this, young Filipinos are being taught the dignity of labor and are learning useful trades.

This photograph, labelled a "Typical Scene in a Trade School," also published by Worcester, communicates some of the chief messages of William Cameron Forbes's "material development" policy, especially its emphasis on Filipinos as laboring bodies and a concern with manual and industrial training over literary or civics education. Here, the workshop of a trade school is made to exemplify strengthening and disciplining of Filipino men through physical labor. Such labor and education, Forbes and others hoped, would orient Filipinos away from political topics such as the question of Philippine sovereignty. From Worcester, Philippines, Past and Present, vol. 1, facing p. 354.

interprovincial road between Nueva Ecija and Nueva Vizcaya, which, according to Forbes, was to have "great benefit to the provinces." It was apparently of less benefit to the forced Ifugao laborers themselves, who were exposed to smallpox and influenza. When they returned to their villages with contagion, the death toll was "appalling."[46]

Facing limited success in converting Filipino villagers into "voluntary" laborers, Forbes turned enthusiastically to the islands' growing prison population for a potential solution to the "labor problem." The sheer number of prisoners had led to what Forbes called a "surplus of labor" beyond the needs of the prisons themselves, and the commission decided to employ prison labor wherever possible, claiming that "all government work involving labor for which the taxpayers were called upon to pay was perfectly proper employment for prisoners." Prisoners repaired the fortress at Corregidor. Repair shops for the maintenance of municipal and insular government transports were moved inside Bilibid prison. Prison industries specialized in "certain types of furniture, silverware, and other objects which had not previously been introduced in the commercial shops of the city." In Bilibid and Bontoc prisons, "about fifty per cent of the prisoners were constantly employed in the shops." Forbes and others found in incarceration and prison labor the ideal formula for physical "upbuilding." Long-term Bilibid prisoners, Forbes boasted, were compelled to live under "hygienic" conditions in the prison and left with stronger physiques than their "free" compatriots outside. Upon release, convicts were found to have a higher capacity for labor than most Filipino workers, "who suffered from drinking the polluted waters and living in unhygienic lives common to the uneducated classes." The prison was also the ideal labor bureau, with "[r]epresentatives of private enterprises . . . always on the lookout for released convicts, who were able to find immediate employment."[47]

Among forms of involuntary labor, prison labor on roads neatly brought together three Forbesian preoccupations: the control and productivity of Filipino bodies, greater efficiency in transportation and communication, and the streamlining of the export economy in the interests of nation-building. In 1905, the insular government established road-building camps "to relieve the overcrowding in the Bureau of Prisons," where "well-behaved prisoners" would labor under military guards. A Scout battalion under Gen. Henry C. Corbin, for example, guarded 500 prisoners charged with building the road between Tabaco and Ligao in the province of Albay, subsequently "one of the most beautiful" in the islands, and one that "tapped a region very productive of Manila hemp." Having failed to secure passage of the *corvee* law, Governor Cailles requested from the insular government 500 prison laborers to show his province "that he was in high favor with the authorities in Manila." When one tried to escape, he was shot, and Cailles had the man's dead body, which was "stripped so as to show the bullet holes," dragged in front of a lineup of prisoners. The road went through successfully, and "there were no further attempts at escape," noted Forbes with satisfaction. A similar experiment in Mindanao undermined some of Forbes's claims for the invigorating effects of prison labor. When Leonard Wood, governor-general of Moro Province, was sent prisoners to improve a military road from Overton to Marahui, beriberi broke out in the prison camp and "the percentage of mortality was high." Such incidents gave dark meaning to Governor Tinio's claim, proudly recorded in Forbes's journal in July 1909, that "from what he could see of the road work, it was the life of the people."[48]

It was a reflection of U.S. colonialists' fears of revolt that, despite controversies over their excesses, the regime's symbolic investments in developing capacity were most frequently placed in the Philippine Constabulary and Scouts. As at St. Louis, both institutions were recognized as the core of an emergent Philippine nation, as U.S. colonialists understood it. Throughout the colonial world, native armies and police forces were heavily charged with gendered and racialized political meanings: often European colonialists imagined themselves to be organizing "martial races" into imperial institutions that might guarantee stability and order, above and against "effeminate," overeducated, nationalist agitators. The selection, training, and deployment of Filipino troops would, U.S. colonial officials imagined, put their capacities on trial. But colonial military institutions might also be a powerful mechanism for radiating these capacities outward into the population at large. "[N]ot the least of the good influence of the Constabulary comes from those who return to civil life after a transforming course of instruction and discipline during their period of enlistment," wrote Charles Lobingier, a U.S. judge in the Philippine courts.[49]

Filipino troops' most important, and hotly debated, capacity was for loyalty: U.S. Army officials, for example, had resented the establishment of a Constabulary under civilian jurisdiction and had often voiced this resentment by challenging assertions of Filipino allegiance to the United States. Here, as in so much else, the specter of revolution haunted the imaginations of colonial state-builders. High-level army officers and many others suspected that armed Constabularymen would either revolt or sell their arms to the ladrones they were paid to fight.

While their loyalty was sometimes suspect, Constabularymen were often made into exemplars of physical strength and laboring capacity. U.S. colonial officials recognized their endurance and valor in weathering the hardships of jungle warfare against ladrones. Constabularymen were not only used to coerce labor but were sometimes used to supplement labor gangs, thereby giving evidence of their capacity for work. In praise of their hygiene, Forbes stated that the Constabulary and Scouts showed "desirable evidences of development and served as object lessons to demonstrate lines along which improvement in the labor situation might be made."[50]

Perhaps most directly, the Constabulary was made exemplary of capacity for self-government. If colonial officials imagined the Constabulary as the nation, it was in part because the Constabulary had colonized so much of the state. Colonial officials and U.S. journalists in the Philippines and the United States often emphasized the sheer breadth of tasks to which the Constabulary had been assigned. At one time or another, Forbes recalled, the Constabulary had "rendered service to practically every branch of government."[51] Col. William C. Rivers, assistant director of the Constabulary, noted that "new responsibilities" were being "constantly added" in the form of "calls to aid other bureaus to fight disease of man and beast, inspect and report upon jails and roads and even to assist village authorities in exterminating locusts."[52] Instead of reading this as the state's overstretch and inefficiency, officials preferred to see it as requiring of a Constabularyman what Rivers, quoting Lord Cromer, called "'sufficient elasticity of mind'" and "'quick[ness] to adopt any local feature of the administration to suit his own reforming purposes.'"[53] Constabulary officers were also, importantly, seen as instructors, finding what Lobingier called "a very practical field of usefulness in assisting and instructing native civilian officials," many of them "with very little training for their tasks."[54]

But a crucial element of capacity, as in the wider politics of recognition, was an insistence on U.S. surveillance and supervision: Filipino soldiers and policemen were only brave and disciplined "under proper supervision," meaning by U.S. officers. Suspicions of the Filipino leadership's capacity endured even as the first Constabulary academy was established in 1904 at the Santa Lucia barracks in Manila, providing a three-month course in Constabulary regulations, law, Spanish, and civil government.

This suspicion centered on the "racial" difference of Filipino recruits. Being "[a]n oriental with an admixture of Latin and Chinese blood in many cases," stated Rivers, it was "natural that the Filipino should have well marked temperamental peculiarities." Specifically, Rivers racialized corruption, distancing Constabulary abuses from both Americans and colonial state structures. "Oriental officials" were "not given to minimizing their own authority," he wrote, and it was "but natural" that "with armed Filipino non-commissioned officers and soldiers in positions of authority, sometimes at a distance from supervision, some abuses should occur." Under supervision by Americans, it was presumed, such corruption could be checked.[55]

American officers were also required in order to maintain Filipino Constabularymen's loyalty and bravery. Forbes stated that when "properly trained, commanded, and led," Filipino enlisted men "performed gallant service in the field, showing intelligence, fidelity, and loyalty." John Roberts White observed that "nothing but the psychic influence of their commander can carry [Filipino Constabularymen] through." Emphasis was perpetually placed on Americans as the sources of discipline and masculinization, rather than on Filipinos' initiative, courage, or skill. One 1904 editorial encapsulated discourses of evolution, assimilation, martial masculinization, and capacity, asserting proudly that "[t]he six thousand little brown men who wear the red-trimmed khaki have in three years grown into an efficient compact body of alert, erect, English-speaking soldiers, who are proud of their service."[56]

As this image suggested, nation-building meant homogenization: the consolidation of a single, insular state, the deepening of English-language education, transportation infrastructure, and other measures, it was hoped, would lead to a Filipino population that was not only loyal and laboring but less internally differentiated. Despite simultaneous efforts to cordon off non-Christians from the control of Hispanicized Filipinos, U.S. officials insisted their policy was to consolidate the two populations, the latter of which, many believed, would ultimately neutralize the former through asymmetrical trade, land seizure, and conversion. Under the rubric of material development, roads were believed to automatically bring about cohesion and homogenization. Filipino military and police units were seen as the most direct means for bringing about the withering away of internal difference, a process essential to future nationality. Col. James G. Harbord reported with surprise in 1904 that divisions between Moro, "pagan," and Christian Constabularymen in Moro Province broke down through common service. While he had believed "unconquerable" the "well-known dislike of the Moro to eat with the Filipino, a feeling which is reciprocated with interest," eight months' experience showed that Muslims, Christians, and animists "amalgamate with but little friction," and separate messes had been abolished. Harbord noted proudly that in the Constabulary, what he called "tribal lines" were "disappearing."[57]

Narratives of upbuilding, capacity, and homogenization within Filipino military units were enfolded in a much-reproduced photographic series generated by Dean Worcester, probably in the early 1910s. Drawing on familiar before-and-after genres common to U.S. reform literature, it featured three successive profile shots of the same Igorot man at progressive stages. In the first, leftmost image, the man slouches shirtless, wearing only a small woven hat on the back of his head. In the second, he sits further upright, dressed in the white cotton uniform of a low-ranking Constabulary officer, ostensibly two years later. In the third, an additional two years later, he sits fully erect in a lieutenant's uniform. The series vividly brought together in a single cartoon the overlapping definitions of imperial progress. It was an image of collaboration as civilization that implicitly referred back to the terrors of the war: here was a "savage" who, far from eluding U.S. soldiers, was becoming one. The series was also a narrative of imperial masculinization, of a child-race developing into erect, martial manhood. As some Filipino nationalists might have noted, it was an image that—as had the popular reception of the Philippine Exposition at St. Louis—dangerously blurred the lines between Christians and non-Christians: read backwards, it suggested that just beneath the surface of every civilized Filipino remained a savage one. Perhaps most subtly, the series put the Constabulary at the center of accounts of the emerging Philippine nation, representing progress among Filipinos as a whole.[58]

Philippine Constabularymen and Scouts were not only representative of an "evolving" Filipino polity but played an increasingly important role in the self-representation of the United States itself. Their symbolic use would reveal the ways that nation-building in the Philippines and the United States were mutually constitutive projects. Philippine Scouts brought from the world's fair in St. Louis, for example, played a notable part in Theodore Roosevelt's inaugural ceremonies on March 4, 1905. The *New York Times* described the day both as unprecedented, with pageants that had "never been equaled in Presidential inaugurations," and as deeply nationalizing, having "attracted the greatest outside crowd to the

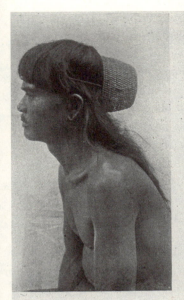

EDUCATIONAL VALUE OF THE CONSTABULARY.

1. Bontoc Igorot on entering the service, 1901.   2. After a year's service, 1902.
3. After two years' service, 1903.

This photographic series, labelled "Educational Value of the Constabulary," taken by Dean Worcester supposedly over several years, crystallizes many of the key elements of the U.S. colonial racial formation in the Philippines, with its progressive, evolutionary sequence; its transformation of "savagery" into "civilization"; its masculinization and "upbuilding" of its slouching subject into an upright man; and its equivalence of civilization and political collaboration, in this case through the Philippine Constabulary. The image works simultaneously through posture, dress, and haircut to reinforce messages of assimilation as well as homogenization; nation-building is represented as the eradication of difference between Philippine peoples. Reproduced from Chamberlin, Philippine Problem, 1898–1913, with permission of The University of Michigan Museum of Anthropology.

Nation's seat of government that has ever been brought here." The event had also been given "[p]icturesqueness and novelty" by the participation of "the representative and armed forces of the countries which Uncle Sam has acquired since the preceding President was inaugurated." Spectators could observe during an elaborate parade, as one headline put it, the "Nation Mirrored in Marching Host," with nearly 35,000 men representing "any considerable type of American life," "all the way from a delegation of conquered Indian chiefs" to "half a hundred Harvard undergraduates."[59]

Somewhere between these in evolutionary terms marched a Puerto Rican regiment and the Philippine Scouts, the "first to earn the President's applause." As the Scout band, marching ahead of a "beautifully drilled and disciplined" unit, played "the highly inappropriate tune of 'The Irish Washerwoman,'" the president had "leaned far out over the railing, and clapped his hands for half a minute." The assembled crowd was "quick to observe the official approval and added its own indorsement." According to the New York Times, Roosevelt had also apparently used the occasion of passing Puerto Rican and Filipino troops to make fun of anti-imperialist colleagues nearby, saying to Senator Augustus Bacon of the Puerto Rican unit, "'They look pretty well for an oppressed people, eh, Senator?'" and of the Scouts, "'The wretched serfs disguise their feelings admirably.'" To Senator Henry Cabot Lodge, he had joked, "'You should have seen Bacon hide his face when the Filipinos came by. The "slaves" were rejoicing in their shackles.'" "'I really shuddered slightly to-day as I swore to obey the Constitution!'" he was reported to say to Bacon at one point "with a merry laugh."[60]

Struggles over Sovereignty

Imperial visions of U.S.-led nation-building and the colonial discourse of capacity did not go uncontested by Filipino advocates of independence, some of whom saw in them malleable instruments for their subjection. Take, for example, Resident Commissioner Pablo Ocampo's address on "The Aspirations of the Filipino" delivered at the October 1908 Lake Mohonk Conference. The question of "the capacity of the Filipinos for independence," Ocampo noted, had become "the subject of systematic controversy . . . around which arguments of varied tones and colors are being adduced orally and written, in the press, in pamphlets and in books, publicly and privately." In most cases, self-governing capacity was "denied [Filipinos] completely," although it was often said to be possible "after fifteen or twenty years." Ocampo charged that the issue of capacity "revolv[ed] round an imaginary axis." He suggested that, by its very nature, the game of recognition that it represented was one that Filipinos must inevitably lose: the question of capacity itself was "a repealer of the capacity actually possessed by the Filipino people."[61]

While challenging U.S. standards of capacity in theory, Ocampo held the Philippines up to them in practice. He argued first for the homogeneity of the islands' peoples. In geography, the Philippines were "a dispersed, separate and scattered country," but "in its constant, latent and uniform aspiration" for independence, it was "a cohesive whole—a people intensely orthodox, compact, homogeneous." Looking for a phrase to capture this unity, he turned strategically to "*e pluribus unum*," applied to "the American Confederation with reference to the plurality of states with which it is composed." The thirteen colonies, he pointed out, had not "indulge[d] in useless arguments" because "Maryland was a Catholic colony, Virginia an Anglican, Massachusetts a Puritan, the Carolinas aristocrats, and Pennsylvania a democrat."[62]

Besides the homogeneity argument, Ocampo had two other issues of capacity to contend with. He answered the material development argument—that "countries not in a flourishing condition, economically," were "doomed to perpetual dependent life"—with the tools of comparison. Were most of the world's independent states prosperous or not? "How often do we find, among the crevices of ruins," he asked, "plants with fragrant flowers shooting forth to reveal that the blessings of the Almighty are for all, in every land and for all races!" While material development hinged on the notion that the Philippines "ought to first upbuild its economic condition in order to insure an independent life," Filipinos were "convinced of the contrary," that "after securing their political independence, they would be in a better position to ameliorate their economic condition." They would also be able to do so in a manner "more suited to their needs, their uses, customs, idiosyncrasies, civilization and laws, not forgetting, though, to mould them after the requirements of modern culture." Had not the United States "attained the position she now enjoys among the foremost nations of the world" after Americans successfully threw off "foreign interference"? Second was the argument that an independent Philippines would lack the capacity for self-defense against outside powers. This Ocampo dismissed as the artifact of an earlier "imperial" age, citing the success of arbitration and neutralization; "the excesses of the chancellories of egotism" had been "repressed by international treaties."[63]

Ultimately, claims against Filipino capacity were unfair comparisons between societies at unlike stages of development, employing criteria "based on the standards of civilization attained by those nations now forming the international powers." Nothing could be so unrealistic, since the ratio of progress between the United States and the Philippines—"say, of 100 to 10 in civilization and culture"—would remain fixed over time; the Philippines would at some point "claim the same degree of civilization and culture" as the present-day United States, only to find itself proportionally surpassed. Given this exponential logic, capacity, then, was a kind of ideological perpetual motion machine for producing empire. Even when Filipinos had progressed, independence would "be denied to them just the same, under pretext of incapacity, a conclusion which will be drawn from the higher standard of advancement attained by the United States in the race for progress and enlightenment."[64]

Ocampo's critique also inverted the closed imperial logic of capacity by arguing that the colonial state had "eloquently shown and proven the capacity of my people" through Filipino collaboration. Flattering his audiences that the Philippine colonial government had "marched onward with insuperable success," Ocampo suggested that it was due either to "the system of government established there by the Americans" or to "the special conditionality of the people of the islands." Both of these alternatives, in Ocampo's hands, were indisputable evidence of Filipino capacity. If the first hypothesis were true, it "proves the actual fitness of the Filipinos," since the successful system had been "entirely assimilated by the inhabitants." If the second were true, it "proves to evidence the capacity I was trying to show." Turning the discourse of tutelage toward his own purposes, Ocampo declared Filipinos successful graduates of a benevolent educational program. "What teacher would not feel proud of his pupils," he inquired, "if he finds that they answer to the requirements of his plan and seem able to carry out the object he had in view in less time than expected?"[65]

Ocampo's speech looked ahead to a much broader set of contests between Filipino and U.S. visions of Philippine nation-building in the years from the first assembly election to the 1912 U.S. presidential election. Filipino nationalists and U.S. colonialists struggled, for example, over the question of who would represent the nation: as the 1911 fight over the appointment of resident commissioners illustrated, the Philippine Assembly and the Philippine Commission had radically different conceptions of what national representation meant in a colonial democracy. Tensions would erupt over the question of which ritual cycle the Philippine nation should celebrate and, most heatedly, over which flag the nation should wave. In the 1907 "flag incident," for example, the Manila American community would mobilize massively to guarantee that Philippine nationalism would only be represented by the U.S. flag, and not Philippine revolutionary banners. There was the question of who the Philippine nation's heroes should be. Here, both Filipino nationalists and U.S. imperialists waged war for the memory of José Rizal, placing him at the foundation of both radical nationalist and imperialist nation-building projects. Finally, there was the question of whether non-Christians were members of the Philippine nation. Here, U.S. imperialists employed the resources of the bifurcated state to wage a politics of divide-and-rule: non-Christians were both outside the Philippine nation and in need of protection from it (and vice versa). Filipino nationalists responded with a nationalist-colonialist politics that saw non-Christians—and the territory they occupied—as integral to the Philippine nation but subordinate to the political agency of Christians. With regard to non-Christian peoples, Philippine nation-building would also be empire-building.

An illuminating struggle over the nation's appropriate representative men emerged during a 1911 stalemate between the commission and the assembly over the selection of resident commissioners, two of whom had, since 1907, been authorized to speak—but not to vote—on behalf of the "Filipino people" in the U.S. House of Representatives. Along with the assembly, the advent of the position illustrated a partial recognition of Filipino agency, giving colonial state authorization to Filipino representatives of the insular population as a whole. But procedures for selecting this figure remained ambiguous and fought-over and became a source of friction when the commission selected Benito Legarda, a Federalista and one of the first three Filipino collaborators to serve on the commission. During the position's first two cycles, each institution had, in practice, selected its own representative; while Legarda had served two terms between 1907 and 1911, his reappointment in 1911 aroused the opposition of the predominantly Nacionalista assembly, prompting the formation of conference committees to settle the matter.

The exchange between these committees, headed by Forbes and Osmeña, was a charged debate on the meanings of national representation.

Forbes stated that Legarda was a legitimate representative because he was "thoroughly acquainted with all the work of the Commission" and was "in entire harmony with the views and the policy of the Administration out here." He was "socially popular and agreeable," a "master of the English language," and a "personal friend of the President." Taft had picked Legarda for the position upon his trip to inaugurate the assembly, and Forbes was aware of "nothing which has transpired since that time which renders him less representative of the Philippine people." Importantly, Legarda represented the Philippine commercial and industrial interests and had "high standing and influence among those engaged in manufacture, transportation, banking, and commerce." He was, in brief, "morally and socially entirely fit to worthily represent the Filipino people in the Capitol." More broadly, Forbes claimed representative powers for the commission since it was charged with looking after the "welfare" of all Philippine peoples, "the great majority of whom by reason of their limited suffrage have no way of expressing their political preferences." Finally, Forbes forcefully retained the power of political recognition for American officials in unusually clear terms. "It should not be forgotten also that, although participation in the Government has been granted to the Filipinos, self-government has not been entirely established in these Islands."[66]

In response, Assembly Speaker Osmeña dismantled Forbes's shallow criteria for national representation. The resident commissioner was not meant to be "a creature of the Administration or a representative of the Commission" but "the mouthpiece and delegate of the Filipino people." While McKinley had charged the commission with looking after the "happiness, peace, and prosperity of the Philippine people," neither he nor Congress could "convert their representatives or agents into representatives or agents of the Philippine people, for the simple reason that their authority did not emanate from that people." The assembly, as "the only genuinely Filipino institution" in the central government, had "taken to its bosom the longings of the people" and as a result been given "exclusive representation" by Filipinos. Osmeña meant "exclusive representation" in more than one sense, accepting "with certain reservations" the theory "admitted among the Americans" that restricted suffrage "raise[d] the standard of those who are to manage the public interests." Even at its broadest, then, assembly representation meant that voters "govern for themselves and for those excluded by the law."[67]

Osmeña also secured representative powers for the assembly through a reinterpretation of North American colonial history. The principle of "territorial representation" had begun in Anglo-American colonial assemblies, he argued, and had been exercised in the United States' own western territories. Proceeding from the "rule" that nations "reproduce in their colonies the types of . . . theory and practice of government prevalent in the sovereign country," Osmeña claimed these rights for Filipinos as well. Finally, the inability of Americans to represent the Philippines was a matter of geographic distance, competing economic interests, and "difference in race and the inequality of population." Reversing the commission's argument that colonial rule was necessitated by the hierarchical racial gap between Americans and Filipinos, Osmeña asserted the commission could not properly represent the Philippine people, "situated as they are at a distance of more than 6,000 miles from the sovereign country [and] placed under the control of a foreign government merely by the fortunes of war." Moreover, "while on the one hand the race that inhabits the Philippines differs entirely from the race in the sovereign country, on the other hand the interests and supreme aspirations of each people may likewise be in complete discord."[68]

Contested Symbols

While they clashed over the procedures for determining the representative men of the Philippine nation, Filipino and U.S. nation-builders also fought over public rituals of sovereignty. Conflict along these lines erupted on Manila streets, for example, in the "flag incident" of August 1907. Understanding that incident requires that attention be paid both to Manila's contested public sphere in general and to the meanings of flags in particular. Manila emerged in the American colonial period as a crowded stage upon which competing rites of sovereignty were performed by asymmetrically empowered actors. Filipino nationalists and revolutionaries invented a ritual calendar keyed to crucial events within the nationalist— and U.S. colonial—cosmology. There were three days of affirmative commemoration: Rizal's martyrdom on December 30, Labor Day on May 30, and the August 26 anniversary of Bonifacio's "Cry of Balintawak," which had inaugurated the Katipunan revolt. There were two days of critical response: the United States' Independence Day—and the anniversary of the Philippine-American War's imaginary ending—on July 4, and the

August 13 "Occupation Day" anniversary of the U.S. takeover of Manila in 1898. These days often featured massive crowds, lavish parades, fiery speeches, and swirling rumors of revolt.[69]

These same streets and those of other major cities were seen by the American colonial regime as stages upon which a theatrics of force would regularly have to be enacted. As in every other colonial setting, there was a lurking fear that "civilization" ended fifty feet out from the railroad tracks. How, with so few Americans and—especially at first—so few traces of civilization, would the "natives" be reminded of the presence of Americans, let alone their dominion? American celebrations of the Fourth of July and Occupation Day provided some occasions for public expressions of U.S. sovereignty and imperial pride. But the almost re-flexive American answer to fears of internal intrigue and foreign inva-sion was massive, regular displays of martial force. To counteract what Forbes called the "false impressions" of U.S. troop withdrawal, spread by "Filipino agitators," U.S. generals had "[m]ore than once" ordered practice marches of "impressive forces of American infantry, cavalry, and artillery through regions where such rumors had been current." In April 1906, Forbes had, as secretary of commerce and police, suggested that "great columns of troops . . . scour the whole country, on practice marches."[70]

In Manila, where fears of insurrection were most palpable, visible asser-tions of U.S. martial power were prominent features. In 1911, Maj. Gen. William P. Duvall, commander of the Military Division of the Philip-pines, used the occasion of the Manila Carnival, when "representative people" converged on Manila from across the archipelago, to parade over 8,000 troops through the city. As Forbes noted with satisfaction, Fili-pinos present "were able from personal observation to carry to the farthest confines of the archipelago word that American troops were still present in force." The martial statement of greatest magnitude was the appearance of the "Great White Fleet" in Manila Harbor in early October 1909. While U.S. navalists aimed the gesture at Japan, U.S. colonial officials hoped it would send a message to imagined Filipino insurrectionists, close to whom the specter of Japan always hovered.[71]

While U.S. colonial holidays provided occasion for expansive public rhetoric on the virtues of U.S. benevolence and, importantly, for intimi-dating displays of martial power, they also provided opportunities for Filipino critics. An *El Renacimiento* editorialist, for example, commented in August 1909 on American preparations for the Occupation Day celebrations "full of pride and satisfaction to the men of the race who proudly planted here the American flag." To the Filipino, he maintained, the occupation had meant "a tremendous change in the conditions of his existence, personal and national." It had been accompanied with "brave promises" but had "concealed many threatening elements." Somewhat disingenuously recalling an earlier period when August 13 had been a symbol of "friendship and mutual co-operation," the holiday now marked the anniversary of "a colonial empire of the United States in the Orient." After more than a decade, "flattering hopes" had disappeared. "What American has left his office after eleven years because a Filipino is able to undertake the work?" he inquired. Given the "handsome profit" achieved by many U.S. officials from business enterprises, "[w]hat inducement has there been . . . to recognize the ability of the Filipinos to take their share of administrative responsibility?"[72]

If marking U.S. sovereignty in time was one dilemma, another was to delineate it in space. It was in answer to this problem that U.S. flags became essential to the cultural politics of American rule, as portable representations of imperial sovereignty and its boundaries. More than one observer noted upon arrival in Manila the almost absurd prevalence of the Stars and Stripes: U.S. flags hung not only from naval vessels and army barracks but from shops, warehouses, private homes, and church pulpits. Maud Huntley Jenks observed that the Escolta was "literally covered with flags, most of them American; but there were also Chinese, Japanese, Spanish, and British flags mixed in." Of a Manila parade in honor of Taft's return, Jenks commented, "I never saw so many American flags before." There were flag-draped arches along the parade route, and a bridge over the Pasig had an arch at each end, "a mass of red, white, and blue." Manila Americans made note of the banner's distinctive meaning in the Philippine context. "[O]ver here the flag means to an American everything that is good," Jenks observed one month into her stay. During the "flag incident," the *Cablenews-American* noted that "[w]e who live far away from the land where Old Glory was born and waves in undisputed triumph, who are exiles in this distant outpost of our nation, feel more keenly our kinship with her sons than did we when in our own land as there was no need of defense."[73]

The U.S. flag became central to the marking of the outer boundary of U.S. sovereignty precisely because its triumph was disputed: Old Glory allowed Americans, against tremendous odds, to recognize American space in the Philippines. Unwilling to refer to the Philippines as a "territory" or a "colony" and increasingly wary of languages of empire, Americans often stated that the Philippines simply fell "beneath the folds of our starry flag." The trope had begun as early as the U.S. occupation of Manila in August 1898; during the Philippine-American War, the flag marked the furthest edge of U.S. imperial power as a bloody frontier and had eventually decorated thousands of crosses on improvised U.S. military graves throughout the islands. In this, as in so much else, the war left its imprint on the postwar period, with the flag at the center of U.S. colonial imagery. In what was an often fractious and internally divided colonial American community, the flag was a kind of symbolic lowest common denominator. Who, asked the *Cablenews-American*, having made the long journey to the islands, upon seeing "the Stars and Stripes float majestically over the buildings in this city, did not feel his very soul burn with patriotic fire?" Having crossed the "desert of the sea" and seen scores of other flags pass, "we were again come into our own." Here was "where America has planted her pennon on the uttermost rampart of the world, and we are sent to keep it." Keeping it, however, meant recognizing that in the Philippines, apparently unlike in the United States, there was "need of defense." The editorial conceded that the flag was "doubly dear" in the islands because there it had "none but enforced respect."[74]

The absence of authentic respect became obvious in the months leading up to the Philippine Assembly elections in August 1907. As part of their electioneering, some Nacionalista supporters had paraded in public with the Katipunan flag, a fact that was "noted with growing indignation" by some Americans. This flag, carried into "every political gathering" of the Liga Nacionalista, represented to at least one American observer the "whole unnatural movement" against everything American. During the campaign's final days, the flag's appearance had become more conspicuous throughout the archipelago; U.S. veterans gathering in Manila at the time of the elections had described local politics as "shifting from bad to worse." The sweeping victory of the Nacionalistas had emboldened the party's supporters to take to the street, "playing insurgent music" and "flaunting" that "best recognized symbol of insurrection." True, the U.S. flag was also featured in some of the processions, "but too often it was either conspicuous by its total absence or by insignificant size as compared with the Katipunan standard." One postelection parade had led to the U.S. veterans' hall, where a "native band lustily played 'Aguinaldo's March,' amid the cheers of hundreds of native on-lookers." According to the *Manila Opinion*, the "groans and moans of the motley horde" had muffled the "Star-

Spangled Banner," which had been followed by the "Funeral March." Channeled by the police, this parade merged with others and, when the Constabulary Band began its concert, "surged into the road with theirs and completely drowned [its music] out" with the "noise and din of their shouting and discordant music." It was here that the "worst crime against constituted authority" had apparently been committed, when one marcher had "trampled" Old Glory in the dirt.[75]

Word of the events ripped through the Manila American community in the coming days, and responses were debated at "many quiet meetings . . . of an impromptu character." For some, the incident was evidence of Filipino "ingratitude." "Thus is our policy of *benevolent assimilation* and tolerance of the frivolities and weaknesses of this people again rewarded," lamented the *Manila Opinion*. The flying of Old Glory in the parades had been to "flatter our vanity," speculated the *Manila Times*, but "we do not feel flattered at having our holy emblem borne in such hands as . . . the ragtag and bobtail which characterized parts of those processions." For some, the incident was readily harnessed to arguments about the incapacity of Filipinos for self-government. Presented the "crucial test" of the election, the *Manila Times* stated, Filipinos had "become childish," and like "the bad boy that makes faces at his master," they had behaved in a manner "that in many countries would be considered evidences of incipient rebellion." The *Cablenews-American* stated that the incident indicated not only the "ingratitude of those who have fed from America's hand" but the "utter unfitness of the Filipino nation to govern itself even as much as it is governing." Some longed for the days before such concessions. The *Cablenews-American* had thought sufficient respect for the U.S. flag had "been taught in these Islands during the days when shot and shell made hideous the land." Inflated with privileges, Filipinos had forgotten the lessons taught them "when ballots were bullets." The *Manila Times* noted, interestingly, that it understood Filipino longings for "nationality" and that "possibly something of the same feeling which animates us toward our flag inspires them toward theirs." But the parades had taken things too far, and the *Times* sternly reminded Filipinos that "[t]he last naked argument in this world is force."[76]

As American-owned newspapers beat the drums for repression, influential Manila Americans pressed the commission for legislative action, which they obtained within days. On August 22, the *Manila Times* reported directives from the customs service that "foreign merchants are not to be permitted to make capital out of the Katipunan flag." The collector of customs had, for example, singled out for special inspection twenty-four cases of cotton goods from the British firm E. W. Duck and Company that he was "inclined to think were seditious in character," based on labels carrying the Katipunan flag. The following day, the governor-general instructed the police to confiscate "all goods bearing marks of which the Katipunan flag or insignia form a part," not only in Manila but "all over the archipelago," in an attempt to "clean up the country of all such matter" before the arrival of the secretary of war. Manila merchants who sold either flags or insignia were "notified to remove all such stock from their shelves and show windows." A political rally was "visited" and its leaders "required to remove the banners they were using." But state repression simultaneously made clear just how ubiquitous the Katipunan banner was. "All cigar rings and cigaret packets bearing this insignia in any form whatever will be seized and destroyed," the *Manila Times* reported, for example.[77]

The culmination of the campaign was a "mass meeting" organized at Manila's Grand Opera House on August 27 to determine, as one newspaper put it, "whether or not the American sovereignty in the Philippines is to be represented by other than the American flag." The event had been initiated by a few "representative Americans of Manila" and organized through an elaborate committee structure involving the American "best men" of the city. It gathered together a standing-room-only crowd of an estimated 3,000 people, "the largest and most representative body of American men and women that has ever been seen in the Islands." The opera house was unsurprisingly draped in the "American colors" and the flag projected in "colored incandescent lights" at the back of the stage; as attendees entered, a military band "discoursed patriotic airs." Along with dozens of committeemen, the stage was filled with "representative business men" of Manila and "one or two" visiting congressmen. The *Cablenews-American* noted that the meeting marked "an era in government here," the awakening of a "civic spirit among the resident Americans," united for the first time on a "common platform of patriotism alone." But this claim itself pointed to fractures in that community that had become evident during the event's planning stages. Some civil servants feared attendance would bring on "the anger of their chiefs"; some "corporate interests" feared participation would be a "deterrent to capital and to the sale of their bonds and stocks."[78]

These tensions were paved over in the event's speeches, which attempted to galvanize those in attendance into a new, unified, aggressive imperial and national politics. To at least some, the event was a counterassembly: if Filipinos would soon fill a room nearby with their sovereignty, so too could Americans. Despite increasing Filipino participation in Philippine government, Capt. Thomas E. Leonard of the 44th U.S. Volunteers stated that *we who are here tonight ARE the Government!,*" officials and nonofficials alike, to which he reportedly received "[g]reat applause." Congressman James McKinney cautioned the audience not to "condemn all the people of a certain race, but to condemn the men who were responsible for the reprehensible acts." But this suggestion was not taken up by other speakers, who saw in the incident a broad metaphor for Filipino incapacity. The event's chair, William H. Anderson, employed the hierarchical familial metaphors within the regime's inclusionary racial formation. Filipinos on the whole were like an "undeveloped child," to be guided and protected; if their "innocent amusements" should not be broken up, neither could the "father" allow them to "adopt a reckless course of dissipation." "While the child remains under the parental roof," he cautioned, "the father will not be downed." Leonard similarly stated that while "a little candy" of self-government was "good for a child," too much "sometimes makes it sick," to which there was "[g]reater laughter and applause."[79]

The meeting's resolutions included a strident assertion of U.S. sovereignty and the derecognition of Filipino cultural and political symbols. The Katipunan flag had "no national status," had "never been adopted by any national assembly," and "represents no people" but rather symbolized, "if anything at all, a spirit of revolt against existing order, or a demand that cannot now be granted." Whereas it had been used to "engender in the minds of the audience feelings of hostility and revolt," and whereas government inaction would "tend to discredit the wisdom of our rules, the extent of our power, and the honesty of our professions," the resolution praised the commission's flag law for defending "national honor" and teaching Filipinos the proper "limitations of freedom of action and speech." At the same time, it called upon Filipinos to work with Americans to make the Philippines the home of liberty, "as it is at present understood by the best of minds among philosophers, statesmen and patriots."[80]

Where Filipinos and Americans had grave difficulty determining which flag would represent the Philippine nation, they were, at least superficially, united in their choice of a "national" hero. José Rizal was inescapable for both Filipino and American nation-builders. Rizal had, almost instantly, emerged as both an elite and popular icon of developing Filipino nationality during the years of the revolution. During the short life of the Philippine Republic, the date of his martyrdom, December 30, had been commemorated in Manila and other major towns. Subsequently, *El Renacimiento* featured colorful descriptions of what it called, in English, "Rizal Day," from all over the archipelago. On February 7, 1905, for example, it reported on Rizal Day celebrations in Davao the previous December, at which "highly patriotic phrases" had been delivered regarding "the civic virtues that adorned the Great Martyr Rizal." A program "appropriate for all" had been developed by local *principales*, and invitations had been sent out to "the youth of both sexes," to which they had eagerly responded. The day's procession had "surpassed all hopes, attended by an infinity of persons who roved around the principal streets of the town." The float bearing "portraits of Rizal and Mackinley [sic]" was "adorned profusely," with an "infinity of crowns dedicated to Rizal by the youth of the town."[81]

While *ilustrado* elites continued to associate Rizal with a politics of education and assimilation, the meanings of his life and martyrdom were reworked by peasants, workers, and radical nationalists, who linked him—through the narrative of Christ's passion—with revolution and the ongoing quest for *kalayaan*. Rizal became a central figure in the period's revolutionary, millenarian movements—the Constabulary's ladrones and tulisanes—with peasant leaders claiming either to be in communication with Rizal or even to be Rizal's reincarnation. One movement attempted to have Rizal's remains interred in a pantheon alongside those of revolutionaries Macario Sakay, Cornelio Felizardo, and possibly Bonifacio before colonial officials persuaded the Rizal family not to. Particularly during election years, when nationalist rhetoric flowed most freely, the approach of Rizal Day saw intensified rumors of revolt. A 1915 report identified the date as one when "occasionally . . . there were rumors for the most part unfounded, but in some cases with conspiracies behind them."[82]

The U.S. colonial regime also struggled to capture Rizal as an icon of the imperial nation-building process. But the U.S. colonial Rizal was one that Rizal himself might have had difficulty recognizing. Gone was the Rizal who had raged against the abuse of his countrymen by callous colonial officialdom, who had threatened revolution as the tragic necessity of the exploited, who had mocked Americans as blindly arrogant. Available for colonial installation was the Rizal who had refused to join the Katipunan and its revolution, who had speculated on American colonial rule over the Philippines, and who had written of Filipinos' character flaws as obstacles to their self-fulfillment. President Theodore Roosevelt had both invoked and reconstructed Rizal along these lines in an April 1903 speech given in Fargo, North Dakota, noting that Rizal's denunciation of revolution "applies with tenfold greater force to those who foolishly or wickedly oppose the mild and beneficent government we were instituting in the islands." Indeed, the U.S. government was attempting "to carry out exactly what the greatest genius and most revered patriot ever known in the Philippines, José Rizal, steadfastly advocated." Roosevelt's Rizal had, unbeknownst to Rizal himself, set forth "the duty of American sovereignty, a duty from which the American people will never flinch."[83]

The effort to seize Rizal for American "benevolence" was undertaken by institutions of U.S. colonial civil society. A December 1912 *Manila Times* editorial entitled "If Rizal Could Come Back," near the anniversary of Rizal's death, described U.S. colonialism as having catapulted the islands miraculously into the imagined future of Rizal's "The Philippines a Century Hence." Returning to the islands, it speculated, Rizal would "find in reality and in practice a score of things that he never dreamed of," including "[f]reedom of religion, speech and press," and "a great system of free public schools." While Americans were "frequently charged with a purpose and a desire to hold and retain the Filipino people in subjection that is tantamount to enslavement," the resurrected Rizal would know that "it never was the custom to educate slaves nor to give them free speech and a free press." Rizal would have seen American benevolence at work even at the bloody birth of U.S. sovereignty. "He would have known," it concluded, draping the glories of the U.S. Civil War over the Philippine-American War, "that Americans fought a great war that men might be free."[84]

It was in the interest of gaining Filipino recognition of the colonial state that colonial officials also energetically pursued and promoted Rizal as representative. By the end of the era of Republican rule, Forbes reported, the colonial government had taken "active steps" to "preserve the memory of the Philippine patriot-martyr." The commission employed Rizal to mark colonial time, establishing Rizal Day as an official holiday. As the prolific Rizal biographer Austin Craig noted, the holiday by 1913 meant the "entire community uniting," since "Spaniards no longer consider [Rizal] to have been a traitor to Spain and the American authorities have founded a government in conformity with his teachings." Craig noted that the fiftieth anniversary of his birth was observed "throughout the Archipelago" in public schools "organized along the lines he wished, to make self-dependent, capable men and women, strong in body and in mind." His mother's funeral in 1911 was "an occasion of public mourning," attended by the governor-general, the assembly, and "chief men of the Islands," with "all public business being suspended by proclamation."[85]

Rizal also played a crucial role in U.S. colonial material culture. His image was ubiquitous on Philippine currency and postage. "[S]uch of his relics as could be protected were gathered and preserved," wrote Forbes. Not surprisingly in the Forbesian era, this "representative man" often appeared in the built environment. A public park was constructed at Dapitan, where Rizal had been exiled, and his relief map of Mindanao was "bordered with cement and fenced around for better preservation." As had other regime symbols, Rizal would also be installed at the spatial core of the nation under construction. By 1910, the commission had established a committee to erect a monument near Rizal's execution site in Manila, funded by popular subscription. According to a description written of the proposed structure, designed by sculptor Richard Kiesling of Zurich, it featured four bronze statues, with Rizal the central icon. The inscription beneath the figures, apparently taken from his writings, emphasized the march of evolutionary time and the shedding of blood (presumably Filipinos') as the precursor to regeneration. "Progress will continue its course," it read, "and from the blood of those who have fallen will spring up new and vigorous shoots."[86]

The most elaborate effort to write Rizal into the prehistory of U.S. colonialism was found in the first full-length English-language biography treating his life, published by the Philippine Education Company in 1913. Its author was Austin Craig, an American colonial schoolteacher and self-conscious champion of the man he called, in an earlier publication, the "greatest man of the brown race." Craig's chief goal was to use Rizal's life to indigenize U.S. colonialism and to give it indisputable historical legitimacy, calling it "A Study of the Growth of Free Ideas in the Trans-Pacific American Territory." In support of this effort, Craig situated Rizal among other "heroes of the free Philippines," with whom he might otherwise have seemed out of place: "Magellan, Legaspi, Carriedo, Rizal and McKinley." Hard against the grain of the Black Legend, Anglo-Saxon racial exceptionalism, and U.S. national exceptionalism, Craig's historical narrative was one of virtually unbroken Philippine progress under successive colonizers, culminating in its present, perfected form. "The American system is in reality not foreign to the Philippines," he wrote, "but it is the highest development, perfected by experience, of the original plan under which the Philippines had prospered and progressed."[87]

Craig's first move made Rizal American and Anglo-Saxon, what he called "America's Forerunner." In order to create a lineage for U.S. colonialism, Craig went to great pains, most highly implausible, to trace the undifferentiated "Americanization" and "Anglo-Saxonism" of the Philippines back to the Spanish colonization. Had not the Philippines been "[c]onquered and colonized from Mexico" and its inhabitants recognized as "Americans" by the Spaniards? Had not the islands been touched by "liberalizing" Anglo-Saxon influences in the shape of English pirates? Paradoxically, perhaps, even Craig's Spaniards had been agents of "Anglo-Saxon" freedom in the islands. Had not the Spaniards been "neighbors of the Anglo-Saxons in the forests of Germany," leading to similarities between "the customs of Anglo-Saxon England and the Gothic kingdom of Castile"? Were not "the New England township and the Mexican, and consequently the early Philippine pueblo," therefore, "nearly related" as units of local government? This dramatic process—Americanization and Anglo-Saxonism by Spanish means—reached its pinnacle in Rizal himself. "These American associations, English influences, and Anglo-Saxon ideals . . . culminated in the life work of José Rizal," Craig wrote, "the heir of all the past ages in Philippine history."[88]

Importantly, Craig's Rizal was the product of multiple races. Like the nation under construction, crisscrossed with roads and bridges, people and goods, the Philippines' internal boundaries were said to have broken down in Rizal, leading to a nation-of-one of special richness and strength. Rizal was a "typical Filipino," for "few persons in this land of mixed blood could boast a greater mixture than his." Rizal's ancestors included "representatives of all the various peoples who have blended to make the strength of the Philippine race." Practically all the "ethnic elements, perhaps even the Negrito in the far past, combined in his blood." Just as Rizal's body brought together the diverse peoples of the Philippines, so his life had united them in political terms, "preparing the way for the union of the various disunited Chinese mestizos, Spanish mestizos, and half a hundred dialectically distinguished 'Indians' into the united people of the Philippines."[89]

Finally, Craig's Rizal was an antirevolutionary, constitutionally committed to gradualist, evolutionary politics: what most proved his Americanness and Anglo-Saxonism was his sense of self-government as self-discipline. Rizal himself was said to have exemplified a manly "self-restraint and freedom from exhibitions of emotion." He was also said to have "inculcated that self-respect which, by leading to self-restraint and self-control, makes self-government possible" and had sought "to inspire in all a love of ordered freedom." When visited in exile and urged to join the revolution, Rizal urged education first and opposed "embarking on a change of government for which the people were not prepared." In these beliefs, Rizal had passed the stiffest U.S. tests of his capacity, the subjection to which also made him a representative Filipino. "Necessarily there had to be careful study of his life and scrutiny of his writings," Craig wrote, "before the head of our nation could indorse . . . the very ideas which Spain had considered a sufficient warrant for shooting their author as a traitor." Rizal's ideas had "stood the test" both of Roosevelt's advisers and his critics.[90]

Nationalist Colonialism

Finally, there was the question of the status of non-Christians with respect to the Philippine "nation" under construction. The struggle was illustrated in microcosm in the controversy over the Jamestown Exposition of 1907 and the question of whether non-Christians should be displayed there. In 1904, the colonial state had committed vast resources to its self-promotion at St. Louis. By 1907, officials were not only unwilling to commit state resources to such projects but were wary of their organization by private individuals. Throughout the colonial state, the temptation to use one's position for personal profit had been, and would continue to be, rampant and frequently indulged. One such opportunity, in the field of exhibitions, had occurred to William Sutherland, a former secretary of Taft's and an official in the Bureau of Education. As superintendent of the *pensionado* program in the United States, Sutherland had long been in the official business of representation, grappling with issues of transportation, immigration, and customs. In 1906, however, Sutherland requested a one-year leave of absence to undertake a quite different kind of "exposition," the mounting of a Philippine display at the upcoming Jamestown Exposition. Taft granted him support, pending commission approval, to "secure the comfort and return of those whom you invite." But Taft's simultaneous cautions suggested how far the state had retreated from the business of exposition:

It must of course be distinctly understood that this exhibition . . . is neither a War Department, an Insular Bureau, or a Philippine Government matter, and we cannot be responsible for it in any way. . . . It is quite possible that there may be some public misconception of who is making this exhibit, and I trust you will always be specific in the statement that it is not a government exhibit, but only one by the Governors of the Jamestown Exposition.[91]

Reaction from the insular government was sharper. While the attorney general claimed in a telegram that "the Philippine government has no right by legislation to restrict going or coming of such natives," Governor-General James Smith reported to Taft in January 1907 that he was inclined to refuse Sutherland's request for a contract under which Smith would have "the right to intervene and protect the interests of the natives" without liability. Smith felt that such a contract would be perceived as official sponsorship. "Agreement asked for by Sutherland would be protection to them," he wrote, "but am quite sure it would be misconstrued."

There is a very pronounced public sentiment in the Islands against taking of Igorrotes to Jamestown Exposition and executing of such agreement by Governor-General will be regarded by the people, irrespective of all explanations to contrary, as Government approval of taking of such Igorrotes. In fact, protests have been made to Governor-General against taking of Igorrotes to Jamestown Exposition.[92]

While they made state/private distinctions, Filipino nationalist editors condemned Sutherland's effort as a misrepresentation of Filipinos before the American public, one they were willing to depict as inadvertent. As early as October, *La Igualdad* noted in an editorial entitled "For the Third Time" (referring to Madrid and St. Louis) that "The Insular Government should not permit the realization of Mr. Sutherland's desires." The following January, an editorial in *El Renacimiento* praised the exposition idea but criticized the display of "Igorots" on nationalist-colonialist grounds. An exposition was to demonstrate "that which is best in a nation and marks its highest degree of progress," it stated. Out of juxtaposition and comparison, "new incentives may be gained for the future progress of each and all." "No nation and no race now considered civilized would think of sending to such exhibitions examples of backwardness, ignorance or savagery which might exist within its borders," it observed. A display of Igorots was objectionable because "they do not represent any of the manifestations of real progress and advance of our people." It would leave the impression that "we were still living divided into tribes, which is untrue." It would be especially damaging at "a critical period," when it was "so desirable that the United States and the world in general may form a correct opinion of the Philippine nation." Americans had already proven themselves likely to "confound" Igorots with "Filipinos in general." It was an "aggravating circumstance" that the fair was to be held in "a place . . . hostile to the colored race—Virginia, which, like all Southern States, is imbued with prejudice against it."[93]

The eventual Jamestown display reflected Sutherland's resourcefulness in confronting the increasingly constrained politics of representation. Having already made extensive arrangements without authorization, he informed the commission that he could not "omit uncivilized people without great loss." But he promised the display would "contain large majority Christians, representing faithfully relative insignificance of uncivilized people." When the commission was unmoved and invited Sutherland to discuss "the advisability of his taking Igorots" "in the face of the feeling of the Filipino people against it," Sutherland promised that "he would take no Igorots to the Exposition." The commission, without authority to prohibit him, in turn promised to lend its "moral support" and not to sanction competing efforts.[94]

But Sutherland's apparent concession was, in fact, a clever sleight-of-hand that traded on rhetorical slippage between "Igorot" and "uncivilized." While there were no actual Igorots at Jamestown, Sutherland was still able to construct "tribal" distinction and evolutionary contrast from his 140 "natives." One May 1907 account of the five-acre display in the *Norfolk Ledger-Dispatch* confirmed Filipino nationalist fears. Each of the four tribes represented—Moros, Bagobos, Ilocanos, and Tagalogs—had "its own village, separate and apart from the others." The description contrasted the Moros, "the most warlike and uncivilized" inhabitants, with Tagalogs, "the tribe to which Aguinaldo belongs"; each tribe had "a different religion, different occupations and different pastimes." The Tagalogs, it noted, "dress more like Americans," eat food "like that of any civilized people," and "look with contempt on their neighbors and do not like to have them referred to as Filipinos." The "greatest attraction" in the Moro village was drawn from recent events: the presence of Prince Sansaluna, son of Datto Ali, "who was killed by the United States troops in the battle of Mount Dajo."[95]

While Filipino nationalists objected to the use of non-Christians as representatives of the Philippine nation, they would also actively seek to extend their control over regions that the commission had insulated as special provinces. U.S. imperial nation-building, importantly, imagined Muslims and animists as permanently outside the Philippine nation that U.S. colonialism was constructing. The institutions of the bifurcated state served to insulate the Mountain Province of Northern Luzon and the Moro Province of the southern archipelago, the latter not only from Washington but from the central, insular government itself. Moro Province was in many ways constructed as an independent state under U.S. military authorities.[96] In fact, its formal detachment was even envisioned in August 1905, when the Zamboanga Chamber of Commerce, made up mostly of U.S. businessmen, presented a resolution to Secretary of War Taft and visiting congressmen asking that Mindanao and Sulu be formed into a separate U.S. territory by an act of Congress. According to the resolution, such an act would open up the region's rich and fertile lands and facilitate the region's civilization, which could "come only with American colonization and enterprise." The region's indigenous population was small and did "not constitute any obstacle to American civilization"; Christian Filipinos, incapable of governing themselves, could not be given control. The resolution went nowhere, but a similar project was advanced in 1909 by Acting Governor Colonel Hoyt, who suggested a similar "permanent detachment" to be named "The Mindanao Plantation," with coaling stations, a naval base, politico-military rule, and land divided into plantations for U.S. agricultural colonization. Muslims and animists were to be entirely excluded from participation; so would Christian Filipinos, for whom the southern Philippines was "an unnecessary burden . . . retarding their progress and postponing the realization of their hopes for the future."[97]

The structures of the bifurcated state were central to the denial of Christian Filipino capacity for self-government. Colonial reports often contrasted the efficient, honest, and self-sacrificial work of U.S. officials in the special provinces with the corruption and wastefulness of governments in regions predominantly ruled by Christian Filipinos at the local level. This discourse defended both the bifurcated state and U.S. imperial sovereignty more generally: as nationalist politics developed, it became increasingly common for U.S. officials to describe their task, for example, as defending Luzon's non-Christians from the destructive rule of incapable Christians. Taft, for example, wrote Worcester in November 1907 to congratulate him on Luzon's special province under "American Governors." "Nothing more clearly shows the inability of the Filipinos really to govern themselves as the mistreatment or utter neglect of treatment with which they visit the Non-Christians," he wrote.[98]

Filipino nationalists actively resisted U.S. efforts to insulate or detach non-Christian regions. The seventh plank on the Nacionalista Party's 1907 platform warned that "[t]he dismemberment of any portion of our territory is a challenge to our national integrity and the Partido Nacionalista will consider it its duty to oppose any such intent or purpose and to work for the conservation of the entire territory for ourselves and our descendents."[99] As early as January 1908, Worcester wrote to Taft reporting that "[t]here has been a vigorous effort on the part of some members of the Assembly to secure the repeal of legislation establishing these [special] governments, thus far without result."[100] Later that year, *El Renacimiento* openly criticized Worcester for his attempt to isolate, dominate, and exploit the Mountain Province for his own purposes. A stinging October 30 editorial entitled "Aves de Rapiña" (Birds of Prey) skewered an unnamed Worcester as part (American) "eagle" and part "vulture," "ascending the mountains of Benguet to classify and measure the skulls of Igorots and study and civilize them, and to espy in his flight, with the eye of a bird of prey, where there are large deposits of gold. . . . Presenting himself on all occasions with the wrinkled brow of the scientist who consumes his life in the mysteries of the laboratory of sciences."[101]

Following the editorial's publication, Worcester used the colonial state's libel laws to brutal effect, suing *El Renacimiento* and winning; the imposed fine of $30,000 crushed the newspaper, and Teodoro M. Kalaw and Martin Ocampo were given prison sentences that were affirmed by the U.S. Supreme Court. But Worcester was only at the beginning of an aggressive, anti-independence politics of divide and rule, as exemplified in a polemical address delivered on October 10, 1910, at the Manila YMCA. While no text of the speech exists, its outlines can be reconstructed by the newspaper reports that swirled around it for days afterwards. In it, Worcester defended both U.S. imperial sovereignty and bifurcated state-building by employing dark fantasies of race war and a novel imperial indigenism in which the colonial state figured as the "protector" of otherwise powerless indigenous people, policing primordial hatreds in which it otherwise had no part. In the event of the United States' withdrawal, he prophesied, there would be an inevitable Christian-Muslim race war in which Muslims would, by virtue of their superior valor—emerge victorious. According to the nationalist newspaper *La Vanguardia*, Worcester—"the supreme chief of the pagan tribes"—stated that "[i]f the immediate independence of these islands were granted . . . as is requested, and if it were possible for us to remove ourselves from here for one moment leaving events to take their own course, and excluding all outside intervention, I believe that the Moros would renew the conquest of the Islands . . . and would carry it forward with great vigor until arriving at a final, complete success."[102]

More outrageous still for nationalist editors, Worcester had stated that Christian Filipinos' claims to sovereignty over the Philippines on the basis of their indigenousness were undermined by the historical precedence of the Negritos. "If the original property is to be the determining factor of the sovereignty of these Islands," Worcester was quoted as saying, "they must be undoubtedly handed over to the Negritos that are recognized universally as the aboriginal inhabitants of the Archipelago."[103] Worcester had found, besides, that the colonial state had had "more success" among the Negritos, as they did not put up "obstacles or hindrances." Some of the Negrito *rancherías* he had visited were "cleaner and more hygienic than many barrios where Christians lived."[104]

Worcester's YMCA address focused Filipino public opinion against him as never before. *La Democracia* believed he had not "stepped close to the truth"; the claim that the Moros would be able to retake the islands was, for example, "utterly ridiculous."[105] Newspaper attacks accompanied political mobilization. A "Comite Contra Worcester" (Anti-Worcester Committee) was formed; the assembly passed a resolution condemning his statements as "false, slanderous, and offensive to the Philippine people." Indeed, Worcester's speech had been "a grave violation" of McKinley's original orders that colonial state officials must "respect the sensibilities, beliefs, and sentiments of the Philippine people." Worcester had, instead, "sow[ed] distrust between the Americans and the Filipinos."[106] One sardonic cartoon applied Worcester's impeccable ethnological premises to the United States itself: it featured Worcester in Washington, D.C., standing next to a stereotyped Native American in a feather headdress. "Mr. Red Skin" says to him: "You have said in Manila that the Negritos, as the earlier inhabitants of the country, are the only ones with territorial rights in the Philippines. My friend, apply this story to America. When are you all leaving?"[107]

This image and the broader response to Worcester's imperial indigenist politics illuminate the status of non-Christians in emerging Filipino nationalist discourse. The dominant accusation was not that Worcester had attempted to divide the nation against itself but that he had "insulted" the nation—identified as "civilized" and "Christian"—by representing it as beneath its "non-Christian" inferiors. In making the Philippines' Negritos the equivalent of Native Americans for ironic purposes, the cartoon had also made Christian Filipinos the equivalent of U.S. imperialists. It said a great deal about the ongoing dialogue between U.S. imperialism and Filipino nationalism that much of the criticism launched against the regime's imperial indigenism took the form of a nationalist-colonialist politics that defined the Filipino nation against its "others." Here, perhaps, was a form of nation-building that Americans could recognize.

IT WAS ONE OF the perversities of colonial politics that Filipino nationalists would recognize, as one of their representative men, New Jersey governor Woodrow Wilson. As a politics professor at Princeton, Wilson had articulated the domestic benefits of U.S. colonial imperialism during the Philippine-American War and Filipinos' morbid incapacity for self-government. Lecturing at Columbia University on "The Place of the United States in Constitutional Development" as Princeton's president in 1907, he had defined self-government in terms of discipline and obedience. Self-government was not "a mere form of institutions, to be had when desired"; it was "a form of character . . . the steadiness and self-control of political maturity." The distinction was "of vital concern to us in respect of practical choices of policy which we must make, and make very soon." Wilson was referring to the United States' "dependencies," specifically the Philippines. The Filipinos, he argued, could not be "given" self-government, because "the self-control of maturity" could only be earned by "a long apprenticeship of obedience." While Wilson was far from an ally of Philippine independence, the Democratic Party had had an anti-imperialist plank in its platform since 1900. In 1912, it had "condemn[ed] the experiment in imperialism" as an "inexcusable blunder" and called for a promise of Philippine independence "as soon as a stable government can be established," qualified by the retention of "such lands as may be necessary for coaling stations and naval bases."[108]

Filipinos had followed U.S. national politics closely since the Philippine-American War, and news of Wilson's presidential victory spread instantly to Manila. "Enthusiastic ratification meetings were held," Charles Elliott recalled, "and the cables were warm with congratulatory messages." An estimated 10,000 people paraded through Manila's streets, and 20,000 gathered on the Luneta, where Osmeña, Quezon, and Aguinaldo spoke of the election's significance. *La Vanguardia* called Wilson a modern Moses who would "preside over our triumphal entrance into the Promised Land after redeeming us from the long captivity to which the imperial Pharaohs reduced us." *El Ideal*'s November 6 editorial heralded "Wilson's Triumph" and audaciously claimed it as a victory for the Philippine people. As the paper had "repeatedly declared," Wilson had been nothing less than the "candidate of the Philippine people." While it reluctantly acknowledged that much of the election had been of "a character exclusively 'American,'" dealing with tariffs and trusts, the editorial nonetheless recognized in Wilson's victory a retreat from the "period of imperial effervescence," when Americans had been "intoxicated with the territorial expansion idea."[109]

Specifically, *El Ideal* interpreted Wilson's statement of the need to hold the Philippines "in trust" and to establish "whatever arrangement of government will be most serviceable to their freedom and development," as a "fundamental condemnation" of the previous fourteen years of Republican policy. But what the paper anticipated as a "change of regime" required not merely a "change of principles" but a "change of men." "In the Philippine Islands," it predicted, "there is going to be, then, a great change, if not a complete one, of the highest officers of the administration." Otherwise, it cautioned, "[t]he triumph of the Democratic Party in this part of the world would be only imaginary."[110]

Manila American opinion was, not surprisingly, full of fear and foreboding: would the great "experiment," with Filipinos endlessly enhancing their capacity for self-government under U.S. tutelage, be allowed to continue? Martin Egan, editor of the *Manila Times* and friend to both Taft and Forbes, cabled the secretary of war reporting the demoralization among official and nonofficial Americans in Manila and urging them to coax Wilson toward a gradualist position. "Authoritative general statements saying Democratic program constructive, changes evolutionary, not revolutionary, all interests protected, would help situation," he suggested.[111]

Wilson would appoint a Democratic governor-general for the islands, and the logic of devolving power to Filipinos would both intensify and be given a name: the policy of "Filipinization." As before, shifts in the boundaries of sovereignty would occasion, and in turn be conditioned by, shifts in the terrain of racial politics. As Filipinos asserted themselves politically by taking over further and further reaches of the state, and as American colonial officials defended their positions and privileges against what appeared to be hostile Democratic policies, the tenor of colonial politics would become yet more acrimonious. What many called a "racial" element in politics would be more pronounced than at any time since the war. Americans would employ the discourse of capacity to brutal effect: even given years of tutelage, Filipinos without U.S. supervision would prove corrupt, incompetent, exploitative, and even savage as a "self-governing" people. The condition of non-Christian peoples would be foregrounded, with Americans taking advantage of the bifurcated racial state—specifically, their own exclusive jurisdiction over non-Christian regions—to make arguments ostensibly in defense of non-Christian peoples against their purported Christian adversaries. Struggles over the rule of non-Christians and over the rule of the islands as a whole would become inseparable. In debates over Philippine sovereignty, Americans would also increasingly confront the reality of an empire they could not confine to their colonies, as Filipino migration stirred fears of a Philippine "invasion" of the United States.

Ending the Philippine Invasion
of the United States

*For the sake of our social and economic welfare we should
release the Philippines and give them complete independence.*
CONGRESSMAN RICHARD WELCH, 1932

*It is unjust to exclude Filipinos from the United States while
Americans assume the right to enter the Philippines without
restriction. . . . Do not exclude Filipinos from the United
States before you have placed us in a position to exclude
Americans from the Philippine Islands.*
MANUEL ROXAS, 1930

Where world's fairs were always draped in rhetorical
grandeur too heavy for them, the Panama-Pacific International Exposition, which opened in February 1915, carried the burden of global interconnection and mutual understanding. This was unsurprising, given its
celebration of the completion of the Panama Canal, an engineering feat
that had achieved what Walter Andrews called "the commerce and intercourse of all nations and all peoples." The exposition—with its foreign
goods spread out enticingly before San Francisco and U.S. markets—was
both an actual global marketplace and an attempt to represent what a
utopian one would look like. It had been what Edward H. Todd, president of the College of Puget Sound, called "a silent yet forceful expression
of the fact of the interlocking of the civilizations of the world." For James
Cox, former Ohio governor, the exposition provided a vivid "demonstration of human interdependence, the one nation upon another, and of one
people upon another people." Cox had witnessed at the exposition "the
weaving in one city of a fabric of art by the looms of the earth, and the
spirit of internationalism that was begotten in the weaving."[1]

One of the exposition's commonplaces was that the accelerating global
circuits of goods necessarily brought about new forms of mutual understanding, enhancing what Joseph H. Apple, president of Hood College,

called the "neighborliness of the world." William McMurray, passenger agent for a West Coast railroad, asserted that "the happy mingling there from day to day of representatives from all nations must have created a world-wide and enduring influence for a united people and a higher civilization." Where the Panama Canal had been called "the marriage of the Great Waters—the blending of those seas whose waves lap the continents of the world," for Henry M. Pindell, owner of a Peoria newspaper, the exposition had brought "all peoples and all races" together "in the celebration of these nuptials." Col. P. Townsley, member of the Coast Artillery Corps and West Point superintendent, hoped that "the commingling of the peoples, like the commingling of the waters," might "knit brother closer to brother, until all nations of men be truly one great Brotherhood."[2]

As the home of the exposition, San Francisco's geographic location on the shores of the Pacific helped organize two related discourses of "connection" between East and West. The event would, by drawing the East Coast's attention to the Pacific, have a powerful nationalizing function, what Helen Balsley, leader of a national sorority, called "a closer relationship and deeper appreciation between the East and West of our own country." The exposition might also bridge that other division of East and West: between the Occident and Orient. Located "on the border line as it were between the Occident and the Orient," wrote Frank J. Goodnow, president of the Johns Hopkins University, the fair "cannot fail to exercise a powerful influence in the direction of maintaining peace between the peoples of the West and the East."[3]

For many observers, these two East/West distinctions were tied to each other: the less the East Coast treated California as a kind of "Orient," the larger Asia and the Pacific loomed. For Lyman Abbott, editor of the *Outlook*, the exposition had brought "to the national consciousness the truth not yet adequately realized, that the Pacific Coast with its western outlook is as important as the Atlantic Coast with its eastern outlook."[4] Observers noted that San Francisco—and California generally—were creations of the U.S. empire on the Pacific. University of California president Benjamin Ide Wheeler called 1898 "the year of the awakening" of California, when there "suddenly awoke in the minds of the people the consciousness of the western sea and its meaning for the Nation." That year had seen "the opening of relations with the Philippines" and "the quickening of life in the Pacific." Where California had once been "the end of a *cul de sac*," San Francisco was now "a station on a main highway around the globe." Expanding Pacific trade had attracted new westward migrants, with "[t]he East and the Far West . . . blending just now with astonishing rapidity." Building a Pacific empire had also begun to reorient the United States as a whole: as America "turn[ed] its face westward," California would emerge as "the outpost of the Occident and the porch of the Nation." As such, it would "face the awakening East for the final meeting of the world-halves."[5]

But this "final meeting" was not as harmonious as high-flown exposition rhetoric might have had it. Indeed, the exposition took place at the very epicenter of U.S. racial nativism. By 1910, the California nativist movement had Chinese exclusion to its credit; San Francisco's segregation of Japanese students in October 1906 had provoked an international crisis leading to Roosevelt's intervention and the negotiation of a "Gentleman's Agreement" that restricted Japanese immigration to elites.[6] One collision between commercial cosmopolitanism and racial nativism occurred during the exposition's planning, when exposition officials eager to attract a Japanese delegation unsuccessfully attempted to pressure nativist state legislators to abandon a proposal to ban "alien" land ownership, an action that would inevitably anger the Japanese government. While the former group saw the Pacific as a realm of commercial empire and, perhaps, "human interdependence," the latter sought to guarantee that the West Coast's "commingling" of Occident and Orient would confine itself to bodies of water. James D. Phelan of the California State Federation of Labor had stated that while the exposition was mounted for only a year, "the white race, I hope, will be here forever."[7]

As this one conflict illuminated, while ties of commerce, migration, and diplomacy "quickened" the life of the Pacific, the interests and understandings that surrounded it also diversified and confronted each other. Both between and within the polities of the United States, China, Japan, and the Philippines, actors offered competing strategies for reordering the Pacific. By 1914, the Pacific politics of the United States was organized around three pillars: informal commercial and naval empire and the "Open Door" in China; formal colonialism in the Philippines, Hawaii, Guam, and Samoa; and racial exclusion from the United States of Chinese and Japanese migrants "ineligible for citizenship." For most American policy makers, there seemed little, if any, conflict between these three projects and, indeed, there was a good deal of convergence: for many, annexing the Philippines had itself been part of a strategy to pursue commercial empire in China, one that was proven effective when

U.S. troops were deployed from the Philippines to suppress the Boxer Rebellion and to secure access to Chinese markets. But after 1905, Chinese and Japanese protesters and officials drove a wedge down the center of U.S. Pacific politics with claims that there was a fundamental contradiction between empire and exclusion. In China, opposition to exclusion led to a boycott of U.S. imports, one that drove U.S. exporters to urge the reform of Chinese exclusion. In more militarily and diplomatically powerful Japan, exclusion prompted military threats and negotiations that yielded a "Gentleman's Agreement" permitting the entry of Japanese elites into the United States. In both cases, Asian polities asserted that empire and exclusion were incompatible: if the United States wanted to maintain its informal empire in the Pacific, it must also recognize the migration rights of other empires and include their subjects.[8]

For all the other contradictions in formal U.S. colonial rule, policy toward the Philippines had been more consistent along these lines. Unlike the Chinese and Japanese, Filipinos as U.S. nationals could obtain passports and migrate to the United States or other territorial possessions. In practice, formal empire had meant that while the United States occupied the Philippines, Filipinos could also occupy the United States. The fact that, prior to 1920, few apart from the *pensionados* had come had not prevented nervous speculation, as early as the Philippine-American War, about the ways the United States' assimilation of Filipinos might inevitably lead to the Filipino assimilation of the United States. After World War I, and especially by the late 1920s, increasing Filipino migration to the United States was opposed by a nativist movement that reasserted the compatibility of empire and exclusion: these efforts, which culminated in the 1930 Welch Bill, sought to exclude migrating Filipinos from the very metropole that simultaneously demanded their allegiance. When that bill failed, nativists joined the movement for Philippine independence: if formal empire precluded racial exclusion, then there would be one policy—nativist self-determination—for the Philippines.

The fortunes of Philippine independence would change after 1912 when, for the first time since the Philippine-American War, a Democratic administration with links to anti-imperialism took power, amenable to the reform or withdrawal of U.S. sovereignty over the Philippines. Taken together, the opening of metropolitan political space and the consolidation of Filipino nationalist politics produced, between 1912 and 1916, the most significant domestic U.S. struggle over sovereignty in the Philippines since the end of the Philippine-American War. The intensifying "Filipinization" of the colonial state under the Democrats and the consideration in Congress of two bills advancing Philippine independence put U.S. colonialists on the defensive for the first time. They responded by updating earlier tropes of Filipino "incapacity," including imperial-indigenist demands for the protection of non-Christians from Christian oppression. As before, Filipino nationalists and their U.S. allies sought recognition of Filipino capacities and accomplishments under U.S. rule, including Filipino demonstrations of loyalty during World War I. Often these claims to capacity involved nationalist-colonialist minimizations of, and political claims over, non-Christian populations.

But Democratic anti-imperialist and Filipino nationalist pressure did not, in the end, produce Philippine independence. In fact, the achievement of Philippine independence occurred almost entirely outside, and in many ways despite, the politics of recognition, calibrated colonialism, and inclusionary racism. By the late 1920s, powerful lobbies in the United States were emerging that were convinced only of Philippine capacities to threaten them. Domestic agricultural producers—of dairy products, sugar, and cordage, especially—blamed declining prices on the "menace" of inexpensive, untaxed Philippine imports. U.S. labor unions and anti-Filipino organizations held a growing influx of Filipino laborers, especially on the West Coast, responsible for lowered wages and racial-civilizational decline. Where U.S. nativists understood Filipinos as dangerous and unassimilable, Filipino migrants often felt surprisingly at home in American environments based on what they had learned of the United States in the Philippines and on their personal experiences with Americans there. Their relative familiarity heightened the shock of encountering U.S. racist nativism; it also suggested the ways in which the Philippines and the United States were becoming "commingled," no longer part of each others' boondocks.

By the early 1930s, nativists and protectionists joined together to terminate what they believed to be a fatal Philippine "invasion" of the United States and directed their arguments and political resources to the "liberation" of the United States from its colony. They were never, by any means, the only domestic U.S. force pushing for independence; geopolitical arguments, especially regarding the perceived indefensibility of the islands from Japanese attack, also played a significant role. To the extent that nativists explicitly aided this effort, however, Philippine independence should be seen less as an exceptionally early moment in the history of "decolonization" than as an episode in what John Higham called "the Tribal Twenties." The architects of colonialism had hoped for Filipino assimilation, in part through migration to the United States, especially for purposes of education and socialization. Like the exposition attendees, they understood empire to be, for better or worse, an inclusionary community, if one whose internal boundaries must therefore be policed. Nativists in support of Philippine independence chose racial exclusion over formal colonialism. Having sought their independence after World War I in the name of Wilsonian principles, Filipino nationalists would have the grimmer satisfaction of achieving instead what might, in part, be called nativist self-determination.

The Politics of Filipinization

In 1913, two years prior to the exposition, Woodrow Wilson's newly appointed governor-general, Francis Burton Harrison, a Democratic politician from New York, arrived in Manila to great fanfare. Following his election, Wilson had made his most definitive statement on the Philippines during a December visit to his birthplace in Staunton, Virginia. It appears to have been a mere aside. "In the days when we had a frontier—," he began, then broke off, "the Philippines are our frontier now. We don't know what is going on out there, and presently I hope to deprive ourselves of that frontier." Despite its fragmentary quality, the statement constituted the president's "Independence Pledge" in what Resident Commissioner Manuel Quezon's personal publication, the *Filipino People*, called "notably clear and unequivocal language." Wilson confirmed his intentions in his instructions to Harrison, who arrived in Manila October 11 to what the *Filipino People* called "unusual manifestations of satisfaction and enthusiasm."[9] Quezon had played, and would widely advertise, a major role in the appointment of Harrison, who was sympathetic to Philippine independence.

Immediately upon arrival, Harrison delivered a public address in English at the Rizal Monument in Manila before tens of thousands, while Quezon translated into Spanish. He bore a message from Wilson that the Americans regarded themselves as "trustees acting not for the advantage of the United States but for the benefit of the Philippine Islands." Every step from then on would be taken "with a view to the ultimate independence of the Islands and as a preparation for that independence." He promised a Filipino majority on the Philippine Commission as "immediate proof" of Filipino "political capacity." He claimed that Democrats did not believe that "Democratic institutions are the exclusive privileges of our race." He also reasserted the politics of recognition, stating that Filipinos were "now on trial before an international tribunal that is as wide as the world," and that Americans expected "that dignity of bearing and that self-restraint which are the outward evidences of daily increased national consciousness." Until independence, he warned, "we shall demand of you unremitting recognition of our sovereignty." Despite these cautions, which resembled those Taft had given the first Philippine Assembly, Harrison announced triumphantly that "a new era is dawning" and that Americans "place within your reach the instruments of your redemption."[10]

In practice, Harrison's rhetoric translated into a policy of what became known as "Filipinization," which accelerated the state employment of Filipinos at the insular and provincial levels.[11] The most immediate and dramatic changes were on the commission. Forbes had been requested by the War Department to resign after Harrison's selection; Worcester bowed to the inevitable. Resignations were requested from Forbes's commissioners, who were replaced with Democrats and Nacionalistas; Filipinos constituted a majority of the commission for the first time. Filipinization at lower levels of the state took place both through selective firings, some of them with partisan overtones, and through attrition. Harrison would also move quickly to end the regime's encouragement of business activity by colonial officials. The combination of withdrawn incentives, attrition, and the cumulative effect of American removals and Filipino employment made for rapid change. Over the next six years, the percentage of Americans in the colonial service would decline from 29 percent to 6 percent.[12]

While Harrison Filipinized the colonial bureaucracy, Democrats in Congress took advantage of their return to power by proposing legislation to fundamentally alter, and even terminate, U.S. sovereignty in the Philippines, the last time such an opportunity would present itself until the 1930s. Even before the 1912 election that would bring Democratic victory, Congressman William A. Jones, Democrat of Arkansas, chair of the House Committee on Insular Affairs, attempted to launch a bill to set a fixed date for Philippine independence, without regard for neutralization efforts or U.S. discretionary criteria. When Jones delayed, Quezon himself drafted the first of what would eventually be two "Jones Bills" that he hoped would boost the Nacionalista Party in upcoming Philippine elections, one that provided for the election of a Philippine Senate as the upper house of the legislature and "independence" eight years afterward, with U.S. troops remaining in the islands to "protect" against outside intervention for twenty years. With Republicans dominating the Senate and with William Howard Taft as president, the first Jones Bill had little chance of passage; while the Philippine election pushed Quezon to seek more radical legislation from Congress, the U.S. election made Democrats cautious about making Philippine independence a priority.[13]

With Democratic electoral success, the appointment of Harrison, and the inauguration of Filipinization, conditions seemed more favorable to new legislation. Eager to see any independence legislation pass, Quezon drafted a second Jones Bill in early 1914 that he believed contained enough flexibility to suit President Wilson, who had informed Quezon of his hostility to any fixed timetable for independence. Under the plan, the president would continue to appoint a governor-general and Philippine Supreme Court justices, but all other legislative authority would reside in a bicameral elected legislature, subject to the vetoes of the governor-general and the president. A census would be held in 1925 and every decade following; when 60 percent of adult Filipino males were literate in English, or 75 percent literate in any language, and peace, order, and financial responsibility were recognized by U.S. authorities, a referendum on independence would be conducted and a constitutional convention held in the case of its passage. These were formidable stipulations, and Quezon was chastened by anti-imperialist opposition, abbreviating the second bill's conditions for "ultimate independence" to "stable government"—a term he borrowed from the 1912 Democratic platform—had been established. While it would inevitably postpone independence, such a bill would advance home rule; Quezon believed it would meet Wilson's standards and thus stand a good chance of passing.

Backed by Harrison, Secretary of War Lindley Garrison, and Wilson, the second Jones Bill passed the House in October and went to the Senate, but a number of senators opposed the preamble's pledge of "ultimate" independence, and the session ended without resolution. The bill's sponsors hoped for passage in early 1916, but in January, Senator John P. Clarke of Arkansas introduced an amendment directing the president to terminate U.S. sovereignty in two years, the most radical proposal for the transfer of Philippine sovereignty yet fielded by Congress. Wilson pressured Clarke to lengthen the transfer to between two and four years, with possible additional extensions. In early February, the Clarke Amendment narrowly passed the Senate, but its promises of neutralization or U.S. military protection had been removed. Jones opposed it, and Quezon expressed fears at the domestic turmoil and foreign intervention that might result from a rapid and unguarded transfer of sovereignty. The Democratic caucus in the House adopted the measure, but twenty-eight Democrats refused to follow the caucus's vote and joined with Republicans to defeat the amendment and to substitute for it the far more conservative second Jones Bill, which became the basis for conference committee negotiations. The bill passed and was signed by Wilson on August 29, 1916.[14]

Leading the charge for independence legislation were Democratic elements in Congress, pushed by Philippine nationalists and anti-imperialist activists. Since 1900, the Democratic platform had contained an anti-imperialist plank criticizing Philippine-American colonialism. In 1912, it had called on the United States to issue an "immediate declaration of the Nation's purpose" to "recognize the independence of the Philippine Islands" as soon as a "stable government" could be established, with this independence "guaranteed" by the United States until the islands had secured neutralization treaties with other powers. While this and earlier planks had played little to no role in Democratic campaigns, Democrats were most responsible for pushing independence bills through Congress after 1912, especially southern and western legislators such as Congressman Jones and Senator Clarke (Arkansas), Senator Gilbert M. Hitchcock (Nebraska), and Congressmen Finis J. Garret (Tennessee), James L. Slayden (Texas), and William P. Borland (Missouri). They were aided by Republicans like Congressman Henry A. Cooper (Wisconsin) and Progressives such as Congressman George Curry (New Mexico), as well as by northern, urban Democrats outside of Congress, such as Boston mayor James Michael Curley.[15]

Remnants of the Anti-Imperialist League, allied with Quezon and other Filipino nationalist politicians, actively pressured Congress. The league had splintered in 1904–5, with some of its original Republican officers breaking off to work with Republican leaders on a gradualist program toward "ultimate" independence; the remaining leadership called for unconditional and immediate independence. Especially with the advent of the resident commissioner position in 1907, anti-imperialists and Filipino nationalists developed a transnational politics of agitation that would play an important role in advancing new legislation. League officers contributed articles to Filipino publications in the United States such as

Quezon's *Filipino People*; Filipino nationalists spoke at the annual meetings of the Anti-Imperialist League. Quezon and anti-imperialists Moorfield Storey and Erving Winslow corresponded frequently throughout the Jones Bill debates. Questions of capacity were not absent from these collaborations: league officers did not wish to appear to be propping up a Filipino nationalism incapable of standing on its own.[16]

While some Democratic politicians who supported new legislation did so out of recognition of Filipino capacities, many more did so explicitly out of recognition of the Philippines as a source of geostrategic weakness. With the rise of Japanese power in East Asia, they maintained, the United States would be unable to defend the Philippines in the case of a Japanese invasion. Such concerns were not new but dated back to the Japanese victory against Russia in 1904–5. Following the San Francisco school crisis of 1906, when the segregation of Japanese schoolchildren had led to international friction, the U.S. Navy had developed War Plan Orange, a plan that anticipated a naval war with Japan, which would, it was assumed, attack U.S. colonial possessions in Asia and the Pacific to prepare the way for its hegemony in East Asia and possibly an assault on the mainland United States. Jones himself declared that the Philippine Islands, costly and difficult to defend, were a menace rather than a boon to U.S. security in the Far East. Senator Albert B. Fall, Republican of New Mexico, speaking in support of the Clarke Amendment, saw the prompt granting of Philippine independence as a defensive war measure, as the Philippines was "a weak point in the line of our defense." Retentionists lost an important ally in Theodore Roosevelt, who as early as August 1907 had privately expressed his concern that the Philippines had developed into the United States' "heel of Achilles." In a 1914 essay in the *New York Times*, Roosevelt notably excluded the Philippines from his map of the Pacific that the U.S. Navy should prepare to defend. Roosevelt held that the United States had "no obligation to guarantee neutrality to "an inherently weak nation which is impotent to preserve order at home, to repel assaults from abroad, or to refrain from doing wrong to outsiders." If Filipinos were "entitled to independence," he wrote, the United States was "entitled to be freed from all the responsibility of staying in the Islands without governing them." Philippine independence, in other words, should be a function of U.S. strategic independence.[17]

It was not just that the Philippines was a strategic liability to the United States but that U.S. possessions actively antagonized Japan in geopolitical terms. While imperialists had imagined the Philippines as part of an "Anglo-Saxon" sea in 1900, U.S. advocates of Philippine independence in the mid-1910s saw it as an increasingly exposed holding in Japan's natural dominion. Senator Willard Saulsbury Jr., Democrat of Delaware, attempted to approximate the perspective of Japan, looking on an empire-building United States that, in just over a century, had pushed westward from the Atlantic coast to take "dominion over lands in Asia," and that might be seen as "encroaching on its proper sphere." Saulsbury thought there was "much reason" in what the Japanese might call, "in contradistinction to what we term the 'yellow peril,' the 'white peril' of the Occident." While U.S. withdrawal should not signal "our intention to essay the role of the dominant power in eastern Asia," it would send clear messages of the United States' peaceful intentions. Withdrawing from the Philippines would help the United States legitimize what for Clarke was its necessary, ongoing exclusion of "Asiatics." "We have just simply got to have a policy that is consistent with itself," he said. The United States could not legitimately hold the Philippines within the Japanese sphere while insisting on the "forcible exclusion from our borders of those Asiatic races." Philippine independence would be a logical, positive step in the broader racial separation of East and West: the United States must "get out of their territory and ask them to let us run our own."[18]

Limiting Independence

The campaign for Philippine independence confronted a determined retentionist campaign whose three main promoters were U.S. colonial officials, the Philippine-American business lobby, and the Catholic Church in the United States. At the center of the effort were actual or former high-level American colonial officials such as Taft, Forbes, and Worcester, whose transfer, firing, or resignation returned them to centers of media and public opinion in the United States, full of resentment for Democratic Filipinization and independence legislation. In some cases, their campaign took place in previously established arenas of colonial debate, such as the Lake Mohonk Conference, which became an increasingly polarized setting where retentionists and Filipino *independistas* confronted each other. The National Geographic Society, which owed much of its success to the Philippine census photographs Taft had provided its magazine, returned the favor by hosting retentionist speakers. Retentionists also took advantage of the robust, middle-class, civic, and literary-intellectual culture of the Progressive-era United States. Dean Worcester, for example, would eventually deliver what would become infamous slide and motion-picture lectures at natural science and geographical societies, institutes, colleges and schools, religious societies, alumni organizations, Republican clubs, private city clubs, and professional academic meetings.

In one case, imperialists formed an ostensibly nonpolitical private organization dedicated to U.S. retention. Late April 1913 saw the formation of the "Philippine Society," with Taft as honorary president, Luke Wright as acting president, and Forbes as honorary vice president. Publicly, the society's aim was "to diffuse among the American people a more accurate knowledge of the Philippine Islands" and "to bring into closer relationship one with another the varied interests concerned in the welfare of the Islands"; it was to be "kept free of all partisanship or sectarianism." Privately, it was a retentionist organization. When Quezon, who had been placed on the society's executive committee, received a private communication that "[t]he personnel of the officers of the society is made up of those in favor of the retention of the Philippines," he dramatically and publicly resigned.[19]

Philippine-American business interests, often closely tied to former colonial officials, also organized to shape public debate and legislation.[20] The American-Philippine Company, for example, incorporated in mid-1912, was a major sponsor of publicity against present or future Philippine independence. The company, capitalized at $5 million, was an umbrella organization created to develop subordinate companies in specific commercial areas in the Philippines. From its beginning, it was also meant to provide a revolving door between the colonial state and private enterprise. Former colonial officials featured prominently in its membership, and it actively recruited U.S. administrators with relevant knowledge, especially in terms of commercial exploitation and labor. At the same time, the company saw itself, particularly in light of Democratic policy shifts, as a lobbying organization. As company president Edward H. Fallows put it at one dinner, the company was one in which "a large number of people of power and prominence, having a personal interest in the Philippines," would "prevent the Government from doing something which might be prejudicial to their interests in the country."[21] There were also close ties between the company and the Philippine Society; the company's first vice president, Richard E. Forrest, for example, had been the society's first secretary.

A third major stakeholder in, and promoter of, the U.S. retention of the Philippines was the American hierarchy of the Catholic Church. Early in the U.S. occupation, Taft had negotiated for the church's sale of the Spanish friar lands to the United States, as well as the Americanization of the church hierarchy in the Philippines. While many prominent Catholic leaders, such as Baltimore's Archbishop James Gibbons, had at first opposed the annexation, the Americanization of the Philippine hierarchy gave them powerful political incentives to support U.S. retention. In controversies ranging from the friar lands to the question of religious education, Gibbons, in particular, had become an important mediator between the church and the administration and had become especially close to Theodore Roosevelt and Taft in the process. When the Democrats had begun to debate early independence prior to their 1912 convention, Archbishop Jeremiah Harty of Manila had written Gibbons asking him to mobilize the American hierarchy against it; among other concerns, Harty feared that the United States' withdrawal would lead to the invasion of the islands by the Japanese, who would "blot out any vestige of Christianity that might be found." One week after the Democratic victory and Wilson's election, President Taft met with Gibbons at the White House and urged him to pressure the American hierarchy against the first Jones Bill; in the Philippines, Forbes had met with Harty along similar lines. On December 2, Gibbons issued a statement to the American hierarchy condemning the bill and urging the church to use all its energies quickly and forcefully against it. Emphasizing the president's support, Gibbons reiterated Taft's claim that the church's power was "sorely needed in the Islands" to prevent upheaval and social disorder. Taft thanked Gibbons for the intervention, and Forbes stated that his instructions would have "immense effect," and if followed, "the bill can be killed in its infancy."[22]

Specifically, church leaders were able to appeal to Democratic voters and legislators in urban, industrial areas and thus weaken the Democrats' support for Philippine independence. When, in early 1916, debate on the Clarke Amendment raged, Taft—now dean of Yale Law School—wrote Gibbons asking him to exert influence on the church hierarchy to prevent it from passing. Gibbons responded that he would be glad to comply in order to protect the church in the islands. Among other efforts, he hired—as did Manila-based business interests—the lawyer and lobbyist William A. Kincaid to pressure Washington officials; Kincaid wrote Wilson himself that the Clarke Amendment was a "threat to every Christian Church in the Philippines" as well as a direct threat to U.S.-owned enterprises. Gibbons's direct and indirect lobbying efforts were widely credited with having pushed crucial Democratic votes away from the majority Democratic support of the Clarke Amendment. With all Republican congressmen opposed to the amendment and Democrats holding a twenty-one-person majority, twenty-eight Democratic congressmen, almost entirely from majority Catholic districts, voted against it, dooming it to failure.[23]

While there was a strong tendency to emphasize the church's role in blocking Philippine independence, Wilson himself played a central and active role in preventing it. In accepting the Democratic nomination in 1912, Wilson had stated that, as the islands' "trustees," the United States must "make whatever arrangement of government will be most serviceable to their freedom and development." During his first year in office, he had drawn up a policy based on the findings of his personal investigator sent to the islands, Henry Jones Ford, and those of Felix Frankfurter, a legal aid at the Bureau of Insular Affairs; it provided for increased self-government through a Philippine Senate, but any concern for independence was limited to promises of what he called, in a December 1913 address to Congress, "ultimate independence," a goal toward which "we must move . . . as steadily as the way can be cleared and the foundations thoughtfully and permanently laid." On January 19, 1914, Wilson met with Quezon and made clear to him that he would not support the earlier Jones Bill, although he would support further movement toward self-government and a congressional declaration of the purpose to grant the Philippines independence. By May, Quezon had prepared the second Jones Bill, which Wilson supported during Senate hearings. When presented with the original Clarke Amendment, Wilson succeeded in insisting that Clarke extend its two-year timetable for independence to four years and that he add provisions that would allow additional congressional reconsideration. Having effectively disarmed the amendment's unconditional independence by conditionalizing it, Wilson still supported it only reluctantly, and this support appears to have been for tactical rather than ideological reasons. Wilson wrote to Secretary of War Garrison that he believed the measure was "unwise at this time," given the other, more important agenda items he was pursuing, but that should the House agree to it, it would be inadvisable for him to dissent. When the amendment was defeated in the House with the twenty-eight-member Democratic defection and the second Jones Bill, containing nothing but a pledge of "ultimate" independence, became the basis for conference committee negotiations, Wilson actively supported it. In signing it, he confidently reasserted the politics of recognition, declaring that it was a "very satisfactory advancement in our policy of extending [Filipinos] self-government and control of their own affairs," the only way "that any people comes into contentment and into political capacity."[24]

Congressional and administration politics had, in turn, fundamentally shaped the actions of Filipino nationalists, especially Manuel Quezon. On the one hand, Quezon's actions should be seen as by-products of personal-political pragmatism: his repeated assertion that the passage of "any" legislation was better than no legislation was carefully keyed to a sense of his own political survival in the Philippines. A willingness to trim his demands to suit administration guidelines was evidenced in the difference between the first Jones Bill he authored in early 1912—which called for unconditional independence in eight years—and the second, written after his January 1914 meeting with Wilson, which contained what he understood to be Wilson's demand for high and adjustable conditions for independence. Indeed, Quezon's desire to see virtually any legislation pass even led him to accept the Senate committee's replacement, in January 1915, of the House preamble containing the minimalist "stable government" provision, with a far harsher statement that Filipinos would be given "the privileges of complete independence . . . when, in the judgement of the United States, the people of the Philippine Islands shall be fitted therefore." When Osmeña was outraged at the new preamble and feared that any Filipino support for it would be "construed as accepting actual incapacity persistently supported by the Republican Party," Quezon responded feebly that he would "say our acceptance does not mean we admit present incapability."[25]

But while Quezon was never out in front of the Wilson administration, as Wong Kwok-Chu argues, he appears to have actively pursued opportunities for "immediate" independence whenever they were accompanied by military and diplomatic "guarantees." In his understanding of the conditions that would sustain Philippine independence, Quezon was also pragmatic: believing that the Philippines would become vulnerable to Japanese aggression in the wake of complete U.S. "abandonment," he responded only to openings in which Philippine independence would be secured by U.S. diplomatic or military means. Quezon supported the amendment when it contained guarantees of neutralization or U.S. defense: in late January 1916, after the Clarke Amendment's introduction, Quezon informed Osmeña that he "strongly recommend[ed] immediate passage [of] joint resolution indorsing the amendment." When, by early February, guarantees had been removed from the amendment, Quezon rejected it and shifted his support back to the second Jones Bill, preferring indefinite colonialism to indefensible independence. At the same time, both Quezon and Osmeña feared the potential political volatility that would result from a Clarke Amendment whose promise of unconditional independence had been undermined at Wilson's insistence. Osmeña feared "the possibility of a revolution in case Congress should decide according to circumstances to postpone independence." Faced with this possibility, he told Quezon, "the well-to-do Filipinos" were "strongly in favor" of the more indeterminate second Jones Bill.[26]

The Jones Act would be the last major congressional adjustment of Philippine-American sovereignty until 1934; while represented as "independence" legislation, measured in terms of longevity, it would be more effective in prolonging U.S. colonialism than Congress's original Organic Act of 1902 had been. Opposition from colonial officials and businessmen, from the Catholic Church, and from Wilson himself had together closed down what Philippine nationalists had imagined as the decisive political opening of Democratic dominance in the metropole. While reducing Philippine independence to a "declaration of purpose," the Jones Act blunted the force of Philippine nationalism and U.S. anti-imperialism. It established new grounds for calibrated colonialism around the United States' eventual recognition of "stability" in the islands. At the same time, it regrounded U.S. national-exceptionalist claims about its colonial empire with what was hailed as a pioneering "promise" of independence, which would shore up the United States' own moral recognition in the international arena. In addressing the issue of Philippine sovereignty, Wilson had made clear that it was subordinate to the larger issue of the United States' moral claims elsewhere. Campaigning in Topeka in 1914, for example, he had stated that "just as soon as we feel that they can take care of their own affairs without our direct interference and protection," the flag of the United States would "again be honored by the fulfillment of a promise." Indeed, Wilson hoped that the Jones Act would vindicate before the Filipino people themselves the colonialism it failed to terminate. The legislation "excites peculiar feelings in me," he said, as "there have been times when the people of the Philippines doubted our intention to be liberal and just to them." Wilson hoped that the legislation would be "sufficient and earnest proof to them of our real intentions." The Jones

Act, with its preamble assuring Filipinos, Americans, and the world of the United States' intention to free the Philippines "ultimately," had sacrificed Philippine political independence to U.S. moral independence.[27]

Arguing for Retention

During both Harrison's transformation of the bureaucracy and the congressional debates surrounding the Jones Bills, the meanings of "Filipinization" had been hotly contested. For Filipino nationalists, it meant a widening range of freedoms and the power to recognize their own leaders. For those appointed or promoted, it meant more lucrative, powerful, and status-bearing employment with implicit recognition of capacity. Quezon cast the policy as the natural extension of earlier promises of "eventual self-government." "If self-government for the Islands has any significance at all," he wrote, "it means that the inhabitants, whether immediately given political independence of the United States or not, are to be permitted to select their own representatives and administrative officers." If what American officials from Taft onward had said was true, "that the inhabitants have shown a material degree of ability to manage their own affairs," then "the process of eliminating Americans and substituting Filipinos must be expected to go forward steadily and perhaps rapidly." Indeed, capacity could "never be developed except through the exercise of opportunity."[28]

For American colonial officials and retentionists, Filipinization meant nothing less than political apocalypse, a "scuttle policy" aimed at sinking the ship of state. Congressman Clarence Miller, Republican of Minnesota, dramatically observed that "[n]ot Attila of the Huns nor Theodoric of the Goths ever laid such destructive hands upon human institutions." Charles Elliott accused Harrison's administration of failing to respect the altruistic sacrifices of "trained and faithful American officials," removing them "to make way for inefficient and even dishonest native politicians."[29] The Philippine state, they held, would inevitably decline in Filipino hands. The *Manila Times* strikingly wound the American colonial project in reverse, stating that Harrison's policy meant the "restitution of the conditions of an older day—when justice halted—when the masses of the people were sunk in ignorance—when disease was rampant and unchecked—when roads were trails and bridges were few—when the seven devils of discontent bred revolution, and progress was a word unknown—when the intolerant few rode roughshod over the many—when the weak staggered and fell, with none to raise them up and help them on."[30]

The widespread sense that the replacement of Americans by Filipinos under any circumstances constituted a loss of "efficiency" revealed how shallow the notion of capacity had been as anything but an ideology of indefinite retention. No matter how long their tutelage, it appeared, any Filipino was an inferior candidate as a state employee to any American. As Nicholas Roosevelt put it, Filipinization meant not only the employment of "men indifferent to [their work's] execution and unversed in technical knowledge" but the introduction of "nepotism and graft, neither of which had existed" previously. It was telling that Roosevelt described the replacement of Americans in terms that called up fears of Filipino savagery. It had become clear, for example, that "any or all Americans might lose their heads," while "those not already decapitated became embittered." Similarly, the *Cablenews-American*, reporting on some of Harrison's earlier firings, noted in a headline that three "stalwart up-builders" had "surrendered their scalps."[31]

As had been true at other times in the American colonial period, possible or actual adjustments in the terms of Philippine sovereignty were observed by experts elsewhere in the colonial world who offered, and were solicited for, their critical opinion of American developments. Forbes reported receiving a letter from Col. Sir Francis Younghusband, "the noted Thibetan explorer," stating that, as a matter of "hard practical fact," "of course you never will be able to leave" the Philippines. In the meantime, though, "the *talk* of leaving will have done an infinity of harm—and harm to the poor Filipinos themselves." A *New York Times* correspondent in the Hague interviewed Hendrick Colijn, "perhaps the greatest living expert in the government of Malay races," who had "practically created the present civil service in the Dutch East Indies." Colijn stated that he did not believe Americans could grant the Philippines complete independence "now, or soon." If they did so, the Americans would confront "disorders" and be forced to retake control, or lose the islands to invasion by other powers. The Americans had been too "democratic," as the "independence" bills demonstrated; if these were to pass, there would be "most serious consequences—not only in the Philippines but all over the Orient in the possessions of European powers." Specifically, if Americans "set the example of giving independence to her Asiatic possessions," nationalists in European colonies would "at once begin to chafe under their own restrictions, and there might be a good deal of trouble in more places than one."[32]

As Colijn suggested, at least some of Europe's colonial subjects used Filipinization for their own purposes. Indian nationalist Lala Lajput Rai, for example, had spent three weeks in the United States in 1905 as the guest of the Anti-Imperialist League in Boston and returned for a longer stay in 1915 during which he traveled throughout the country. He found American problems "very similar to those that face us in India," and his 1916 account, *The United States: A Hindu's Impressions and a Study*, highlighted subjects with an eye toward "their particular usefulness for our own development." Rai dedicated an entire chapter to the progress of the Philippines under U.S. rule, basing his account less on the anti-imperialists than on interviews with Frank McIntyre of the Bureau of Insular Affairs; Rai appears to have been eager enough to criticize British rule in India that he accepted many official dogmas of U.S. national exceptionalism without skepticism. He affirmatively quoted a letter from McIntyre to the colonial secretary in England, for example, that stated Filipinos had been "given more power in his government than is exercised by any oriental people," that "all the agencies which are supposed to work for the advancement of a people in popular self-government are being used to the greatest possible extent." Rai praised the U.S. colonial taxation system and found the Americans performing "the most interesting and most promising piece of original work in education now in progress anywhere in the world." He also italicized legislative provisions dealing with due process and freedom of expression that "should be read with interest in India." Nonetheless, Rai asserted, disingenuously, that he had "made no comparison with India," which he would "leave to my readers."[33]

During the 1912–16 Jones Bill debates and Filipinization process, retentionists' arguments drew upon both novel realities and older imperial themes. In the context of the European war and the overrunning of small countries by aggressive imperial powers, they intensified the use of what by that time had become a commonplace threat, that of Japanese aggression against the Philippines. But they reversed Theodore Roosevelt's argument, stating that the very "weakness" of a hypothetically independent Philippines meant that the United States must maintain its military presence there.[34] An independent Philippines, they argued, would inevitably lack the capacity for self-defense suitable for fending off such incursions. They rehearsed more than a decade of accomplishment in areas of benevolence and industrial progress, showcasing schools, sanitation projects, and roads; these projects were, however paradoxically, both fully realized miracles and vulnerable undertakings merely in their infancy. They emphasized Filipino incapacity for self-government in terms of education and political morality, suggesting that additional—and indefinite—tutelage remained to be carried out.

As they had before, retentionists also mobilized imperial-indigenist arguments: the Philippines' peoples, they maintained, sharply divided into Christians and non-Christian tribes, required U.S. retention to guarantee internal stability. The most notorious example of imperial-indigenist argument in the retention campaign was Dean Worcester's lecture tour between 1913 and 1915 under American-Philippine Company propulsion. Fallows had called on Worcester during a Philippine tour to inquire about the islands' cattle resources and to interest him in possibly joining the company; Worcester had accepted the following day and almost immediately signed a contract making him vice president and development manager of the company, with a healthy salary and stock benefits. Worcester had pushed the idea of a publicity campaign in the United States sponsored by the company, and Fallows had agreed to pay for the production of necessary films and slides. It was, in many ways, a perfect match: Fallows crowed that securing Worcester "wound the whole thing up so far as the Philippines were concerned"; Worcester, who knew he was politically a marked man, was pleased that the new position would allow him to leave his "political job" in economic security. Neglecting his own official responsibilities, Worcester used his last months in office, from April to September, employing colonial state resources on behalf of the American-Philippine Company's development efforts and the beginnings of his publicity campaign. While he still had access to state files and a stenographer, he began drafting *The Philippines, Past and Present*, a massive, two-volume broadside against his and the regime's critics. Among other images, the work featured a photograph of a Cordilleran warrior standing next to a recently severed head, identifying the man as "A Possible Office-Holder" under the Jones Bill.[35]

As a retentionist campaigner, Worcester focused almost exclusively on non-Christians, completely melding arguments for continuing American rule and descriptions of non-Christians and their "progress." Whether in publication, lecture, or film, Worcester's imperial indigenism in many ways projected onto non-Christians the evolutionary, tutelary narratives that had been used to describe U.S. relations with Christian lowlanders. As with Christian Filipinos, the U.S. colonial regime was gradually con-

This photograph of a supposed headhunter, taken by Dean Worcester, resembles earlier wartime cartoons and quickly became notorious. It attempts to defeat Filipino claims to self-government on the basis of civilization by warning that a headhunter such as the one depicted would be "A Possible Office-Holder" in the Philippine legislature under the Jones Act. Such imperial indigenism conveyed the image of non-Christians as both fierce and barbaric (as here) or as vulnerable and in need of protection; in either case, permanently incapable of self-government and in need of indefinite tutelage. From Worcester, Philippines, Past and Present, vol. 2, facing p. 972.

verting toward civilization the savages it had encountered; that project was being moved forward by the building of schools, roads, and police forces; it was a process well under way but that nonetheless required an indefinite future to realize itself. But if imperial indigenism echoed "benevolent assimilation," it also displaced it in important ways. For one, non-Christians were often figured as "noble savages," where Christian Filipinos had never been imagined in this way. Christian Filipinos' partial absorption into Hispanic Catholic civilization was itself a sign of their weakness; the absorption had led to further degeneration. On the contrary, non-Christians' success in fighting off Spanish control and influence, whether in Luzon or in the south, was the sign of a manly spirit of "independence." On another score, this imperial indigenism cast Christian Filipinos in the role formerly played by the Spanish: as a corrupting and weakening invasion that must be resisted with aggressive U.S. assistance. While it often contained praise for non-Christians as the moral, masculine, and military superiors of Christian Filipinos and calls for their "protection," imperial indigenism also represented them as formerly (and prospectively) savage peoples in need of stern outside control. Noble savages required empires to preserve their nobility.[36]

After November 1913, Worcester's campaign would be waged in the metropole from what he would call "the Philippine Lyceum Bureau," conveniently located in the New York offices of the American-Philippine Company. Worcester had contemplated releasing a motion picture through a commercial film distributor, but ultimately, company sponsorship enabled him greater control over setting and tone. In format, he would mix the traditional lyceum lecture and the novel motion-picture feature, allowing him to narrate and interpret the film to his audience. Worcester's descriptions of the film's goal would combine hopes for non-Christian uplift, retentionist argument, and commercial boosterism. He would target "the people who really count" and thus influence public opinion so that "it will not be possible for the succeeding administration to drop the work for the non-Christian tribes which has already attained so large a degree of success." At the same time, he would "educate the people of the United States as to the resources and commercial importance of the Islands, the political condition of their people and the utter absurdity of believing that they can at this time maintain a just and stable independent government of their own." The imperial spectacle opened at Carnegie Hall on December 30, 1913, to astonished reviews. The *New York World*'s headline stated that Worcester's presentation "Shows Regeneration of Filipinos in Movies; Head Hunters Transformed into Soldiers of Peace and Savages Become Workers Are Portrayed." Worcester had been introduced by Bishop Fallows of Illinois as "the highest living authority on all that relates to the Philippines." Fallows also claimed that America's beneficial influence in the islands was "without parallel, transcending the fable of Aladdin's Lamp and the romances of Jules Verne."[37] As the *World* related dramatically the following day, the film reproduced a narrative similar to that contained in Worcester's photographic series of an "evolving" Constabularyman:

> Motion pictures showed the head hunters during the earlier days of American occupation and as they are now. The one portrayed life in its most savage form, breech-clouted and tattooed warriors armed with spears, bows and arrows, and their primitive dwelling places; the other showed a transformation almost unbelievable, uniformed soldiery maneuvering with precision, young men in duck, canvas shoes and Panama hats who looked as though they had strolled out of Newport churches, hospitals, schools and public buildings of stone and brick built by native labor.[38]

Throughout 1914 and 1915, Worcester presented his spectacle before a wide cross section of early twentieth-century U.S. civil society. He focused primarily on organizations of "cultivation" and "influence": alumni clubs, lyceums, high schools, museums of natural history, geographical societies, historical associations, universities, war-relief committees, and Republican clubs. He also performed in the halls of power. On December 30, 1914, he delivered a lantern slide address before the Senate Committee on the Philippines in the capitol's designated "Philippine Room."[39]

Challenging Retention

Worcester's propaganda efforts, both before and after his resignation, also attracted the attention of Filipinos in the United States and the Philippines, who charged that his motion picture was a sinister "exposition" by other means. The *Filipino People* noted that Worcester had "long perceived the significance of popular treatment of the Philippine situation, interspersed with photographs of savages." These images left the impression that the islands were "inhabited by 'primitive' peoples who can not for a moment be left to their own devices but must be kept under constant surveillance by American authorities." Following an evening's lecture on "savage customs" and after "viewing motion pictures portraying the most uncivilized of the 'wild tribes,'" it stated, "the idea of independent self-government for the Islands seems absurd, and very naturally so." An editorial in *El Ideal* called on the Philippine Assembly to establish a "publicity bureau" in the United States, "for the purpose of offsetting and retarding the progress of the tactics followed by the enemies of the Filipino people."[40] The editors found the campaign most offensive for the innocence of its stated motives:

> This campaign to besmear our national honor is the more infamous because it is done under the cloak of philanthropy and its promoters and accomplices are so steeped in hypocrisy that they invariably invoke the welfare of the Filipinos as the only motives of their actions, when it is as clear as the light of day that their intention is to bring an outrage on the dignity of our people who are held up to the eyes of the unknowing as a lot of "cut-throats" and savages.[41]

Filipino leaders had, in fact, attempted to affect the United States' perception of the Philippines for some time. As resident commissioner, for example, Quezon had proven to be every bit as dogged a public campaigner as Worcester. Alongside the direct lobbying of Congress, he inaugurated a monthly journal based in Washington, the *Filipino People*, in September 1912, funded by subscriptions, advertising, and government resources. It was primarily a vanity publication composed by Quezon and his aides in Washington, carrying his editorials, recounting his speeches, and chronicling his political successes. But the journal also counted among its contributors prominent anti-imperialists like Moorfield Storey and congressmen sympathetic to Philippine independence. It also followed legislative developments such as the Jones Bill, argued for Philippine independence, and carried running commentary on, and criticism of, the retentionist campaign. Its stated goals were "[t]o promote the great cause of Philippine independence, to clear away current misconceptions respecting the character of the Filipino people and their capacity for self-government; to show the practicability and desirability of setting up an independent Republic."[42] It says a great deal about divided Filipino-American government that, in early 1913, prior to Worcester's resignation, resources of the colonial state were employed by both Worcester's retentionist and Quezon's antiretentionist campaigns.

As illustrated in the *Filipino People*, Filipino nationalists and their American allies exposed retentionist propaganda and answered its arguments point by point. Where retentionists argued that the United States was "protecting" the Philippines, that an independent state would simply be invaded by another power, Filipino editorialists countered that the United States should negotiate neutralization agreements that would bind other powers to preserve an independent Philippines' territorial integrity. The nationalists also fought on the terrain of "capacity." First, they recognized the last decade's progress as a demonstration of Filipino capacity, rather than, as was commonly done, as one of American expertise, benevolence, virtue, and sacrifice. Advances in education and infrastructure were due to the discipline, intelligence, and labor of the Filipinos who had collaborated in them. The journal also sought recognition for Filipino capacities in such new institutions as an "All-Filipino Baseball Team" that toured the United States in 1913. "The Americans who have seen them play with American teams have to acknowledge another proof of the capacity and adaptability of the Filipinos to modern sports," read a note in the *Filipino People*. "Indeed to those fans who consider Walter Johnson and Ty Cobb the greatest men in the United States, our team will be the strongest argument in favor of Philippine independence."[43]

Second, the journal argued that Filipino capacity could only be truly revealed through completely independent Philippine government. While Filipinos were recognized as capable and in need of independence to demonstrate their capacities more fully, American officials were said to be incapable, corrupt, and incompetent, a drag on progress that Filipinos might have achieved more quickly on their own. One editorial complained that appointees under Roosevelt and Taft had "proved themselves incapable of handling the situation in the Islands in any satisfactory way." The Philippines was "tired of political hangers-on," "drones and idlers" for whom there was "no place at home" and "who see only what those who sent them want them to see."[44]

American allies of the campaign were especially eager to subvert the politics of recognition by turning imperialist notions of insufficient capacity on the United States. "Some people may think that a country where the practice of lynching prevails is not fit for self-government," wrote Horace White, a New York editor, in the *Filipino People* in January 1914, pointing to forty-five lynchings over the previous six months, many of them unpunished. "If this practice of wholesale murder with impunity prevailed in the Philippines the nations of the old world might say that they were incapable of self-government," he stated, "but what could we say?" Winfred Denison, a Progressive New York Democrat and Worcester's replacement as secretary of the interior, delivered one striking reversal along these lines when he applied the notion that inferior political capacity warranted colonization of the United States itself. Commentators such as James Bryce had long pointed out the "scandalous maladministration and wasteful inefficiency" of U.S. municipal governments, he noted. What if the Germans, acting on Bryce's description, had said to themselves, "'We are the acknowledged experts in the world in the operation of municipal governments. . . . Therefore we have come to do it for you.'"? "Would we welcome them?" he asked rhetorically. "Would we be grateful to them?"[45]

Inevitably, there was the "non-Christian" question. Confronted with an onslaught of imperial indigenism, Filipino nationalists and their U.S. allies often responded with nationalist colonialism. In doing so, they revealed the impact of the regime's bifurcated racial formation on emerging Filipino nationalism. Some sought to exceptionalize the Philippines within Asia, stating, as Rafael Palma did at an October 1912 banquet in Manila, that the mind of the "Filipino race" had "long ceased to be an Oriental mind." Filipinos, he said, were in "their religious ideas, in their customs, in their thoughts and feelings . . . more like the Occident than any other Oriental nation." Specifically, what made Filipinos "Occidental" was Christianity. Lecturers and writers in the United States supporting Philippine independence constantly emphasized the predominance of Christianity among the population. Manuel Quezon cited the islands' 1903 census to demonstrate that the Philippines contained nearly 7 million "civilized" people who were "all Christians and their ancestors have been Christian for three centuries," possessing "the fundamentals of occidental civilization." Palma saw the Philippines as a Christian bulwark against "heathen" China and Japan, calling for independence so that the islands might defend themselves against those nations' "spirit of expansion." "We have to defend the Philippines not only for the interests of our race and civilization," he stated, "but also for the great interest of Christianity in the Islands."[46]

Making the Philippines Christian meant both distinguishing non-Christians from Filipinos and minimizing them as a population. The Philippines, stated Quezon, was home to "a people homogeneous in race, one in religion—with the exception of a proportionately small number of uncivilized non-Christians—welded together into a common nationality." Ralph Woolley took the making of difference even further than Quezon,

Ball at a Private Residence In Manila.
The Interior of a Typical Filipino Home.

This photograph in the March 1913 issue of the *Filipino People* depicts the ornate home of an elite Manila family as a "Typical Filipino Home" in the effort to convey Filipino civilization to U.S. audiences. It represents Manuel Quezon's salvo in the heated representational contests of the post-1912 era when, in the aftermath of Democratic victories, Philippine independence was again hotly debated in the United States. This willingness to generalize both urban-elite and Catholic identities was consistent with larger nationalist-colonialist premises.

describing "the hill tribes" as "a wholly different race from the Filipinos or Malays." According to the anonymous writer "American," the term "Filipino" was "properly applied only when used to designate the civilized 90 per cent of the population of the archipelago." While Americans in the metropole often misunderstood the term, its meaning was "never misunderstood in the Philippines." Any resident there "would no more think of calling an Igorot, or a Negrito, a Filipino, than he would of applying the term American to an Eskimo." As "American" had done, clarifying the "civilization" of Filipinos often involved making analogies to Americans' relationship to Native Americans: Christian Filipinos were the equivalent of white American settlers, and non-Christians the Indians for whom they should not be mistaken. Anti-imperialist Winslow Warren, responding to what he called "The 'Barbarous Tribes' Bugaboo" in a speech by Taft, accused him of "magnifying the number of barbarous tribes," which bore "about the same relation to the Christian Filipinos that a few years ago the North American Indians did to our people."[47]

Not only were Christian Filipinos distinct and predominant, but they had the capacity and right to rule over non-Christians. "It is said that if let alone the Christian Filipinos could not govern the non-Christian," wrote Quezon, and that if they could, "they would not have a right to govern their non-Christian brethren." He doubted that what he—unlike most—called "non-Christian Filipinos" would be denied the right to choose representatives "on account of their lack of ability." But the "general government" would have "the right to govern them"; Quezon cited "the case of the Indians in this country, who have been governed by the American people through their national government and yet the Indians are not represented in the National Government."[48]

When it came to the Moros, specifically, Quezon was confident that an independent Philippines "could support a standing army of at least 30,000 men and could place in Mindanao one third of this force to keep order among the Moros." He was also certain that Moros would favor Filipino rule over U.S. rule, since "[t]here is, at least, the common tie of kinship." The "Filipino Moros," he pointed out, belonged to the "same race as the Christian Filipino," namely the Malay.[49]

The politics of imperial indigenism and nationalist colonialism fundamentally shaped Philippine participation in the Panama-Pacific International Exposition, as Filipino nationalists in charge of the display foregrounded the islands' capacity for production and completely eliminated non-Christian exhibits. On February 6, 1912, the Philippine legislature passed Act No. 2163, which authorized the governor-general to appoint a commission to arrange an exhibit for the exposition, with an appropriation of $250,000 to assemble ethnological, agricultural, and industrial displays; Quezon would serve as on-the-ground director in the United States. "The opportunity for us is unique," he wrote to a Bureau of Insular Affairs official. "St. Louis was nothing as compared to this."[50] In 1904, Filipino criticisms of the Philippine exhibit had been largely confined to editorials and private resentments. By 1912, Filipino legislators were directly empowered to shape their self-representation overseas. During the collection process, La Democracia urged members of the Panama-Pacific Exposition Board to "take the necessary precaution to avoid exhibits at the Panama-Pacific show that will mislead foreign opinion concerning the real condition of the Filipino people." In particular, the fiasco of St. Louis ought to be avoided. "No more Igorots should be sent to the United States," it stated, "the majority of Americans who saw them at St. Louis having arrived at the conclusion that the Filipinos are largely dog-eaters and savages."[51]

The effort to minimize "negative" representations of Filipinos as either "naked" or "savage" found its way into legislation. In October 1913, a Manila municipal board member proposed an ordinance "prohibiting people from appearing in the streets unless fully dressed." One article stated that it was not clear how the ordinance would affect thousands of urban cargadores, "three-quarters naked men running on the streets of Manila with loads on their backs." In February of the following year, the Philippine Assembly passed a bill outlawing the taking, exhibiting, or possession of photographs of "naked" Filipinos entirely, under penalty of fine and imprisonment. Such pictures, it was argued, "tended to make it appear that the Philippines were inhabited by people in the nude." Europeans and Americans, upon viewing such images, "might go away with the opinion that the members of the august Assembly gathered together to legislate in the typical make up of the well known 'Senator from Bontoc,'" a reference to Worcester's "head-hunter" photograph.[52]

Within a month after the passage of this second law, the legal prohibitions received their first challenge. On March 24, a man identified only as "indio Miller," either English or American, a former resident of the cordillera, was found to have smuggled twelve Igorots onto a ship in Manila, with intentions to set sail for Hong Kong and from there to the United States. When Manila police and the customs service learned of this, they detained the party and scrambled to find legal authorization to stop them in the hours before their scheduled departure. Authorities concluded, however, that "no law existed which prohibited it [and that] the Igorrotes should be allowed to sail with their contractor or 'impresario.'" The ship was allowed to sail.[53]

As the Filipino press noted with shock, this "definitely establishes the precedent that Igorrotes may be recruited wih [sic] impunity at any time and on any occasion to take them abroad for the ends which may be desired." At the same time, it appeared that Miller was not working on his own but had been "commissioned by an enterprise of the metropolis." The *Renacimiento Filipino* saw the hand of Worcester, whom Miller was said to have known in the highlands. It was understood that the twelve were merely "the advance guard of a large band to be taken to the Panama-Pacific exposition, and exhibited throughout the middle and eastern states, the project being financed by a former official of the insular government and a society recently formed, whose membership consists of former residents of the islands."[54]

Governor-General Harrison and the Philippine Assembly reacted quickly. Harrison declared two days later that he was "'very much opposed to shipping out these people for exhibition purposes . . . and if there is no law at present to stop this, I will see that one is passed.'" That same day, the commission passed an act prohibiting the removal of "Igorots" from the islands, with a fine of 10,000 pesos and a penalty of five years' imprisonment. The act had been introduced by Secretary of the Interior Winfred Denison, who claimed that it did not prohibit Igorots from leaving the islands but only targeted those who would remove them for exhibition purposes. "'I believe . . . since these exhibitions are against the true interests of the Philippines and the Igorots themselves,'" he stated, "'that there can be no constitutional objection to the bill.'"[55]

As a result of these efforts to limit the display of non-Christians, the Philippine exhibits at San Francisco diverged sharply from those of St. Louis just over a decade earlier. Their social vision reflected elements of the "material development" policy: if the exhibits at the St. Louis exposition had, in a sense, been a bustling, bifurcated schoolroom, at San Francisco, the Philippines was put on display as a vast and almost depopulated warehouse of commodities, showcasing the islands' capacity for labor and production. Exhibits were both gathered in a Philippine Building (its interior made of Philippine hardwoods) and scattered in buildings such as the Palace of Education and Social Economy. This palace contained health and education displays, the latter featuring "motion pictures and lantern slides [to] bring the exposition visitors to the boys and girls of the Philippines."[56]

According to one description, the Philippine exhibits provided "as complete and thorough a representation of the commercial and industrial possibilities of the Islands as possible." Displays included, for example, exhibits of coconuts and other nuts and their oils, marble and brick-making materials, and lumber and other forest products, including "a film showing native and modern methods of logging and manufacturing in the Philippine Islands." Many exhibits provided market information on, and put up for sale, Philippine handicrafts such as needlework, wood carvings, and hats, increasingly coordinated through industrial education programs in the public school system. The only Filipinos displayed were diligent laborers, with "from thirty to forty artisans engaged in making these articles during the time of the exposition." The section on "ethnology," importantly, contained no actual persons but rather "objects in daily use among the Filipinos," such as "household objects, baskets, implements, [and] tools."[57]

In their public remarks, Filipino speakers made explicit their goal of seeking U.S. and international recognition for Filipino accomplishments. At the exposition's opening, Quezon telegraphed his comments in from Washington, where he was undertaking negotiations over the Jones Bill. The Philippine government had decided to participate, despite a "world-wide commercial depression," he wrote, because "the Filipinos are an enterprising and progressive people" and were "fully aware that the only way by which they can occupy a place in international affairs such as they are entitled to, is that of mingling with other peoples and of showing them what they themselves are." Filipinos remained "among the least known people of the world" despite fifteen years of American rule. "There still prevails in many minds the idea that the majority of them are uncivilized."[58]

Quezon would also explore this theme during his dedicatory remarks on "Philippine Day," held on November 3. American "misapprehensions" about Filipinos were due "probably, as much as anything else, to the exhibition of the native Igorote village at the St. Louis Exposition ten years ago." It was actually believed "by many, if not most, Americans that the Islands were inhabited only by naked savages before the United States took possession." Quezon then distinguished himself and other Christians from non-Christians, stating that while "[g]reat things have been done by the United States in the Philippine Islands . . . no government could have converted a savage, naked people, in ten years, into such citizens as you see represented here in the persons, say, of the Philippine Commission." Filipinos, he said, using remarkably Forbesian tropes, had been "building on the solid foundation of the three hundred years of Spanish dominion and you (the people of the United States) are still building."[59] After touring the pavilions to "examine our exhibits in arts and in science, in agriculture, in industry, and in commerce," he had telegraphed, "you must come to the conclusion that a people capable of accomplishing such results is not altogether foreign to civilization."[60]

Filipinizing the "White Man's Burden"

While imperial indigenism triggered efforts to minimize the Philippines' non-Christian population, the new Democratic regime transformed U.S. colonial policy toward non-Christians in ways that undercut the earlier "dual mandate." Until 1914, Harrison observed, "an aggressive effort was made to keep the Filipinos from all interference with or control over these pagans of the mountains, and to accentuate in every way possible the separation between the races." Harrison was also keenly aware of the ongoing ideological uses of non-Christians, noting that "their situation has been frequently used in argument by those Americans who were campaigning against Philippine independence, in an effort to prove that the Filipinos would abuse or exploit these primitive peoples if put in charge of them." In a direct jab at Worcester, he astutely noted the effort "to maintain the mountain tribes like ethnological specimens in a vast reserve or like an interesting anthropological collection within a glass case." Harrison's policy would intentionally break down some of its walls. "The time had now arrived," he wrote, "to train the mountaineers for gradual participation in the main body of Philippine citizenship." But non-Christians were still politically unlike Christian Filipinos in their capacities and would need a period of tutelage not unlike that to which Christian Filipinos themselves had been subjected. Indeed, Harrison's policy amounted to a kind of Filipinization of the white man's burden vis-à-vis non-Christians. Lowland Filipinos, he observed, "can and do manage the destinies of the mountain tribes with generosity and conscientious consideration" and "have a keen sense of responsibility toward their wards."[61]

This particular aspect of Filipinization was set in place by Secretary of the Interior Denison. On June 30, 1914, Denison laid out his plan to reverse Worcester's non-Christian policy in an address at the City Club of Manila. The crux of his speech was that Filipinos' taxes were being misspent on priorities that did not benefit them. To make his point about fiscal irresponsibility clear, Denison ridiculed two classic Worcesterian projects: the expense of 500 pesos "for the photographing of molluscs" and of 14,000 pesos "for printing the results of ethnological research into the habits of the Bukidnons and other non-Christian tribes." Was it better to enlighten "the outside scientific world" about Bukidnon customs, he inquired, or "to send school teachers to teach the Bukidnons the ways of the outside world?" If non-Christians should receive the same benefits that Christians did, they were also not dissimilar from Christians as political subjects. Having toured Northern Luzon and met with non-Christians, Denison had found that "even the most uncivilized people know what they want" and could be guided toward it with "a little leadership."[62]

That leadership would increasingly be provided by Christian Filipinos, who would take over formerly American-held positions in the government of non-Christians in the late 1910s and 1920s. The bifurcated state was becoming Filipinized: nationalists who had argued for their capacity to rule over non-Christians since the founding of the special provinces would begin to replace U.S. appointees. As early as October 1913, Joaquin Luna had been made the first Filipino governor of the Mountain Province, and Filipinos would serve as provincial governors there until 1924. In December, the Harrison administration ended the hard-won military monopoly on the southern archipelago by eliminating Moro Province as a special province and replacing it with a new, civilian-run Department of Mindanao and Sulu under Frank Carpenter, former executive secretary of the insular government. Carpenter would oversee a rapid Filipinization of the new government, remaining the only American in a key position within a year of his appointment.[63] But the Filipinization of these regions in terms of personnel preceded their complete normalization as part of the Philippine state. The insular government did extend the jurisdiction of many of its departments, such as health, education, and justice, to non-Christian areas from which they had largely been cut off. But as Filipinization proceeded, non-Christian areas would still remain administratively "special" in some ways. When the Jones Act abolished the Philippine Commission, jurisdiction over non-Christians was not handed over to the new bicameral Philippine legislature but was retained by the American governor-general, who appointed proportional representatives for these regions to the Philippine Senate and House of Representatives.[64]

When it was reconstituted in 1917 as a policy-making entity, the Bureau of Non-Christian Tribes, directed by Hispanicized Filipinos, would rein-scribe the difference between Christians and non-Christians, even as it advanced an aggressive project in assimilation, to

> continue the work for advancement and liberty in favour of the regions inhabited by non-Christian Filipinos, and foster by all adequate means, and in a systematic, rapid, and complete manner, the moral, material, economic, social, and political development of those regions, always having in view the aim of rendering permanent the mutual intelligence between, and complete fusion of, the Christian and non-Christian elements populating the provinces of the Archipelago.[65]

As Christian Filipinos gradually assumed administrative control over non-Christians, some criticized U.S. colonial policy for its failure to transform non-Christians, a project that, it was claimed, Christian Filipinos would undertake with greater success. According to a March 1913 editorial in *La Democracia*, while American officials were "ever disposed to sacrifice all on the altars of civilization and the progress of humanity," the Igorots of Baguio remained "in the same state morally as when they were beside the Spanish, dirty, indecently clad, without any idea of what is required to keep up with the onward procession of humanity." *La Democracia* was especially scandalized by the *cañaos* (feasts) sponsored by visiting American officials, and Worcester in particular, which sanctioned and even promoted Igorot "savagery." The very people "who should educate them and direct their intelligence along the roads of progress," the editorial asserted, in fact "[took] advantage of their state of ignorance to amuse themselves to the full, by their presence countenancing their feasts that the unfortunate people organize of a decidedly savage character."[66] Christian Filipinos would, presumably, "direct their intelligence" down better paths.

The Christian Filipinization of the "white man's burden" was nowhere more enthusiastically embraced than in a prize-winning speech by F. R. Ventura, given at the Seventh Annual Oratorical Contest of the College of Law in December 1918, entitled "The Problem of the Non-Christian Tribes." Ventura represented the Philippines nervously seeking recognition before the searching eyes of other nations, while "the censuring finger of the world" pointed out "contemptuously" that "in this Christian country of ours, the blind idol of paganism still reigns over a portion of our land." Ventura was critical of the exploitative display of non-Christians, who had been made the "helpless objects of a magnified, distorted and calumnious representation," and when "fully exposed to the world," had been "the targets of its disdainful jeers." Such "lurid descriptions of the biased press" had been "calculated to reflect on our customs and traditions to belittle our civilization, and to stain our national honor." The non-Christians merited not disdain but hierarchical sympathy and obligation. "Yonder in the north in the pine-clad mountains of Luzon," he stated, dwelt "a simple, semi-civilized people . . . [u]tterly wanting in the treasures of civilization." In the south, there lived the Moros, "a sturdy and spirited people, our brothers in blood and in race, born with us in the same land endeared to our hearts and worshipping but before a different altar." Moros were, however, also "[i]ntolerant and fanatic, garbed in a civilization dyed in the Moslem faith and strangers yet to the blessings of liberty and democracy."[67]

American colonial rule, Ventura claimed, had widened the gulf between these groups and "Filipinos." "[I]n the onward march of our progress," he stated gloomily, the non-Christians had been "shamelessly left to limp behind us." But the fate of Filipinos was bound up inexorably with that of the non-Christians. For the Philippines to "attain to that consummate civilization which will command the respect of the world for ages to come," the Filipinos, "as a people and as a nation," must "shoulder, in the fullness of its weight and responsibility, the sacred trust handed down to us through centuries for its final discharge and execution." This trust was nothing less than the "uplift" of non-Christians to "the heights of our civilization" and their "redemption" from "the fetters of ignorance and superstition." The Americans had bequeathed to Filipinos the tools for civilizing their own internal others, tools Filipinos now had the capacity to employ. More than the palliative measures the Americans had undertaken, this task required a "crusade," led by an "army of the torch-bearers of learning and the host of the messengers of Christ" that would "obliterate forever every vestige of ignorance and idolatry."[68]

To achieve this end required the same civilizing methods Filipinos themselves had been subjected to by the Americans. "[L]et us lavish upon them all that have made us happy and prosperous," said Ventura, until Mindanao and the Cordillera were "netted with roads," with a school on every mountaintop "builded as the shrine of peace and order for the intolerant Moro and as a beacon-light to guide the benighted Igorot." In those schools, Filipinos must "impart to them the knowledge we have in all industries; to instruct them in all the scientific ways that bid the soil yield its riches in abundant harvests. Ours is the duty to train them in the exercise and enjoyment of a democratic government; to stand by them and vindicate their honor against the calumnies of their enemies." The connection between the "progress" of Philippine nation-building and the United States' civilizing mission was seamless here. Ventura felt the Filipino crusade for the non-Christians would pay homage to "the noble sons of America" who had dedicated themselves to "opening the homes of our Non-Christian tribes to the light of civilization, and who have laid the foundation for us." Philippine nationalism would earn the recognition of the United States and the world, in other words, based on Hispanicized Filipinos' success at nationalist colonialism with respect to non-Christians. "Should we repudiate this trust," Ventura warned, "the world will brand us as unequal to the task nobly begun for us by America."[69]

War and Self-Determination

If Filipino nationalists attempted to use the political opening of Democratic rule in the United States to assert their rights to recognition and to demonstrate their political capacities, they would also take advantage of the context of World War I. When war erupted in Europe in late 1914, Filipino nationalists read in the cataclysm powerful forces in their favor. While "almost the whole of Europe flashes into a war flame," read one editorial in the *Filipino People*, lessons were emerging regarding "the general world struggle or conflict of races as some describe it." Most of all, the war challenged the politics of recognition, as "a stinging rebuke to those who have been in the habit of prating about 'stable government,' 'western civilization,' and other shibboleths of the same sort." News reports suggested that the conflict would "rival, in brutality and destructiveness, if it does not surpass, any war of human history." The Balkan struggle had already shown "the lengths to which 'civilized' men would go in their infliction of cruelties and barbarities not only upon their opponents, but upon non-combatants as well." With strong European states collapsing, many an attack on Filipinization appeared ridiculous. "The cant expressions of fear lest independent government, when bestowed upon a people of less than first-class military rank, would lead to 'instability' and war become ridiculous." The more one considered the war, the more it became clear "that the boasted superiority of the Western peoples in civilization, the asserted stability of their governments, and the alleged capacity to make and abide by treaty agreements" were "largely figments of the imagination." In this way, the war would make it difficult for colonial powers "to put forward such arguments in support of their 'mission' to pacify and civilize all countries which differ from themselves in the character of their customs or culture."[70]

If the war undermined the politics of recognition by revealing the inner savagery of Europe, it was also providing what the *Filipino People* called "an impulse to nationalism such as [has] never before been administered." An editorial in the *Philippine Review* observed that the "sentiment of nationality" was being "profoundly stimulated in consequence of developments that are now in progress." The piece defined "nationalism" as the belief that "the true basis of stability in Europe and everywhere else is found in national self-government and the abandonment of outside control." It was unsurprising that this nationalism was of "particular interest to the peoples of the Orient," for it was there that "the aggressions of European nations based upon the alleged 'mission of civilization,' but in fact directed by greed of territory or trade, have been most obnoxious." According to the piece, nationalist movements were spreading across Asia in the war's wake. "The nationalism of Japan, the awakening of China, the national aspirations of the Philippines" were "all parts of a general movement" being pushed along by the currents of war. The postwar world, the piece prophesied, would "make the nation the basis of the state," rather than "force different peoples of differing languages, race, religion, or custom to adopt or accept one another's way of living." Such an outcome, by "ending once and for all the progress of the vicious imperialistic nations," might make the war worth fighting.[71]

Filipinos used the occasion of the United States' entry into the war in April 1917 to seek recognition by demonstrating both their loyalty and capacities for self-government. The U.S. declaration of war was followed by expressions of support in the Philippines. In Manila, large demonstrations were held, with Filipino leaders declaring their allegiance to the United States, culminating in an early May march of thousands to Malacañang Palace. Filipinos responded enthusiastically to war campaigns, exceeding their quotas in Liberty Bond drives and campaigns to grow food. When the Philippine Assembly convened in October 1917, its first act was the unanimous passage of a proclamation of support for the United States and its war effort. Filipino nationalists and their allies in the Harrison administration were also eager to make sure that Filipinos did at least some of the fighting: a well-organized Philippine division in the U.S. Expeditionary Force, they believed, would achieve recognition of Filipino loyalty, capacity, and martial masculinity before the United States and the world. In December 1917, Congress authorized the president to call Philippine militia units into the federal service, prompting Harrison and Quezon to volunteer as commanders. Efforts to mobilize Philippine troops appear to have been stalled by the U.S. Army high command, however, which held Filipino troops in contempt; the Philippine division would be mustered into federal service only on Armistice Day and never leave the islands.[72]

Filipino attempts to gain recognition by participating in the U.S. Navy were curtailed in illuminating ways. One month following its declaration of support, the Philippine Assembly authorized the governor-general to arrange for the building of a submarine and a destroyer to be contributed to the war effort, using Philippine government revenues, at a cost of $2 million. The project was conceived as an expression of Filipino nationalism, fidelity to the United States, and capacity: the assembly placed on its donation the stipulation that the crew of the destroyer, tellingly named the uss *Rizal*, must be entirely Filipino. Following the ships' construction in a San Francisco ironworks, the U.S. Navy accepted the vessels and agreed to follow the assembly's requirement; the destroyer was launched in June 1918 and commissioned on May 20, 1919. The unsuccessful career of the *Rizal* as an all-Filipino vessel, however, reflected the politics of Filipinization in miniature. Despite U.S. Navy promises of a Filipino command, the ship was—not unlike the Philippine state as a whole—given an American commanding officer, Edmund S. Root. Root, who would later serve as the governor of Guam, reported that the Filipino crew was lacking in capacity, its members insufficiently trained, unable to communicate in English, and wanting in character, leadership, and initiative. An all-Filipino crew, he asserted, would only be possible after a long period of tutelage. Believing that the crew endangered both the ship and their own lives, Root requested an increase in the number of American petty officers, and the navy soon abandoned its agreement. The ship, with its predominantly Filipino crew under U.S. command, would enter the Asiatic Fleet in 1920 and tour ports in Japan, China, the Philippines, and Guam throughout the 1920s.[73]

While both the Filipino army division and naval crew failed, however, Filipinos would be recruited in large numbers into the U.S. Navy during and after the war. The earliest Filipino recruits to the navy dated back to shortly after the Philippine-American War. By 1917, there were some 2,000 Filipinos in the U.S. Navy, a number that would spike to over 5,700 by the war's end, stabilizing around 4,000 in the 1920s and 1930s, providing about 5 percent of total navy personnel. Prior to and during the war, the navy allowed Filipino enlistees to serve in a wide range of occupational ratings, including petty officers, band masters, machinists, and firemen. Following the war, however, the navy issued new rulings that restricted Filipinos, even those with a college education, to the positions of officers' stewards and mess attendants.[74]

Even as Filipinos attempted to demonstrate their loyalty to the United States, Filipino nationalists were inspired by postwar languages of self-determination to push the Jones Act's promise of independence toward its ultimate point. Opposition Democrats, supported by Governor-General Harrison, favored taking an independence petition directly to the peace conference in Paris, asking the United States and allied powers to grant the Philippines a seat. Quezon cautioned against it, noting that Wilson was afraid of possible embarrassment from the Philippines at the conference; the majority Nacionalistas instead favored submitting the question first to the U.S. government. In March 1919, the Nacionalista-dominated legislature established the first of several "Commissions of Independence" to promote the cause of independence in the Philippines and through a "mission" to Washington. In anticipation of the mission's departure, Harrison cabled the secretary of war asking that its independence message be taken seriously and that the mission itself be given proper recognition "to show the Filipino people our appreciation of their loyalty" during the war.[75]

The first mission found to its dismay, however, that Wilson was too busy "liberating" the colonies of Germany and the Ottoman Empire to liberate the Philippines. The mission's plans to leave before the end of 1918 were frustrated when it received word in November that Wilson would be unable to meet with it due to the Paris Peace Conference. Quezon was apparently enraged, writing a confidential memorandum to Harrison that the "indefinite postponement" of independence would frustrate Filipino hopes and "reopen . . . in their trusting minds the grave doubts and the dark pessimism of years gone by." Harrison sent a caution along to Washington, noting that while it was "of course, out of the question to think that these people, once disappointed, could present a serious military problem to the United States," his own position would become untenable in the absence of an independence pledge.[76]

Following a three-month delay, the first mission did depart for the United States, its expectations trimmed by a Republican-controlled Congress and Wilson's preoccupation with Europe. But the mission missed the boat to self-determination, arriving in Washington just under a month after Wilson had sailed for Europe. Quezon presented its case instead to Secretary of War Newton Baker, stating that independence was the "great national ideal of the Filipino people" and should be granted since "stable government" was the reality there, as the Jones Act had stipulated. In his conclusion, Quezon ably used Wilsonian premises to advantage, holding up a contradiction between the United States' colonialism in Asia and its insistence on self-determination elsewhere. It was only through Philippine independence that the moral superiority of the United States would be recognized by the world. When Philippine national independence had been granted, "the world will know that the people of America are indeed bearers of good will . . . a liberating rather than a conquering nation." The world the United States hoped to remake along self-determining lines would learn that "it is our liberty and not your power, our welfare not your gain you sought to enhance in the Philippines." Baker responded feebly that while the Philippines was "almost independent" already, he believed "the time has substantially come, if not quite come," when the Philippines could be allowed to sever "the mere formal political tie remaining."[77]

The mission made little additional headway in Congress when presented with the opportunity to appear on June 2–3, 1919, before a joint meeting of the Senate Committee on the Philippines and the House Committee on Insular Affairs. It presented a memorial asking for the granting of an early independence to the Philippines in explicitly Wilsonian language, veiling its grievances in a new language of rights. "For the first time in the history of colonial relations," it declared, "a subject and alien race comes to ask the severance of their political connection with the sovereign nation without recounting any act of injustice" but rather with "a feeling of gratitude and affection." Independence was requested "based not on the injustice which might be found in the forcible subjection of the Filipinos" but on "the justice of our claim that the national sovereignty of our people be fully recognized." An independent Philippines would advance the cause of Americanism and civilization in Asia, "contribut[ing] to the spread and establishment of democracy and Christian institutions in the Far East."[78]

Acting as chairman of the hearing, Congressman Horace M. Townes, Republican of Iowa, responded by lecturing the mission to the effect that the United States was "overwhelmed with the process of reconstruction and rehabilitation" elsewhere, with many "pressing matters" before it. In July, Republican leaders postponed any question of Philippine independence, pending "convincing proof" of Filipino capacities for self-government; it was also deemed "inadvisable" to adjust the condition of "those wards of the American Republic until the equilibrium of world conditions was restored." The mission returned to the Philippines, determined to turn failure into success. Its report concluded that the U.S. administration had at least recognized the Philippine desire for independence and that the U.S. public, "as far as we can ascertain," had been won over. Furthermore, the mission had set a "precedent new in the history of democracy" wherein "the relationship between a dependent people and their sovereign nation" could be settled "not by force and unconditional subjection" but by "peaceful conference." The last triumph achieved by the mission was continuous with a campaign that went deep into the Spanish period. The mission itself, in presenting "a large number of distinguished Filipinos," had "erased the erroneous impression hitherto current among many Americans" that the islands were "inhabited by a backward race unaccustomed to the ways of civilization."[79]

In eight years of power, with two decades of anti-imperialist campaign planks behind them, the Democrats had by 1919 failed to "deprive ourselves of that frontier" in the Philippines, as Wilson had put it. In the Jones Act, they had managed, with substantial Filipino nationalist impetus, to advance home rule in the Philippines through Filipinization and to extend a promise of "ultimate independence" to Filipinos once conditions of "stable government" had been established. The timidity of Democrats unwilling to raise the "Philippine question" in election years, the lobbying of U.S. political and economic interests committed to retention, and Wilson's preoccupation with a post–World War I settlement that did not include alterations to U.S. colonialism together closed down the Philippines' opportunity for independence at the moment of greatest metropolitan possibility. As a result, the Jones Act regrounded the politics of recognition around the new question of Philippine "stability," which would emerge as a novel, malleable standard interpreted and fought over by nationalists and retentionists.

Wilson turned to the Philippine question only after the Democrats' serious defeat in November 1920. Just before the end of his term in office, he would publicly call for the granting of Philippine independence, the first sitting president to do so. Wilson might have made this demand in the name of self-determination, which he had championed in Europe in the postwar settlement. But the Philippines would not be allowed to partake of self-determination; its status continued to depend upon the recognition of Philippine achievement using U.S. imperial benchmarks; Wilson believed that at last these benchmarks had been met. At the very end of his annual address in December, Wilson called Congress's attention to "the fact that the Philippine Islands have succeeded in maintaining a stable government" since the Jones Act and "thus fulfilled the condition set by Congress" as necessary for "a consideration of granting independence" to the islands. This "condition precedent having been fulfilled," it was "our liberty and our duty" to "keep our promise" to Filipinos "by granting them the independence which they so honorably covet."[80]

Retrenchment and Disillusionment

As Wilson surely knew, the Republican victory doomed any effort to alter the Philippines' status. Indeed, throughout the 1920s, Republican presidents sought to halt or reverse the Filipinization process that had intensified under the Democrats, in an effort to shore up U.S. rule in the Philippines. They would justify this retrenchment through missions of "investigation" that would expose and diagnose the failings of Filipinization and urge greater "Americanization" of the colonial state and longer timetables of retention. President Harding would send Gen. Leonard Wood and William Cameron Forbes to the islands in 1920–21: the Wood-Forbes Report they submitted cleaved closely to the accounts of their surviving American and Filipino friends in the regime and hung horrific details on the *Manila Times'* prophecy of cataclysmic reversals. Under Filipino auspices, they reported, public health projects had eroded and epidemic disease rates soared; the justice system had caved in before special interests; the Philippine National Bank had loaned extravagantly and corruptly and soon after had collapsed.[81] When President Coolidge sent Carmi Thompson to investigate the islands in 1926, he would similarly find that Filipinos lacked the financial resources, "common language," and "homogeneity and solidarity" necessary for "a strong, democratic nation." It was also "unwise" to grant Philippine independence in light of "international relations in the Orient" and "American commercial interests in the Far East."[82]

On the strength of the Wood-Forbes Report, Leonard Wood was appointed by Harding to succeed Harrison as governor-general and in this capacity attempted to reverse Filipinization, Americanizing and militarizing the state and expanding his executive powers at the expense of Filipino legislators he believed were incurably corrupt and incompetent. Where

Wilson had ultimately declared the Philippines "stable" and deserving of independence, Wood reasserted that Filipinos must have their capacities for industrial and agricultural production and efficient government recognized by Americans before independence could be considered. Wood's politics led to direct collisions with the Philippine legislature and ultimately a crisis when Wood's cabinet officers resigned.[83] During this period, Americans gained familiarity with Wood's Philippines through middlebrow publications solicited by, and sympathetic to, the governor-general, like Katherine Mayo's sensationalist, muckraking 1925 *Isles of Fear: The Truth about the Philippines*. Based on the author's travel to the islands, it was a damning imperial-indigenist indictment of Filipinization as the will to power of a treacherous "cacique mestizo" elite in a war from above against the peasantry. Mayo had her peasants, ventriloquized in long, verbatim passages, plead for continued U.S. protection; one claimed the islands would be ready for independence only in "two or three hundred years."[84]

Wood's tenure in office brought about a critical tension in Philippine-American relations. Since the advent of U.S. rule, Filipino elites' cooperation had been predicated on calibrated colonialism, the promise of gradually devolved power that—with or without independence—would guarantee their own political progress. While perceived by their opponents as radical, both Filipinization and the Jones Act had been highly effective hegemonic strategies for preserving the tense compromises between ongoing colonialism and deferred independence. Both had recognized Filipino accomplishment while establishing new, as yet unfulfilled, criteria for further advancement; both had provided Filipino elites with concrete measures of their own increasing power.

The regime's inclusionary racial formation, which promised assimilation through a progressive, if open-ended, process of tutelage, had been central to calibrated colonialism. But with Wood and his Republican allies, calibration had begun to collapse. The game of recognition was over, but not as Wilson had hoped in December 1920. There would be no Filipino assimilation and U.S. recognition: Wood recognized only Filipino failings in an increasingly exposed project of indefinite retention. The political gap between Filipinos and the Americans was widening into what Spanish imperialist Pablo Feced had once called an unbridgeable "abyss between *them* and *us*." Shortly before Quezon's departure on an "independence mission" to the United States in mid-1924 to criticize Wood's administration, Wood sought him out and ordered him to end his "campaign of abuse." In the "very frank" conversation that followed, Wood asserted that "the real problem out here was biological and not political." Quezon appeared to Wood "rather emotionally stirred by this." As his eyes "filled up," Quezon had conceded that this was "the real trouble, biological and not political, that of different races."[85] However strategic these utterances may have been, they reflected a willingness of both parties to express their doubts about Filipino-American collaboration in terms of a racial problematic that the politics of recognition could not resolve.

Filipino rejection of the politics of recognition was also registered by Maximo Kalaw in his 1916 book, *The Case for the Filipinos*, a political brief on what he referred to as the "so-called Philippine question." By that date, he conceded, "volumes enough to fill a library" had been written on the subject. Kalaw divided these works into two categories, both of them invested in the politics of recognition. There were those by retentionists, which after a few pages on the annexation as "an inevitable God-sent incident of the Spanish-American War," breathlessly recounted U.S. improvements in education, sanitation, and roads and depicted Filipinos in "the darkest colors . . . exaggerating, if not entirely creating new, native vices and shortcomings." Then there were works by advocates of independence, which affirmed the Philippine Republic and enumerated in detail "the unmistakable signs of capacity manifested by the Filipinos during the American occupation" as arguments for independence.[86]

In one sense, Kalaw's book, which criticized Americans' failure to recognize Filipinos' traits and accomplishments, clearly belonged to the latter school. U.S. officials had, for example, "belittled, if not completely ignored," Filipino responsibility for what beneficial results there were from U.S. colonialism, the "splendid materials" Filipinos had brought to bear upon the project, "the inherent capacity of the Filipinos to advance, their thirst for knowledge, [and] the money they pay for all the boasted improvements." U.S. colonialists neglected the islands' "Christian culture and civilization," while "slandering the entire Filipino people, picturing them as a mere conglomeration of contemptible savage tribes separated from one another by age-long jealousies and hatreds."[87]

But even as he held the Philippines up to U.S. standards of civilization, Kalaw simultaneously challenged the politics of recognition. In the name of tutelage, assimilation, and eventual self-government, he asserted, the Philippines was being held to standards that other countries were not. When it decided that Cuba should be "free and independent" following the Spanish-Cuban-American War, he claimed, the United States "did not have to know the characteristics and the skulls of the people of Santiago de Cuba" or "whether the city of Havana could honestly use the Australian ballot." The decision had been made, he claimed, without a politics of recognition, "[w]ithout stopping to learn the racial differences separating the inhabitants of the Islands or the great ignorance of the masses." In the Cuban case, it had been enough that "an entire people were desperately fighting for liberty."[88]

This raised the question of why the Philippines had been singled out for special recognition. Kalaw's answer was that the politics of recognition as a whole, and the specific criteria through which it was exercised, had been generated by the Americans to serve their immediate political needs. From Taft through Forbes, he wrote, the colonial regime's "central theme" had been "the incapacity of the Filipinos to carry on any decent form of government." This "theme" had been a structural precondition of colonial service. Upon assuming their posts, U.S. colonial officials "must of necessity, consciously or unconsciously, accept the theory of Filipino incapacity," because "the only excuse for the Government they were serving was the incapacity of the inhabitants of the Philippines." Upholding the Republican policy of "indefinite retention," they had "their minds already prepared to see and deal with an incapable people."[89]

Arriving in search of Filipino incapacity, U.S. officials had also actively generated evidence of it to make their own case before U.S. publics. "What must be the necessary instrument," Kalaw asked, to make colonialism acceptable to Americans, "whose revered and traditional political doctrine" was to "respect the right of self-government of all peoples"? Advocates of U.S. colonialism would "necessarily paint that people in the color that will best suit their purposes." Where that purpose was denying Filipinos political power, it meant the "humiliation of being calumniated and described as a mere conglomeration of warring tribes or a coterie of naked savages, incapable of any form of national self-government."[90]

For Kalaw, the imperial generation of race had not only been about ideology but about practice. Rituals of empire and the actual exercise of imperial power had helped give life to the very racial hierarchies that, in turn, were used to legitimize U.S. colonial rule. In the minds of American colonialists, what Kalaw called a preexisting "Anglo-Saxon assumption of superiority" had been "strengthened by the sense of political mastery over a subject and 'incapable' people." As long as Americans exercised "mastery," Filipinos must, despite their partial recognition, by definition ultimately be found incapable. "Race prejudice," Kalaw concluded, "had found a natural breeding place in such an atmosphere."[91]

Exclusion and Protectionism

Philippine independence was formally promised by the U.S. Congress with the passage of the Tydings-McDuffie Act in 1934, which ushered in the Philippine Commonwealth, and was granted only after World War II and the end of the Japanese occupation, in 1946.[92] Given the United States' promises that colonialism would be a progressive process of tutelage, assimilation, and the building of capacity, one might expect that the years leading up to the passage of the act would have been especially intense periods for the politics of recognition. Within that framework, Americans had committed themselves to relinquishing control of the Philippines when Filipinos met various sociocultural criteria, among them English-language competence, a capitalist work ethic, and disciplined political behavior. If these promises were true, it might be expected that Philippine independence would be achieved through the United States' ultimate recognition of Filipinos' capacity for self-government. Both sides would have fulfilled the obligations of the colonial compact: the Americans would have selflessly tutored, the Filipinos eagerly assimilated, and the Americans acknowledged their progress by handing over to Filipinos the self-government they could only now responsibly exercise. This, indeed, is how many came to understand the process of Philippine independence: the United States, either "ambivalent" about colonialism to begin with, or the home of an exceptional, "democratic" form of colonialism, had been more than willing to conclude its nation-building project and grant the Philippines independence once Filipinos had adequately proven themselves.

But, in fact, the politics of recognition that had organized U.S. colonialism since the Philippine-American War retreated in the decade leading up to the Tydings-McDuffie Act and had little to do with the granting of independence. The failure of the Democrats to fulfill their pledge to grant the Philippines independence once stable government was established and the Republicans' insistence over three decades on the unchanging weakness of Filipino capacity together confirmed what at least some Filipino nationalists had long suspected: that the politics of recognition had never been intended to grant greater freedom or independence at all but had been constructed to provide U.S. colonialists a set of almost infinitely malleable criteria for denying it. The illusion of recognition had been highly functional to the illusion of impermanence. Filipinos would never—indeed could never—gain their independence laboring to have their capacities recognized by the United States. To the extent that the politics of recognition had been actually embraced by Filipinos, it appeared, the capacity U.S. colonialism had been most successful in developing was a capacity for self-deception.

Philippine independence would be born not from the politics of recognition but from the politics of exclusion. Unlike recognition, which involved complex exchanges between Filipinos and Americans, these new projects were almost completely metropolitan, predominantly the result of U.S. political agency. They came in at least two varieties that, while they diverged, had a common starting point: a palpable sense of the United States' victimization by the Philippine Islands. Beginning in the late 1920s, large agricultural interests would argue that the decline of prices—especially the price of sugar—was directly due to Philippine imports allowed in under U.S. tariff barriers since 1909. At the same moment, organized U.S. workers and patriotic organizations formed vocal lobbies aiming to exclude Filipino migrant workers from the West Coast and from the United States as a whole, workers they believed fatally threatened white labor rights and the racial and sexual integrity of the nation. The dreams of harmonious global integration expressed by visitors to the Panama-Pacific Exposition were here overtaken by nightmares of race war and white surrender.

The combined force of these two political projects—protectionist and racial-nativist—generated much of the political will for Philippine independence. Ironically, their exponents were more affirmative of Filipino capacities than the politicians of recognition had ever been, but these capacities—the very Filipino labor and production displayed at San Francisco—were now the problem. It was the Philippines' rising capacity for sugar production that was believed to threaten domestic sugar interests; it was the very capability of the migratory Filipino labor force—the objects of the colonial state's upbuilding and tutelage in manual labor—that seemed to pose a racial and economic threat to whites. By the late 1920s and early 1930s, the two projects converged around a common, powerful determination: after three decades, the Philippine invasion of the United States must be brought to an end.

Domestic U.S. agricultural producers had not expressed concerns about possible competition from Philippine imports during the granting of partial free trade to the islands in 1909 or full free trade in 1913. Indeed, domestic U.S. and Philippine sugar lobbies had joined together to fight, unsuccessfully, for the maintenance of sugar tariffs against other producers, especially those in Cuba, after 1916. World War I dramatically changed the economic relations of metropole and colony in this regard: the war rapidly increased world demand for most of the Philippines' key exports—copra, coconut oil, sugar, cordage—while scarcity of supply meant booming prices (a doubling of sugar prices, for example) and unprecedented growth, with increases in sugar cane and coconut acreage and the construction of new cordage mills and sugar centrals. With protected access to U.S. markets, Philippine sugar exports more than doubled during the war. Coconut products expanded most rapidly, with the United States in 1918 importing more than thirty-two times what it had in 1910 (and more than sixteen times what it had following the postwar decline).[93]

Domestic U.S. farm groups blamed postwar slumps in dairy and cottonseed oil prices on the free entry of Philippine coconut and copra, what they called "Oriental and foreign oils," and pushed for the imposition of tariffs against them in 1921 tariff negotiations. So, too, did U.S. cordage manufacturers: a representative of the Cordage Association, speaking before the House Ways and Means Committee, called competition with Philippine cordage "a very serious menace." These demands were neglected; indeed, the 1921 Fordney-McCumber Tariff, by raising rates on imports, favored Philippine products, which weathered a postwar depression and grew massively in the 1920s: sugar exports to the United States increased by 450 percent, coconut oil exports (including copra) by 223 percent, and cordage by more than 500 percent.[94]

The same decade saw the drop of agricultural prices and farm incomes in the United States, increases in the cost of living, and a related intensification of militant organizing and lobbying by farmers. The earliest bloc to identify Philippine exports as the cause of agricultural depression was one made up of domestic vegetable oil and dairy producers, who vehemently opposed the importation of Philippine coconut oil. In the early 1920s, producers of cottonseed oil allied with the National Dairy Union, the National Co-operative Milk Producers' Federation, and the National Grange to form a joint "Tariff Defense Committee of American Producers of Oils and Fats." The lobby argued before Congress and the Tariff Commission that, as a congressman from Minnesota put it, the Philippine Islands constituted "the greatest single menace" to their industries. Conveniently exaggerating the interchangeability of cottonseed, animal fats, and coconut oils in the making of products like soap, the producers argued that declining prices due to inexpensive Philippine imports were driving American workers to accept an "Oriental" standard of living.[95]

Interested protectionists also depicted Philippine products as filthy and dangerous. Dairy producers, for example, implausibly hoped to use tariffs to raise the price of margarine enough to close a nearly eighteen-cent gap between butter and its inexpensive competitor. Closing out Philippine coconut oil would, they believed, make margarine more costly to produce and shift demand toward butter. In their effort to discredit Philippine coconut oil products that went into margarine, U.S. dairy producers employed racial tropes that connected the hygiene and safety of Philippine imports to the race of the workers who produced and transported them. In August 1929, the *Butter and Cheese Journal* approvingly quoted an article that depicted a Philippine shipment of copra, which was "impossibly filthy" and smelled "like stable manure or worse." When ready for transport, "swarms of half-naked Malays" loaded it onto ships, "trampling it in the holds of vessels with bare feet." In the interests of protectionism, the dairy journal's nightmare vision joined dark visions of bodily corruption and racial invasion: "An army of naked Malays sweating under the tropical heat, tramping copra that is going to be made into the poor man's butter. Think of it!"[96]

U.S. sugar producers were among the most active lobbyists for tariffs against Philippine products, connecting in cause-and-effect fashion the growth of the Philippine sugar industry and the simultaneous drop in U.S. sugar prices in the late 1920s. This was a questionable theory, given the multiple sources of U.S. sugar imports, which could easily satisfy demand. The Philippines supplied only about 20 percent of the U.S. market in 1933, while Cuba already supplied more than 25 percent.[97] Furthermore, due to the shorter U.S. growing season and other factors, U.S. domestic beet sugar was far more expensive to produce and was only competitive with imported sugars, especially Cuban and Philippine sugars, in regional U.S. markets reachable by inexpensive transport. It was in the East Coast's urban markets, not those near sugarcane regions, that 90 percent of Philippine sugar was consumed. This did not prevent the Nebraska State Senate from passing a resolution stating that Philippine sugar imports constituted a "grave menace" to U.S. beet sugar and the "agricultural prosperity of the state of Nebraska," and that tariffs should be imposed on the former so that the latter could be "adequately safeguarded against this hazard."[98]

By the end of the decade, proposals for Philippine independence would emerge from these lobbies, proposals entirely subordinate to the politics of protectionism. Their efforts to erect barriers against Philippine imports had failed in the early 1920s and again in the 1929–30 Smoot-Hawley Tariff debates. But by that later date, the lobbies were far more organized; when tariff reform failed and Philippine free entry was preserved, they would direct their attention powerfully to independence politics. A December 1929 resolution by the American Farm Bureau Federation called for "immediate independence" for "our so-called colonies or dependencies," but "in the event that such independence cannot be granted," insisted "most strenuously" that their exports be subject to tariffs "applicable to similar products from foreign nations."[99]

The American Association of Creamery Butter Manufacturers backed into its independence politics reluctantly, informing its members that since it appeared that a tariff could not be placed on imports from the Philippines as long as it was a "possession," "it would seem that we should support a movement to give the Philippine Islands their independence." Senator James Heflin, Democrat of Alabama, gave new meaning to the "white man's burden," calling the Philippines "a millstone about the necks of the cotton producers." Philippine independence would mean liberation: for Alabama's cotton oil producers. While freeing Filipinos, it would, more importantly, "free our American farmers from the unfair and destructive competition to which they are subjected." Philippine independence meant that "hereafter when their cheap and inferior stuff comes in to swamp our American farmers," the United States could place a tariff on it "and preserve the home market for our American home people."[100]

The political influence of the U.S. farm lobby on the question of Philippine independence was, in part, due to the comparative weakness of American interests dedicated to preserving U.S. sovereignty in the Philippines and Philippine free-entry status. While both the Philippine Commission and American-Philippine Company had actively sought U.S. capital investment for Philippine agricultural exports, capital had not willingly followed the flag into Asia. U.S. investments in Philippine sugar, for example, were small compared with those made in Cuban, Puerto Rican, and Hawaiian sugar, whose investors were powerful and stood to benefit from Philippine tariff exclusion.[101] Indeed, the biggest commercial interests opposing the exclusion of Philippine products were those who exported U.S. goods to the Philippines, organized in the Philippine-

American Chamber of Commerce. Their influence was dwarfed by the combined power of the domestic agricultural lobbies.[102]

Filipino Migration

The other looming Philippine "invasion" of the United States was not by imports but by Filipino laborers. Apart from the *pensionados*, there had been few Filipino immigrants to the United States before World War I, but their numbers had grown steadily in the 1920s and particularly toward the end of the decade. Just as U.S. agricultural producers had blamed falling prices on Philippine imports, white workers and their allies would blame their precarious position and racial-civilizational decline on the latest wave of "Asiatics." Against the inclusionary racial formation of the Philippine colonial state, racial nativists of the 1920s and 1930s would represent Filipinos as "aliens" who were unassimilable to American institutions, and they would contribute their energy and resources to the broader effort to exclude them from the United States. The nativists appear to have been marginal to the Philippine independence movement until after the failure of the 1930 Welch Bill, which would have excluded Filipinos from migration to the mainland United States within an imperial framework by redefining them—alone among the U.S. colonial subjects—as aliens. Thereafter, the nativists cast their hopes with the Philippine independence movement and supported its efforts to free the United States from its colony. As with the protectionists, nativists believed that independence should not be granted out of recognition of Filipinos' capacities for self-government but only out of recognition of the threat they posed to the United States.

Filipino migration to the mainland United States increased steadily in the years after World War I. Migrants were pushed out of the islands by land pressure resulting from rising populations and unreformed, concentrated landholdings. They were drawn by two staggered but rising sources of demand. First, there was the Hawaiian Sugar Planters' Association, which had brought Filipinos to Hawaii's expanding sugar plantations as contract laborers as early as 1907, when Japanese exclusion had gone into effect. By 1920, there were over 20,000 Filipinos in Hawaii, more than four times the Filipino population of the mainland United States, one sector of a complex agricultural working class. Second and somewhat later, there was increasing demand for labor in the mainland United

States as a result of intensified wartime agricultural and industrial production and the military enlistment of thousands of domestic laborers.[103] One not insignificant source of new migration had derived directly from the war. Under 1917 regulations, Filipino enlistees in the navy were eligible for naturalization as U.S. citizens. Many had been discharged in continental ports, taking service in navy yards or the merchant marine. During the 1920s, and especially during the second half of the decade, Filipino migration to the United States rose dramatically, with a 66 percent increase to Hawaii and 88 percent increase to the mainland, much of it via Hawaii. By 1930, Filipinos occupied an increasingly important economic and demographic place in both the sugar plantations of Hawaii, with an estimated 75,000 Filipinos, and in the asparagus and lettuce farms and salmon canneries of the West Coast of the United States, with an estimated 60,000 Filipinos.[104]

What made this migration legally possible was the colonial state's legal definition of Filipinos as U.S. nationals and its inclusionary racial formation, which represented Filipino migrations to the United States positively, as pilgrimages in the interest of "assimilation." Filipinos traveled to the United States under passports issued by the insular government; before World War I, the majority had been *pensionados*, few in number, geographically scattered, and attracting little notice. Nativists would complain that it was difficult to gather statistics on Filipino migrants because the state did not monitor them as a legally and racially distinct stream, as it did Chinese, Japanese, and South Asian migrants. Most illuminating of the colonial state's strategies of legal and racial "inclusion" of Filipinos for migration purposes was the geographical boundary of the "Asiatic Barred Zone" initiated in 1917, which expansively contained China, Japan, and South and Southeast Asia, but which was carefully gerrymandered around the Philippines. Into the 1930s, Filipinos would be neither "Asiatic" nor "barred" for state purposes.

Filipino migrations played a limited role in the making of U.S. immigration policy before the mid-1920s. But the occupied Philippines as a problem of immigration dated back to the advent of U.S. colonialism. During the annexation debates, racist anti-imperialists, especially from labor-nativist backgrounds, had feared that the islands would inevitably prove the gateway to hordes of "Asiatics." As the U.S. occupation unfolded, that sense of threat grew more immediate and more complex, first taking shape around the question of Chinese immigration to the Philippines. On September 26, 1898, just over one month into the U.S. occupa-

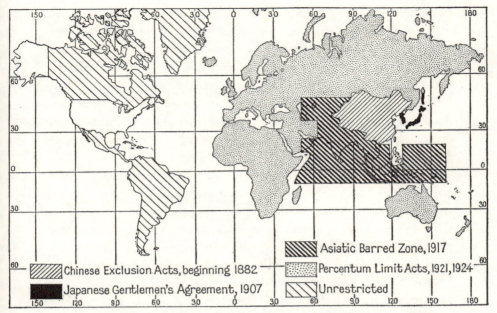

This 1928 world map of exclusionary zones within U.S. immigration law illustrates the way that the colonial state's inclusionary racism was institutionalized at this moment. The "Asiatic barred zone," inaugurated in 1917 and brought into the 1924 Johnson-Reed Immigration Act, comprehensively excluded the immigration of all "Asiatics" but permitted the immigration of Filipinos. As Filipino migration grew in the late 1920s and early 1930s, U.S. nativists responded by redefining Filipinos as "Asiatics." The Tydings-McDuffie Act of 1934 imposed an annual quota of fifty persons on Filipino immigration; following independence in 1946, the nativists would achieve their goal, extending the "barred zone" to the Philippines and making self-determination and exclusion synonymous. Reproduced from Bowman, The New World, 783.

tion of Manila, General Otis had given orders to block all Chinese in-migrants except former residents who had left the islands after December 31, 1895, and those who belonged to elite, exempt classes under U.S. exclusion law. When Congress considered adjustments to exclusion in mid-1902, its members debated whether to extend the laws formally to the Philippines or to allow the Philippine Commission greater flexibility in developing regulations that would allow the entry of select Chinese immigrants, especially skilled laborers, whose talents were believed necessary for economic development.[105]

In a sense, it was a choice between empire—the East Asian commercial empire the United States hoped an economically robust Philippines would facilitate—and exclusion. Congressman Julius Kahn, Republican of California, pushed to have the Chinese exclusion acts amended to "incorporate" the United States' new, otherwise "unincorporated" territories: in doing so, he extended the nativist sympathy normally accorded only to white U.S. workers to Filipinos. Was it not the United States' stated goal to "preserve the islands for the natives thereof?" Better to "retard exploitation" and "allow the natives ultimately to participate in the development of their own land" than to crush them by "opening the gates" to Chinese merchants who would "aggrandize themselves at the expense of the population." Kahn rehearsed the concerns of colonial officials in the islands who, citing long-standing Filipino hostility to the Chinese, feared that a failure to exclude the latter would foment further upheaval: Filipinos would recognize in Chinese exclusion the United States' good intentions.[106]

Others were less concerned with the question of Filipino welfare than the issue of whether, by allowing the Chinese into the Philippines, the United States would open a gaping hole in policies aimed at "protecting" Americans. "Manila must not be permitted to exist as a gateway through which Chinese immigrants can find entrance into the United States," stated Senator Boies Penrose, Republican of Pennsylvania. Senator Henry Heitfeld, Populist of Idaho, conceded that, because of geographical proximity, it was inevitable that the Philippines would be "invaded" by Chinese migrants, regardless of U.S. regulatory efforts there. Thus, it was "all important" to "legislate in anticipation of the rush from the islands into this country." Certain "corporate interests" hoped to find ways around the exclusion laws in order to introduce "Chinese coolly [sic] labor" into the United States; the new possessions gave them a "splendid opportunity to do by indirection what cannot otherwise be accomplished." If this "gap" were left open, it would afford "the open door through which the yellow horde can reach the United States." Those who wished to "incorporate" the Philippines into the United States for purposes of Chinese exclusion triumphed in April 1902, when Congress passed its new law, "to prohibit the coming into and to regulate the residence within the United States, its territories, and all territory under its jurisdiction . . . of Chinese and persons of Chinese descent." The following March, the Philippine Commission would implement Chinese exclusion through Act No. 702, although it would prove difficult if not impossible to enforce.[107]

While it was Chinese transmigrants rather than Filipinos that first preoccupied U.S. nativists, Filipino officials had concerned themselves with the impact of migrants on the politics of recognition even prior to the arrival of large numbers of Filipinos to the United States. As early as 1911, Quezon had inquired of the Bureau of Insular Affairs whether it had the power to ship out of the United States and back to the Philippines "those Filipinos who are either unable to find work or unwilling to do some work." Quezon complained that "there are nearly one thousand Filipinos" in the United States and singled out those who came down from Alaska who "do nothing but all sorts of scandals." He felt that the forced repatriation of these workers was "worthy of the consideration of our Government" and took as his model the insular government in the Philippines and its treatment of poor or disreputable whites who might damage American colonial prestige. "[W]e ought to do with the bad Filipinos here what is done with bad Americans in the Philippines," he wrote, "send them home."[108]

Filipino attitudes toward out-migration were complex, crosscut with both economic politics and the politics of colonialism. Especially among self-consciously modernizing elites, migration to both Hawaii and the mainland United States was seen as a form of tutelage, an experience through which young Filipino men would acquire necessary skills and economic reserves with which to return and develop the Philippines. The right to migrate was also viewed as a matter of recognition and national honor whose restriction or elimination would constitute a serious affront. For many, however, Filipino migration was the object of criticism. According to Resil Mojares, the Cebuano press attacked the Hawaii migrations for the deceptive premises of recruitment, the hyperexploitation of Filipino laborers, the loss of labor necessary for Philippine development, and the lack of "patriotism" among migrants.[109] Filipino landowners had long attempted to restrict labor migrations within the Philippines; some elites quietly favored the restriction of Filipino out-migration through measures exercised by the Philippine state itself, such as passports, literacy tests, or a "Gentleman's Agreement." Exclusion, they hoped, would increase available agricultural labor in the islands and drive down wages, while ending the reputed "spoiling" of Filipino returnees from American sojourns.

Filipino-American Encounters

For many Filipinos arriving in the United States, the country was surprisingly familiar, undermining stark dichotomies between "East" and "West."[110] Many had learned of the United States in the colonial education system in the Philippines. "Native," for example, one of the persons interviewed in a Fisk University social science study, had been "the brightest pupil in Geography" in his English-language public school, and being "most interested in North American geography" had, among other things, "learned by heart the name of the capital and the most important city of every state in the union." "Filipino," another interviewee, had been taught geography and the "history, government, and the institutions of America" by American missionaries, who had also converted him to Protestantism. Some Filipinos reported having studied glowing accounts of the United States, which had served as powerful magnets. It was the "beautiful life and kind attitude" of the missionaries that had convinced Native that "America must be like heaven." Filipino had read from textbooks featuring "the big buildings, beautiful streets and parks, big factories, great men, etc." and had come to picture it "as a land of Paradise." Furthermore, "[t]he results of the American administration in the Philippines showed us the greatness of America," and "we typified all the American people in the United States as [being] like those missionaries and teachers who are working with the spirit of love among my people." In some cases, the colonial state apparently promoted the United States as a destination quite directly. "Foreigner," a third interviewee, reported that "[i]n the office of American consuls in Manila, and all over [the] Philippine Islands, also Europe, when I was there," he had seen "big posters . . . displayed on the walls inviting people to emigrate to America, promising them work, good salaries and shelter."[111]

In many ways, Filipino migrants already recognized much of what they saw in the United States: as nativists feared, the Philippine and American worlds were becoming "commingled," neither one part of the other's boondocks. Filipino reported that his countrymen felt "perfect strangers in this country just for the first week or so," but they "could easily adjust themselves" and soon felt "at home, especially some of us who have been in contact with Americans back home." The similarity of California's climate for those who arrived there was a help. For others, the urban environments of the West Coast felt familiar. Native noted that "[h]aving lived in the city of Manila, which is an American city, there was very little change or difference that was called to my attention when I first got into either the city of San Francisco or Los Angeles." When he had difficulty catching a streetcar, Native at first attributed it to the racism of a white conductor, but after pulling himself on board, he learned that he was merely hailing it incorrectly. The conductor had asked him his origins and then revealed that he himself had been in the Philippines and "had the same experience as I had when he was in Manila." Native "felt quite at home with him," and from then on the two had "a good time" whenever he would ride the car, with the driver talking to him now and then "in broken Tagalog or Spanish." Multilingual migrants were best able to gather improvised new communities together. Native, for example, knowing six languages, had been able to enter a diverse Filipino community in Los Angeles. Although many of the other migrants "looked strange to me at first, somehow I felt at home with them, being able to speak to them in any of the native dialects."[112]

Given their utopian hopes and sense of familiarity, Filipino migrants often registered shock and alienation over the sharp contrast between their expectations of American benevolence, nurtured by U.S. colonial education, and American metropolitan realities. "Upon landing on United States soil," wrote "R. S." to a sociologist, "I began to encounter another new life which I had never thought of before." R. S.'s "impressions as to how some of the American people feel toward the Filipinos" had been "very discouraging." "After I am known as a Filipino," reported Native, "there is an absolute change in the attitude of the white man or woman towards me." Foreigner observed that migrants like himself were disappointed to find that "the American hospitality they have heard about" failed to materialize. Filipino migrants experienced widespread job discrimination: Filipino reported that only the jobs of "dishwashing, porter, etc." were available to Filipinos, with "[m]any of my country-men . . . telling me that they could not get any office work at all," although some had finished college. Public accommodations were closed to Filipinos; one man reported that he and others had been "debarred from some amusements such as dance halls, swimming pools, and other similar places of amusement." When Manuel Buaken was denied housing for being Filipino, his "personal pride was entirely subdued," and he was "wounded deeply in heart and soul!" In that moment, Buaken "had tasted more pangs of life's bitterness and all the sordidness of this world than I [had] ever known before." He had "learned what calamity and what tragic consequences race prejudice can inflict upon a man's life!"[113]

Many Filipinos reported being misrecognized as Chinese or Japanese migrants and facing the various harassments that followed. Native reported that "being mistaken for either a Chinese or Japanese in California . . . made and still makes it difficult in finding my way about and getting adjusted to America." Filipino said he was refused a haircut when a barber had asked him hoarsely, "'Are you a Jap?'" Some of the employment agencies he had consulted in New York "would not give me any job because I am an Oriental." R. S. had been confined, as an "Oriental," to jobs which he was neither prepared for nor willing to perform. He had been "debarred" from one household, for example, "on account of the fact that I didn't know about 'laundry business.'" Filipinos, he corrected, "are not all used to any domestic work."[114]

In other cases, Filipinos grappled with specifically colonialist stereotypes. R. S. lamented that many Americans "think that the Filipinos are yet uncivilized and wild people." Filipino had met a woman whose uncle had "been among the mountain tribes in the Philippines" and sent her pictures of them; the woman had asked him "if the Filipinos are all headhunters," prompting him to warn against developing "our opinions about a certain nation by induction." He related that it "breaks my heart to think that many of the good Americans who have been in my country have misrepresented my people to their own people." He had seen "exhibitions in museums and in the windows of the banks and big stores of the primitive utensils, furniture, implements, etc., of the backward and ignorant Filipinos." There were books "full of pictures of the naked Igorots and their primitive ways of living—people who only number about one-twentieth of the whole population." A Protestant, he complained that even missionaries, in their lectures and articles, "talk of the dark side of the Filipino life."[115]

U.S. racism came as a shock to some Filipino immigrants. Although he had suspected the conductor of "not car[ing] for me because I was not white" on his second day in the United States, Filipino also related that "I have never known or heard the phrase, 'race prejudice' in my life." Initially,

This photograph, taken in Stockton, California, in 1930, vividly represents the explicitly anti-Filipino nativist mobilizations of the Great Depression on the West Coast, which included legalized discrimination and extralegal violence. For nativists, imperialism was wreaking racial havoc by allowing one element of the "yellow peril" through U.S. immigration barriers; for antinativists, the United States' quest for a commercial "open door" in Asia was hypocritical in light of closed doors like this one. The sign also shows how U.S. racial formations had themselves, by 1930, been transformed by empire even at a grassroots level. From Cordova, Cordova, and Acera, Filipinos.

he "had a difficult time getting over the thought that I was a different individual in color and race from the people I came in contact with." "Western people are brought up to regard Orientals or colored peoples as inferior," wrote Carlos Bulosan in 1937, "but the mockery of it all is that Filipinos are taught to regard Americans as our equals." This sense of equality had been nurtured by promises of benevolent assimilation. "Adhering to American ideals, living American life," he wrote, "these are contributory to our feeling of equality." If Bulosan and others had perhaps taken the "brotherhood" in "little brown brother" further than expected, however, they were rudely awakened in the United States itself. "The terrible truth in America shatters the Filipinos' dream of fraternity," he wrote. Had he not "studied about American institutions and racial equality in the Philippines," Bulosan noted, he would "never have minded so much the horrible impact of white chauvinism." As it was, he was left "completely disillusioned" and would "never forget what I have suffered in this country because of racial prejudice."[116]

Filipino migrants were frustrated and sometimes furious at what they perceived as Americans' arrogance. "The Americans are stupid when it comes to understanding foreign people because they think themselves at their best and the foreigners at their worst," reported Native. "They do not take any time to stop and think that foreigners, especially my people, have a different psychology and civilization." "N. F." had been barred from a swimming pool and snubbed by churchgoers but had learned to hide his outrage in the face of what he called "the American psychology of flattery." Criticize an American, he stated, and "they will hate you." One professor had told him, "'Mr. X, do not pick out our bad side. See our good qualities only.'" He had therefore decided not to "expose my feeling to the American people in printed words" while in the United States. "If I let myself go," he said, "I know that your people will not like it."[117]

Some immigrants pointed up the apparent contradiction between Americans' attitudes regarding foreigners living abroad and those in their midst. Native concluded that "the white race is superior in either doing good or bad for others than any of the dark or colored races." Americans, for example, "can be the most generous people on earth towards other people and at the same time be unkind or unchristian in their dealings with the same, when they come face to face with each other." Along these same lines, Filipino observed with some irony that in Sunday school classes and Christian religious services he had attended, he had seen American congregations "greatly moved with sympathy and they give their last penny to help the foreign field work whenever the pitiful conditions of the unchristian world are pictured to them." However, when "the actual foreign persons are here mingling with them, they feel indifferent to them."[118]

Anti-Filipino Racial Politics

Something deeper than "indifference" was revealed in emerging U.S. nativist attitudes toward Filipinos. These partly borrowed from specifically anti-Filipino racial formations that had grown out of the colonial experience and "commingled" with racial formations of the domestic United States. In California, a San Francisco Municipal Court judge referred to Filipinos in January 1936 as "scarcely more than savages," and the North Monterey Chamber of Commerce's anti-Filipino resolutions of late 1929, which triggered an anti-Filipino race war at Watsonville, referred to them as but "ten years removed from a bolo and a breechclout." Newspaper reports covering the pogrom quoted white racist terrorists referring to Filipinos as "goo-goos."[119]

In a more social-scientific vein, C. M. Goethe, president of the Immigration Study Commission, referred in 1931 to Filipino laborers in the United States as "jungle folk," whose "primitive moral code accentuates the race problem," in part because of reproduction rates that endangered "our American seed stock." At least one survey respondent reported around 1929 that his/her first contact with Filipinos—at the St. Louis fair—had fundamentally shaped his/her subsequent vision of them. "Although I did not talk with them," the respondent recalled, "I was definitely impressed unfavorably," considering them "practically on the same level as the American Indians." The respondent believed they were "uncivilized" and "should not be admitted to the United States." The sociologist conducting the survey observed that the "head-hunting proclivities" of "certain wild Filipinos" had made a similarly "permanent impression on many people."[120]

Some anti-Filipino nativism drew, by contrast, on longer trajectories of anti-Oriental racist politics, making Filipinos into a "third invasion" of "Asiatics," proving true Rizal's earlier observation that "ignorant Americans" tended to "confuse" different Asian peoples. To the extent that these attitudes were promoted by nativist organizations, ideological continuities were, in large measure, due to contiguous institutions and leadership, as Filipinos inherited the veterans of earlier Asiatic exclusion efforts. The "Orientalization" of Filipino migration was reflected among respondents to a 1929 survey by sociologist Emory Bogardus. Like earlier Chinese and Japanese immigrants, Filipinos were believed to be "displacing Americans" economically, especially as seamen in coastwise shipping and in urban occupations like elevator attendant, bellboy, and hotel maid. Where Filipinos did not compete with whites in employment—in backbreaking agricultural labor—farmers compared them unfavorably with the Japanese and Mexican laborers next to whom they did work, finding that Filipinos "organize quickly," strike "at inopportune moments," and "seek the city." Like other "Orientals"—and yet apparently more extremely than others— Filipinos were said to pose a racial-sexual threat to white women, proving, to one woman, both aggressive and "smart-Alecky" in their approaches.[121]

As this woman suggested, Filipino migrants were most feared for their sexual attraction and agency with respect to white women. Here, there were echoes of St. Louis, where white mobs had also attempted to racially police both colonial subjects and white women on metropolitan ground. Prior to the Great Depression, attacks on Filipino migrants had taken place almost exclusively in landscapes of troublesome intimacy. In August 1926, for example, Filipino youths had been harassed for attempting to attend a local street dance in Dinuba, California, and a local American Legion chapter formed a patrol to prevent such interactions. The principal racial-sexual flash point, however, was taxi dance halls, where working-class women sold dances to working-class men, many of them immigrants. Within the feverish imaginaries of racist nativists, the dance halls were places of vice, immorality, disease, and miscegenation, where the borders between home and abroad and between metropole and colony dissolved. It was here that the exposition's hopes for a "commingling of the peoples" was, for nativists, darkly realized. As at St. Louis, the coupling of Filipino men and white women threatened to collapse crucial and fragile racial and geographic markers. On December 5, for example, just before the opening of a new taxi dance hall, the *Watsonville Evening Pajaronian* would run a front-page photograph of Esther Schmick, a sixteen-year-old from Salinas, with her Filipino fiancé Perfecto Bandalan, beneath the headline, "There's No East, There's No West When . . ." Where in the early years after the Philippine-American war, elite, interracial cultures of dancing in Manila had cemented colonial politics, in the late 1920s, dancing between working-class Filipino men and white women would contribute to colonialism's undoing.[122]

These anxieties animated the rapid growth of state-level anti-Filipino political nativism on the West Coast toward the end of the 1920s. Proba-

This photograph of Esther Schmick and Perfecto Bandalan on the front page of the Watson-ville *Evening Pajaronian* in December 1929, entitled "There's No East, There's No West When . . . ," expressed anxieties about the racial-sexual implications of Filipino migration to the United States. As at the St. Louis fair, nativist sentiment against Filipino migrants commonly took the form of fears of sexual immorality and racial degeneracy through Filipino-American coupling. By 1929, the most visible target for these fears was the taxi dance hall, where Filipinos hired white women to dance with them; it was such a dance hall that triggered a massive anti-Filipino "race war" in Watsonville the month following the publication of this photograph. Reproduced courtesy of the *Watsonville Register-Pajaronian*.

bly due to the relatively small numbers of pre-1920 Filipino migrants to the West Coast, where anti-Oriental politics was concentrated, nativists appear not to have objected to the Philippine exemption in the 1917 and 1924 immigration restriction acts. By the mid-1920s, however, Filipino migrants were a larger mainland presence, and nativists were flush with victory from the sweeping European and Asiatic exclusions of 1924. For organized nativists, the late 1920s was dedicated to maintaining their momentum by plugging dangerous holes in the edifice of exclusion, especially from Mexico and the Philippines.[123] Each year between 1927 and 1929, the California State Federation of Labor conventions sought to refocus the line between "East" and "West" by passing resolutions calling for the exclusion of Filipinos, resolutions supported by organizations such as the California Joint Immigration Committee, the American Legion, the Grange, and the Native Sons of the Golden West. In 1929, the California Assembly passed Joint Resolution No. 15, a proposal to limit Filipino immigration. The state developed its own anti-Filipino politicians, like Republican congressman Richard Welch, who would push anti-Filipino politics onto the national level.[124]

Such mobilizations led to the successful alteration of the U.S. racial state as Filipinos' racial and legal status was contested in U.S. courts. Leti Volpp relates that as Filipino migrants applied for California marriage licenses, county clerks were faced with the question of whether or not Filipinos were to be barred as "Mongolians," prohibited by sections 60 and 69 of the California Civil Code, along with many other nonwhite groups, from marriage with whites. In 1921, a Los Angeles County counsel reasoned that Filipinos who were neither Negritos nor Chinese should be exempted from the ban. The issue came up again in the 1925 Yatko murder trial in Los Angeles, when the state sought permission for a white woman married to a Filipino man to testify against him by annulling their marriage on racial grounds; the judge in the case legally voided the union, finding that "the Filipino is a Malay and that the Malay is a Mongolian." In cases that followed, however, courts refused such racial annulments. In the March 29, 1933, *Roldan v. Los Angeles County* decision, a Filipino man won in an appeal to the California Supreme Court, allowing him to marry a white woman, having persuaded the court that he was "Malay," as separate from "Mongolian." This was a dangerous distinction for California's nativists: just prior to the *Roldan* decision, State Senator Herbert Jones introduced bills to amend the state's antimiscegenation statute to explicitly include "Malays." Supported by the state's nativist lobbies, the bills passed, retroactively voiding all Filipino-white marriages. Nearly four decades after Rizal had read a lack of "civil liberty" in the United States from antimiscegenation laws directed at African Americans, Filipinos had been "incorporated" into them.[125]

These nativist political mobilizations would, in more than one case, have deadly implications: even where Filipino men could not yet be separated from white women by law, they would be separated by extralegal violence. The years 1929–30 saw at least twenty outbreaks of racial violence against Filipinos in Western states.[126] In December 1929, for example, Judge D. W. Rohrback of the Pajaro Township proposed a resolution to the North Monterey County Chamber of Commerce condemning the Filipino migrant population. When it passed unanimously, the resolution apparently sent a powerful message to local whites about the Filipinos in their midst. So, too, did inflammatory editorials in the *Watsonville Evening Pajaronian*. On January 11, when a new taxi dance hall opened in Palm Beach, local whites attacked Filipinos in what became a five-day race war. Between the nineteenth and the twenty-third, mobs of between 200 and 700 whites hunted Filipinos in the streets, raiding the new dance hall and attacking ranches that employed Filipinos. When one gang of eight fired a machine gun into a bunkhouse occupied by Filipinos at the John Murphy ranch, it killed twenty-two-year-old Fermin Tobera.[127]

In the wake of the upheaval, leaders such as A. Antenor Cruz and A. E. Magsuci mobilized the Filipino community, condemning the violence and urging organized resistance to the white mobs; leading whites also began to crack down on the vigilantes. Local police apparently dispersed white mobs and incarcerated Filipinos to "protect" them during the violence but were reluctant to press for a full investigation into Tobera's death. Edsel Frey, the gang's leader, was the son of a local merchant who apparently informed the police that his son had not been involved, despite the finding of his son's shoe at the scene of the murder. The eight were convicted and given suspended sentences of two years, each serving one month in jail.[128]

The nativist attacks at Watsonville echoed quickly to Manila, the *Manila Times* reporting "[v]irtual racial warfare" in California as early as January 24. The dark news met a vigorous response from labor organizations, civic groups, and nationalist leaders. Labor unions, among which the attacks had "created quite a stir," had already met to forge a response by the twenty-fourth. According to the *Manila Times*, Governor-General Dwight Davis had responded by cabling the Bureau of Insular Affairs "urging protection for the Filipino laborers." But colonial authorities in the

United States had already been alerted by Filipino migrants themselves, who had immediately cabled the resident commissioners in Washington "asking for aid." The commissioners had, in turn, contacted the Bureau of Insular Affairs, which had called on the governor of California to "ascertain the full facts" and to "extend all protection necessary" to Filipinos. The governor had confidently responded that "the situation was well in hand."[129]

Immediately, competing groups on both sides of the Pacific vied to interpret the origins and meaning of the violence. U.S. colonial officials and the Manila commercial establishment claimed that its roots were economic, which enabled them to argue for the continued viability of colonial empire. Violence due to labor competition, they asserted, was periodic rather than structural and could be addressed by "protections" or immigration bars. The *Manila Times* editorialized that the attacks presented "no insult to the Filipino people, no attack upon the dignity of the Filipino nation." While race had undoubtedly been a factor, the principal cause was "economic," the perennial "resentment" caused by an influx of workers willing to labor for lower wages. The *Times* reported that Governor-General Davis also saw the violence as "a result of economic competition" rather than as a "racial agitation." Speaker of the House Manuel Roxas similarly dismissed racial interpretations, calling accusations that Filipino men had tempted white women into "vice dens" "incendiary and misleading."[130]

But many argued that the violence had, at base, been racial and that its occurrence pointed to deeper, more fundamental incompatibilities between Filipinos and Americans. One editorial in the *New York Times* suggested darkly that it had taken more than economic tension to spur white mobs to "burn the little brown brothers in their beds." For one, there was no white competition for the jobs Filipinos took: the existence of Filipino "housemen or elevator operators" could "hardly be said to have created an economic crisis." Rather, the attacks had been a symptom of what the author called "a third attack of 'neurosis orientalis,'" a periodic "rash" that caused a self-styled "superior white race" to assault "Asiatics" who "threaten our treasured Anglo-Saxon civilization." Evidence in support of this thesis came from California politicians. The *Manila Times* reported that Congressman Arthur M. Free, Republican of California, whose district included Watsonville, planned to testify in Washington that the "so-called rioters," "even though they acted without the law," had been "socially tried by the vicious practices" of Filipinos, who were "luring young white girls into degradation."[131]

For many, interpretations of the violence as racial suggested the necessity of Philippine independence. In some cases, independence was seen as the only way to halt the arrival of Filipino migrants, whose in-migration "caused" racial hatred and violence. According to the *Manila Times*, Senator Millard Tydings, Democrat of Maryland—cosponsor of the legislation that would inaugurate the commonwealth—had stated that the United States "already has race questions" and that "Filipino immigration would make the problem more difficult while the freedom of the islands is postponed."[132]

Filipino nationalists also took up arguments for abiding race tensions as the rationale for independence. Where Tydings and others saw Philippine independence as a necessary step to prevent racial turmoil in the United States, Filipino nationalists saw the violence as an indication that the United States' vaunted hopes for colonial "uplift" had run aground on shoals of natural history. Camilo Osias informed the press that "race incompatibility" was "one of the greatest reasons for the United States to grant us political freedom."[133] In a speech memorializing Tobera, Jorge Bocobo, dean of the Philippine Law School, hoped the ongoing "race war" in California might be "part of the inscrutable designs of Providence." That Philippine and American "economic interests clash" and that "our racial feelings are far from harmonious" were "grim, relentless realities." Filipinos and Americans should not be forced to continue what he called "an unnatural association," especially one that came with "such dire results." The Watsonville race war was biology's spasmodic rebellion against empire.[134]

Nationalizing Anti-Filipino Nativism

By the time of the Watsonville attacks, anti-Filipino nativism had begun to take hold on a national scale. As early as 1928, the American Federation of Labor had passed resolutions at its annual conventions condemning Filipino migration, stating that a "sufficient number" of Filipinos was "ready and willing to come to the United States" and that if allowed to continue, it would "create a race problem equal to that already here." The National Grange and other farm organizations demanded that action be taken against the "increasing immigration . . . of undesirable immigrants who can never be assimilated." The Advisory Board of the American Coalition of Patriotic Societies—which comprised over forty U.S. nationalist societies—adopted a resolution demanding immediate Filipino exclusion.[135] These groups were emboldened by President Hoover's temporary ban on Filipino migration in 1929, when an outbreak of meningitis was attributed to incoming Filipino laborers.[136]

Politicians responded to, and in turn inspired, the intensification of anti-Filipino sentiment. In 1928, Congressman Richard Welch, Republican of California, introduced an amendment to the 1924 Immigration Act in the form of a bill to "exclude certain citizens of the Philippine Islands from the United States." Welch's proposal was to expand the legal definition of the term "alien" in subdivision b of section 28 of the existing law: an alien would now be anyone who was not "a native-born or naturalized citizen," excepting Native Americans and "citizens of the islands (except the Philippine Islands) under the jurisdiction of the United States."[137] As had been true under Spanish law, the Philippines would again be the legal exception even among U.S. colonies. Where Asian polities from the beginning of the century had asserted, in diverse ways, the incompatibility of empire and exclusion, the Welch Bill was the latest effort to bind them together, excluding from one side of the Pacific those the United States was, ostensibly, attempting to assimilate on the other.

Hearings on the Welch Bill began just three months after the Watsonville race war. Held in the House Committee on Immigration and Naturalization in April and May 1930, they brought together a motley assortment of interested parties in a wide-ranging debate over the meanings of race, migration, and sovereignty. The proceedings recalled the strange bedfellows of the Philippine-American War, when agents of the Philippine Republic and U.S. anti-imperialists—some of them racial exclusionists—had both opposed colonial conquest and annexation. But the landscape of Philippine-American relations was dramatically different by the early 1930s: powerful agricultural lobbies had made Philippine independence a viable policy; U.S. nativists were far more organized, national, and successful than they had been in 1900; and Filipino nationalists were positioned to shape the debate far more effectively, with a leadership far more familiar with U.S. political institutions and idioms.

The nativists' main argument in favor of the Welch Bill was that Filipinos were "ineligible for citizenship" and therefore legally subject to exclusion. This term, which relied on the 1790 naturalization law's application only to "free white persons," had been the chosen euphemism with which all other Asians had been excluded by 1924.[138] V. S. McClatchy, secretary of the California Joint Immigration Committee, openly admitted the term's political functions, stating that in employing it, "[w]e endeavored to avoid the charge of discrimination by claiming we were urging passage of a law which would be applicable equally to all aliens, ineligible to citizenship, without exception."[139]

Nativists believed that Filipinos had unjustly been made such an exception but were, in fact, "ineligibles," for two different, if seldom distinguished, reasons. The first of these had been their legal disposition in the Treaty of Paris. According to California attorney general U. S. Webb, Filipinos (apart from those who chose otherwise) had "lost" their Spanish citizenship upon U.S. annexation of the islands. But they did not simultaneously "gain a citizenship in the United States, nor did they gain the right to become in any fashion citizens of the United States, except as that right might be extended to them."[140] While it was in Congress's power to determine the legal status of Filipinos, it had never—apart from Filipinos who had served in the U.S. Navy during World War I—granted Filipinos naturalization rights. They were, therefore, "ineligible for citizenship" and subject to the 1924 restrictions originally intended for the Japanese.[141]

The other way to establish Filipinos' legal excludability was by establishing their race as nonwhite. Legally transforming Filipinos into "aliens" meant racially recasting them as "Orientals." "All the white people of all the world are eligible for [U.S.] citizenship to-day," noted Webb, while "all the colored people of all the world except negroes are ineligible to citizenship here." Confronted with the claim by the Bureau of Insular Affairs that Filipinos could not be excluded from the U.S. mainland because they were, in terms of sovereignty and allegiance, "our own people," Webb answered sharply that Filipinos were, in racial terms, "not and never were our own people." Establishing this fact required nativists to fold recent Filipino migrations into earlier "Oriental" ones, making what might otherwise be seen as legally distinct migrations into a single, unbroken stream. McClatchy quoted former U.S. colonial educator David Barrows, a "good friend of the Filipinos," as saying that U.S. race "problems" were complicated enough without introducing "'a fourth element from the continent of Asia.'"[142] Like other "Asiatics," Filipinos were "unassimilable"; indeed, contrary to the colonial state's governing ideology, McClatchy referred to what he called the "extreme unassimilability of the Filipino people."[143]

It was Filipinos' biological "unassimilability" that most preoccupied nativist witnesses during the Welch Bill hearings. As in earlier anti-Chinese and anti-Japanese nativism, themes of rape, sexual depravity, and miscegenation—often understood as synonymous—were at the core of the restrictionist argument. "It was not intended that the Asiatic blood should mix with the Caucasian blood," stated Welch axiomatically, in a reversal of the Spanish colonial "blood compact" narrative. But even among Asiatics, Filipinos were imagined as an exceptional sexual threat. Statistics showed that Filipino immigrants were predominantly young, single men, who were represented as especially "aggressive" in sexual terms. In a frequently quoted passage from an article in the *Transactions of the Commonwealth Club of California* bulletin, Barrows referred to Filipino vices as "almost entirely based on sexual passion," a passion "inordinately strong" in Malays and one "rarely directed into the right channels or restrained by custom or by individual will." Chief among these wrong "channels" were Filipino men's reputed sexual preference for white women and the increasing visibility of Filipino-American social-sexual encounters in clubs and taxi dance halls. Quoting a California editorial that expressed thinly veiled support for recent anti-Filipino racial terrorism, McClatchy asked rhetorically, "What would our southern fellow Americans say if the southern negroes were to open halls with white entertainers saying they preferred white women to negresses? There would not be a riot in the South, there would be a massacre." Closing a demographic loophole, McClatchy noted that if single Filipino men raised the specter of miscegenation, married Filipino couples were also problematic: a married female Filipino migrant would obstruct assimilation, as "her influence and standards will naturally retard possible partial assimilation of their children."[144]

One rhetorically powerful way to represent Filipinos as part of a broader Asiatic migration was through metaphors of invasion. Welch, for example, called Filipino migrants "the Third Asiatic invasion of our Pacific coast." This usage was, in many ways, unsurprising. By 1930 such tropes, organized around notions of the Yellow Peril in its various incarnations, were at least five decades old and had significant legislative successes to their name. But the specifics of Philippine-American history, begun in large measure by a U.S. military invasion the other way, gave this discourse the eerie character of a return of the repressed. According to Webb, the Filipino question was "not a new one" for those who "of necessity" occupied "the front line trench in every racial conflict between the whites and the Asiatics." California nativists appearing before the House committee did so not as "agitators" but rather as people "driven here because the invasion started on our shore." McClatchy similarly noted that California was not a "beggar" in its protest but acted in the racial defense of the nation as a whole. California was, in fact, "really acting as a border State, where the wars of invaders must be fought and where the victory may be won with least loss of life and revenues."[145]

As these apologetics indicated, this discourse of "invasion" was in part about "invading" national politics with what might otherwise be perceived as provincial, regional concerns. West Coast nativists repeatedly emphasized the easterly—and nationalizing—direction of Filipino migration. "[A]n injury to the State of California at this time means destruction of the United States if it is continued," McClatchy observed. Picking up on the work of Lothrop Stoddard, J. S. Cassidy of the American Coalition of Patriotic Societies stated that the Rocky Mountains "would be no bar if these States should be allowed to be submerged in the rising tide of color from the Philippines." Welch warned that Filipinos were "colonizing here in the East," drawn to an absence of antimiscegenation laws. It was "our problem to-day, but it will be yours to-morrow." To make the point sharpest—particularly to Southern legislators with regional sensitivities to invading armies and Jim Crow racial anxieties—Welch represented the estimated Filipino population as marching south from Washington:

> Imagine an army of 46,000 troops, approximately 40 regiments, 46,000 young Filipinos from the ages of 17 to 25 in mass formation.
> If they were here and their leader started them across the Potomac into the State of Virginia, what would occur? Would the good people of Virginia accept them?[146]

Representations of the "invasion" cast it as an unwinnable war whose inevitable victims were whites. For examples of it, Webb urged the House committee to look no farther than San Francisco. Unlike Americans, Filipinos, it seemed, had "colonies." In that now-occupied city, there were "blocks and blocks of dwellings that 20 years ago were the homes of the whites that are now occupied by the Japanese exclusively, and we have other sections more recently given over to the Filipinos, and as they come in the whites move out." The most apocalyptic scenario, however, was Hawaii. With two-thirds of its population "Asiatic," McClatchy called Hawaii "a terrible example of the penetration of colored races," a territory "hopelessly lost to the white race." Without Filipino restriction, however, the Hawaiian present would be the American future, "bring[ing] to California the condition which you now have in Hawaii."[147]

For Webb, whites confronted with what he called "the invasion of the colored people" had the choice either to fight or to retreat. Whether in Pacific islands, San Francisco neighborhoods, or the North American continent as a whole, Webb was witnessing the "only instance in history where the whites have retreated without firing a shot"; apparently, the shots fired at Watsonville did not count. In a turn of phrase that hauntingly recalled an earlier war's refugees, Webb described retreating whites as the beaten survivors of race war, going forth "as sad as any defeated army." Instinctually withdrawing to preserve their purity, white refugees "realized they are leaving their homes and possessions" but were "driven out by an unendurable contact that is more dangerous and more deadly than the weapon of the battle field."[148]

Against Colonial Exclusion

If nativists saw Filipino exclusion as the only way to stop the Philippine invasion of the United States, U.S. colonial officials—those, in a sense, committed to the ongoing U.S. invasion of the Philippines—asserted Filipinos' claims as "nationals," their loyalty during the war, and the potential political turmoil that might result in the colony itself from the passage of exclusionary legislation. Brig. Gen. F. L. Parker, director of the Bureau of Insular Affairs, who had been in the Philippines for five years (two of them as an aide to Forbes), attempted to shift the debate, arguing that this was "a question, not of aliens, but of people who owe allegiance to our government, who are entitled to the protection of that government." Filipinos were, technically, "our own nationals." When asked whether that usage was "intentional," Parker stated that Filipinos "owe their allegiance to our National Government, and they are wards of the United States." "We are the only Government they can look to," he said. "They have no other."[149]

Parker saw himself acting in the hypothetical role of a Philippine consular official. Where other potentially excluded immigrants "have diplomatic representatives here to present their cause," the Filipinos "have no such representative to present their grievances." Filipinos' status as U.S. nationals was bolstered by their "whole-hearted loyalty and patriotism to the United States in the great war," as evidenced by the offer of approximately 25,000 men "as volunteers for the defense of our institutions." Parker qualified abstract claims of U.S. responsibility and Filipino entitlement with the relative insignificance of Filipino migration; Filipinos constituted what he called "a minor case, under our general immigration policy." Even 10,000 migrants a year, he stated, was not "a big drop in the bucket."[150]

Parker largely, if not completely, steered clear of counterargument on questions of race. "[W]ithout pretending to know the ethnological features of it," however, he attempted to indigenize Filipinos to North America, noting a "probable racial connection between certain races of this continent and Asiatics," such that there was "no sound reason . . . for a distinction between the inhabitants of the Philippine Islands and the inhabitants of Mexico from that point of view." (Parker abruptly abandoned this line of defense when he was informed of an upcoming bill to restrict Mexican immigration.) Parker did try to undermine charges of Filipino sexual immorality, stating that "there is some misunderstanding of the character of the Filipino." If Filipino laborers were licentious, they were not alone in it. After all, "[w]hen we sent our American soldiers into the Philippines," did Americans not "sen[d] a sex problem with them"? Nor were Filipinos necessarily agents of immorality. It was not clear, for example, that the "particular women" Filipinos associated with "would have been of a high type even if the Filipinos had not come."[151]

Parker was especially concerned about the impact of exclusion on the colonial state's stability, urging "that we consider the sensibilities of these Asiatic people." What he called "radical legislation" would likely cause "resentment," especially given that "the acuteness of this situation has been brought to the attention of the people of the islands through the prominence given to it recently." Parker suggested subterfuge and other, more subtle policy instruments as an alternative to exclusion. When it came to "excluding the Filipino as an undesirable Asiatic," Parker believed "the less it is discussed in this country . . . the more probability there is of the working out of a relatively unofficial arrangement which will get the results you want," especially through the imposition on would-be migrants of head taxes, literacy tests, and bars against radicals.[152]

Two Filipino nationalists at the hearings, Speaker of the House Manuel Roxas and Camilo Osias, educator, resident commissioner, and former *pensionado*, took issue with what they believed to be legal inconsistencies in the Welch Bill and demanded Filipinos' recognition as U.S. colonial subjects bearing certain rights. "[T]he amendment places on the term 'alien' a wholly arbitrary meaning," stated Roxas. "The citizens of the Philippine Islands are not aliens in the legal and accepted meaning of that word," because "they owe allegiance to the United States." They were "subjects of this country, and not citizens of a foreign State." Why were Europeans being given immigration quotas, but not "the people whom you call your wards under the American flag?" he asked. If immigration constituted a "labor problem," Roxas believed it a matter of "justice and fairness" that "curtailment should start with countries and peoples not under the American flag." He suggested that geopolitics wrongly contributed to U.S. immigration policy, noting that if restriction could not be inflicted on "these other peoples because they are strong," that "should not induce you to do it against us because we are weak."[153]

Roxas turned to comparisons to make the case that, to the contrary, empires often gave special migration rights to their colonial subjects. Restrictions such as those proposed in the Welch Bill had, for Roxas, "no precedent in the annals of colonization since the birth of time." "No country," he claimed, "however imperialistic, however commercialistic its policy in its dealings with its colonies, has ever prohibited the citizens of its colonies from migrating to the mother country." Indians were not prohibited from traveling to metropolitan Britain, he noted; even Spain— "selfish, imperialistic power!"—had done better by Filipinos in the late nineteenth century by allowing them to travel and live in the metropole. "America that went to the Philippines to give us a more humane and just government than we had under Spain," he said, "certainly can not refuse to grant us rights and privileges which Spain accorded us."[154]

Roxas took especially strident exception to the racial logic of the bill, having listened "with a great deal of attention" to the "serious, careful, studiously phrased indictment made against the Filipino people as a whole, as a race, during these hearings." While "not phrased in offensive language," he said, "no Filipino can hear what has been said of them here without deep resentment." Filipinos had been attacked as "unassimilable," where they were "in many respects assimilable and would make . . . desirable citizen[s] of the United States." Nativists had claimed, drawing on decades-old colonial discourses, that Filipinos were "divided and fighting among themselves," especially between "[t]hree tribes" of Tagalogs, Visayans, and Ilocanos; unable to "mix together" in the Philippines, migrating Filipinos would therefore "create disturbances" inside the United States. Using the example of the regionally diverse Philippine delegation itself, Roxas noted that there was more unity in the Philippines than "between the North, South, East, and West of the American Union."[155]

When McClatchy employed the logic of divide and rule, suspecting that Philippine independence would lead to "trouble" between Christians and "the hill groups of the so-called uncivilized and un-Christian Moros," Roxas countered that "such a possibility is very remote." Indeed, Roxas "resent[ed] . . . very sincerely" the very mention of "headhunters." He recalled that a few headhunters had once been "brought in by imperialists, men determined to maintain permanently American sovereignty over the Philippines for their selfish ends," who had "exhibited them all over the United States as typical Filipinos." These headhunters had worn "an apparel which is not the ordinary and common apparel used in the Philippines," although they had been presented as "expositions of our civilization; and we resented it." Due to Philippine Assembly legislation since that time, "[n]o head hunters come from the Philippine Islands to the United States." In the Philippines itself, head-hunting was now a criminal act and punished as such. "If 'head hunters' means criminals, we have them there," he admitted, but lest Americans judge too harshly, recent records showed that "criminality in many localities here exceeds that of any other country in the world." Roxas observed that Filipinos were "just as human being [sic] as are Americans" and urged the committee chairman not to consider "the people of the Philippines as different from those belonging to any other race upon this earth."[156]

While they struggled to defend Filipino "unity" and "civilization," Filipino nationalists were compelled to deflect the "social" question—that of miscegenation. Roxas approached the question with "unconcealed diffidence." The social question involved "a consideration of races, race biology, characteristics, virtues, propensities, weaknesses, pride, antipathies," he said. "It is a most delicate subject. It burns the hand that touches it." He first minimized miscegenation in the present and future. Barrows's claim of Filipino sexual excess was, for Roxas, "contagiously humorous," but "as a scientific formula," it was "sublimely ridiculous." "Aside from the existence of a public opinion here against Filipino marital incursions into the nordic circle," he noted wryly, there was little desire among Filipino men for sex or marriage with white women. The Filipino man saw himself as a temporary sojourner eager to return and build a household in the Philippines with a woman "who can understand him and in whom he can find complete identity in custom, manner, desire, education, habits, religion, etc." Against the hopes of many of those who had seen visions of global commingling at the Panama-Pacific Exposition, the time was "far distant" when "humankind shall have become one great family"; in the present, humanity was "composed of various great families denominated races whose tendency is to isolate themselves from one another."[157]

Filipino nationalists also tried to displace accusations of miscegenation away from the Filipino people as a whole and onto a specific, and lower-class, segment of Filipino laborers in the United States. "We are not proud of all the Filipinos who come here," stated Roxas, "just as you can not be proud of all your own people." Referring to an incident in which a Filipino man had been arrested with two young, white women in his bed, Roxas claimed that no indictment should be "indiscriminately hurled against a whole race on the basis of a single, solitary incident." Indeed, if such an indictment were reversed, "unhappy would be this land of yours." Roxas was specifically referring to the fact that while there were far fewer Americans in the Philippines than Filipinos in the United States, they had managed to leave behind "a wake of shame and sorrow, written large upon the lives of 20,000 children abandoned by their fathers."[158]

In their attempt to legitimate Filipino migration and to distinguish it from earlier Asiatic ones, opponents of the Welch Bill recast it not as part of a continuous "invasion" but as the unique, natural, and expected by-product of U.S. colonial tutelage. The policy of attraction—of conciliating Filipino elites in the Philippines—had become, quite literally, a policy of attraction to the United States. For Parker, exclusion constituted a "very sudden reversal" of thirty years of U.S. colonial policy, in which "the Filipinos have been encouraged, rather than discouraged, to come to this country . . . to take advantage of the exceptional opportunities offered by our educational institutions." "Back in the Philippines the Filipinos are told of the greatness of America," stated Roxas. From the beginning of U.S. rule, he observed, "it has been the aim of the American Government, using a common expression, to sell America to the Filipinos." English-language public schools, "where the text-books used picture America as a land of promise aglow with brilliance," had been the main sales agencies. In them, Filipinos learned about "Washington, about Bunker Hill, York-town, and Gettysburg," as well as "the great industrial activities taking place in this country."[159]

They also, importantly, learned "about Chicago, and about Memphis, Tenn., and of what occurred in Salinas Valley," said Roxas, places where "men have taken the law into their own hands." Despite these lapses, "[a]dmiration for American achievements, civilization, and government [has] been studiously aroused in the hearts of the Filipino people." Filipinos had learned the transpacific lessons of Horatio Alger: that the United States was "a country of untrammeled opportunity where many a struggling youth with nothing but a stout heart and a lofty purpose has scaled the heights of wealth and power." Given these factors, was it any wonder, then, that "there should have been created among the young men and young women of the Philippines, not to speak of the older people, a real ambition to come to the United States?"[160]

Roxas addressed the question of the Philippine "invasion" of the United States by making clear exactly whose invasion was at issue. "History," Roxas said, "speaks truths which sometimes are unpleasant." Revisiting the question of U.S. sovereignty would "carry us back 32 years to recall events of bloodshed, of blighted hopes, and disappointments." Roxas then did so, recounting the backdrop of the Philippine-American War, when Filipinos had had "American sovereignty imposed upon us." Set against a superior force, Filipinos had fought a "determined struggle for freedom" in an "expression of deep and sincere national aspiration." The costs had been high: "Towns were burned; whole villages completely wiped out."[161]

But with sovereignty imposed, the United States had been bound to the Philippines by ties of reciprocity that Americans had often failed to respect. The Filipino people "occupy a peculiar relationship with the United States," said Roxas, one that "creates certain duties and responsibilities, as well as privileges and rights, both on the part of the United States and of the Philippine Islands." While respect for these responsibilities had allowed "harmonious relations" over three decades, the current bill ruptured them, since it empowered one side to cut off migrations but not the other. If American nativists remade Filipino migrations into invasions, Filipino nationalists in turn made U.S. colonialism into a kind of mass migration by "undesirables," which Filipinos should also have the power to curtail. "It is unjust to exclude Filipinos from the United States while Americans assume the right to enter the Philippines without restriction," Roxas stated. ". . . Do not exclude Filipinos from the United States before you have placed us in a position to exclude Americans from the Philippine Islands."[162]

Nativist Self-Determination

The Welch Bill failed: Filipinos would not yet be made aliens within the U.S. empire. Its failure was almost simultaneous with the protectionists' failure to impose tariffs on Philippine exports in the Smoot-Hawley Act. In response, both protectionists and nativists joined, and quickly became powerful stakeholders in, the movement for Philippine independence: "self-determination" would be exclusion by other means.

By early 1932, the political openings for Philippine independence had widened, as pressure on Republicans in farm states undercut a long-standing Republican resistance. In January, Senator Harry Hawes, Democrat of Missouri, and Senator Bronson Cutting, Republican of New Mexico, introduced independence legislation, as did Congressman Butler B. Hare, Democrat of South Carolina, in the House. Both the Hawes-Cutting and Hare Bills authorized the Philippine legislature to call for an immediate constitutional convention, followed by a gradual transition to independence under a U.S.-supervised "commonwealth" government, which would culminate in a Philippine plebiscite on the question of independence, although the bills differed in their proposed timetables. After extended struggles over the length of transition and the phasing in of tariffs, the joint Hare-Hawes-Cutting Act passed the Senate and House in December 1932, providing for a ten-year transition period, limits on the import of Philippine coconut oil, sugar, and cordage, and no plebiscite. Hoover vetoed the bill in January, but the veto was overturned; in the Philippines, however, the bill was jeopardized by rivalries within the Nacionalista Party. The bill was credited to the Osmeña-Roxas mission, and Quezon feared its passage would threaten his chances of winning election as the first president of the commonwealth; he maneuvered to have the bill rejected by the Philippine legislature and negotiated instead for a virtually identical substitute bill, authored by Senator Millard Tydings, Democrat of Maryland, and Congressman John McDuffie, Democrat of Alabama. With Democratic majorities behind it, the bill passed both houses of Congress in March 1934 and was signed into law on March 24 by President Franklin Roosevelt.[163] "Our nation covets no territory," Roosevelt stated, "nor sovereignty over a people gained through war against their will." For nearly two decades, he stated, the U.S. government had promised the Philippines "ultimate independence" pending "a suitable government capable of maintaining that independence among the nations of the world." For Roosevelt, the Filipinos had, at last, proven their capacity.[164] On May 1, the Philippine legislature accepted the act, thirty-six years after the Battle of Manila Bay.

The Tydings-McDuffie Act's provisions suggested not an early act of decolonization, however, but yet another moment in the unfolding of calibrated colonialism. Its stated goal was to provide what it called "the complete independence of the Philippine Islands," but the act contained numerous "mandatory provisions" that suggested something less. Unlike the U.S. colonial government that had preceded it, the Philippine Commonwealth must have a constitution that was "republican in form" and would contain a "bill of rights." Pending "the final and complete withdrawal" of U.S. sovereignty, all Philippine citizens would "owe allegiance to the United States," and all officers would take an oath recognizing the United States' "supreme authority." All officials presently serving would continue to exercise their authority "as if elected directly under such a government." The U.S. president exercised veto power over the islands' legislation "affecting currency, coinage, imports, exports, and immigration." As U.S. producers had hoped, Philippine exports were placed under a far more restrictive tariff. The U.S. Supreme Court would review all decisions by the commonwealth's courts. The Philippines' foreign affairs would be under the United States' "direct supervision and control," and the president reserved the right to seize Philippine property, to maintain military facilities in the Philippines, and to deploy the Philippines' armed forces. The Philippine government would take responsibility for paying any debts incurred by the prior regime, and "such obligations shall be a first lien on the taxes collected in the Philippine Islands." Ultimately, the U.S. president would have veto power over the Philippine Constitution itself. On July 4, ten years after the inauguration of the new constitution, the president would, by proclamation, "withdraw and surrender all right of possession, supervision, jurisdiction, control and sovereignty then existing and exercised by the United States in and over the territory and people of the Philippines." This included "all military and other reservations" of the present government, with the exception of certain "naval reservations and fueling stations"; pending negotiations, these would remain in their "present status."[165]

The independence campaigns of the early 1930s provided recently joined exclusionists the opportunity to articulate their hopes for what might be called "nativist self-determination." Some nativist spokesmen at congressional hearings tried to obscure the exclusionary motivations beneath their advocacy of Philippine independence. Confronted with the suggestion that organized labor's lobbying for independence was simply a means toward exclusion, AFL legislative representative William Hushing insisted that "when we first stood for their independence, it was not on that ground." Congressman Joe Crail, Republican of California, was not for independence "merely for the purpose of excluding" Filipinos but believed that exclusion was "vitally important to our welfare in the United States." Others were less bashful. Congressman Ralph Horr, Republican of Washington, concerned about high-school children "debauched" by

Filipinos, preferred, as in the Welch Bill, to give Filipinos neither sovereignty nor migration rights; this was fair because the United States had already "repaid them" with "protection" and "in our teaching, in the establishment of industry there, etc." He conceded, though, that independence was "preferable to the condition that is prevailing now."[166]

Nativist self-determination reached its height in Congressman Welch's statement before the House. "For the sake of our social and economic welfare we should release the Philippines and give them complete independence," he stated outright. Congress had wisely denied Filipinos U.S. citizenship because they were not meant "to merge with our population" and "remain under the same government permanently." While Welch claimed that he had "no racial prejudices," he stated that God himself had given "the nonassimilable Asiatics a place in the sun," and "that place is the Orient." Turmoil naturally erupted where East trespassed upon West. White Californians confronting labor competition with Filipinos, for example, had resorted to "unlawful violence and bloodshed," which, while "deeply deplore[d]," was also "inevitable"; only Filipino exclusion provided the "real solution of this problem." Afraid of a protracted transition, Welch suggested that any independence bill should come with strict exclusion provisions "to take effect 30 days after its enactment."[167]

Debate had raged on the proper number of Filipino migrants that should be allowed into the United States under the commonwealth. Filipino nationalists had asserted that if the United States were to exclude Filipinos, it must also provide them independence, which included the reciprocal right to exclude Americans. But on questions of immigration, the Tydings-McDuffie Act followed the earlier Welch Bill, which made Filipinos aliens while preserving U.S. sovereignty over them. Hard-core nativists had argued that the United States had no special responsibility to treat Filipinos as other than Asiatics and should exclude them completely, as it did Chinese, Japanese, and South Asian migrants. Filipino nationalists countered that if the United States hoped to recognize Philippine sovereignty, it must grant the Philippines at least one hundred immigrants annually, consistent with the 1924 quota system.

Sections 8 and 14 of the act dealt with immigration by declaring that Filipinos, while not yet citizens of an independent polity, were now aliens within the U.S. empire. While it had been defeated as legislation, the Welch Bill's logic—of separating Filipinos from their rights as U.S. nationals prior to separating the Philippines from U.S. colonialism—had triumphed in the Tydings-McDuffie Act. For purposes of immigration, it declared that "the Philippine Islands shall be considered to be a foreign country," and citizens of the Philippines who were not also citizens of the United States "shall be considered as if they are aliens." The Philippines' quota would be halfway between a sovereign, quota country and an Asiatic, excluded one, with only fifty immigrants permitted annually. According to Section 14, upon independence, U.S. immigration laws would apply to the Philippines, "including all the provisions relating to persons ineligible to citizenship."[168] Where the Welch Bill had failed, the Tydings-McDuffie Act had realized nativist self-determination and exclusionary independence.

Where Filipino migrants blurred the boundaries between East and West, between metropole and colony, state governments would undertake to repatriate them after 1933. "Repatriation" referred specifically to the sponsorship of transpacific travel back to the Philippines for indigent Filipinos who, it was believed, were less expensive to ship home than to support on the welfare rolls. Ironically, for purposes of exclusion only, the term implicitly recognized that Filipinos had a "patria" to return to, well in advance of political independence. While the first such bill was introduced in 1933, it was Congressman Welch's bill that was ultimately signed into law in July 1935. It provided that any Filipino in the United States who wished to return to the islands by the end of 1936 (then 1938, after extensions), could apply to the secretary of labor and, if approved, receive free passage to a West Coast port and from there to Manila; the Bureau of Labor would arrange transportation contracts. Participants could not return to the United States except as quota immigrants. Welch made it clear, however, that repatriation was not deportation but "a voluntary act" undertaken by Filipinos wishing to take advantage of the U.S. government's "generous offer."[169]

Filipino responses to repatriation varied. One man in New York believed that returnees should be grateful to the U.S. government and would be "of great help to the Philippine Commonwealth in the development of her social, economic and political status." Others were more skeptical. One writer feared that returnees would be "[s]horn of wealth they have earned and acquired; equipped with experiences they could not utilize in their own country; possessed of education but no place to fit in." Some migrants were reluctant to return to the Philippines impoverished or to take advantage of government "charity"; others feared even more limited prospects in the Philippines. Approximately 2,000 Filipinos repatriated through the federally sponsored program. Many complained of the horrible conditions of transport, including shipboard confinement during stops at ports. One group petitioned against the "shabby, shameful and almost inhuman treatment" they had received.[170] The Philippine business press suggested that repatriates might best serve the nation by applying the agricultural skills and resources they had gained in the U.S. West to the Philippines' own "frontier" in Mindanao: rejected in the United States as "invaders," they could participate in "civilizing" missions closer to home.

OUR STORY ENDS, prematurely, with one such repatriate. After his murder during the Watsonville attacks, Fermin Tobera's long odyssey back to Manila in late January 1930 traced a path across a U.S. imperium and a Filipino diaspora that had not existed when Rizal had first expressed frustration at the needless and politically motivated quarantine of "Asiatics" at San Francisco. His first stop was Honolulu; after debating the possibility of a mass protest, Filipino organizations there had instead held church memorial services, and delegates "went to the ship and laid wreaths on the dead boy's coffin." On February 2, however, mass rallies were held on both sides of the Pacific. In Los Angeles, Pablo Manlapit organized a march of 1,000 sympathizers protesting Tobera's murder. In Manila, a simultaneous "necrological service" was conducted on the Luneta in Manila, as part of the rites of a "National Humiliation Day," with coordinated events planned in the provincial capitals of Bulacan, Nueva Ecija, Pampanga, Rizal, Laguna, Cavite, and Batangas. The *Manila Times*, unsympathetic to the protest, nonetheless anticipated that it would be "one of the biggest gatherings ever assembled on the Luneta."[171]

The Manila ceremony vividly illustrated the mutual constitution of U.S. colonialism and Filipino nationalism across transpacific space. Carried out concurrently with ceremonies in California and in the provinces of the Philippines, its organizers asked attendees to unite around a "national" tragedy that had occurred half a world away; it also marked the California pogroms as examples of colonial violence, another battle in a race war not yet ended. Speakers now accepted that war as natural and inevitable and thus toppled the edifice of inclusionary racism upon which U.S. colonial rule had been predicated: Watsonville showed that there could only be peace through separation. "The cherished theories of the American government," Jorge Bocobo stated at the ceremony, had been "swept away by the mighty current of the human condition." To-

This photograph from the January 31, 1930, *Manila Times* shows Filipino students at the University of the Philippines protesting the racist-nativist pogrom against Filipino migrant laborers in Watsonville, California, that had begun twelve days earlier. Signs read: "We Protest against the Watsonville Outrage!" "We Want Fairness," and "Can't the Flag to Which We Have Sworn Allegiance Give Us Protection?" Philippine protest politics against nativist violence in the United States shows the ways that U.S. colonialism had helped give rise to a transpacific Filipino consciousness.

gether, racial repulsion and economic tension mandated that Philippine-American ties "be severed at once." How could Filipinos accept their current status under the U.S. flag, "[d]espised as an inferior race and deprived of equal opportunities"? If Tobera's death symbolized the false promises of the United States, it also announced the perpetual rebirth of the Filipino nation in tragedy. Representative Confesor stated that despite the organizers' desire to "lay bare the bleeding heart of the Filipino people" before "the eyes of the world" and the "Supreme Ruler of all humanity," it was "not amiss" to declare the day a "glorious" one for Filipinos. Remembering the attacks at Watsonville, he said, "you and I, our children and children's children," would reaffirm "our faith and confidence in ourselves to live a successful independent national life."[172]

Attendees at San Francisco's Panama-Pacific Exposition in 1915 had hoped that global integration would produce harmony and commingling, realizing promises of the "neighborliness of the world." During the first third of the twentieth century, those forces had indeed operated to profoundly embed the worlds of the United States and the Philippines into each other. The United States had been altered by its occupation of the islands—in the projection of power into Asia and the Pacific that the colony had facilitated, in the national-exceptionalist languages of benevolence and assimilation Americans had cast over their project and into U.S. foreign policy more broadly, and in their imperial-indigenist representations of Filipinos and articulation of criteria of recognition Filipinos would have to achieve in order to earn "self-government." The Philippines had also been remade under U.S. colonialism, more deeply integrated into global politics and commerce than ever before, with Filipinos seeking recognition of their "capacities" for self-government before American and world audiences. Included among these efforts at recognition were nationalist-colonialist premises of Filipinos' distinction from, superiority to, and rights to govern the islands' "non-Christians."

But the "weaving" together of the nations on "the looms of the earth" had not produced the "blending" of "all peoples and races." Rather, global integration could heighten racial fears, as older hierarchies of space and difference were undermined, as colony and metropole became indistinguishable, and East and West dissolved into each other. When forces of transpacific empire, commerce, and migration had entangled the U.S. and Philippine worlds, they had set formal colonialist, inclusionary racial dreams of assimilation against visions of anti-imperialist racial exclusion in a political struggle in which the latter had triumphed. It was not an exceptional ambivalence about colonialism but economic protectionism and racist nativism that had "liberated" the Philippines and the United States from their shared formal colonial history. After nearly fifty years, the United States had achieved "independence" from its colony; formal Philippine independence would be born as an act of American racial insularity.

We conclude with two travelers to the United States, their voices separated by nearly sixty years. Writing in 1889, José Rizal had found himself frustrated, parked for days on a ship just offshore from San Francisco, awaiting quarantine inspectors to examine Chinese immigrants suspected of disease. Rizal was certain that the Chinese passengers, completely free from illness, had been targeted for racial political reasons: to appease the racist anger of California's nativist electorate. Over the course of his train ride across the country, Rizal had witnessed the caricatured "Indians" that fronted cigar stores; he had carefully observed that the country had no "civil freedom," as African American men were denied the right to marry white women. But interestingly, Rizal jotted no notes about his own racial position vis-à-vis the Americans. Even given the brevity of his travelogue, one might have suspected Rizal—a sharp critic of Spanish racial politics toward the Philippine peoples, and one who astutely perceived the United States' racism toward other groups—to have made note of any racial insults or mistreatment he had received. The contrast is striking: where the Chinese were blocked, Rizal passed into the country, even exercising a kind of colonial prerogative on the way, noting that the Great Plains could use irrigation in order to "improve" it. The racial term Rizal would take away from the United States would not be one imposed on him by others but one he took for himself. In choosing, for the name of his Filipino solidarity organization, "Los Indios Bravos"—which literally meant "the brave natives"—Rizal was associating himself with the United States' colonized peoples rather than identifying himself as a Philippine-born "overseas Spaniard," who was owed political rights by virtue of language, culture, and civilization.

The second traveler was merely described as "a Filipino" by a sociology interviewer at Fisk University in 1946. His encounter with the United States, almost six decades after Rizal's, could not have been more different. The title given him by the interviewer, which he was also quoted as using himself, was itself telling: Rizal had traveled to the United States as an *indio* and an *ilustrado* but would not yet have used the term "Filipino" to describe himself. The name "Filipino," then, was itself a significant marker of the historical space between them: Rizal was not yet a Filipino in 1889; by 1946, this had emerged as the term for the Philippine-born population and for its national identity, molded by colonial institutions. The interviewee Filipino had known a great deal about the United States before his arrival, having encountered many Americans in the colonial Philippines; among other influences, he had been converted to evangelical Protestantism. Unlike Rizal, for whom the United States seems to have been a large obstacle on the path to European learning, Filipino had seen America as the proper destination for those seeking modernity and progress. He believed this because the United States had already come to the Philippines in the form of the colonial administration, which embodied benevolence and uplift for him. Those Filipinos who had encountered Americans in the Philippines, he reported, felt at home in the United States within a week. But if Filipinos were familiar with Americans, Americans were also "familiar" with Filipinos. Filipino had met Americans who had seen photographs of "mountain tribes" and had himself seen books, museum displays, and commercial exhibits that emphasized what he called the "dark side" of Filipino life. Where Rizal had identified with America's *indios*, Filipino drew stark lines between himself and the Philippines' non-Christian peoples. That his plea for Filipino recognition—as distinct from this "dark side"—came in 1946, the same year the United States granted the Philippines formal independence, suggests the ways in which colonial frameworks would be extended into a formally "postcolonial" era.

Colonialism had made a difference. The two travelers' experiences would not have been so different had the United States encountered the Philippines by simply projecting or exporting its racial formations to the islands. Had Americans merely treated the Filipinos as they had the Chinese or the Japanese, Filipino would not have been in the United States in the first place. Had they treated Filipinos like African Americans or Native Americans, he would likely not have been so shocked to encounter racial hostility upon his arrival in the United States. By contrast, Filipino's experience revealed many of the traces of a distinct, colonial racial formation that owed its outlines to both transnational forces and local contingencies. It had been molded in the crucible of revolution and war: the term "Filipino" had been imagined from "within" for purposes of seeking reform and independence from Spain and from "without" by both Spanish and U.S. invaders who cast the islands' population as a united enemy. But it had also been shaped by the complex structures of collaboration: an elastic politics of recognition, with a distinct evolutionary and tutelary framework, had accommodated elite Filipino demands for political participation while forestalling broader and deeper questions of independence. The colonial state's bifurcation of the Philippine population at Catholicism—putting Christians and non-Christians on parallel tracks of development—had racialized religion and, through the inauguration of special provinces, territorialized race. This racial-administrative grid had given U.S. imperialists effective arguments for the ongoing necessity of U.S. rule. Imperial-indigenist arguments displaced discourses of savagery onto non-Christians, representing them as both vulnerable populations in need of "protection" from exploitative Christians and, simultaneously, as a violent threat to Christians that could only be contained by U.S. power. It was not, as during the Philippine-American War, that Filipinos could not govern themselves because they were savages but that they could not rule morally, safely, and effectively over "their" savages. Arguments of this kind encouraged nationalist-colonialist counterarguments that Catholic Filipinos could, indeed, control and uplift the non-Christians. The symmetry between imperial indigenism and nationalist colonialism suggests the ways in which the new racial formation was the product of intense contestation and dialogue, a joint American-Filipino venture situated inside a broader, evolving colonial project.

Some critics of empire at the turn of the century had been frightened by the prospect that the U.S. annexation of new colonies in the Caribbean and the Pacific would lead to America's own racial "corruption." An empire, they suggested, was a society of distended racial frontiers in which the appropriate lines between races could no longer be maintained (as they liked to imagine they were maintained in the continental United States). The racial-political angst of these anti-imperialists reflected a profound truth: that the very racial formations upon which American politics was grounded at that moment were themselves plastic. The epistemological foundations of race were "sliding scales" that shifted with historical and political circumstance: for these anti-imperialists, the advent of empire, just as it would sunder the republic, would collapse the racial foundations upon which it was built. Imperialists would try to assuage these anxieties with aggressive narratives of assimilation: that colonialism would be a one-way road along which American ideas and institutions would be projected without being transformed. Philippine-American history proved them wrong. In both the Philippines and the United States, colonial rule had involved adapting racial idioms to suit local realities in ways that suggested the Americans themselves were being "assimilated" to their own empire. For imperialists on the ground, the flexibility of race, sometimes seen as an obstacle, was also embraced as an opportunity: when held against other racial formations, narratives of assimilation might even be made to approximate an empire without race. But their simultaneous sense that U.S. empire simply meant the "export" of America would not be sustained. By 1946, there was—for better or worse—a racial place in the United States for a traveler like Filipino that Rizal had not occupied in 1889. Like other empires, the United States had gone out into the world in the twentieth century, only to find itself remade by it. Long after the end of formal U.S. imperial sovereignty, struggles over the terms of Philippine-American colonialism, embedded in Philippine and U.S. national and racial formations, would continue to haunt the way each society approached its global history.

Notes

Abbreviations

DWP   Dean C. Worcester Papers, Bentley Historical Library, University of Michigan, Ann Arbor

ERSI   Exposition Records of the Smithsonian Institution and U.S. National Museum, Record Unit 70, Smithsonian Institution Archives, Washington, D.C.

SAWS   Spanish-American War Series, U.S. Military History Institute, Carlisle, Pennsylvania

Introduction

1. Beveridge, "The March of the Flag," in *Meaning of the Times*, "distance," 51, "separate," 52, "inaccessible," 51, "world duties," 57, "imperial," 47, "broaden" 48, "consent," 49, "humane,"49.

2. Speech by Albert Beveridge before the U.S. Senate, Jan. 9, 1900, 56th Cong., 1st sess., *Congressional Record* 33, pt. 1 (1899–1900), "mangled," "assaults," 708, "deeper," "elemental," "English-speaking," 711; Beveridge, "March of the Flag," "blood of government," 50; Speech by Beveridge, "remember," "hundreds," "alchemy," 708.

3. For a rich account of the advent of "global history" in this period, see Geyer and Bright, "World History in a Global Age." The present work hopes to contribute to the "internationalization" of U.S. history, suggesting that, alongside many other processes—migration, social movements, cultural and institutional transfer—formal and informal empire should play a central role in such a history. For debates surrounding this development, see, especially, Bender, *Rethinking American History*; Tyrrell, "American Exceptionalism"; McGerr, "Price of the 'New Transnational History'"; and Tyrrell, "Ian Tyrrell Responds."

4. On the tense, mutual constitution of metropolitan and colonial societies, see Cooper and Stoler, "Between Metropole and Colony." For a useful critique of modes of narrating the interconnection of metropole and colony, see Coronil, "Beyond Occidentalism."

5. The fundamental elements of a pre-1898 Philippine-American history consist of the presence of Philippine migrants in Louisiana, as well as U.S. commercial companies in the Philippines. On the latter, see Legarda, *After the Galleons*; and Hackler, "United States Presence," pts. 1 and 2.

6. The present study draws inspiration from a number of works that have approached the transnational processes through which national identities have taken shape in the modern world. Exemplary of this literature in the Asian-American context is Iriye, *Across the Pacific*; and Bradley, *Imagining Vietnam and America*. On Cuban-American exchanges and identity formations, see Pérez, *On Becoming Cuban*.

7. For an overview of the congressional politics of race in Philippine-American colonialism, see Weston, "American Imperialism in the Philippine Islands." On visual imagery and racialized representations of the Philippines, see Vergara, *Displaying Filipinos*.

8. Evidence suggests that national-exceptionalist imaginations of U.S. colonial rule in the Philippines, for example, provided a template for subsequent U.S. foreign policy formations, especially with respect to the failings of European colonialism and proper approaches to "decolonization." See, for example, Franklin Delano Roosevelt's use of the analogy in Bradley, *Imagining Vietnam and America*, 77–79; and Gardner, "How We 'Lost' Vietnam," 124.

9. McCoy and De Jesus, *Philippine Social History*.

10. Schumacher, *Propaganda Movement*.

11. José Rizal y Alonso, "Las Filipinas Dentro de Cien Años," pt. 1, *La Solidaridad* 1, no. 16 (Sept. 30, 1889), 377 (all quotations from *La Solidaridad* are translations from the original Spanish by the author.)

12. Ibid., pt. 2, *La Solidaridad* 1, no. 18 (Oct. 31, 1889), "inhabitants," "forces," "abroad," "sailors," 436, "affront," 432.

13. José Rizal to A. B. Meyer, Dec. 1, 1889, Edward E. Ayer Collection, Newberry Library, Chicago (translation from the original Spanish by the author).

14. Rizal y Alonso, "Las Filipinas Dentro de Cien Años," pt. 3, *La Solidaridad* 1, no. 21 (Dec. 15, 1889), "autonomy," 510; ibid., conclusion, *La Solidaridad* 2, no. 24 (Feb. 1, 1890), "dominion," 32; ibid., pt. 2, "destroy," 436; ibid., pt. 3, "serve," 510.

15. Ibid., conclusion, 33.

16. Ibid.

17. On interimperial connections see, for example, Bönker, "Admiration, Enmity, and Cooperation." For discussions of linkages between Philippine-American colonial history and the histories of European colonial empires, see Go, "Introduction"; and Adas, "Improving on the Civilizing Mission?" For one account of the United States' ongoing "colonial" relationship to Europe, see Lodge, "Colonialism in the United States."

18. See Kramer, "Empires, Exceptions, and Anglo-Saxons.

19. On Kipling's Anglo-American connections, see Gilmour, *Long Recessional*.

20. Kipling, "White Man's Burden."

21. Du Bois, *Souls of Black Folk*, 45. On Du Bois during this period, see Lewis, *W. E. B. Du Bois*.

22. Du Bois, "Present Outlook," "color line," "race question," 95, "world problem," 104, "centre," 95, "congeries," 97–98, "masses," 98.

23. Ibid., "expansion," "German," 107, "significant," 103, "colored," "attitude," "sympathy," "Negro," 102.

24. There are numerous recent exceptions to this "insulation," which have richly integrated Philippine, U.S., and world histories. For some of the best of this literature, which attempts to connect Philippine-American colonial state-building outward in diverse ways, see Go and Foster, *American Colonial State in the Philippines*. Some of the most promising efforts involve the bridging of literatures on colonialism and migration, traditionally distinct sets of inquiry. See, especially, Choy, *Em-*

pire of Care; Fujita-Rony, *American Workers, Colonial Power*; and Alidio, "Between Civilizing Mission and Ethnic Assimilation."

25. On the historiography of exceptionalism, see Rodgers, "Exceptionalism." For probing discussions of the intersection of U.S. national exceptionalism and the denial of empire, see Kaplan, "Left Alone with America"; Pérez, *War of 1898*; Campomanes, "New Empire's Forgetful and Forgotten Citizens"; and Winks, "American Struggle with 'Imperialism.'"

26. On the mutual imbrication of U.S. national exceptionalism and imperial ideologies, see Stephanson, *Manifest Destiny*.

27. For critical reassessments of the historiography of late nineteenth-century foreign relations, see, especially, Crapol, "Coming to Terms with Empire"; J. Fry, "Imperialism, American Style"; De Santis, "Imperialist Impulse and American Innocence"; and Field, "American Imperialism."

28. This view is most closely associated with Richard Hofstader's "psychic crisis" thesis, in "Cuba, the Philippines, and Manifest Destiny." A similar interpretation can be found earlier, in Pratt, *Expansionists of 1898*. In more recent work, the crisis has been figured as one of masculinity, one with a decisive causal role in overseas formal empire-building. See, especially, Hoganson, *Fighting for American Manhood*.

29. William Williams, *Tragedy of American Diplomacy*; LaFeber, *New Empire*.

30. See, for example, McCormick, *China Market*.

31. Robin Winks criticizes assumptions of exceptionalism but effectively declares U.S. imperialism exceptional on the basis of its "republicanism," impermanence, and "makeshift" character; see "Imperialism." More recently, Michael Adas argues that Philippine-American colonialism was exceptional for its commitment to principles of "self-rule" and Filipino "capacity," as well as its developmentalism; see "Improving on the Civilizing Mission?"

32. My understanding of the politics of recognition is related to Uday Mehta's understanding of nineteenth-century British liberalism, which placed "behind the capacities ascribed to all human beings . . . a thicker set of social credentials that constitute the real bases of political inclusion." Mehta, "Liberal Strategies of Exclusion."

33. See, for example, M. Hunt, *Ideology and U.S. Foreign Policy*; Kennedy, "Race and American Expansion" and "Racial Overtones of Imperialism"; and Lasch, "Anti-Imperialists."

34. Matthew Frye Jacobson argues, for example, that the domestic disenfranchisement of immigrants and of diverse colonial subjects were identical, in *Barbarian Virtues*. Walter Williams argues for the "export" of U.S. Indian policy as the basis of U.S. colonial rule in the Philippines, in "United States Indian Policy." For a more recent elaboration, see Paulet, "Only Good Indian Is a Dead Indian." Each of these accounts, in different ways, narrates the connection of colony and metropole as what Fernando Coronil has called "the dissolution of the Other by the Self," in "Beyond Occidentalism." Marilyn Young cautions historians of U.S. empire to pay attention to the voices of those on the other side of U.S. power, to prevent the historiographic rearticulation of imperial processes, in "Age of Global Power."

35. Scholarship on colonial discourse often begins from premises set out in Edward Said's foundational work *Orientalism*. For works that hold up the effort

to understand the representational politics of colonialism, while challenging the monolithic framework, dualism, and ahistoricism of much scholarship on colonial discourse, see Lowe, *Critical Terrains*, especially ch. 1; Thomas, *Colonialism's Culture*; and Clifford, "On Orientalism."

36. My thinking on race here brings together, necessarily in highly condensed form, insights from diverse critical approaches on race, including Balibar, "Racism and Nationalism"; Holt, *Problem of Race*; Stoler, "Sexual Affronts"; Fields, "Ideology and Race in American History"; S. Hall, "Race, Articulation and Societies"; and Hodes, "Mercurial Nature."

37. Stoler, "Racial Histories."

38. Omi and Winant, *Racial Formation in the United States*.

39. On the multiplicities of colonial discourse in specific colonial settings see, especially, Thomas, *Colonialism's Culture*.

40. See, especially, Sinha, *Colonial Masculinity*; Burton, *Burdens of History*; and Stoler, "Sexual Affronts." On gender and U.S. empire, see Hoganson, *Fighting for American Manhood*; Renda, *Taking Haiti*; Wexler, *Tender Violence*; and Briggs, *Reproducing Empire*.

41. Sinha, *Colonial Masculinity*.

42. "Sr. Don Juan Macleod [*sic*]," in Jackson, *Representative Men of the Philippines*, 65.

43. MacLeod, preface.

44. MacLeod, "Sliding Scale," "bright lad," 5, "enveloped," 10, "contrasted," 11.

45. Ibid., "glimpse," 13, "Pepe," 17.

46. Ibid., "English wife," 21, "ignorance," 22–23, "suffer," 27.

47. Ibid., 30.

48. For a provocative reading that emphasizes fears of racial-imperial inversion, see Arata, "Occidental Tourist."

49. See, for example, Robinson, "Non-European Foundations of European Imperialism."

50. See, especially, Chatterjee, *Nationalist Thought and the Colonial World*.

51. The problematic of colonial migration to the metropole was one that cut across empires, as were proposals for its resolution. For the British Empire, see, for example, Huttenback, *Racism and Empire*.

52. For comparisons of the Philippines and Puerto Rico under U.S. rule, see Go, "Chains of Empire" and "Transcultured States"; and L. Thompson, "Imperial Republic."

Chapter 1

1. On the exposition's form during this period, see Greenhalgh, *Ephemeral Vistas*, 67. On challenges to Spanish commercial hegemony, see Salazar, "British and German Passivity." On the 1887 exposition and Spanish colonial knowledge, see Sánchez Gómez, *Un Imperio en la Vitrina*, and "Etnografía de Filipinas." Balaguer, *Islas Filipinas*, 6 (translation from the original Spanish by the author).

2. Aguirre quoted in Sánchez Gómez, "Salvajes e Ilustrados," 148 (translation from the original Spanish by the author).

3. On Philippine political economy during the Spanish colonial period, see Mc-Coy and De Jesus, *Philippine Social History*. On the political structure of nineteenth-century Spanish colonialism, see Fradera, *Gobernar Colonias*.

4. On the race and class structures of the urban Philippines under Spanish rule, see Reed, "Hispanic Urbanism." On the Chinese, see Wickberg, *Chinese in Philippine Life*. On Chinese mestizos, see Wickberg, "Chinese Mestizo in Philippine History."

5. Reed, "Hispanic Urbanism"; penal code quoted in Bankoff, *Crime, Society, and the State*, 96–97.

6. Schumacher, *Propaganda Movement*, ch. 1.

7. Ibid., 5–9; Schumacher, *Father Jose Burgos*.

8. José Burgos, "Manifesto of Filipinos," in Schumacher, *Father Jose Burgos*, 73.

9. Cullinane, *Ilustrado Politics*, ch. 1; Majul, "Principales, Ilustrados."

10. José Rizal y Alonso, "A La Juventud Filipina," reprinted in Retana, *Vida y Escritos*, 32–33 (translation from the original Spanish by the author). The biographical literature on Rizal is extensive. For provocative essays, see A. Ocampo, *Rizal without the Overcoat*; and B. Anderson, "The First Filipino," and "Hard to Imagine," in *Spectres of Comparison*, 227–34, 235–62.

11. Schumacher, *Propaganda Movement*, 35.

12. Corpuz, *Roots of the Filipino Nation*, 2:45.

13. José Rizal y Alonso, "Los Viajes," *La Solidaridad* 1, no. 7 (May 15, 1889), 160. The essay was originally published in 1882 in *Diariong Tagalog*.

14. Rizal Diary, July 4, 1889, in Rizal y Alonso, *Reminiscences and Travels*, 153–55.

15. Ibid., 155.

16. "Movimiento Colonial," *La Solidaridad* 6, no. 126 (Apr. 30, 1894), "English newspaper," 182; "Nuestros Propósitos," *La Solidaridad* 1, no. 1 (Feb. 15, 1889), "British press," 5.

17. Feced, *Filipinas*, "familiarize," 131, "not well-known," 148 (translation from the original Spanish by the author); Ferdinand Blumentritt, "¡Que Viva la Leña!," *La Solidaridad* 2, no. 36 (July 31, 1890), "fix everything," 336.

18. On the popular journalistic representation of the Philippines in Spanish journal graphics, see, for example, Vidal, "Filipinas en la Ilustración." On colonialism and Spanish theater, see O'Connor, *Representations of the Cuban and Philippine Insurrections*.

19. Taga-Ilog [Antonio Luna], "Impresiones Madrileñas de un Filipino," *La Solidaridad* 1, no. 18 (Oct. 31, 1889), "dictionary," 446, "pronounced," "head," "Chinese," 444, "theaters," 444–46, "doubting," 446.

20. "Carta de Filipinas," *La Solidaridad* 1, no. 4 (Mar. 31, 1889), 86.

21. Schumacher, *Propaganda Movement*, ch. 9.

22. On *La Solidaridad*, see Valenzuela, *History of Journalism*, 92–94.

23. Balaguer, *Islas Filipinas*, 18; D. E. Maisonnave, in *Exposición de Filipinas*, 211; Manuel Antón, "La Raza Negrita," in ibid., "insignificant," 84; Manuel Antón, "La Raza Micronesia," in ibid., "four distinct races," 111 (all quotations from *Exposición de Filipinas* are translations from the original Spanish by the author).

24. Taga-Ilog [Luna], "Impresiones Madrileñas," 446; José Rizal to his family, Jan. 29, 1883, quoted in Bernad, *Rizal and Spain*, 67; Graciano López Jaena, "Los Indios de

Filipinas," in López Jaena, *Discursos y Artículos Varios*, 138 (all quotations from *Discursos y Artículos Varios* are translations from the original Spanish by the author).

25. On Feced and his exchange with López Jaena, see Sánchez Gómez, "'Ellos y Nosotros.'"

26. Feced quoted in ibid., "Spaniard," "foot," "anthropoid," 315, "abyss," 316 (translation from the original Spanish by the author).

27. Feced quoted in ibid., "accustomed," "propaganda," "no idea," 317, "conventional," "unopposable," 316.

28. On *ilustrado* engagements with racial science, see Aguilar, "Tracing Origins"; and Dumol, "Rizal contra European Racism." While not without his own agenda, Ferdinand Blumentritt identified the Propaganda movement closely with the Filipino criticism of Spanish racism; see "Race Questions in the Philippine Islands" and "Views of Dr. Rizal."

29. Editorial response to Eduardo P. Casal y Ochoa's pamphlet "Philippine Affairs," *La Solidaridad* 1, no. 3 (Mar. 18, 1889), "genius," 63; Marcelo Del Pilar, "The Assimilation of the Philippines," *La Solidaridad* 1, no. 16 (Sept. 30, 1889), 379.

30. Del Pilar, "Assimilation of the Philippines," 379; Rizal quoted in Schumacher, *Propaganda Movement*, 71–72.

31. "Filipinos Celebres," *La Solidaridad* 2, no. 24 (Feb. 1, 1890), 34.

32. "Mr. Frederik [*sic*] Douglass," *La Solidaridad* 7, no. 152 (May 15, 1895), "savagery," 252, "succeeded," 254.

33. López Jaena quoted in Schumacher, "Propaganda Movement," 121. On Philippine arts and notions of civilization at the 1887 exposition, see Sánchez Gómez, "Indigenous Art at the Philippine Exposition."

34. Rizal quoted in Schumacher, *Propaganda Movement*, 50–51.

35. Rizal to Blumentritt, Aug. 7, 1888, quoted in Dumol, "Rizal contra European Racism," "Heaven," 7; Rizal to Blumentritt, Nov. 8, 1888, quoted in ibid., "educated," 7, "visiting," 9.

36. Ferdinand Blumentritt, "Un Aniversario," *La Solidaridad* 1, no. 6 (Apr. 30, 1889), "Malay dialects," 132; Ferdinand Blumentritt, "La Representación Parlamentaria de Filipinas: Observaciones de un Cosmopolita Sedentario," *La Solidaridad* 1, no. 17 (Oct. 15, 1889), "Bulgaria," 405.

37. Graciano López Jaena, "Los Indios de Filipinas," in López Jaena, *Discursos y Artículos Varios*, 140; Sancianco quoted in Schumacher, *Propaganda Movement*, 28.

38. José Rizal y Alonso, "Sobre la Indolencia de los Filipinos," pt. 1, *La Solidaridad* 2, no. 35 (July 15, 1890), "blamed," "instead," 322, "surrounded," 324; ibid., pt. 3, *La Solidaridad* 2, no. 37 (Aug. 15, 1890), "fatal," 362, "graves," 366; ibid., pt. 1, "pretensions," 324.

39. Del Pilar quoted in Schumacher, *Propaganda Movement*, 150.

40. Rafael, *Contracting Colonialism*; Gaerlan, "Politics and Pedagogy of Language Use," 78–89.

41. Rafael, "Translation and Revenge," 219; Taga-Ilog [Antonio Luna] quoted in ibid., 233.

42. Owen, "Masculinity and National Identity"; López Jaena, "Los Indios de Filipinas," 138. On López Jaena's challenge, see Schumacher, *Propaganda Movement*, 194.

43. On gender and early *ilustrado* nationalism, see Rafael, "Nationalism, Imagery and the Filipino Intelligentsia"; López Jaena, "Los Indios de Filipinas," 138–39.

44. On the nineteenth-century "invented tradition" in Europe, see Hobsbawm and Ranger, "Mass-Producing Traditions." On the San Agustín letter, see Bernad, *Christianization of the Philippines*, ch. 13, quoted on 165.

45. On the *ilustrado* reconstruction of the Philippine past, see Schumacher, "Propagandists' Reconstruction"; Paterno, *La Antigua Civilización Tagalog*; Morga and Rizal y Alonso, *Sucesos de las Islas Filipinas*. On Rizal's use of Morga's text, see A. Ocampo, "Rizal's Morga"; and Schumacher, "Propagandists' Reconstruction."

46. On De los Reyes, see three essays by Scott in *Cracks in the Parchment Curtain*: "Isabelo de los Reyes, Father of Philippine Folklore," "Isabelo de los Reyes, Provinciano and Nationalist," and "A Minority Reaction to American Rule"; Kramer, "Pragmatic Empire," ch. 2; and B. Anderson, "Rooster's Egg." De los Reyes, introduction to *El Folk-Lore Filipino*, "European nations," 8, "ways," 6 (all quotations from *El Folk-Lore Filipino* are translations from the original Spanish by the author).

47. On mestizo-native tensions, see Schumacher, *Propaganda Movement*, 64–65; "En Tinieblas," *La Solidaridad* 1, no. 6 (Apr. 30, 1889), "Partisans," 118; Rizal to Blumentritt, Apr. 13, 1887, in Rizal y Alonso, *Rizal-Blumentritt Correspondence*, 1.72.

48. "Cosas de Manila," *La Solidaridad* 1, no. 20 (Nov. 30, 1889), "accusing," 476; Hecrnr H. Astfeld, "¿Correrá Sangre?" *La Solidaridad* 1, no. 22 (Dec. 31, 1889), "adore Spain," 560; "Algo Sobre las Colonias," *La Solidaridad* 1, no. 15 (Sept. 15, 1889), "Our Filipinos," 358.

49. Aguilar, "Tracing Origins."

50. De los Reyes, "Folklore Terminology," in *El Folk-Lore Filipino*, "forest-dwellers," 20; De los Reyes, "Origen de las Razas Filipinas," quoted in Scott, "Isabelo de los Reyes, Provinciano and Nationalist," in *Cracks in the Parchment Curtain*, 274. De los Reyes would be criticized by *ilustrado* readers, especially Tagalogs, who pointed out his strong *provinciano* tendency to imagine "Filipinos" as Ilocanos, using the terms interchangeably and drawing disproportionately on Ilocano materials. In exchange, De los Reyes challenged Rizal for romanticizing the pre-Hispanic past.

51. Taga-Ilog [Luna], "Impresiones Madrileñas," 445.

52. López Jaena, "La Exposición de Filipinas," in López Jaena, *Discursos y Artículos Varios*, "deny," 165; López Jaena, "Filipinas en Madrid," in ibid., "place of honor," 155–56.

53. López Jaena, "La Exposición de Filipinas," 165–66.

54. On the display of "non-Christian" peoples and *ilustrado* responses, see Sánchez Gómez, "Salvajes e Ilustrados"; and Scott, "Igorots Who Went to Madrid."

55. Rizal to Blumentritt, June 19, 1887, quoted in Scott, *Discovery of the Igorots*, 276.

56. Barrado quoted in Schumacher, *Propaganda Movement*, 75.

57. *El Resumen* quoted in ibid., 73; D. Emilio Castelar, "Prologo," in *Exposición de Filipinas*, 15.

58. Payo and Font quoted in Schumacher, *Propaganda Movement*, 76.

59. López Jaena, "Filipinas en Madrid," 156.

60. Graciano López Jaena, "Una Visita a la Exposición," in López Jaena, *Discursos y Artículos Varios*, "barrack," 155, "repression," 158.

61. Editorial quoted in Schumacher, *Propaganda Movement*, "idea," 75, "collectivity," 76.

62. Schumacher, *Propaganda Movement*, 197–99.

63. Ibid., 199–205.

64. Taga-Ilog [Luna] quoted in ibid., 216; Del Pilar quoted in ibid., 217.

65. Rizal quoted in ibid., 251.

66. Rizal quoted in ibid., "propagation," 237, "knowledge," 240.

67. On the Buffalo Bill show, see Slotkin, "Buffalo Bill's 'Wild West.'"

68. Rizal quoted in Schumacher, *Propaganda Movement*, 257.

69. On petty crime in the late nineteenth-century Philippines, see Bankoff, *Crime, Society, and the State.* On revolutionary movements, see Ileto, *Pasyon and Revolution*; and Sturtevant, *Popular Uprisings in the Philippines.*

70. Ileto, *Pasyon and Revolution.*

71. "Katipunan, Last Instructions concerning Admission into the Society," Exhibit 11b, in J. Taylor, *Philippine Insurrection,* 1:215–16.

72. Andaya, "Ethnicity in the Philippine Revolution," "Long live," 66; De los Reyes quoted in ibid., 67; Sakay quoted in ibid., 70.

73. Aguinaldo quoted in ibid., 73–74; Mabini quoted in ibid., 69.

74. Hintze quoted in Wionzek, "Lt. Commander Paul Hintze's Visit," 168.

75. Aguinaldo quoted in T. Agoncillo, *Malolos,* 13.

76. Alhama quoted in O'Connor, *Representations of the Cuban and Philippine Insurrections,* 104; Trigo quoted in ibid., 105.

77. *Filipinas por España* quoted in ibid., 96; Taboada quoted in ibid., 97–98.

78. Comerge quoted in Foreman, *Philippine Islands,* 549.

79. Unamuno, "Epilogo," in Retana, *Vida y Escritos,* 480. On class differences within the revolution, see T. Agoncillo, *Revolt of the Masses.*

80. Ibid., 56–57.

81. See Trask, *War with Spain*; and Pérez, *War of 1898.*

82. For accounts of the rise of a U.S. Pacific commercial empire in the nineteenth century, see Pletcher, *Diplomacy of Involvement*; and Van Alstyne, *Rising American Empire.*

83. Aguinaldo quoted in T. Agoncillo, *Malolos,* "avenging," 62–63, "motives," 67–68.

84. Rizal to Mariano Ponce, July 27, 1888, in Rizal y Alonso, *Reminiscences and Travels,* 303.

85. Rizal to his parents, Apr. 29, 1888, in ibid., "in sight," 293; Rizal to Ponce, July 27, 1888, in ibid., "Negro," 303.

Chapter 2

1. "The Status of the Filipinos," *New York Times,* Feb. 9, 1899, 6.

2. On the U.S. military in the Pacific after 1898, see Linn, *Guardians of Empire*; Braisted, *United States Navy in the Pacific*; and Flint, "United States Army on the Pacific Frontier."

3. On race war in other U.S. historical settings, see Dower, *War without Mercy*; and Grimsley, "'Rebels' and 'Redskins.'"

4. Stuart Creighton Miller puts racism at the center of his account of U.S. troop conduct in *"Benevolent Assimilation."* For a differing account that minimizes the role of racism and atrocity in the war, see Linn, "Taking Up the White Man's Burden."

5. Many histories of the war use letters attributed to U.S. soldiers republished in "anti-imperialist" pamphlets and newspapers—without tracing them back to original materials. The most commonly misused of these sources is *Soldiers' Letters: Being Materials for the History of a War of Criminal Aggression* (Boston: Anti-Imperialist League, 1899), which is questionable as a primary document. In attempting to reconstruct soldiers' mentalities and practices here, I rely primarily on archival sources or those quoted by other historians.

6. For the purposes of this essay, "exterminism" is the wartime use of force against entire populations—combatant and civilian—as a military tactic. "Racial exterminism" is the wartime use of force against entire populations whose racialized status facilitates the blurring of combatant and civilian. Racial exterminism differs from genocide, pursuing violence against a racialized population toward the ultimate goal of postwar rule and coexistence, whereas genocide takes the elimination of that population as its goal, subordinates tactics to that end, and imagines neither postwar rule nor coexistence. On the concept of exterminism, see Bönker, "Militarizing the Western World." Other historians have discussed whether or not the Philippine-American War constitutes a "total war," a much-debated concept. See May, "Was the Philippine-American War a 'Total War'?" For an intriguing comparative approach that properly situates the Philippine-American War alongside German colonial violence, see H. Smith, "Logic of Colonial Violence." Arthur MacArthur, Report to Adjutant General of the Army, Oct. 1, 1900, in *Annual Report of Major General Arthur MacArthur*, 6.

7. For historiographic debates on late nineteenth-century U.S. foreign relations, see Crapol, "Coming to Terms with Empire"; and De Santis, "Imperialist Impulse and American Innocence."

8. See Grenville, "American Naval Preparations."

9. T. Agoncillo, *Malolos*, 96.

10. Nozaleda quoted in ibid., 93.

11. Aguinaldo quoted in ibid., 98.

12. Circular quoted in ibid., 103.

13. Long quoted in ibid., 119.

14. Dewey quoted in ibid., 119.

15. Aguinaldo quoted in ibid., 109.

16. Williams quoted in ibid., 110.

17. "Act of the Proclamation of Independence of the Filipino People," Exhibit 28, in J. Taylor, *Philippine Insurrection*, 3.103–4.

18. Ibid., 106.

19. De Santos quoted in T. Agoncillo, *Malolos*, 111.

20. *Straits Times* quoted in ibid., 112.

21. Wildman quoted in ibid., 122–23.

22. On preprofessional diplomacy of this kind, see Beisner, *From the Old Diplomacy to the New*, chs. 2–3.

23. Day quoted in T. Agoncillo, *Malolos*, 120–21.

24. Anderson quoted in ibid., 140–41.

25. Anderson quoted in ibid., 150.

26. Ibid., 165.

27. Markey, *From Iowa to the Philippines*, 141.

28. McKinley's instructions quoted in T. Agoncillo, *Malolos*, 137–38.

29. On the links between "print-capitalism" and nationalist "imagined community," see B. Anderson, *Imagined Communities*, especially ch. 3. On the press during the Philippine-American War, see Lent, "Philippine Press"; and Valenzuela, *History of Journalism*.

30. On the structure of the Malolos government, see T. Agoncillo, *Malolos*, ch. 8.

31. Ibid., 232.

32. Aguinaldo quoted in ibid., 231.

33. Otis quoted in S. Miller, *"Benevolent Assimilation,"* 47.

34. On one element of these sanitary campaigns, the politics of prostitution and its regulation during the Philippine-American War, see Kramer, "Darkness That Enters the Home."

35. F. Agoncillo, *Memorial to the Senate*, "continuously," "countrymen," 2, map, 6, "notable," 7.

36. See F. Agoncillo, "Are the Filipinos Civilized?"

37. "Nuestro Programa," *La Independencia* 1, no. 1 (Sept. 3, 1898) (all quotations from *La Independencia* are translations from the original Spanish by the author).

38. Advertisement for *La Independencia* 1, no. 2 (Sept. 5, 1898).

39. "La Cultura de los Filipinos," *La Independencia* 1, no. 9 (Sept. 14, 1898); "Nuestro Pueblo," ibid., no. 52 (Nov. 5, 1898); "Campaña de Odio," ibid., no. 92 (Dec. 23, 1898); "Odios de Raza," ibid., no. 4 (Sept. 7, 1898).

40. See, for example, "El Espíritu de la Asociación," *La Independencia* 1, no. 5 (Sept. 9, 1898); "De Higiene Pública," ibid., no. 36 (Oct. 17, 1898); "Los Presupuestos," ibid., no. 41 (Oct. 22, 1898); "Apuntes sobre Enseñanza," ibid., no. 47 (Oct. 29, 1898); "Moralización," ibid., no. 63 (Nov. 18, 1898).

41. "Al Público," *La Independencia* 1, no. 180 (Aug. 11, 1899), "union"; "Lo Indispensable," ibid., no. 2 (Sept. 5, 1898), "savage," "govern."

42. Dewey quoted in S. Miller, *"Benevolent Assimilation,"* 41.

43. Anderson quoted in ibid., 40.

44. King quoted in ibid., 41.

45. [Unsigned] quoted in *Wisconsin Weekly Advocate*, May 17, 1900, in Gatewood, *"Smoked Yankees,"* 279.

46. On martial masculinity in this period, see Hoganson, *Fighting for American Manhood*; and Mrozek, "Habit of Victory."

47. On "passionate" masculinity, see Rotundo, *American Manhood*; and Higham, "Reorientation of American Culture."

48. Irving Speer Diary, late August and Nov. 6, 1898, Folder: "Irving Speer, 1898-W-448, Co. I, Diary, Clipping," Box 18: Colorado Infantry, 1st Regiment, SAWS.

49. Myers to "Dear Parents," Jan. 10, 1899, Folder: "Myer, Claude F. 1898–119, Co. C, 1st Tennessee Vol. Infantry," Box 170: Tennessee Infantry, 1st Regiment, SAWS.

50. Speer Diary, Nov. 6, 1898.

51. Speer Diary, [date illegible].

52. Faust, *Campaigning in the Philippines*, 125.

53. "General McReeve's Interview," *Anti-Imperialist* 1, no. 3 (July 4, 1899), 18.

54. U.S. Senate, *Report of Tour through the Island of Luzon*, 20.

55. Quoted in Johnson, *History of Negro Soldiers*, 131.

56. Palmer, "White Man and Brown Man," 79.

57. Quoted in Saum, "Western Volunteer," 22.

58. Brace, "Itamo, the Insurrecto," 16–19.

59. Ibid., 19–20.

60. Sargent, "In Aguinaldo's Realm," 2477.

61. U.S. Senate, *Report of Tour through the Island of Luzon*, 13.

62. Wilcox, "In the Heart of Luzon," 2475; Sargent, "In Aguinaldo's Realm," 2479.

63. Sargent, "In Aguinaldo's Realm," 2480–81.

64. U.S. Senate, *Report of Tour through the Island of Luzon*, 20.

65. Sargent, "In Aguinaldo's Realm," 2481.

66. U.S. Senate, *Report of Tour through the Island of Luzon*, 16.

67. On McKinley's much-debated role in the decision to seize the Philippines, see E. Smith, "William McKinley's Enduring Legacy."

68. McKinley quoted in S. Miller, *"Benevolent Assimilation,"* 24.

69. Quoted in ibid.

70. William McKinley to the Secretary of War, Dec. 21, 1898, "Message from the President of the United States," 56th Cong., 1st sess., 1899–1900, S. Doc. 208, 82–83.

71. Vest Resolution quoted in S. Miller, *"Benevolent Assimilation,"* 26.

72. "Future Work in the Philippines," *New York Times*, Feb. 7, 1899, 6.

73. On the conventional war, see Linn, *Philippine War, 1899–1902*, chs. 3–8; and Jamieson, *Crossing the Deadly Ground*, ch. 8.

74. Osborne quoted in Chapman, "Taking Up the White Man's Burden," 35.

75. MacArthur quoted in Gates, *Schoolbooks and Krags*, 83.

76. Lawton quoted in ibid.

77. On the politics of Filipino-American collaboration, see Paredes, *Philippine Colonial Democracy*; Owen, *Compadre Colonialism*; and Salamanca, *Filipino Reaction to American Rule*.

78. "Letter of Transmittal," Jan. 31, 1900, in *Report of the Philippine Commission* (1900), 1:1–2.

79. Quoted in Gates, *Schoolbooks and Krags*, 82.

80. Rhodes, "Utilization of Foreign Troops," 3.

81. On the Scouts, see Laurie, "Philippine Scouts"; Wollard, "Philippine Scouts"; and McCoy, "Colonial Origins."

82. On the "tribalization" of the Scouts, see McCoy, "Colonial Origins," 98; Wollard, "Philippine Scouts," 67; "To Whom Shall We Surrender?" *New York Times*, Oct. 4, 1899, "hereditary enemies," 8; "The Macabebe Scouts: Interesting Story of the Little Men Who Hate the Tagalogs," newspaper clipping, Folder: "Maj. Matt. A. Batson, 9th U.S. Cav., Messages/Orders," Box 1, Matthew Batson Papers, U.S. Military History Institute, Carlisle, Pennsylvania, "wonderful."

83. Batson and Otis quoted in "The Scout," memorandum dated Aug. 23, 1908, Folder 9: "Major Matt. Batson, 1898–186.45, 9th Cav., Originals of Letters," Box 1, Batson Papers.

84. Apacible, "Al Pueblo Americano," "civilized," "weigh," 3, "impartial," 3–4 (all quotations from this document are translations from the original Spanish by the author).

85. Ibid., 4.

86. Ibid., "cannons," 4, "applauded," "time," 8, "boastful," 5, "conditions," 6–7.

87. "To the Filipino People," Exhibit 992, in J. Taylor, *Philippine Insurrection*, 5:96. Taylor speculates that its author was Emilio Aguinaldo; a more likely candidate is Apolinario Mabini.

88. Mabini quoted in T. Kalaw, *Philippine Revolution*, 176–77.

89. On the domestic U.S. politics of the war, see Welch, *Response to Imperialism*; Schirmer, *Republic or Empire*; and Tompkins, *Anti-Imperialism in the United States*.

90. Heretofore in this work, I have used quotation marks around the terms "anti-imperialism" and "anti-imperialist" to distinguish my own definition of "imperialism" from that employed by many so-called anti-imperialists. As New Left historians demonstrated long ago, most anti-imperialists defined "imperialism" narrowly, as military conquest and colonial state-building, either neglecting or promoting other processes of empire-building, especially commercial-capitalist ones.

91. For readings that emphasize the abolitionist roots of anti-imperialism, see McPherson, *Abolitionist Legacy*; Schirmer, *Republic or Empire*; and Salman, *Embarrassment of Slavery*.

92. On U.S. anti-imperialism, see Schirmer, *Republic or Empire*; Beisner, *Twelve against Empire*; Tompkins, *Anti-Imperialism in the United States*; and Zwick, "Anti-Imperialist League." On the personnel of anti-imperialism, see Zimmerman, "Who Were the Anti-Imperialists?" On the gender politics of anti-imperialism, see Hoganson, *Fighting for American Manhood*. On anti-imperialism in the early twentieth century more generally, see Zwick, "Anti-Imperialist Movement." On its importance to twentieth-century U.S. foreign policy, see Ninkovich, *United States and Imperialism*.

93. Blumentritt quoted in *Facts about the Filipinos* 1, no. 1 (May 1901), "Christianized," 9, "gifted," 16, "self-control," 14; "Intellectual Attainments and Education of the Filipinos," *Facts about the Filipinos* 2, no. 2 (Dec. 1901), 52–64. Blumentritt was forthright about Filipino exceptionalism—his sense of the "Malays and mestizos" as "susceptible to cultivation" above and beyond other "colored races"—in "Race Questions in the Philippine Islands," 473–74.

94. For examples of anti-imperialist argument, see Zwick, *Anti-Imperialism*; Foner and Winchester, *Anti-Imperialist Reader*; and Bresnahan, *In Time of Hesitation*.

95. On the racial politics of anti-imperialism, see Lasch, "Anti-Imperialists."

96. Schurz, "American Imperialism."

97. J. Davis, "Why We Do Not Want the Philippines," 235–36.

98. Gompers, "Imperialism, Its Dangers and Wrongs," 207.

99. For black public opinion on the war, see Gatewood, *Black Americans and the White Man's Burden*; and Marks, *Black Press*.

100. "Negroes Opposed to Treaty of Paris," *Washington Bee*, Feb. 11, 1899, quoted in Marks, *Black Press*, 114.

101. "Annexation Questioned," *Indianapolis Recorder*, Jan. 28, 1899, quoted in ibid., 110.

102. "Negroes against McKinley's Philippine Policy," *Richmond Planet*, July 22, 1899, quoted in ibid., 135.

103. "Filipinos Should Have Republican Form of Government," *Washington Bee*, Dec. 10, 1898, quoted in ibid., 106.

104. "North Carolina Imperialism," *Washington Bee*, Aug. 11, 1900, reprinted in the *Chicago Inter-Ocean* [undated], quoted in ibid., 177.

105. "Declaration of Independence Applies to All Peoples," *Chicago Broad Ax*, Oct. 21, 1899, quoted in ibid., 153.

106. "Negroes Should Not Fight in China," *Cleveland Gazette*, Aug. 13, 1900, quoted in ibid., 178.

107. "Civilization Should Begin at Home," *Indianapolis Recorder*, Apr. 1, 1899, quoted in ibid., 120.

108. "Filipino Struggle Admired," *Washington Bee*, Mar. 11, 1899, quoted in ibid., 117.

109. "A World Movement among Darker Races Has Begun," *A.M.E. Church Review*, Oct. 1899, quoted in ibid., 154.

110. "Against Blacks Fighting Filipinos," *Cleveland Gazette*, July 8, 1899, quoted in ibid., 133.

111. "Disagreement with New England Anti-Imperialists' Attack on McKinley's Administration," *Indianapolis Freeman*, May 26, 1900, quoted in ibid., 170.

112. "The Philippine War Is No Race War," *Indianapolis Freeman*, Oct. 7, 1899, quoted in ibid., 150.

113. Kramer, "Empires, Exceptions, and Anglo-Saxons." Anglo-Saxonists themselves conceded that the United States' "Anglo-Saxonism" was compromised by diverse European immigrants. As Matthew Frye Jacobson shows, these groups actively debated the politics of imperial conquest in the Philippines; imperialists among them compromised any strict, essentialist connection between Anglo-Saxonism and empire. See Jacobson, *Special Sorrows*, ch. 5.

114. On contemporary social-evolutionary theory, see Stocking, *Race, Culture, and Evolution*; Hinsley, *Smithsonian and the American Indian*; Haller, *Outcasts from Evolution*; and Hofstader, *Social Darwinism in American Thought*.

115. On ideological uses of the concept of "tribe" in other contexts, see M. Friend, *Notion of Tribe*.

116. "The Native Peoples of the Philippines," *Report of the Philippine Commission* (1900), 1:11.

117. Ibid.

118. Ibid.

119. Ibid.

120. Ibid., 12.

121. "Preliminary Report: Capacity for Self-Government" (Nov. 2, 1899), ibid., 1:182.

122. "Native Peoples," "extremely," 14–15, "not a nation," 15.

123. On Lopez's efforts in the United States, see Jim Zwick, foreword to Eyot, *Story of the Lopez Family*, 5–13. S. Lopez, *"Tribes" in the Philippines*, "native," 3, "incorrect," 1, "imagination," "Americans," 3, "absurd," 7, "exception," 6.

124. S. Lopez, *"Tribes" in the Philippines*, "belong," 5, "so-called 'tribes,'" 1, "religion," 4; Charles Francis Adams quoted in Zwick, foreword, 10.

125. Chas. L. Lisle, "How I Killed an Insurgent," *Manila Times*, July 4, 1899, 3.

126. Andrew Wadsworth to sister, July 20, 1898, Folder 158, Hussey-Wadsworth Papers, Clements Library, University of Michigan, "bright and intelligent"; Wadsworth to Anna M. Wadsworth, Oct. 14, 1898, Folder 163, "like a negro"; Wadsworth to sister, Feb. 19, 1899, Folder 172, "hot time"; Wadsworth to Jennie Wadsworth [Aunt], Mar. 8, 1899, Folder 173, "commenced to chase niggers." On Wadsworth's correspondence, see Reilly, "Andrew Wadsworth."

127. Earl Pearsall Diary, Folder: "Pearsall, Earl, 1898-W-1521, 1st Neb. Vol. Inf., Diary for 1899," Box 97: Nebraska Infantry, 1st Regiment, SAWS, "not been as friendly lately" (Jan. 5, 1899), "dusky fellows" (Feb. 4, 1899), "black rascals" (Feb. 24, 1899), "attacked" (Mar. 6, 1899).

128. William Henry Barrett Diary, Folder: "Pvt. William Henry Barrett, 1898–39, 2nd Oregon Volunteer Infantry," Box 137: Oregon Infantry, 2nd Regiment, SAWS, "natives driven" (Feb. 9, 1899), "chased out the niggers" (Feb. 23, 1899).

129. Louis Hubbard letters to "My dearest Mother," Folder: "Louis W. Hubbard, 1898-W-987, 1st Regt. Band, 1st S.D. Vol. Inf., Newspaper, map letters," Box 169: South Dakota Infantry, 1st Regiment, SAWS, "finest clarinetist" (Dec. 20, 1898), "like any savage" (Feb. 20, 1899), "gugos" (Mar. 17, 1899).

130. John F. Bass, "The Fall of Manila" (dispatch of Aug. 30, 1898), *Harper's Weekly* 42 (Oct. 15, 1898), 1008.

131. Wells quoted in Welch, "American Atrocities," 241.

132. On the term "gook," see also Roediger, "Gook."

133. Freeman, "Yankee Music in the Far East," 31.

134. For this interpretation, see Roth, *Muddy Glory*, 223.

135. Freeman, "Yankee Music in the Far East," 31. The original song was written by John Queen and Hughie Cannon and first published in 1900.

136. Peter Lewis to "Friend Tom," Nov. 25, 1900, in Lewis and Kells, *Foot Soldier*, 96.

137. Nelson quoted in Schirmer, *Republic or Empire*, 240.

138. Palmer, "White Man and Brown Man," 81.

139. William Eggenberger to "Dear Mother and all," Mar. 25, 1899, Folder: "Wm Eggenberger, 1898–120, Col. K, 3rd U.S. Inf.," Box 214: U.S. Infantry, 3rd Regiment, SAWS.

140. John L. Jordan to "My dear Mother," Oct. 19, 1900, in Folder: "John L. Jordan, 1898–1920, 38th U.S. Vol. Inf, 37 letters," Box 279: U.S. Volunteer Infantry, 38th Regiment, SAWS.

141. Peter Lewis to "Dear Brother," Jan. 20, 1902, in Lewis and Kells, *Foot Soldier*, 124.

142. [Unsigned] quoted in *Wisconsin Weekly Advocate*, May 17, 1900, in Gatewood, *"Smoked Yankees,"* 280.

143. On black troops in the Spanish-Cuban-American War and the Philippine-American War, see Gatewood, *Black Americans and the White Man's Burden.*

144. Mason quoted in *Cleveland Gazette*, Nov. 19, 1899, in Gatewood, *"Smoked Yankees"* 257; Galloway quoted in *Richmond Planet*, Nov. 16, 1899, in ibid., 235; Simms quoted in ibid., 237.

145. Paula Pardo to Rozalia Magdalo, Aug. 23, 1899, quoted in Diokno, *Voices and Scenes of the Past*, 55.

146. *Richmond Planet*, Nov. 11, 1899, quoted in Gatewood, *"Smoked Yankees,"* 259. In at least one prominent case, a black soldier switched sides and fought alongside Filipino soldiers; see Robinson and Schubert, "David Fagen."

147. MacArthur quoted in Gates, *Schoolbooks and Krags*, 112.

148. Otis quoted in ibid.

149. On the guerrilla war, see Linn, *Philippine War, 1899–1902*, pt. 2.

150. Wagner quoted in Linn, "Intelligence and Low-Intensity Conflict," 90.

151. See, for example, "Las Espías," *La Independencia* 2, no. 258 (Nov. 21, 1899); and Francisco Jalandoni, "Guerrilla Warfare" (June 1, 1900), in J. Taylor, *Philippine Insurrection*, 5:584.

152. Isabelo de los Reyes, introduction to J. Rodriguez, "La Guerra de Guerrillas," *Filipinas ante Europa* 2, no. 20 (Mar. 10, 1900), 81–82 (translation from the original Spanish by the author). On De los Reyes's revolutionary activism, see Scott, "Minority Reaction to American Rule," in *Cracks in the Parchment Curtain.*

153. Villamor, *Inédita Crónica*, 81 (translation from the original Spanish by the author).

154. On class tensions between the republic and Filipino peasants during the Philippine-American War, see Guerrero, "Luzon at War."

155. On late nineteenth-century Filipino masculinity and codes of honor, see Owen, "Masculinity and National Identity."

156. Concepción, *Memorias de un Revolucionario*, 57 (translation from the original Spanish by the author).

157. Lyon quoted in S. Miller, *"Benevolent Assimilation,"* 185.

158. Quoted in Lent, "Philippine Press," 318.

159. "Bryan Subordinates Silver: In His Notification Speech He Will Treat Imperialism as the Paramount Issue," *New York Times*, July 28, 1900, 3. John Gates argues that U.S. anti-imperialists persuaded Filipinos to continue their fighting, in "Philippine Guerillas."

160. E. Aguinaldo, "To the Filipino Generals, Field and Line Officers and Soldiers," Oct. 29, 1900, Exhibit 1013, in J. Taylor, *Philippine Insurrection*, 5:130.

161. William Eggenberger to "Dear Mother and all," Sept. 29, 1900, Folder: "Wm

Eggenberger, 1898–120, Col. K, 3rd U.S. Inf.," Box 214: U.S. Infantry, 3rd Regiment, SAWS.

162. William Carey Brown to "My dear Helen," Jan. 26, 1901, in Folder: "William Carey Brown: Letter to Brown from Headquarters 42nd U.S. Volunteers, Theoretical Instruction; W. C. Brown diary 1900; letter from Inspector General; Correspondence with sisters Grace and Helen," Box 1, William Carey Brown Papers, U.S. Military History Institute, Carlisle, Pennsylvania.

163. *New York Tribune*, Oct. 22, 1901, 1, quoted in Gates, *Schoolbooks and Krags*, 184.

164. *Republican Campaign Text-Book 1900*, 64–65.

165. S. B. M. Young to Henry Corbin, Nov. 28, 1900, in Letterbook, Box 12: "Philippine Insurrection: Scattered Items Relating to Demobilization after the Spanish-American War, 1898–1902," Samuel B. M. Young Papers, U.S. Military History Institute, Carlisle, Pennsylvania.

166. Young to Theodore Roosevelt, Nov. 10, 1900, in ibid.

167. See, for example, Dickson, *War Slang*, 28.

168. Percy Hill, "The Anting-Anting," *American Old-Timer* 1, no. 12 (Oct. 1934), 12.

169. Garrett, *My Bunkie, and Other Ballads*, 18.

170. Isselhard, *Filipino in Every-Day Life*, 99–100.

171. On Mabini, see Majul, *Apolinario Mabini, Revolutionary* and *Mabini and the Philippine Revolution*. On contrasting American and Filipino definitions of "peace," see Diokno, "Perspectives on Peace."

172. James F. Bell to Apolinario Mabini, Aug. 28, 1900, in Mabini, *Letters of Apolinario Mabini*, 265–66.

173. Mabini to Bell, Aug. 31, 1900, in ibid., 259–60.

174. Ibid.

175. Mabini to Felipe Buencamino, July 20, 1900, in ibid., 254.

176. Mabini to Buencamino, Aug. 31, 1900, in ibid., 260.

177. Arthur MacArthur, "Proclamation," in *Annual Report of the Secretary of War*, 1901, 57th Cong., 1st sess., H. Doc. 2, vol. 1, pt. 4, "most essential," 91, "instruct all classes," 92; "General MacArthur's Proclamation," Official Supplement to the *Manila Times*, Dec. 20, 1900. The *Manila Times* had been inaugurated Oct. 11, 1898, by Thomas Gowan, an English resident in the Philippines, to cater to U.S. soldiers.

178. MacArthur, "Proclamation," 93.

179. Ibid., "rejected," 91, "secret communities," 92.

180. Ibid., 91.

181. Ibid., 92.

182. Ibid., "martial environment," 92, "prisoners of war," 95, "prominent," 96.

183. On the General Orders No. 100 in the context of Civil War combat regulations, see Grimsley, *Hard Hand of War*.

184. "Instructions for the Government of Armies of the United States in the Field," in Lieber and Hartigan, *Lieber's Code and the Law of War*, "inoffensive citizen" (Article 25), "internecine wars" (Article 28).

185. MacArthur, "Proclamation," 92.

186. Root quoted in Storey and Codman, *Secretary Root's Record*, 54.

187. General Hughes, "Diary of Events from December 14 to December 29, received by the War Department February 9, 1901," quoted in *Facts about the Filipinos* 1, no. 10 (Sept. 15, 1901), 33.

188. MacArthur, Report to Adjutant General of the Army, Oct. 1, 1900, in *Annual Report of Major General Arthur MacArthur*, "unity," 5, "ethnological," 6.

189. Young quoted in "Gen. Young on Filipinos: The Cavalry Leader Makes a Speech in Pittsburg [*sic*]," *New York Times*, Apr. 28, 1901, 3.

190. Perry Thompson to "Dear Folks," Aug. 21, 1901, Folder: "Perry E. Thompson, 1898–192, Co. L, 30th U.S. Infantry," Box 241: U.S. Infantry, 30th Regiment, SAWS.

191. Lewis and Kells, *Foot Soldier*, 110.

192. William Eggenberger to "Dear Mother and all," Sept. 29, 1899, Folder: "Wm Eggenberger, 1898–120, Col. K, 3rd U.S. Inf.," Box 214: U.S. Infantry, 3rd Regiment, SAWS.

193. Eggenberger to "Dear Mother and all," Feb. 5, 1900.

194. "The Soldiers' Song," in Dolph, "*Sound Off!*," 200–202. The song was sung to the tune of "Tramp, Tramp, Tramp, the Boys Are Marching," a Union Army song in the Civil War.

195. Frank Johnson to parents, Jan. 17, 1899, quoted in Saum, "Western Volunteer," 23.

196. Henry Hackthorn to "Dear Mother," June 24, 1899, in Grant, "Letters from the Philippines," 174.

197. Jackson quoted in Linn, "Taking Up the White Man's Burden," 140.

198. Eggenberger to "Dear Mother and all," Mar. 26, 1900.

199. The issue of prisoner abuse during the war has been one of its most ideologically charged aspects. Indeed, heated controversy during the war itself came to generate the sources, and many of the paradigms, for contemporary historical debate. The fact that the vast majority of these sources were American—reports from U.S. military commanders, records of interrogation, military tribunals against suspected Filipinos—should raise special caution to the historian. From what can be safely reconstructed, it is clear that both American and Filipino soldiers tortured and killed prisoners during the conflict. U.S. soldiers tortured and killed Filipino civilians they believed were collaborating with the revolutionaries; Filipino revolutionaries tortured and killed those they believed were collaborating with the invading U.S. Army. Much more research remains to be done on the scale of atrocities on both sides. See Welch, "American Atrocities"; and D. Smith, "American Atrocities in the Philippines."

200. "Odds and Ends: A Testimonial, 1902," in Notebook, Folder: "Albert E. Gardner, 1898-W-851, Troop B., 1st U.S. Cav., Scrapbook, Booklets, Letters, Soldiers' Manual," Box 194: U.S. Cavalry, 1st Regiment, SAWS.

201. Ibid.

202. Ibid.

203. "The Water Cure in the P.I.," in Gardner Notebook.

204. Ibid.

205. Ibid.

206. Arthur C. Johnson to *Rocky Mountain News*, Feb. 21, 1899, quoted in G. Hunt, "First Colorado Regiment," 235; Willis Platts Diary, Feb. 6, 1899, quoted in McEnroe, "Oregon Soldiers," 92; George Telfer to Family, Mar. 28, 1899, in Telfer and Bunnett, *Manila Envelopes*, 147.

207. Osborne quoted in Poplin, "Letters of W. Thomas Osborne," 164.

208. Osborn quoted in Roth, *Muddy Glory*, 53.

209. William Eggenberger to "Dear Mother and all," Jan. 28, 1900, Folder: "Wm Eggenberger, 1898–120, Col. K, 3rd U.S. Inf.," Box 214: U.S. Infantry, 3rd Regiment, SAWS.

210. Eggenberger to "Dear Mother and all," Mar. 25, 1901.

211. On Samar, see S. Miller, *Benevolent Assimilation*, ch. 2; Schott, *Ordeal of Samar*; and Linn, "'We Will Go Heavily Armed.'"

212. Chriss Bell Diary, Apr. 12, 1899, quoted in McEnroe, "Oregon Soldiers," 90.

213. Bell Diary, Feb. 6, 1899, quoted in ibid., 89; Albert Southwick quoted in ibid., 84; Willis Platts Diary, Feb. 23, Apr. 18, 1899, quoted in ibid., 93, 95.

214. On martial masculinity during the Spanish-Cuban American War and Philippine-American War, see Hoganson, *Fighting for American Manhood*. On the period more broadly, see Mrozek, "Habit of Victory." On "passionate" or "savage" masculinity among middle-class men, see Rotundo, *American Manhood*, ch. 10; and Higham, "Reorientation of American Culture."

215. Louis Hubbard to "My dearest Mother," Feb. 12, 1899, Folder: "Louis W. Hubbard, 1898-W-987, 1st Regt. Band, 1st S.D. Vol. Inf., Newspaper, map letters," Box 169: South Dakota Infantry, 1st Regiment, SAWS.

216. Bright quoted in Chapman, "Taking Up the White Man's Burden," 33.

217. S. B. M. Young to H. C. Corbin, Nov. 28, 1900, in Letterbook, Box 12: "Philippine Insurrection: Scattered Items Relating to Demobilization after the Spanish-American War, 1898–1902," Young Papers.

218. Wells quoted in Welch, "American Atrocities," 241; Hubbard to "My dearest Mother," Feb. 20, 1899, Folder: "Louis W. Hubbard," SAWS.

219. Osborn quoted in Roth, *Muddy Glory*, 54.

220. George Telfer to Lottie, Apr. 7, 1899, in Telfer and Bunnett, *Manila Envelopes*, 151.

221. U.S. Senate, *Trials of Courts-Martial in the Philippine Islands*, 2; Harold Kinman to Sister, Dec. 23, 1901, quoted in Linn, "'We Will Go Heavily Armed,'" 280.

222. *Modesto Bee*, May 31, 1965, quoted in Linn, "'We Will Go Heavily Armed,'" 280.

223. Testimony of Capt. David D. Porter quoted in ibid.

224. Lent, "Philippine Press," 316–18. Military censorship was openly criticized by journalists; see Martin, "Manila Censorship"; "Protest of the Newspaper Correspondents at Manila," in Ballard, *Liberty, Independence and Self-Government*, 159; and "Robert M. Collins on Otis' Censorship," in ibid., 160.

225. See Storey and Codman, *Secretary Root's Record*.

226. Quoted in Welch, *Response to Imperialism*, 136.

227. Parker quoted in Gates, *Schoolbooks and Krags*, 190–91.

228. Rawlins and Hughes quoted in Graff, *American Imperialism and the Philippine Insurrection*, 65.

229. On the attribution of racial conflict to colonized people more broadly, see Füredi, *Silent War*.

230. In 1899, General Otis created the Insurgent Records Office, later the Bureau of Insurgent Records, to translate and annotate captured documents. It was eventually headed by Capt. John Rogers Meigs Taylor, who would travel to Washington in 1901 and receive an estimated three tons of "insurgent records," which he would selectively translate for use by the War Department and imperialist senators defending the war. See Constantino, "Historical Truths from Biased Sources"; and Farrell, "Abandoned Approach to Philippine History."

231. John F. Bass, "The Philippine Revolt—Manila's Night of Terror" (dispatch of Mar. 9, 1899), *Harper's Weekly* (Apr. 22, 1899), 401; "Chicago Hears Roosevelt: Immense Throngs Greet the Vice Presidential Candidate," *New York Times*, Oct. 7, 1900, 1; *Republican Campaign Text-Book 1900*, 337–39. Sixto Lopez refuted charges of "race war" in "The Filipino Position," *Springfield Republican* (Oct. 11, 1900).

232. S. B. M. Young, "Our Soldiers in the Philippines," 1, 2, Folder: "Speech 'Our Soldiers in the Philippines,'" Box 10, Young Papers.

233. Ibid., 4.

234. Speech by Henry Cabot Lodge, May 5, 1902, 57th Cong., 1st sess., *Congressional Record* 35, 57-1 (1901–2), 5035.

235. Ibid.

236. U.S. Senate, *Charges of Cruelty, etc.*, pt. 1, 1–57.

237. Ibid., pt. 2, 1–370.

238. "Major Batson, the Macabebe Leader: Interesting Sketch of the Organizer of the First Native Filipino Soldiers in Uncle Sam's Uniform . . ." clipping, Folder: "Maj. Matthew A. Batson, 9th U.S. Cavalry, Personal/Family," Batson Papers.

239. Wheaton quoted in May, *Battle for Batangas*, 259–60.

240. Exhibit A, Letter from Frederick Funston to the Adjutant-General, Feb. 2, 1902, in U.S. Senate, *Charges of Cruelty, Etc.*, pt. 1, 3.

241. On contemporary discourse about "degeneration," see Chamberlin and Gilman, *Degeneration*; and Pick, *Faces of Degeneration*.

242. On "degeneration" in the annexation debate, see Hoganson, *Fighting for American Manhood*, ch. 8.

243. Rowland, "Fighting Life in the Philippines," "obedient fulfillment," 241, "seized," 244.

244. Ibid., "unsuspected," 243, "unaccustomed conditions," 244.

245. Ibid., "hacked," "equal," "pacification," 244, "*parts*," 246, "vermin," 244.

246. Ibid., 247.

247. Bigelow, "How to Convert a White Man," "blue-eyed," 1159, "brutal," "whole population," 1160, "gaudy," 1161.

248. Taft quoted in "The First Civil Governor," *Manila Times*, July 3, 1901, 1.

249. "Inauguration of His Excellency Governor Taft," *Manila Times*, July 5, 1901, 1.

250. "The Day We Celebrate," *Manila Times*, July 5, 1901, 4.

251. "Inauguration of His Excellency," 1.

252. On Bell's "reconcentration" policy, see May, *Battle for Batangas*, ch. 9; and Dery, "General Bell."

253. U.S. House, *Papers Relating to the Foreign Relations*, 12.

254. "Mr. Churchill on the War," *New York Evening Herald*, Dec. 9, 1900.

255. "A Boer Concentration Camp," *Public Opinion* 31, no. 18 (1901), 555. On the ways in which the Anglo-Boer War and Philippine-American War were debated in tandem, see Kramer, "Empires, Exceptions, and Anglo-Saxons."

256. J. F. Bell, "Telegraphic Circulars Issued by Brig. Gen. J. F. Bell to Station Commanders in the Provinces of Tayabas, Batangas, and Laguna," in Senate Committee on the Philippines, *Affairs in the Philippine Islands*, 1607.

257. Bell, Telegraphic Circular No. 3 (Dec. 9, 1901), 1608.

258. Ibid., 1607.

259. Proclamation, in General Orders No. 69, in U.S. Senate, *Mabini Case*, 8–9.

260. Pomeroy, "American 'Pacification,' " 438–43.

261. *Washington Post* quoted in Francisco, "First Vietnam," 18.

262. On the Philippine Constabulary, see Coats, "Philippine Constabulary, 1901–1917."

263. Coolidge, "Roosevelt Indignant," *Boston Morning Journal*, May 31, 1902; T. Roosevelt, *Address*.

264. T. Roosevelt, *Address*. Roosevelt here connected genocide and world-historical progress as did a wide variety of European and American thinkers during this period. See Lindqvist and Tate, *Exterminate All the Brutes*; and Brantlinger, *Dark Vanishings*.

265. Statement of David J. Gilmer, *Colored American*, Jan. 19, 1901, reprinted in Gatewood, *"Smoked Yankees,"* 292–93.

266. Millett and Maslowski identify 1,004 U.S. battle deaths, 3,161 U.S. deaths by noncombat causes, and 2,911 wounded during the Philippine-American War, of a total 126,468 U.S. soldiers who served. This was approximately three times the U.S. mortality rate during the Spanish-Cuban-American War. Millett and Maslowski, *For the Common Defense*, Appendix A, 653. For other estimates, see Gates, "War-Related Deaths in the Philippines."

267. On the postwar cholera epidemic, see Smallman-Raynor and Cliff, "Philippines Insurrection, Part I" and "Philippines Insurrection, Part II."

268. May, "150,000 Missing Filipinos."

269. De Bevoise, "Compromised Host."

Chapter 3

1. "Santa Cruz Bridge Open to the Public: Event Successfully Celebrated Yesterday Afternoon; Monument to American Enterprise, a Blaze of Glory, Military and Civil Represented in the Parade; American and Native Police Cheered by the Members of the American Chamber of Commerce; Pacific Oriental Trading Co. Entertains," *Manila American*, Mar. 2, 1903.

2. Ibid.

3. On Lugard and the concept of the "dual mandate," see Mamdani, *Citizen and Subject*.

4. L. Thompson, "Imperial Republic."

5. Coudert quoted in ibid., 548.

6. Lowell quoted in ibid., 550; White quoted in ibid., 551. On the Insular Cases, see Burnett and Marshall, *Foreign in a Domestic Sense*; and Kerr, *Insular Cases*.

7. Edwards, "Work of the Bureau of Insular Affairs," 239.

8. Ibid., "clearinghouse," 244, "uninterrupted," 243.

9. Ibid., 244.

10. Ibid., "government," 244, "responsible," 240. Root's statement was made in his annual report of Nov. 27, 1901.

11. *Philippine Organic Act*, 57th Cong., 1st sess. (July 1, 1902), ch. 1369, *U.S. Statutes at Large* 32: 691.

12. Ibid., 692.

13. On the debates surrounding colonialism and the civil service system, see Kramer, "Efficiency, Expertise."

14. "The Civil Service," *Report of the Philippine Commission* (1900), "very difficult," 1.23; De la Torre, *History of the Philippine Civil Service*, "competitive," "regulated," 41; *Report of the Philippine Commission* (1900), 1:112–13.

15. See table in De la Torre, *History of the Philippine Civil Service*, 47.

16. William H. Taft, in Senate Committee on the Philippines, *Affairs in the Philippine Islands*, "venturesome," 9, "gentlemen," 59.

17. David P. Barrows to [?] Bailey, Jan. 9, 1902, Folder: "Jan.–Nov. 1901," Correspondence Box 1, David P. Barrows Papers, Bancroft Library, University of California, Berkeley.

18. *Manila Sunday Sun* quoted in De la Torre, *History of the Philippine Civil Service*, 50. For involuntary terminations, see table in ibid., 65; Mrs. Taft quoted in ibid., 50; officials quoted in ibid., "spectacle," 51, "rumor of injustice," 53.

19. On the "Thomasites" and the U.S. colonial school system, see May, *Social Engineering*, chs. 5–7; Hollnsteiner and Ick, *Bearers of Benevolence*; and Pecson and Hollnsteiner, *Tales of the American Teachers*.

20. Adeline Knapp, "A Notable Educational Experiment," in Gleason, *Log of the "Thomas,"* "white ship," "carry," 11, "chasm," 11–12, "people," 11.

21. There were extensive social and ideological exchanges between U.S. schoolteachers and Protestant missionaries in the Philippines. On the latter, see Clymer, *Protestant Missionaries*.

22. "Notes of the Voyage," in Gleason, *Log of the "Thomas,"* "pioneer spirit," 49; Knapp, "Notable Educational Experiment," "armed force," 12.

23. Aggressive public health campaigns directed at "regeneration" as well as sanitary order would become some of the colonial state's defining projects. See Ileto, "Cholera"; and the work of Warwick Anderson, especially "Colonial Pathologies," "Immunities of Empire," and "Excremental Colonialism."

24. Moses, *Unofficial Letters*, "sensational," 329, "all parts," "almost," "prosperous," 323.

25. On the disease crisis that accompanied the war, see De Bevoise, "Compromised Host."

26. On the structure of local governance, see Hutchcroft, "Colonial Masters."

27. On early Federalista-American collaboration, see Cullinane, *Ilustrado Politics*, chs. 2–3; and Paredes, "Origins of National Politics."

28. Bellairs, *As It Is in the Philippines*, 24; Taft quoted in Pomeroy, *American Neo-Colonialism*, "coldness," "recognition," 140. On the commission offices, see Minger, "Taft, MacArthur," 313.

29. Report of Maj. Cornelius Gardener to the Civil Governor of the Philippines, Dec. 16, 1901, in Senate Committee on the Philippines, *Affairs in the Philippine Islands*, 885; Bellairs, *As It Is in the Philippines*, "reins," 24–25.

30. Taft, "Duty of Americans"; Sedition Act, in "First Annual Report of the Secretary of Finance and Justice to the Philippine Commission from October 15, 1901 to September 30, 1902," in *Report of the Philippine Commission* (1902), 2:693.

31. Bellairs, *As It Is in the Philippines*, "centre," 208, "distinctively," 209, "qualifications," 210, "scarcely," 215–16. On club life in a nostalgic vein, see Gleeck, *Over Seventy-Five Years* and *American Institutions in the Philippines*.

32. Taft, in Senate Committee on the Philippines, *Affairs in the Philippine Islands*, 270. The double reportage of this fragment calls for caution: Taft had an interest in representing Filipino fears that his regime could address; the *ilustrado* had an interest in revealing himself to be a suitable mediator between Taft and the Filipino masses. The incident does, however, suggest the Philippine Commission's sense of the kinds of popular suspicions to which it was responding.

33. Bellairs, *As It Is in the Philippines*, 160–61.

34. On *El Renacimiento*, see Cullinane, *Ilustrado Politics*, 89–96; and Valenzuela, *History of Journalism. Muling Pagsilang* was the title of the Tagalog-language edition.

35. On the "Seditious Plays," see Rafael, "White Love"; and Lapeña-Bonifacio, *"Seditious" Tagalog Playwrights*. Fernandez, introduction, "unlawful purposes," xv–xvi.

36. Fernandez, introduction, xiv.

37. On the experiences and perceptions of white women in the Philippines during this period, see Rafael, "Colonial Domesticity."

38. Stevens, *Yester-days in the Philippines*, 219.

39. Worcester, *Philippine Islands and Their People*, 87.

40. Ibid., "lump," 472, "eighty," 473, "amiable," 482.

41. *Outlook* quoted in Sullivan, *Exemplar of Americanism*, 34.

42. Sullivan, *Exemplar of Americanism*, 36–39.

43. "A Philippines Commission," *New York Times*, Jan. 17, 1899, 1.

44. On the regime's scientific work, see Van Hise, "American Contributions."

45. Rizal quoted in Schumacher, *Propaganda Movement*, 240; Taft, *Duty of Americans in the Philippines*.

46. On Pardo, see "T. H. Pardo de Tavera," in Manuel and Manuel, *Dictionary of Philippine Biography*, 1.317–47. On the Pardo family, see Paredes, "Ilustrado Legacy."

47. On Pardo's ideas on Philippine modernity, see Gaerlan, "Pursuit of Modernity."

48. Taft quoted in Pomeroy, *American Neo-Colonialism*, 141; Report of Maj. Cornelius Gardener, in Senate Committee on the Philippines, *Affairs in the Philippine Islands*, 884; David P. Barrows to Bernard Moses, Dec. 7, 1901, National Archives and Records Administration (NARA), Record Group (RG) 350, Stack 150, Entry 5A, #3833 (Box 368), 1.

49. *Report of the Philippine Commission*, 1900–1916.

50. "Philippine Report."

51. Griffiths, "Philippine Insurrection," 497.

52. "Will What Visiting Congressman Saw Influence Future Legislation?" *Manila American* 1, no. 39 (Oct. 9, 1901).

53. Ibid.

54. Moses, *Unofficial Letters*, "more 'pacifying,'" 343, "difficult to make," 355, "shyness," 87.

55. LeRoy, "Race Prejudice," 101–2. LeRoy remains an intriguing and understudied figure. For a celebratory biography, see Gleeck, *Nine Years to Make a Difference*.

56. LeRoy, "Race Prejudice," 102.

57. Moses, *Unofficial Letters*, "table etiquette," 79, "society speeches," "distant pueblos," 232, "too offhand," 215, "obliged to drink," 29, "gracious manner," "always flattering," 157.

58. Ibid., "compelling," 42, "turning or turned," 86, "insurrecto general," 126, "bolo makers," 66–67, "rumors of uprisings," 47; "Socials in the Gate City of the Orient: Golf and Tennis and Drives Will Be Popular Fall Amusements," *Freedom* 3, no. 19 (Oct. 9, 1899), "attempted insurrection," 6.

59. Moses, *Unofficial Letters*, 47.

60. Ibid., 124.

61. Ibid., "Goddess of Liberty," "an interior town," 124, paraphrasing Taft, 124–25, "patriotic songs," 38–39.

62. Michael Adas argues that the colonial state's evolutionary time lines and scientistic ethos are a linear precursor to subsequent "modernization" theory. Adas, "Improving on the Civilizing Mission?"

63. LeRoy, *Philippine Life*, 99.

64. Bellairs, *As It Is in the Philippines*, 219; Taft, in Senate Committee on the Philippines, *Affairs in the Philippine Islands*, 89; LeRoy, "Race Prejudice," 104; Morrison quoted in Minger, "Taft, MacArthur," 321–22.

65. LeRoy, "Race Prejudice," 100. This formation resembles the broader, and somewhat later, development of a "new racial etiquette" in the Anglo-American colonial world that sought to mask overtly racial expressions in order to preserve colonial hierarchies, described in Füredi, *Silent War*.

66. LeRoy, "Race Prejudice," 100–101.

67. Ibid., "studied attitude," 109, "upon force," 105.

68. Dauncey, *Englishwoman in the Philippines*, "colour-distinction," 62, "Equality," 13, "friendly," 62, "heavily fined," 297.

69. Taft quoted in Alfonso, "Taft's Early Views," "ambitious," "tricky," 54, "magnificent liars," 52, "perquisite," 54.

70. On the construction of the "cacique," see Ileto, "Orientalism and the Study of Philippine Politics," in *Knowing America's Colony.*

71. Taft quoted in ibid., 53; Barrows, Note on "Manila in 1901," Aug. 9, 1901, Folder: "Vol. 13. Notes/Trip to China & Japan/Aug. 4th to Sept. 1901 [diary]," Box 2, Barrows Papers; Maud Huntley Jenks to Family, Aug. 10, 1902, in M. Jenks, *Death Stalks the Philippine Wilds,* 25.

72. Riggs, *Filipino Drama, 1905,* table of contents.

73. Ibid., "cohesiveness," "no Filipino literature," 1, "genuine," 6, "native character," 20.

74. Ibid., "bleakness," 1, "mental nakedness," 10, "educated men," "emotional," 14, "involutions," 15, "greater value," 49 n. 14, "defects," 49, "evolution," 23, "pagan," 36, "services," 33, "hardy," 27.

75. Taft quoted in Alfonso, "Taft's Early Views," "unfitness," 58, "training," 52.

76. On social-evolutionary theory in the late nineteenth century, see Stocking, *Race, Culture and Evolution.*

77. On evolutionary thought of this kind in U.S. colonial education, see Ileto, "The Philippine Revolution and U.S. Colonial Education," in *Knowing America's Colony.*

78. On educational institutions' response to perceived demands for new "imperial" knowledge and its limits, see Ng, "Knowledge for Empire."

79. On the Anglo-Saxonist ideological context for U.S. colonial state-building, see Kramer, "Empires, Exceptions, and Anglo-Saxons."

80. E. Thompson, "Exhibit C," 262.

81. "Filipino Students in the United States," in *Census of the Philippine Islands,* 3:669. On the *pensionados,* see Alidio, "Between Civilizing Mission and Ethnic Assimilation," especially ch. 3.

82. Taft quoted in Salamanca, *Filipino Reaction to American Rule,* 78–79; Sutherland, *Not by Might,* 28.

83. See, for example, Pardo de Tavera, Legarda, and De Luzuriaga, "Filipino Views of American Rule."

84. Pardo de Tavera, "Filipino Soul," "preserve," 171, "trustee," 178. The speech was first published in *El Renacimiento,* May 17, 1906.

85. Pardo de Tavera, "Filipino Soul," "race-inferiority," 174, "striking example," 184.

86. Ibid., "new spirit," 175, "Filipinos educated," "Philippinism," "respect the race," 177, "oneness," 186, "heterogeneity," "fellowship," 185.

87. R. Taylor, "Disposition of the Philippine Islands," 48–49.

88. Ibid.

89. Ibid., 50.

90. In employing the concept of the "bifurcated state," I draw on Mahmood Mamdani's conceptualization of the African colonial state in *Citizen and Subject.*

91. The term "non-Christian" was sometimes applied only to animists and sometimes encompassed Muslims as well; the Bureau of Non-Christian Tribes, for example, sponsored ethnographic research on both animists and Muslims.

92. Moses, *Unofficial Letters,* 344.

93. Keesing and Keesing, *Taming Philippine Headhunters*, "dual task," 26, "dependency," 94.

94. On continuities and discontinuities between Spanish and U.S. legal codes, see W. Thompson, *Introduction of American Law*. On the Taft mission, see Alvarez, "Purely a Business Matter." On the religious politics of education, see Raftery, "Textbook Wars."

95. LeRoy, *Philippine Life*, 177; Taft quoted in *Census of the Philippine Islands*, 1:31.

96. On the Bureau of Non-Christian Tribes, see Kramer, "Pragmatic Empire"; and Hutterer, "Dean Worcester and Philippine Anthropology."

97. Act No. 253, "An Act Creating a Bureau of Non-Christian Tribes for the Philippine Islands," enacted Oct. 2, 1901, NARA, RG 350, Stack 150, Entry 5A, #3833 (Box 368).

98. Worcester, "Non-Christian Tribes," 791; David P. Barrows, "The Peoples of the Philippines," in *Census of the Philippine Islands*, 1:453–54.

99. Barrows, "Peoples of the Philippines," 453.

100. Pardo de Tavera, *Etimologia de los Nombres*, 3–4 (translation from the original Spanish by the author).

101. Pardo de Tavera to José Tupas (Pasig), Nov. 12, 1901, Correspondence Books, Trinidad H. Pardo de Tavera Papers, Rizal Library, Ateneo de Manila University, Quezon City.

102. Root quoted in H. Fry, *History of the Mountain Province*, 16. On Barrows, see Clymer, "Humanitarian Imperialism."

103. David P. Barrows to Dean C. Worcester, Apr. 7, 1902, Folder: "Jan.–Sept. 1902," Box 1: "Letters by Barrows, 1892–1910," Barrows Papers. On the reservation system, see David P. Barrows, "Report of the Chief of the Bureau of Non-Christian Tribes for Year Ending Aug. 31, 1902," in *Report of the Philippine Commission* (1903), 1:684. On the debates surrounding the Dawes Act and Indian reform, see Hoxie, *Final Promise*.

104. Township Act quoted in H. Fry, *History of the Mountain Province*, 41.

105. The subprovinces were Benguet, Amburayan, Lepanto, Bontoc, Kalinga, Apayao, and Ifugao. Ibid., 51.

106. Bartlett quoted in H. Fry, *History of the Mountain Province*, 52.

107. Worcester quoted in ibid., 52.

108. Forbes quoted in ibid., 86–87.

109. Abinales, "American Colonial State." On Moro Province, see also Gowing, *Mandate in Moroland*.

110. On accusations of slavery in the southern Philippines, see, for example, Salman, *Embarrassment of Slavery*, pt. 3.

111. Quoted in Abinales, "American Colonial State," 55.

112. On Bud Dajo, see Gowing, *Mandate in Moroland*, 160–66. Wood and Roosevelt quoted in ibid., 162.

113. On the census, see Rafael, "White Love"; Vergara, *Displaying Filipinos*, ch. 4; and Gealogo, "Beyond the Numbers."

114. *Census of the Philippine Islands*, 1:11.

115. Ibid., 16.

116. Ibid., 17.

117. Ibid., 19.

118. Ibid., "army," 14, "assailants," "fact," 22, "detested," 14.

119. Ibid., "notoriously," 13, "attempts," 22, "sultans," "feared," "illustrate," 25.

120. Ibid., 35–36.

121. Ibid., 39–40.

122. Ibid., "recognition," 11, "not inhabited," 12, "wide difference," 23, "dealing," 13, "caution," "instructed," "hostile," 23.

123. Ibid., "dwelt," "sincerity," 36, "guidance," 40.

124. Ibid., 47–48.

Chapter 4

1. Daniel Folkmar, "Some Philippine Physical Types, Manila, 1903," Folder 758: "Philippines, Folkmar mss.," Box 66: "Paris Exposition, Philippine Islands," National Anthropological Archives, U.S. Natural History Museum. The fact that Folkmar crossed out the term "tribes" and replaced it with "peoples" in his original draft suggests the ongoing debates on the relevance of the term to the Philippines, as discussed in the previous chapter.

2. Ibid. The result of Folkmar's investigation was his *Album of Philippine Types*. The volume was available for sale at the exposition but sold poorly.

3. In his pathbreaking work on world's fairs and racial ideology, Robert Rydell sees the expositions as hegemonic efforts by domestic U.S. elites to promote seamless visions of U.S. racial and imperial superiority before American audiences; see *All the World's a Fair*. In this chapter, I attempt to examine both the colonial agendas that informed the making of an exposition display, as well as the tensions and misreadings that characterized the communication of racial and imperial messages. For other treatments of the Philippine exhibit, see Vostral, "Imperialism on Display"; and Vergara, *Displaying Filipinos*, ch. 6.

4. Hoffman, "Philippine Exhibit," 119.

5. On the McGee era at the Smithsonian, see Hinsley, *Smithsonian and the American Indian*.

6. W J McGee to S. P. Langley, Sept. 7, 1898, McGee Letterbooks (microfilm), National Anthropological Archives, National Museum of Natural History, Smithsonian Institution; J. W. Powell to S. P. Langley, Jan. 28, 1899, ibid. On the broader response of scholarly institutions to the advent of colonialism, see Ng, "Knowledge for Empire."

7. F. F. Hilder to J. D. Pennybacker, Mar. 25, 1899, McGee Letterbooks. For correspondence on McGee's arrangements between the Smithsonian and the Pan-American Exposition, see Series 14, Box 52, Record Unit 70, ERSI.

8. J. B. Guthrie to F. W. True, Jan. 3, 1900, ERSI, Folder: "E–G."

9. On lack of mobility, see P. L. Sherman to F. F. Hilder, May 31, 1900, ERSI, Folder: "P. L. Sherman"; Sherman to Hilder, Feb. 15, 1901, ibid., "bad time"; Memorandum by F. F. Hilder, ERSI, Folder: "Exhibits," "great danger"; Sherman to Hilder, Nov. 13, 1900, ERSI, Folder: "P. L. Sherman," "sorry to hear."

10. Hilder to F. W. True, Mar. 31, 1900, ERSI, Folder: "H–J," "war relics"; Sherman to True, Mar. 9, 1901, ERSI, Folder: "P. L. Sherman," "curio crazy"; Sherman to Hilder, May 31, 1900, ERSI, Folder: "H–J," "more expensive"; Sherman to Hilder, May 14, 1900, ibid., "every officer."

11. Hoffman, "Philippine Exhibit," "upwards," 119; Memorandum by J. B. Guthrie, quoted in Sherman to Arthur MacArthur, May 17, 1900, ERSI, Folder: "P. L. Sherman," "trophies"; Hilder to True, May 17, 1900, ERSI, Folder: "H–J."

12. On the acquisition of skulls, see Sherman to Hilder, Apr. 30, 1900, ERSI, Folder: "H–J"; Sherman to Hilder, May 14, 1900, ibid., "eight skulls," "Manila or suburbs"; Sherman to Hilder, Nov. 13, 1900, ERSI, Folder: "P. L. Sherman," "ought to be done."

13. Hoffman, "Philippine Exhibit," 119–20. On the Pan-American Exposition, see Rydell, *All the World's a Fair*.

14. Spahr, "Philippine Educational Exhibit."

15. Taft quoted in "The Philippine Display: To Be One of the Greatest Features of the St. Louis World's Fair," *World's Fair Bulletin*, May 1902, 20. On the initial appropriation, see Niederlein, "Brief Chronological Sketch," 9.

16. Taft quoted in "Philippine Display," 21.

17. "The World's Fair Abroad: Diplomatic Commissioners for the Louisiana Purchase Exposition," *World's Fair Bulletin*, Sept. 1901, 21.

18. On exposition culture and Euro-American colonialism, see Mitchell, *Colonising Egypt*; Coombes, *Reinventing Africa*; Greenhalgh, *Ephemeral Vistas*; and Yengoyen, "Culture, Ideology and World's Fairs." On connections between imperialism and popular culture more generally, in the British context, see Mackenzie, *Imperialism and Popular Culture*.

19. "World's Fair Abroad," "invited men," 21; "Notifying the Nations: Plans to Induce Foreign Nations to Take an Interest in the St. Louis Fair," *World's Fair Bulletin*, Aug. 1901, 17. On the growing U.S. influence in Asia, see Thomson, Stanley, and Perry, *Sentimental Imperialists*; and Van Alstyne, *Rising American Empire*.

20. "Departure of John Barrett: Commissioner-General to Asia and Australia," *World's Fair Bulletin*, Apr. 1902, 19; "World's Fair Abroad," "recognized authority," 24. On Barrett's diplomatic career, see Prisco, *John Barrett*.

21. "Asia at St. Louis: Review of the Work of Commissioner-General Barrett," *World's Fair Bulletin*, July 1903, 10–11.

22. On the Philadelphia Commercial Museum, see Conn, "Epistemology for Empire."

23. "Dr. W. P. Wilson, Special Commissioner for the Philippine Government," *World's Fair Bulletin*, Oct. 1902, 23; "Dr. Gustavo Niederlein, Special Commissioner of Philippine Islands for the World's Fair," ibid., 30.

24. Niederlein, "Outline of the Proposed Exhibit," 24–25.

25. Niederlein, "Exhibit Q," "requesting them," 407, "order all men," 409.

26. Ibid., 408.

27. Niederlein, "Brief Chronological Sketch," 11.

28. *Circular Letter of Governor Taft*, 22–23.

29. Ibid., 16.

30. Niederlein, "Brief Chronological Sketch," 12.

31. William N. Swarthout, "A Descriptive Story of the Philippine Exhibit," *World's Fair Bulletin*, June 1904, 49.

32. Niederlein, "Exhibit Q," 408.

33. Professor Lyon quoted in ibid., 406.

34. Ibid.

35. Ibid., 409.

36. Niederlein, "Brief Chronological Sketch," 14. For a description of the ceremonies and initial exhibits, see "Permanent Museum: Opened in the Presence of the Governor and Commission," *Manila Times*, Feb. 24, 1903, 1.

37. Niederlein, "Brief Chronological Sketch," 14.

38. Niederlein, "Exhibit Q," 409–11.

39. Ibid.

40. David Francis to the Secretary of War, Dec. 15, 1902, NARA, RG 350, Stack 150, Entry 5A—General Classified Files #7395 (Box 494).

41. George Davis to Adjutant General, Feb. 7, 1903, ibid.; Taft to Secretary of War, Feb. 12, 1903, ibid. On the Scouts' participation at the fair, see Laurie, "Oddity of Empire."

42. Davis to Adjutant General, Feb. 7, 1903.

43. Col. E. J. McClernand to Clarence Edwards, June 13, 1903, NARA, RG 350, Stack 150, Entry 5A—General Classified Files #7395 (Box 494).

44. *Circular Letter of Governor Taft*, 6.

45. Cullinane, *Ilustrado Politics*, 104–5.

46. On the display of "Igorots," see Vaughan, "Ogling Igorots."

47. Niederlein, "Exhibit Q," "furnish the student," 415, "feasibility," 411.

48. Mataas, "¿Otra Exposición del 'Retiro'?" (translation from the original Spanish by the author).

49. Ibid.

50. Ibid.

51. Mataas, "¿Otra Exposición del 'Retiro'?"

52. "World's Fair Abroad," 21.

53. Quoted in "Dr. Gustavo Niederlein," 30.

54. "Philippine Exhibit Opens with Native Parade," *St. Louis Post-Dispatch*, June 18, 1904, 7.

55. Taft quoted in *World's Fair Bulletin*, June 1904, 20.

56. Hale quoted in "Big Chiefs Join in Celebrating Fall of Manila," *St. Louis Post-Dispatch*, Aug. 14, 1904, 1; "U.S. Generals Meet Old Foes Filipino Day" and "Filipinos See Impressive Array," *St. Louis Post-Dispatch*, Aug. 13, 1904, 1.

57. "Big Chiefs," "showed their delight," 1; "U.S. Generals Meet," "Filipino students," 1; "Big Chiefs," "stockades," 1; "U.S. Generals Meet," "former enemies," 1; "Big Chiefs," "Felicitate[d]," 1.

58. "Scouts Will Give Real Sample of Philippine Fight," *St. Louis Post-Dispatch*, Aug. 4, 1904, 15.

59. Quoted in Laurie, "Oddity of Empire," 52.

60. *St. Louis Post-Dispatch*, Apr. 18, 1902, quoted in Laurie, "Oddity of Empire," 52; Munro quoted in ibid.

61. "Filipino Students Come with a Yell," *St. Louis Post-Dispatch*, Aug. 5, 1904, 8. On the *pensionados* at the fair, see Alidio, "Between Civilizing Mission and Ethnic Assimilation," ch. 3.

62. "Filipino Students Come with a Yell."

63. W. P. Wilson quoted in "Igorrotes in Dress Parade Omit Clothes," *St. Louis Post-Dispatch*, June 19, 1904, 4.

64. Niederlein quoted in "Dr. Gustavo Niederlein," 30. For a map of the proposed layout, see "Ground Plan for Philippine Village, World's Fair Grounds," in John Lebens, "Philippine Exhibit: Forty Acres Covered with Native Buildings," *World's Fair Bulletin*, Oct. 1903, 7.

65. Francis, *Universal Exposition of 1904*, 567.

66. Allen, *Pilgrimage of Mary Commandery No. 36*, "Filipino exhibition," 178; Dauncey, *Englishwoman in the Philippines*, 137; Philibert quoted in Clevenger, "Indescribably Grand," 86; Schneiderhahn quoted in Clevenger, "Indescribably Grand," "Considered," 70, "delight," 50, "proved," 70.

67. Holley, *Samantha at the St. Louis Exposition*, "sings," 280, "complexioned," 275, "doorstep," 276, "disgraceful," 276–77.

68. "Philippine Exposition" (guide booklet), NARA, RG 350, Stack 150, Entry 5A, #8753 (Box 530); Newell, "Philippine Peoples," 5128; Bennitt, *History of the Louisiana Purchase Exposition*, 465.

69. For an excellent collection of wartime political cartoons that surveys this imagery, see Ignacio et al., *Forbidden Book*.

70. George H. Allen, *Among the Filipinos: A Story for Very Young Folks, Older Folks Will Not Care to Read It*, Box: "Polish," Warshaw Collection of Business Americana, National Museum of American History, Smithsonian Institution. My thanks to Fath Ruffins for her assistance in finding this source.

71. "Asia at St. Louis," *World's Fair Bulletin*, July 1903, 11. On the class segmentation of popular culture more generally in this period, see Levine, *Highbrow/Lowbrow*.

72. "World's Fair Abroad," "tended to make," 24; "Objects to Proximity of Saloon," *St. Louis Globe-Democrat*, May 8, 1904, "unsightly," 11; McGee quoted in "The Uncivilized Races: Will Be Better Represented at St. Louis World's Fair than Ever Heretofore," *World's Fair Bulletin*, Sept. 1901, 26.

73. "Igorrotes in Dress Parade," 4; Mataas, "¿Otra Exposición del 'Retiro'?"

74. Clarence Edwards to William H. Taft, June 22, 1913, NARA, RG 350, Stack 150, Entry 5A, #7395 (Box 494).

75. "All Roads Led to Filipinos, Thoughts of Visitors Thronged about and through the Reservation All Day," *St. Louis Post-Dispatch*, May 1, 1904, 6.

76. "Big Rush to See Igorrotes Unclad," *St. Louis Post-Dispatch*, June 26, 1904.

77. "Minstrel Show Shadows Pike," *St. Louis Post-Dispatch*, Sept. 20, 1904, 3. For revenue figures, see "Philippine Exhibit at the World's Fair, St. Louis," in *Report of the Philippine Commission* (1906), 1:28.

78. "Scanty Attire of the Igorrotes Shocks Chief Big Horn and Wife," *St. Louis*

Globe-Democrat, May 2, 1904, "first exchange," 3; "Igorrotes Suffer Social Setback, Compelled to Decline Invitation to Ice Cream Festival at Borromeo Church," *St. Louis Post-Dispatch*, June 10, 1904, 11; "Oh, Say! But Won't This Be the Limit? Visiting Manufacturers Will Partake of an 'Igorrote Breakfast' This Morning," *St. Louis Post-Dispatch*, Aug. 7, 1904, "dogwood blossoms," 6.

79. Sutherland, "Philippine Exposition," 14; "Publicity and Exploitation," in *Report of the Exposition Board*, p. 33.

80. The St. Louis fair prided itself specifically on its display of "processes" rather than just finished goods. See "Exposition of Processes: How the Louisiana Purchase Will Differ from Other World's Fairs," *World's Fair Bulletin*, Aug. 1901, 17.

81. Newell, "Philippine Peoples," 5130; Sutherland, "Philippine Exposition," 14; "Filipino Students Come with a Yell," 8.

82. Dauncey, *Englishwoman in the Philippines*, 137.

83. "Called 'Savages,' Now Visayan Girls Won't Go to School," *St. Louis Post-Dispatch*, Aug. 20, 1904, 1.

84. "Filipino Youths Enjoying Jolly Student Life Here," *St. Louis Post-Dispatch*, Aug. 10, 1904, pt. 2, 1.

85. "Igorots and Americans," *Filipino* 1, no. 2 (Mar. 1906): 4.

86. Nepomuceno quoted in "Filipinos as Preposterously Misrepresented," *St. Louis Post-Dispatch*, July 19, 1904, 1. For a biography of Nepomuceno, see Ferguson and Hardeman, *Brief Biography*, 7.

87. "Filipinos as Preposterously Misrepresented," 1.

88. Ibid. On tensions between the Federalistas and the commission over tax reform, see Stanley, *Nation in the Making*, ch. 5.

89. Legarda quoted in "Filipino Exhibit Fulfills Object, Fellow Commissioner of Vicente Nepomuceno Says He Greatly Exaggerated Conditions," *St. Louis Post-Dispatch*, July 20, 1904, 9.

90. "Filipino Students Come with a Yell," 8; "St. Louis Color Line Problem at the Fair: Filipino Soldiers Aspire to Figure in Society," *St. Louis Post-Dispatch*, July 3, 1904 (Sunday magazine), 2.

91. "St. Louis Color Line Problem," 2.

92. Ibid. While this was only the board's reported response, it is also telling that the board apparently placed no limits on Scout or Constabulary fraternization during the fair prior to the outbreak of violence.

93. On racial politics in St. Louis, see Christensen, "Race Relations in St. Louis"; Bourgois, "If You're Not Black You're White"; and "Proposes Bureau for Negro Races: Vexatious Fair Question," *St. Louis Globe-Democrat*, June 2, 1904, 3. On Jim Crow, race, gender, and sex, see J. Hall, "'Mind That Burns'"; and Gilmore, *Gender and Jim Crow*.

94. "St. Louis Color Line Problem," 2.

95. "Police Separate Filipinos and White Women, Brown Scouts Are Forbidden to Pass through Gate," *St. Louis Post-Dispatch*, July 17, 1904, 8. This was not the end of violence relating to the Philippine Exposition. On a July knife-fight in the exposition's "Luzon Café," see "White Man Is Fatally Stabbed by Filipinos, in Battle between Constabulary and Attaches of Luzon Cafe," *St. Louis Post-Dispatch*, July 24,

1904, 1. On the October murder of a young woman by her jealous boyfriend for corresponding with a departed Philippine Scout, see "She Died for Love of Filipino Soldier," *St. Louis Post-Dispatch*, Oct. 3, 1904, 1.

96. "Igorrotes to Stay It Out, War Department However Is Worried about the Slump in Paid Attendance," *St. Louis Post-Dispatch*, Nov. 6, 1904, "very much disappointed," 1; A. L. Lawshe to C. E. Edwards, Feb. 17, 1905, NARA, RG 350, Stack 150, Entry 5A, #10076 (Box 598); W. P. Wilson to Edwards, Feb. 17, 1905, ibid.

97. "Fleeing Disgrace, Soldier Captain Hints at Death," *St. Louis Post-Dispatch*, Sept. 13, 1904, 1.

98. Edwards quoted in "Philippine Show Has Cost $600,000," *St. Louis Post-Dispatch*, Nov. 18, 1904, 4; "Filipino Houses for Wealthy Only, Philippine Exhibits at the World's Fair to Be Sold by Government Agents," *St. Louis Post-Dispatch*, Nov. 2, 1904, "pictures and statuary," 5.

99. Contract between the exposition board and the American Museum of Natural History, Jan. 12, 1905, Box 69, Folder 2: "Lists of Specimens and Objects Collected from Exhibit, 1903–6," ERSI.

100. Merton Miller, Appendix M: "Report of the Ethnological Survey," *Report of the Philippine Commission* (1905), 2:422.

101. On commercial exploitation of Igorots after the exposition, "Ogling Igorots."

102. On the National Geographic Society in the broader context of U.S. geography, see Schulten, *Geographical Imagination in America*.

103. Grosvenor, *National Geographic Society*, 43.

104. Grosvenor, "Revelation of the Filipinos"; Taft, "Philippines," 361. Taft's address was delivered before the society on May 5, 1905.

Chapter 5

1. On the Lake Mohonk Conference, see Burgess, "Lake Mohonk Conferences."

2. M. Kalaw, "Filipino Youth," "rising generation," 158, "no common aims," 160, "thoughts," 158, "compact," "dissemination," "national feelings," 159, "animated," 160.

3. Ibid., "battle-cry," 160, following quotes, 161.

4. Partridge, "America as Seen by a Filipino," 18–19.

5. Ibid., 19–20.

6. Ibid., 21.

7. On the crisis, see Cullinane, *Ilustrado Politics*, chs. 4–5; and Paredes, "Origins of National Politics."

8. H. Wilson, *Reconcentration in the Philippines*, 3.

9. On the corruption case, see Golay, *Face of Empire*, 95.

10. "La Teoría de Baker," *El Renacimiento*, Mar. 3, 1902 (translation from the original Spanish by the author).

11. "La Concentración en Kabite," *El Renacimiento*, June 30, 1905, 1 (translation from the original Spanish by the author).

12. H. Wilson, *Reconcentration in the Philippines*, "abuses," 3, "war measure," 4–5, "evidences," 7, "Cuba," 7–8, "recent result," 8, "conceptions," 10, "idleness," "destitute," 11.

13. Parsons, "American Snobbishness in the Philippines," 332. See also J. Jenks, "Some Difficulties, 88.

14. LeRoy, "Conditions in the Philippines To-Day," "lost ground," "displaying," 103, "proportion," 101, "dependent," 100, "patience," 102, "getting hold," 101, "sympathetic contact," 99, "concessions," 101.

15. J. Jenks, "Some Difficulties," 88–89.

16. Horne, "Race from Power"; Gallicchio, *African American Encounter*, 13–16.

17. Elliott, *Philippines to the End*, 410. On Japan as a threat to white supremacy, see Horne, "Race from Power."

18. W. E. B. Du Bois quoted in Gallicchio, *African-American Encounter*, 8–9.

19. "Ante la Guerra," *El Renacimiento*, Feb. 10, 1904, 1 (translation from the original Spanish by the author). On the School of Law message, see Goodman, "Problem of Philippine Independence," 169.

20. Forbes quoted in Goodman, "Problem of Philippine Independence," 188 n. 18. See also Goodman, "General Artemio Ricarte and Japan."

21. Streible, "Race and Reception."

22. Pedro Quinto, "El bofetón de Reno," *Renacimiento Filipino* 1, no. 2 (July 14, 1910), "given over," 16–17; "A través de siete días," *Renacimiento Filipino* 1, no. 2 (July 14, 1910), "punches thrown," 21 (translations from the original Spanish by the author).

23. Quinto, "El bofetón de Reno," 17.

24. Jenista, "Conflict with the Assembly," 80.

25. On the emergence of the Nacionalista-American bloc, see Cullinane, *Ilustrado Politics*, chs. 6–11; and McCoy, "Quezon's Commonwealth."

26. Ileto, "Orators and the Crowd"; Osmeña, *Discurso Pronunciado*, 3–4.

27. Osmeña, *Discurso Pronunciado*, 5–6.

28. Taft, "Inauguration of the Philippine Assembly," 85.

29. Ibid., "into the hands," 90, "sullenness," 86, "agitation," 88, "educational process," 86.

30. Ibid., "ladronism," 89, "dependence," 87, "numerous," 92, "qualifications," "useful," "franchise," 90.

31. Ibid., "intervals," 105, "emphatically," "execration," "irreconcilables," 103, "neglect," "responsibility," 105.

32. Artigas y Cuerva, *Glorias Nacionales*, 5–6 (translations from the original Spanish by the author). On Artigas, see Manuel and Manuel, *Dictionary of Philippine Biography*, 1.68–79.

33. Artigas y Cuerva, *Glorias Nacionales*, 7; Stangl, "Filipino Nationality," 49. Stangl appears to have been a German living in Manila and working as a pharmacist, having published a 1910 guide entitled "Elementos de farmacia."

34. Stangl, "Filipino Nationality," "forget," "splendid," "perfect," 49, "low German," "fire," "break," 50.

35. Ibid., "speech," "national," 50, "district," 50–51, "exotic," 51.

36. Ibid., 51.

37. "Panteón de Filipinos Ilustres," *El Renacimiento*, Jan. 14, 1905, 1 (translation

from the original Spanish by the author); Tuohy, *Albúm Histórico*; Artigas y Cuerva, *Galería de Filipinos Ilustres* (translation from the original Spanish by the author).

38. Forbes, "What Had Best Be Done," 120. On Forbes, see Stanley, "William Cameron Forbes." For a celebratory account, see Spector, "W. Cameron Forbes." On Forbes as governor-general, see Gleeck, *American Governors-General*.

39. Forbes, *Philippine Islands*, 1:387. The regime's hill station at Baguio was exemplary in this regard. See Reed, *City of Pines*.

40. Jackson, *Representative Men of the Philippines*, editor's note.

41. Forbes, *Philippine Islands*, "immense amount," 1:176, "rarely portray," 215, "educational," 334; Forbes, "What Had Best Be Done," "model and refine," 117; Forbes, "Decade of American Rule," "step by step," 208; Forbes, *Philippine Islands*, "advanced," 1:442.

42. Forbes, *Philippine Islands*, 1:455.

43. Ibid., 2:535.

44. Ibid., 166–67.

45. Forbes, "Decade of American Rule," 205–6. On similar discourses throughout Southeast Asia, see Alatas, *Myth of the Lazy Native*.

46. Forbes, *Philippine Islands*, "less offensive," 1:370, "not a single," 370–71, "earnest effort," 371, "freely used," 380, "always suspect," 380 n. 1, "great benefit," "appalling," 341.

47. Ibid., "surplus," 495, on Corregidor, 490, "furniture," "fifty per cent," 495, "suffered," "private enterprises," 496.

48. Ibid., "relieve," "beautiful," 384, "high favor," 385, "stripped," "escape," 386, "mortality," 385, "road work," 383–84.

49. Lobingier, "Peacekeepers," 313. On similar gendered political tropes in the context of British India, see Sinha, *Colonial Masculinity*.

50. Forbes, *Philippine Islands*, 1:518.

51. Ibid., 213.

52. Rivers, "Maintenance of Order," 128.

53. Cromer quoted in ibid., 130.

54. Lobingier, "Peacekeepers," 314. See also Forbes, *Philippine Islands*, 1:213; and Rivers, "Maintenance of Order," 128–30.

55. Rivers, "Maintenance of Order," 130–31.

56. Forbes, *Philippine Islands*, 1:235; John Roberts White, "With the Philippine Constabulary," *Boston Evening Transcript*, May 31, 1913, quoted in ibid., 222–23 n. 3; 1904 editorial quoted in ibid., 218.

57. Harbord quoted in Forbes, *Philippine Islands*, 1:214.

58. See, for example, Chamberlin, *Philippine Problem*.

59. "Roosevelt Hero of Brilliant Day," *New York Times*, Mar. 5, 1905, "equaled," "[p]icturesqueness," 1; "Nation Mirrored in Marching Host," *New York Times*, Mar. 5, 1905, "any considerable type," 2; "Roosevelt Hero of Brilliant Day," "all the way," 1.

60. "Nation Mirrored in Marching Host," "first to earn," "beautifully drilled," "quick to observe," 2; Roosevelt quoted in "Roosevelt Hero of Brilliant Day," 1.

61. P. Ocampo, "Aspirations of the Filipino," 79. On Pablo Ocampo, see Manuel and Manuel, *Dictionary of Philippine Biography*, 1.291–94.

62. P. Ocampo, "Aspirations of the Filipino," "dispersed," "*e pluribus unum*," 78, "indulge," 80.

63. Ibid., "flourishing," "crevices," 80, "upbuild," "attained," 81, "excesses," 82.

64. Ibid., 79.

65. Ibid., 82–83.

66. Forbes quoted in *Election of Resident Commissioners*, "acquainted," "socially popular," 9, "transpired," 10, "high standing," 32–33, "morally," 10, "limited suffrage," 33, "forgotten," 39.

67. Osmeña quoted in ibid., "creature," 14, "happiness," 45, "genuinely," 54, "reservations," "govern," 57.

68. Osmeña quoted in ibid., "territorial representation," 36, "reproduce," 49, "difference," 38, "situated," 39.

69. See Ileto, "Orators and the Crowd."

70. Forbes, *Philippine Islands*, 1:192.

71. Ibid., 192–93. On the Great White Fleet stopover in the Philippines, see Golay, *Face of Empire*, 142–43. On the larger voyage, see Hart, *Great White Fleet*.

72. "Occupation Day," *El Renacimiento*, Oct. 12, 1909, in *Report of the Eleventh Annual Meeting of the Anti-Imperialist League* (Boston: Anti-Imperialist League, 1909), in Zwick, *Anti-Imperialism*.

73. M. Jenks, *Death Stalks the Philippine Wilds*, 25–26; "Why No Other Flag Shall Fly," *Cablenews-American*, Aug. 21, 1907, quoted in Westcott, *Exaltation*, 40.

74. "Why No Other Flag Shall Fly," 40–41.

75. Westcott, introduction, *Exaltation*, "indignation," "gathering," 6, "bad to worse," 7, "music," "conspicuous," 4, "lustily," 5, "groans," 14, "surged," "worst crime," 15.

76. "Would Compel More Respect," *Manila American*, Aug. 17, 1907, in Westcott, *Exaltation*, "impromptu," 19; "Our Humiliation," *Manila Opinion*, Aug. 17, 1907, in ibid., "our policy," 17; "El Renacimiento and 'the Flag,'" *Manila Times*, Aug. 20, 1907, in ibid., "flatter," 36; "No Time for Hysteria," *Manila Times*, Aug. 18, 1907, in ibid., "crucial test," 25; "Drunk with Triumph," *Cablenews-American*, Aug. 18, 1907, in ibid., "ingratitude," 31; "Respect for the Flag," *Cablenews-American*, Aug. 18, 1907, in ibid., "hideous," 27; "Why No Other Flag Shall Fly," "bullets," 43; "El Renacimiento and 'the Flag,'" "animates," "naked argument," 37.

77. "Debars Traffic in Flag," *Manila Times*, Aug. 22, 1907, in Westcott, *Exaltation*, 45; "Sweeping Order Given: Revolutionary Flags Are Taboo," *Manila Times*, Aug. 23, 1907, in ibid., "insignia," 56; "Katipunan Emblem to Be Quietly Suppressed," *Manila American*, Aug. 23, 1907, in ibid., "notified to remove," 62, "required," 64; "Sweeping Order Given," "cigar rings," 56.

78. "Mass Meeting Friday Night," *Manila American*, Aug. 20, 1907, in Westcott, *Exaltation*, "sovereignty," 39; introduction, ibid., "best men," 8, "representative body," 10; "The Meeting Tonight," *Cablenews-American*, Aug. 23, 1907, in ibid., "era in government," 60.

79. Leonard quoted in Westcott, *Exaltation*, "*we who are here*," 119; McKinney quoted in ibid., 114; Anderson quoted in ibid., 76; Leonard quoted in ibid., "little candy," 118.

80. Resolutions of the Mass Meeting, quoted in Westcott, *Exaltation*, 139–40, 145.

81. "El 'Rizal Day' en Davao," *El Renacimiento*, Feb. 7, 1905, 2 (translation from the original Spanish by the author).

82. Quoted in Ileto, "Orators and the Crowd," 142–44.

83. Theodore Roosevelt, Address of Apr. 7, 1903, quoted in Craig, Rizal y Alonso, and Mabini, *Filipinos' Fight for Freedom*, 349–52. On the literary reception of Rizal, see Hosillos, *Philippine-American Literary Relations*, 127–37.

84. "If Rizal Could Come Back," *Manila Times*, Dec. 28, 1912, quoted in Forbes, *Philippine Islands*, 2:509.

85. Forbes, *Philippine Islands*, 2:178; Craig, *Lineage, Life and Labors*, "community," 263, "Archipelago," "mourning," 265.

86. Forbes, *Philippine Islands*, "bordered," 2:178; Salt and Heistland, *Introduction to History of Manila*, "progress."

87. Craig, *Story of José Rizal*; Craig, *Lineage, Life and Labors*, "Study of the Growth," title page, "heroes," 13, "American," 20. A U.S. edition of the book was published by the World Book Company in 1914. On Craig, see Manuel and Manuel, *Dictionary of Philippine Biography*, 2.131–53.

88. Craig, *Lineage, Life and Labors*, "Forerunner," 1, "Mexico," 14, "neighbors," "New England," "associations," 18.

89. Ibid., 64.

90. Ibid., "self-restraint," 92, "inculcated," 11, "embarking," 225, "careful," 19, "test," 20.

91. William H. Taft to William Sutherland, Aug. 28, 1906, NARA, RG 350, Stack 150, Entry 5A, #15000 (Box 725). For Sutherland's account of his work and the *pensionado* program, see Sutherland, *Not by Might*.

92. James Smith to Secretary of War, Jan. 12, 1907, NARA, RG 350, Stack 150, Entry 5A, #15000: Jamestown Exposition (Box 725).

93. "For the Third Time," translation of article appearing in *La Igualdad*, Oct. 16, 1906, in ibid.; "The Filipinos Do Not Want the 'Wild Tribes' Exhibited," *El Renacimiento*, Jan. 3, 1907, reprinted in *The Public* 9 (Mar. 9, 1907), in Zwick, *Anti-Imperialism*.

94. Sutherland quoted in cablegram from Governor-General James Smith to William Howard Taft, Jan. 12, 1907, NARA, RG 350, Stack 150, Entry 5A, #15000 (Box 725); Excerpt from minutes of the Philippine Commission hearings, Jan. 24, 1907, in ibid.

95. "The Philippine Reservation: A Hundred and Forty of the Natives Now at the Jamestown Exposition," *Norfolk Ledger-Dispatch* May 7, 1907, in Zwick, *Anti-Imperialism*.

96. Abinales, "American Colonial State."

97. Gowing, *Mandate in Moroland*, "colonization," "obstacle," 205, "Mindanao

Plantation," 206, "burden," 207. One of the most ambitious efforts along these lines was the 1926 Bacon Bill, which would have detached Mindanao as a separate U.S. colony. See H. Fry, "Bacon Bill."

98. Taft to Worcester, Nov. 30, 1907, in Folder: "Correspondence 1907–1911," DWP.

99. Quoted in Sullivan, *Exemplar of Americanism*, 159.

100. Worcester to Taft, Jan. 27, 1908, in Folder: "Correspondence 1907–1911," DWP.

101. "Aves de Rapiña" (editorial), *El Renacimiento*, Oct. 30, 1908, translation in Guillermo, "Worcester Libel Case," 35.

102. "El Insulto Final," *La Vanguardia*, Oct. 12, 1910, in Folder: "Lecture, 1910, given at the YMCA," Box 2, DWP.

103. "El Insulto Final."

104. "Los Infieles y Worcester," *El Ideal*, Oct. 11, 1910, in Folder: "Lecture, 1910, given at the YMCA," Box 2, DWP.

105. Editorial, *La Democracia*, Oct. 13, 1910, in ibid.

106. Resolution quoted in Blount, *American Occupation of the Philippines*, 584.

107. "Worcester en Washington" (cartoon), *Alipatos*, Nov. 9, 1910, in Folder: "Lecture, 1910, given at the YMCA," Box 2, DWP.

108. Woodrow Wilson, "The Place of the United States in Constitutional Development," excerpted in Forbes, *Philippine Islands*, Appendix 26, 2:511–12. On Wilson's advocacy of colonialism in the context of Princeton during and after 1898, see Kramer, "Princeton University." For the Democratic and Republican "Philippine" planks from 1900 to 1928, see ibid., 566–70.

109. Elliott, *Philippines to the End*, 417; on the Manila parade and *La Vanguardia*, see Ileto, "Orators and the Crowd," 149; "Wilson's Triumph," *El Ideal*, Nov. 6, 1912, in Zwick, *Anti-Imperialism*.

110. "Wilson's Triumph."

111. Egan quoted in Stanley, *Nation in the Making*, 185.

Chapter 6

1. Andrews quoted in Barr, *Legacy of the Exposition*, 6–7; Todd quoted in ibid., 162; Cox quoted in ibid., 34. On the exposition generally, see Rydell, *All the World's a Fair*, ch. 8; and Benedict, *Anthropology of World's Fairs*.

2. Apple quoted in Barr, *Legacy of the Exposition*, 6; McMurray quoted in ibid., 108; Pindell quoted in ibid., 129; Townsley quoted in ibid., 165.

3. Balsley quoted in ibid., 15; Goodnow quoted in ibid., 68.

4. Abbott quoted in ibid., 4.

5. B. Wheeler, "Forecast for California," "year," 170, "opening," 168, "end," "blending," 170, "face the awakening," 174.

6. On the West Coast nativist movement against the Japanese, see Daniels, *Politics of Prejudice*; Almaguer, *Racial Fault Lines*; and Daniels and Olin, *Racism in California*.

7. Phelan quoted in Roger Daniels, "The Progressives Draw the Color Line," in Daniels and Olin, *Racism in California*, 129–30.

8. On the Chinese boycott and U.S. responses, see Lorence, "Business and Reform."

9. "Wilson Renews Independence Pledge during Staunton Visit," *Filipino People* 1, no. 5 (Jan. 1913), 4; "Governor Harrison's Policy," *Filipino People* 2, no. 4 (Dec. 1913), 4.

10. "Governor Harrison's Policy," 4.

11. On Wilson's Philippine policy, see Curry, "Woodrow Wilson and Philippine Policy." For overviews of the Harrison administration and "Filipinization," see Stanley, *Nation in the Making*, ch. 8; and Golay, *Face of Empire*. For one account of the Harrison administration, see Gleeck, *American Governors-General*. For Harrison's own account of his administration, see Harrison, *Corner-Stone of Philippine Independence*.

12. Golay, *Face of Empire*, 176.

13. On the politics of the first Jones Bill, see Stanley, *Nation in the Making*, 172–75.

14. On the politics of the second Jones Bill and the Clarke Amendment, see ibid., 212–25.

15. Democratic platform quoted in Kwok-Chu, "Jones Bills," 254 n. 7. On congressional support for the new legislation, see Beadles, "Debate in the United States," 432.

16. Zwick, "Anti-Imperialist League."

17. E. Miller, *War Plan Orange*; Beadles, "Debate in the United States," on Jones, 432; Fall quoted in ibid., 435; Theodore Roosevelt to William H. Taft, quoted in Alfonso, *Theodore Roosevelt and the Philippines*, 74–75; Theodore Roosevelt, "The Navy as a Peacemaker," *New York Times Sunday Magazine*, Nov. 22, 1914, 5.

18. Willard Saulsbury Jr., 64th Cong., 1st sess., *Congressional Record*, 2109–10; James P. Clarke, ibid., 2108.

19. "A New Philippine Society—What Is Its Purpose," *Filipino People* 1, no. 9 (May 1913), 6–7; "Commissioner Quezon Resigns from Philippine Society," *Filipino People* 1, no. 10 (June 1913), 3–9.

20. On the Manila-based business lobby, see Golay, "'Manila Americans.'"

21. Fallows quoted in Sullivan, *Exemplar of Americanism*, 167–68. On the American-Philippine Company, see ibid., chs. 7–8.

22. Harty quoted in Ellis, *Life of James Cardinal Gibbons*, 133; Gibbons quoted in ibid., 134; Forbes quoted in ibid., 135. Gibbons also broadcast retentionist messages in a newspaper interview, "Cardinal Gibbons on 'Our Duty in the Philippines,'" *Boston Evening Transcript*, Feb. 19, 1913. On Gibbons, his relationship to Roosevelt and Taft, and his approach to the Philippines and Puerto Rico, see Ellis, *Life of James Cardinal Gibbons*, ch. 17.

23. On Gibbons's lobbying, see Beadles, "Debate in the United States," 426; Kincaid quoted in Curry, "Woodrow Wilson and Philippine Policy," 448. On Quezon's sense that Catholic pressure was dooming the Clarke Amendment, see M. Kalaw, *Development of Philippine Politics*, 347.

24. Wilson quoted in Curry, "Woodrow Wilson and Philippine Policy," "service-able," 435, "steadily," 436, "unwise," 447; Wilson quoted in "Philippine Measure Now a Law, Army and Navy Bills Signed," *Manila Times*, Aug. 30, 1916, "satisfactory," 1.

25. On the Senate preamble and Quezon's response, see Kwok-Chu, "Jones Bills," 260. Other Filipino nationalist politicians pushed for more aggressive measures: Sergio Osmeña sought legislation that would have allowed a self-authorizing Philippine independence through a constitutional convention; to his left, the Partido Democrata Nacional under Teodoro Sandiko agitated against the second Jones Bill.

26. Kwok-Chu, "Jones Bills," "strongly," 261–62, "well-to-do," 263. Quezon's work against the postneutralization Clarke Amendment alienated him from the Anti-Imperialist League, which broke with him; see Gripaldo, "Quezon-Winslow Correspondence." The league itself, frustrated at what it perceived as the lack of authentic independence politics among its Filipino nationalist counterparts, disbanded in 1920; see Zwick, "Anti-Imperialist League."

27. Wilson quoted in Curry, "Woodrow Wilson and Philippine Policy," "just as soon," 450; Wilson quoted in "Philippine Measure Now a Law, Army and Navy Bills Signed," *Manila Times*, Aug. 30, 1916, "excites," 1.

28. Manuel Quezon, "Filipinization of the Insular Service," *Filipino People* 3, no. 1 (Sept. 1914), 11.

29. Miller quoted in Forbes, *Philippine Islands*, 2:232; Elliott, *Philippines to the End*, 420.

30. *Manila Times*, Apr. 28, 1914, quoted in Forbes, *Philippine Islands*, 2:248–49.

31. N. Roosevelt, *Philippines*, 26; *Cablenews-American* quoted in Stanley, *Nation in the Making*, 208.

32. Younghusband quoted in Forbes, *Philippine Islands*, 2:253; "Foresees Disaster in Philippine Bill," *New York Times*, Feb. 14, 1916, 4.

33. Rai, *United States*, "very similar," "usefulness," iii, "more power," 314, "most interesting," 323, "should be read," 310–11, "no comparison," 324. On U.S. anti-imperialists and India, including Rai's trips to the United States, see Raucher, "American Anti-Imperialists," 83–110.

34. On U.S. Navy fears about the exposure of the Philippines, see Braisted, *United States Navy in the Pacific*.

35. On Worcester's campaign, see Sullivan, *Exemplar of Americanism*, ch. 7; Fallows quoted in ibid., 169. The image that came to be known as the "Senator from Bontoc" was printed in Worcester, *Philippines, Past and Present*, vol. 2, facing 972.

36. As part of his broader retentionist campaign, Worcester produced a report alleging that peonage and the enslavement of "non-Christians" persisted in the Philippines under assembly rule. On Worcester's report and the critical Filipino response, see Salman, *Embarrassment of Slavery*, chs. 11–13.

37. Dean Worcester to M. Douglas Flattery, Sept. 21, 1913, Folder: "Correspondence July–Dec. 1913," Box 1, DWP; "Shows Regeneration of Filipinos in Movies," *New York World*, Dec. 31, 1913, Folder: "Newspaper clippings, 1913–4, concerning lectures," Box 2, DWP, "highest"; "We're Civilizing 'Our Newly-Caught Sullen People,'" *New York World*, Jan. 11, 1914, "without parallel," ibid.

38. "Shows Regeneration of Filipinos in Movies."

39. Worcester to Gilbert Grosvenor, Dec. 21, 1914, Folder: "Correspondence, July–Dec. 1914," Box 1, DWP.

40. "Worcester Again to the Front," *Filipino People* 2, no. 5 (Jan. 1914), 16; Editorial, *El Ideal*, Dec. 5, 1913, quoted in "Demand that the Assembly," *Manila Daily Bulletin*, Dec. [?], 1913, in vol. 3, no. 29: "Exhibition of Igorots" (clippings and documents), Dean C. Worcester Papers, Hatcher Library, University of Michigan.

41. Editorial, *El Ideal*, Dec. 5, 1913.

42. "Foreword," *Filipino People* 1, no. 1 (Sept. 1912), 12. On Quezon's campaigning in the United States, see Gopinath, *Manuel L. Quezon*. For his own account, see Quezon, *Good Fight*. Quezon also conducted his campaign outside the United States and the Philippines, speaking in July 1911 at the First Universal Races Congress in London, which promoted "fuller understanding, the most friendly feelings, and a heartier co-operation" between "the peoples of the West and those of the East." Quezon apparently reviewed the accomplishments of the Philippine Republic and Wilcox's and Sargent's late-1898 "recognition" of its merits. *Record of the Proceedings*, 3, 38.

43. "The All-Filipino Baseball Team Touring the United States," *Filipino People* 1, no. 11 (July 1913), 13.

44. "Inexperienced Men for the Philippines," *Filipino People* 1, no. 8 (Apr. 1913), 13.

45. Horace White, "Not Capable of Self-Government," *Filipino People* 2, no. 5 (Jan. 1914), 11; Winfred Denison, "Democracy's Mission in the Philippines," *Filipino People* 2, no. 12 (Aug. 1914), 4.

46. "How the Filipinos Feel toward Americans," *Filipino People* 1, no. 7 (Mar. 1913), 9; Manuel Quezon, "The Right of the Filipinos to Independence," *Filipino People* 1, no. 2 (Oct. 1912), 2; "How the Filipinos Feel," 10.

47. "Filipinos Demand Independence," *Filipino People* 3, no. 3 (Nov. 1914), 6; Ralph Woolley, "Americans as Colonists," *Filipino People* 2, no. 2 (Oct. 1913), 6; American [pseud.], "Some Phases of the Philippine Problem, II: The National Character of the Filipinos," *Filipino People* 1, no. 3 (Nov. 1912), 18; Winslow Warren, "Disputes Taft's Philippine Arguments," *Filipino People* 2, no. 7 (Mar. 1914), 4.

48. Quezon, "Right of the Filipinos to Independence," 4–5.

49. Ibid.

50. Quezon to "Col." [McIntyre], Sept. 9, 1911, NARA, RG 350, Stack 150, Entry 5A, #20823 (Box 857).

51. *La Democracia* quoted in *Manila Daily Bulletin*, Feb. 24, 1914, in "Exhibition of Igorots."

52. "Nude and Semi-Nude to Be Taboo," *Cablenews*, Oct. 13, 1913, in "Exhibition of Igorots"; "Photographing of Igorots and Negritos Taboo," *Cablenews*, Feb. 26, 1914, in ibid.

53. "Los 12 Igorrotes que Salieron Ayer en el 'Taming,'" *Renacimiento Filipino*, Mar. 25, 1914, in "Exhibition of Igorots."

54. Ibid., "establishes," "commissioned"; "Bontoc Igorots Evade Authorities" [translation], *Renacimiento Filipino*, Mar. 25, 1914 in "Exhibition of Igorots," "advance guard."

55. Harrison quoted in "Harrison Indignant at Igorot Episode," *Manila Daily Bulletin*, Mar. 27, 1914, in "Exhibition of Igorots"; Denison quoted in "Igorots May Not Be Taken from Islands," *Manila Times*, Mar. 27, 1914, in ibid.

56. "The Philippines at the Panama Exposition," *Filipino People* 3, no. 7 (Mar. 1915), 6.

57. Ibid., "complete," 4, "film," 6, "thirty," 5, "objects," 4.

58. Quezon quoted in ibid., 7–8.

59. Quezon quoted in "Philippine Day and the Panama Exposition," *Filipino People* 3, no. 8 (Dec. 1915), 7, 23.

60. Quezon quoted in "The Philippines at the Panama Exposition," 8.

61. Harrison, *Corner-Stone of Philippine Independence*, "aggressive," 124, "maintain," 126.

62. Denison, "Democracy's Mission," 3–4.

63. Gowing, *Mandate in Moroland*, 272.

64. Keesing and Keesing, *Taming Philippine Headhunters*, 31.

65. Quoted in ibid., 32.

66. *La Democracia*, quoted in Finin, "Regional Consciousness", 127.

67. F. R. Ventura, "The Problem of the Non-Christian Tribes," *Revista Filipina/ Philippine Review* 4, no. 1 (Jan. 1919), "censuring," 72, "helpless," "lurid," 72–73, "yonder," "sturdy," "intolerant," 72.

68. Ibid., "onward," "attain," "uplift," 72, "crusade, 73.

69. Ibid., "lavish," 73, "impart," "noble," 74, "repudiate," 73.

70. "Some Aspects of the European War," *Filipino People* 2, no. 12 (Aug. 1914), 16–17. On World War I as a crisis of European self-understanding that overturned notions of "civilization" and "savagery," see Adas, *Machines as the Measure of Men*.

71. "The War and Nationalism," *Filipino People* 3, no. 4 (Dec. 1914), 13.

72. Harrison quoted in Golay, *Face of Empire*, 210. See Jose, "Philippine National Guard."

73. On the USS *Rizal*, see Harrod, *Manning the New Navy*, 62.

74. Espiritu, *Filipino American Lives*, 15–16.

75. Churchill, *Philippine Independence Missions*, 302 n. 2; Harrison quoted in ibid., 11.

76. Quezon and Harrison quoted in ibid., 12.

77. Quezon and Baker quoted in ibid., 16.

78. Quoted in ibid., 19.

79. Ibid., "overwhelmed," 21, "inadvisable," 24, "ascertain," "distinguished," 25.

80. Woodrow Wilson, 66th Cong., 3rd sess., *Congressional Record* 60, pt. 1, 26.

81. On the Philippine National Bank Scandal, see Yoshiko Nagano, "American Colonial Discourse: 'The Scandal of the Philippine National Bank' in 1919–1922," paper presented at the International Conference of Asia Scholars, Singapore, Aug. 2003.

82. Thompson quoted in Churchill, *Philippine Independence Missions*, 156.

83. On Republican policy in the 1920s and Wood as governor-general, see G. Wheeler, "Republican Philippine Policy"; Tan, *Critical Decade*; Gleeck, *American Governors-General*; Golay, *Face of Empire*; and Stanley, *Nation in the Making*.

84. Mayo, *Isles of Fear*, 76. On Mayo, see Sinha, introduction.

85. Feced quoted in Sánchez Gómez, "'Ellos y Nosotros,'" 316; Wood quoted in Churchill, *Philippine Independence Missions*, 97.

86. M. Kalaw, *Case for the Filipinos*, xi–xii.

87. Ibid., 153.

88. Ibid., xiii.

89. Ibid., 153, 154.

90. Ibid., 172.

91. Ibid., 173.

92. On the politics of independence legislation, see Friend, *Between Two Empires*.

93. Kirk, *Philippine Independence*, 73–74.

94. Ibid., 75–76.

95. Ibid., "single menace," 79, "Oriental," 80.

96. Quoted in ibid., 88 n. 29.

97. Ibid., 90.

98. Nebraska State Senate quoted in ibid., 89.

99. American Farm Bureau Federation quoted in ibid., 94.

100. American Association of Creamery Butter Manufacturers and Heflin quoted in ibid., 95–96.

101. Ibid., 90.

102. Ibid., 100–101.

103. Melendy, "Filipinos in the United States," 521–23.

104. Ibid., 523; Lasker, *Filipino Immigration*, 324.

105. On Otis's exclusion order, see Jensen, *Chinese in the Philippines*, 44.

106. Julius Kahn, 57th Cong., 1st sess., 1902, *Congressional Record* 35, 3692.

107. Boies Penrose, in ibid., 4159; Henry Heitfeld, in ibid., 4149–50; Jensen, *Chinese in the Philippines*, "to prohibit," 65. On problems of enforcement, see ibid., 66–77.

108. Quoted in Lasker, *Filipino Immigration*, 82–83; Manuel Quezon to "Col." [McIntyre], Sept. 9, 1911, NARA, RG 350, Stack 150, Entry 5A, #20823 (Box 857).

109. Mojares, *Cebuano Perceptions*, 5.

110. Quotations in this section are from three anonymous testimonies taken in a Fisk University social study, respectively entitled "A Native Filipino's Impression of America," "Experiences and Opinions of a Filipino," and "I Am Only a Foreigner." For reference purposes, I have assigned the narrators the following names: "Native," "Filipino" and "Foreigner." See Social Science Institute, *Orientals and Their Cultural Adjustment*.

111. "Native Filipino's Impression," "brightest pupil," 111; "Experiences and Opinions of a Filipino," "history," 127; "Native Filipino's Impression," "beautiful life," 112; "Experiences and Opinions of a Filipino," "big buildings," "results," 128; "I Am Only a Foreigner," "American consuls," 123–24.

112. "Experiences and Opinions of a Filipino," "perfect strangers," 132, "California," 129; "Native Filipino's Impression," "American city," 114, "same experience," "quite at home," 115, "looked strange," 116.

113. R. S. quoted in Bogardus, "Filipino Immigrant Attitudes," 472; "Native

Filipino's Impression," "absolute change," 119; "I Am Only a Foreigner," "American hospitality," 122; "Experiences and Opinions of a Filipino," "different customs," "dishwashing," 130–31; Bogardus, "Filipino Immigrant Attitudes," "debarred," 473; Buaken, *I Have Lived with the American People*, 70.

114. "Native Filipino's Impression," "being mistaken," 116; "Experiences and Opinions of a Filipino," " 'Jap,' " 131–32; R. S. quoted in Bogardus, "Filipino Immigrant Attitudes," 472–73.

115. R. S. quoted in Bogardus, "Filipino Immigrant Attitudes," 473; "Experiences and Opinions of a Filipino," "mountain tribes," 136, "breaks my heart," "exhibitions," "Igorots," "dark side," 128–29.

116. "Native Filipino's Impression," "not white," 116, "difficult time," 113; Bulosan quoted in Melendy, "California's Discrimination," 3.

117. "Native Filipino's Impression," "stupid," 119; N. F. quoted in Bogardus, "Filipino Immigrant Attitudes," 474.

118. "Native Filipino's Impression," "white race," 119; "Experiences and Opinions of a Filipino," "greatly moved," 132.

119. Melendy, "California's Discrimination," "scarcely more," 5; Bogardus, "Anti-Filipino Race Riots," "ten years," 53, "goo-goos," 59.

120. Goethe, "Filipino Immigration Viewed as Peril," 73; Bogardus, "American Attitudes," "impressed unfavorably," "proclivities," 64.

121. Bogardus, "American Attitudes," "organize quickly," 65, "smart-Alecky," 67–68.

122. On Dinuba, see DeWitt, *Violence in the Fields*, 33. For a contemporary social-scientific account of the taxi dance halls, see Cressey, *Taxi-Dance Hall*. On the taxi dance halls and their study by Chicago sociologists, see Alidio, "Between Civilizing Mission and Ethnic Assimilation," ch. 4. On social scientists and sex between whites and "Orientals," see Yu, "Mixing Bodies and Cultures." "There's No East, There's No West When . . . ," *Watsonville Evening Pajaronian*, Dec. 5, 1929, 1. Schmick was very likely Jewish, suggesting the ways that, for purposes of racial nativism, Jews—themselves a concern for nativists—could also become "white," or representative of the "West."

123. On the nativist movement in the 1920s, see Higham, *Strangers in the Land*. On anti-Filipino nativism, see Ngai, *Impossible Subjects*, ch. 3.

124. On the Federation of Labor resolutions and Section 60, see Melendy, "California's Discrimination," 8–9. On Joint Resolution No. 15, see Kirk, *Philippine Independence*, 99. On the rise of an anti-Filipino nativist movement more generally, see Lasker, *Filipino Immigration*, ch. 5; and Saniel, *Filipino Exclusion Movement*.

125. On these cases, see Volpp, "American Mestizo."

126. Bruno Lasker identifies twenty separate incidents of attacks on Filipinos, including one by Mexican laborers, involving two Filipino mortalities, in the states of California, Oregon, Washington, Idaho, and Utah during this period. Lasker, *Filipino Immigration*, ch. 2. See also Bogardus, "Anti-Filipino Race Riots."

127. On the Watsonville race war, see DeWitt, *Violence in the Fields*.

128. Ibid., 38–45.

129. "Two Wounded in Attack on Filipinos," *Manila Times*, Jan. 24, 1930, "racial

warfare," 1; "California Rioting Stirs Comment; Differences Are Economic Is Opinion Here," *Manila Times*, Jan. 26, 1930, "quite a stir," "urging protection," 1; "Labor Dispute in California Well in Hand," *Manila Times*, Jan. 27, 1930, "asking for aid," 1.

130. "Calm Judgment [*sic*]," *Manila Times*, Jan. 27, 1930, "no insult," 6; "California Rioting Stirs Comment," "economic competition," 1; "Independence Proponents Urge Early Separation of Philippines on Basis of Racial and Immigration Problems," *Manila Times*, Jan. 30, 1930, "incendiary," 1.

131. "Golden State Again Goes Anti-Oriental," *New York Times*, Feb. 2, 1930, 52; "Labor Dispute in California Well in Hand," "so-called rioters," 1.

132. Tydings quoted in "Independence Proponents Urge Early Separation," 1.

133. Osias quoted in "Labor Dispute in California Well in Hand," 1.

134. Bocobo quoted in "Several Hundred Persons Attend Luneta Services," *Manila Times*, Feb. 3, 1930, 2.

135. AFL, Grange, and American Coalition resolutions quoted in Kirk, *Philippine Independence*, 99. The AFL had been concerned with the underselling of U.S. goods by cheaper Philippine goods due to the lower cost of Filipino labor since as early as 1923. See Lawrence, "American Federation of Labor"; and Pivar, "American Federation of Labor."

136. On the meningitis ban, see Lasker, *Filipino Immigration*, 106–8.

137. House Committee on Immigration and Naturalization, *Exclusion of Immigration*, 1.

138. On the 1924 act, see Ngai, "Architecture of Race." On immigration law and Asian American history, see Hing, *Making and Remaking Asian America*; and Ngai, *Impossible Subjects*.

139. McClatchy quoted in House Committee, *Exclusion of Immigration*, 32.

140. Webb quoted in ibid., 60–61.

141. For contemporary discussions of Filipinos and U.S. immigration law, see "Status of Filipinos"; and Manzon, *Strange Case of the Filipinos*. For a more recent perspective, see McClain, *Asian Indians*.

142. McClatchy, in House Committee, *Exclusion of Immigration*, 11.

143. McClatchy, in ibid., 32.

144. Welch, in ibid., 7–8; Barrows quoted in ibid., 35; McClatchy, in ibid., 38, 14. For the article, see Barrows, "Desirability of the Filipino."

145. Welch, in House Committee, *Exclusion of Immigration*, 3; Webb, in ibid., 58, 60; McClatchy, in ibid., 29.

146. The expression "rising tide of color" came from Lothrop Stoddard's 1920 racist tract *The Rising Tide of Color against World White-Supremacy*, which foretold the global downfall of white domination through anticolonial rebellion and nonwhite immigration. McClatchy, in ibid., 29; Cassidy, in ibid., 86; Welch, in ibid., 7, 4.

147. Webb, in ibid., 70; McClatchy, in ibid., 30.

148. Webb, in ibid., 70.

149. Parker, in ibid., "special question," 88, "our own nationals," 93, "owe their allegiance," 94.

150. Parker, in ibid., "diplomatic representatives," 94, "loyalty," 88, "just treatment," 89, "big drop," 96.

151. Parker, in ibid., "ethnological features," 93, "some misunderstanding," 98.

152. Parker, in ibid., "sensibilities," 93, "radical legislation," 97, "excluding," 96.

153. Roxas, in ibid., "amendment," "subjects," 102, "curtailment," "against," 107, "wards," 108.

154. Roxas, in ibid., 110–11.

155. Roxas, in ibid., "great deal," 108, "assimilable," 109, "divided," 113, "create disturbances," 114.

156. Roxas, in ibid., "hill groups," 114, "very sincerely," 113, "imperialists," 115, "criminals," 113, "human being," 106.

157. Roxas, in ibid., "unconcealed," "consideration," 115, "contagiously humorous," "incursion," "understand," "distant," 128.

158. Roxas, in ibid., "not proud," 113, "indiscriminately hurled," 112.

159. Parker, in ibid., 89; Roxas, in ibid., 112.

160. Roxas, in ibid., 112.

161. Roxas, in ibid., "speaks truths," 103, "American sovereignty," 105.

162. Roxas, in ibid., "peculiar relationship," 102, "unjust," 106.

163. On the politics of independence legislation, see T. Friend, *Between Two Empires*, chs. 8–11; and Churchill, *Philippine Independence Missions*, chs. 11–12.

164. Roosevelt quoted in Kirk, *Philippine Independence*, 127.

165. *Philippine Independence Act*, "complete," "mandatory," "republican," "final," "allegiance," "supreme," 456, "as if elected," "currency," "direct supervision," 457, "obligations," 458, "withdraw," "military," 463.

166. Hushing, in Senate Committee on Territories and Insular Affairs, *Independence for the Philippine Islands*, 116; Crail, in House Committee on Insular Affairs, *Independence for the Philippine Islands*, 124; Horr, in ibid., 272, 274.

167. Welch, in House Committee, *Independence for the Philippine Islands*, 378–79.

168. Tydings-McDuffie Act quoted in Kirk, *Philippine Independence*, "foreign country," 246, "aliens," on fifty-immigrant quota, 245, "including," 248.

169. Welch quoted in Coloma, *Study of the Filipino Repatriation Movement*, 37.

170. Ibid., "of great help," 42–43, "wealth," 44, "shabby," 48.

171. Lasker, *Filipino Immigration*, Appendix E, "wreaths," 364; "Protest Rites in Provinces," *Manila Times*, Jan. 31, 1930, 4; "Luneta Service Early Sunday," *Manila Times*, Jan. 31, 1930, "biggest," 2.

172. Quoted in "Several Hundred Persons Attend Luneta Services," *Manila Times*, Feb. 3, 1930, 2.

Bibliography

Archival Sources

Balaguer Library, Vilanova i La Geltrú, Spain
Bancroft Library, University of California, Berkeley
    David P. Barrows Papers
Bentley Historical Library, University of Michigan, Ann Arbor
    Dean C. Worcester Papers
Biblioteca Nacional, Madrid, Spain
Clements Library, University of Michigan, Ann Arbor
    Hussey-Wadsworth Papers
Hatcher Library, University of Michigan, Ann Arbor
    Dean C. Worcester Papers
Lopez Memorial Museum, Manila, Philippines
National Archives and Records Administration, College Park, Maryland
    Bureau of Insular Affairs, Record Group 350
Newberry Library, Chicago
    Edward E. Ayer Collection
Rizal Library, Ateneo de Manila University, Quezon City, Philippines
    American Historical Collection
    Trinidad H. Pardo de Tavera Papers
Smithsonian Institution, Washington, D.C.
    National Museum of American History
        Warshaw Collection of Business Americana
    National Museum of Natural History
        National Anthropological Archives
    Smithsonian Institution Archives
        Exposition Records of the Smithsonian Institution and U.S. National
           Museum, Record Unit 70
U.S. Military History Institute, Carlisle, Pennsylvania
    Matthew Batson Papers
    William Carey Brown Papers
    Spanish-American War Series
    Samuel B. M. Young Papers

Newspapers and Periodicals

American Old-Timer
Boston Morning Journal
La Democracia
Facts about the Filipinos

Filipino People
La Independencia
Manila Times
New York Times
El Renacimiento
Renacimiento Filipino
Revista Filipina / Philippine Review
La Solidaridad
Springfield (Mass.) Republican
St. Louis Globe-Democrat
St. Louis Post-Dispatch
La Vanguardia
Washington Post
Watsonville Evening Pajaronian
World's Fair Bulletin

Government-Published Primary Sources

Annual Report of Major General Arthur MacArthur, U.S. Volunteers, Commanding
    Division of the Philippines. Vol. 1. Manila, 1900.
Census of the Philippine Islands. 4 vols. Washington, D.C.: U.S. Bureau of the
    Census, 1905.
Circular Letter of Governor Taft and Information and Instructions for the Preparation
    of the Philippine Exhibit for the Louisiana Purchase Exposition to Be Held at St.
    Louis, Mo., U.S.A., 1904. Manila: Bureau of Public Printing, 1902.
Election of Resident Commissioners to the United States, Philippine Assembly, Second
    Legislature, First Session, Document No. 250—A.38. Manila: Bureau of Public
    Printing, 1911.
Ferguson, A. W., and Thomas Hardeman. Brief Biography of the Members of the
    Honorary Board of Filipino Commissioners to the Louisiana Purchase Exposition.
    Washington, D.C.: Government Printing Office, 1904.
Niederlein, Gustavo, Leon M. Guerrero, and Pedro A. Paterno. "Exhibit Q:
    Annual Report of the Exposition Board." In Report of the Philippine Commission
    to the Secretary of War, 1.406–24. Manila: Bureau of Public Printing, 1904.
Philippine Autonomy Act (Jones Act), Aug. 29, 1916, Public Law 240, 64th Cong.,
    Ch. 416; 39 Stat. 545.
Philippine Exposition Board. Report of the Philippine Exposition Board in the United
    States for the Louisiana Purchase Exposition. Washington, D.C.: Bureau of
    Insular Affairs, War Department, 1905.
Philippine Independence Act (Tydings-McDuffie Act), Mar. 24, 1934, Public Law
    127, 73rd Cong., Ch. 84; 48 Stat. 456.
Philippine Organic Act (Lodge Act), July 1, 1902, Public Law 235, 57th Cong., Ch.
    1369; 32 Stat. 691.
Report of the Philippine Commission to the Secretary of War. Washington, D.C.:
    Government Printing Office, 1900–1916.

Thompson, Everett E. "Exhibit C: Civil Service in Oriental Possessions." In *4th Annual Report of the Philippine Civil Service Board: Report of the Philippine Commission to the Secretary of War for 1904*, 259–68. Washington, D.C.: Government Printing Office, 1905.

U.S. Congress. House. *Annual Report of the Secretary of War*. 57th Cong., 1st sess., 1901. H. Doc. 2, vol. 1, pt. 4.

——. *Papers Relating to the Foreign Relations of the United States with the Annual Message of the President*. 55th Cong., 2nd sess., 1898. H. Doc. 1.

——. Committee on Immigration and Naturalization. *Exclusion of Immigration from the Philippine Islands*. 71st Cong., 2nd sess., 1930.

——. Committee on Insular Affairs. *Independence for the Philippine Islands*. 72nd Cong., 1st sess., 1931.

U.S. Congress. Senate. *Charges of Cruelty, etc., to the Natives of the Philippines*. 57th Cong., 1st sess., 1902. S. Doc. 205.

——. *The Mabini Case*. 57th Cong., 2nd sess., 1902. S. Doc. 111.

——. *Report of Tour through the Island of Luzon*. 56th Cong., 1st sess., Feb. 23, 1900. S. Doc. 196.

——. *Trials of Courts-Martial in the Philippine Islands in Consequence of Certain Instructions*. 57th Cong., 2nd sess., 1903. S. Doc. 213.

——. Committee on Territories and Insular Affairs. *Independence for the Philippine Islands*. 71st Cong., 2nd sess., 1930.

——. Committee on the Philippines. *Affairs in the Philippine Islands*. 57th Cong., 1st sess., 1902. S. Doc. 331.

Other Published Primary Sources

Agoncillo, Felipe. "Are the Filipinos Civilized?" *Frank Leslie's Popular Monthly* 43 (1899): 75–85.

——. *Memorial to the Senate of the United States*. N.p., 1899.

Allen, Clifford Paynter. *Pilgrimage of Mary Commandery No. 36, Knights Templar of Pennsylvania to the Twenty-Ninth Triennial Conclave of the Grand Encampment U.S. at San Francisco, Cal*. Philadelphia: Thomson Printing, 1904.

Apacible, G. "Al Pueblo Americano / To the American People." Anti-Imperialist League, 1900.

Artigas y Cuerva, Manuel. *Galería de Filipinos Ilustres: Biografías á Contar Desde los Primeros Tiempos de la Dominación Hispana, de los Hijos del Pais Que en Sus Respectivas Profesiones Descollaron o Hayan Alcanzado Algún Puesto de Distinción en Sociedad*. 2 vols. Manila: Renacimiento, 1917–18.

——. *Glorias Nacionales: Los Sucesos de 1872; Reseña Histórica-Bio-Bibliográfica*. Vol. 2. Manila: Imp. de la Vanguardia, 1911.

Balaguer, Victor. *Islas Filipinas: Memoria*. Madrid: R. Angeles, 1895.

Ballard, Everett Guy, ed. *Liberty, Independence and Self-Government*. Chicago, 1900.

Barr, James A., ed. *The Legacy of the Exposition: Interpretation of the Intellectual and Moral Heritage Left to Mankind by the World Celebration at San Francisco in 1915*. San Francisco: J. H. Nash, 1916.

Barrows, David P. "The Desirability of the Filipino." *Transactions of the Commonwealth Club of California* 24 (1929): 231–36.

Buaken, Manuel. *I Have Lived with the American People.* Caldwell, Idaho: Caxton Printers, 1948.

Bellairs, Edgar. *As It Is in the Philippines.* New York: Lewis, Scribner, 1902.

Bennitt, Mark, ed. *History of the Louisiana Purchase Exposition.* 1905. New York: Arno Press, 1976.

Beveridge, Albert J. *The Meaning of the Times and Other Speeches.* Indianapolis: Bobbs-Merrill, 1908.

Bigelow, Poultney. "How to Convert a White Man into a Savage." *Independent* 54, no. 2789 (1902): 1159–61.

Blount, James H. *The American Occupation of the Philippines, 1898–1912.* New York: G. P. Putnam's Sons, 1912.

Blumentritt, Ferdinand. "Race Questions in the Philippine Islands." *Appleton's Popular Science Monthly* 55 (1899): 472–80.

——. "Views of Dr. Rizal, the Filipino Scholar, upon Race Differences." *Popular Science Monthly* 61 (1902): 223–28.

"A Boer Concentration Camp." *Public Opinion* 31, no. 18 (1901): 555.

Bogardus, Emory Stephen. "American Attitudes towards Filipinos." *Social Science Review* 14, no. 1 (1929): 59–69.

——. "Anti-Filipino Race Riots." In *Letters in Exile: An Introductory Reader on the History of Pilipinos in America,* 51–61. Los Angeles: UCLA Asian American Studies Center, 1975.

——. "Filipino Immigrant Attitudes." *Sociology and Social Research* 14, no. 5 (1930): 469–79.

Bowman, Isaiah. *The New World: Problems in Political Geography* (Yonkers-on-Hudson, N.Y.; Chicago, Ill.: World Book Co., 1928).

Brace, H. M. "Itamo, the Insurrecto: A Story of the Philippines." *Soldier's Letter* 1, no. 1 (1898): 16–20.

Bresnahan, Roger J. *In Time of Hesitation: American Anti-Imperialists and the Philippine-American War.* Quezon City, Phil.: New Day Publishers, 1981.

Chamberlin, Frederick Carleton. *The Philippine Problem, 1898–1913.* Boston: Little, Brown, 1913.

Clevenger, Martha R., *"Indescribably Grand": Diaries and Letters from the 1904 World's Fair.* Saint Louis: Missouri Historical Society Press, 1996.

Concepción, Epifanio. *Memorias de un Revolucionario.* Iloilo, Phil.: J. M. Basa, 1949.

Condict, Alice. *Old Glory and the Gospel in the Philippines: Notes Gathered during Professional and Missionary Work.* Chicago: F. H. Revell Co., 1902.

Craig, Austin. *Lineage, Life and Labors of José Rizal, Philippine Patriot: A Study of the Growth of Free Ideas in the Trans-Pacific American Territory.* Manila: Philippine Education Publishing Co., 1913.

——. *The Story of José Rizal, the Greatest Man of the Brown Race.* Manila: Philippine Education Publishing Co., 1909.

——, ed. *Rizal's Political Writings: Nation Building, Race Differences, Basic Principles of Good Government.* Manila: Oriental Commercial Co., 1933.

Craig, Austin, José Rizal y Alonso, and Apolinario Mabini. *The Filipinos' Fight for Freedom*. Manila: Oriental Commercial Co., 1933.

Cressey, Paul Goalby. *The Taxi-Dance Hall: A Sociological Study in Commercialized Recreation and City Life*. Chicago: University of Chicago Press, 1932.

Dauncey, Campbell. *An Englishwoman in the Philippines*. New York: E. P. Dutton, 1906.

Davis, Mrs. Jefferson. "Why We Do Not Want the Philippines." In *The Anti-Imperialist Reader: A Documentary History of Anti-Imperialism in the United States*, edited by Philip Sheldon Foner and Richard C. Winchester, 1.235–36. New York: Holmes and Meier, 1984.

De los Reyes, Isabelo. *El Folk-Lore Filipino*. 1889. Translated by Salud C. Dizon and Maria Elinora P. Imson. Diliman, Quezon City, Phil.: University of the Philippines Press, 1994.

Dickson, Paul. *War Slang: American Fighting Words and Phrases from the Civil War to the Gulf War*. New York: Pocket Books, 1994.

Dolph, Edward Arthur. *"Sound Off!": Soldier Songs from the Revolution to World War II*. New York: Farrar and Rinehart, 1942.

Du Bois, W. E. B. "The Present Outlook for the Dark Races of Mankind." *A.M.E. Church Review* 17, no. 2 (1900): 95–110.

———. *The Souls of Black Folk*. Edited and with an introduction by David W. Blight and Robert Gooding-Williams. Boston: Bedford Books, 1997.

Edwards, Clarence R. "The Work of the Bureau of Insular Affairs." *National Geographic Magazine* 15, no. 6 (1904): 239–55.

Elliott, Charles B. *The Philippines*. Vol. 2. *To the End of the Commission Government*. Indianapolis: Bobbs-Merrill, 1917.

Exposición de Filipinas: Colección de Artículos Publicados en El Globo, Diario Ilustrado Político, Científico y Literario. Madrid: El Globo, 1887.

Eyot, Canning, ed. *The Story of the Lopez Family*. 1904. With a foreword by Jim Zwick. Manila: Platypus Publishing, 2001.

Fabella, Maximo P., ed. *A Portable Rizal Reader*. Orange Park, Fla.: Philippines Research Center South, 1998.

Faust, Karl Irving. *Campaigning in the Philippines*. San Francisco: Hicks-Judd Co., 1899.

Feced, Pablo. *Filipinas: Esbozos y Pinceladas*. Manila: Establecimiento Tipográfico de Ramirez y Co., 1888.

Folkmar, Daniel. *Album of Philippine Types Found in Bilibid Prison in 1903: Christians and Moros (Including a Few Non-Christians)*. Manila: Philippine Exposition Board, Bureau of Public Printing, 1904.

Foner, Philip Sheldon, and Richard C. Winchester, eds. *The Anti-Imperialist Reader: A Documentary History of Anti-Imperialism in the United States*. New York: Holmes and Meier, 1984.

Forbes, W. Cameron. "A Decade of American Rule in the Philippines." *Atlantic Monthly* 103, no. 2 (1909): 200–209.

———. *The Philippine Islands*. 2 vols. Boston: Houghton Mifflin, 1928.

———. "What Had Best Be Done for the Material Advancement of the Philippines."

In *Proceedings of the Twenty-Sixth Annual Meeting of the Lake Mohonk Conference of Friends of the Indian and Other Dependent Peoples*, 117–23. New York: Lake Mohonk Conference of Friends of the Indian and Other Dependent Peoples, 1908.

Foreman, John. *The Philippine Islands: A Political, Geographical, Ethnographical, Social and Commercial History of the Philippine Archipelago and Its Political Dependencies, Embracing the Whole Period of Spanish Rule*. New York: C. Scribner's Sons, 1899.

Francis, David R. *The Universal Exposition of 1904*. St. Louis: Louisiana Purchase Exposition, 1913.

Garrett, Erwin Clarkson. *My Bunkie, and Other Ballads*. Philadelphia: J. B. Lippincott, 1907.

Gatewood, Willard, ed. *"Smoked Yankees" and the Struggle for Empire: Letters from Negro Soldiers, 1898–1902*. Urbana: University of Illinois Press, 1971.

Gleason, Ronald P., ed. *The Log of the "Thomas," July 23 to August 21, 1901*. 1901.

Goethe, C. M. "Filipino Immigration Viewed as Peril." In *Letters in Exile: An Introductory Reader on the History of Pilipinos in America*, 72–73. Los Angeles: UCLA Asian American Studies Center, 1975.

Gompers, Samuel. "Imperialism, Its Dangers and Wrongs." In *The Anti-Imperialist Reader: A Documentary History of Anti-Imperialism in the United States*, vol. 1, edited by Philip Sheldon Foner and Richard C. Winchester. New York: Holmes and Meier, 1984.

Graff, Henry F., ed. *American Imperialism and the Philippine Insurrection*. Boston: Little, Brown, 1969.

Grant, H. Roger. "Letters from the Philippines: The 51st Iowa Volunteers at War, 1898–1899." *Palimpsest* 55, no. 6 (1974): 162–77.

Griffiths, Arthur Llewllyn. "The Philippine Insurrection: Why?" *Arena* 22 (1904): 496–500.

Grosvenor, Gilbert H. *The National Geographic Society and Its Magazine*. Washington, D.C.: National Geographic Society, 1957.

——. "A Revelation of the Filipinos." *National Geographic Magazine* 16, no. 4 (1905): 139–92.

Harrison, Francis Burton. *The Corner-Stone of Philippine Independence*. New York: Century, 1922.

Hoffman, D. O. Noble. "The Philippine Exhibit at the Pan-American Exposition." *National Geographic Magazine* 12 (1901): 119–22.

Holley, Marietta. *Samantha at the St. Louis Exposition, by Josiah Allen's Wife*. New York: G. W. Dillingham, 1904.

"Igorots and Americans." *Filipino* 1, no. 2 (1906): 4.

Isselhard, Jacob. *The Filipino in Every-Day Life: An Interesting and Instructive Narrative of the Personal Observations of an American Soldier during the Late Philippine Insurrection*. Chicago: Privately printed, 1904.

Jackson, Frank E. *The Representative Men of the Philippines*. Manila: E. C. McCullough, 1906.

Jenks, Jeremiah W. "Some Difficulties in the Administration of Dependencies." In

Proceedings of the Twenty-Third Annual Meeting of the Lake Mohonk Conference
of Friends of the Indian and Other Dependent Peoples, 80–91. New York: Lake
Mohonk Conference of Friends of the Indian and Other Dependent Peoples,
1905.

Jenks, Maud Huntley. Death Stalks the Philippine Wilds: Letters of Maud Huntley
Jenks. Minneapolis: Lund Press, 1951.

Johnson, Edward Augustus. History of Negro Soldiers in the Spanish-American War,
and Other Items of Interest. Raleigh, N.C.: Capital Printing Co., 1899.

Kalaw, Maximo M. The Case for the Filipinos. New York: Century Co., 1916.

——. The Development of Philippine Politics (1872–1920): An Account of the Part
Played by the Filipino Leaders and Parties in the Political Development of the
Philippines. Manila: Oriental Commercial Co., 1926.

——. "The Filipino Youth and the Independence of the Philippinos [sic]." In
Report of the Thirtieth Annual Lake Mohonk Conference of Friends of the Indian
and Other Dependent Peoples, 158–61. New York: Lake Mohonk Conference of
Friends of the Indian and Other Dependent Peoples, 1912.

Kalaw, Teodoro M. The Philippine Revolution. Manila: J. B. Vargas Foundation,
1969.

Keesing, Felix Maxwell, and Marie Martin Keesing. Taming Philippine
Headhunters: A Study of Government and of Cultural Change in Northern Luzon.
Stanford, Calif.: Stanford University Press, 1934.

Kipling, Rudyard. "The White Man's Burden." McClure's Magazine, Feb. 1899,
240–41.

LeRoy, James A. "Conditions in the Philippines To-Day." In Proceedings of the
Twenty-Third Annual Meeting of the Lake Mohonk Conference of Friends of the
Indian and Other Dependent Peoples, 99–105. New York: Lake Mohonk
Conference of Friends of the Indian and Other Dependent Peoples, 1905.

——. Philippine Life in Town and Country. New York: G. P. Putnam's Sons, 1906.

——. "Race Prejudice in the Philippines." Atlantic Monthly, July 1902, 110–12.

Lewis, Peter, and H. R. Kells. Foot Soldier in an Occupation Force: The Letters of
Peter Lewis, 1898–1902. Manila: Linguistics Office, De La Salle University, 1999.

Lobingier, Charles Sumner. "The Peacekeepers of the Philippines." American
Review of Reviews 42 (Sept. 1910): 310–14.

Lodge, Henry Cabot. "Colonialism in the United States." Atlantic Monthly, May
1883, 612–27.

Lopez, Sixto. The "Tribes" in the Philippines. Boston: New England Anti-
Imperialist League, 1900.

López Jaena, Graciano. Discursos y Artículos Varios por Graciano López Jaena.
Manila: Bureau of Public Printing, 1951.

Mabini, Apolinario. The Letters of Apolinario Mabini. Manila: National Heroes
Commission, 1965.

MacLeod, John T. Preface to The Sliding Scale and Other Philippine Sketches.
Manila: I. R. Morales, 1910.

——. "The Sliding Scale." In The Sliding Scale and Other Philippine Sketches, 3–34.
Manila: I. R. Morales, 1910.

Martin, Harold. "The Manila Censorship." *Forum* 31 (June 1901): 462.

Mataas, Lauro. "¿Otra Exposición del 'Retiro'?" *El Renacimiento*, Mar. 18, 1903, 1.

Mayo, Katherine. *The Isles of Fear: The Truth about the Philippines*. New York: Harcourt, 1925.

Morga, Antonio de, and José Rizal y Alonso. *Sucesos de las Islas Filipinas*. Paris: Garnier Hermanos, 1890.

Moses, Edith. *Unofficial Letters of an Official's Wife*. New York: D. Appleton, 1908.

Neely, Frank Tennyson. *Fighting in the Philippines: Authentic Original Photographs*. Chicago: F. T. Neely, 1899.

Neland, Charles. *Cartoons of Our War with Spain*. New York: F. A. Stokes Co., 1898.

Newell, Alfred C. "The Philippine Peoples." *World's Work* 8 (Aug. 1904): 5128–45.

Niederlein, Gustavo. "Brief Chronological Sketch of the Organization of the Philippine Exposition Board and the Collection and Installation of the Philippine Exhibit." In *Official Handbook of the Philippines and Catalogue of the Philippine Exhibit*, 1.9–20. Manila: Bureau of Public Printing, 1904.

——. "Outline of the Proposed Exhibit at the Louisiana Purchase Exposition Held at St. Louis, Mo., U.S.A., in 1904." In *Circular Letter of Governor Taft and Information and Instructions for the Preparation of the Philippine Exhibit for the Louisiana Purchase Exposition to Be Held at St. Louis, Mo., U.S.A.*, 1904, 24–26. Manila: Bureau of Public Printing, 1902.

Ocampo, Pablo. "Aspirations of the Filipino." In *Proceedings of the Twenty-Sixth Annual Lake Mohonk Conference of Friends of the Indian and Other Dependent Peoples*, 72–83. New York: Lake Mohonk Conference of Friends of the Indian and Other Dependent Peoples, 1908.

Osmeña, Sergio. *Discurso Pronunciado por el Hon. Sergio Osmeña, Speaker de la Asamblea Filipina, en el Banquete en su Honor Ofrecido por el Pueblo de San Miguel de Mayumo, Provincia de Bulacan, el Dia 7 de Mayo de 1910*. Manila: Imp. de "El Mercantil," 1910.

Palmer, Frederick. "White Man and Brown Man in the Philippines." *Scribner's Magazine* 27 (1900): 76–86.

Pardo de Tavera, T. H. *Etimologia de los Nombres de Razas de Filipinas*. Manila: Establecimiento Tipográfico de Modesto Reyes, 1901.

——. "The Filipino Soul." 1928. In *Thinking for Ourselves: A Collection of Representative Filipino Essays*, edited by Vicente M. Hilario and Eliseo Quirino, 170–86. Metro Manila: Cacho Hermanos, 1985.

Pardo de Tavera, T. H., Benito Legarda, and José de Luzuriaga. "Filipino Views of American Rule." *North American Review* 174 (1902): 73–84.

Parsons, Elsie Clews. "American Snobbishness in the Philippines." *Independent* 60, no. 8 (1906): 332–33.

Partridge [pseud.]. "America as Seen by a Filipino." *Filipino* 1, no. 6 (1906): 18–21.

Paterno, Pedro. *La Antigua Civilización Tagalog (Apuntes)*. Madrid: Tipog. de M. G. Hernández, 1887.

"The Philippine Report." *Harper's Weekly* 43, no. 2239 (1899), 1154.

Poplin, Richard R. "The Letters of W. Thomas Osborne, a Spanish-American

War Soldier of Bedford County." *Tennessee Historical Quarterly* 22, no. 2 (1963): 152–69.

Quezon, Manuel Luis. *The Good Fight.* New York: D. Appleton-Century, 1946.

Rai, Lajput. *The United States: A Hindu's Impressions and a Study.* Calcutta: R. Chatterjee, 1916.

Record of the Proceedings of the First Universal Races Congress, July 26–29, 1911. London: P. S. King and Son, 1911.

Republican National Committee. *Republican Campaign Text-Book 1900.* Milwaukee: Press of the Evening Wisconsin Co., 1900.

Retana, W. E. ed. *Vida y Escritos del Dr. José Rizal.* Madrid: Librería General de Victoriano Suárez, 1907.

Rhodes, Charles D. "The Utilization of Foreign Troops in Our Foreign Possessions." *Journal of the Military Service Institution of the United States* 30, no. 140 (1902): 1–22.

Riggs, Arthur Stanley. *The Filipino Drama, 1905.* Manila: Ministry of Human Settlements, Intramuros Administration, 1981.

Rivers, William C. "The Maintenance of Order in the Philippine Islands." In *Proceedings of the Twenty-Ninth Annual Lake Mohonk Conference of Friends of the Indian and Other Dependent Peoples,* 124–31. New York: Lake Mohonk Conference of Friends of the Indian and Other Dependent Peoples, 1911.

Rizal y Alonso, José. *Reminiscences and Travels of José Rizal.* Vol. 1. Manila: José Rizal National Centennial Commission, 1961.

———. *The Rizal-Blumentritt Correspondence.* Manila: José Rizal National Centennial Commission, 1961.

Roosevelt, Nicholas. *The Philippines: A Treasure and a Problem.* New York: Sears Publishing, 1933.

Roosevelt, Theodore. *Address of President Roosevelt at Arlington, Memorial Day, May 30, 1902.* N.p., 1902.

Rowland, Henry C. "Fighting Life in the Philippines." *McClure's Magazine,* July 1902, 241–47.

Salt, Alexander E. W., and H. O. S. Heistland. *An Introduction to the History of Manila.* Berkeley: University of California, n.d.

Sargent, L. R. "In Aguinaldo's Realm." *New York Independent,* Sept. 14, 1899, 2477–81.

Schurz, Carl. "American Imperialism: An Address Opposing Annexation of the Philippines, January 4, 1899." In *American Imperialism in 1898,* edited by Theodore P. Greene, 77–84. Boston: D. C. Heath, 1955.

Social Science Institute, Fisk University. *Orientals and Their Cultural Adjustment: Interviews, Life Histories and Social Adjustment Experiences of Chinese and Japanese of Varying Backgrounds and Length of Residence in the United States.* Nashville, Tenn.: Social Science Institute, Fisk University, 1946.

Soldiers' Letters: Being Materials for the History of a War of Criminal Aggression. Boston: Anti-Imperialist League, 1899.

Spahr, Charles B. "The Philippine Educational Exhibit." *Outlook* 69 (Sept. 7, 1901).

Stangl, P. L. "Filipino Nationality." *Philippine Historical Review/Revista Histórica Filipina* 1, no. 4 (1905): 49–51.

"The Status of Filipinos for Purposes of Immigration and Naturalization." *Harvard Law Review* 42 (Apr. 1929): 810–12.

Stevens, Joseph Earle. *Yester-days in the Philippines.* 1898.

Stoddard, Lothrop. *The Rising Tide of Color against World White-Supremacy.* New York: Scribner, 1920.

Storey, Moorfield, and Julian Codman. *Secretary Root's Record: "Marked Severities" in Philippine Warfare: An Analysis of the Law and Facts Bearing on the Action and Utterances of President Roosevelt and Secretary Root.* Boston: G. H. Ellis Co., 1902.

Sutherland, William A. *Not by Might: The Epic of the Philippines.* Las Cruces, N.M.: Southwest Publishing, 1953.

———. "The Philippine Exposition and the Jamestown Tercentennial Exposition in 1907." *Filipino* 1, nos. 4–5 (July–Sept. 1906): 14–15.

Taft, William H. *The Duty of Americans in the Philippines: Address before the Union Reading College of Manila, December 17, 1903.* 58th Cong., 2nd sess., 1903, S. Doc. 191.

———. "Inauguration of the Philippine Assembly." In *Four Aspects of Civic Duty; and, Present Day Problems,* 83–105. Athens: Ohio University Press, 2001.

———. "The Philippines." *National Geographic Magazine* 16, no. 8 (1905): 361–75.

Taylor, J. R. M., ed. *The Philippine Insurrection against the United States: A Compilation of Documents with Notes and Introduction.* 5 vols. Pasay City, Phil.: Eugenio Lopez Foundation, 1971.

Taylor, Rebecca J. "Disposition of the Philippine Islands." *Arena* 29 (1903): 48–50.

Telfer, George F., and Sara Bunnett. *Manila Envelopes: Oregon Volunteer Lt. George F. Telfer's Spanish-American War Letters.* Portland: Oregon Historical Society Press, 1987.

"The Truth about the Concentration Camps." *Public Opinion* 31, no. 25 (1901): 780.

Tuohy, Anthony R. *Álbum Histórico de la Primera Asamblea Filipina.* Manila: N.p., 1908.

Villamor, Juan. *Inédita Crónica de la Guerra Americano-Filipina en el Norte de Luzon, 1899–1901.* Manila: Imprenta Juan Fajardo, 1924.

Villard, Oswald Garrison. *Fighting Years: Memoirs of a Liberal Editor.* New York: Harcourt, Brace, 1939.

Westcott, Robert B., ed. *The Exaltation of the Flag: Proceedings at the Patriotic Mass Meeting Held by the Americans of the Philippine Islands, August 23, 1907.* Manila: Edgar and Co., 1907.

Wheeler, Benjamin Ide. "A Forecast for California and the Pacific Coast." *Outlook* 99 (1911): 167–74.

Wilcox, W. B. "In the Heart of Luzon." *New York Independent,* Sept. 14, 1899, 2475.

Wilson, H. C. *Reconcentration in the Philippines, and Statistical Table Showing Results of "Benevolent Assimilation" on Population, Production and Prosperity in the Philippines.* Boston: Anti-Imperialist League, 1906.

Worcester, Dean Conant. "The Non-Christian Tribes of Northern Luzon."
  Philippine Journal of Science 1, no. 8 (Oct. 1906): 791–876.
——. *The Philippine Islands and Their People: A Record of Personal Observation and
  Experience, with a Short Summary of the More Important Facts in the History of the
  Archipelago.* New York: Macmillan, 1899.
——. *The Philippines, Past and Present.* 2 vols. New York: Macmillan, 1914.

Secondary Sources

Abinales, Patricio. "An American Colonial State: Authority and Structure in
  Southern Mindanao." In *Images of State Power: Essays on Philippine Politics from
  the Margins*, 1–52. Diliman: University of the Philippines Press, 1998.
Adas, Michael. "Improving on the Civilizing Mission? Assumptions of United
  States Exceptionalism in the Colonisation of the Philippines." *Itinerario* 22, no.
  4 (1998): 44–66.
——. *Machines as the Measure of Men: Science, Technology, and Ideologies of Western
  Dominance.* Ithaca, N.Y.: Cornell University Press, 1989.
Agoncillo, Teodoro A. *Malolos: The Crisis of the Republic.* Quezon City, Phil.:
  University of the Philippines, 1960.
——. *The Revolt of the Masses: The Story of Bonifacio and the Katipunan.* Quezon
  City, Phil.: University of the Philippines, 1956.
Aguilar, Filomeno V., Jr. "Tracing Origins: Ilustrado Nationalism and the Racial
  Science of Migration Waves." *Journal of Asian Studies* 64, no. 3 (Aug. 2005).
Alatas, Hussein. *The Myth of the Lazy Native: A Study of the Image of the Malays,
  Filipinos and Javanese from the 16th to the 20th Century and Its Function in the
  Ideology of Colonial Capitalism.* London: F. Cass, 1977.
Alfonso, Oscar M. "Taft's Early Views on the Filipinos." *Solidaridad* 4 (1969): 52–
  58.
——. *Theodore Roosevelt and the Philippines, 1897–1909.* Quezon City, Phil.:
  University of the Philippines Press, 1970.
Alidio, Kim. "Between Civilizing Mission and Ethnic Assimilation: Racial
  Discourse, U.S. Colonial Education and Filipino Ethnicity, 1901–1946." Ph.D.
  diss., University of Michigan, 2001.
——. "'When I Get Home, I Want to Forget': Memory and Amnesia in the
  Occupied Philippines, 1901–1904." *Social Text* 59, no. 2 (Summer 1999): 105–22.
Almaguer, Tomás. *Racial Fault Lines: The Historical Origins of White Supremacy in
  California.* Berkeley: University of California Press, 1994.
Alvarez, David. "Purely a Business Matter: The Taft Mission to the Vatican."
  Diplomatic History 16, no. 3 (1992): 357–70.
Andaya, Leonard Y. "Ethnicity in the Philippine Revolution." In *The Philippine
  Revolution of 1896: Ordinary Lives in Extraordinary Times*, edited by Florentino
  Rodao García and Felice Noelle Rodriguez, 49–82. Manila: Ateneo de Manila
  University Press, 2001.
Anderson, Benedict R. O'G. *Imagined Communities: Reflections on the Origin and
  Spread of Nationalism.* London: Verso, 1983.

———. "The Rooster's Egg," *New Left Review* 2 (2000): 47–62.

———. *Spectres of Comparison: Nationalism, Southeast Asia, and the World*. London: Verso, 1998.

Anderson, Warwick. "Colonial Pathologies: American Medicine in the Philippines, 1898–1921." Ph.D. diss., University of Pennsylvania, 1992.

———. "Excremental Colonialism: Public Health and the Politics of Pollution." *Critical Inquiry* 21, no. 3 (Spring 1995): 640–69.

———. "Immunities of Empire: Race, Disease and the New Tropical Medicine, 1900–1920." *Bulletin of the History of Medicine* 7, no. 1 (1996): 94–118.

———. "'Where Every Prospect Pleases and Only Man Is Vile': Laboratory Medicine as Colonial Discourse." *Critical Inquiry* 18, no. 3 (1992): 506–29.

Arata, Stephen D. "The Occidental Tourist: Dracula and the Anxiety of Reverse Colonization." *Victorian Studies* 33, no. 4 (1990): 621–45.

Balibar, Etienne. "Racism and Nationalism." In *Race, Nation, Class: Ambiguous Identities*, edited by Etienne Balibar and Immanuel Maurice Wallerstein, 37–67. London: Verso, 1991.

Bankoff, Greg. *Crime, Society, and the State in the Nineteenth-Century Philippines*. Quezon City, Phil.: Ateneo de Manila University Press, 1996.

Beadles, John A. "The Debate in the United States concerning Philippine Independence." *Philippine Studies* 16, no. 3 (1968): 421–41.

Bederman, Gail. *Manliness and Civilization: A Cultural History of Gender and Race in the United States, 1880–1917*. Chicago: University of Chicago Press, 1995.

Beisner, Robert L. *From the Old Diplomacy to the New, 1865–1900*. Arlington Heights, Ill.: Harlan Davidson, 1986.

———. *Twelve against Empire: The Anti-Imperialists, 1898–1900*. New York: McGraw-Hill, 1968.

Bender, Thomas, ed. *Rethinking American History in a Global Age*. Berkeley: University of California Press, 2002.

Benedict, Burton. *The Anthropology of World's Fairs: San Francisco's Panama Pacific International Exposition of 1915*. Berkeley: Lowie Museum of Anthropology, Scolar Press, 1983.

Bernad, Miguel. *The Christianization of the Philippines: Problems and Perspectives*. Manila: Filipiniana Book Guild, 1972.

———. *Rizal and Spain: An Essay in Biographical Context*. Manila: National Bookstore, 1986.

Bönker, Dirk. "Admiration, Enmity, and Cooperation: U.S. Navalism and the British and German Empires before the Great War." *Journal of Colonialism and Colonial History* 2, no. 1 (2001), <http://muse.jhu.edu/journals/cch/v002/2.1bonker.html>. Jan. 7, 2005.

———. "Militarizing the Western World: Navalism, Empire and State-Building in Germany and the United States before World War I." Ph.D. diss., Johns Hopkins University, 2002.

Bourgois, Phillipe. "If You're Not Black You're White: A History of Ethnic Relations in St. Louis." *City and Society* 3, no. 2 (1989): 106–31.

Bradley, Mark. *Imagining Vietnam and America: The Making of Postcolonial Vietnam, 1919–1950.* Chapel Hill: University of North Carolina Press, 2000.

Braisted, William Reynolds. *The United States Navy in the Pacific, 1897–1909.* Austin: University of Texas Press, 1958.

Brantlinger, Patrick. *Dark Vanishings: Discourse on the Extinction of Primitive Races, 1800–1930.* Ithaca, N.Y.: Cornell University Press, 2003.

Briggs, Laura. *Reproducing Empire: Race, Sex, Science, and U.S. Imperialism in Puerto Rico.* Berkeley: University of California Press, 2002.

Brown, Charles Henry. *The Correspondents' War: Journalists in the Spanish-American War.* New York: Scribner, 1967.

Burgess, Larry E. "The Lake Mohonk Conferences on the Indian, 1883–1916." Ph.D. diss., Claremont Graduate School, 1972.

Burnett, Christina Duffy, and Burke Marshall, eds. *Foreign in a Domestic Sense: Puerto Rico, American Expansion, and the Constitution.* Durham: N.C. Duke University Press, 2001.

Burton, Antoinette. *Burdens of History: British Feminists, Indian Women, and Imperial Culture, 1865–1915.* Chapel Hill: University of North Carolina Press, 1994.

Campomanes, Oscar V. "The New Empire's Forgetful and Forgotten Citizens: Unrepresentability and Unassimilability in Filipino-American Postcolonialities." *Critical Mass* 2, no. 2 (1995): 145–200.

Chamberlin, J. Edward, and Sander L. Gilman. *Degeneration: The Dark Side of Progress.* New York: Columbia University Press, 1985.

Chapman, Gregory Dean. "Taking Up the White Man's Burden: Tennesseans in the Philippine Insurrection, 1899." *Tennessee Historical Quarterly* 47, no. 1 (1988): 27–40.

Chatterjee, Partha. *Nationalist Thought and the Colonial World: A Derivative Discourse?* London: Zed Books, 1986.

Choy, Catherine Ceniza. *Empire of Care: Nursing and Migration in Filipino American History.* Durham, N.C.: Duke University Press, 2003.

Christensen, Lawrence O. "Race Relations in St. Louis, 1865–1916." *Missouri Historical Review* 78, no. 2 (1983): 123–36.

Churchill, Bernardita Reyes. *The Philippine Independence Missions to the United States, 1919–1934.* Manila: National Historical Institute, 1983.

Clifford, James. "On Orientalism." In *The Predicament of Culture: Twentieth-Century Ethnography, Literature, and Art.* Cambridge, Mass.: Harvard University Press, 1988.

Clymer, Kenton J. "Humanitarian Imperialism: David Prescott Barrows and the White Man's Burden in the Philippines." *Pacific Historical Review* 45, no. 4 (1976): 495–518.

——. *Protestant Missionaries in the Philippines, 1898–1916: An Inquiry into the American Colonial Mentality.* Urbana: University of Illinois Press, 1986.

Coats, George Yarrington. "The Philippine Constabulary, 1901–1917." Ph.D. diss., Ohio State University, 1968.

Coloma, Casiano Pagdilao. *A Study of the Filipino Repatriation Movement.* San Francisco: R and E Research Associates, 1974.

Conn, Steven. "An Epistemology for Empire: The Philadelphia Commercial Museum, 1893–1926." *Diplomatic History* 22, no. 4 (1998): 533–63.

Constantino, Renato. "Historical Truths from Biased Sources." In *The Philippine Insurrection against the United States: A Compilation of Documents with Notes and Introduction*, edited by John R. M. Taylor, 1.ix–xiii. Pasay City, Phil.: Eugenio Lopez Foundation, 1971.

Coombes, Annie E. *Reinventing Africa: Museums, Material Culture, and Popular Imagination in Late Victorian and Edwardian England.* New Haven: Yale University Press, 1994.

Cooper, Frederick, and Ann Laura Stoler. "Between Metropole and Colony: Rethinking a Research Agenda." In *Tensions of Empire: Colonial Cultures in a Bourgeois World*, edited by Frederick Cooper and Ann Laura Stoler, 1–56. Berkeley: University of California Press, 1997.

Cordova, Fred, Dorothy Cordova, and Albert A. Acera. *Filipinos: Forgotten Asian Americans; A Pictorial Essay, 1763–circa 1963.* Dubuque, Iowa: Kendall/Hunt Publishing, 1983.

Coronil, Fernando. "Beyond Occidentalism: Towards Nonimperial Geohistorical Categories." *Cultural Anthropology* 11, no. 1 (1996): 51–86.

Corpuz, Onofre D. *The Roots of the Filipino Nation.* 2 vols. Quezon City, Phil.: Aklahi Foundation, 1989.

Crapol, Edward P. "Coming to Terms with Empire: The Historiography of Late-Nineteenth-Century American Foreign Relations." *Diplomatic History* 16, no. 4 (1992): 573–598.

Cruz, Romeo V. *America's Colonial Desk and the Philippines, 1898–1934.* Quezon City, Phil.: University of the Philippines Press, 1974.

Cullinane, Michael. *Ilustrado Politics: Filipino Elite Responses to American Rule, 1898–1908.* Quezon City, Phil.: Ateneo de Manila University Press, 2003.

———. "Playing the Game: The Rise of Sergio Osmeña." In *Philippine Colonial Democracy*, edited by Ruby R. Paredes, 70–113. Quezon City, Phil.: Ateneo de Manila University Press, 1989.

Curry, Roy Watson. *Woodrow Wilson and Far Eastern Policy, 1913–1921.* New York: Bookman Associates, 1957.

———. "Woodrow Wilson and Philippine Policy." *Mississippi Valley Historical Review* 41, no. 3 (1954): 435–52.

Daniels, Roger. *The Politics of Prejudice: The Anti-Japanese Movement in California, and the Struggle for Japanese Exclusion.* Berkeley: University of California Press, 1962.

Daniels, Roger, and Olin, Spencer C., eds. *Racism in California: A Reader in the History of Oppression.* New York: Macmillan, 1972.

De Bevoise, Ken. "The Compromised Host: The Epidemiological Context of the Philippine-American War." Ph.D. diss., University of Oregon, 1986.

De la Torre, Visitacion R. *History of the Philippine Civil Service.* Quezon City, Phil.: New Day Publishers, 1986.

Dery, Luis Camara. "General Bell and America's 'Benevolent Assimilation' Policy in Batangas, 1901–1902." In *The Army of the First Philippine Republic and Other Historical Essays*, edited by Luis Camara Dery, 123–32. Manila: De La Salle University Press, 1995.

De Santis, Hugh. "The Imperialist Impulse and American Innocence, 1865–1900." In *American Foreign Relations: A Historiographical Review*, edited by Gerald K. Haines and J. Samuel Walker, 65–90. Westport, Conn.: Greenwood Press, 1981.

DeWitt, Howard A. *Violence in the Fields: California Filipino Farm Labor Unionization during the Great Depression*. Saratoga, Calif.: Century Twenty One, 1980.

Diokno, Maria Serena I. "Perspectives on Peace during the Philippine-American War of 1899–1902." *South East Asia Research* 5, no. 1 (1997): 5–19.

——. *Voices and Scenes of the Past: The Philippine-American War Retold*. Quezon City, Phil.: Jose W. Diokno Foundation, 1999.

Dower, John W. *War without Mercy: Race and Power in the Pacific War*. New York: Pantheon Books, 1986.

Dumol, Paul A. "Rizal contra European Racism: An Autobiography of José Rizal Embedded in Blumentritt's Obituary of Rizal." In *European Studies: Essays by Filipino Scholars*, edited by Vyva Victoria Aguirre. Quezon City, Phil.: University of the Philippines Press, 1999.

Ellis, John Tracy. *The Life of James Cardinal Gibbons: Archbishop of Baltimore, 1834–1921*. Vol. 2. Milwaukee: Bruce Publishing, 1952.

Espiritu, Yen Le. *Filipino American Lives*. Philadelphia: Temple University Press, 1995.

Farrell, John T. "An Abandoned Approach to Philippine History: John R. M. Taylor and the Philippine Insurrection Records." *Catholic Historical Review* 39, no. 4 (1954): 385–407.

Field, James A., Jr. "American Imperialism: The Worst Chapter in Almost Any Book." *American Historical Review* 83, no. 3 (1978): 644–68.

Fields, Barbara J. "Ideology and Race in American History." In *Region, Race, and Reconstruction: Essays in Honor of C. Vann Woodward*, edited by C. Vann Woodward, J. Morgan Kousser, and James M. McPherson, 143–78. New York: Oxford University Press, 1982.

Finin, Gerard A. "Regional Consciousness and Administrative Grids: Understanding the Role of Planning in the Philippines' Gran Cordillera Central." Ph.D. diss., Cornell University, 1991.

Flint, Roy K. "The United States Army on the Pacific Frontier, 1899–1939." In *The American Military and the Far East, Proceedings of the Ninth Military History Symposium*, edited by Joe Dixon, 139–59. Colorado Springs: United States Air Force Academy and Office of Air Force History, 1980.

Fradera, Josep Maria. *Gobernar Colonias*. Barcelona: Ediciones Península, 1999.

Francisco, Luzviminda, "The First Vietnam—The Philippine-American War of 1899–1902." In *Letters in Exile: An Introductory Reader on the History of Pilipinos in America*, 1–22. Los Angeles: UCLA Asian American Studies Center, 1975.

Freeman, Charles A. "Yankee Music in the Far East." *American Old-Timer* 3, no. 1 (1935): 31.

Friend, Morton H. *The Notion of Tribe*. Menlo Park, Calif.: Cummings Publishing, 1975.

Friend, Theodore. "American Interests and Philippine Independence, 1929–1933." *Philippine Studies* 2, no. 4 (Oct. 1963): 505–23.

———. *Between Two Empires: The Ordeal of the Philippines, 1929–1946*. New Haven: Yale University Press, 1965.

Fry, Howard Tyrrell. "The Bacon Bill of 1926: New Light on an Exercise in Divide-and-Rule." *Philippine Studies* 26, no. 3 (1978): 257–73.

———. *A History of the Mountain Province*. Quezon City, Phil.: New Day Publishers, 1983.

Fry, Joseph. "Imperialism, American Style, 1890–1916." In *American Foreign Relations Reconsidered, 1890–1993*, edited by Gordon Martel, 52–70. London: Routledge, 1994.

Fujita-Rony, Dorothy B. *American Workers, Colonial Power: Philippine Seattle and the Transpacific West, 1919–1941*. Berkeley: University of California Press, 2002.

Füredi, Frank. *The Silent War: Imperialism and the Changing Perception of Race*. New Brunswick, N.J.: Rutgers University Press, 1998.

Gaerlan, Barbara. "The Politics and Pedagogy of Language Use at the University of the Philippines: The History of English as the Medium of Instruction and the Challenge Mounted by Filipinos." Ph.D. diss., University of California at Los Angeles, 1998.

———. "The Pursuit of Modernity: Trinidad H. Pardo De Tavera and the Educational Legacy of the Philippine Revolution." *Amerasia Journal* 24, no. 2 (1998): 87–108.

Gallicchio, Marc S. *The African American Encounter with Japan and China: Black Internationalism in Asia, 1895–1945*. Chapel Hill: University of North Carolina Press, 2000.

Gardner, Lloyd C. "How We 'Lost' Vietnam, 1940–1954." In *The United States and Decolonization*, edited by David Ryan and Victor Pungong, 121–39. New York: St. Martin's Press, 2000.

Gates, John M. "Philippine Guerillas, American Anti-Imperialists, and the Election of 1900." *Pacific Historical Review* 46, no. 1 (1977): 51–64.

———. *Schoolbooks and Krags: The United States Army in the Philippines, 1898–1902*. Westport, Conn.: Greenwood Press, 1973.

———. "War-Related Deaths in the Philippines, 1898–1902." *Pacific Historical Review* 53, no. 3 (1984): 367–78.

Gatewood, Willard B. *Black Americans and the White Man's Burden, 1898–1903*. Urbana: University of Illinois Press, 1975.

Gealogo, Francis A. "Beyond the Numbers: Colonial Demography and the Representation of the Native in the Philippines." Paper presented at the "Bridging the Agenda Gap" workshop, Antipolo, Philippines, Dec. 2002.

Geyer, Michael, and Charles Bright. "World History in a Global Age." *American Historical Review* 100, no. 4 (1995): 1034–60.

Gilmore, Glenda Elizabeth. *Gender and Jim Crow: Women and the Politics of White Supremacy in North Carolina, 1896–1920.* Chapel Hill: University of North Carolina Press, 1996.

Gilmour, David. *The Long Recessional: The Imperial Life of Rudyard Kipling.* London: J. Murray, 2002.

Gleeck, Lewis E. *The American Governors-General and High Commissioners in the Philippines: Proconsuls, Nation-Builders and Politicians.* Quezon City, Phil.: New Day Publishers, 1986.

——. *American Institutions in the Philippines, 1898–1941.* Manila: Historical Conservation Society, 1976.

——. *Nine Years to Make a Difference: The Tragically Short Career of James A. LeRoy in the Philippines.* Manila: L. E. Gleeck, 1996.

——. *Over Seventy-Five Years of Philippine-American History: The Army and Navy Club of Manila.* Manila: Carmelo and Bauermann, 1976.

Go, Julian. "Chains of Empire, Projects of State: Political Education and U.S. Colonial Rule in Puerto Rico and the Philippines." *Comparative Studies in Society and History* 42, no. 2 (2000): 333–62.

——. "Introduction: Global Perspectives on the U.S. Colonial State in the Philippines." In *The American Colonial State in the Philippines: Global Perspectives,* edited by Julian Go and Anne L. Foster, 1–42. Durham, N.C.: Duke University Press, 2003.

——. "Transcultured States: Elite Political Culture in Puerto Rico and the Philippines during U.S. Colonial Rule (c. 1898–1912)." Ph.D. diss., University of Chicago, 2000.

Go, Julian, and Anne L. Foster, eds. *The American Colonial State in the Philippines: Global Perspectives.* Durham, N.C.: Duke University Press, 2003.

Golay, Frank. *Face of Empire: United States-Philippine Relations, 1898–1946.* Madison, Wisc.: Center for Southeast Asian Studies, 1997.

——. "'Manila Americans' and Philippine Policy: The Voice of American Business." In *The Philippine Economy and the United States: Studies in Past and Present Interactions,* edited by Norman G. Owen, 1–35. Ann Arbor: Center for South and Southeast Asian Studies, University of Michigan, 1983.

Gong, Gerrit W. *The Standard of "Civilization" in International Society.* Oxford: Clarendon Press, 1984.

Goodman, Grant K. "General Artemio Ricarte and Japan." *Journal of Southeast Asian History* 7, no. 2 (1966): 48–60.

——. "The Problem of Philippine Independence and Japan: The First Three Decades of American Colonial Rule." *Southeast Asia* 1, no. 3 (1971): 165–96.

Gopinath, Aruna. *Manuel L. Quezon, the Tutelary Democrat.* Quezon City, Phil.: New Day Publishers, 1987.

Gowing, Peter G. *Mandate in Moroland: The American Government of Muslim Filipinos, 1899–1920.* Quezon City, Phil.: New Day Publishers, 1983.

Greenhalgh, Paul. *Ephemeral Vistas: A History of the Expositions Universelles, Great Exhibitions and World's Fairs, 1851–1939.* Manchester: Manchester University Press, 1988.

Grenville, John A. S. "American Naval Preparations for War with Spain." *Journal of American Studies* 2 (1968): 33–47.

Grimsley, Mark. *The Hard Hand of War: Union Military Policy toward Southern Civilians, 1861–1865.* New York: Cambridge University Press, 1995.

———. "'Rebels' and 'Redskins': U.S. Military Conduct toward White Southerners and Native Americans in Comparative Perspective." In *Civilians in the Path of War,* edited by Mark Grimsley and Clifford J. Rogers, 137–62. Lincoln: University of Nebraska Press, 2002.

Gripaldo, Rolando M. "The Quezon-Winslow Correspondence: A Friendship Turned Sour." *Philippine Studies* 32 (1984): 129–62.

Guerrero, Milagros C. "Luzon at War: Contradictions in Philippine Society, 1899–1902." Ph.D. diss., University of Michigan, 1977.

———. *Under Stars and Stripes.* Vol. 6 of *Kasaysayan.* Manila: Asia Publishing; Pleasantville, N.Y.: Reader's Digest, 1998.

Guillermo, Artemio R., "The Worcester Libel Case and Philippine Journalism." *Bulletin of the American Historical Collection* 3, no. 3 (July 1975): 22–50.

Hackler, Rhoda. "The United States Presence in the Northern Philippines prior to 1898." Pts. 1 and 2. *Bulletin of the American Historical Collection* 17, no. 4 (Oct.–Dec. 1989): 22–49; 18, no. 1 (Jan.–Mar. 1990): 49–72.

Hall, Jacqueline Dowd. "'The Mind That Burns in Each Body': Women, Rape and Racial Violence." In *Powers of Desire: The Politics of Sexuality,* edited by Ann Snitow, Christine Stansell, and Sharon Thompson, 328–49. New York: Monthly Review Press, 1983.

Hall, Stuart. "Race, Articulation and Societies Structured in Dominance." In *Sociological Theories: Race and Colonialism,* 305–45. Paris: UNESCO, 1980.

Haller, John S. *Outcasts from Evolution: Scientific Attitudes of Racial Inferiority, 1859–1900.* Urbana: University of Illinois Press, 1971.

Harrod, Frederick S. *Manning the New Navy: The Development of a Modern Naval Enlisted Force, 1899–1940.* Westport, Conn.: Greenwood Press, 1978.

Hart, Robert A. *The Great White Fleet: Its Voyage around the World, 1907–1909.* Boston: Little, Brown, 1965.

Higham, John. "The Reorientation of American Culture in the 1890s." In *Writing American History: Essays on Modern Scholarship,* 73–102. Bloomington: Indiana University Press, 1972.

———. *Strangers in the Land: Patterns of American Nativism, 1860–1925.* New Brunswick, N.J.: Rutgers University Press, 1955.

Hing, Bill Ong. *Making and Remaking Asian America through Immigration Policy, 1850–1990.* Stanford, Calif.: Stanford University Press, 1993.

Hinsley, Curtis M. *The Smithsonian and the American Indian: Making a Moral Anthropology in Victorian America.* Washington, D.C.: Smithsonian Institution Press, 1994.

Hobsbawm, E. J., and T. O. Ranger. "Mass-Producing Traditions: Europe, 1870–1914." In *The Invention of Tradition,* edited by E. J. Hobsbawm and T. O. Ranger, 263–307. Cambridge, Eng.: Cambridge University Press, 1983.

Hodes, Martha. "The Mercurial Nature and Abiding Power of Race: A Transnational Family Story." *American Historical Review* 18 (Feb. 2003): 84–118.

Hofstader, Richard. "Cuba, the Philippines, and Manifest Destiny." In *The Paranoid Style in American Politics and Other Essays*, 145–87. New York: Knopf, 1965.

——. *Social Darwinism in American Thought*. Boston: Beacon Press, 1944.

Hoganson, Kristin L. *Fighting for American Manhood: How Gender Politics Provoked the Spanish-American and Philippine-American Wars*. New Haven: Yale University Press, 1998.

Hollnsteiner, Mary Racelis, and Judy Celine A. Ick. *Bearers of Benevolence: The Thomasites and Public Education in the Philippines*. Pasig City, Phil.: Anvil Pub., 2001.

Holt, Thomas C. *The Problem of Race in the Twenty-First Century*. Cambridge, Mass.: Harvard University Press, 2000.

Horne, Gerald. "Race from Power: U.S. Foreign Policy and the General Crisis of White Supremacy." *Diplomatic History* 23, no. 3 (1999): 437–61.

Hosillos, Lucila V. *Philippine-American Literary Relations, 1898–1941*. Quezon City, Phil.: University of the Philippines Press, 1969.

Hoxie, Frederick E. *A Final Promise: The Campaign to Assimilate the Indians, 1880–1920*. Lincoln: University of Nebraska Press, 1984.

Hunt, Geoffrey Roland. "The First Colorado Regiment in the Philippine Wars." Ph.D. diss., University of Colorado, 1997.

Hunt, Michael H. *Ideology and U.S. Foreign Policy*. New Haven: Yale University Press, 1987.

Hutchcroft, Paul D. "Colonial Masters, National Politicos, and Provincial Lords: Central Authority and Local Autonomy in the American Philippines, 1900–1913." *Journal of Asian Studies* 59, no. 2 (2000): 277–306.

Huttenback, Robert A. *Racism and Empire: White Settlers and Colored Immigrants in the British Self-Governing Colonies, 1830–1910*. Ithaca, N.Y.: Cornell University Press, 1976.

Hutterer, Karl L. "Dean Worcester and Philippine Anthropology." *Philippine Quarterly of Culture and Society* 6 (1978): 125–36.

Ignacio, Abe, Enrique de la Cruz, Jorge Emmanuel, and Helen Toribio. *The Forbidden Book: The Philippine-American War in Political Cartoons*. San Francisco: T'Boli Publishing, 2004.

Ileto, Reynaldo Clemeña. "Cholera and the Origins of the American Sanitary Order in the Philippines." In *Imperial Medicine and Indigenous Societies*, edited by David Arnold, 125–48. Manchester: Manchester University Press, 1988.

——. *Knowing America's Colony: A Hundred Years from the Philippine War*. Honolulu: Center for Philippine Studies, School of Hawaiian, Asian and Pacific Studies, University of Hawaii at Manoa, 1999.

——. "Orators and the Crowd: Independence Politics, 1910–1914." In *Filipinos and Their Revolution*, edited by Reynaldo Clemeña Ileto, 135–64. Quezon City, Phil.: Ateneo de Manila University Press, 1998.

——. *Pasyon and Revolution: Popular Movements in the Philippines, 1840–1910.* Quezon City, Phil.: Ateneo de Manila University Press, 1979.

Iriye, Akira. *Across the Pacific: An Inner History of American-East Asian Relations.* New York: Harcourt, Brace, 1967.

Jacobson, Matthew Frye. *Barbarian Virtues: The United States Encounters Foreign Peoples at Home and Abroad, 1876–1917.* New York: Farrar, Straus and Giroux, 2000.

——. *Special Sorrows: The Diasporic Imagination of Irish, Polish, and Jewish Immigrants in the United States.* Berkeley: University of California Press, 2002.

Jamieson, Perry D. *Crossing the Deadly Ground: United States Army Tactics, 1865–1899.* Tuscaloosa: University of Alabama Press, 1994.

Jenista, Frank L. "Conflict with the Assembly." In *Compadre Colonialism: Studies on the Philippines under American Rule,* edited by Norman G. Owen, 77–101. Ann Arbor: Center for South and Southeast Asian Studies, University of Michigan, 1971.

——. *The White Apos: American Governors on the Cordillera Central.* Quezon City, Phil.: New Day Publishers, 1987.

Jensen, Irene. *The Chinese in the Philippines during the American Regime, 1898–1946.* San Francisco: R and E Research Associates, 1975.

Jose, Ricardo. "The Philippine National Guard in World War I." *Philippine Studies* 36 (1988): 275–99.

Kaplan, Amy. "Left Alone with America: The Absence of Empire in the Study of American Culture." In *Cultures of U.S. Imperialism,* edited by Amy Kaplan and Donald E. Pease, 3–21. Durham, N.C.: Duke University Press, 1993.

Kennedy, Philip W. "Race and American Expansion in Cuba and Puerto Rico, 1895–1905." *Journal of Black Studies* 1, no. 3 (1971): 306–15.

——. "The Racial Overtones of Imperialism as a Campaign Issue, 1900." *Mid-America* 48, no. 3 (1966): 196–205.

Kerr, James Edward. *The Insular Cases: The Role of the Judiciary in American Expansionism.* Port Washington, N.Y.: Kennikat Press, 1982.

Kirk, Grayson, *Philippine Independence: Motives, Problems, and Prospects.* New York: Farrar and Rinehart, 1936.

Kramer, Paul A. "The Darkness That Enters the Home: The Politics of Prostitution during the Philippine-American War." In *Haunted by Empire: Race and Colonial Intimacies in North American History,* edited by Ann Laura Stoler. Durham: Duke University Press, forthcoming.

——. "Empires, Exceptions, and Anglo-Saxons: Race and Rule between the British and United States Empires, 1880–1910." *Journal of American History* 88, no. 4 (2002): 1315–53.

——. "Making Concessions: Race and Empire Revisited at the Philippine Exposition, St. Louis, 1901–1905." *Radical History Review* 73 (Winter 1999): 74–114.

——. "The Pragmatic Empire: U.S. Anthropology and Colonial Politics in the Occupied Philippines, 1898–1916." Ph.D. diss., Princeton University, 1998.

——. "Princeton University and the Academic Life of Empire." *PLAS Cuadernos,* no. 1. Princeton, N.J.: Princeton University Program in Latin American Studies, 1998.

——. "The Spoils of Empire: Debating Corruption, State-Building, and Colonialism in the Early 20th Century." Paper presented at the Joint Neale and Commonwealth Fund Conference on Anglo-American Relations, University College of London, Feb. 2005.

Kwok-Chu, Wong. "The Jones Bills, 1912–1916: A Reappraisal of Filipino Views of Independence." *Journal of Southeast Asian Studies* 13, no. 2 (1982): 252–69.

LaFeber, Walter. *The New Empire: An Interpretation of American Expansion, 1860–1898.* Ithaca, N.Y.: Cornell University Press, 1963.

Lapeña-Bonifacio, Amelia. *The "Seditious" Tagalog Playwrights: Early American Occupation.* Manila: Zarzuela Foundation of the Philippines, 1972.

Lasch, Christopher. "The Anti-Imperialists, the Philippines, and the Inequality of Man." *Journal of Southern History* 24, no. 3 (1958): 319–31.

Lasker, Bruno. *Filipino Immigration to Continental United States and to Hawaii.* Chicago: University of Chicago Press, 1931.

Laurie, Clayton. "An Oddity of Empire: The Philippine Scouts and the 1904 World's Fair." *Gateway Heritage* 15, no. 3 (1994–95): 44–55.

——. "The Philippine Scouts: America's Colonial Army, 1899–1913." *Philippine Studies* 37, no. 2 (1989): 174–91.

Lawrence, James R. "The American Federation of Labor and the Philippine Independence Question, 1920–1935." *Labor History* 7, no. 1 (1966): 62–69.

Legarda, Benito, Jr. *After the Galleons: Foreign Trade, Economic Change, and Entrepreneurship in the Nineteenth-Century Philippines.* Madison: University of Wisconsin Press, 2004.

Lent, John. "The Philippine Press during the Revolution and the Filipino-American War." *Asian Thought and Society* 3, no. 9 (1978): 308–21.

Levine, Lawrence W. *Highbrow / Lowbrow: The Emergence of Cultural Hierarchy in America.* Cambridge, Mass.: Harvard University Press, 1988.

Lewis, David L. *W. E. B. Du Bois: Biography of a Race, 1868–1919.* New York: H. Holt, 1994.

Lieber, Francis, and Richard Shelly Hartigan. *Lieber's Code and the Law of War.* Chicago: Precedent, 1983.

Lindqvist, Sven. *Exterminate All the Brutes.* New York: New Press, 1996.

Linn, Brian M. *Guardians of Empire: The U.S. Army and the Pacific, 1902–1940.* Chapel Hill: University of North Carolina Press, 1997.

——. "Intelligence and Low-Intensity Conflict in the Philippine War, 1899–1902." *Intelligence and National Security* 6, no. 1 (1991): 90–114.

——. *The Philippine War, 1899–1902.* Lawrence: University Press of Kansas, 2000.

——. "Taking Up the White Man's Burden: The U.S. Military in the Philippines, 1898–1902." In *1898: Enfoques y Perspectivas,* 111–42. San Juan: Academia Puertorriqueña de la Historia, 1997.

——. "'We Will Go Heavily Armed': The Marines' Small War on Samar, 1901–1902." In *New Interpretations in Naval History: Selected Papers from the Ninth*

Naval History Symposium Held at the United States Naval Academy, 18–20 October 1989, edited by William R. Roberts, Jack Sweetman, and United States Naval Academy, 273–92. Annapolis, Md.: Naval Institute Press, 1991.

Lorence, James J. "Business and Reform: The American Asiatic Association and the Exclusion Laws, 1905–1907." *Pacific Historical Review* 39, no. 4 (1970): 421–38.

Lowe, Lisa. *Critical Terrains: French and British Orientalisms.* Ithaca, N.Y.: Cornell University Press, 1991.

Mackenzie, John M., ed. *Imperialism and Popular Culture.* New York: Manchester University Press, 1992.

Majul, Cesar Adib. *Apolinario Mabini, Revolutionary.* Manila: National Heroes Commission, 1964.

——. *Mabini and the Philippine Revolution.* Quezon City, Phil.: University of the · Philippines, 1960.

——. "*Principales, Ilustrados,* Intellectuals and the Original Concept of Filipino National Community." *Asian Studies* 15 (1977): 1–20.

Mamdani, Mahmood. *Citizen and Subject: Contemporary Africa and the Legacy of Late Colonialism.* Princeton, N.J.: Princeton University Press, 1996.

Manuel, E. Arsenio, and Magdalena Avenir Manuel. *Dictionary of Philippine Biography.* 4 vols. Quezon City, Phil.: Filipiniana Publications, 1955–.

Manzon, Maximo C. *The Strange Case of the Filipinos in the United States.* New York: American Committee for the Protection of the Foreign Born, 1938.

Markey, Joseph Ignacious. *From Iowa to the Philippines: A History of Company M, Fifty-first Iowa Infantry Volunteers.* Red Oak, Iowa: T. D. Murphy Co., 1900.

Marks, George P., ed. *The Black Press Views American Imperialism (1898–1900).* New York: Arno Press, 1971.

May, Glenn A. *Battle for Batangas: A Philippine Province at War.* New Haven: Yale University Press, 1991.

——. "150,000 Missing Filipinos: A Demographic Crisis in Batangas, 1887–1903." *Annales de Démographie Historique* (1985): 215–43.

——. *Social Engineering in the Philippines: The Aims, Execution, and Impact of American Colonial Policy, 1900–1913.* Westport, Conn: Greenwood Press, 1980.

——. "Was the Philippine-American War a 'Total War'?" In *Anticipating Total War: The German and American Experiences, 1871–1914,* edited by Stig Forster, Roger Chickering, and Manfred F. Boemeke, 437–57. Cambridge, Eng.: Cambridge University Press, 1999.

McClain, Charles J. *Asian Indians, Filipinos, Other Asian Communities, and the Law.* New York: Garland, 1994.

McCormick, Thomas J. *China Market: America's Quest for Informal Empire, 1893–1901.* Chicago: Quadrangle Books, 1967.

McCoy, Alfred W. "The Colonial Origins of Philippine Military Traditions." In *The Philippine Revolution of 1896: Ordinary Lives in Extraordinary Times,* edited by Florentino Rodao García and Felice Noelle Rodriguez, 83–124. Manila: Ateneo de Manila University Press, 2001.

——. "Quezon's Commonwealth: The Emergence of Philippine Authoritarianism." In *Philippine Colonial Democracy*, edited by Ruby R. Paredes, 114–60. Quezon City, Phil.: Ateneo de Manila University Press, 1989.

McCoy, Alfred W., and Ed C. de Jesus. *Philippine Social History: Global Trade and Local Transformations*. Quezon City, Phil.: Ateneo de Manila University Press, 1982.

McCoy, Alfred, and Alfredo Roces. *Philippine Cartoons: Political Caricatures of the American Era, 1900–1941*. Manila: Vera-Reyes, 1984.

McEnroe, Sean F. "Oregon Soldiers and the Portland Press in the Philippine Wars of 1898 and 1899: How Oregonians Defined the Race of Filipinos and the Mission of America." M.A. thesis. University of Oregon, 2001.

McGerr, Michael. "The Price of the 'New Transnational History.'" *American Historical Review* 96, no. 4 (1991): 1056–67.

McPherson, James M. *The Abolitionist Legacy: From Reconstruction to the NAACP*. Princeton, N.J.: Princeton University Press, 1975.

Mehta, Uday Singh. "Liberal Strategies of Exclusion." In *Tensions of Empire: Colonial Cultures in a Bourgeois World*, edited by Frederick Cooper and Ann Stoler, 59–86. Berkeley: University of California Press, 1997.

Melendy, H. Brett. "California's Discrimination against Filipinos, 1927–1935." In *The Filipino Exclusion Movement, 1927–1935*, edited by Josefa M. Saniel. 3–10. Quezon City, Phil.: University of the Philippines Press, 1967.

——. "Filipinos in the United States." *Pacific Historical Review* 43 (1974): 520–47.

Miller, Edward S. *War Plan Orange: The U.S. Strategy to Defeat Japan, 1897–1945*. Annapolis, Md.: Naval Institute Press, 1991.

Miller, Stuart Creighton. *"Benevolent Assimilation": The American Conquest of the Philippines, 1899–1903*. New Haven: Yale University Press, 1982.

Millett, Allan R., and Peter Maslowski. *For the Common Defense: A Military History of the United States of America*. New York: Free Press, 1994.

Minger, Ralph Eldin. "Taft, MacArthur, and the Establishment of Civil Government in the Philippines." *Ohio Historical Quarterly* 70, no. 4 (1961): 308–31.

Mitchell, Timothy. *Colonising Egypt*. Cambridge, Eng.: Cambridge University Press, 1988.

Mojares, Resil B. *Cebuano Perceptions of the Hawaii Migration, 1909–1934*. Cebu City, Phil.: R. B. Mojares, 1981.

Mrozek, Donald J. "The Habit of Victory: The American Military and the Cult of Manliness." In *Manliness and Morality: Middle-Class Masculinity in Britain and America, 1800–1940*, edited by J. A. Mangan and James Walvin, 220–41. New York: St. Martin's Press, 1987.

Ng, Frank. "Knowledge for Empire: Academics and Universities in the Service of Imperialism." In *On Cultural Ground: Essays in International History*, edited by Robert David Johnson. Chicago: Imprint Publications, 1994.

Ngai, Mae M. "The Architecture of Race in American Immigration Law: A Reexamination of the Immigration Act of 1924." *Journal of American History* 86, no. 1 (1999): 67–92.

———. *Impossible Subjects: Illegal Aliens and the Making of Modern America.* Princeton, N.J.: Princeton University Press, 2004.

Ninkovich, Frank A. *The United States and Imperialism.* Malden, Mass.: Blackwell Publishers, 2001.

Ocampo, Ambeth R. "Rizal's Morga and Views of Philippine History." *Philippine Studies* 46, no. 2 (1998): 31.

———. *Rizal without the Overcoat.* Manila: Anvil Publishing, 1990.

O'Connor, D. J. *Representations of the Cuban and Philippine Insurrections on the Spanish Stage, 1887–1898.* Tempe, Ariz.: Bilingual Press/Editorial Bilingue, 2001.

Omi, Michael, and Howard Winant. *Racial Formation in the United States: From the 1960s to the 1980s.* New York: Routledge & Kegan Paul, 1986.

Owen, Norman G., ed. *Compadre Colonialism: Studies on the Philippines under American Rule.* Ann Arbor: Center for South and Southeast Asian Studies, University of Michigan, 1971.

———. "Masculinity and National Identity in the 19th Century Philippines." *Illes I Imperis* 2 (1999): 23–47.

Paredes, Ruby R. "Ilustrado Legacy: The Pardo De Taveras of Manila." In *An Anarchy of Families: State and Family in the Philippines*, edited by Alfred W. McCoy, 347–427. Quezon City, Phil.: Ateneo de Manila University Press, 1998.

———. "The Origins of National Politics: Taft and the Partido Federal." In *Philippine Colonial Democracy*, edited by Ruby R. Paredes, 41–69. Quezon City, Phil.: Ateneo de Manila University Press, 1989.

———, ed. *Philippine Colonial Democracy.* Quezon City, Phil.: Ateneo de Manila University Press, 1989.

Paulet, Anne. "The Only Good Indian Is a Dead Indian: The Use of United States Indian Policy as a Guide for the Conquest and Occupation of the Philippines, 1898–1905." Ph.D. diss., Rutgers University, 1995.

Pecson, Geronima T., and Mary Racelis Hollnsteiner. *Tales of the American Teachers in the Philippines.* Manila: Carmelo and Bauermann, 1959.

Pérez, Louis A., Jr. *On Becoming Cuban: Identity, Nationality, and Culture.* Chapel Hill: University of North Carolina Press, 1999.

———. *The War of 1898: The United States and Cuba in History and Historiography.* Chapel Hill: University of North Carolina Press, 1998.

Pick, Daniel. *Faces of Degeneration: A European Disorder, c. 1898–1918.* Cambridge, Eng.: Cambridge University Press, 1989.

Pivar, David J. "The American Federation of Labor and Filipino Exclusion, 1927–1934." In *The Filipino Exclusion Movement, 1927–1935*, edited by Josefa M. Saniel, 30–39. Quezon City, Phil.: University of the Philippines Press, 1967.

Pletcher, David M. *The Diplomacy of Involvement: American Economic Expansion across the Pacific, 1784–1900.* Columbia: University of Missouri Press, 2001.

Pomeroy, William J. *American Neo-Colonialism: Its Emergence in the Philippines and Asia.* New York: International Publishers, 1970.

———. "American 'Pacification' in the Philippines, 1898–1913." *France-Asie* 21, nos. 189–90 (1967): 427–46.

Porter, Theodore. *Trust in Numbers: The Pursuit of Objectivity in Science and Public Life.* Princeton, N.J.: Princeton University Press, 1995.

Pratt, Julian W. *Expansionists of 1898: The Acquisition of Hawaii and the Spanish Islands.* Baltimore: Johns Hopkins University Press, 1936.

Prisco, Salvatore. *John Barrett, Progressive Era Diplomat: A Study of a Commercial Expansionist, 1887–1920.* Tuscaloosa: University of Alabama Press, 1973.

Rafael, Vicente L. "Colonial Domesticity: White Women and United States Rule in the Philippines." *American Literature* 67 (1995): 639–66.

——. *Contracting Colonialism: Translation and Christian Conversion in Tagalog Society under Early Spanish Rule.* Ithaca, N.Y.: Cornell University Press, 1988.

——. "Nationalism, Imagery and the Filipino Intelligentsia in the Nineteenth Century." *Critical Inquiry* 16, no. 3 (1990): 591–612.

——. "Translation and Revenge: Castilian and the Origins of Nationalism in the Philippines." In *The Places of History: Regionalism Revisited in Latin America,* edited by Doris Sommer, 214–35. Durham, N.C.: Duke University Press, 1999.

——. "White Love: Surveillance and Nationalist Resistance in the U.S. Colonization of the Philippines." In *Cultures of United States Imperialism,* edited by Amy Kaplan and Donald E. Pease, 185–218. Durham, N.C.: Duke University Press, 1993.

Raftery, Judith. "Textbook Wars: Governor-General James Francis Smith and the Protestant-Catholic Conflict in Public Education in the Philippines, 1904–1907." *History of Education Quarterly* 38, no. 2 (1998): 143–64.

Raucher, Alan. "American Anti-Imperialists and the Pro-India Movement, 1900–1932." *Pacific Historical Review* 43, no. 1 (1974): 23–110.

Reed, Robert Ronald. *City of Pines: The Origins of Bagio as Colonial Hill Station and Regional Capital.* Berkeley: Center for South and Southeast Asian Studies, 1976.

——. "Hispanic Urbanism in the Philippines: A Study of the Impact of Church and State." *University of Manila Journal of East Asiatic Studies* 11 (1967): 1–222.

Reilly, Margaret Inglehart. "Andrew Wadsworth: A Nebraska Soldier in the Philippines, 1898–1899." *Nebraska History* 68, no. 4 (1987): 183–99.

Renda, Mary A. *Taking Haiti: Military Occupation and the Culture of U.S. Imperialism, 1915–1940.* Chapel Hill: University of North Carolina Press, 2001.

Reuter, Frank T. *Catholic Influence on American Colonial Policies, 1898–1904.* Austin: University of Texas Press, 1967.

Robinson, Michael C., and Frank N. Schubert. "David Fagen: An Afro-American in the Philippines, 1899–1901." *Pacific Historical Review* 44, no. 1 (1975): 68–83.

Robinson, Ronald. "Non-European Foundations of European Imperialism: Sketch for a Theory of Collaboration." In *Studies in the Theory of Imperialism,* edited by Roger Owen and Robert B. Sutcliffe, 117–40. London: Longman, 1972.

Roces, Alfredo. *Felix Resurrección Hidalgo and the Generation of 1872.* Pasay City, Phil.: Eugenio Lopez Foundation, 1995.

Rodgers, Daniel T. *Atlantic Crossings: Social Politics in a Progressive Age.* Cambridge, Mass.: Belknap Press of Harvard University Press, 1998.

——. "Exceptionalism." In *Imagined Histories: American Historians Interpret the*

Past, edited by Anthony Molho and Gordon S. Wood, 21–40. Princeton, N.J.: Princeton University Press, 1998.

Roediger, David R. "Gook: The Short History of an Americanism." In *Towards the Abolition of Whiteness: Essays on Race, Politics, and Working Class History*, edited by David R. Roediger, 117–20. New York: Verso, 1994.

Roth, Russell. *Muddy Glory: America's "Indian Wars" in the Philippines, 1899–1935.* West Hanover, Mass.: Christopher Pub. House, 1981.

Rotundo, E. Anthony. *American Manhood: Transformations in Masculinity from the Revolution to the Modern Era.* New York: Basic Books, 1993.

Rydell, Robert W. *All the World's a Fair: Visions of Empire at American International Expositions, 1876–1916.* Chicago: University of Chicago Press, 1984.

Said, Edward W. *Orientalism.* New York: Pantheon Books, 1978.

Salamanca, Bonifacio S. *The Filipino Reaction to American Rule, 1901–1913.* Hamden, Conn.: Shoe String Press, 1968.

Salazar, Wigan. "British and German Passivity in the Face of Spanish Neo-Mercantilist Resurgence in the Philippines, c. 1883–1898." *Itinerario* 21, no. 2 (1997): 124–53.

Salman, Michael. *The Embarrassment of Slavery: Controversies over Bondage and Nationalism in the American Colonial Philippines.* Berkeley: University of California Press, 2001.

Sánchez Gómez, Luis Angel. " 'Ellos y Nosotros' y 'Los Indios de Filipinas': Artículos de Pablo Feced y Graciano López Jaena (1887)." *Revista Española del Pacífico* 8 (1998): 309–21.

——. "La Etnografía de Filipinas desde la Administración Colonial Española (1874–1898)." *Revista de Indias* 47, no. 179 (1987): 157–85.

——. *Un Imperio en la Vitrina: El Colonialismo Español en el Pacífico y la Exposición de Filipinas de 1887.* Madrid: Consejo Superior de Investigaciones Científicas, Instituto de Historia, 2003.

——. "Indigenous Art at the Philippine Exposition of 1887: Arguments for an Ideological and Racial Battle in Colonial Context." *Journal of the History of Collections* 14, no. 2 (2002): 283–94.

——. "Salvajes e Ilustrados: Actitudes de los Nacionalistas Filipinos ante la Exposición de 1887." In *Imperios y Naciones en el Pacífico*, edited by María Dolores Elizalde Pérez-Grueso, Josep Maria Fradera, and L. Alonso Alvarez, 145–72. Madrid: Asociación Española de Estudios del Pacífico, Consejo Superior de Investigaciones Científicas, 2001.

Saniel, Josefa M., ed. *The Filipino Exclusion Movement, 1927–1935.* Quezon City, Phil.: University of the Philippines Press, 1967.

Saum, Lewis O. "The Western Volunteer and 'the New Empire.' " *Pacific Northwest Quarterly* 57, no. 1 (1966): 18–27.

Schirmer, Daniel B. *Republic or Empire: American Resistance to the Philippine War.* Cambridge, Mass.: Schenkman Pub. Co., 1972.

Schott, Joseph L. *The Ordeal of Samar.* Indianapolis: Bobbs-Merrill, 1965.

Schulten, Susan. *The Geographical Imagination in America, 1880–1950.* Chicago: University of Chicago Press, 2001.

Schumacher, John N. *Father Jose Burgos: A Documentary History with Spanish Documents and Their Translation.* Quezon City, Phil.: Ateneo de Manila University Press, 1999.

——. *The Propaganda Movement, 1880–1895: The Creators of a Filipino Consciousness, the Makers of Revolution.* Manila: Solidaridad Pub. House, 1973.

——. "The Propaganda Movement, Literature, and the Arts." In *The Making of a Nation: Essays on Nineteenth-Century Filipino Nationalism,* edited by John N. Schumacher, 119–25. Quezon City, Phil.: Ateneo de Manila University Press, 1991.

——. "The Propagandists' Reconstruction of the Philippine Past." In *The Making of a Nation: Essays on Nineteenth-Century Filipino Nationalism,* edited by John N. Schumacher, 102–18. Quezon City, Phil.: Ateneo de Manila University Press, 1991.

Scott, William Henry. *Cracks in the Parchment Curtain and Other Essays in Philippine History.* Quezon City, Phil.: New Day Publishers, 1985.

——. *The Discovery of the Igorots: Spanish Contacts with the Pagans of Northern Luzon.* Quezon City, Phil.: New Day Publishers, 1974.

——. "The Igorots Who Went to Madrid." In *History on the Cordillera: Collected Writings on Mountain Province History.* Baguio City, Phil.: Baguio Printing and Pub. Co, 1975.

Sinha, Mrinalini. *Colonial Masculinity: The 'Manly Englishman' and the 'Effeminate Bengali' in the Late Nineteenth Century.* Manchester: Manchester University Press, 1995.

——. Introduction to *Mother India,* by Katherine Mayo, 1–62. Ann Arbor: University of Michigan Press, 2003.

Slotkin, Richard. "Buffalo Bill's 'Wild West' and the Mythologization of the American Empire." In *Cultures of United States Imperialism,* edited by Amy Kaplan and Donald E. Pease. 164–81. Durham, N.C.: Duke University Press, 1993.

Smallman-Raynor, Matthew, and Andrew Cliff. "The Philippines Insurrection and the 1902–4 Cholera Epidemic, Part I: Epidemiological Diffusion Processes in War." *Journal of Historical Geography* 24, no. 1 (1998): 69–89.

——. "The Philippines Insurrection and the 1902–4 Cholera Epidemic, Part II: Diffusion Patterns in War and Peace." *Journal of Historical Geography* 24, no. 2 (1998): 188–210.

Smith, D. H. "American Atrocities in the Philippines: Some New Evidence." *Pacific Historical Review* 55, no. 2 (1986): 281–83.

Smith, Ephraim K. "William McKinley's Enduring Legacy: The Historiographical Debate on the Taking of the Philippine Islands." In *Crucible of Empire: The Spanish-American War and Its Aftermath,* edited by James C. Bradford, 205–49. Annapolis, Md.: Naval Institute Press, 1993.

Smith, Helmut Walser. "The Logic of Colonial Violence: Germany in Southwest Africa (1904–1907); the United States in the Philippines (1899–1902)." In *German and American Nationalism: A Comparative Perspective,* edited by Hartmut Lehmann and Hermann Wellenreuther, 205–31. New York: Berg, 1999.

Spector, Robert M. "W. Cameron Forbes in the Philippines." *Journal of Southeast Asian History* 7, no. 2 (1966): 74–92.

Stanley, Peter W. *A Nation in the Making: The Philippines and the United States, 1899–1921.* Cambridge, Mass.: Harvard University Press, 1974.

———. "William Cameron Forbes: Proconsul in the Philippines." *Pacific Historical Review* 35, no. 3 (1966): 285–301.

Stephanson, Anders. *Manifest Destiny: American Expansionism and the Empire of Right.* New York: Hill and Wang, 1995.

Stocking, George, Jr. *Race, Culture, and Evolution: Essays in the History of Anthropology.* Chicago: University of Chicago Press, 1982.

Stoler, Ann. "Racial Histories and Their Regimes of Truth." *Political Power and Social Theory* 11 (1997): 183–206.

———. "Sexual Affronts and Racial Frontiers: European Identities and the Cultural Politics of Exclusion in Colonial Southeast Asia." *Comparative Studies in Society and History* 34 (1992): 514–51.

Streible, Dan. "Race and the Reception of Jack Johnson Fight Films." In *The Birth of Whiteness: Race and the Emergence of U.S. Cinema,* edited by Daniel Bernardi, 170–200. New Brunswick, N.J.: Rutgers University Press, 1996.

Sturtevant, David Reeves. *Popular Uprisings in the Philippines, 1840–1940.* Ithaca, N.Y.: Cornell University Press, 1976.

Sullivan, Rodney J. *Exemplar of Americanism: The Philippine Career of Dean C. Worcester.* Ann Arbor: Center for South and Southeast Asian Studies, University of Michigan, 1991.

Tan, Samuel. *The Critical Decade, 1921–1930.* Diliman, Phil.: University of the Philippines and the National Commission on Culture and the Arts, 1993.

Thomas, Nicholas. *Colonialism's Culture: Anthropology, Travel, and Government.* Princeton, N.J.: Princeton University Press, 1994.

Thompson, Lanny. "The Imperial Republic: A Comparison of the Insular Territories under U.S. Dominion after 1898." *Pacific Historical Review* 71, no. 4 (2002): 535–74.

Thompson, Winfred Lee. *The Introduction of American Law in the Philippines and Puerto Rico, 1898–1905.* Fayetteville: University of Arkansas Press, 1989.

Thomson, James Claude, Peter W. Stanley, and John Curtis Perry. *Sentimental Imperialists: The American Experience in East Asia.* New York: Harper and Row, 1981.

Tompkins, E. Berkeley. *Anti-Imperialism in the United States: The Great Debate, 1890–1920.* Philadelphia: University of Pennsylvania Press, 1970.

Trask, David F. *The War with Spain in 1898.* Lincoln: University of Nebraska Press, 1996.

Tyrrell, Ian R. "American Exceptionalism in an Age of International History." *American Historical Review* 96, no. 4 (1991): 1031–55.

———. "Ian Tyrrell Responds." *American Historical Review* 96, no. 4 (1991): 1068–72.

Valenzuela, Jesús Z. *History of Journalism in the Philippine Islands.* Manila: Privately printed, 1933.

Van Alstyne, Richard Warner. *The Rising American Empire*. Oxford, Eng.: Blackwell, 1960.

Van Hise, J. B. "American Contributions to Philippine Science and Technology, 1898–1916." Ph.D. diss., University of Wisconsin, 1957.

Vaughan, Christopher A. "Ogling Igorots: The Politics and Commerce of Exhibiting Cultural Otherness, 1898–1913." In *Freakery: Cultural Spectacles of the Extraordinary Body*, edited by Rosemarie Garland Thomson, 219–33. New York: New York University Press, 1996.

Vergara, Benito M. *Displaying Filipinos: Photography and Colonialism in Early 20th Century Philippines*. Quezon City, Phil.: University of the Philippines Press, 1995.

Vidal, Agustín Muñoz. "Filipinas en la Ilustración Gráfica de la Segunda Mitad del Siglo XIX en España." *Revista Española del Pacífico* 8 (1998): 289–307.

Volpp, Leti. "American Mestizo: Filipinos and Antimiscegenation Laws in California." *U.C. Davis Law Review* 33, no. 4 (Summer 2000): 795–835.

Vostral, Sharra. "Imperialism on Display: The Philippine Exposition at the 1904 World's Fair." *Gateway Heritage* 13, no. 4 (1993): 18–31.

Welch, Richard E., Jr. "American Atrocities in the Philippines: The Indictment and the Response." *Pacific Historical Review* 43, no. 2 (1974): 233–53.

——. *Response to Imperialism: The United States and the Philippine-American War, 1899–1902*. Chapel Hill: University of North Carolina Press, 1979.

Weston, Rubin Francis. *Racism in U.S. Imperialism: The Influence of Racial Assumptions on American Foreign Policy, 1893–1946*. Columbia: University of South Carolina Press, 1972.

Wexler, Laura. *Tender Violence: Domestic Visions in an Age of U.S. Imperialism*, Chapel Hill: University of North Carolina Press, 2000.

Wheeler, Gerald E. "Republican Philippine Policy, 1921–1933." *Pacific Historical Review* 28, no. 4 (1959): 377–90.

Wickberg, Edgar. *The Chinese in Philippine Life, 1850–1898*. New Haven: Yale University Press, 1965.

——. "The Chinese Mestizo in Philippine History." *Journal of Southeast Asian History* 5, no. 1 (1964): 62–99.

Williams, Walter L. "A Southerner in the Philippines, 1901–1903." *Research Studies* 39, no. 2 (1971): 156–65.

——. "United States Indian Policy and the Debate over Philippine Annexation: Implications for the Origins of American Imperialism." *Journal of American History* 66, no. 4 (1980): 810–31.

Williams, William Appleman. *The Tragedy of American Diplomacy*. Cleveland: World Pub. Co., 1959.

Winks, Robin W. "The American Struggle with 'Imperialism': How Words Frighten." In *The American Identity: Fusion and Fragmentation*, edited by Rob Kroes, 143–77. Amsterdam: Amerika Instituut, Universiteit van Amsterdam, 1980.

——. "Imperialism." In *The Comparative Approach to American History*, edited by C. Vann Woodward, 253–70. New York: Basic Books, 1968.

Wionzek, Karl-Heinz. "Lt. Commander Paul Hintze's Visit to the Philippine Revolution's Headquarters." In *The Philippine Revolution of 1896: Ordinary Lives in Extraordinary Times*, edited by Florentino Rodao García and Felice Noelle Rodriguez. 165–78. Manila: Ateneo de Manila University Press, 2001.

Wollard, James Richard. "The Philippine Scouts: The Development of America's Colonial Army." Ph.D. diss., Ohio State University, 1975.

Yengoyen, Aram A. "Culture, Ideology and World's Fairs: Colonizer and Colonized in Comparative Perspective." In *Fair Representations: World's Fairs and the Modern Worlds*, edited by Robert Rydell, Nancy Gwinn, and James Gilbert, 62–83. Amsterdam: VU University Press, 1994.

Young, Marilyn B. "The Age of Global Power." In *Rethinking American History in a Global Age*, edited by Thomas Bender, 274–94. Berkeley: University of California Press, 2002.

Yu, Henry. "Mixing Bodies and Cultures: The Meaning of America's Fascination with Sex between 'Orientals' and 'Whites.'" In *Sex, Love, Race: Crossing Boundaries in North American History*, edited by Martha Hodes, 444–63. New York: New York University Press, 1999.

Zimmerman, James A. "Who Were the Anti-Imperialists and Expansionists of 1898 and 1899? A Chicago Perspective." *Pacific Historical Review* 46, no. 4 (1977): 589–601.

Zwick, Jim. "The Anti-Imperialist League and the Origins of Filipino-American Oppositional Solidarity." *Amerasia Journal* 24, no. 2 (1998): 65–85.

——. "The Anti-Imperialist Movement, 1898–1921." In *Whose America? The War of 1898 and the Battles to Define the Nation*, edited by Virginia Marie Bouvier, 171–92. Westport, Conn.: Praeger, 2001.

——, ed. *Anti-Imperialism in the United States, 1898–1935*, <http://www.boon docksnet.com/ai/>. Jan. 7, 2005.

Index

Page numbers in italics refer to illustrations.

Abbott, Lyman, 348
Aetas, 68, 249, 250. *See also* Negritos
Africa, 9–10, 13
African Americans, 415, 434; as potential allies of colonized peoples, 13–14; racism against as presumed Philippine model, 19, 21; Filipinos' uses of history of, 56–57, 104; Rizal observes racism against, 86, 411, 433; compared with Filipinos, 102, 125; as soldiers in Philippines, 102; "Negro problem" as parallel to "Philippine problem," 117, 119; editors address imperialism, 119–21; solidarity with Filipinos debated, 120–21; U.S. soldiers compare Filipinos to, 125; black soldiers on U.S. war, 129–30; black soldier defends war, 156–57; army racism dismissed as holdover of racism against, 194–95; Holley contrasts Philippine "uplift" with situation of, 261; image of, in wartime cartoons of Filipinos, 263; as not representative of Americans, 265; Filipinos mistaken for, at St. Louis, 269; as attendees at St. Louis fair, 278; views of Russo-Japanese War, 296; Filipinos inspired by activism of, 297; anti-Filipino nativists employ racism against, 416; Roxas criticizes racism against, 422. *See also* Douglass, Frederick; Jim Crow; Johnson, Jackson; Lynching; Minstrelsy, blackface
Agoncillo, Felipe, 82, 100
Agricultural interests, U.S., 351, 393–96, 414

Aguinaldo, Emilio, 78, 79, 81, 82, 84, 93, 94, 95, 96, 97, 98, 99, 100, 104, 111, 121, 125, 130, 131, 132, 133, 147, 156, 182, 184, 189, 190, 244, 256, 330, 340, 345; declares Philippine independence, 95; captured, 151–52
Aguirre, Evaristo, 36
Agustín, Basilio, 91
Alejandrino, José, 93
Algue, José, 212, 264
Alhama, Manuel, 79
Allen, George H., 263
Alvarez-Guerra, Juan, 69
American Chamber of Commerce, 160, 396–97
American Club, 175
American Federation of Labor, 413, 425
American Museum of Natural History, 280–81
American-Philippine Company, 358, 366, 368, 396
Anderson, Thomas, 96, 97, 102
Anderson, William H., 333
Andrews, Walter, 347
Angell, James Burrill, 180
Anglo-Boer War, 131, 153, 261
Anglo-Saxonism, 199, 336, 391, 412; as rationale for U.S. colonialism, 11; as contrast to *mestizaje*, 27; colonial natives as racial threat to, 117; racialization of Americans as, 121; criticized by *Renacimiento*, 177; English language as element of, 204; Pardo desires for Philippines, 206; Pacific as "Anglo-Saxon," 357. *See also* Anglo-Saxons; English language
Anglo-Saxons, 295; Americans as, 89–90, 206; Rizal represented as, 337–

38. *See also* Anglo-Saxonism; English language

Animists, 28, 30, 37, 39, 67, 68, 71, 73, 113, 131, 320; displayed at Madrid, 36; as outside "civilization," 67, 68, 85; included in Filipino polity, 100; minimized by Lopez, 124; as "tribal," 211–14. *See also* Non-Christians

Anthropology: Spanish colonial, 51; Feced relies upon, 53; used by Rizal to observe Europeans, 57; as goal of Madrid Exposition, 71; Bilibid as site of, 229–31; as element of Philippine Exposition, 241; as element of European expositions, 248; at St. Louis Fair, 264; avoided at Panama-Pacific Exposition, 377; Worcester's policy criticized as, 378; used in defense of Filipino migration, 419. *See also* Bureau of Non-Christian Tribes; Ethnological Survey

Anti-imperialism, 2; extension of recognition to Filipinos in, 116–17; racial, 117–19, 161, 265, 435; as element of 1900 presidential race, 132; colonial knowledge directed against, 183–84; problematics of term, 448 (n. 90). *See also* Anti-imperialists; Anti-Imperialist League

Anti-Imperialist League, 114, 116, 236, 365; pushes for Philippine legislation, 355; transnational politics of, 355–56; breaks with Quezon, 474 (n. 26). *See also* Anti-imperialism; Anti-imperialists

Anti-imperialists, 1, 90, 116, 154, 171, 184, 185, 191, 200, 225, 226, 237, 304, 322, 351, 387, 414; in U.S. Senate, 110–11; blamed for outbreak of war, 111; answer charges of "tribalism," 123–24; accused of "treason," 133–34; 147; investigate atrocities, 145–46; colonial "expertise" directed at, 179; investigate of reconcentration, 292, 293–94; oppose conditional Jones

Bill, 354; push for Philippine legislation, 355–56; promote Philippine independence, 370; oppose Filipino migration, 398. *See also* Anti-imperialism; Anti-Imperialist League

Antón, Manuel, 51

Apacible, Galiciano, 114

Apple, John H., 347

Architecture, U.S. colonial: as project and metaphor, 159–60, 309–10, 311

Arellano, Cayetano, 113

Arlington National Cemetery, 155

Army and Navy Club, 175, 184

Art: prizes won by Filipinos for, 56; as sign of civilization and "capacity," 85, 117; Filipino, praised by Mataas, 249; Hidalgo, commission for St. Louis, 254

Artigas y Cuerva, Manuel, 306, 308

Asiatic Barred Zone, 398–99

Asiatics: atrocities attributed to, 148; Filipinos represented by nativists as, 416–17. *See also* Orientals

Asociación Hispano-Filipino, 50, 74

Assimilation, 5, 31, 56, 66, 76, 79, 85, 122, 199, 203, 211, 220, 226, 227, 289, 321, 334, 350, 389, 390, 392, 430, 435; criticized by Feced, 53; Propagandists as advocates for, 54; as element of inclusionary racial formation, 161, 201–5; symbolized through Americanisms, 190; friars as successful at, 198, 209, 211; *pensionados* as undergoing, 204–5; Pardo affirms, 205–7; Taylor fears Filipino-American, 207–8; of Native Americans, 214; exposition as means of, 232; demonstrated at exposition, 257–61; Scout socializing as, 276–78; reversing logic of, 307; migration seen as, 352; of "non-Christians" sought, 380; Filipino migrants as incapable of, 415, 416, 426; Filipino migrants as capable of, 420; United States as undergoing, 435–36. *See also* "Benevolent Assimilation" address; Propaganda movement

Atrocities: investigated, 145–46; defended on racial grounds, 146–51; minimized by Roosevelt, 156; source problems regarding, 445 (n. 5), 453 (n. 199). *See also* Prisoners of war: killing of; Torture; Water Cure

Aves de Rapiña, 342

Bacon, Augustus, 322
Baker, D. J., 292–93
Baker, Newton, 386
Balaguer, Victor, 35, 36, 51, 71
Balsley, Helen C., 348
Bandalan, Perfecto, 408–9, *409*
Bandholtz, Harry, 302
Banditry: Filipino resistance declared, 130, 293
Bandolerismo. See Banditry
Barcelona, 43, 50, 53
Barrado, Pascual, 71
Barrett, John, 239–40, 243
Barrett, William H., 125
Barrows, David P., 167–68, 183, 197, 229–30; as first chief of Bureau of Non-Christian Tribes, 212; denies existence of "tribes," 212–13; rejects Indian policy, 214; on Filipino migration, 415, 416, 421
Bartlett, Dean, 216
Bass, John F., 127, 147
Bates Agreement, 217
Batson, Matthew, 113, 114
Battle of Manila Bay, 3, 93, 424
Becerra, Manuel, 74
Bell, Alexander Graham, 282
Bell, Chriss, 143
Bell, James F.: debates Mabini on guerrilla war, 134–36; reconcentration of Batangas by, 153–54, 170; in fiesta politics, 186
Bellairs, Edgar, 159, 173–74, 175, 176, 192, 194

"Benevolent Assimilation" address, 109–10; Taylor satirizes, 207–8. *See also* Assimilation
Bennitt, Mark, 262
Beveridge, Albert, 1–2
Biak-na-Bato, Pact of, 81
Bifurcated state: Philippine colonial state as, 5–6, 30, 161–62, 208–20, 226, 289, 341, 435; marked in Census, 224–25; as structuring exposition, 258–61, 264; as framework for assembly, 300–301; used in divide-and-rule retentionist politics, 325; used to deny Hispanicized Filipino "capacity," 341; nationalists challenge, 342; Filipinization of, 379–82. *See also* Imperial Indigenism
Bigelow, Poultney, 151
Big Horn, Chief, 268
Bilibid Prison, 168, 280; as anthropological lab, 229–32; labor in, 316
Blood compact, 29, 37, 60, 61, 74; legend described, 59–61; used in Katipunan, 77; emergency use by Spanish, 92; use in fiesta politics, 189; Welch rejects, 416
Blumentritt, Ferdinand, 57, 65, 66, 67, 68, 69, 75; theories of, used by anti-imperialists, 116–17; theories of, used by Philippine Commission, 122–23; identifies eighty-two tribes, 212; theories of, used by Pardo, 213
Bocobo, Jorge, 413, 428, 430
Body: blood compact as making single, 59–61; colonialism as corrupting U.S., 207–8; up-building of Filipinos', sought, 312, *315*, 316; Filipino migration as threatening U.S., 407–13
Boers, 131, 153
Bogardus, Emory, 408
Bones, collection of, 236
Bonifacio, Andrés, 77, 78, 81, 327, 334
Boondocks, 33–34, 351, 402–3
Borland, William P., 355

Bourns, Frank, 180, 182
Boxer Rebellion, 120, 350
Brigandage Act, 155
Bright, John F., 144
British empire, 9, 13, 131, 159, 234, 287, 295, 365; as source of U.S. inspiration, 11, 15, 18; as critical comparison for *ilustrados*, 46–47; Spanish colonial envy of, 47, 80; use of indigenous armies cited, 113; U.S. as tied to by Anglo-Saxonism, 121; Mabini cites American war against, 136, 205; as proper model of colonial racism, 195–96; permits colonial migration, 420. *See also* Anglo-Boer War; Anglo-Saxonism; Anglo-Saxons; Comparison, inter-imperial; Connection, inter-imperial
Brown, William Carey, 133
Bryan, William Jennings, 110, 119, 132, 133
Bryce, James, 372
Buaken, Manuel, 404
Bud Dajo, 218, 219, 340
Buencamino, Felipe, 79, 113, 308
Buffalo Pan-American Exposition, 233–37
Bulosan, Carlos, 406
Bureau of American Ethnology, 233
Bureau of Insular Affairs, 164, 166, 256, 264, 339, 360, 365, 375, 401, 411, 412, 415
Bureau of Non-Christian Tribes, 229; founded, 212; Filipinos involved in, 213–14; rejects Indian policy, 214; surveys Cordillera, 215; reconstituted under Filipinos, 380. *See also* Ethnological Survey
Burgos, José, 41, 42

Caciques, 161, 196, 243, 389
Cailles, Juan, 314, 317
Calibrated colonialism: defined, 191; special provinces cut off from archipelago-wide, 215; practiced in

microcosm in Mountain Province, 216; nation-building as ultimate goal of, 288, 300; assembly as embedded in, 305; not source of Philippine independence, 351; Jones Act reconfigures, 362; Wood's regime undermines, 389–90; Tyding-McDuffie Act as, 424–25. *See also* Assimilation; Capacity; Evolution; Maturation as colonial metaphor; Tutelage
California, 1, 404, 405, 407, 411, 412, 413, 414, 415, 416, 425, 426, 428; as creation of empire, 348–49; as familiar to Filipino migrants, 403; as front-line of Filipino "invasion," 417
Cánovas, Antonio, 74
Capacity, 304, 346, 363, 384, 389, 392, 430; as colonial discourse, 5, 31, 199, 288; LeRoy defends Filipino, 294; as subject of calibrated colonialism, 300, 310, 311–12, 311; Ocampo addresses, 322–24; "flag incident" as evidence of absence of, 331, 333; mistreatment of "non-Christians" as evidence of lack of, 341–42; Woodrow Wilson denies Filipino, 344; lack of, used in retentionist campaign, 351; denied in U.S. Senate preamble, 361; Wilson sees as precondition for independence, 361; as serving indefinite retention, 364; Filipino nationalists argue for Filipino, 370–71; Europeans as lacking, 382; Filipino participation in World War I to demonstrate, 383–84; Kalaw criticizes evaluation of Filipino, 390–92; threat to United States of Filipino, 393; Roosevelt claims Filipinos have proven, 424. *See also* Calibrated colonialism
Carpenter, Frank, 379
Cassidy, J. S., 417
Castelar, Emilio, 71
Casualties, Philippine-American War: Filipino civilian, 112, 157; Filipino

military, 157; U.S. military, 157, 456 (n. 266)

Catholic Church: Taft negotiates with, over friar lands, 209; as retentionist lobby, 357, 358–60, 362; Americanization of Philippine, 359

Catholicism, 77, 197, 373; as "civilizing agent," 192; as element of bifurcated racial formation, 208–14, 226, 435; influence on education, 209; as anti-rational, 312. *See also* Catholics; Christianity

Catholics: as no longer "tribal," 211–12; as invisible at St. Louis, 268, 269, 270, 271; claim right to represent Philippines at St. Louis, 271, 273; foregrounded by Sutherland at Jamestown, 340. *See also* Catholicism; Christianity

Censorship, U.S. military, 133, 137, 145, 147, 184, 287, 299

Census: Spanish, 223. *See also* Philippine Census

Chaffee, Adna, 251, 254

Chicago Field Columbian Exposition, 271

China, 8, 17, 38, 52, 84, 91, 238, 239, 250, 261, 296, 307, 349, 372, 383, 384

Chinese: Antonio Luna mistaken for, 48, 68; Lopez Jaena takes credit for repulsion of, 63; boycott U.S. goods in response to exclusion, 350; exclusion from Philippines of, 398, 400–401

—mestizos, 25–26, 39, 40, 78, 337

—migrants to United States, 83, 86, 398, 408; U.S. nativism against, 349–50, 415, 426, 433, 434; Filipinos in U.S. mistaken for, 404; anti-miscegenation laws against, 410

—Philippine, 25–27, 28, 79, 117, 225; discrimination against, 40; as guides for U.S. forces, 143; as subcontractors, 167–68; as "foreign influence" on Filipino culture, 197

Christianity, Philippine, 116, 124; Christians as opposed to "non-Christians," 161–62; as civilizing force, 201; as element of nation-building, 286; as threatened by Philippine independence, 359; as sign of "weakness" of lowlanders, 368; as argument for independence, 372, 386, 390. *See also* Catholicism

Churchill, Winston, 153

Citizenship, Philippine: Filipinos given, 165; colonialism as education in, 203; Filipinos as achieving, 224. *See also* Incorporation, legal doctrine of; Nationals

Citizenship, U.S.: Asian migrants as "ineligible" for, 349; U.S. navy service as means to, 398; Treaty of Paris as not granting Filipinos, 415. *See also* Incorporation, legal doctrine of; Nationals

Civilization, 21; as imperial discourse, 13; as Catholicism under Spanish rule, 39; as *ilustrado* self-definition, 42, 44; pre-Hispanic Filipinos as possessors of, 64; defined as Hispanic-Catholic influence, 67–68; advertised by Philippine Revolution, 79; Agoncillo promotes Philippine, 100; prewar campaigns in defense of Philippine, 100–101; wartime defenses of Philippine, 114–16; anti-imperialists advertise Filipino, 116–17; Philippine Commission on varied levels of Philippine, 123; defined in terms of hospitality, 188; U.S. as "trustee" for, 206; "non-Christians" as lacking, 212; Bureau of Non-Christian Tribes as promoting, 212; highland militias as promoting, 217; on display at exposition, 258, 261. *See also* Civilized warfare; Imperial indigenism

Civilized warfare, 90, 154; urged against Spain by Aguinaldo, 94; urged against Filipinos by MacArthur and

Lawton, 112; Aguinaldo fears to abandon, 132; Mabini and Bell debate meanings of, 134–36

Civil service. *See* Philippine Civil Service

Clarke, John P., 354, 357

Clarke Amendment, 354–55, 356, 359–60, 361, 362, 474 (n. 26); Wilson conditionalizes, 360

Class: race as undermining politics of, 4; commission consults only upper, 112; civilian officials as elevated, 178; *ilustrados* as suspicious of civilian officials' social, 178, 295; *pensionados* selected for, 205; Filipinos of elevated, as source of Philippine nationalism, 206; poorer, as victims of reconcentration, 293; of colonized elites as superior to that of colonizers, 295; repatriation of lower, Americans and Filipinos, 401; miscegenation blamed on Filipinos of lower, 421–22

Cobb, Ty, 371

Codman, Julian, 146

Cody, Buffalo Bill, 76

Colijn, Hendrick, 364–65

Collaboration, 24, 29, 160–61, 162, 181, 191, 196, 211, 226, 434; as central principle of colonial state, 171, 173; opposed by Manila Americans, 175; "expertise" facilitates, 179; as mutual cultural construction, 190–91; put at risk by "nigger theory," 195; tested by census, 221–22; enlisted for exposition, 241–42, 243, 246–47; Wright alters terms of, 248; as "civilization," 320. *See also* State-Building, Colonial

Collection of Philippine materials: by tourists, 185; for Pan-American Exposition, 235–37; for St. Louis Fair facilitated by state, 241–42; difficulties in, for St. Louis Fair, 243–45. *See also* Bones, collection of

Colonial discourse, 5, 21–22

Comerge, Rafael, 80–81

Commerce. *See* Trade

Comparison, inter-imperial: Rizal's, 9; as *ilustrado* strategy, 46–47; in terms of language policy, 204; *pensionado* program within, 205; Rai's implied, 365

Concepción, Emilio, 132

Connection, inter-imperial: Kipling's poem as, 11–12; Churchill's advice on reconcentration as, 153; Hilder's career as, 234; colonial exposition genres as, 238–39, 241; Filipino enthusiasm for Japan as, 296–97; Younghusband's caution as, 364; Colijn's caution as, 364–65

Conrad, Joseph, 149

Contractors, 167–68; among Manila Americans, 174–75. *See also* Corruption

Coolidge, Calvin, 388

Cooper, Henry A., 355

Corbin, Henry, 133, 316

Corruption, 167–68, 304; Filipino elites accused of, 196, 198, 388; in exposition, 279–80; by Constabulary, 292; racialized, 319; said to characterize Filipino rule, 341, 346, 364; Americans accused of, 371; as sign of American "incapacity" for self-government, 372

Coudert, Frederic, 163

Cox, James, 347

Craig, Austin, 335–38

Crail, Joe, 425

Cruz, A. Antenor, 411

Cuba, 3, 9, 11, 14, 36, 38, 48, 55, 87, 91, 92, 96, 162, 164, 290, 390–91; as source for Philippine constitution, 81, 82; revolution in, 82; Filipinos compared to people of, 102; as model of guerrilla war, 131; reconcentration in, 153, 293–94; status under Insular Cases of, 163; as producer of sugar, 394, 395, 396

Curley, James Michael, 355
Curry, George, 355
Cutting, Bronson, 424

Dancing: as part of Filipino-American
   sociability, 105, 106, 185–87; as sym-
   bol of racial inclusion, 196; of "sav-
   ages" in Madrid, 249; declines under
   Wright, 294; Filipino-American, as
   racial-sexual threat, 408, 411. *See also*
   Music; Fiesta politics
Dauncey, Mrs. Campbell, 195, 261, 271
Davis, Dwight, 411, 412
Davis, George, 246
Davis, Mrs. Jefferson, 117
Day, William R., 96
Degeneration: as rationale for atrocity,
   149–51; as obstacle to white settlement, 163; as opposite of "regeneration," 170; assimilation as, 207–8
Delgado, Juan José, 63
De los Reyes, Isabelo: as folklorist, 65;
   includes "non-Christians" as Filipinos, 68, 73; expansive use of "Tag-
   alog," 78; on guerrilla war, 131; leads
   strike, 176
De los Santos, Antonia, 72
Del Pilar, Marcelo H., 48, 50, 54, 61,
   74, 75, 77
De Luzuriaga, José, 182
Democratic Party, 31, 110, 116, 345, 351,
   353, 357, 358, 359, 360, 372, 373, 378,
   382, 385, 388, 396, 413; as Jim Crow
   party, 119; anti-imperialist plank of,
   344, 354, 355; victory for, opens
   spaces, 350, 351, 362; new Philippine
   legislation of, 353–56; fails to realize
   Philippine independence, 387, 392;
   Philippine independence legislation
   by, 424
De Morga, Antonio: chronicle by, 8;
   cited by anti-imperialists, 117
Denison, Winfred, 372, 376, 378
Department of Mindanao and Sulu,
   379

De Rivera, Primo, 43, 81
De San Agustín, Gaspar, 63
De Santos, Isidoro, 95
Dewey, George, 17, 84, 91, 92, 93, 94,
   95, 96, 102, 115, 180
Disease, 157, 234, 244, 304, 316, 318, 363,
   408, 414, 433; cattle, 170, 388; epi-
   demics, postwar, 170; in reconcentra-
   tion camp, 293. *See also* Sanitation
Douglass, Frederick, 55–56
Dracula, 27
Du Bois, W. E. B., 7, 13–14, 296
Dutch empire, 9, 287, 295, 364–65
Duvall, William P., 328

Education, 365, 376, 379; as source of
   Filipino consciousness, 9; under
   Spanish rule, 42; *ilustrado* quests for,
   43; campaigns for Spanish-language,
   61–62; as metaphor for U.S. war, 111;
   wartime Filipino invocations of, as
   "civilization," 115; as exemplary of
   U.S. colonial state, 168–70, 390; as
   colonial metaphor, 201–5, 304;
   Pardo on, 205–7; as source of Philippine nationalism, 207, 287; Cath-
   olic influence on, 209; Rizal as sym-
   bol of, 334, 338; advances in, claimed
   by Filipinos, 371; as attracting Filipino migrants, 402–3. *See also*
   English Language; *Pensionados*;
   Schools; Thomasites; Tutelage
Edwards, Clarence, 164, 264, 265, 266,
   280
Egan, Martin, 345
Eggenberger, William, 128, 133, 139, 140,
   143
Elections
—Philippine (1907), 220, 222
—U.S. (1900): as factor in guerrilla
   resistance, 133
—U.S. (1912), 343–44, 353, 359
Elliott, Charles, 296, 344, 363
El Pacto de Sangre, 60. *See also* Blood
   compact

El Renacimiento, 177, 249, 264, 271, 290, 292, 296, 297, 308, 328, 334, 339; challenges Worcester, 342; crushed by lawsuit, 342

Empire: transforms race, 2–3, 4–7, 391–92, 433; Rizal surveys global, 9–10; expands scope of race, 13; U.S. as expanding, 82–84; as characterizing U.S. history, 121, 253; exclusion as incompatible with, 349–50, 418–23; exclusion as compatible with formal, 414–18

English language, 334, 352, 422; as element of Anglo-Saxonism, 2; used in civil service exams, 166–67; *presidente* address in, 190; as sign of "progress," 201, 225, 236, 257; decision for education in, 203–4; as element of nation-building, 203–4, 285, 287, 319, 392; as vehicle for "liberty," 203–4, 287; taught in model schoolhouse, 273; mandatory for officials, proposal to make, 275; as qualification for suffrage, 301; as condition in Jones Bill, 354

España en Filipinas, 50, 72

Ethnological Survey, 162, 198, 281; originally Bureau of Non-Christian Tribes, 212

Evolution, 5, 121, 161, 198, 200–201, 226, 299, 336, 337, 345, 366, 434–35; narrative of exposition, 253, 258, 265, 269, 271; illustrated in photographic series, 320

Exceptionalism
—racial, 90, 121
—temporal, 16
—U.S. national, 5, 83, 88, 90, 365, 430; as framework for Philippine-American colonial history, 15, 17–18, 21; colonial education as supporting, 169–70, 202; colonial "expertise" in defense of, 179; English language as element of, 204; inclusionary racism as element of, 192, 195–96; resonates with Philippine exceptionalism, 211; nation-building as sign of, 288; Jones Act as shoring up, 362; in accounts of Philippine independence, 392; leads to application of Philippine model, 438 (n. 8)

Exclusion: of Chinese and Japanese immigrants from U.S., 349; Asiatic, to be aided by Philippine independence, 357; Philippine independence as project of, 393; Chinese, extended to Philippines, 398, 400–401; Filipinos included as "Asiatics" for purposes of, 407–8; Welch Bill as anti-Filipino, 414; Roxas calls for, of Americans, 423

Exclusion, social: of Filipinos, 186, 188, 403–7; migrants encounter, 403–7

Expansion as exceptionalist euphemism, 15, 162

Expertise, 205, 364; as civilian discourse, 178–79; Worcester as possessing, 179–81; Filipino, 181–82; U.S. travelers invested with, 184–85; Riggs's reliance on, 198; Ethnological Survey as, 212; census as, 220, 226; Niederlein and Wilson's exposition, 240–41; Filipinos as limited in, 312–13, 364

"Export" as analytic, 3, 5, 19–20, 89, 435–36, 439 (n. 34)

Exposition, 35, 227, 238–39; historiography of, 230, 231, 462 (n. 3); anthropology as element of, 248; Taft rejects official sponsorship of, 339. *See also* Buffalo Pan-American Exposition; Chicago Field Columbian Exposition; Jamestown Exposition; Lewis and Clark Exposition; Panama-Pacific International Exposition; Paris Exposition; Philippine Exposition, Madrid

Exterminism, 445 (n. 6). *See also* Racial exterminism

Fall, Albert B., 356
Fallows, Edward H., 358, 366
Family as colonial metaphor, 161, 198, 199–200, 226, 333. *See also* Fraternalism, colonial; Maturation as colonial metaphor; Paternalism, colonial
Faust, Karl Irving, 103
Feced y Temprano, Pablo, 47, 52–54, 389. *See also* Quioquiap
Federalista Party, 160, 173, 177, 182, 242, 248, 287, 291, 300, 325; opposes Wright, 292; political shift away from, 299, 301
Felizardo, Cornelio, 293, 334
Femininity: Propaganda movement characterizes Philippines in terms of, 49–50, 62–63; Filipino men accused of, 62. *See also* Gender; Masculinity
Fiesta politics, 159, 185–91, 244; as element of inclusionary racism, 192; rejected by Wright, 248, 291; decline in, 294
Filipinization, 31, 215, 357, 382, 387; deferred by Forbes, 313; accelerated by Harrison, 345, 351, 354; meanings of, debated, 363–69; of "white man's burden," 378–82; on USS *Rizal*, 384; reversed by Republicans, 388–89; as hegemonic strategy, 389. *See also* Harrison, Francis Burton
Filipino: boundaries of category, 37, 66–73, 79, 85; term spreads in revolutionary discourse, 78; defined by Mabini, 78–79; Worcester denies existence of category, 122; emergence of term, 433–34
Filipino migrants to United States, 351
Filipino People, 352, 356, 370
Flag, Katipunan: shown in plays, 177; flown, 330; declared to have no national status, 333
Flag, Philippine: raised on U.S. vessel, 94; adopted, 95; as missing, 302
Flag, Spanish: lowered, 97
Flag, U.S., 85, 95, 105, 152; raised over

Philippines, 97; in Senate debate over annexation, 110, 111; Constitution as "following," 162–63; taken down in plays, 177; used in fiesta politics by Filipinos, 190; as marker of American sovereignty, 191; Bud Dajo as victory for, 220; as imperial marker, 329–30; trampling of, during "flag incident," 325, 331–33; fails to protect Filipino migrants, 430
Folklore, Philippine, 64–65, 182
Folkmar, Daniel, 229–31, 248
Font, Salvador, 71
Forbes, William Cameron, 217, 297, 309, 313, 314, 315, 316, 335, 336, 345, 353, 364, 391, 418; uses metaphors of "construction," 310; condones forced labor, 314; on "representation," 325–26; as retentionist campaigner, 357–58, 359; investigates Filipinization, 388
Ford, Henry Jones, 360
Forrest, Richard E., 358
Francis, David, 245, 260
Frankfurter, Felix, 360
Fraternalism, 348
Fraternalism, colonial, 194, 200, 312; Filipinos as participants in, 105, 215. *See also* Family as colonial metaphor; Maturation as colonial metaphor; Paternalism, colonial
Free, Arthur M., 412
Freeman, Charles A., 127
French empire, 9, 239, 241
Frey, Edsel, 411
Friars, 35, 40–41, 55, 61, 64, 74, 85, 182, 291; blamed for Philippine "backwardness," 58, 72–73; blamed for Philippine Revolution, 79; praised for civilizing Filipinos, 198; Taft negotiates for lands of, 209, 304, 359
Funston, Frederick, 149, 254

Galloway, John W., 129
Gardener, Cornelius, 174, 183

Gardner, Albert, 140–41
Garret, Finis J., 355
Garrett, Edwin, 134
Garrison, Lindley, 354, 360
Gender: and imperialism, 23; of *ilustrados*, 62–63, 76; of civilian colonial state, 178; and Filipino-American sociability, 186; of Filipinos as "boys," 199, 312; of "martial races" as against that of effeminate agitators, 317. *See also* Femininity; Masculinity
General Orders No. 100, 136, 138, 154. *See also* Civilized warfare; Guerrilla warfare
German empire, 9
Gibbons, James, 359–60
Gilmer, David J., 156
Goethe, C. M., 407
Gompers, Samuel, 119
Goodnow, Frank J., 348
Gook. *See* Gu-Gu
Griffiths, Arthur L., 184–85
Grosvenor, Gilbert, 281–83
Guam, 349, 384; deportation of Filipinos to, 137
Guerrero, Fernando Maria, 177
Guerrero, Leon Maria, 242
Guerrilla warfare, 29, 90, 147, 150; inaugurated by Philippine Republic, 130–31; Filipino interpretations of, 131–33; U.S. interpretations of, 134; Mabini and Bell debate meanings of, 134–36; racialization of, 137–39; as racial justification for atrocities, 146–47. *See also* Civilized Warfare; General Orders No. 100
Gu-Gu, 29, 125, 139; origins of term, 127–28; used in Watsonville attacks, 407

Hackthorn, Henry, 140
Hale, Irving, 253
Harbord, James G., 319
Harding, Warren G., 388
Hare, Butler B., 424

Hare-Hawes-Cutting Act, 424
Harrison, Francis Burton, 363, 364, 376, 378, 385; declares "new era" and Filipinization, 352–53, 354; seeks Filipino participation in World War I, 383–84
Harty, Jeremiah, 359
Hawaii, 32, 84, 163, 238, 349, 396, 428; Filipino migrations to, 397–98, 401; as zone of race war, 417
Hawes, Harry, 424
Head-hunting, 262, 269, 367, 369, 375, 420–21
Heart of Darkness, 149
Heflin, James, 396
Heitfelt, Henry, 400
Hilder, Frank, 400
Hintz, Paul, 79
Historiography: Spanish colonial, of Philippines, 8; by Rizal, 8–9; Propaganda uses of, 63–64; used in Philippine nation-building, 305–8
Hitchcock, Gilbert M., 355
Hoar, George, 146
Holidays, 327–28. *See also* Occupation Day; Rizal Day
Holley, Marietta, 261
Hong Kong, 10, 47, 51, 75, 77, 81, 82, 91, 92, 93, 101, 108, 129, 131, 375
Hoover, Herbert, 414, 424
Horr, Ralph, 425–26
Hose, Sam, 130
House Committee on Immigration and Naturalization, 414
House Committee on Insular Affairs, 353, 386
Hubbard, Louis, 125, 144
Hughes, Robert, 138, 146
Hunting, U.S. combat as, 144
Hushing, William, 425

Ide, Mrs. Henry, 160
Igorots, 39, 52, 58, 68, 71, 254, 273, 276, 320–21, 342, 374, 380; Antonio Luna mistaken for, 48; displayed at Ma-

drid, 69–70, *70*; as sharply distinct from Tagalogs, 209; exchanges established for, 216; bones of, sought, 236; sought for Philippine Exposition, 248; display of, at St. Louis condemned, 249–50; exposition controversies over, 252, 264–65; village of, at St. Louis, *259*, 267; contrasted with Scouts at exposition, 262; in Cedarine advertisement, *263*; "nudity" of, as spectacle, 265–66, 268; dog-eating of, as spectacle, 266, 268, 269; conflated with "Filipinos," 269, 271; *pensionados* lament display of, 274; exploited on vaudeville, 281; exposition display of, protested, 339–40; Sutherland agrees not to display, 340; opposition to display of, at Panama-Pacific, 375; smuggled from Manila, 375–76; display of, blamed for misunderstanding, 377, 404

Ilustrados, 36, 37, 63, 65, 66, 67, 68, 69, 71, 72, 73, 75, 76, 110, 123, 171, 176, 181, 206, 291, 299, 301, 334, 433, 458 (n. 32); defined, 42; confront Spanish racism, 47–48; criticize Spanish ignorance, 51–52; Spanish-language ability of, 61–62; masculinity of, 62–63; as exemplars of Hispanic-Catholic "civilization," 67; exclude Igorots from "civilization," 68; criticize Madrid Exposition, 71–73; alienated from Spain, 74–75; cultivated by U.S. military, 99; "attracted" by Philippine Commission, 112, 113; in Federalista Party, 173; suspect civilian class standing, 178; and fiesta politics, 186; exposition board enlists, 242–43, 251, 284

Imperial indigenism, 23, 73, 430, 435; Spanish, 52, 63; wartime U.S., 121–24; of civilian regime, 161; novel, required by civilian regime, 196–98; bifurcated, 208–14; casts "non-

Christians" as prey of Christians, 216; emphasizes "war-like" Moros, 218; emphasizes Christian/non-Christian antagonism, 289, 342; used in retentionist campaign, 351, 366–69, 372, 374, 378, 389. *See also* Nationalist colonialism

Imperialism: in debate over Philippine annexation, 110–11; as opposed to "expansion," 162

Inclusionary racism, 5–6, 29–30, 192–96, 226; at odds with exterminist racism, 192–93; discursive elements of, 198–208; Pardo's thought as congruent with, 206; denigrates Filipino capacities, 196–98, 223–24; rejected by white St. Louis mobs, 278–79; not source of Philippine independence, 351; needed for calibrated colonialism, 389; opposed by racial-nativists, 397; promotes Filipino migration to United States, 398; exemplified by Asiatic Barred Zone, 398–99; Watsonville attacks undermine, 428

Incorporation: legal doctrine of, 162–63; Taylor satirizes, 207–8. *See also* Citizenship, U.S.; Nationals

Independence missions, 385–87

India, 15, 204, 205, 239, 287, 293, 295, 365, 420

Indians. *See* Native Americans

Indolence: Filipinos accused of, by Spanish, 53, 58, 64; Rizal's discussion of, 58–59; reconcentration as promoting, 294; Filipinos accused of, by Americans, 313. *See also* Labor; Material development

Informal empire, 16–17, 88; as element of U.S. Pacific policy, 349–50

Insular Cases, 163

Insularity of Philippine-American history, 7, 14–18; exceptions to, 438 (n. 24)

Invasions: U.S. fears of Filipino racial,

32, 33, 393, 397–402, 416, 422; Philippine history as series of, 67; U.S. fear of Chinese, 400–401; Roxas criticizes notion of Philippine, 423

Isselhard, Jacob, 134

Jackson, Frank, 140
Jackson, Frank E., 310
Jamestown Exposition, 338–40
Japan, 10, 15, 27, 52, 84, 205, 206, 239, 250, 299, 307, 349, 372, 383, 384; as imperial threat, 296, 328, 356–57; fears of invasion by, 297, 359, 361, 365; negotiates for "Gentleman's Agreement," 350; Philippines invaded by, 392
Japanese migrants to Philippines, 225, 297
Japanese migrants to United States: 83, 398, 408; nativism directed against, 349–50, 397, 415, 417, 426, 434; Filipinos in U.S. mistaken for, 404
Java, 204, 287, 294, 307
Jeffries, Jim, 297–99
Jenks, Albert E., 198, 281
Jenks, Jeremiah, 295
Jenks, Maud Huntley, 197, 199
Jim Crow, 21; fear of extension of, to Philippines, 119–21; imposed on Scouts at St. Louis, 278; criticized by *pensionados*, 291; appealed to by anti-Filipino nativists, 417
Johnson, Arthur C., 141
Johnson, J. M., 95
Johnson, Jackson, 297–99
Johnson, Walter, 371
Johnson-Reed Immigration Act, 399, 414
Jones, Herbert, 410
Jones, William A., 353–55, 356
Jones Bills, 363, 365, 370, 385, 386, 387, 388; summary of passage of, 353–55; opposed by Gibbons, 359; Wilson on, 360–61; Quezon and making of, 361–62; preserves U.S. colonialism,

362, 389; preserves "special" character of "non-Christians," 379
Jordan, John, 128
Junoy, Emilio, 74

Kahn, Julius, 400
Kalaw, Maximo, 285–87, 289, 390–92
Kalaw, Teodoro M., 177, 297, 342
Katigpak, José, 308
Katipunan, 59, 76–77, 78, 81, 134, 177, 327, 334; connected to Propaganda movement, 77; ideology of, 77; as guerrilla network, 130; flag flown, 330; flag declared to have no national status, 333
Katsura, Taro, 296
Keesing, Felix, 209
Keesing, Marie, 209
Keithley, Ira, 280
Kiesling, Richard, 336
Kincaid, William A., 359–60
King, Charles, 102
Kipling, Rudyard, 7, 11–12, 121, 158; Feced as comparable to, 53
Kiram, Jamal-ul, II, 217
Knapp, Adeline, 168–70
Knowledge-production, 5; by Philippine Commission, 113, 122–23, 178–81; by Filipino nationalists, 123–24; civilians undertake, versus army, 182–83; by Bureau of Non-Christian Tribes, 212–14; Philippine census as colonial, 220–26; exposition as colonial, 234; Kalaw criticizes colonial, 390–92
Korea, 84, 296
Ku Klux Klan, 120

Labor, 37, 53, 181, 358, 371, 376; as sign of "progress," 201; coerced, used for road-building, 216, 217; Filipino "capacities" for, evaluated, 288, 313–17; reconcentration as bad for, 294; system of *corvee*, established, 314, 315; prisons as sources of, 316–17; Filipino, as threat to United States, 393. *See also* Indolence; Labor movement, Philippine; Labor movement, U.S.; Material development

Labor movement, Philippine, 176

Labor movement, U.S.: racial anti-imperialism of, 119; anti-Filipino nativism of, 351

La Democracia, 177, 182, 242, 343, 375

Ladronismo, 155, 244, 304, 318, 334; against census, 222

La Independencia, 98, 101–2

Lake Mohonk Conference of Friends of the Indian and Other Dependent Races, 285–86, 294, 295, 309, 322, 357

Language: Philippine pluralism in, as nonobstacle to nationality, 124, 196, 306–7; regime decisions about, 203; single, needed for "nationality," 203–4, 388; literacy in any, as Jones Bill condition, 354. *See also* English language; Spanish language; Tagalog language; Translation

La Solidaridad, 47, 50–51, 54, 55, 66, 74, 75

Law: place of Philippines in American, 162–63; U.S. adoption of Spanish colonial, 209. *See also* Citizenship, U.S.; Nationals

Lawshe, A. L., 279

Laws of war, 136. *See also* Civilized warfare; General Orders No. 100; Guerrilla warfare

Lawton, Henry, 112

Legarda, Benito, 113, 182, 248, 275, 325–26

Legazpi, Miguel López de, 59, 60, 211, 336

Leonard, Thomas E., 333

LeRoy, James, 186; declares impossibility of "color line," 192; sees army as "racist," 194; as exponent of inclusionary racism, 194–95, 214; praises Spanish colonialism, 211; condemns "race prejudice" of Wright regime, 294–95

Lewis, Peter, 128, 139

Lewis and Clark Exposition, 281

Literature: competitions, 42–43; as sign of "capacity," 85; Riggs denies existence of Filipino, 197–98

"Little Brown Brother" metaphor, 194, 200, 226, 406. *See also* Family as colonial metaphor; Fraternalism, colonial; Maturation as colonial metaphor

Lobingier, Charles, 317, 318

Lodge, Henry Cabot, 91, 146, 147, 322

Long, John D., 94

Lopez, Sixto, 123–24, 212

López Jaena, Graciano, 52, 56, 58, 62, 63, 68–69, 73; criticizes Madrid Exposition, 72

Los Angeles, 403, 410, 428

Los Indios Bravios, 76, 433

Lowell, Abbott, 163

Luna, Antonio, 48, 51, 62, 66, 68, 74, 131, 290

Luna, Joaquin, 379

Luna, Juan, 56, 63; as painter of *El Pacto de Sangre*, 59, 60; work of, used by anti-imperialists, 117

Lynching, 104, 120; as evidence of U.S. "incapacity" for self-government, 371–72

Lyon, Samuel, 132

Mabini, Apolinario, 78, 113, 116; debates Bell on guerrilla war, 134–36; deported, 137

Macabebe Scouts, 113, 114, 140; atrocities by, 148–49

MacArthur, Arthur, 90, 112, 130, 138, 183, 194; December 1900 proclamation by, 136–37, 152; fails to recognize commission, 174

MacLeod, John T., 25–27

Madrid, 35, 50, 52, 53, 59, 75, 80, 82, 101; *ilustrados* in, 36; Luna's views on, 48, 62, 68, 74, 101, 290

Magellan, Ferdinand, 307
Magsuci, A. E., 411
Maisonnave, D. E., 51
Malolos Congress, 99, 182, 301
Malvar, Miguel, 92, 154
Manila, 25, 26, 35, 38, 40, 41, 42, 50, 57, 65, 66, 72, 75, 77, 80, 81, 93, 94, 108, 111, 129, 131, 169, 170, 181, 203, 209, 221, 223, 226, 234, 235, 241, 248, 290, 299, 317, 318, 334, 342, 343, 349, 373, 375, 379; occupied by U.S. forces, 1, 3, 5, 28, 97, 98, 100, 109, 111, 182, 229; as insular metropole, 44, 68; plan for U.S. occupation of, 91; instructions for U.S. military governance of, 98; illegible to U.S. soldiers, 102; site of competitive sociability, 104–6; as site of commission hearings, 112; supposed Filipino "race war" in, 147; "end" of war celebrated in, 151–52; rituals of state-building in, 159–60; American community in, 174; divided civil society of, 175–76; labor organizing in, 176; congressional visitors to, 184; site of fiesta politics, 185; Filipinos excluded from social life of, 188; perceived dangers of, 189; no official "color line" in, 192, 196; Spanish rule memorialized in, 211; Mindanao cut off from, 217, 218; first U.S. schools in, 236; Permanent Museum in, 244; occupation of, celebrated at St. Louis, 251; simulated at St. Louis, 258–59, 273; breakdown of Filipino-American sociability in, 294; fears of uprising in, 295; bans Johnson-Jeffries film, 298; Nacionalista base outside of, 301; call for pantheon for, 308; as stage for conflicts over nation, 327–33; Rizal monument in, 336; Wilson victory celebrated in, 344–45; Harrison declaration in, 352–53; World War I demonstrations in, 383; Chinese exclusion in, 400; U.S. migration advertised in, 402; as similar to U.S. cities, 403; repatriation to, 427; Tobera memorialized in, 428, 430
Manila Americans, 174–75, 177, 296; host congressmen, 184–85; favor colonial paternalism, 200; preferred by Wright, 291; LeRoy blames, 294; and "flag incident," 325, 329–31; fear Wilson's election, 345
Manlapit, Pablo, 428
Markey, Joseph, 97
Martial races, 317
Masculinity: and imperialism, 23; of *ilustrados*, 62–63, 76; U.S. martial, 103; U.S. army "hunting" as, 144; U.S. officers as promoting, of Filipino troops, 319, 320–21; non-Christians as superior in, 368; Filipino service in World War I as proving, 383. *See also* Femininity; Gender
Mason, Patrick, 129
Masonry, 50, 65, 74
Mataas, Lauro, 249–51
Material development, 31, 288, 376; independence politics as bad for, 304; policy of, defined, 309; as technocracy, 312–13; homogenization as goal of, 319; Ocampo challenges rationale of, 323
Maturation as colonial metaphor, 5, 199–200, 331
Mayo, Katherine, 389
McClatchy, V. S., 414, 415, 416, 417, 420
McClernand, E. J., 246–47
McDuffie, John, 424
McGee, W J, 233–34, 264
McIntyre, Frank, 365
McKinley, William, 1, 91, 93, 110, 180, 190, 207, 242, 326, 334, 336; gives instructions to Merritt, 97–98, 106, 110, 134, 136; decision to acquire Philippines by, 109; condemns reconcentration, 153; invoked by Filipinos against Worcester, 343

McKinney, James, 333

McMurray, William, 348

Merchants, U.S., in Philippines, 174, 179; Taft enjoins, to study Filipinos, 181. *See also* Manila Americans; Trade

Merritt, Wesley, 97, 254

Mestizaje, 5, 25–27, 28, 39; among overseas *ilustrados*, 66, 67; emergency use by Spanish, 92; Rizal as product of, 337

Mestizos, 79, 389. *See also* Chinese—mestizos; Spanish mestizos

Mexico, 8, 38, 80, 280, 419; migrant laborers from, 408; nativism directed at, 410

Meyer, A. B., 9

Migrants: European, 83. *See also* Chinese—migrants to United States; Filipino migrants to United States; Japanese migrants to United States

Migration: as imperial problem, 24, 31; Filipino, to United States, 6, 346, 397–402; as colonial right, 420

Miller, Clarence, 363

Mindanao, 85, 222, 229, 292, 307, 317, 336, 374, 379, 381, 428; not incorporated into Spanish Philippines, 217; efforts to detach, from Philippines, 218, 341; Rizal's map of, 336; repatriates urged to develop, 428

Minstrelsy, blackface: and origins of term "gu-gu," 127; in wartime cartoons of Filipinos, 263; Igorots incorporated into, 266, 268

Mir Deas, Celso, 62

Miscegenation, 27, 415, 417; Rizal notes U.S. laws against, 86; fears of, between Scouts and white women at St. Louis, 276–79; fears of, at taxi dance halls, 408; Filipino nationalists address question of, 421–22

Missionaries, 83, 84, 163, 166, 172, 285, 402; Thomasites as, 169–70, 178; Taft praises Spanish, 211

Monroe Doctrine, 99

Monuments, 211; to Rizal, 336, 352

Moro Province, 5, 161–62, 209, 317, 319, 341; formation of, 215–20; elimination of, 379

Moros, 39, 71, 154, 155, 166, 180, 217, 218, 254, 273, 319–20, 343, 381; U.S. adoption of term, 211; terms for assembly exclude, 224; sought for Philippine Exposition, 248; display at St. Louis condemned, 249–50; village of, at St. Louis, 259, 267; conflated with "Filipinos," 269; as possessing "Filipino" identity, 307; displayed at Jamestown, 340; Worcester anticipates Philippine takeover by, 343; Quezon anticipates rule over, 374; Philippine independence as leading to Christian war with, 420. *See also* Muslims

Morrison, Robert F., 194, 200

Mosely, Beauregard F., 120

Moses, Edith, 159, 170, 186, 188, 189, 209

Motion pictures: of Johnson-Jeffries fight banned in Manila, 298; retentionist, of Worcester, 358, 366–69; criticism of Worcester's, 370; use at exposition, 377

Mountain Province, 5, 161–62, 209, 210, 341; formation of, 214–18; Worcester's rule over, criticized, 342; Filipinization of, 379

Muñoz, Calvo, 73–74

Munro, James, 257

Museum, Insular, 281

Music: Philippine national anthem adopted, 95; U.S. diplomat serenaded, 95; part of prewar Filipino-American sociability, 105, 106, 108, 125, 130; minstrel song among U.S. soldiers, 127; racist U.S. marching songs, 139; "patriotic" songs in fiesta politics, 191; Constabulary band at exposition, 253, 266; Scout band at exposition, 257, 261; Visayans sing

U.S. national anthem, 273; Scout band at inauguration, 322; "insurgent music" during campaign, 330–31; "patriotic" music at U.S. flag event, 332. *See also* Dancing; Fiesta politics

Muslims, 28, 30, 37, 39, 67, 68, 73, 75, 121; Moro Province for, 5; displayed at Madrid, 36, 69, 71; as outside of "civilization," 67, 69, 85; included in Filipino polity, 100; minimized by Lopez, 124; as "tribal," 211–14; ruled by *datus*, 217; anticipations of warfare with Christians, 218, 342; as outside Philippine nation, 341

Myers, Claude, 103

Nacionalista Party, 287, 299–300, 325, 330, 353, 385, 424; swept into assembly, 301, 303; ambivalent about independence, 302; resists detachment of "non-Christian" provinces, 342

National Geographic Magazine, 282–83

National Geographic Society, 282–83, 357

National Humiliation Day, 428

Nationalism, Philippine, 6, 8, 28; as teleology of Philippine history, 15; and U.S. colonial ideologies, 30–31; "official," 15, 33; education as source of, 206–7; Kalaw explains, 286–87; U.S. attempts to control, 288; Japanese victory as catalyst for, 296; U.S. attempts to cultivate, 300; as transcending language, 306–7; intensified by World War I, 383

Nationalist colonialism, 6, 32, 85, 249, 351, 382, 430, 435; defined, 73; used in response to "non-Christians" at exposition, 271, 273–75; as response to divide-and-rule politics, 325; used in criticism of Igorot displays, 339–40; used in response to Worcester, 343–44, 372, 374

Nationals: Filipinos as U.S., 6, 350, 398, 418; Filipinos stripped of migration

rights of, 426. *See also* Citizenship, U.S.

Nation-building, 31, 201; U.S., put at risk by assimilation, 208; Philippine, out of "tribes," 211–12; U.S. attempts to monopolize Philippine, 288, 299–300; Filipino historical efforts at, 305–6; as achieved through empire-building, 308; as physical "upbuilding," 314–15; role of Filipinos in U.S., 320, 322; memory of Rizal enlisted in U.S., 334

Native Americans, 10, 83, 250, 407, 414, 433, 434; racism against, as presumed Philippine model, 19, 21; in Buffalo Bill show, 76; as inspiration for *Los Indios Bravos*, 76; history of, used by Filipinos, 104; Indian Scouts invoked, 113; as analogous to Philippine "tribes," 124; Filipinos as not possessing "tribes" like, 213; "non-Christian" policy rejects policies towards, 214; all Americans mistaken for part–, 237; as nonrepresentative of Americans, 265; policy regarding, discussed at Lake Mohonk, 285; Filipinos challenge Worcester using image of, 343–44; used to distinguish "Filipinos" from "non-Christians," 374

Nativism: anti-Filipino, 32, 33, 119, 350, 351, 352, 393, 405; anti-Chinese, 86, 119, 349; California-based, 349; ideologies of anti-Filipino, 407–8; anti-Filipino political, 408, 410–11; nationalization of, 413–18; arguments within anti-Filipino, 414–18; as one cause of Philippine independence, 431

Nativist self-determination, 350, 352, 425, 426, 427

Neely, Frank T., 126

Negritos, 117, 213, 236, 264, 273, 337, 374, 410; as first migration wave, 67, 122; as "lowest" of Philippine "tribes,"

180; displayed at St. Louis, 248; conflated with "Filipino," 269; as recent past of "civilized" Filipinos, 272; Worcester refers to, as indigenous rather than Christians, 343

Neland, Charles, *118*

Nelson, Henry Loomis, 128

Nepomuceno, Vicente, 229, 274–75

Newell, Alfred, 262, 269

New Left historians, 16–17

Newspapers: of Philippine Republic, 98–102; of "attracted" *ilustrados*, 113, 182; black, on imperialism, 119–21; first U.S., in Manila, 136; U.S., culled for news of atrocities, 145; established by Manila Americans, 174–75; Filipino workers strike, 176; critical Filipino, 177, 299; U.S., publicize commission report, 183–84; cover Philippine Exposition, 266; Manila Americans', on "flag incident," 331, 332; Filipino, respond to Worcester, 342–43

Niederlein, Gustavo, 229, 239, 241–45, 248, 249, 252, 258

"Nigger" epithet: applied to Filipinos prewar, 102, 104; use in describing Filipinos transformed during Philippine-American War, 125, 128–29; used during guerrilla war, 139–44; "theory" condemned by civilians, 195–96; applied to Philippine Scouts at St. Louis, 278

Noli Me Tangere, 75

Non-Christians, 5, 30, 32, 39, 161, 162, 166, 201, 220, 226, 257, 279, 319, 320; as element of bifurcated racial formation, 208–14; origins of term, 211, 460 (n. 91); as "tribal," 211–14; Indian policy rejected for, 214; "special provinces" for, 214–20; terms for assembly exclude, 224; demarcated by census, 224–25; controversy over display of, at St. Louis, 248–51, 264–65, 271, 284; Philippine-

American War displaced onto, 254, 256; in bifurcated exposition, 258–60, 265, 272; as highlight of Philippine Exposition, 265–66, 267, 270; in *National Geographic*, 283; question of status of, in nation-building, 289, 325, 338–44; nationalists resist political separation of, 342; Christian treatment of, as evidence of "incapacity," 346, 351; used by retentionists, 366–69; minimization of, by Filipino nationalists, 372–76; Harrison's new policy towards, 378–80; Hispanicized Filipinos' duty to assimilate, 380–82

Nozaleda, Bernardino, 92

O'Brien, E. F., 175

Ocampo, Martin, 342

Ocampo, Pablo, 322

Occupation Day: celebrated at St. Louis, 251; as holiday in Manila, 328; used for critical purposes, 329

Orientals: Filipinos as not being, 372; nativists recast Filipinos as, 415

Osborn, George, 143

Osborne, Thomas, 112, 141, 143

Osias, Camilo, 413, 419

Osmeña, Sergio, 299, 301, 345, 361, 362, 424, 474 (n. 25); gives meaning to assembly, 302; on "representation," 325–27

Otis, Elwell S., 1, 100, 111, 114, 130, 131, 235, 400, 455 (n. 23)

Pacific Ocean, 83, 84, 85, 238; Panama-Pacific Exposition draws attention to, 348; pillars of U.S. policy regarding, 349

Palma, Rafael, 177, 372

Palmer, Frederick, 104, 128

Panama Canal, 347–48

Panama-Pacific International Exposition, 375, 376; as global harmony, 347–48, 421, 430; racial conflicts over, 349; Philippine exhibit at, 374–78

Pardo, Paula, 129

Pardo de Tavera, Trinidad H., 60, 113, 181–82, 248, 299; assimilationist ideology of, 205–7; involvement with Bureau of Non-Christian Tribes, 213–14

Paris Exposition, 76, 250

Parker, F. L., 418–19, 422

Parker, John H., 146

Parsons, Elsie Clews, 294

Partridge, 289–91

Pasyon, 77; Rizal incorporated into, 334

Paternalism, colonial, 162, 200, 294, 312; "non-Christians" as objects of, 215; at Lake Mohonk, 285–86; emphasized during "flag incident," 333. *See also* Family as colonial metaphor; Fraternalism, colonial

Paterno, Pedro, 56, 64, 71, 81, 242

Payo, Pedro, 71

Pearsall, Earl, 125

Pelaez, Pedro, 41

Penrose, Boies, 400

Pensionados, 204–5, 268, 281, 338, 350, 397, 398, 419; at exposition, 254, 257–58; unrecognizable at St. Louis, 269; express nationalist colonialism, 273–74, 284; alienated by U.S. imperialist pretension, 289–91

Permanent Museum, 244, 280

Perry, Matthew, 84

Phelan, James D., 349

Philadelphia Commercial Museum, 240–41, 280

Philippine-American War, 1, 11, 15, 28, 161, 162, 182, 217, 229, 233, 263, 301, 306, 330, 335, 344, 350, 351, 384, 392, 408, 435; fictitious end of, 32; historical persistence of, 32, 89; importance of, as transition, 88–89; outbreak of, 111; as extension of U.S. continental empire, 121; first fictitious end declared, 130; second fictitious end

declared, 151–52; Roosevelt's amnesty order in, 154; third fictitious end declared, 154, 327; declared over by census, 220; neutralized by exposition, 253–54, 255, 256, 279; Constabulary fights remnants of, 292; Roxas reminds Congress of, 423

Philippine Assembly, 31, 286, 289, 309, 310, 330, 353, 370, 375, 376, 421; terms for, in Organic Act, 165–66, 220; terms for, exclude "non-Christians," 224; inauguration of, 287; as core of colonial democracy, 300–301; competing interpretations of, 302, 303–5; fights bifurcated state, 342; supports U.S. in World War I, 383–84

Philippine Bureau of Education, 295, 338

Philippine Bureau of Health, 310

Philippine Census, 212, 220–27, 229, 231, 241, 372; Taft publicizes, through *National Geographic*, 281–83, 357; publication of, enables assembly, 300; as part of Jones Bill, 354

Philippine Civil Service, 164, 166–68, 180, 332; English as language of, 204; *pensionado* program trains for, 204; Filipino criticism of, 275, 329; rules of, suspended for exposition, 279; Americanization of, 313; Filipinization of, 313; private business activities of members of, 338

Philippine Commission, 5, 29, 31, 116, 160, 161, 165, 166, 179, 182, 226, 231, 244, 260, 275, 286, 287, 289, 299, 326, 335, 376, 378, 396, 400, 401, 455 (n. 32); establishment of, 112; wartime "tribalization" of Philippines by, 122–23; transfer of power to, 151–52; piecemeal transfer of power to, 155; establishes civil service, 166; builds "postwar" order, 171; knowledge-production by, against anti-imperialists, 183–84; holds rituals of collaboration, 185–91; as exponent of inclusionary racism, 192–93; as favoring colonial fraternalism, 200; extends control over Cordillera, 215; creates Moro Province, 217; Moro Province as outside control of, 218; calls for assembly election, 220; bans Katipunan flags, 331–32; Harrison promises Filipino majority on, 353

Philippine Commonwealth, 392, 424–25, 426, 427

Philippine Constabulary, 33, 160, 173, 217, 295, 301, 302, 310, 334; at St. Louis Fair, 30, 246, 251, 252–53, 254, 266, 269, 280; as partial replacement for U.S. Army, 32, 155; abuses of, criticized, 177, 247, 292–94, 304; as census enumerators, 221–22; Wright defends, 248, 291; as exemplars of assimilation, 257; use of reconcentration by, 292–93, 301; compels forced labor, 314, 315; as core of Philippine "nation-building," 317, 320; loyalty of, suspected, 317–19; broad state tasks of, 318; as exemplars of physical "up-building," 318; as homogenizing "tribes," 319–21; as "civilizing," 320–21; band interrupted, 331

Philippine Education Company, 336

Philippine Exposition, Madrid, 35, 51, 254, 339; as symbol of assimilation policy, 53, 68–69; criticisms of human displays at, 69–73; as point of reference for St. Louis, 248–50, 271

Philippine Exposition, St. Louis, 30, 230, 252, 254, 256, 320, 338, 352, 376; process of collection for, 237–45; imagined as "pacification," 238; Barrett's difficulty in promoting, 240; controversies surrounding representation at, 245–51; "Philippine Day" at, 251; as isolated, 251–52; opening day at, 252; Taft incorporates, into U.S., 253; map of, 259; as political

failure, 260–61; as widely attended, 261; attempt to separate, from midway, 264; non-Christians as chief attraction at, 265–68; as financial failure, 279–80; exhibits from, sold in U.S., 280–81

Philippine Exposition Board, 229, 232, 243, 244, 247, 271, 279; established, 240; organizes collection, 241–42; de-emphasizes non-Christians, 268–70

Philippine independence: declared by Aguinaldo, 95; Nacionalista Party ambivalent about, 302; Democratic plank calls for, when Philippines "stable," 344; movement for, joined by nativists, 350; possibilities for, opened by Democrats, 350; unachieved by Democrats, 351; role of geopolitics in, 351, 356–57; Jones Bill promises "ultimate," 354; Wilson hostile to fixed timetable for, 354; Clarke Amendment promises unconditional, in two years, 354–55; as shoring up Asiatic exclusion, 357; opposed by retentionists, 357–60; Jones Act declares "purpose" to grant, 362; as needed to reveal "capacity," 371; needed for defense of Christianity in Asia, 372; missions to lobby for, 385–87; Democratic opening fails to achieve, 387; as byproduct of exclusion, 393, 431; promoted by U.S. agriculture, 393–97, 423; promoted by U.S. racial nativists, 397, 423, 425–26; Watsonville race war as argument for, 413; as leading to Christian-Muslim war, 420; as necessary for U.S. welfare, 426

Philippine insurrection, 15, 88, 89. *See also* Philippine-American War

Philippine Lyceum Bureau, 368–69

Philippine National Bank, 388

Philippine Organic Act, 165, 362; establishes census, 220; establishes assembly, 300

Philippine Republic, 1, 28, 89, 90, 100, 117, 233, 274, 334, 390, 414, 475 (n. 42); declared at Biak-na-Bato, 81; forces of, prohibited from entering Manila, 97; not mentioned in McKinley's instructions, 98; government of, under construction, 98–102; class politics within, 99, 101–2; recognized by Wilcox and Sargent, 106, 108–9; excluded from Treaty of Paris, 109; erased by "Benevolent Assimilation" address, 110; as "single tribe," 121, 122, 288; as evidence of Philippine nation, 288

Philippine Revolution, 77, 79, 85, 100, 109, 157, 182, 206, 233, 306; as antiracial, 79; problem of status for United States, 87–88; negotiates with U.S. diplomats, 92–93; suspects U.S. intentions, 93; resumed, 94–95; as evidence of Philippine nation, 288, 300; assembly as continuation of, 302

Philippines: limited contacts with United States before 1898, 3; history of, as global history, 7–14; history of, as insulated, 14–18; as political exception in Spanish empire, 36–37, 38–39; as object of Spanish ridicule, 48; Spanish ignorance of, 51–52; as united to Spain by "blood," 59, 60; history and folklore of, 63–64; declared independent, 95; McKinley declares sovereignty over, 97–98; McKinley pushes for annexation of, 109; Senate ratifies annexation of, 110; as immigration floodgate, 119; as "unincorporated territory," 162–63; Organic Act for, 165–66; commission develops "expertise" on, 178–81; as lacking own culture, 197–98; as bodily threat to U.S., 207–8; as bifurcated state, 208–20; desire to represent, at St. Louis, 237–38; as symbolically isolated at exposition, 251–52; added to Lake Mohonk purview, 285; as naturally united, 286; struggles over representation of, 324–38; as element in broader U.S. Pacific policy, 349; as threat to U.S., 393

Philippine Scouts, 155, 173, 292; at St. Louis Fair, 30, 246, 251, 252, 254, 261, 269, 272, 284; established by U.S. Army, 113–14; as census enumerators, 222; in mock battles, 256; as exemplars of assimilation, 257; police non-Christians at exposition, 258–59; as racial-sexual danger at St. Louis, 276–79; as guards for prison labor, 316–17; as core of Philippine "nation-building," 317; participate in Roosevelt inauguration, 320, 322

Philippine Senate, 354, 360, 379

Philippine Society, 358

Philippine Supreme Court, 354

Photography, 49, 126, 142, 172, 187, 219, 219–20, 234, 236, 267, 270, 315, 379, 404, 405, 409, 429; anthropological, in Bilibid, 230–31, 231; in commission reports, 265; used to show "progress," 272, 321; in National Geographic, 282–83; of assembly, 303, 311, 308; used in Worcester campaign, 366–69; used by Quezon, 373; of "naked" Filipinos banned, 375

Pindell, Henry M., 348

Platts, Willis, 141, 144

Ponce, Mariano, 49, 85

Porter, David D., 145

Powell, John Wesley, 234

Pratt, E. Spencer, 92, 95, 96

Principalía, 42, 81, 108, 130, 171, 173, 301; use of Spanish by, 61; employed in U.S. colonial state, 182; as electors of local governments, 215; as census enumerators, 221–22

Prisoners of war: killing of, 141, 142;

torture of, 140–42, 142, 149, 150, 195.
See also Atrocities; Water cure

Prisons, 318; as source of labor, 316–17.
See also Bilibid Prison

Propaganda movement, 28, 37, 47, 55,
59, 61, 62, 64, 66, 67, 72, 75, 77, 85,
89, 90, 91, 110, 115, 116, 117, 122, 124,
182, 249, 271; criticized by Feced, 53–
54; as critical of Spanish colonial
racism, 54–65; use of Spanish language by, 61–62; use of historiography by, 63; connected to Katipunan,
77; Pardo connects U.S. colonialism
to, 206

Protection: colonial state as, 6, 32, 289,
341, 342, 351, 368, 389, 426; of Filipinos through Chinese exclusion,
400

Protectionism, 351, 393–97; as one
cause of Philippine independence,
431

Puerto Rico, 9, 11, 14, 33, 36, 38, 55, 87,
162, 165, 285, 322, 396; status under
Insular Cases, 163

Quezon, 299, 301–2, 345, 352, 356, 358,
360, 372, 373, 374, 375, 377, 384, 385,
386, 389–90, 401, 424, 475 (n. 42);
promotes Jones Bills, 353–55; maneuvers of, 360–61; defines "Filipinization," 363; anti-retentionist campaign of, 370; Anti-Imperialist
League breaks with, 474 (n. 26)

Quinto, Pedro, 298–99

Quioquiap, 59, 62, 63, 75, 76. *See also*
Feced y Temprano, Pablo

Race: intersections with empire, 4; as
site of Filipino-American struggle, 4;
as transnational system of power,
12–14; and politics of recognition,
19–20; as contingent system of
power, 22; as reconstructed in imperial contexts, 22–23; and gender, 23;
in Spanish colonial rule, 28, 39–40;

Feced as proponent of, 52–54; Propaganda movement as critics of, 54–
65; breakdown of categories of, by
overseas *ilustrados*, 66; blamed for
Spanish decadence, 75; opposed by
Katipunan, 77; in Spanish colonial
theater, 80; Rizal observes, in United
States, 86; Filipino suspicion of U.S.
for, 104, 116; Filipino opposition to,
116; in Philippine annexation debate,
116–24; used by anti-imperialists,
116; in new civilian formation, 161–
62; civilian representations of, in
military, 192, 194–95; redefined as
etiquette, 194–95; Wright regime
perceived in terms of, 294–95; as
inherent to colonial situations, 295;
class arrogance of "natives" as, 295;
Jack Johnson as obliterating, 298–
99; Osmeña uses, to argue for "representation," 327

Race war, 5, 28, 158; advocated by Comerge, 80–81; defined, 89; Philippine-
American War as, 89; promotion
between Filipinos of, 114; denied by
African American editors, 120–21;
exploited by Filipinos, 129; observed
by black soldiers, 129; denied by Filipinos, 136; Filipinos accused of,
146–47; Roosevelt rationalizes
using, 155–56; Gilmer denies, 156–
57; Christian/"non-Christian" relations cast as, 216, 289, 342; suspicions
of impending Filipino-American,
295; Russo-Japanese War as, 296–97;
Johnson-Jeffries fight as, 297–99;
Watsonville attacks as, 411–13, 428;
Filipino migration as anti-white,
416–18. *See also* Racial exterminism

Racial exterminism, 90, 158, 161; during
guerrilla war, 139–45; at odds with
inclusionary racism, 192–93; at Bud
Dajo, 218–20; distinguished from
genocide, 445 (n. 6)

Racial formation: novel, produced by

Philippine-American colonialism, 4–7; inclusionary, 161; bifurcated, 161–62; shaped in part by Filipinos, 213–14; as embodied in census, 220–26; impossible to "import" to St. Louis, 261; impact upon Filipino nationalism, 372. *See also* Imperial indigenism

Racialization: in Beveridge's addresses, 2; as process in Philippine-American history, 4–7; in Philippine-American War, 5, 28, 89, 90; of Americans by U.S. imperialists, 121; of Filipinos by U.S. imperialists, 121–22; of Filipinos by U.S. soldiers during Philippine-American War, 124–28, 158; observed by U.S. journalists, 125, 127; during guerrilla war, 137–39

Racial state, 5; U.S. colonial Philippines as bifurcated, 208–14; U.S., transformed by anti-Filipino nativism, 410

Rai, Lala Lajput, 365

Ramirez, Teresa, 271, 273

Rawlins, Joseph, 146

Recognition: politics of, 18–19, 20, 430, 434; sought by Propaganda movement, 37; *ilustrado* quests for, 48–51, 54; in Philippine-American War, 89–90; ambiguities of, between Aguinaldo and Dewey, 94; sought for Philippine "civilized war," 94; granted to Philippine Revolution by U.S. diplomats, 95–96; sought by Philippine Republic through diplomacy, 100–101; sought for U.S. forces, 109–10; "policy of attraction" as, 112; politics of, continued into Philippine-American War, 112; collaboration as, 159–61; of Filipino elites by commission, 171, 173; rituals of, held, 185–91; calibrated colonialism as hinging on, 191; in elements of inclusionary racism, 199; imperiled by colonial assimilation, 207–8; of

Hispanicized Filipinos as partly civilized, 208–14; exposition participation as, 232; role of expositions in extending, 247–48; difficulties of, at St. Louis, 269, 276; measuring of "capacities" as mode of, 288; Filipinos deny Americans, 291; assembly as self-, 302; assembly as stage in U.S., 304–5; extended to "national" heroes, 308; "capacity" as part of politics of, 323; resident commissioner as partial, 325; Filipino support in World War I in search of, 351, 383–85; not source of Philippine independence, 351; Harrison reasserts, 353; Jones Bill independence through, 354; Wilson reasserts logic of, 361; Jones Act gains U.S., 362; "Filipinization" as, 363, 382; Philippine exhibit at San Francisco as search for, 377; Hispanicized Filipino treatment of "non-Christians" as earning, 380–82; politics of, undermined by World War I, 382–83; regrounded by Jones Act, 387; Wilson approaches Philippine independence through, 388; breaks down under Wood, 389; criticized by Kalaw, 390–92; retreats in lead-up to Philippine independence, 392; as mode of indefinite retention, 392–93; migration as a matter of, 401

Reconcentration, 29, 129, 145, 157, 170, 176; implemented in Philippines, 152–54; Reconcentration Act, 155; criticized by *Renacimiento*, 177, 292–93; used by Constabulary, 292–94

Reconcentration Act, 155

Religion, racialized construction of, 208; studied by Bureau of Non-Christian Tribes, 212. *See also* Animists; Catholicism; Christianity, Philippine; Muslims

Reorganization Act, 308

Repatriation of Filipinos to Philippines, 401, 427–28

Representation: Filipinos denied, in Spanish Cortes, 38–39, 73–74; debated regarding commissioners, 325–27

Republican Party, 1, 110, 116, 120, 147, 345, 354–55, 358, 360, 361, 363, 369, 385, 386, 388, 391, 392, 400, 412, 414, 425; opened to Philippine independence by farm bloc, 424

Resident commissioners, 166, 286, 322, 355, 412, 419; struggle over appointment of, 324–27; Quezon's publicity as, 370–71

Resurreccion Hidalgo, Felix, 56, 63, 254, 255

Retentionism: "material development" as, 309, 312–13; campaign of, against Jones Bills, 357–60; arguments for, 365–66; Worcester's campaigns as, 366–69, 474 (n. 36); Filipino nationalists oppose, 369–78

Rhodes, Charles, 113

Ricarte, Antonio, 297

Riggs, Arthur Stanley, 197–98

Rivers, William C., 318, 319

Rizal Day, 327, 334; made official holiday, 335

Rizal y Alonso, José, 7–8, 12, 35, 45, 49, 55, 56, 60, 63, 66, 69, 74, 75, 77, 81, 181, 242, 297, 303, 306, 434; literary competitions of, 42–43; on travel, 44; on Americans, 45–46; as *Solidaridad* contributor, 50; as editor of *Los Sucesos*, 64; observes United States' racism, 85–86, 411, 428, 433; struggle over memory of, 325, 333; Filipino celebrations of, 327, 334; U.S. imperial usages of, 334–38

Roads, 216, 217, 310, 318, 337, 363, 365, 368, 381; as element of "material development," 309; forced labor on, 314, 316–17

Rohrback, D. W., 411

Roldan v. Los Angeles County, 410

Roosevelt, Alice, 294

Roosevelt, Franklin D., 424

Roosevelt, Nicholas, 364

Roosevelt, Theodore, 87, 91, 133–34, 146, 147, 154, 165, 237, 242, 266, 304, 359, 365, 371; rationalizes war as war for civilization, 155–56; congratulates Wood on Bud Dajo, 220; escorted by Scouts, 257; Scouts in inauguration of, 320, 322; uses Rizal to justify U.S. rule, 335; and "Gentleman's Agreement," 349; says Philippines "heel of Achilles," 356

Root, Edmund S., 384

Root, Elihu, 109, 138, 148, 165, 183, 197, 237

Rowland, Henry C., 149–51, 207

Roxas, Manuel, 347, 412, 424; opposition to Welch Bill by, 419–22

Rumors: of U.S. racism, 104; of Filipino revolt, 190, 328, 334; regarding census, 223

Russo-Japanese War, 296–97, 356

St. Louis Louisiana Purchase Exposition. *See* Philippine Exposition, St. Louis

Sakay, Macario, 78, 334

Samoa, 84, 349

Sancianco, Gregorio, 58, 59

Sandiko, Teodoro, 147, 474 (n. 25)

San Francisco, 86, 91, 93, 127, 234, 246, 347, 384, 428, 430; as meeting point of "East" and "West," 348; as creation of empire, 348–49; and segregation of Japanese students, 349, 356; as familiar to Filipino migrants, 403; as zone of race war, 417

Sanger, J. P., 221–27

Sanitation, 293, 309, 365–66; and U.S. military in Manila, 99, 106; postwar, in Manila, 159; as evidence of "regeneration," 170; as sign of "progress," 201, 390; hill station for, 215; in reconcentration camp, 293; as explanation for "indolence," 314; Worcester praises Negrito, over Christian, 343

Sargent, L. R., 130, 132; trip through Luzon by, 106, 108–9, 475 (n. 42)

Saulsbury, Willard, Jr., 357

Schmick, Esther, 408–9, *409*

Schneiderhahn, Edward, 261

Schools, 170, 201–3, 315, 335, 336, 365, 368, 381, 422; opened by U.S. soldiers, 203; displayed at Pan-American Exposition, 236; model, at St. Louis, 260, 271, 273; buildings as metaphor, 311. *See also* Education; English language; Thomasites

Schurman, Jacob Gould, 112

Schurz, Carl, 117

Science, 242, 251, 281, 342, 358, 381; Steere expedition, 179–80; commission's sponsorship of, 181; in Pardo's ideology, 182; in Worcester's authority, 184; as language of "race prejudice," 195; *Philippine Journal of Science*, 212; census as expression of, 220; Bilibid Prison as site of, 230; as goal of Hilder expedition, 236; used to attract *ilustrados* to exposition, 242–43; Taft taps into Washington community of, 281–83; Filipinos as lacking, 313. *See also* Anthropology; Expertise; Knowledge-production

Sedition Act, 165, 175, 177

Segregation: of Chinese in Manila under Spanish rule, 40; of Japanese schoolchildren, 356; of Filipino migrants to United States, 403–4, 405

Senate Committee on Insular Affairs, 146

Senate Committee on the Philippines, 361, 369

Sex, 102; fear of, between Scouts and white women at St. Louis, 276–79; fear of, between Filipino migrants and white women, 408–11, 412, 416;

arguments against, as grounds for anti-Filipino exclusion, 419; between U.S. soldiers and Filipinas, 422

Sherman, Penoyer, 234–36

Sikatuna, Rajah, 59

Simms, William, 129

Singapore, 92, 101

Slayden, James L., 355

Smith, Jacob H., 144–45

Smith, James, 339

Smithsonian Institution, 233–34, 236, 280

Sociability, Filipino-American, 104–6, 185–91. *See also* Fiesta politics

Sonnichsen, Albert, 126

Sousa, John Philip, 154

Southwick, Albert, 143

Spahr, Charles, 236–37

Spain: colonial racial formation of, 5, 39–41, 52–54; as colonial power, 8, 38–39; *ilustrados* campaign in, 36–38; as inferior colonial power, 46–47; as ignorant of Philippines, 51–52; "blood compact" binds Philippines to, 59–61; fails to grant Philippine representation, 73–74; *ilustrado* alienation from, 74–75; suspected in *Maine* disaster, 91; Filipino forces fight, 94; Filipinos declare independence from, 95; fights U.S. soldiers for Manila, 97; U.S. treaty with, 109; colonial rule of, praised, 209, 211; permits colonial migration, 420

Spanish-Cuban-American War, 1, 3, 15, 103, 157, 169, 239, 253, 390; anticipated by Filipino revolutionaries, 8; U.S. declares war in, 92; U.S. mobilization for, 93

Spanish language, 10, 77, 78, 213, 234, 242, 257, 290, 352, 403; retained as exclusive by Spanish friars, 61; use by nineteenth-century *principalía*, 61–62; McKinley orders in, 97; MacArthur proclamation printed in, 136; used in civil service exams, 166–67;

in *Renacimiento*, 177; spoken by few Americans, 203; as possible official language, 203–4; as language of census, 221; as element of nation-building, 286; as qualification for suffrage, 301

Spanish mestizos, 78, 337

Special Provincial Government Act, 216

Speer, Irving, 103

Stangl, P. L., 306–7

State-building, Philippine, 29–30, 162–70; competitive Philippine-American, 98–102; by civilian government, 171–77; as bifurcated, 208–20; census as, 220–26; exposition as, 232, 241–42; through changed alliances, 299; through government reorganization, 308–9

Steere, J. B., 179

Stevens, Joseph Earle, 179

Stoddard, Lothrop, 417

Stoker, Bram, 27

Storey, Moorfield, 146, 356

Suez Canal, 43

Sugar: Hawaiian, 84, 398; Philippine, as threat to U.S. production, 393–97, 424

Sutherland, William, 205, 268, 269; and Jamestown Exposition, 338–40

Taboada, Luis, 80

Taft, William H., 112, 151, 152, 167, 175, 179, 181, 183, 186, 194, 199, 200, 201, 202, 205, 222, 225, 242, 246, 248, 251, 254, 264, 265, 275, 291, 300, 326, 338, 341, 342, 345, 354, 359, 363, 371, 374, 391, 458 (n. 32); on civil-military tensions, 173–74; on Filipino character, 196–97; praises Spanish colonialism, 211; as promoter of exposition, 237–38, 241; as secretary of war, 247–48; introduces Philippine Exposition, 253; promotes census through *National Geographic*, 281–83; investiga-

tive mission of, 292, 299; gives meaning to assembly, 302, 304–5, 353; rejects official sponsorship for exposition, 339; as retentionist campaigner, 357, 358

Taft, Mrs. William H., 168

Tagalog language, 68, 77, 78, 134, 242; McKinley orders in, 97; MacArthur proclamation printed in, 136; in *Renacimiento*, 177; exposition pamphlets in, 242

Tagalogs, 8, 42, 56, 57, 68, 80, 117, 260; as "Filipinos," 78; revolution as exclusively by, 90, 113, 121–22; Macabebe "racial" animosity toward, 114; as closer to Americans than Igorots, 209; seek to differentiate "blacks," 213–14; Scout company of, sent to St. Louis, 246; displayed at Jamestown, 340

Tariffs, 345; reform of, sought through exposition, 237, 241, 260; criticism of U.S., on Philippines, 275; calls for reduced U.S., 309; U.S. agriculture pushes for higher Philippine, 394–97, 423; raised with Philippine Commonwealth law, 424, 425

Taylor, John R. M., 455 (n. 23)

Taylor, Rebecca, 207

Teachers, 178, 188, 197, 201, 204, 310. *See also* Education; Thomasites

Telfer, George, 141

Teller Amendment, 92

Theater: Spanish treatment of Philippines in, 48, 80; Filipino resistance through, 177; Filipino, as site of colonial race-making, 197–98. *See also* Seditious plays

Thomasites, 168–70, 178. *See also* Education; Teachers

Thompson, Carmi, 388

Thompson, Everett, 204

Thompson, Perry, 139

Through Peace and Liberty, 254, 255, 303

Tobera, Fermin, 411, 413, 428

Todd, Edward H., 347

Tolentino, Aureliano, 177

Torture, 140. *See also* Water cure

Townes, Horace M., 386

Township Act, 216

Townsley, P., 348

Trade: U.S.-Pacific, 83, 239; promoted by Philadelphia Commercial Museum, 240; Philippine-American, as goal of exposition, 241; U.S., interests seek retention, 357, 358. *See also* Protectionism; Tariffs

Translation: use by friars, 61; as *ilustrado* power, 62; of McKinley's instructions, 97

Transnational history: in Philippine-American encounters, 2–4; in past voices, 7; scholarship in, 437 (nn. 3, 6)

Transportation: improves between Spain and Philippines, 43–44; transatlantic, 83. *See also* Travel

Travel: as influence on *ilustrado* consciousness, 9, 43–44; as U.S. colonial "expertise," 184–85. *See also* Migration

Treaty of Paris, 87, 108, 155; Filipino representatives excluded from, 109; negotiations of, 109; ratified by U.S. Senate, 111; leaves Filipinos' status to Congress, 162, 165; as not granting Filipinos U.S. citizenship, 415

Tribes, 5, 90, 196, 201, 203, 211, 245, 246, 254, 374, 390; Philippine Republic as "single tribe," 113, 121; Philippine Scouts organized as, 114; racial anti-imperialist references to, 117; as anti-nation, 121–22, 212; Lopez criticizes use of concept, 123–24; in Worcester travelogue, 180; Riggs on Filipino, 197; debates on boundaries of, 212–13, 462 (n. 1); domestic U.S. model of, rejected, 214; Cordillera governance adapted to, 215–16; as outside of Hispanicized Filipinos' control, 216; Moro Province governance

adapted to, 217; as vanishing under U.S. rule, 225; displayed at exposition, 259, 259–60, 262; homogenized by Constabulary, 319–21; nationalists deny existence of, 340; Sutherland represents Philippines as, 340; as part of nativist argument, 420

Trigo, Felipe, 79

Tutelage, 5, 161, 199, 201–5, 207, 211, 220, 226, 227, 288, 294, 313, 345, 346, 364, 366, 384, 389, 390, 392, 393, 434–35; census as, 225; exposition as, 247; at model schoolhouse, 260; assembly as example of, 305; Ocampo uses language of, 324; non-Christians also in need of, 378; migration to United States as, 401, 422

Tydings, Millard, 413, 424

Tydings-McDuffie Act, 392, 399, 426–27

U.S. Army, 229, 233, 246, 253, 262, 292, 317; initial force of, sent to Philippines, 93; occupation of Manila by, 97–98; prewar abuse of Filipinos by, 102–3; masculinity of, 103; prewar tensions between, and Filipino troops, 103–4; establishes Filipino Scout units, 113–14; adapts to guerrilla war, 131; conflicts with civilians, 160; contractors with, 167; conflict with commission, 171, 173–74, 179, 226, 237; Board of Health, 182; represented as "ignorant," 183; censorship by, 184; officers of, as racially excluding of Filipinos, 186, 188; imagines indefinite retention, 191; represented as "racist," 194; controls Moro Province, 217; fears invasion of Philippines, 217; as guarantor of Muslim-Christian peace, 218; as census enumerators, 221–22; as exposition collectors, 242; at St. Louis, 254; marches in Manila, 328; suggestion

of Filipino troops for, in World
War I, 383–84

U.S. Congress, 162, 164, 166, 237, 239,
245, 304, 326, 361, 362, 370, 384, 385,
386, 388, 400, 401, 415; sightseers
from, sent to Philippines, 184–85;
considers Philippine independence
bills, 351; considers new Philippine
legislation, 353–54; passes Tydings-
McDuffie Act, 424

U.S. Constitution, 162–63, 322

U.S. Geological Survey, 282

U.S. House of Representatives, 286,
325, 354–55, 361

U.S. Marines, 84, 278–79

U.S. National Museum, 234, 236

U.S. Navy, 11, 82, 84, 197, 349; bases for,
88, 341, 344; plans of, for war with
Spain, 91; Asiatic Squadron of,
destroys Spanish fleet, 93; officers
Wilcox and Sargent of, 106, 108–9;
bombardment of Iloilo by, 112; Great
White Fleet of, stops in Manila, 328;
war plans of, against Japan, 356; Filipino service in, 384–85; Filipino
service in, as means to U.S. citizenship, 398, 415; bases of, as remaining
under Commonwealth, 425

U.S. Navy Department, 240

U.S. Senate, 1, 2, 87, 88, 109, 110, 111,
167, 194, 354–55; Agoncillo's memorial to, 100; ratifies Treaty of Paris,
111; hearings of, on Philippine-
American War, 146

U.S. State Department, 82, 96, 234,
239, 240

U.S. Supreme Court, 163, 342

U.S. War Department, 93, 146, 164,
235, 239, 240, 256, 266, 279, 281, 339,
353, 455 (n. 23)

USS Maine, 82, 91

USS Rizal, 384

USS Thomas, 168

Unamuno, Miguel de, 81

Urdaneta, Andrés de, 211

Ventura, F. R., 380–82

Villamor, Juan, 131

Visayans, 420; Scout company of, sent
to St. Louis, 246; village of, at St.
Louis, 260; as "invisible" at St. Louis,
268, 269, 270; imagined as recent
"savages," 271, 273

Wadsworth, Andrew, 125

Wagner, Arthur, 131

Waller, Littleton, 143, 144–45

War Plan Orange, 356

War rebels, 136–37

Warren, Winslow, 374

Water cure, 140–42, 142, 149, 150, 195

Watsonville Evening Pajaronian, 409, 411

Watsonville race war, 407, 409, 418,
428; meanings of, debated, 412–13;
protested by students, 429; as firing
Filipino nationalism, 430

Wave migration theory, 67, 122–23,
200–201, 213

Webb, U. S., 415, 416, 417, 418

Weeks, Edgar, 184–85, 290

Welch, Richard, 347, 410, 414, 415, 417,
426, 427

Welch Bill, 350, 397, 414, 426; arguments in favor of, 414–18; arguments
against, 418–23

Wells, H. L., 87, 127

Welsh, Herbert, 145

Weyler, Valeriano, 170, 293

Wheaton, Loyd, 149

Wheeler, Benjamin Ide, 348

White, Edward, 163

White, John Roberts, 319

"White Man's Burden" (Kipling), 11–12,
121, 195, 227, 378

Wilcox, William, 130, 132; trip through
Luzon, 106, 108–9, 475 (n. 42)

Wildman, Rounseville, 82, 93, 95, 96

Williams, O. F., 94

Wilson, Helen C., 292, 293–94

Wilson, William P., 240, 264, 279

Wilson, Woodrow, 31, 287, 359, 387;

election of, hailed by Filipinos, 344–45; appoints Harrison, 352; initial statement by, on Philippines, 352; hostile to fixed timetable for independence, 354; signs Jones Act, 355; role in blocking Philippine independence, 360–61, 362; uses Jones Act to vindicate U.S., 362–63; Filipino "self-determination" not a priority for, 385; independence missions use language of, 386; approaches Philippines independence through recognition, 387–88, 389

Winslow, Erving, 356

Wood, Leonard, 202, 317; and "Battle of Bud Dajo," 218–20; investigation by, 388; appointed Governor-General, 388–90

Woolley, Ralph, 372, 374

Worcester, Dean C., 122, 183–84, 214, 234, 311, 315, 321, 341, 342, 353, 372, 375, 376, 378, 379; pre-1898 Philippine "expertise" of, 179–81; defends Philippine use of "tribes," 212–13; casts "non-Christians" as vulnerable,

216; sues *Renacimiento*, 342; speech by criticized by Filipino press, 342–43; as retentionist campaigner, 357–58, 366–69, 370

World War I, 31, 365, 387; as start of large-scale Filipino migration to U.S., 350, 397; Filipino support for U.S. in, 351, 352; Filipinos question European "civilization" in, 382–83; as beginning of "independence missions," 385; leads to boom in Philippine exports, 394; Filipino loyalty during, as argument for migration rights, 418

World War II, 392

Wright, Luke, 248, 275, 289, 291, 299, 358

"Yellow peril," 357, 405, 416

Young, S. B. M., 133–34, 138, 144, 147

Young Men's Christian Association, 342–43

Younghusband, Francis, 364

Zamora, Pilar, 260